Canadian Advertising in Action

Canadian Advertising in Action

11th Edition

Keith J. Tuckwell

Pearson

Editorial Director: Claudine O'Donnell
Acquisitions Editor: Darcey Pepper
Marketing Manager: Leigh-Anne Graham
Program Manager: John Polanszky
Project Manager: Susan Johnson
Manager of Content Development: Suzanne Schaan
Developmental Editor: Christine Langone
Production Services: Rajiv Sharma, iEnergizer Aptara, Inc.
Permissions Project Manager: Shruti Jamadagni
Photo Permissions Research: Photo Affairs, Inc.
Text Permissions Research: Photo Affairs, Inc.
Interior Designer: Anthony Leung
Cover Designer: Anthony Leung
Cover Image: Mrs_ya/Shutterstock
Vice-President, Cross Media and Publishing Services: Gary Bennett

---

Pearson Canada Inc., 26 Prince Andrew Place, Don Mills, Ontario M3C 2T8.

ISBN 13: 978-0-13-422884-6

10 9 8 7 6 5 4 3 2 1

Library and Archives Canada Cataloguing in Publication

Tuckwell, Keith J. (Keith John), 1950-, author
Canadian advertising in action / Keith J. Tuckwell. — Eleventh edition.

ISBN 978-0-13-422884-6 (paperback)

1. Advertising—Textbooks. 2. Advertising—Canada—Textbooks.
I. Title.

HF5823.T82 2016 659.1 C2016-905667-8

To Esther . . . for your patience, understanding, love,
and support over the years

Brief Contents

Contents

Preface

© Mrs_ya/Shutterstock

The Eleventh Edition of *Canadian Advertising in Action* has been revised according to feedback from peer reviewers and current users. Their primary request was to ensure that content reflected the changing nature of advertising, specifically the gradual yet continuous shift by advertisers of placing more emphasis on digital media in their campaigns. This request has been met. There is much new discussion about online media, social media, and mobile communications in Chapters 1, 4, 7, and 12. Since the textbook places an emphasis on advertising planning, every attempt has been made to demonstrate the impact of data usage, technology transitions in traditional media, the rise of video content and sponsored content, and automated media buying techniques on advertising decisions.

The core structure of the book remains unchanged. Similar to previous editions, the book remains student friendly. Key concepts are presented in easy-to-read language, and numerous examples and illustrations, written and visual, are included to demonstrate key concepts and related advertising and marketing communications strategies.

To encourage students to read this book, my objectives in preparing this edition were as follows:

1. Present content in a clear, concise, yet engaging manner
2. Provide well-known examples and illustrations (both text and visual) so that students can quickly relate theoretical marketing communications concepts to applied situations
3. Present the most up-to-date material possible while recognizing that change in this industry is happening at lightning speed
4. Retain an appropriate balance between theory and practice and maintain the strategic planning focus that was offered in previous editions
5. Maintain a strong focus on advertising while recognizing the relationship advertising has with other components of the marketing communications mix

Is This Book for Your Students?

This book is ideal for courses that focus primarily on advertising while introducing students to the broader topic of integrated marketing communications. In the context of strategic planning, the core content focuses on creating and communicating the message in all forms of media. Media-oriented chapters are presented in a balanced manner to demonstrate their usefulness in planning broad-reaching or narrowly focused campaigns. Print media, broadcast media, out-of-home media, and interactive media (including social media and mobile communications) are given equal attention.

Additional content that covers sales promotion, public relations, and experiential marketing broadens the focus to integrated marketing communications.

Adopters and reviewers clearly acknowledge the **strengths and benefits** of *Canadian Advertising in Action*. The Eleventh Edition of *Canadian Advertising in Action*

- Is the only truly Canadian advertising textbook full of examples with which your students will readily identify
- Is written in an enjoyable and engaging reading style that students appreciate
- Presents all advertising illustrations and photographs in a vivid four-colour format, with each illustration clearly demonstrating how an important marketing communications concept is applied
- Offers a strong focus on strategic planning in all creative and media chapters; it is an essential resource for courses in which students develop their own advertising plans. Chapter 5 (Creative Planning Essentials) and Chapter 7 (Media Planning Essentials) are always mentioned by reviewers as being the strongest chapters in the book
- Provides media rate card information and numerous media buying illustrations; students can apply these media buying procedures in their own media and marketing communications plans
- Includes a sample marketing communications plan that demonstrates the relationships between various components of the marketing communications mix
- Offers three unique Canadian cases (included in the Instructor's Manual); these cases are ideal for assignments in which students must develop their own advertising or marketing communications plans

Canadian Advertising in Action is the most up-to-date book on the subject. It includes discussion on all of the latest trends and practices and shows the important role that advertising plays in the integrated marketing communications mix. All statistical information has been updated, and most of the stories in the Advertising in Action boxes are new.

Examine the content of this book carefully; you will find it to be a unique and contemporary presentation of advertising and marketing communications practice. You will discover that *Canadian Advertising in Action* is clear, concise, and colourful, a potent combination that should have an impact on you and your students.

New to This Edition

This edition focuses on essential issues that are shaping contemporary communications practice. With so much growth in interactive creative and media spending there is no longer any need to differentiate traditional media from new media. All media alternatives are equal partners in the media mix, and any combination of the various components can be employed to resolve a unique marketing problem or opportunity. Media planners approach the media this way and devise effective and efficient plans for their clients.

Planners are now more concerned about how engaged people are with the media and how much time they spend with various media. When devising a media strategy, planners must give engagement and time spent the same attention as more common variables such as reach, frequency, continuity, and market coverage. This different way of thinking is integrated into various sections of the textbook. Planners must also consider the potential impact of sales promotion techniques, public relations, and experiential marketing programs on consumers and include them in integrated plans that help achieve an organization's objectives.

The Eleventh Edition retains its primary focus on advertising and its strong emphasis on strategic planning. The goal is to present planning strategies in the context of how plans fit together. For example, what are the connections between marketing plans, marketing communications plans, and advertising plans? What are the links between advertising plans (creative and media), sales promotion plans, public relations plans, and social media plans? In keeping with past editions, all material is presented with a Canadian perspective. The concepts developed here are relevant to business, marketing, and advertising students, as well as to future managers who are embarking on a career in marketing communications.

Key Features

Among the more important and exciting changes and additions are the following:

1. Throughout the book, there is much discussion about the strategic nature of advertising planning and the role that advertising plays in the context of the bigger picture, specifically, integrated marketing communications planning. Clients now look for **total solutions** when trying to resolve problems. The role that advertising and marketing communications play in this process is discussed throughout the book.
2. Chapter 1 presents all components of the **integrated marketing communications** mix and presents some key issues facing the industry today. There is new discussion on how technology is influencing media consumption habits and becoming the central hub for all media. New insights into how analytics is having an impact on advertising decisions are also presented.
3. Chapter 2, The Advertising Industry, reflects the most current practices and procedures employed by different kinds of advertising and marketing communications agencies. The **relationship between client and agency**, including the roles and responsibilities of each party, remains a focal point of the chapter. More emphasis is placed on client–agency relationships and the trend toward the use of specialist agencies by clients.
4. Chapter 7, Media Planning Essentials, presents the latest trends on data usage, technology transitions by traditional media, and the shift to digital media usage in campaigns. It also emphasizes the need for creative planners and media planners to collaborate early in the planning stages of a project.
5. Chapter 8, Print Media, and Chapter 9, Broadcast Media, present new forms of advertising available to organizations. Since print and broadcast media are slowly losing ground to digital media, options such as sponsored content and branded content (content marketing) are being offered by print and broadcast media companies.
6. Chapter 12, Interactive Media, has been updated to include the most recent data about interactive media consumption and how it is influencing advertising decisions. There is new discussion on click fraud and the lack of viewing of digital ads—two key issues that digital advertising participants are grappling with. The chapter also includes new discussion on programmatic media buying and real-time bidding, a fully automated system that eliminates human input in the media buying process. Finally, all information about social media and mobile media usage has been updated.

7. Most of the **Advertising in Action** vignettes are new. These vignettes reflect newsworthy stories about advertisers or agencies and embrace a cross-section of companies and industries. These stories demonstrate the use of key planning concepts presented in the book (see next section for details).
8. Advertising remains the primary focus of the book but, since companies are looking for **total communications solutions**, the various components of the marketing communications mix are discussed. All forms of media and marketing communications techniques are given equal consideration in resolving business problems.
9. **Appendix I** includes a **marketing communications plan** for the Schick Quattro razor. It neatly shows how various components of marketing communications are integrated together. Advertising plays a key role in this plan.
10. The focus for this book clearly remains on **communications processes** and **strategic planning principles** that should apply to any and all industries. The examples and plans embrace business-to-consumer situations, business-to-business situations, product situations, and service situations.
11. **New visual illustrations** give the Eleventh Edition a **colourful**, fresh look. New ads from a multitude of well-known advertisers aptly demonstrate important advertising and marketing communications concepts. Presented in colour, all of the figures are visually striking!

The text is presented in a **practical**, **student-oriented style** and provides good **balance between theory and practice**. It is written from a Canadian perspective that your students will appreciate, especially if they become employed in the Canadian communications industry.

Success Stories Dramatize Advertising Practice

The best way to show how advertising plans become reality is to present stories that include the initial insights upon which a campaign was based and to link together the objectives, strategies, and tactics of a campaign. The **Advertising in Action** feature stories demonstrates the application of key advertising concepts. By way of example, students will learn how

- Molson Canadian effectively employs a patriotic theme to grow the brand in the competitive beer market
- A campaign aimed at various ethnic groups to attract new customers was successfully planned and implemented by Scotiabank
- McCain's assessment of its external environment led to several new products to meet new consumer needs; new advertising campaigns were launched to introduce these products
- Hyundai repositioned itself in the minds of new car consumers with its all-new "H-Factor" advertising campaign
- Canadian Tire effectively integrated a commercial titled "Ice Truck" into its "Tested for Life in Canada" advertising platform; products are tested in unexpected ways to demonstrate their reliability
- ING Bank transformed and rebranded itself to Tangerine with the help of an intensive and carefully phased-in communications campaign

- Honda effectively used outdoor advertising to demonstrate how much space was actually available in one of its subcompact vehicles
- McDonald's effectively uses sales promotion techniques to build its market share in the restaurant coffee market
- The Stratford Festival effectively used a social media campaign to boost ticket sales

Other companies and brands that appear in feature stories include Boston Pizza, Budweiser, President's Choice, Apple, Mr. Clean, Chevrolet Silverado, and the Canadian Tourism Commission, among others.

Pedagogy

- ***Learning objectives*** Each chapter starts with a list of learning objectives directly related to the key concepts presented in the chapter.
- ***Advertisements, figures, charts, and graphs*** Throughout each chapter, key concepts and applications are illustrated with strong visual material. Sample advertisements augment the Canadian perspective and demonstrate key aspects of communications strategy and execution.
- ***Key terms*** Key terms are highlighted within the text and defined in the glossary at the end of the text.
- ***Review questions and discussion questions*** Both sets of questions allow students to review material and apply concepts learned in the chapter.
- ***Appendix I: Marketing Communications Plan*** *Schick Quattro* An extremely useful model for reviewing the format of marketing communications plans, the Schick Quattro plan shows how the various models presented in the text are adapted to a real planning situation and how various marketing communications components are integrated into one plan.
- ***Appendix II: Advertising Regulations*** This section provides a useful reference tool for students.
- ***Appendix III: Glossary*** A glossary of key terms and definitions appears at the end of the text.

Organization

This book is organized into five sections.

PART 1—ADVERTISING AND MARKETING COMMUNICATIONS TODAY

The initial section presents an overview of today's advertising industry and the organizations that compose it. The relationship between agency and client is explored along with some of the controversial issues facing the industry. The relationship between advertising and other components of the integrated marketing communications mix is explored.

PART 2—MARKETING COMMUNICATIONS PLANNING

The first chapter in this section presents key topics related to consumer behaviour, market segmentation and identification of target markets, and market positioning strategies. Knowledge of these topics provides essential input for strategic planning. The second chapter examines the relationships between corporate planning, marketing planning, and marketing communications planning, illustrating how each type of plan contributes to achieving organizational objectives.

PART 3—CREATING THE MESSAGE

A detailed discussion of creative planning is presented in this section. The initial chapter focuses on the creative development process by examining the content of a creative brief. The roles of creative objectives and creative strategies are discussed in detail along with research techniques and creative evaluation processes. The next chapter focuses on creative execution and presents various alternatives regarding design, layout, and production of advertising.

PART 4—COMMUNICATING THE MESSAGE: PLANNING MESSAGE PLACEMENT

Chapter 7, the initial chapter in this section, is devoted to media planning and gives consideration to the development of media budgets, objectives, strategies, and tactics. The next five chapters evaluate the use and effectiveness of the various media alternatives. The strengths and weaknesses of television, radio, magazines, newspapers, out-of-home media, and interactive media (including social media and mobile media communications) are presented, along with media buying practices for each medium.

PART 5—COMMUNICATING THE MESSAGE: INTEGRATED MEDIA CHOICES

This section focuses on media alternatives beyond the traditional mass media. In the quest to reach customers more efficiently and to entice them to buy, organizations are embracing integrated marketing opportunities that include sales promotion, public relations, experiential marketing, event marketing, and sponsorships. The role and impact of these communications alternatives are examined in detail.

The format of chapters is consistent throughout the book. Chapters start with a list of learning objectives directly related to key concepts presented. Chapter summaries are located at the end of each chapter, along with review questions and discussion questions, which serve two purposes: to reinforce key concepts and to stimulate discussion on issues and problems confronting practitioners today.

The Appendices contain a sample marketing communications plan, a selection of laws and regulations that govern Canadian advertising, and an advertising lexicon that defines key terms.

Supplements

The following instructor supplements are available for download from a password-protected section of Pearson Education Canada's online catalogue (http://catalogue.pearsoned.ca). Navigate to your book's catalogue page to view a list of supplements available. See your local sales representative for details and access.

Instructor's Resource Manual This invaluable resource not only includes chapter-by-chapter teaching strategies, but also features notes about the PowerPoint slides and the video cases.

Test Item File This test bank in Microsoft Word format contains over 1 000 questions in multiple choice, true/false, short answer, and essay formats.

PowerPoint® Presentations PowerPoint slides are available with this edition and include up to 25 slides per chapter that help bring marketing concepts to life.

Image Library The Image Library contains various full-colour images from the textbook, such as photos, ads, and figures. Instructors can integrate these images in their own presentations.

Acknowledgments

For undertaking the task of reviewing the textbook at various stages of development, and for the time and energy she put into the review process, I would like to thank Linda C. Jay, School of Business, North Island College.

From Pearson Education Canada and its external suppliers I would like to sincerely thank Darcey Pepper, Acquisitions Editor; Karen Townsend, Program Manager; Christine Langone, Developmental Editor; Susan Johnson, Project Manager; Rajiv Sharma with Aptara; Leanne Rancourt, Copy Editor; Sally Glover, Proofreader; Julie De Adder, Photo and Permissions Researcher; Sarah Horsfall, Permissions Manager; and Anthony Leung, Designer.

As always, I would like to thank my family for their support over the past year. For her unwavering support over so many years of writing, a very special thank you to my wife, Esther. Another book is complete!

Keith Tuckwell

PART 1 Advertising and Marketing Communications Today

© Mrs_ya/Shutterstock

Part 1 focuses primarily on advertising and its role within the integrated marketing communications mix.

Chapter 1 examines the role of advertising and its relationship to other marketing and marketing communications activities, discussing the forms of advertising, the elements of integrated marketing communications, the factors conducive to investing in advertising, and some of the key trends and issues that have an impact on the nature of advertising planning today.

Chapter 2 introduces the key organizations that constitute the marketing communications industry, describing the roles and responsibilities of client organizations and various communications companies in planning and implementing marketing communications programs.

CHAPTER 1

Advertising in a Marketing Communications Environment

© nopporn/Shutterstock

Learning Objectives

After studying this chapter, you will be able to

1. Assess the role of advertising and its relationship to marketing and other elements of marketing communications
2. Identify distinctions among the various forms of advertising
3. Identify and define the various components of integrated marketing communications
4. Explain basic conditions for using advertising effectively
5. Identify critical trends and issues that have an impact on advertising and marketing communications planning
6. Describe the role that laws and regulations play in guiding marketing communications programs in Canada

Advertising Today

Advertising is undoubtedly the most visible form of marketing and marketing communications today, and it is an industry that is continuously evolving due to rapid changes in technology. It will continue to be an exciting and dynamic career field for students. The growth that has occurred in digital media has created new career opportunities for young, digitally savvy people. Further, traditional agencies have evolved and now offer a full range of employment opportunities that embrace all media. It's a great time to get involved in this fast-paced and rewarding business.

Advertising is all around us, and we as consumers underestimate the influence it has on us. Have you ever really thought about the influence that advertising has on you? Consciously or subconsciously, advertising messages reach us each day because we spend so much time with the media. Canadians 18 years and older spend 24 hours a week watching television, 21 hours a week online, 17 hours listening to radio, and only 2 hours a week reading newspapers. Among adults 18 to 34 years old, online media consumption can be as much as 33 hours a week.[1] Collectively, these statistics indicate that media play an important role in our lives. If we are exposed to the media, we are also exposed to advertising messages.

Just recently the internet became the largest advertising medium in Canada, surpassing television in terms of revenue. The internet now accounts for $3.9 billion in revenue in Canada each year.[2] Advertisers have followed consumer trends in terms of their media consumption and adjusted their budget allocations accordingly, causing a shift away from print media to online media in terms of advertising investment.

Because Canadians between the ages of 18 and 34 spend so much of their media time online, social media platforms such as Facebook, Twitter, Instagram, and others must also be given equal consideration when planning an advertising campaign. This younger group of consumers will carry their media habits forward as they age. In the future, digital media will play an even more prominent role than it already does. Procter & Gamble (P&G), for example, now spends one-third of its North American marketing budget on digital media.[3] P&G has made this bold move based on the consumer migration to digital media and its own desire to increase the effectiveness of the money it spends on marketing.

Advertising in Canada is big business. In fact, in 2014 (the latest data available at the time of publication) the amount spent on advertising was estimated to be $14 billion.[4] Within that framework of spending, certain trends are occurring. As previously indicated, spending on internet advertising is growing rapidly, while television and out-of-home advertising are only growing marginally. Radio is holding its own in terms of revenue, but both newspaper and magazine advertising are declining on an annual basis, reflecting consumers' movement away from print media. Refer to Figure 1.1 for additional details about media advertising revenues.

The largest advertising categories in Canada are retail, automotive, food, financial and insurance services, and entertainment. Several large and successful companies are the biggest advertising spenders on an annual basis. Among these leaders are P&G, Rogers Communications, General Motors, BCE Inc., Ford, Chrysler, and McDonald's.

DEFINING ADVERTISING AND ITS ROLE IN BUSINESS

Let's now clearly define what advertising is. Advertising is best defined in terms of its purpose. **Advertising** is a paid form of marketing communication through the media that is designed to influence the thought patterns and purchase behaviour of a target audience. A good advertisement will make the customer aware of a brand and the benefits it offers. Exposing the same customer to the message with some planned frequency will, advertisers

FIGURE 1.1

Net advertising revenues by media in Canada (millions of dollars)

Medium (Actual $)	2014 $	% of Total
Online	3793	30.8
Television	3361	27.3
Newspaper	2590	21.0
Radio	1589	12.9
Magazines	472	3.8
Out-of-Home	521	4.2
Total Reported Media	**12326**	**100.0**

Medium (Unreported Estimates)	2014 $	% of Total
Catalogues/Direct Mail	1181	60.3
Yellow Pages	435	22.2
Miscellaneous	341	17.5
Total Estimated Media	**1957**	**100.0**

Notes: Newspapers include daily newspapers, community newspapers, and online newspapers (digital editions). Online media includes mobile media and video gaming revenue.

Source: Canadian Media Directors' Council *Media Digest*, 2014-2015. Printed with permission.

hope, increase the interest level in the product, ultimately leading to the desired action—a positive purchase decision. Remember that competitors are trying to impress the same target audience with their advertising message.

Although advertising can accomplish specific tasks, such as increasing the public's awareness of a product or service or inducing trial purchase through a trial incentive, its primary role is to influence the behaviour of a target market in such a way that members of the target market view the product, service, or idea favourably. Once consumers hold a favourable attitude, advertising attempts to motivate them to buy the product or service or act on the idea. Essentially, advertising is a game of persuasion. Message and media are combined to persuade people to take action. Throughout the pages of this text, you will learn how message and media combine to persuade people to take action.

Advertising plays a major role in helping an organization achieve its business objectives. When carefully planned, advertising will attract new customers (and new revenues) to an organization and generate more loyalty (and additional revenues) from current customers. The nature of contemporary advertising is now more targeted and is based on database management and interactive marketing techniques. New opportunities tend to be more micro-based (e.g., direct response techniques, internet communications, mobile communications) than macro-based (mass advertising on television and in newspapers and magazines). Nonetheless, the purpose is the same—to help a brand or company grow.

The challenge for advertisers is how to select the right combination of media to effectively reach and have an impact on their target market. In that regard, there has been a change in how advertising plans are devised. Previously, the creative component (the message) dominated planning meetings—the emphasis was always on coming up with the big idea for a campaign. Now, in a rapidly changing media environment, it is essential that creative planners and media planners work closely together to devise the right advertising ideas for their clients. Successful advertising today is about getting the right message into the right medium at the right time. That requires careful strategic thinking across disciplines in an advertising agency. Good ideas are good ideas regardless of where they originate!

ADVERTISING AND INTEGRATED MARKETING COMMUNICATIONS

Advertising is not a stand-alone discipline. Rather, it is part of a bigger strategic environment referred to as *integrated marketing communications*. For an organization to grow, it must be operating on all cylinders, meaning that advertising alone will not influence the consumer's decision-making process. It is the convergence of many different yet related forms of marketing communications that influences consumer attitudes and perceptions about an organization or brand. Advertising is simply one component of the process—it is part of a package of communications variables that helps drive sales.

As you will learn, different situations require different marketing communications strategies. In some situations, advertising may be the driving force behind the entire strategy; in other situations, it may simply be a complementary activity. For example, the launch of a new product historically called for a mass-reach multimedia advertising strategy, the goal of which was to create widespread awareness of the product. In that scenario, media advertising played a lead role.

Now organizations are looking at alternative and more cost-efficient communications strategies. Many organizations are even getting significant benefits from word-of-mouth marketing communications. Social media platforms such as Facebook and Twitter, for example, are proving to be significant buzz-builders for new product launches. Through social media, an organization can plant its message well in advance of a product launch and create excitement and demand for the product when it is launched.

Social media have changed the nature of communications between an organization and the public. Formerly, communications were a one-way affair—the message was intended to interrupt the consumer and make him or her pay attention. In contrast, social media communications are a two-way affair where the goal is to engage consumers in an organization's message so they respond to it as they see fit—advertisers hope they will pass it on to friends in their social network. Is social media important? You bet! Some 20 million Canadians used social media monthly in 2015.[5]

Molson Coors Canada has been working with social media for years and promotes its brands through websites, community blogs, Facebook pages, and Twitter feeds. The company sees social media as an essential part of overall brand communications—a form of communication that can help build buzz and brand loyalty.

Scotiabank is also using social media as a means to reach younger consumers—consumers it sees as critical to its future growth. The bank recently joined a wave of advertisers on Instagram in Canada. Aimed directly at 18- to 24-year-olds, the series of posts included content related to movies. Clinton Braganza, senior vice-president of marketing at Scotiabank, says "the investment in the current series of Instagram ads is small compared to the company's overall media spend, but the spots have reached over 675 000 Canadians aged 18 to 22."[6] Refer to the illustration in Figure 1.2.

The nature of communications generally, and advertising specifically, continues to change. In fact, the combination of changes in consumer behaviour and new media technologies is changing the way people receive advertising messages. Therefore, advertising campaigns must be designed in the context of a bigger picture, a picture that embraces all forms of marketing communications, a picture in which each form of communication plays a role in helping the organization achieve its overall objectives.

Integrated marketing communications (IMC) involves the coordination of all forms of marketing communications into a unified program that maximizes the impact on customers. It embraces many unique yet complementary forms of communication: media advertising (the primary focus of this textbook), interactive communications and social media, direct response communications, public relations, sales promotions, personal selling, and experiential marketing (which includes events and sponsorships). The

FIGURE 1.2

Scotiabank reaches a millennial target through advertisements on Instagram.

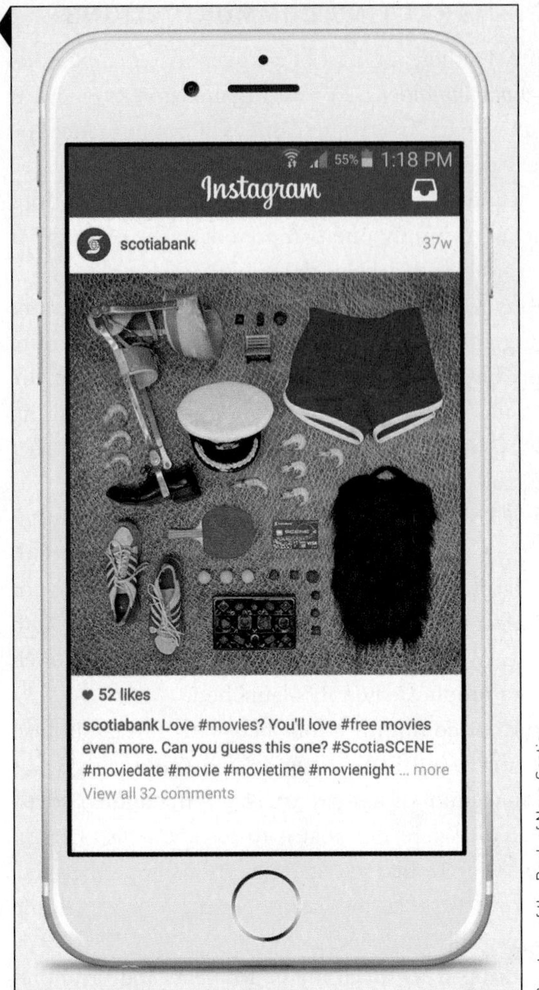

Courtesy of the Bank of Nova Scotia

goal of IMC is to coordinate the various components of the marketing communications mix so that components relevant to a certain marketing situation work together to achieve common objectives. Refer to Figure 1.3 for a visual illustration of the position of IMC in the marketing mix.

The thrust toward IMC has forced traditional advertising agencies to rethink their roles and relationships with clients. Whereas once agencies were solely responsible for advertising, they are now also responsible for providing input into any aspect of the marketing communications mix, or they must work more closely with communications specialists in other fields who provide the necessary expertise. Many traditional advertising agencies have been transformed into marketing communications companies. These changes are presented in more detail in Chapter 2.

Let's introduce briefly each component of the marketing communications mix. Refer to Figure 1.4 for an illustration of the components of the marketing communications mix.

ADVERTISING Advertising was introduced and defined in the previous section. This section will introduce you to some different types of advertising. Advertising is classified based on who the message is directed at. If directed at consumers, it is referred to as *consumer advertising*. If directed at business customers, it is referred to as *business advertising* or *business-to-business advertising*.

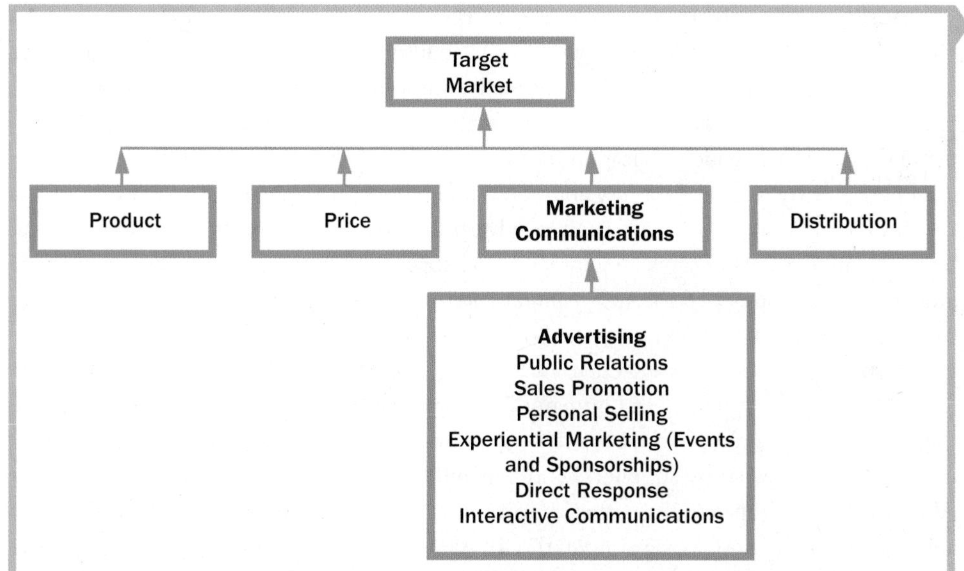

FIGURE 1.3

Marketing communications: its position and role in the marketing mix

Consumer advertising refers to persuasive communications designed to elicit a purchase response from consumers. Such advertising may be from a nationally branded product such as Coca-Cola, Honda automobiles, or Colgate toothpaste. Typically such ads communicate the brand name, the benefits offered, and the availability of the product or service. The services offered by financial institutions such as RBC Financial or BMO Financial Group fall into this classification, as does retail advertising from companies such as Hudson's Bay, Walmart, and Old Navy.

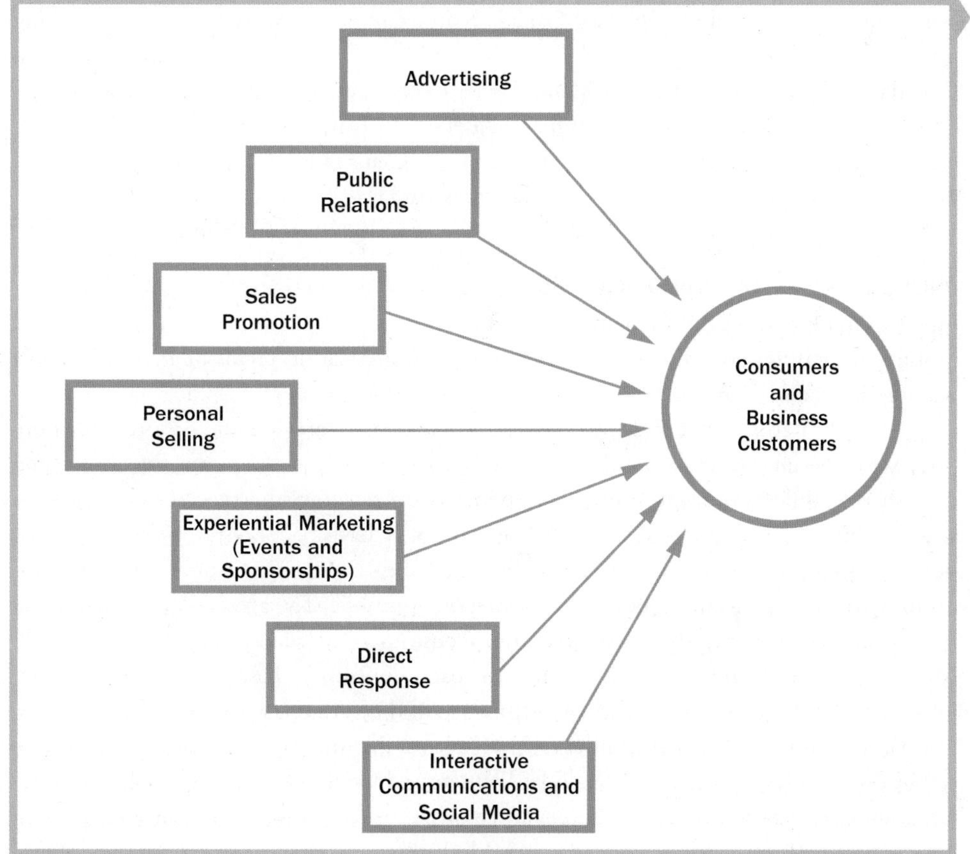

FIGURE 1.4

The concept of integrated marketing communications

"A chain is only as strong as its weakest link." This famous expression applies to integrated marketing communications. IMC programs are successful when all components of the communications mix complement each other. Regardless of the medium used or activity undertaken, the customer must receive a unified message.

Business advertising (or business-to-business advertising) refers to advertising directed by business and industry at business and industry. For example, many manufacturing companies sell consumer products to consumers, but to reach consumers they pass through a channel of distribution. *Trade advertising* encourages distributors to carry a manufacturer's product. There are many trade publications in Canada—*Canadian Grocer* and *Food in Canada,* for example, serve the needs of grocery and household product manufacturers and distributors.

Industrial companies have a need to advertise their products and services to industrial buyers. Manufacturers of capital equipment, accessory equipment, and fabricated parts create awareness for their products through *industrial advertising*. Sending advertising messages directly to companies (direct response advertising) is one option for industrial advertisers, as are publications such as *Equipment Journal, Canadian Packaging,* and *Materials Management and Distribution.*

There are occasions when companies or organizations have a need to communicate with a variety of publics at the same time. These publics include consumers, business customers, governments, suppliers, and the public at large. Often, the intent of such advertising is to improve the organization's image or alter a perception the public has about the organization. For example, the message could focus on an important issue the company shares with the public, or it could inform the public about the organization's social responsibility efforts. Refer to the illustration in Figure 1.5. Such advertising is often referred to as **corporate advertising**. Very often, the organization's public relations department is responsible for this type of advertising.

Both profit and not-for-profit organizations may be involved with advocacy advertising. **Advocacy advertising** is any public communication paid for by an identified sponsor that presents information or a point of view on a publicly recognized, controversial issue. The purpose of advocacy advertising is to influence public opinion. This form of advertising can also be referred to as **cause marketing**—a form of advertising that supports causes that benefit society. Bell Canada is an example of an organization supporting a worthwhile cause. Since 2010 Bell has been associated with mental health issues in Canada through its "Let's Talk" program. Bell actively advertises Let's Talk Day, an annual event, through a multimedia campaign. On Let's Talk Day, 5 cents is donated for every text or long distance call made by Bell customers. Clara Hughes, one of Canada's most distinguished athletes, suffered from mental illness and is the cornerstone of the campaign. In 2015, $6.1 million was raised in 24 hours. Refer to the illustration in Figure 1.6.[7]

ONLINE (INTERACTIVE) COMMUNICATIONS The future of interactive communications is the future of marketing. A bold statement, but it is very true. The combination of online and mobile advertising has eclipsed television and taken the lead in terms of advertising revenue generated in Canada.

The internet is direct and interactive, and consumers are spending more and more time with it—an attractive situation for advertisers. The next big area for advertising growth is mobile communications. The penetration rate for smartphones continues to rise, reaching 68 percent early in 2015. Smartphones have become the preferred access point for the online world.[8] Carriers such as Bell and Rogers are bringing new live TV options to their customers (both companies offer mobile TV apps). When customers access mobile content, they will become accustomed to seeing advertising as well. Mobile media offer marketers the ability to reach consumers based on where they are located at any point in time—perhaps a time when they are ready to buy!

Various advertising opportunities are available on the internet, including search advertising, display advertising (which includes banners and video advertising), publisher-based email, and video game advertising. Similar formats are available for mobile communications.

Social media advertising is also growing. Marketers are seeing the benefit of the engagement opportunities that social media present. Historically, one of the most potent forms of

Courtesy of Suncor

FIGURE 1.5

An example of corporate advertising designed to create goodwill for an organization

influence on brand decisions has been word of mouth, a situation marketers have little control over. However, on a social network such as Facebook, Twitter, or LinkedIn, word of mouth advances to a new level—people like to pass on relevant information to their friends. The participative nature of social media provides marketers the opportunity to converse with customers (a situation where they can listen and gather information about how consumers feel about the company or its brands). Further, social media networks now reach all age segments of the population. Granted, penetration is lower in older age groups, but it is growing!

FIGURE 1.6

Bell actively supports a cause that will benefit Canadian society.

The development of appropriate advertising models for these media remains a work in progress, but organizations are experimenting with social media opportunities.

A recent survey among advertising and marketing decision makers conducted by *Advertising Age* reveals some of the challenges that organizations face with social media communications. Nearly 86 percent of respondents said they use Facebook as a marketing tactic, but only 55 percent say they advertise on Facebook. The general feeling among respondents is that measuring return on investment is difficult, and it is hard to compare social media investment with traditional media channels.[9]

For more insight into how various components of the marketing communications mix can work together to deliver an effective message, read the Advertising in Action vignette **Scotiabank Adds Hockey to Its Seasonal Mix.**

DIRECT RESPONSE COMMUNICATIONS **Direct response communications** is a form of marketing in which messages are delivered directly to potential customers on an individual basis. Direct mail is the most common means of delivering these messages, but other forms of communication such as direct response television, direct response print, and telemarketing also play a role. Organizations that maintain and use databases implement customer relationship management (CRM) programs. Through CRM, a company is capable of communicating unique offers to individual customers in a cost-efficient manner. The cost efficiency of direct communications, when compared to the high costs of mass media advertising, makes direct response an attractive option for marketing communications decision makers.

ADVERTISING IN ACTION

Scotiabank Adds Hockey to its Seasonal Mix

Scotiabank is well known for its "You're richer than you think" advertising campaign. The campaign has enjoyed a successful run using a communications mix that includes television, print, digital, and social media to deliver the message. In addition to advertising, Scotiabank has been active with hockey sponsorships at the community and professional levels in recent years.

It was Scotiabank's extensive involvement with hockey that spawned the idea for a new advertising campaign. Scotiabank sponsors 5000 minor hockey teams and leagues, is the official bank of the National Hockey League, and has sponsorship agreements with all seven Canadian NHL franchises. Scotiabank also has naming rights for Rogers's Wednesday night NHL broadcasts.

Research conducted by the bank revealed that 89 percent of Canadians are involved in hockey in some way—anything from coaching to simply watching NHL games. Being Canadian, it seems, is about eating, sleeping, and breathing hockey. The bank's goal was to tap into that involvement in a manner that would be perceived as different from other brands that also use hockey as a campaign foundation.

The new campaign proposed that Canada has five seasons—the fifth season being "hockey season." One of the commercials features a young girl at a science fair making a passionate speech about Canada's fifth season. In the commercial subtle humour and an emotional tone effectively combine to impact the viewing audience. Another commercial features a little boy trying to decide what number he should have on his team hockey sweater. He asks his father a series of questions, including "How many games did his team lose last year?" (all of them was the answer) and "What number did he wear when he was a kid?" The boy decides to use the number his father wore—another emotional connection!

The commercials were carefully crafted and based on solid consumer research. According to Clinton Braganza, the bank's senior vice-president of marketing, "Canadians told us to keep it authentic and that charming moments are okay." Such insights offered great guidance to the creative team at Bensimon Byrne, the advertising agency that created the commercials.

Associating a brand with a sport is about image transfer. When it is done right, consumers will transfer their feelings about an event onto the brands that sponsor them. Good emotional advertising like Scotiabank's also has an impact. People start to connect brands to the values they care about (in this case hockey), which will affect their attitudes and determine how they will spend their money. This is a concept that Scotiabank clearly understands.

Courtesy of the Bank of Nova Scotia

Adapted from Susan Krashinsky, "Blood, Sweat and Tears: Selling Hockey's Softer Side," *The Globe and Mail*, October 8, 2014, p. B7 and Michelle Dipardo, "Scotiabank Celebrates Hockey with the Fifth Season," *Marketing*, October 7, 2014, www.marketingmag.ca.

Shoppers Drug Mart operates one of the largest consumer databases in Canada. If you possess an Optimum card, you are part of that database, and every time you make a purchase Shoppers is collecting data about you. That data can be used to develop unique offers and messages tailored specifically to your historical buying behaviour. These messages can be efficiently sent to customers by email. Refer to the image in Figure 1.7.

PUBLIC RELATIONS **Public relations** includes a variety of activities that an organization undertakes to influence the attitudes, opinions, and behaviours of interest groups toward

FIGURE 1.7

The Shoppers Optimum card collects data about customer buying patterns.

an organization. For example, a company might issue press releases announcing the launch of a new product. The release would include all of the virtues of the product and the way it will be advertised. The objective is to generate free publicity through the media (e.g., stories about the product will appear on newscasts or in newspapers). These positive news reports make the product or company credible in the eyes of the public. Digital communications, specifically company websites and social media, now play a key role in the execution of public relations strategies.

A brand like Red Bull is a master at planning events while using public relations to effectively promote the event and garner publicity. A recent social media event by Red Bull saw millions of people watch on the internet as Felix Baumgartner jumped from the edge of space (a 39-kilometre jump)—the viewers were literally there with him! Some 40 television stations in 50 countries carried the live feed, and there were 8 million simultaneous views on YouTube—now that's publicity for a brand![10] Refer to the illustration in Figure 1.8.

SALES PROMOTION **Sales promotion** is an activity that encourages an immediate response from consumers and distributors of a product or service. On the consumer side, strategies such as coupons, cash refunds, and contests are offered by manufacturers to encourage buying activity; refer to the illustration in Figure 1.9. Among distributors, a company will offer a variety of price discounts to encourage volume buying or seasonal buying, or to encourage merchandising activity in retail stores. Such strategies are frequently implemented in conjunction with an advertising campaign.

FIGURE 1.8

Red Bull's jump from space produced significant publicity for the brand.

Photo by Keith J. Tuckwell

FIGURE 1.9

Promotion incentives encourage consumers to take more immediate action.

PERSONAL SELLING **Personal selling** is a personalized form of communication that involves a seller presenting the features and benefits of a product or service to a buyer for the purpose of making a sale. To illustrate the importance of personal selling, consider how a product such as Tide to Go (an instant stain remover) or Minute Maid Simply Orange (100 percent orange juice in a carafe-shaped bottle) arrives on the shelf at your local supermarket. The sales representative for these products would have to present the merits of these brands to a buyer at the supermarket's head office. If the buyer doesn't accept the offer that is put forth (e.g., if both the quality of the sales promotion and the price discounts are unacceptable), these products will not be available in the supermarket, even though they may be supported with an introductory advertising campaign that creates brand awareness. The goal of personal selling is to secure widespread distribution of the product, one retail account at a time.

EXPERIENTIAL MARKETING **Experiential marketing** is a blend of marketing communications disciplines that engage people with a brand in a more personal way; often the communication is done face to face or through another form of communication that reaches a person directly. The core components of experiential marketing are events and sponsorships. The customer experience could be anything from attending an event where a sponsor's product is freely distributed to being part of a unique branded event that becomes the focal point of an IMC campaign.

Rather than plan a unique event, an organization may choose to sponsor an existing event. A sponsor provides money to an event in return for specified marketing and advertising privileges. Some research indicates that consumers respond positively to companies and brands that sponsor events—they have a more favourable impression of them. One recent study identified Molson and Visa as the most active Canadian sponsors. Visa was the brand mentioned most often by respondents.[11] Such a result would indicate that Visa's investment in sponsorship activity is paying dividends.

Marketers see events and sponsorships as useful vehicles for reaching their target market directly and for improving brand awareness. Sports sponsorship is an important

FIGURE 1.10

Worthwhile events and sponsorships help build a company's image and allow consumers to engage with the company.

© Hand-out/Canadian Tire Jumpstart/Newscom

ingredient in Canadian Tire's marketing strategy. In 2013, Canadian Tire signed an eight-year sponsorship deal to be a premier national sponsor for the Canadian Olympic team. Canadian Tire also partnered with Hockey Canada to help break down the barriers for kids who want to play. The company's "Jump Start" program helps kids of low-income families cover the costs of playing youth sports. Well-known hockey stars such as Jonathan Toews and Hayley Wickenheiser are featured in communications for this program.[12] Refer to the image in Figure 1.10.

Using Advertising Effectively

Prior to investing any amount of money in advertising, a wise manager will assess conditions in the marketplace. An assessment of market conditions, product life-cycle status, competitive activity, and an organization's commitment to advertising will allow the manager to make better decisions about how to advertise and how much to spend on it. Such an assessment may indicate that advertising is not always the right solution.

MARKET (PRODUCT CATEGORY) DEMAND

One of the first considerations to review is the basic demand for all products in a category. Is the product category (market) growing, and if so, at what rate of growth? Or is the overall category mature or in decline? If, for example, a product category is relatively new, a significant investment in advertising is necessary to educate and inform consumers about the product's benefits. The introduction of a new product concept is quite challenging, since the marketing communications must first make customers recognize a need and then stimulate a purchase response based on that recognition.

When Molson Coors Canada launched a product called Mad Jack, a beverage that combines beer with cider, it was the first of its kind on the market. Granted, many new beer beverages have been launched in recent years, but the immediate advertising challenge was to create interest in a sweet, apple-flavoured beer. The beverage was aimed at consumers who don't like the bitterness of traditional beers. The launch campaign included media advertising, social media, and in-store sampling. Refer to the image in Figure 1.11.

Courtesy of Molson Coors Canada

FIGURE 1.11

Advertising and other forms of marketing communications played a key role in the launch of Mad Jack apple cider beer.

Conversely, if a market is more mature and all competing products are firmly established, other marketing and marketing communications activities may take precedence over advertising. For example, companies like Coca-Cola and PepsiCo, which market cold beverages in a variety of product categories, have difficult choices to make regarding the nature and intensity of advertising. Sales in soft drinks (the core of each company) are declining as consumers migrate to healthier or alternative beverages (a lifestyle consideration) such as fruit juice, water, and energy drinks. Each company will invest in advertising but may give less support to its core soft drink beverages and provide more dollars to growing categories. In this way, the companies balance their investment according to the stage the market is in and the life-cycle stage of each product. See the next section for product life-cycle considerations.

PRODUCT LIFE CYCLE

The stage of a brand in its product life cycle also influences decisions on advertising. A **product life cycle** is defined as the movement of a product through a series of four stages, from its introduction to its eventual withdrawal from the market. According to traditional life-cycle theory, a product starts out slowly in the introduction stage, experiences rapid sales increases in the growth stage, experiences marginal growth or decline each year as it matures, and then enters the decline stage in which sales drop off at an increasing rate each year. The conditions and characteristics that are present in each stage of the life cycle are quite different. Therefore, different strategies and tactics are used in each stage.

INTRODUCTION STAGE The critical stages for advertising are the introduction and growth stages. The *introduction stage* is typically a period of slow sales growth as a new product idea is introduced to the market. Losses are frequently incurred because of the high initial investment required to launch a product. For example, Unilever faced a big challenge when it launched a new men's grooming line called Dove Men+Care (a range of deodorants and shower gels). Dove is a successful brand in female-grooming categories, so the brand is perceived as feminine. One of the objectives of the launch campaign was to alter male perceptions of the brand—a difficult task. Beyond that, Dove had to communicate the core benefits of the product lines and give men a strong reason to buy. To do so, the brand used basketball stars (former and present) such as Magic Johnson, Larry Bird, and Dwayne Wade to discuss being comfortable in their own skin, which, along with the common meaning of the expression *self-assurance,* was meant more literally to convey the moisturizing properties of Dove Men+Care's soaps and shower gels. Results have been positive—Dove Men+Care quickly achieved a 4 percent market share, a figure that exceeded company expectations.[13]

Trial purchase is another objective in an introductory campaign. Therefore, promotional incentives such as coupons or trial-size samples are common. The combination of media advertising and sales promotions requires a sizable budget and a powerful message—the marketing team must do it right the first time out. This short-term financial commitment enables the brand to grow before new and competing innovations occur. Profits will be generated at a later stage of the life cycle.

GROWTH STAGE The product's *growth stage* is the period of rapid consumer acceptance. Several competitive brands will enter the market to get a piece of the action, which means that the original product must continue to invest aggressively in advertising to build market share. In the growth stage, marketing communications performs a dual role. There is still ample opportunity to attract new users, so creating awareness remains a priority; but because competitors have entered the market, objectives must also focus on brand preference. A brand must clearly distinguish itself from competing brands (i.e., give customers a valid reason why they should buy one brand over another). For example, there are several brands available in the toothpaste category that are geared toward people with sensitive gums and teeth. Colgate Sensitive Pro-Relief differentiates itself by stating that it actually repairs exposed nerves to help repair teeth—quite a compelling message. Refer to the image in Figure 1.12.

The competitive nature of the growth stage requires that an advertiser maintain a strong advertising presence; the financial investment will remain high. Deciding how much to spend is often difficult. It is possible that competitors with less market share but with ambitious growth plans will force another company to spend more on marketing communications than it desires. In terms of strategy, the advertiser should be looking at more cost-efficient media vehicles that reach its target market more directly. The investment in advertising should produce a financial return. Unlike the introduction stage, sales are rising rapidly and profits materialize.

MATURITY STAGE The *maturity stage* is characterized by a slowdown in sales growth (marginal growth and marginal decline); the product has been accepted by most of its potential buyers. Profits stabilize and begin to decline because of the expenses incurred in defending the brand's market share position.

When a product is in the mature stage, advertising tends to give way to other forms of marketing communications. Assuming that new strategies are not implemented to

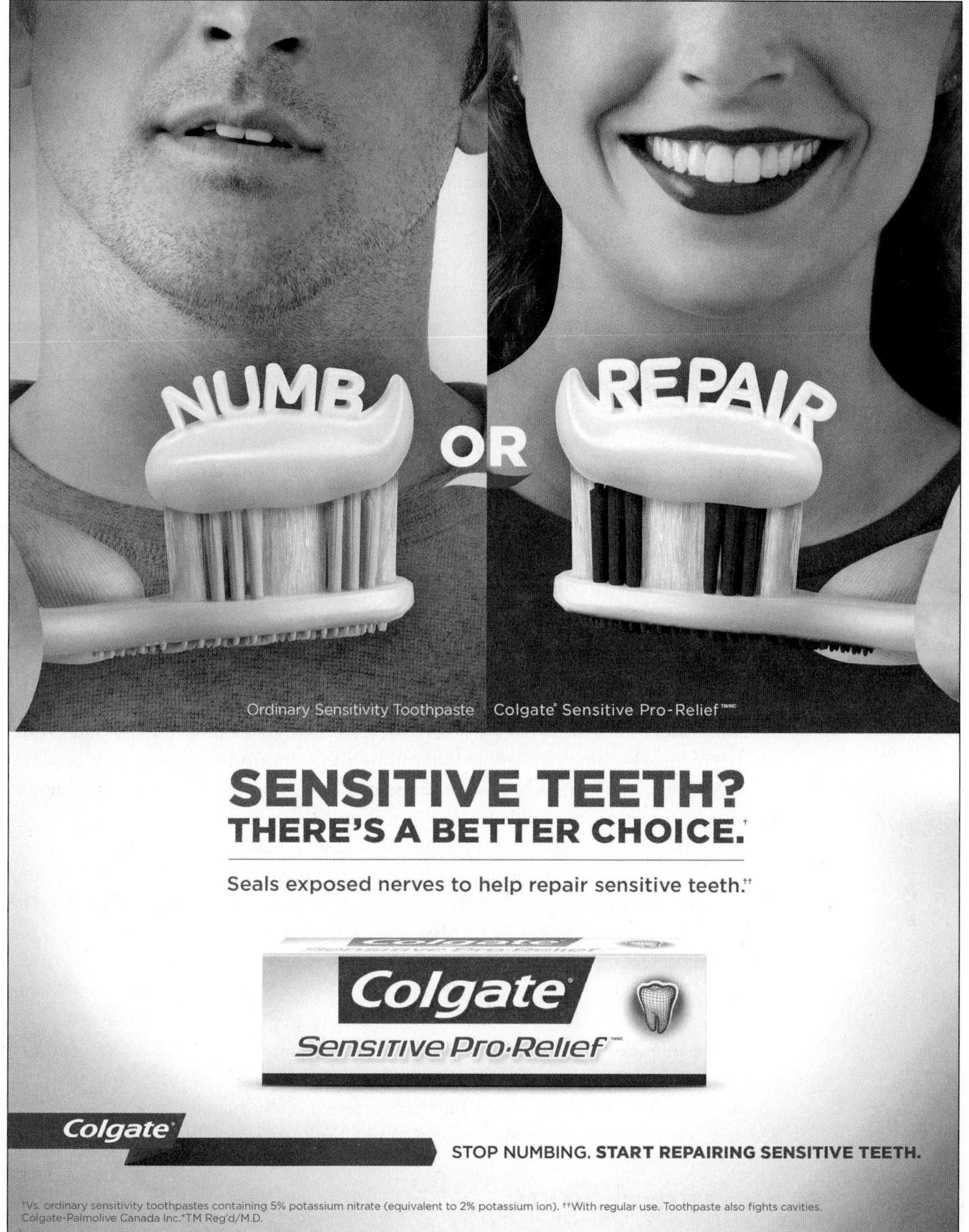

Courtesy of Colgate-Palmolive

FIGURE 1.12

Colgate Sensitive Pro-Relief differentiates itself from competitors by emphasizing that it seals exposed nerves to help repair sensitive teeth.

rejuvenate the product, funds formerly allocated to advertising the product may be shifted into other areas, such as sales promotion and price discounting. In the mature stage, the objective is to conserve money rather than spend it. There are exceptions to every rule, however, since this is a period in which the only way to grow is to steal business from the competitor(s).

In Canada's beer market, for example, sales are declining modestly from year to year—an aging population that drinks less beer and a consumer shift toward wine and mixed drinks has had a negative effect on market volume. But that doesn't mean the big brands have stopped advertising! Rather, marketing managers must make tough decisions on which brands should get advertising support and at what level of spending. It wasn't long ago that Molson Canadian and Labatt Blue were market leaders, and each brand received significant advertising support. Now the owners of these brands have shifted their priorities and are spending more advertising dollars on American brands, such as Coors Light and Budweiser. Molson Canadian is making a comeback, however, another sign of shifting priorities. This illustration shows that companies invest in brands where the opportunity (financial return) is greatest. For more insight into a successful campaign for Molson Canadian, read the Advertising in Action vignette **The Beer Fridge: Molson Canadian's Patriotic Advertising Campaign.**

Maturity is the time when many brands try to reposition themselves in the market. Given the nature of competitor activity, the abundance of brand alternatives, and changing consumer preferences, there is an opportunity to rejuvenate a brand. When trying to rejuvenate a brand, a company will spend heavily in the short term to implement direction. For example, Mountain Equipment Co-op was originally positioned as a store selling products for hard-core adventurers. Confronting an aging target market with new, more relaxed recreation endeavours in mind, the company altered its product mix to appeal to a broader cross-section of the population. Advertising played a key role in introducing the change to the marketplace.

Maturity is also a time when a brand adopts a defensive strategy and tries to protect market share by spending only what is absolutely necessary on advertising. Promotions that encourage brand loyalty are popular at this stage (e.g., cash refunds, contests, premium offers) since they are designed to encourage repeat purchases and multiple purchases.

DECLINE STAGE The *decline stage* occurs when sales begin to drop rapidly and profits erode. Products become obsolete as many consumers shift to more innovative products entering the market. Price cuts are a common marketing strategy at this stage, as competing brands attempt to protect their share in a declining market.

Objectives involve planning and implementing withdrawal from the market, because the costs of maintaining a product in decline are quite high. A rather exaggerated illustration of product withdrawal was Suzuki's decision to stop selling cars in Canada. The company had been "monitoring market conditions carefully and, after reviewing the long-term viability of automotive product for Canada concluded it was no longer feasible to produce and sell cars in the Canadian market."[14] At the time of the decision (March 2013), Suzuki's unit sales were down 30 percent compared with the year before.

Companies do not have the resources to support all products equally. Therefore, a wise company has products at various stages of their life cycles so that marketing strategies can be managed effectively within financial constraints. In Suzuki's case, the company decided to concentrate on its motorcycles, ATVs, and other recreational vehicles.

COMPETITIVE ADVANTAGE

Prior to investing in marketing communications, a brand must offer something unique and desirable to a market segment—a competitive advantage. A distinctive message must be planted in the consumer's mind. The most common way to show advantage is to *demonstrate the superiority* of a given product by comparing it to a similar product or by simply making significant claims about what the product will do. Product claims must be meaningful to consumers. In the illustration that appears in Figure 1.12, Colgate clearly identifies the competitive advantage that separates it from other brands on the market.

ADVERTISING IN ACTION

The Beer Fridge: Molson Canadian's Patriotic Ad Campaign

When you're competing in a huge but declining market and your market share is flat, you have to try something unique to turn things around. That's the situation Molson Canadian faced. Younger beer drinkers who traditionally were the heaviest consumers of beer are gravitating to other alcoholic drinks, such as cider, bourbon, wine, and craft beers—a key factor affecting beer sales and Molson Canadian's position in the market. What unique idea would help turn things around? Molson's ad agency, Rethink, was given that challenge.

Rethink came up with the idea of using a bright red beer fridge adorned with the maple leaf (how Canadian is that!) that would be dropped in the middle of public squares in England, France, and Belgium. The locked fridge would invoke a lot of curiosity, and it could only be opened with a Canadian passport. We won't go into the technical details of how it worked, but those details were considerable.

According to Rethink, the spot was based on insight that the farther Canadians travel, the more Canadian they get. Apparently Canadians react well to validation from outside Canada. Originally planned as a short-term campaign starting on Canada Day in 2013, the fridge's popularity forced a change in long-term advertising strategy.

To reach the younger target, social media would play a key role. Digital videos that can be shared among friends go a long way in rebuilding confidence in a brand. The first video of the fridge's European excursion received more than 6 million views and an estimated $50 million in free media exposure from press coverage in Canada and abroad. Suddenly the phone was ringing, and Canadians living in other parts of Europe and the world wanted the fridge to come to their country!

The Molson Canadian beer fridge went on to fame and fortune during the Sochi Olympics (Molson is a sponsor of the Canadian Olympic team) and was also part of Canada Day celebrations in 2014. For that day the fridge would only open by singing "O Canada." Other media components of the campaign included television, out-of-home, and print.

The beer fridge campaign was a huge success for Molson Canadian. Return on investment was significant. In a $9 billion industry, market share grew by 0.1 percent. That may not seem like a lot, but it's the equivalent of about 7.6 million bottles of beer and a profit increase of about $6 million. There was absolutely no increase in advertising spending from previous years—a sure sign the advertising had a significant impact!

© Neil Davidson/The Canadian Press

Adapted from Susan Krashinsky, "Cheers, to a Winning Ad Campaign," *The Globe and Mail*, February 20, 2015, p. B7 and Raeann Fera, "Molson Canadian Beer Fridge," *Marketing*, August 2013, p. 19.

Another way of showing advantage is to communicate **product innovation**—the idea that the product is on the cutting edge of technology or research and development. Innovation is extremely important in the smartphone market category. Apple and Samsung position their brands on the cutting edge of technology whenever a new version of their phones is launched. Innovation is often directly linked to the design of the product (the combination of the exterior appearance with what's inside is what innovation is about in this market). When Samsung launched the Galaxy S6, the marketing emphasis was on a multitude of benefits, such as its slim design, large high-definition screen, better

© imagebroker/Alamy Stock Photo

FIGURE 1.13

Red Bull advertising images appeal to the active and adventurous instincts of the target market it is pursuing.

camera, being waterproof and dust proof, dual speakers, and fingerprint scanning capabilities. Samsung's advertising said, "The future is here."

A more recent phenomenon in advertising is the progressive use of **lifestyle advertising** to differentiate among products. In this type of advertising, the advertiser targets lifestyle aspirations by appealing to the emotional side of the purchase decision and associating a product with the lifestyle of a certain market segment. The exhilaration and adventure of driving certain automobiles as portrayed in television commercials is often enough to get the target market to buy the vehicle. In the beverage industry, brands such as Red Bull and Mountain Dew associate themselves with lifestyles attractive to the young target market they are pursuing. The images in their ads portray action, adventure, and a certain element of risk. Refer to the image in Figure 1.13.

COMPETITIVE ENVIRONMENT

Keeping track of what competitors are doing and how much they are investing in advertising and marketing communications is important. In many product categories, it is common for the brand leader and the brand challenger (a strong number two in market share) to invest heavily in advertising to build market share. Followers or lower-ranking brands would not have the financial resources to emulate such spending. The quick-serve restaurant market offers a good example. McDonald's and Tim Hortons are big spenders every year, but what about Wendy's, A&W, Harvey's, and KFC? Brands that rank further down the list do advertise, but they need to evaluate more efficient spending alternatives to protect their market share.

PRODUCT QUALITY

It is essential that a product live up to the promise advertising makes. Advertising messages focus on the unique selling points of the product and the benefits the customer will derive from them. Getting the customer to try a product once, at great expense to the company, only to be disappointed in the quality or whatever the primary benefit was supposed to be (e.g., performance or durability) is a waste of money. It is imperative that the brand meet consumer expectations (e.g., deliver as promised) so that repeat purchases occur in the longer term. Product quality issues are inconsistent with the CRM programs that many companies are now implementing. The long-term objective is to build brand loyalty, and when customers are satisfied with the quality of a product, it is more difficult for a competitor to get them to switch brands.

MANAGEMENT COMMITMENT

How management perceives the value of advertising is also important. A management group that possesses a short-term view (e.g., advertising is an expense item on a profit-and-loss statement) of how advertising will benefit the company will not be committed to a plan that requires a long time period to achieve the desired results. When such a view persists, budget cuts are likely to occur during the course of a year, and since advertising spending is a highly visible item on the profit-and-loss statement, it is one of the first items reviewed in a profit-squeeze situation. Any kind of reduced budget support while a plan is in midstream will mean objectives won't be achieved. The entire plan must be reassessed, and objectives might need to change. In the long term, cutbacks to the advertising budget have harmful effects on brand development in the marketplace.

Conversely, a senior management team that views advertising and other forms of marketing communications as a long-term investment is usually more willing to commit funds to see a campaign through to completion. Obviously such an attitude provides a preferable operating environment for managers responsible for developing advertising plans and to external organizations that prepare and implement various components of a marketing communications plan.

Issues and Trends Influencing Contemporary Advertising Planning

The advertising industry often faces controversy with the public over the images and messages that some advertisers deliver—do something out of the ordinary or in an unexpected way, and you can face the wrath of the public! As well, the industry must continually adapt to new technology, a changing media landscape, and lifestyle changes among consumers—specifically how they consume media. This section examines some of the key issues and trends faced by today's practitioners.

TRANSITION TO INTEGRATED MARKETING COMMUNICATIONS

Organizations today are searching for complete solutions for their communications needs. There was a time when various plans were developed separately by distinct organizations that operated independently and specialized in certain areas. As indicated earlier, the environment has changed. Advertisers are looking at different ways of delivering messages and are embracing new opportunities presented by public relations techniques, experiential marketing, and social media communications. Public relations (PR) already enjoys a much higher profile as organizations search for less expensive yet still powerful ways to communicate. Effective PR strategies can secure independent third-party endorsements by the media—endorsements that have more impact on buying decisions than media advertising does. For example, if a blogger who is an expert in computer technology endorses a new Apple product, the endorsement will help create initial demand for the product—at no expense to Apple!

Essentially, there is a gradual shift away from traditional forms of advertising. To illustrate, it is now common for branded products to appear in television shows and movies, a concept referred to as *product placement*. Going a step further, many organizations are now producing their own content for placement directly in the media, be it a YouTube video or a feature story about a product that will appear on a television show or in the print media. This form of communication is referred to as content marketing or native advertising—concepts that will be presented in more detail later in the text. Finding the best solution for any particular marketing problem now involves much creative thinking regarding the best means of communication to employ.

LIFESTYLE CHANGE AND ITS IMPACT ON MEDIA CONSUMPTION

Keeping track of how consumers' lifestyles are changing and how consumers engage with the media is a constant challenge for advertisers. Consumers today are less reliant on traditional media (television, radio, newspapers, and magazines) and more reliant on digital communications (online and mobile) for receiving content and commercial messages. For example, people still watch a lot of television but are doing so on their laptop, tablet, or mobile phone. A recent report titled "4-Screen Canadians: A Glimpse into Multi-Screen Media Behaviour" revealed that 17 percent of Canadian internet users currently have access to four screens. While the computer remains a key device, the report stated that Canadians are increasingly relying on portable devices for activities such as social networking and reading online news.[15] Such switches in allegiance force advertisers to evaluate different media choices. The goal of communications now is to deliver the same message through a variety of media to reach and influence the target audience effectively.

Breaking through the clutter of advertising and reaching the intended target will be a more daunting prospect for advertisers. Clouding this challenge even further is the multitasking behaviour of people, particularly young people. With customers watching television while chatting with friends on a cellphone or socializing on Facebook, it is difficult for an advertising message to break through.

TECHNOLOGY: THE INTERNET AS CONTENT DISTRIBUTOR FOR ALL MEDIA

In the future, no single media delivery channel will drive the marketing industry, but the internet will become the hub for content and the mobile phone will be the means of distribution. If you leave home without your phone, you will probably go back and get it! That demonstrates the daily importance of this device. It's your connection to the world.

Technology has forced traditional media to adapt, and publishers and broadcasters are delivering more content online than ever before. Newspapers and magazines offer digital editions, radio stations broadcast online, and television networks stream shows online, all of which present new advertising challenges and opportunities. Publishers and broadcasters are following their readers', listeners', and viewers' behaviour patterns.

The television industry, for example, is losing viewers as consumers prefer to view their favourite shows online and at a time that suits them, a concept referred to as **on-demand viewing**. Newspapers and magazines are losing subscribers each year, and the future outlook of hardcopy editions is bleak. They have responded by creating their own digital content. Right now the average weekly reach of digital newspapers is as high as 39 percent of readers for some daily newspapers.[16] For broadcasters and publishers, the advertising challenge is to recover lost advertising revenue in their traditional offerings by encouraging advertisers to place ads in their digital offerings. That transition has been slow, and as a result the print media has suffered immensely from a financial standpoint.

With each passing year, consumers are spending more time online, so it's relatively easy to predict what lies ahead. Factor in our insatiable appetite for digital gadgets like smartphones and you quickly see why the internet and how we access it will become the epicentre of the media universe. Many believe the smartphone will be the hub of everything—not to mention the budding influence of wearable devices that are hitting the marketplace. These trends create challenges and opportunities for media planners who make recommendations to clients on how best to spend their advertising dollars.

ADVERTISING IS BECOMING MORE ANALYTIC IN NATURE

Having access to good information has been the foundation for wise decision making by advertisers and the organizations (communications agencies) that produce advertising campaigns for them. Sound market research provides insight into consumer attitudes and behaviours that can be used to create effective messages. As well, the abundance of data available regarding media consumption trends have guided the development of media placement strategies—how much to spend, where to spend, and in what media.

The shift to digital media has presented new opportunities and challenges for decision makers. The process for buying and selling media space is completely different for digital media than for broadcast and print media. Advertisers are gradually adjusting to the change. In the past, media decisions were carefully planned by an advertising agency, presented to the client for approval, and rates and placements were then negotiated and confirmed with the media outlets—print, broadcast, out-of-home, and so on. This is a time-consuming process with many decisions made along the way.

In contrast, the digital media buying and selling process is completed in real time using a process called **programmatic media buying**. This concept will be discussed in detail in Chapter 12. For now, simply consider that digital media placement is determined by software and algorithms instead of by a person doing it manually. The system operates in real time with no advance planning and no negotiation (which sounds frightening to an executive accustomed to making such decisions). The automated system is structured so that the message (ad placement) reaches the intended target audience (based on current data available). The process considers the advertiser's objectives, the advertising inventory available, consumer data, and various ad formats. It delivers an effective media placement plan almost instantaneously—a rather dramatic change in process!

This system offers unprecedented efficiency and is becoming a mainstream marketing tool that will undoubtedly expand into other media. It is a system ideally suited for reaching today's consumers, who are constantly on the move and connected to their electronic devices.

THE ISSUE OF PRIVACY

Organizations are collecting a lot of information about consumers—anything from how much we spend, how often we shop, where we shop, and what we buy to how much time we spend online and where that time is spent. As young people reading this text, you may want to be careful of the information you post on your Facebook page. A lot of the stuff that excites you right now may be embarrassing later on!

The ever-expanding ways computers can search, store, and archive information about us means that the notion of privacy is becoming obsolete. Everyone must now recognize that businesses (and the social media networks are a business) have the technology to track their customers and develop detailed profiles of their preferences to generate profits.[17] The programmatic media buying system described in the previous section is based on such data. To demonstrate, you may not object to the fact that the customer loyalty card you possess collects and keeps information on your purchases, but you must recognize that the information will be used to try and sell you something at a time when you are most likely to buy.

People are showing concern for how their personal information is being used. A survey among 37 000 US and Canadian online adults revealed that 70 percent were concerned about their social security/insurance numbers and credit cards. The survey also revealed that younger people are more open. For example, 47 percent of 55- to 64-year-olds were concerned about access to behavioural data, while among 18- to 24-year-olds only 33 percent were concerned.[18] Marketers like data, and if they use that data properly it will help their businesses grow. That said, marketers must not let the data go awry or be used improperly; marketers don't want to face the wrath of an angry public in the social media.

SOCIAL MEDIA AND ITS INFLUENCE

Social media is not just about young people anymore. All age groups are on social media to some degree, with baby boomers being the fastest-growing segment of users. Canada has the highest social media network penetration in the world as some 82 percent of Canadians use a social network. Further, 55 percent of online Canadians (19 000 000 people) are active on Facebook, the top social network in the country. In terms of time spent with social media, Canadians spend an average of 2 hours on social networks each day—that leaves much less direct time for conventional media like television, radio, and newspapers.[19] Other popular social media sites include Twitter, Google+, LinkedIn, Pinterest, and Instagram.

With so many important target audiences using social media, a logical extension of a brand's marketing communications strategy must be to include social media. The more popular sites mentioned above are excited about their future financial prospects once their advertising models are more finely tuned. They all have advertising models in place, but they are constantly experimenting with new techniques to find a model that is financially prosperous for the advertisers and themselves.

The challenge for marketers is to find a way to capitalize on the popularity of social media. Thus far, marketing executives have expressed mixed opinions on the medium's effectiveness in building a brand's profits. Marketing organizations seek a return on investment for their advertising expenditures, but the medium's inability to measure this is the biggest problem facing social media advertising campaigns, according to a study among marketing and advertising executives. Forty percent of these executives said measuring or defining return on investment was the biggest challenge.[20]

Marketing executives in another research study offered some good news about the impact of social media. These executives perceive social media to be an effective marketing and advertising channel and define effectiveness differently. The large majority of respondents agreed that social media were effective in building market share and improving sales when customers started talking about their brands positively online.[21] But the executives say it's more about the conversation a brand can have with customers that pays dividends. Effective two-way communication between customers and an organization produces positive word of mouth, an intangible that can't be underestimated in brand buying decisions.

THE DELIVERY OF INAPPROPRIATE OR CONTROVERSIAL MESSAGES

The impact of a commercial message is always subject to review by critics of advertising. Rightly or wrongly, planned or unplanned, advertisers sometimes deliver commercial messages that spark controversy. Many advertisers tolerate the controversy as long as the campaign is delivering sales. Other advertisers bow to public pressure and remove the offending message. Key issues often focus on using sex and sex-role stereotyping in advertising, presenting dangerous or inappropriate situations in commercial messages, and misleading the public with confusing messages.

SEX IN ADVERTISING A common complaint about advertising revolves around the use of sex to sell something. As an old saying goes, "Sex sells!" So what's the beef among members of contemporary Canadian society? Using sex appeal in an appropriate manner and

© Rudi Von Briel/PhotoEdit

FIGURE 1.14

Sexual appeals are a popular yet sometimes controversial means of attracting a target audience.

for appropriate products seems natural, but gratuitous sex is something consumers shouldn't have to tolerate.

Product categories such as cosmetics, lingerie, and fashion use sex as an effective motivator. Occasionally, though, an advertiser will step over some line and use an image that sparks controversy. There is a common belief that if core customers (as opposed to the general public) don't find the use of sexual imagery offensive, they may be on to something. Calvin Klein ads, for example, show lots of skin and couples enjoying each other's company; their ads are provocative and attention grabbing (refer to the image in Figure 1.14). In the age of enlightenment, this type of imagery should be acceptable, but you can be the judge of that.

DANGEROUS OR DISTURBING MESSAGES The strategy of depicting dangerous or disturbing situations in advertising messages has come under much scrutiny in recent years. Automakers are under the gun for showing unsafe driving practices in ads. In some cases dangerous driving practices are glamorized. Brands such as Red Bull and Mountain Dew tend to live on the edge. The Mountain Dew "Do the Dew" campaign presents all kinds of risky and adventurous images, and it does so for a good reason—these images attract eyeballs! To many people in the advertising industry, this style of ad fits with a young, contemporary lifestyle. Is there anything wrong with that? Parents may object to the imagery, but such imagery does suggest that advertising has some impact on shaping attitudes and behaviours.

ING Direct (now Tangerine) was forced to pull an ad called "Are You Suffering" (part of an retirement savings plan campaign) that showed an image of a man sitting forlornly on a chair outside and another lying motionless on a couch. The men were "cured" when their wives directed them to ING. ING did not anticipate a negative response, but there were many complaints from mental health professionals accusing ING of reinforcing negative stereotypes about mental illness. ING ultimately made the right decision about the advertisement.[22]

MISLEADING ADVERTISING Sometimes ads can mislead the public or simply misrepresent the brand. Sometimes the public misinterprets the advertiser's message and the campaign backfires. Control over misleading advertising is the responsibility of Advertising Standards Canada. (More information about its role in the advertising industry appears later in this chapter.)

The most common complaints about misleading ads concern the accuracy and clarity of the message. To demonstrate, consider how some food products make claims related to grains on their product labels and in their advertisements. In the snack aisle, do you buy original or multigrain versions of a product? You may get the impression that some salty snack foods are actually healthy for you! Terms like *multigrain* and *whole wheat* can mislead consumers. Brands claim they are made with whole grains, but they also contain a significant amount of refined flour—these products are not necessarily better for you.[23] Food for thought the next time you buy a package of Tostitos or Goldfish Crackers made with whole grain.

A survey released by Advertising Standards Canada revealed that 42 percent of Canadians have recently been exposed to an ad they found unacceptable. The top reason for being unacceptable was the misleading or unrealistic depiction of the advertised product or service. Among survey respondents, 65 percent said they have stopped purchasing a product because they deemed its advertising unacceptable.[24] These findings should be a wakeup call for advertisers and the potential claims they make about their products.

Laws and Regulations

The marketing communications industry in Canada is highly regulated. Regulation and control come from three primary sources: the Canadian Radio-television and Telecommunications Commission (CRTC), which governs all broadcasting laws, including advertising; Advertising Standards Canada, which administers regulations based on codes of practice that are voluntarily established; and the Competition Bureau (a federal agency), which works through the Competition Act, an act that establishes laws and regulations for all marketing activity in Canada.

CANADIAN RADIO-TELEVISION AND TELECOMMUNICATIONS COMMISSION (CRTC)

The CRTC is an independent public authority in charge of regulating and supervising Canadian broadcasting and telecommunications. It serves the public interest and is governed by the Broadcasting Act and the Telecommunications Act. The Broadcasting Act ensures that Canadians have access to a wide variety of high-quality Canadian programming. The Telecommunications Act ensures access to reliable telephone and other telecommunications services at affordable prices. Generally, the role of the CRTC is to maintain a delicate balance, in the public interest, among the cultural, social, and economic goals of the legislation on broadcasting and telecommunications.[25]

Canadian content is the cornerstone of the Broadcasting Act. It addresses several key issues:

- The creation and production of Canadian programs and music
- Financial support for the broadcasting system for the creation of Canadian content
- The way of determining how much Canadian content must be aired on radio and television
- The ratio of Canadian and non-Canadian content distributed by Canadian cable companies and satellite providers
- Canadian ownership and control of the broadcasting system

In addressing these issues, the CRTC has the overall mandate of enforcing Parliament's intent that the national broadcasting system serve a national purpose. There are numerous broadcasting and telecommunications regulations that the CRTC is also responsible for.

For a complete listing of these regulations and more information about the role of the CRTC, visit the CRTC website at www.crtc.gc.ca.

ADVERTISING STANDARDS CANADA

Advertising Standards Canada (ASC) is the industry body committed to creating and maintaining community confidence in advertising. Its mission is to ensure the integrity and viability of advertising through industry self-regulation. ASC members include advertisers, agencies, media organizations, and suppliers to the advertising sector.

Through ASC Clearance Services, ASC reviews advertising to facilitate compliance with specific laws and regulations in five regulated categories: alcoholic beverages, children's advertising, consumer drugs, cosmetics, and nonalcoholic beverages.

ASC also conducts ongoing research to gain insight into consumer perspectives on advertising and advertising standards. Standards are articulated in the Canadian Code of Advertising Standards (the Code). Some key findings of ASC's research include the following:[26]

- 86 percent of Canadians believe advertising offers them some value
- 52 percent of Canadians agree that advertising helps shape society
- 83 percent of Canadians feel it is important to have rules and regulations for advertising
- 65 percent of Canadians say they are likely to stop buying a product if an advertisement is unacceptable to them

The Code is the principal instrument of self-regulation. It was developed to promote the professional practice of advertising and forms the basis upon which advertising is evaluated in response to consumer complaints. The Code is supplemented by other codes and guidelines, including gender portrayal guidelines, which are intended to help advertising practitioners develop positive images of women and men in their commercial messages. The Code also addresses the following concerns about advertising:

- Accuracy and clarity of messages
- Disguised advertising techniques
- Price claims
- "Bait and switch"
- Guarantees
- Comparative advertising
- Testimonials
- Professional and scientific claims
- Imitation
- Safety
- Superstitions and fears
- Advertising directed at children and minors
- Unacceptable depictions and portrayals

For more complete details about the role of Advertising Standards Canada, see Appendix II of this textbook and visit the ASC website at www.adstandards.com.

As discussed in the previous section of this chapter, advertisers are often accused of using inappropriate sexual or other portrayals or showing situations that encourage people to take risks, but rarely is that their intention. Most campaigns focus on a particular target who understands more clearly the advertiser's intent. Nonetheless, complaints do get raised. In 2014, ASC received 1286 complaints for 1075 advertisements. ASC upheld 79 complaints regarding 50 ads. The majority of the upheld complaints (95 percent of them) were about misleading advertising, omitting relevant information, and not clearly stating all pertinent details of an offer.[27]

COMPETITION BUREAU

The Competition Bureau is responsible for the administration and enforcement of the Competition Act, a law that governs business conduct and marketing practices in Canada. The Competition Act contains criminal and civil provisions to address false, misleading, and deceptive marketing practices. Among the practices that come under scrutiny are deceptive telemarketing, deceptive notices of winning prizes, and pyramid selling schemes. Other provisions prohibit representations that are not based on adequate and proper tests, misleading warranties and guarantees, false or misleading price representations, and untrue testimonials.

Organizations that violate these laws and regulations are subject to financial penalties and other actions. Even the most respected Canadian companies violate certain laws at one time or another. Just recently the bureau determined that Bell Canada was violating the Do Not Call List (a set of regulations that all marketing organizations must follow) and fined the company a record-setting penalty of $1.3 million. The CRTC, the body that regulates telecommunications companies, had been besieged with calls from frustrated citizens complaining about calls that interrupted dinner conversations with unwanted sales pitches.[28] Breaking advertising laws does have consequences! For more insight into the Competition Bureau, visit its website at www.competitionbureau.gc.ca.

SUMMARY

Advertising is any paid form of marketing communication designed to influence the thought patterns and purchase behaviour of a target audience. The specific role of advertising is to influence potential customers to respond favourably to a product by communicating relevant information about the product, such as how the product will satisfy a need. It is the combination of message and medium that influences a consumer to buy. In terms of media usage, advertisers are moving toward digital media and away from traditional media such as television, magazines, and newspapers. Today, the internet is the largest and fastest-growing advertising medium in Canada. As well, the amount of time Canadians spend with social media strongly suggests that social media communications will become a key component of any marketing communications strategy, if it is not already.

The nature of communications has changed. Companies now plan and implement IMC programs that embrace strategies beyond advertising. An IMC strategy involves the coordination of advertising with other strategies, such as interactive communications and social media, direct response communications, public relations, sales promotion, experiential marketing, and personal selling. All of these elements combine to achieve common objectives.

Advertising is one element of marketing communications; granted, it is the most visible and probably the most costly. Advertising is divided into two broad categories: consumer advertising and business advertising. Consumer advertising is used by companies that produce national brands and by retailers. Advertising by national brands, retailers, and service organizations is designed to communicate unique benefits and differentiate one brand from another. Consumer advertising also includes corporate advertising and advocacy advertising. Corporate advertising is usually designed to enhance an organization's image. Advocacy advertising aims to influence public opinion by presenting a perspective on a controversial issue. Business advertising includes trade, industrial, service-industry, and corporate advertising.

Before a company invests in advertising, it must determine if market conditions are favourable or unfavourable. If favourable, the investment in advertising should proceed. There must be market and product demand, the product must be at an appropriate stage in the product life cycle, the product should have a competitive advantage, the competitive environment must be conducive for investment, the product must be of adequate quality, and management must be committed to investing in communications over the long term. Finally, advertising must be combined with other IMC elements to produce a coordinated and consistent message for customers.

In planning effective advertising campaigns, practitioners must adapt to a changing media environment. Some of the key trends that must be considered include the ongoing transition to IMC, consumer lifestyle changes and their impact on media consumption, the increasing role of technology in terms of how to best communicate messages and other advertising decisions, the analytical nature of advertising in a data-driven marketplace, and the public's general concern for its privacy. Planners are experimenting with social media advertising opportunities and are seeing good results for brands that effectively implement two-way dialogue with consumers in a social media setting. However, many advertisers remain skeptical of social media because measuring return on investment is difficult.

The advertising industry also faces several ethical issues as it finds ways to communicate messages. Consumers often complain about the use of sex in advertising (too blatant) or ads that use dangerous or disturbing imagery to dramatize a product's benefits. Ads that mislead the public are also subject to complaints.

Regulation and control of the advertising industry comes under the jurisdiction of the federal government through the CRTC and through the laws and regulations established and enforced by the Competition Bureau. The voluntary regulations administered by Advertising Standards Canada also serve to control the industry.

KEY TERMS

advertising 3
advocacy advertising 8
business advertising (business-to-business advertising) 8
cause marketing 8
consumer advertising 7
corporate advertising 8
direct response communications 10
experiential marketing 13
integrated marketing communications (IMC) 5
lifestyle advertising 20
on-demand viewing 22
personal selling 13
product innovation 19
product life cycle 15
programmatic media buying 23
public relations 11
sales promotion 12

REVIEW QUESTIONS

1. What is the primary role of advertising? How is advertising related to marketing and marketing communications decisions?
2. What is IMC, and what role does it play in solving business problems today?
3. Identify and briefly explain the various components of IMC.
4. Identify and briefly explain the various types of consumer advertising.
5. Identify and briefly explain the various types of business-to-business advertising.
6. What is the primary role of corporate advertising?
7. How do market demand and the product life cycle influence the decision to invest in or not invest in advertising?
8. How does a product communicate its competitive advantage? Identify the various options, and provide an example of each option (one that is not included in the text).
9. How important is product quality when making the decision to invest in advertising? Briefly explain.
10. What roles do the CRTC and ASC play in the advertising industry?

DISCUSSION QUESTIONS

1. The balance of power in advertising is shifting from traditional media to digital media. Will this shift continue, and how significant will digital media be in future advertising campaigns? Conduct some research on this issue, and present an opinion on it.
2. What is your opinion of lifestyle advertising? Is it effective in motivating someone to buy a particular brand? Conduct some research on this appeal technique, and present an opinion on it.
3. Some industry analysts are predicting the demise of television advertising, at least in its present format. Do you agree with this prediction? Evaluate the issue, and present an opinion on it.
4. Advertising on social media such as Facebook and Twitter has met with some resistance among many marketing organizations. Will social media play a more dominant role in the communications mix in the future? Conduct some research on the effectiveness of social media advertising, and present an opinion on this issue.
5. Is the use of sex and sexual innuendo in advertising acceptable, or should advertisers be more sensitive to the values of the viewing audience? Refer to the chapter for some insight. For what kinds of products are sexual appeals appropriate? Provide examples to defend your position.

NOTES

1. TVB Television Bureau of Canada, "TV Basics, 2014–2015," p. 26, **www.tvb.ca/page_files/pdf/infocentre/tvbasics.pdf**.
2. Chris Powell, "Digital Now Close to One Third of All Major Media Spending," *Marketing*, July 22, 2015, **www.marketingmag.ca**.
3. "P&G Shifts Marketing Dollars to Online, Mobile," *Wall Street Journal*, August 1, 2013, **http://online.wsj.com**.
4. Canadian Media Directors' Council, *Media Digest*, 2015–2016, p. 19.
5. "Social Scanner: Why Marketers Still Struggle with Pinterest," *Marketing*, January 22, 2015, **www.marketingmag.ca**.
6. Val Maloney, "Scotiabank Makes a Play for Millennials through Instagram," *Media in Canada*, January 27, 2015, **www.mediaincanada.com**.
7. Bell Canada, "A Spectacular Day for Canada's Mental Health," press release, January 29, 2015, **http://letstalk.bell.ca/en/news**.
8. Brett Langlois, "The Canadian Mobile Market in 2015," Catalyst Canada, March 2015, **http://catalyst.ca/2015canadian-smartphone-market**.
9. Michael Learmonth, "Marketers Unsure of Facebook Ad Value: Survey," *Marketing*, June 27, 2012, **www.marketingmag.ca**.
10. Chris Pow, "Branded Content Offers High Growth Opportunity for Canadian Producers: Study," *Marketing*, September 13, 2013, **www.marketingmag.ca**.
11. Matthew Chung, "What Consumers Think about Sponsorships," *Media in Canada*, January 27, 2015, **http://mediaincanada.com**.
12. Hollie Shaw, "Canadian Tire Strikes Sponsorship Deal with Olympic Team in Bid to Bolster Sports Ties," *Financial Post*, January 23, 2013, www.business.financialpost.com.
13. Andrew Newman, "Dove Shows Athletes Off the Court," *New York Times*, March 6, 2011, **www.nytimes.com**.
14. Printed with permission of Suzuki Canada, Inc.
15. Chris Powell, "Nearly 20% of Canadians Now Have Four-Screen Internet Access (Study)," *Marketing*, November 12, 2014, **www.marketingmag.ca**.
16. Newspapers Canada, **www.newspaperscanada.ca**.
17. Carly Weeks, "Can You Know Too Much about Your Customers?' *Globe and Mail*, June 8, 2011, p. B18.
18. Josh Bernoff, "Does Data Collection Affect Consumer Behaviour?" *Marketing*, January 25, 2012, **www.marketingmag.ca**.
19. Melody McKinnon, "Canadian Digital, Social and Mobile Statistics on a Global Scale," **CanadiansInternet.com** Business, January 23, 2014, **http://canadiansinternet.com/canadian-digital-social-mobile-statistics**.
20. Erik Sass, "ROI Is Top Concern for Marketing Execs," *Social Graf*, July 12, 2012, **www.mediapost.com**.
21. Erik Sass, "Brand Execs Like Social Media, but Can't Measure It," *Social Graf*, May 2, 2012, **www.mediapost.com**.
22. Chris Powell, "ING Direct Pulls RSP 'Suffering' Ad over Complaints," *Marketing*, January 22, 2013, **www.marketingmag.ca**.
23. Carly Weeks, "The Whole-Wheat, Whole-Grain, Multigrain Conundrum," *Globe and Mail*, August 6, 2012, pp. L1, L6.
24. Chris Powell, "Majority of Canadians Believe Ads Provide Value: Ad Standards Canada," *Marketing*, November 12, 2014, **www.marketingmag.ca**.
25. CRTC, **www.crtc.gc/ca/eng/background**.
26. Advertising Standards Canada, "ASC's 2014 Consumer Research Shows Canadians View Advertising through a Sharp Lens," press release, November 11, 2014.
27. Advertising Standards Canada, "Truth in Advertising Matters," 2014, **http://adstandards.com/reports/2014/en/year-at-a-glance/highlights.html**.
28. Iain Marlow, "Bell Fined $1.3 Million for Violating No-Call Rules," *Globe and Mail*, December 2, 2010, p. A9.

CHAPTER 2
The Advertising Industry

Learning Objectives

After studying this chapter, you will be able to

1. Identify the organizations that constitute the advertising industry
2. Identify and describe the various advertising management systems used by clients
3. Identify the roles and responsibilities of clients in the advertising development process
4. Describe the roles and responsibilities of agencies in the advertising development process
5. Discuss the nature of relationships between clients and agencies
6. Distinguish among the various types of advertising agencies
7. Outline the organizational structure of agencies and the functions of agency personnel
8. Identify the key concepts associated with managing a client's business
9. Identify the methods of compensating advertising agencies

This chapter focuses on the relationships between advertisers (the clients) and advertising agencies. Once the primary groups that constitute the industry have been identified, discussion will focus on the relationships between clients and agencies as they develop and implement advertising campaigns.

The management of advertising does vary from company to company. Depending on the size and nature of the company, responsibility for communications programs could be with the advertising manager, the marketing manager, or even the owner of a small business. Or a product manager or brand manager may be entirely responsible for communications activities for his or her brands. While recognizing these title variations, this chapter will use the term *advertising manager.*

Advertising agencies exist to help companies communicate with the public and to help market a company's product. The agency is a service company that provides an essential link between the client (advertiser) and the public. An agency provides expertise that a client itself does not possess. Specifically, the client company gains access to creative, media, and other forms of marketing communication specialists who will be responsible for planning and implementing vital components of the overall marketing plan.

In recent times, advertising agencies have had to adapt to our fast-paced and ever-changing marketplace. Technology has fuelled change. The internet, social media, and mobile technology; shifting demographics; and tech-savvy consumers have forced agencies to look at different creative and media opportunities. To meet clients' needs in this environment, agencies are now responsible for developing a wider range of communications solutions than in the past.

Composition of the Advertising Industry

The Canadian advertising industry comprises six primary groups: advertisers, advertising agencies (which can also be called marketing communications agencies), the media, advertising support companies, media support services, and research and audience measurement companies. Collectively, these companies have an economic impact of $19 billion in Canada annually.[1] All advertising revenues generated in Canada result from advertisers' print, broadcast, out-of-home, and online ads placed by advertising agencies in the media. Advertisers are the companies whose investment in advertising is largely responsible for keeping the component groups in business.

ADVERTISERS (THE CLIENTS)

Canadian advertisers include manufacturers, retailers, service firms, technology companies, governments, and not-for-profit organizations. In Canada, the largest advertisers in terms of advertising dollars spent are Procter & Gamble, Rogers Communications, BCE Inc., Ford Motor Company of Canada, and General Motors. Companies of all sizes use advertising to their advantage, be they small, independent retailers that use the local newspaper to reach nearby residents or large conglomerates like Procter & Gamble that use multimedia campaigns that are national in scope.

The Association of Canadian Advertisers (ACA) is a national association exclusively dedicated to serving the interests of companies that market and advertise their products and services in Canada. The ACA's primary goal is to "help our members maximize the full value of their [marketing communications] investments." As the voice for Canadian advertisers, the ACA "represents the views and concerns of our members before government and industry bodies."[2] For more information about the ACA, visit its website at www.acaweb.ca.

ADVERTISING AGENCIES

Advertising agencies (marketing communications agencies) are service organizations responsible for creating, planning, producing, and placing advertising messages for clients. Most of the larger advertising agencies in Canada are subsidiaries of large American or other international agencies. Large agencies continue to grow through the acquisition of domestic agencies (many in Canada).

Essentially, four multinational marketing communications conglomerates—Omnicom Group (American), WPP (British), Interpublic Group (American), and Publicis Groupe (French)—control the advertising agency business worldwide. These conglomerates operate networks of agencies offering a variety of marketing communications services in every country in which they operate. In Canada, for example, Omnicom Group has three full-service agencies (BBDO Canada, DDB Canada, and Juniper Park/TBWA), two interactive agencies (Tribal DDB and Proximity Canada), two media planning and buying agencies (PHD Canada and OMD Canada), two public relations agencies (DDB Public Relations and Ketchum Public Relations), and two branding and design companies (Karacters Design Group and Interbrand Canada). This is only a partial list of Omnicom's Canadian agency network. The other three communications conglomerates have similar types of agencies operating in Canada.

Advertising and marketing communications agencies can be classified as full-service agencies that provide a complete range of services to their clients, such as the agencies described earlier, or specialists that offer limited services in certain areas of expertise.

There are all kinds of smaller, regional advertising agencies that serve the needs of local and regional clients. In Atlantic Canada, for example, M5 is the region's biggest and perhaps most successful agency. M5's clients include GM Canada, Irving, University of New Brunswick, Enbridge Gas NB, Atlantic Lottery, the Government of New Brunswick, and the Government of Newfoundland and Labrador. M5 offers its clients a full range of marketing communications services.

The Institute of Communication Agencies (ICA) is the national association representing full-service advertising agencies. The ICA's mission is to "champion commercial creativity, amplify our economic impact, embrace and drive change."[3] The ICA is responsible for promoting higher standards and best practices and serves as the largest source of information and training for the industry. For more insight into the ICA, visit its website at www.icacanada.ca.

THE MEDIA

The Canadian media are divided into numerous categories: *broadcast*, which includes radio and television; *print*, which includes newspapers and magazines; *out-of-home*, which includes transit and outdoor advertising; *direct response*, which includes direct mail and direct response television companies; and *digital*, which embraces all things related to the internet, including social media and mobile communications. We are living in an era in which new forms of interactive advertising communications are growing at a much faster rate than traditional forms of advertising.

According to the latest revenue data available, net advertising revenue in Canada from all sources (the amount actually spent on media) totals $14 billion. This figure includes actual spending on the internet (including mobile), television, newspapers, radio magazines, and out-of-home media, which totals $12 billion. The remaining $2 billion comes from catalogues, direct mail, yellow pages, and miscellaneous media. The internet is the largest medium, with revenues of $3.9 billion.[4]

Much of Canada's media is controlled by a few large corporations that have acquired smaller media companies over the years, a concept referred to as **media convergence**. The two largest companies are Bell Media and Rogers Media. Bell owns two television networks embracing 30 conventional stations across the country, 35 specialty/digital channels, 106 radio stations, and more than 9500 outdoor boards. Prominent among Bell's holdings are the CTV Network, TSN/RDS, CHUM radio and television, and numerous related websites. Bell Media generates $2.6 billion in revenue annually. Rogers owns 12 conventional stations, 19 specialty/digital channels, 51 radio stations, 57 consumer and trade magazines, and a host of related websites. This combination of media outlets generates $1.7 billion annually for Rogers.[5]

ADVERTISING SUPPORT COMPANIES

This group includes research companies that measure and evaluate the effectiveness of advertising messages. Other support firms are photographers, radio and television commercial production houses, print production specialists, music and sound production and editing companies, software development companies, and media representatives who sell time and space for particular media.

The nature of advertising is changing: The most progressive advertising now borders on entertainment and is increasingly viewed as content—storytelling so compelling consumers will actually want to watch it, even share it. Live events, short television shows, and video content that can be viewed online via YouTube all form part of this innovative advertising. Such change has spawned a new group of specialist agencies that develop communications strategies for digital and social media. Traditional agencies were initially slow to react to this trend but have adapted their operations in recent years by hiring digital experts and by partnering with or acquiring successful digital specialist communication companies.

MEDIA SUPPORT SERVICES

All major media in Canada have a support group whose primary mandate is to educate potential advertisers about the merits of their particular medium. Acting as a resource centre of information, each organization attempts to increase its medium's share of advertising revenue in the marketplace. Where appropriate, these organizations also liaise with governments and the public on matters of interest. This group includes the Television Bureau of Canada (TVB), Newspapers Canada (a joint effort of the Canadian Newspaper Association and the Canadian Community Newspaper Association), Magazines Canada, the Out-of-Home Marketing Association (OMAC), and the Interactive Advertising Bureau of Canada (IAB Canada).

RESEARCH AND AUDIENCE MEASUREMENT COMPANIES

Advertising planners working with limited budgets are constantly evaluating various media alternatives to develop the most effective and efficient media mix. To make sound media decisions requires a factual and objective information base. Media research, therefore, is concerned with quantitative measures of media exposure. In Canada, numerous independent organizations compile and publish reliable measurement data.

Among the organizations involved in audience measurement and other analytics are Numeris and Nielsen Media Research. Both are involved in verifying broadcast audience data. The Alliance for Audited Media independently verifies print and digital circulation, mobile apps, website analytics, social media, and technology platforms for newspapers, magazines, and digital media companies. The Print Measurement Bureau and NADbank recently merged operations and is now called Vividata. Vividata is responsible for collecting audience data for magazines and newspapers in Canada. The services provided by Vividata are discussed in more detail in appropriate media chapters later on.

Client-Side Advertising Management

Management of the advertising function usually falls under the jurisdiction of the marketing department in an organization. Thus, it is common for numerous managers to be directly or indirectly involved with the task of advertising. The number of managers involved depends on the size and nature of the organization and on the relative importance that advertising plays in the marketing of the products. For example, in a large organization where brand managers are employed, numerous managers may be involved in advertising. Junior-level managers are active in the day-to-day affairs of their brands, while senior-level managers are active in the approval process for advertising strategies of all company brands.

A **brand manager (product manager)** formulates and implements marketing strategies for assigned brands. In the context of advertising and other forms of communications, the manager deals directly with the agencies on creative and media assignments, sales promotion programs, experiential marketing activities, direct response and interactive communications, and public relations.

In larger organizations, the brand manager may report to a **category manager** who is responsible for developing marketing strategies for all products in a particular market. The category manager adopts a more generalized view of the business than does an individual brand manager. Consequently, trade-offs among brands are the decision of the category manager (i.e., determining which brands receive more or less advertising support).

To illustrate the concept of brand and category management, consider how Procter & Gamble divides its business into four main categories: beauty and hair care; baby, feminine, and family care; fabric and home care; and health and grooming. In the beauty and hair care category, brand managers are assigned to brands such as Olay, Old Spice, Head & Shoulders, and CoverGirl. In the health and grooming category are brands such as Gillette, Crest, Oral-B, and Braun.

Canada is a diverse country, both geographically and culturally. Therefore, some organizations employ a **regional management system** and implement regional advertising campaigns. Molson Coors, for example, has a three-region structure that affects marketing communications: Western Canada, Ontario/Atlantic, and Quebec. In addition, a national marketing team manages a group of brands referred to as *strategic* *national brands*; Canadian and Coors Light are in this group. Each region has a staff of marketing, sales, and promotion personnel who develop marketing and communications strategies and implement plans for strategic regional brands. According to Molson Coors, such a system allows the company to build on its strengths and chip away at its weaknesses.[6]

Companies operating on a global scale now view the world as one market and are switching to **international management systems** that divide the globe on a continental basis. "Think globally and act locally" is a common refrain among multinational marketers. The objective of a global system is to develop a global campaign that can be tweaked where necessary to meet local market conditions. The McDonald's "I'm lovin' it" campaign, for example, originated in Germany and was implemented globally. The campaign is tweaked on a country-by-country basis.

Durex, the world's leading condom manufacturer with a 34 percent market share in 130 countries, thinks globally and acts locally as well. How do they advertise such a taboo product? They play it safe (a joke!). All countries are connected to a universal platform, and managers from different countries discuss what's best for the brand. Anne Vale, head of global marketing, says the system "helps share the global vision, to engage, and be more consistent."[7] It results in good local campaigns with an overarching global brand personality that is generally described as risqué.

Titles vary for the person responsible for the advertising function in an organization. Regardless of the title, this individual is responsible for coordinating plans for all components of the marketing communications mix. Typically, such an individual possesses analytical, planning, and leadership skills and has knowledge and experience in the operation of the advertising industry. The next section examines the specific responsibilities of the client organization in developing communications strategies.

Client Responsibilities in the Advertising Planning Process

BRIEF AGENCY ON ASSIGNMENTS

The **advertising manager** works within the client organization and compiles and presents all information relevant to a specific advertising assignment to the advertising agency. It is important for agency personnel to fully understand the nature of the assignment, particularly the challenges they will face. Although the amount of information and the nature of it varies from one company to another (an organizational preference), some of the key information that gets transferred includes basic market information, competitor information (e.g., unique selling points and market shares), target market profiles, a positioning strategy statement, key selling points about the product to be advertised, and the budget. Typically, the client and agency personnel meet to discuss the briefing document so that both parties agree on the basic direction before the agency begins work on the assignment.

COORDINATE ADVERTISING STRATEGIES WITH OTHER MARKETING COMMUNICATIONS STRATEGIES

In the age of integrated marketing communications (IMC), it is important that the advertising manager assess the benefits of other activities, such as experiential marketing, public relations, and social media. Specialist agencies in these areas will have to be briefed when a new assignment is undertaken. How various components of the marketing communications mix work together to achieve common business goals is the challenge.

It is quite common for promotional activities to become part of the advertising communications process. Coupons and contests, for example, are often the focal point of an advertisement and are included to achieve trial or repeat purchases by consumers. Public relations can be used for new product launches to help create initial demand. Experiential marketing techniques—something as simple as having street teams distribute product samples in public squares—encourages consumers to engage directly with a brand.

Effective integration and strategic continuity across all activities and plans will produce a more effective plan, one that achieves objectives. Perhaps the expression "A chain is only as strong as its weakest link" applies here. Once advertising and other communications plans are finalized, the advertising manager must distribute plan details to sales management personnel. Communicating advertising details to the salesforce is vital, since the information can be used to inform trade customers of programs that will help them resell company products.

MONITOR THE ADVERTISING PROGRAM

In this area, the advertising manager ensures that advertising execution is in accordance with the actual plan. For example, the manager may request a post-buy media analysis to ensure that desired reach levels were achieved. Also, the manager carefully reviews budgets and planned media expenditures throughout the year, making changes when necessary. A change in competitive activity might dictate an increase in spending, so the manager must know what options are available on short notice. Or a company may be facing a profit-squeeze situation, and spending on advertising might have to be reduced. In this case, the manager must know what flexibility there is for cancellation of advertising in various media.

EVALUATE THE ADVERTISING PROGRAM

The advertising manager is accountable for the success or failure of company advertising programs. Most advertising plans are based on quantifiable objectives, and whether these objectives are achieved can be determined through some form of **advertising research**. For example, a campaign may be designed to increase consumers' awareness of a product to a certain level, to generate sales leads, or to alter a brand's image. To measure the success of a campaign, the manager may conduct research at various stages (such as pre-test and post-test research). The evaluation process is critical, because the advertising manager must make recommendations for changes in advertising direction if research information so dictates. Also, for any campaign, research at carefully timed intervals helps in identifying potential trouble spots before they become problems.

Rightly or wrongly, investment in advertising is often directly linked to its impact on sales and market share of a brand. Failure to improve in these areas often leads to a rocky relationship between clients and agencies, to the point where they eventually part ways.

LIAISE WITH THE ADVERTISING AGENCY

An advertising manager is the direct link with the advertising agency and is in constant contact with agency personnel, checking the status of assignments and projects that the agency may be working on. As liaison, the manager has several key responsibilities, including providing the agency with appropriate information when new assignments occur (see the "Brief Agency on Assignments" section). As the intermediary, the advertising manager is often in the hot seat, because individuals and their egos must be satisfied at both ends of the advertising spectrum (client side and agency side). The manager is responsible for developing advertising that will be acceptable to all stakeholders who must approve the program.

Let's examine this situation more closely. From the viewpoint of the agency, the advertising manager is the person it must satisfy first. If the manager does not like a particular creative or media recommendation, the chances that it will be seen, let alone approved, by others on the client side are minimal. As an experienced critic, and knowing client personnel and their expectations, the advertising manager will provide the agency with feedback so that changes to the proposal can be made before the corporate approval stage.

On the client side, once the creative or media assignment meets the specifications outlined in the marketing plan or briefing document, the advertising manager must carry the agency proposal through the corporate approval network. At this stage, the idiosyncrasies of senior executives often come to the forefront. These executives offer opinions on how the advertisement or media proposal could be improved. When assessing executive feedback, the advertising manager must ensure that any suggestions stay on strategy. The ongoing requests for changes to the proposal that result from the corporate approval process (and from attempting to satisfy each individual manager) often have a negative impact on client–agency relations. Client–agency relations are discussed later in this chapter.

Advertising Agency Roles and Responsibilities

An advertising agency will perform various functions, tailoring its services to meet the specific needs of individual clients. The actual degree of the agency's involvement and responsibility may vary among clients, depending on factors such as the size and expertise of the client company. For example, large advertisers such as Procter & Gamble, Kraft Canada, and Coca-Cola are typically staffed with marketing managers whose expertise is used for devising marketing strategies. In this case, the agency's role will likely be confined to advertising and other forms of marketing communications. For small advertisers, many of whom may lack marketing skills, agencies can provide not only advertising but also marketing planning assistance that will complement overall client operations.

The essential services that an agency offers are experience and expertise in communications, strategic planning assistance, and objectivity in the planning process.

PROVIDE EXPERIENCE AND EXPERTISE IN COMMUNICATIONS

Clients normally develop a comprehensive marketing plan that embraces all elements of the marketing mix (product, price, distribution, and marketing communications). The agency will develop, in more detail, elements from the communications component of the plan. Specifically, the agency will use the guidelines and objectives established in the marketing plan to develop and execute an advertising plan that will contribute to the achievement of the client's objectives. This information is provided to the agency in the briefing process discussed under client responsibilities. The agency's advertising plan (or marketing communications plan) will include recommendations on creative (message), media, and any other form of marketing communications deemed relevant to the situation—public relations, sales promotion, experiential marketing, and so on.

In some cases, several agencies might work on one client's business at the same time but in different capacities. For example, a traditional advertising agency might work on creative and media plans, a digital agency can develop online and mobile creative, and an experiential marketing agency might work on a consumer engagement strategy. Clients often require specialized expertise when trying to find the right solutions to their problems. The different types of agencies are discussed later in the chapter.

PROVIDE PLANNING ASSISTANCE

The agency, through its **account services group** (account executives, account supervisors, and account director), provides assistance not only in advertising but also in other areas of marketing. Depending on the internal structure of the client, the account group might be used as an external planning group. Such external planning may be used in the areas of marketing research, sales promotion, public relations, and other aspects of marketing strategy. Account managers must look at the bigger picture, not just advertising, when it comes to solving a client's problems. If other elements of the marketing communications mix can play a vital role, then they too should be recommended as part of the solution.

PROVIDE OBJECTIVITY IN THE PLANNING PROCESS

Many advertisers tend to use advertising that suits the company's established style or image. Often, clients view a change in direction as a risk. The use of familiar-looking campaigns is a safe strategy, but it is not necessarily the most effective means of communicating with a target market. In advertising, safe usually means ineffective. Since the agency is not directly associated with the internal environment of the client, it can provide an objective perspective that might offer alternative directions for communicating with target markets. This external position can result in the development of customer-oriented campaigns rather than company-oriented campaigns.

Taking risks and adopting new directions are more important than ever, considering the time-pressed nature of consumers as well as their ever-changing media consumption habits. To illustrate, consider a campaign that the agency Bleublancrouge recommended to its client Bristol-Myers Squibb. The client adopted an eye-popping, some say risky, creative for a campaign titled "One life"—a campaign that dealt with safe sex and HIV. How does an advertiser dramatize safe sex without showing some sex? Some visual images in the print media showed almost naked partners entwined in a variety of sexual positions. The provocative imagery wasn't something the client had used in the past, but they believed it was appropriate for delivering the message.[8] Calvin Klein is another brand known for provocative images in its advertising. Risky ads do grab attention, which typically is the objective! Refer to the image in Figure 2.1.

PROMOTE ACTIVE LIAISON WITH CLIENTS

It is important for agencies and clients to communicate regularly with each other. The account executive is the primary link between the agency and the client. An account executive channels vital information from the client into the agency and takes recommendations that are prepared by various agency departments back to the client for review. It is also appropriate for employees at similar management levels to be communicating with each other. For example, a director of account planning (agency) should keep in touch with the director of marketing (client), and the presidents of both organizations should meet periodically to discuss matters. Ongoing and open communication between the parties fosters an environment in which both parties can prosper. It helps build a better partnership.

FIGURE 2.1

Calvin Klein uses provocative images to convey its message.

© Stacy Walsh Rosenstock/Alamy Stock Photo

FIGURE 2.2

A summary of the roles and responsibilities of clients and agencies

Regardless of roles and responsibilities, if the client–agency partnership is to be successful, there must be effective two-way communication between the partners. The partners must share a similar vision and agree to achievable objectives.

KEY CLIENT RESPONSIBILITIES:

- Provide appropriate background information and a budget for the advertising assignment
- Coordinate advertising strategies with other marketing communications strategies
- Monitor the implementation of advertising programs
- Evaluate the effectiveness of advertising programs
- Liaise with advertising agency

KEY AGENCY RESPONSIBILITIES:

- Provide experience and expertise in specialized areas: mainly creative and media strategies and executions
- Offer strategic planning assistance to solve clients' marketing problems
- Produce objective, customer-focused advertising strategies
- Liaise regularly with clients to encourage solid client–agency relationships

For a summary of the roles and responsibilities of clients and advertising agencies, refer to Figure 2.2.

Client–Agency Relationships

The quality of advertising produced is the outcome of a sound business and personal relationship between a client and an agency. Good advertising is the result of two separate organizations working together as partners. True partners have a long-term relationship in which both partners prosper.

Perhaps a marriage is an appropriate analogy for the client–agency relationship. The often-cited ingredients of a good marriage are open and honest communication, trust and respect for each other, and a willingness to accept constructive feedback. If these fundamental principles are applied in a client–agency environment, a productive partnership will prevail.

However, the connection between client and agency is often delicate and can be broken for various reasons. Deteriorating relationships contribute significantly to the amount of account shifting that occurs in Canada each year. **Account shifting** refers to the movement of a client's account from one agency to another. Clients are attracted to agencies that produce good creative and develop campaigns that achieve business objectives. It's not uncommon for clients to fire their agency if business results are not achieved.

Clients choose to move to new agencies for a variety of reasons. Most of these reasons have to do with the client–agency relationship—or lack thereof. In simple terms, where there's marriage, there's divorce. The following are some of the more common reasons for account shifting:

- Clients are dissatisfied with the quality of the advertising or any of the other services provided by the agency.
- The agency can't meet the new communications demands the client requires (e.g., new media or other aspects of IMC or deadlines imposed by the client).
- There are philosophical differences between the client and agency in management style and approach, detected only after the association has begun. For example, the two parties might disagree on the direction the advertising should take.
- The relationship deteriorates based on chemistry problems between the two organizations. Sometimes the players on the teams change during the relationship, upsetting the chemistry that had existed.
- Clients decide to consolidate their business (a cost-savings measure) by using fewer agencies (multiproduct advertisers). In this case, an agency can be dismissed even though it is doing good work for the client.
- Conflict situations arise owing to account realignments at the parent company (shifts at a US parent agency often create shifts in Canadian subsidiaries). Also, agency mergers, in Canada or internationally, can bring competing accounts under one roof, which creates a need for one account to switch to another agency.

Client defections are a fact of life that agencies have to contend with. For example, Juniper Park, a Toronto-based agency, had an excellent performance record with Quaker Foods North America, producing award-winning campaigns for Lay's, SunChips, Cheetos, and various Quaker cereals. Quaker decided to consolidate its agency roster (based on a desire to work with fewer agencies) and awarded the account to Energy BBDO in Chicago.[9] The quality of Juniper Park's work had little do with their demise. Such is life in the ad business!

When things aren't going well for the client (e.g., sales or market share are down), it is quite common for the agency to take the fall. Clients, rightly or wrongly, link their investment in advertising to sales and market share results. Instead of dissolving the partnership, clients and agencies must look squarely at each other, acknowledge any shortcomings in the relationship, and devise strategies to correct them.

To encourage the best possible relationships between clients and agencies, and to clearly review the expectations of parties, clients must conduct agency evaluations at planned intervals. The agency should also have the opportunity to review the client's

ADVERTISING IN ACTION

The Naked Truth

One of the ironies of the advertising business, particularly the advertising agency business, is the often fickle nature of the relationship between a client and the agency. The success of both organizations relies on trust and how well the partnership prospers over the long haul. Yet it is not uncommon for clients to pull the trigger on the partnership, fire the agency, and move on to a new relationship.

There are a variety of reasons why client–agency relationships turn sour: The chemistry between the people involved suddenly wanes, personalities and egos clash over creative direction, or philosophical differences in strategy become a source of concern. What has to be irksome, though, is when an agency is fired for no apparent reason—they are doing a good job, haven't had any complaints about the quality of their work, but suddenly find themselves on the outside looking in.

This is the precise situation that ad agency Leo Burnett was in when Molson Coors consolidated its power brands (Canadian, Coors Light, and Rickard's) with one agency. Burnett had only secured the Coors Light business in 2013, but less than two years later they were out. In announcing the news, Molson Coors said Burnett was a world-class agency doing great work in Canada and that the divorce was not a slight on them. Really! Rethink would be the new agency. Of them, Molson Coors said they really understand the nuances of the business and Molson's marketing model, and they have done great work on Molson Canadian. You will have to read between the lines here to understand there may have been reason to drop Burnett, but it was news to them.

In another case, Ogilvy & Mather was suddenly dropped by Kraft Canada. Ogilvy was handling the lucrative Maxwell House coffee brand and doing a good job. Without even conducting an agency review, the Maxwell House business was handed over to TAXI. Both agencies are highly respected in the industry. In announcing the move, Kraft alluded to the fact that TAXI was doing great work on other brands and specifically mentioned how successful the TAXI launch of MiO (a flavoured beverage) had been. TAXI was perceived as a great fit to continue the momentum on an iconic brand like Maxwell House. Again, you can read between the lines.

Based on these examples, you may observe that the agency business is a rough one to be in. But it is an exciting business as well, in part because it is unpredictable! Perhaps it shows that an agency can never be complacent; they must constantly strive to turn out great creative and media strategies that build a client's business. It's frustrating, though, if you are doing that and are still shown the door. However, good agencies always bounce back!

Adapted from Chris Powell, "Molson Shifts Coors Light to Rethink," *Marketing*, October 28, 2014, www.marketingmag.ca and Kristen Laird, "Kraft Moves Maxwell House to Taxi," *Marketing*, June 12, 2014, www.marketingmag.ca.

performance. Dissolving a business partnership shouldn't be a quick decision. The ICA produces evaluation materials for use by clients and agencies. A booklet titled "Client/Agency Evaluation: A Guide to Best Practice, with Evaluation Formats" is available free of charge through the ICA website, www.icacanada.ca.

For more insight into the dynamics of client–agency relationships, read the Advertising in Action vignette **The Naked Truth**.

Types of Advertising Agencies

The type of agency a client chooses to work with can be a difficult decision. When choosing an agency, the client aims to find the one that will recommend and produce cost-efficient, effective advertising that achieves the desired results. The client must consider factors such as agency size, the service mix and expertise the agency is capable of providing, and compatibility of personnel. Essentially, an agency can be a generalist or a specialist. The generalist is referred to as a full-service agency. The specialist offers services in a specific area of advertising such as creative, media planning and buying, direct response communications, or digital communications (online, mobile, and social media). Let's examine the various types of advertising agencies operating in Canada.

FULL-SERVICE AGENCIES

Full-service agencies appeal strongly to advertisers that need a wide variety of services or require international connections for global advertising campaigns. Services provided by full-service agencies must embrace all of the possible demands a client may place on them. Therefore, the services list is diverse and may include creative planning, creative development and execution, media planning and placement, sales promotion, public relations and direct response, and interactive communications. In other words, a full-service agency must offer IMC solutions to its clients. Figure 2.3 illustrates the internal structure of a typical full-service advertising agency.

Large agencies such as MacLaren McCann, DDB Canada, Ogilvy & Mather, and Saatchi & Saatchi Canada are full-service agencies. Full-service agencies are usually part of the agency conglomerates that were discussed earlier in the chapter. Typically, full-service agencies have offices in many major cities across Canada and attract large national or regional advertisers. There is a tendency for big advertisers to work with big agencies. Often, clients such as Coca-Cola and McDonald's will use the same full-service agency in Canada that they use in the United States. Similarities between the two countries mean that working with the same agency can be cost efficient. For example, if MacLaren

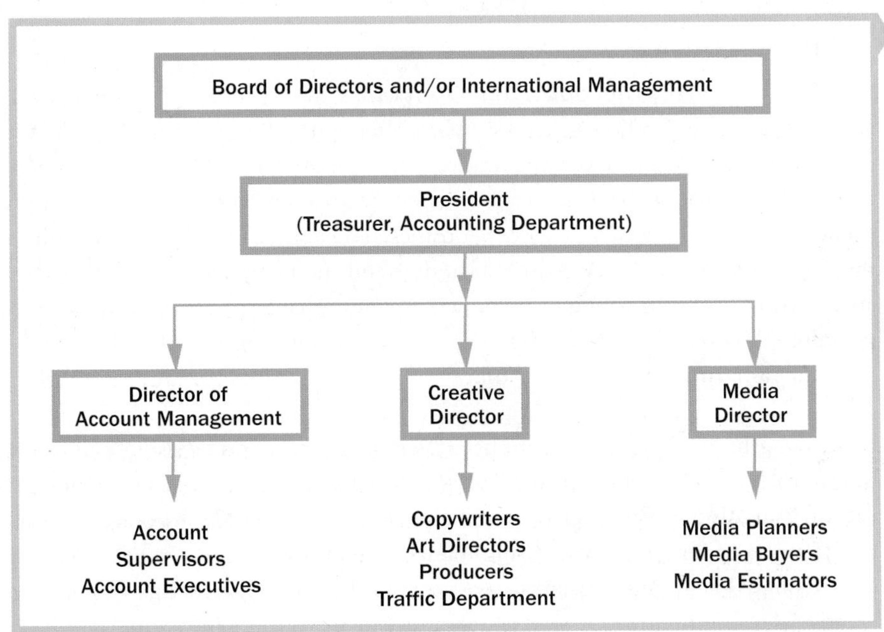

FIGURE 2.3

Organizational structure of a full-service agency

Source: Institute of Communication Agencies.

FIGURE 2.4

Primary functional areas of an advertising agency

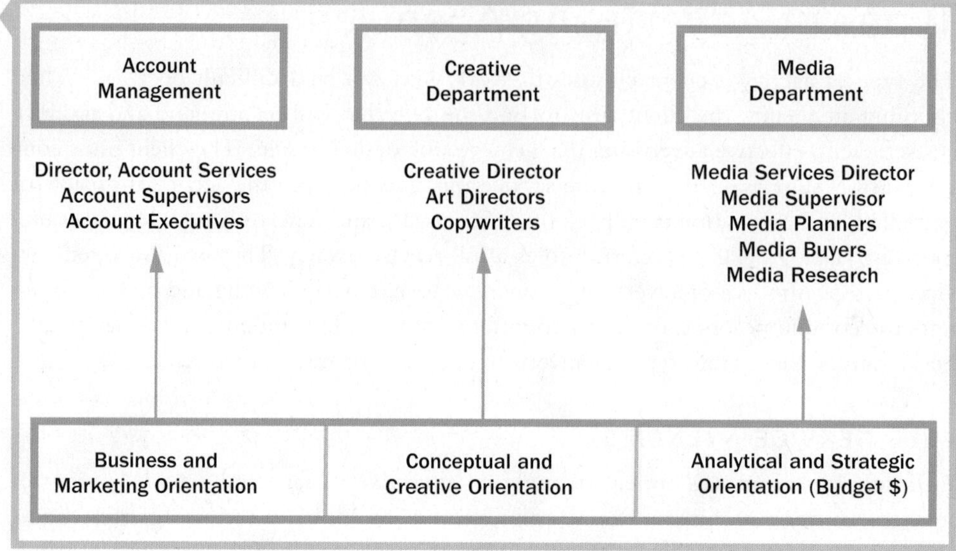

McCann has a great ad for Coca-Cola in the United States, the Canadian agency might run the same ad if it is in the best interests of the client.

Full-service advertising agencies are acquiring or affiliating with specialists in other areas of marketing communications so they have access to the services their clients want. Under the MacLaren McCann umbrella, for example, is the original agency MacLaren McCann, which offers a full range of services with a focus on account planning and creative services; M2 Universal, which offers media planning and media buying services; and MRM//McCann, which offers interactive, direct, and digital services.

From a purely traditional advertising perspective, full-service agencies such as MacLaren McCann and DDB Canada offer three essential services (functions) to clients: account management, creative services, and media services. See Figure 2.4 for more detail on functional areas. Large agencies may include additional departments, embracing functions such as marketing research, interactive communications, sales promotion, and public relations, or they have access to these services from sister companies in their ownership network.

ACCOUNT MANAGEMENT

As the name implies, **account management** staff are responsible for managing the affairs of the agency's clients. Account personnel perform a dual function: They are both consultants and coordinators. Account personnel must fully understand the client's business so they can advise the client on a variety of strategic marketing issues, motivate the agency's personnel to build the client's business, and coordinate communications between the client and agency. They must also understand the needs and wants of the consumers an advertiser (client) is trying to influence. Account managers are actively involved in the planning process and in presenting agency work to the client.

The **account executive** (sometimes referred to as an **account planner**) is responsible for facilitating ongoing communications with the client, planning projects, controlling budgets, preparing annual advertising plans, and advising clients on strategic issues. The account executive liaises between the client and agency and communicates frequently with the personnel in the client organization who are responsible for the advertising function (advertising manager, brand manager). In the development of advertising, the account executive represents the consumer (target audience) in the creative development process. The account executive must fully understand the needs and expectations of the consumers an advertiser is trying to influence. In this role, the executive is a bridge between the business side of the business and the creative side of the business.

Some of the specific roles of an account executive include conducting research on the needs and preferences of a target market, defining the advertising task, providing information to creative personnel to facilitate the creation of ads, participating in the creative process by representing the consumer (e.g., thinking about how the consumer may react to an ad), presenting ads to the client for approval, and tracking how well ads performed (e.g., conducting research to get actual consumer reactions to ads). The working relationship between the agency account executive and the client brand manager is a close one.

Above the account executive in the agency management structure is the **account supervisor**. The supervisor manages a group of account executives and is therefore responsible for an expanded list of clients. Job functions include performing strategic planning, analyzing the market, analyzing competitive activity, and investigating and capitalizing on business-building opportunities.

An **account director** is the senior manager in the account management department. Specific responsibilities include long-term planning, deployment of agency personnel, and overall account profitability. Also, the account director works with senior agency executives from other functional areas in seeking new business for the agency.

CREATIVE DEPARTMENT

The **creative department** is responsible for developing the idea or concept, often referred to as the "big idea," for an advertising campaign. Once the nature of the message (often referred to as the *creative concept*) has been established, members of the creative team must sell it to the client; once the client approves the concept, the creative team must execute the creative.

Heading the creative department is the **creative director**, who oversees the development of all creative generated by the agency. The creative director is ultimately responsible for the quality of creative developed by the agency. In such a position, the creative director must motivate the copywriters and art directors under his or her charge, who are the ones who work directly on client assignments.

The responsibility or challenge facing the **copywriter** is to convert information provided by the client and account managers (e.g., information concerning unique selling points, target market profiles, and purchase motivations) into an effective, persuasive sales message, a message that stands out and is relevant to potential customers. The copywriter develops the main idea of the advertisement in conjunction with an art director, and then creates its various textual components: headlines, body copy, scripts for television and radio commercials, or video content for YouTube and other social media outlets.

Working directly with a copywriter, an **art director** is responsible for developing a visual communication that elicits a favourable reaction from the target market. Art direction requires knowledge in specialized areas such as graphic design, photography, and digital publishing. An art director need not be an artist, but he or she must understand the production process and be able to direct artists and technical production specialists.

While the jobs of copywriters and art directors are separate, individuals in these positions usually work as a team on client assignments. Over a period of time, such a working relationship provides continuity and consistency in the creative product, something that clients are usually looking for. As clients and agencies increasingly look to creative plans that combine traditional media with digital media (two separate areas of creative expertise), the team concept has been emphasized. *Production artists* (artists who transform an art director's vision into reality) and *web designers* can be part of the creative team. Web design is a specialization that can also be outsourced on an as-needed basis.

Production managers are responsible for preparing advertisements for all media recommended in a marketing communications plan. Since production is an activity that involves execution, it requires coordination with numerous external suppliers, such as acting agencies and film production houses. In the case of a television commercial, for example, production managers commission scripts (seek quotes from several suppliers) and recruit models and actors (usually through agents), film crews, musicians, and support services such as costumes and catering.

The production manager ensures that all activities are completed within scheduled time frames—publishers' material deadlines or television air dates, for example. A **traffic manager** is responsible for ensuring that the final product (print, digital, or broadcast commercial) reaches the media destination on time.

MEDIA DEPARTMENT

The media department is responsible for the planning and placement of advertising time and space. The proliferation of media forms, the fragmentation within specific media (e.g., the large number of television channels available to viewers and the fact that people click from one website to another while using the internet), the escalating cost of media, and the uncertainty regarding the accuracy of audience measurement in digital media have all added to the complexity of the media department's responsibility. The essential functions of the media department are media planning, media buying, and media research.

Media planning involves documenting how the client's money will be spent to achieve advertising objectives. Planners devise a media plan that is presented to the client for approval. Once the plan is approved, the **media buying** process begins. The objective of a media buy is to maximize impact on a target audience at the lowest possible cost to the client. The final media plan will document media recommendations that deliver the right target audience, at the right time, in the right place, and with the right number of messages. Media buying in conventional media such as television, radio, magazines, and out-of-home is a negotiated process between agencies or media buying services and the media. Buying time and space in volume yields preferred rates for the advertiser.

The **media research** department of an ad agency plays a key role in the planning and buying of media time and space. Having access to up-to-date information regarding media consumption trends, audience sizes, circulation, and who's watching what and when, for example, is key to devising effective and efficient media plans. This type of information is used to determine the best combination of media to use to reach a brand's target audience. Media research has a strong analytical orientation. External databases containing audience measurement information are available online, or alternatively an agency can hire an independent research company to tap into these databanks and provide media analysis. As well, there is an abundance of analytical data available from digital publishers and social media outlets such as Facebook, YouTube, and Twitter.

By title, the key people in the media department are the media planner, media buyer, and media director.

A **media planner** assesses the strengths, weaknesses, cost efficiencies, and communications potentials of various media to develop a media plan. Since the client's money is on the line, planners must be prepared to address all of the client's concerns. Media plans may go through many revisions before receiving client approval. One of the major challenges of a media planner today is how to develop strategies that effectively blend traditional media together with digital media. The end goal never changes, however: Whatever is recommended must efficiently deliver the message to either a collective target (through mass media) or an individual target (through direct response and interactive media).

A **media buyer** is responsible for developing an intimate knowledge of the media marketplace and being aware of all developments affecting media buying. Buyers must evaluate and make decisions on the competitive claims of the various media to make the most efficient and effective buys for their clients. Good negotiating skills are vital to be successful in a media buying role. The buyer's objective is to get the best possible deal for the client.

A **media director** is the senior manager in the media department. The responsibilities of the media director depend on the size of the agency. In smaller agencies, the director is involved in planning and buying media. In a larger agency, the director is ultimately responsible for all media plans developed by his or her staff. Obtaining the director's approval is essential before presenting the plans to the client. Working with other senior executives, the media director usually plays an active role in business presentations to new clients.

Media planning and media buying are highly specialized fields. Consequently, many agencies have established separate companies within their agency network to handle this function.

CREATIVE BOUTIQUES

Creative boutiques are smaller agencies specializing in the development of creative ideas and their execution for clients' advertising campaigns. Creative boutiques are usually formed and staffed by personnel previously employed by the creative departments of full-service agencies. Many a creative director has chosen to branch out on his or her own to avoid the bureaucracy often associated with full-service agencies or simply to do what he or she does best: create ads for clients. It is quite common for experienced account managers to join forces with copywriters and art directors in the formation of a creative boutique.

A creative boutique concentrates on producing the single most important component of a campaign—the sales message. To illustrate how creative boutiques can move from a startup operation to become a larger successful agency, consider the accomplishment of three well-respected advertising personalities who left the security of Palmer Jarvis DDB to form their own agency called Rethink Communications. It was a bold and risky step for Chris Staples, Tom Shepansky, and Ian Grais. Perhaps tired of big agency bureaucracy, their objective was to stay close to their clients and produce advertising that works for them. Rethink positioned itself as an "ideas company," not an ad agency. Rethink has grown to become a mid-size agency with offices in Vancouver, Toronto, and Montreal. Several new partners with a creative background have joined the company along the way. Clients include A&W, Mr. Lube, Coast Capital Savings, Molson Coors, Shaw Communications, and Sobeys.

There are many other creative specialists in Canada who have produced award-winning and results-oriented campaigns for their clients. Among the leaders in this agency category are John St., TAXI, Sid Lee, and The Hive. Visit their respective websites for insight into their activities and campaigns. Often, successful creative boutiques are acquired by much larger agency networks—another fact of life in the ad business! John St. and TAXI, for example, are part of the WPP network.

MEDIA BUYING SERVICE

A **media buying service** is a specialist agency responsible for planning and purchasing the most cost-efficient media for a client—that is to say, responsible for gaining maximum exposure to a target audience at minimum cost. In addition, a media buying service often obtains government and other clearances for advertisements, ensures that each ad runs as scheduled, and generally takes care of administrative work associated with the media buying transaction.

Since efficiency is important, the use of a media buying service might generate cost savings that can be reinvested in the creative product. Often a client will have creative matters handled by several agencies but have the media planning coordinated and implemented by a media buying service. Placing advertising through one media buying service leads to bigger discounts, since the service has more leverage with the various media suppliers.

In Canada, there are several large media buying companies. The WPP Group, through its subsidiary, GroupM, operates Mediacom, MEC Canada, and Mindshare; the Omnicom Group operates OMD Canada and PHD Canada; and the Interpublic Group of Companies operates M2 Universal. OMD Canada is the largest media agency in Canada, having billed $1.08 billion in 2013. Ranking second was ZenithOptimedia, with billings of $1.01 billion.[10] **Media billings** refer to the total dollar volume of advertising, in terms of time and space, handled by an agency in one year. There is a trend toward relatively few but very large media companies placing the majority of advertising in Canada.

MARKETING COMMUNICATIONS SPECIALISTS: DIRECT RESPONSE, DIGITAL, AND EXPERIENTIAL

Other options are available for clients who like to work with specialists. In today's cluttered media environment, clients demand efficiency and, as a result, are moving toward direct response and online communications and away from the mass media. Such movement calls for a different kind of specialization. Consequently, agencies specializing in direct response, digital communications and social media, and experiential marketing are in greater demand.

Given the technology that is available, it is possible to direct messages at individuals instead of at a large target audience. Reaching an audience of one with a unique message is attractive to advertisers today; hence, there is a need for agencies specializing in direct response communications. Digital agencies differentiate themselves by offering clients a variety of web-based services such as web design and development, search engine marketing, online communications strategies (e.g., banner ads and video display ads), and even ecommerce capabilities. Among the larger digital agencies in Canada are Proximity Canada, Blast Radius, Twist Image, and Critical Mass.

Twist Image of Montreal is an example of a digital agency that established a solid reputation before traditional agencies adapted to digital media. Today, Twist Image is known as an expert in new media and integrated marketing solutions. Working closely with clients, the agency uncovers ways to apply technology to marketing and

Courtesy of Dairy Farmers of Canada

FIGURE 2.5

Twist Image designed this interactive website for Dairy Farmers of Canada.

communications, be it on laptops, tablets, smartphones, or gaming platforms. Some of its clients include Walmart, Dairy Farmers of Canada, TD Bank, and the Montreal Canadiens. A sample of Twist Image's work appears in Figure 2.5.

The increase in competition from digital specialist agencies has been so dramatic that full-service agencies and other specialists have had to acquire digital expertise (either through ownership or strategic alliance) to meet the ever-changing demands of their clients. All of the digital agencies mentioned above were acquired by agency conglomerates. Proximity and Critical Mass are part of the Omnicom Group, and Blast Radius and Twist Image are part of WPP. DDB Canada (a full-service agency) operates Tribal DDB (a digital agency), and Young & Rubicam (full service) operates Wunderman (direct response).

Agencies that specialize in more personalized forms of communications are making headway in the industry. Referred to as *experiential marketing agencies*, they devise strategies that establish two-way dialogue and communicate one to one with people to build brands. Sales promotions, event marketing, retail visits, and social strategies play a key role in the activities recommended by experiential agencies. Mosaic Marketing and Tigris are among Canada's leading experiential marketing agencies.

The growth in popularity of digital agencies is attributed to the rising popularity of web-based social networking sites such as Facebook, Twitter, and YouTube. With so much fragmentation in traditional media, marketers are searching for more effective ways to reach consumers.

INDUSTRY AND MARKET SPECIALISTS

Other specialists focus on product categories or niche market segments that are identified as profitable opportunities. Pharmaceutical marketing, for example, is a highly specialized product category in which laws and regulations governing advertising are very different from other product categories. Consequently, it is an area that not many agencies get involved in. A few prominent agencies that do include FCB Health (a member of the Interpublic Group) and Ogilvy CommonHealth (a division of Ogilvy & Mather Canada and part of the WPP Group).

There are also agencies that focus on reaching specific target markets, such as ethnic groups and specific age groups (e.g., baby boomers). Canada's ethnic population is growing—Statistics Canada predicts that Canada's South Asian population will reach 3.2 million and the Chinese population 2.4 million by 2031.[11] Marketers see value in reaching such targets with original advertising, hence the creation of specialized agencies to meet this need. Toronto-based agency BlueBand recently launched a new ethnic division called Blue Dot, which is dedicated to reaching a multicultural audience.[12] The Zoomer Agency dedicates itself to reaching Canadians 45 years and older, a segment that comprises 14.5 million people and accounts for 60 percent of all consumer spending—a target worth pursuing.

THE GENERALIST OR THE SPECIALIST

Clients tend to go in two directions when selecting the type of agency they would like to work with. Some migrate to the large multinational agencies, while others prefer to work with boutique-style shops. Lately, clients are trending toward specialist agencies, particularly for special projects, new product launches, and digital media requirements. Alternatively, clients may choose to work with full-service agencies on an ongoing basis but decide to farm out specific projects to specialists. Various combinations exist in client–agency relationships.

Creative boutiques and media specialists offer clients a unique advantage. The highly experienced creative and media people who started the boutique or specialist service usually work directly with the clients. Ironically, these creative and media people generally honed their craft at much larger agencies, where various layers of management get involved in the process.

The shift toward specialization is due in part to the rapid growth in digital communications. It caught a good many full-service agencies off guard, and specialists moved in to gain a foothold on that communications segment. Clients themselves had to adapt to the digital environment. Instinctively, they sought the necessary expertise to guide them. Combining the talents of specialists could provide the best of both worlds for advertisers. However, full-service agencies argue that they can handle a collection of services equally well for their clients—and all under one roof, too.

For insight into a new type of agency, read the Advertising in Action vignette **Agency Model of the Future**.

Managing the Client's Business

This section will describe how an agency manages a client's account and how a client compensates the agency for the services it provides. Several factors influence the professional relationship between the client and the agency.

AGENCY TEAMS

The amount of time an agency spends with a client and the personnel it allocates to serve the needs of the client affect the client–agency relationship. Agency management will form teams to work together on a client's business. The employees who constitute a team vary among agencies, depending on factors such as the size of the agency, the various levels of personnel resources available, and the services offered. For the purpose of illustration, a full-service agency typically forms an account group composed of the following personnel:

- Account executive and account supervisor
- Art director and copywriter
- Media planner and media buyer

ADVERTISING IN ACTION

Agency Model of the Future

Advertising agencies come in all shapes and sizes and with varying degrees of specialization. Certainly clients have myriad options to choose from when deciding what type of agency partners to work with. In a larger agency, there are some cost issues to consider. More management layers (administrators and the like) mean overhead costs rise and, ultimately, clients may have to pay more for the services they receive.

Enter a new agency model, a model sparked by four successful agency veterans and one that is very light on extras—it's four guys and an army of freelancers ready to tackle any marketing communications challenge. Even the name of the agency is unique – 123W—which happens to be the longitude of Vancouver, where the agency is located. Scot Keith, one of the founders, describes the agency as an "on-demand" model where a roster of freelance talent can be hired on a project-by-project basis. Different projects get different talent. Keith says, "We can assemble and mobilize a team literally in an hour of some of the finest talent in Canada."[13]

Two key factors prompted this startup agency. First, the recession of 2008 left a lot of agency talent on the sidelines as massive restructuring took place in the industry. Second, advertising budgets are shrinking and marketers are trying to achieve more with less—they are looking for better value from their business suppliers.

The four partners know the traditional model well—all were key players. Scot Keith was general manager at Lowe Roche and Zulu Alpha Kilo. Jeff Harrison was a creative director and partner at Rethink, and Bryan Collins and Rob Sweetman are well-regarded, award-winning creative directors who worked at Rethink and Dare.

Most of the freelancers have similar backgrounds, so the level of expertise available is significant. Alan Russell is one of them. Russell recently made *Advertising Age*'s list of top 10 creatives in North America and has worked with full-service agencies such as Palmer Jarvis, Grey Advertising Canada, and BBDO Canada. At 61 years of age, the level of experience he brings isn't available to a lot of clients at established and larger agencies.

Russell is sold on the new model. Although he believes there will always be large accounts that want multinational agencies, people in the current market want flexibility and creative products at a much lower cost.

How is the new agency doing? Canadian Pacific Railway, one of its first clients, is very pleased. "They demonstrated a hair-trigger responsiveness," says Robert MacLean, director of customer and integrated communications at Canadian Pacific. MacLean liked the streamlined operations. "At some agencies you meet an army of foot soldiers: creative directors, associate creative directors, account directors. With 123W I know who's doing the work, and they don't charge me $350 per hour."

You be the judge. Is this the future model for advertising agencies?

Courtesy of One Twenty Three West

Courtesy of One Twenty Three West

Susan Krashinsky, "A New Kind of Agency, a Nod to Steve Jobs," *The Globe and Mail*, April 10, 2013, p. B5.

Keeping an account team together over a number of assignments benefits both the client and the agency. Familiarity with the products and the way the client operates are obvious benefits. The agency team can draw upon past experiences with the client when considering new directions to pursue. Another benefit involves consistency in approach. The account team develops a strategy that will work over an extended period. Within that long-term strategy will be the flexibility to develop and execute new plans when needed. Clients who are subjected to changing personnel within an account group may question whether the agency values their business. Conversely, the agency may, by keeping an account team together, imply that a client's business is important and that it is trying to serve the client more effectively.

In recent years, the team concept has gone a step further. Now that digital media are a key component of the communications mix, new and unique expertise is required. New job titles such as *digital strategist* and *community manager* have emerged. A **digital strategist** focuses on technology and is responsible for developing strategies for all forms of new media, be it on laptops, tablets, or smartphones, or in video games. Digital strategists don't operate in a silo. They must fully understand the bigger communications picture and work effectively with other planners more focused on traditional media when pursuing new opportunities for a client.

What has emerged is the **hybrid team**, a concept that calls for account planners, creative planners (copywriters and art directors), and media planners from all media to work together on a client's business. By working together in the initial planning stages, the combined team can search out and evaluate concepts that complement all forms of media. When the client briefs the agency on an assignment, it is important that all of these team members participate in the discussion—good ideas can come from anywhere! This briefing process must occur several times if a client works with a number of agencies specializing in different areas of communication.

From a staffing perspective, many agencies now look for employees who have multiple areas of expertise and an appreciation for the bigger picture of how effective interaction among the disciplines should occur. Creative directors and media directors and those job functions that report directly to them must have the right expertise to match the expectations of their clients—expectations that are constantly changing. Keeping up with change is a constant challenge for advertising agency personnel.

COMPETING ACCOUNTS

Agencies are exposed to extremely confidential client information when developing advertising plans. As a consequence, agencies will not, as a rule, accept assignments from an advertiser who is in direct competition with a current client. Numerous conflicts develop as an agency seeks new business. When agencies merge to form larger agencies, competing accounts are often brought together. In such a case, one of the clients (usually the smaller, in terms of media dollars) will take its business elsewhere, or the agency will resign the client's business.

AGENCY OF RECORD

Many large advertisers (companies with numerous divisions or multiproduct lines) distribute their advertising assignments among several advertising agencies. Others consolidate their advertising under a single roof. Both options have their benefits and drawbacks. From the client's perspective, dividing the business among several agencies is advantageous in that the different products or services required will receive more attention than would be possible if all assignments were given to one agency. It also encourages competition between agencies that could influence how new projects are assigned. Dividing the assignments, in other words, should positively affect the quality of the work. Clients that employ a one-agency approach on a national or international scale are searching for cost efficiencies—dealing with only one agency should reduce costs.

On the media side of things, the client often appoints one agency to be the **agency of record (AOR)**. The AOR is a central agency responsible for media negotiation and placement and is one of the agencies (usually a full-service agency or a media buying specialist) employed by multiple-product advertisers. An AOR facilitates efficiency in the media buying process, often making greater discounts available to the client by purchasing all media on a corporate (large-volume) basis. The AOR is responsible for corporate media contracts under which other agencies will issue their placement orders. Also, the AOR records all advertising placed and is responsible for final allotment of time and space in a media schedule. The AOR usually receives slightly more compensation than the other agencies a client works with.

Agency Compensation

How an advertising agency is paid and how much money it makes is an issue frequently on the minds of both client marketing executives and agency managers. Marketing executives often argue that the agency is asking for too much money, or they feel they are paying for unnecessary services. Agency managers, on the other hand, believe that the profit margins on some of their accounts are too low in relation to the amount of resources allocated to the client. Needless to say, compensation is a primary area where clients and agencies are at odds.

There are three basic methods of compensating an advertising agency for the services it provides: an agency commission based on the dollar volume of media placed; a fee that considers the resources an agency allocates to servicing a client; or payment by results, a reduced-rate commission with incentives based on performance standards. A summary of the advantages and disadvantages of each system appears in Figure 2.6.

THE COMMISSION SYSTEM

The original method for compensating agencies was to pay them a **commission** based on how much the advertiser invested in advertising. Traditionally, advertising agencies earned 15 percent of the dollar value of the media time and space they purchased for their clients. For example, if an agency invested $1 million in time and space, the advertiser would pay out $1 million. The agency would retain 15 percent, or $150 000, and the media (say a television network or print media company) would receive $850 000. Under this system, the agency receives a discount from the media for bringing business their way. This discount is granted to accredited agencies for their work in analyzing client research, preparing the overall strategy, creating and producing the advertising material, performing media planning and buying, billing the client, and doing research in support of recommendations and discounts for prompt payment.[14]

The production of advertising materials is also paid for by the client with a provision of commission for the agency. Typically, a profit margin of 17.65 percent is added to the production costs incurred by the agency. For example, if the cost of producing a single 30-second television commercial is $250 000, the agency will receive $44 125 (17.65 percent of $250 000) for its services. The agency would bill the client $294 125, and from these funds the external suppliers who produced the commercial would be paid.

This is a comfortable system for all parties involved, but one can quickly see its weakness. The more the client spends on advertising, the more revenue the agency generates for itself. The agency might not have to do any additional work, yet it will earn much

FIGURE 2.6

The advantages and disadvantages of agency compensation methods

Clients are gradually moving toward the payment-by-results method. They are asking their agencies to be accountable for the strategies and executions being recommended. At the same time, agencies are asking their clients to take more risks instead of retreating to familiar ideas. Agencies want to prove to their clients that their ideas will work in the marketplace.

COMMISSION SYSTEM

Pros:

- Simple to implement
- All services are provided at no additional cost
- Pressure on agency to keep costs down

Cons:

- Profit on some brands (larger budgets); losses on others (smaller budgets)
- Agency recommendations for higher expenditures may be self-serving
- Payment is based on media cost, not the work provided

FEE SYSTEM

Pros:

- Client pays only for services provided
- Agency is accountable for all time devoted to the client's account

Cons:

- High administration costs
- Difficult for agency to forecast workload

PAYMENT-BY-RESULTS SYSTEM (LOWER COMMISSION AND INCENTIVES)

Pros:

- Encourages neutral media recommendations involving a variety of media
- Additional revenue to agency for successful campaigns

Cons:

- Accountability; potential loss on account if results are not achieved
- Influences beyond the control of agency could negatively affect advertising

more. The commission system has fallen out of favour with clients because the system fuelled a perception that some agencies were making too much profit from easy media buying assignments or by recommending more expensive media options.

THE FEE SYSTEM

In its truest form, the **fee system** avoids any form of commission and rewards an agency for the time, effort, and energy it puts into servicing the client. There are several ways in which the fee system can work. An agency could work on a *retainer* basis, in which an annual fee is agreed to and the agency bills the client on a monthly basis. If unforeseen circumstances arise during the year, the financial arrangement can be amended accordingly. Another option is to establish an *hourly fee* for the time an agency spends on a client's business. The client would be billed for the agency services at the end of each month. An agency can determine its hourly rates by estimating the costs of serving a client and building in a profit margin. The fee system is ideally suited for clients who work with many agencies and clients who assign different communications tasks to specialist agencies.

There has been a movement toward fees in recent years because so much of the work in advertising today is not traditional advertising. You can't calculate a commission on activities such as sales promotions, public relations, or experiential marketing. The fee system is more complex and requires lots of administration and paperwork. Critics of the fee system say it doesn't recognize the quality of work; it only considers the time an agency spends on an account. The agency is paid simply for performing various tasks.

PAYMENT BY RESULTS (PBR)

The **payment-by-results (PBR) system** is relatively new and is increasing in popularity with clients and agencies. One of the first advertisers to experiment with performance-based compensation was Procter & Gamble. Its rationale for moving away from the straight commission and fees was to encourage agencies to recommend a variety of media and to rely less on 30-second television ads, which are more expensive than other forms of media and thus garner larger commissions. Under the PBR system, agencies are paid a higher commission percentage for good business results and a lower percentage for poor results. The system is incentive-based and keeps the client and the agency focused on the end goal: to increase brand sales.

Moving to performance-based compensation eliminates media bias (i.e., recommending media that generate hefty commissions) and encourages holistic, media-neutral recommendations from the agency. Coca-Cola has moved to a performance-based system that "promises agencies nothing more than recouped costs if they don't perform—but profit markups as high as 30% if their work hits top targets." Coca-Cola's director of worldwide media and communication operations, Sarah Armstrong, explains: "We want our agencies to earn their profitability, but it's not guaranteed."[15]

In an incentive-based system, the client and agency must agree on what the targets are. Agencies are intrigued by this system but cite a major drawback. Directly linking the performance of a brand to advertising is tricky because sales can be affected by a host of factors, many of which are beyond the control of the advertising agency. In other words, if a market share objective isn't met, advertising is blamed for the shortfall. However, the incentives the system offers should stimulate agency personnel to do their best work possible—with the right creative and media strategies in place, this system will reward them handsomely.

The latest trends in agency compensation indicate the fee system dominates with 80 percent of client–agency partnerships using it. Performance- and incentive-based systems are growing in popularity, as 15 percent of client–agency partnerships now use this method. Getting agencies on board is a challenge. Agencies have a business to run and fixed costs to consider, so the risks for them are significant in this system. The commission system continues to drop in popularity and now only accounts for 5 percent of agency compensation methods.[16]

For more insight into some of the criteria that are included in a performance-based compensation system, see Figure 2.7. Additional information about this compensation system is available free through the ICA website under "Publications" (www.icacanada.ca).

FIGURE 2.7

Performance criteria included in a payment-by-results compensation model

Business Performance	Advertising Performance	Agency Performance
Sales volume	Advertising awareness	Agency service delivery
Volume growth	Brand image shifts	Relationship management
Relative brand performance	Attitude ratings	Functional competencies
Composite performance	Ad enjoyment	Contribution to "branding"
Market share	Brand personality	Project management
Customer loyalty	Predisposition to buy	Administration
Brand equity	Ad scores	Cost efficiency
Brand profitability	Persuasion index	Proactivity

The ICA Study on PBR shows the weighting emphasis was balanced as follows: Agency 41%, Advertising 30%, and Business Results 29%. Further, 83% of Canadian PBR programs include business performance criteria, 65% include advertising performance criteria, and 78% include agency performance criteria.

Source: Payment by Results 2: Advertising Agency Remuneration Best Practices, Institute of Communication Agencies, www.icacanada.ca. Printed with permission.

SUMMARY

In the ever-changing world of advertising, advertising and marketing communications agencies are constantly challenged to develop innovative campaigns that will have an impact on a target audience. As well, agencies are now responsible for complete IMC campaigns. To remain on top of their game, agencies have to adapt to change quickly and always ensure they have the necessary resources available to meet the needs of demanding clients.

The Canadian advertising industry comprises six primary groups: the advertisers (clients), advertising agencies, the media, advertising support organizations, media support services, and research and audience measurement companies.

Advertising management usually comes under the jurisdiction of the marketing department. The size and marketing sophistication of the organization often dictate how advertising is managed. It could be the responsibility of a brand manager or category manager, or it could be the responsibility of many individuals. With marketing and communications strategy becoming more continental and global in scope (i.e., using strategies and executions that are effective for multiple audiences), managers are redefining targets and implementing campaigns on a regional, national, or global scale.

In the advertising development process, the roles and responsibilities of the client include briefing the agency on new assignments, coordinating advertising with other marketing and marketing communications activities, monitoring the implementation of communications activities, liaising with the advertising agency, and securing executive approval to implement advertising plans. Once plans are implemented, the manager is responsible for evaluating advertising, for which he or she is held accountable.

Advertising agencies provide a variety of services to their clients, but their primary role is to provide experience and expertise in the communications process. In this area, the agency provides planning assistance and contributes an objective viewpoint to that planning process. Agency recommendations must be cost effective and have an impact on the intended target.

The goal of a client–agency relationship is to have a long-term partnership in which both parties prosper. However, relationships between clients and agencies are often volatile, and account shifting is a common occurrence in the industry. Such shifting occurs for reasons such as client dissatisfaction with the quality of work, philosophical differences in creative and media direction, and the absence of a team concept. Lasting relationships depend on open and honest communication among the parties, mutual respect, and agreement on common goals. Each party should evaluate the other in a constructive manner.

Advertisers must evaluate the services provided by agencies and decide whether to use a full-service agency or hire a specialist that may or may not offer all of the services required. Specialists include creative boutiques, media buying services, direct response companies, interactive communications companies, and industry-specific agencies. Generally, there has been a trend toward using more specialist agencies.

Traditional, full-service agencies are divided into specific functional areas: account management, creative, and the media. Account management personnel consult with clients and coordinate activity within the agency. The creative department develops communication concepts, and the media department plans and places advertising time and space.

The services that an agency provides to a client are usually handled by an account team that includes personnel from each functional area. A recent trend is the formation of hybrid teams, a practice that brings all parties together in the initial planning stages of a campaign. Collaboration across all functions (account planning, creative, and media) is seen as an effective means of generating good ideas.

A major factor in client–agency relationships is the method by which the agency is paid. There are three systems used to compensate agencies: a commission system, under which the agency receives a percentage of the value of media purchased by an agency for a client; a fee system, which is based on the services requested by the client; and a payment-by-results system, in which agencies are compensated based on how well they meet predetermined performance criteria. The latter system usually involves a lower rate of commission and a bonus system.

KEY TERMS

account director 45
account executive 44
(account planner) 44
account management 44
account services group 39
account shifting 41
account supervisor 45
advertising agency 33
advertising manager 36
advertising research 37
agency of record (AOR) 53
art director 45
brand manager (product manager) 35
category manager 35
commission 53
copywriter 45
creative boutique 47
creative department 45
creative director 45
digital strategist 52
fee system 54
full-service agency 43
hybrid team 52
international management system 36
media billings 48
media buyer 47
media buying 46
media buying service 48
media convergence 34
media director 47
media planner 47
media planning 46
media research 46
payment-by-results (PBR) system 55
production manager 46
regional management system 35
traffic manager 46

REVIEW QUESTIONS

1. What are the six primary groups that constitute the advertising industry?
2. What are the alternative management systems used by clients to manage the advertising function? Briefly explain each system.
3. Identify and explain the roles and responsibilities of the client in the creation of advertising.
4. What are the key roles and responsibilities of advertising agencies in the advertising process?
5. What is meant by the phrase *client–agency relations*? What factors have a negative influence on the relationship? What factors have a positive influence on the relationship?
6. What does *account shifting* refer to? Why does account shifting occur?
7. How do a full-service agency, a creative boutique, and a media buying service differ from one another?
8. What are the primary functions of the following agency departments? Who are the key people in each area?
   a) Account management
   b) Creative department
   c) Media department
9. Explain the concept of agency teams. Why is the team concept important to clients?
10. What is an agency of record (AOR)?
11. What are the three primary methods of compensating an advertising agency? Briefly describe each method.
12. A client spends $3 million on network television advertising, $450 000 on magazine advertising, and $250 000 on outdoor posters. The cost of producing two television commercials was $400 000, and the production charges for the magazines and outdoor posters were $60 000. How much commission does the client's advertising agency earn, given that the agency is compensated using the traditional rate of commission? What does the client pay in total? How much do the media receive in total?

DISCUSSION QUESTIONS

1. Assume you are the director of marketing for PepsiCo Canada. Will you work with a full-service advertising agency, or will you divide your work among various specialists, such as creative boutiques, media buying services, digital agencies, and other types of specialists? Justify your position. What factors determine the use of generalists versus specialists?
2. Given that the client hires an agency to develop creative strategies, how involved in the creative development process should the client be? Where do the client's responsibilities end?
3. "The client–agency relationship is a partnership." Discuss the significance of this statement in the context of today's business environment. Is the statement true? What are the ingredients of a successful relationship?
4. Conduct some additional research on the payment-by-results system for compensating advertising agencies. Is it a good system or a bad system (for the client, for the agency)? Present an informed opinion on this compensation model.

NOTES

1. Institute of Communications Agencies, **www.icacanada.ca**.
2. Association of Canadian Advertisers, **www.acaweb.ca/en/what-we-do**.
3. Institute of Communication Agencies, **www.icacanada.ca**.
4. Newspapers Canada, *Net Advertising Volume Canada Interim Report 2005–2014*, **www.newspaperscanada.ca/sites/default/files/Net_Advertising_Volume_Report_All_Media_TRENDING_20150720.pdf**.
5. Canadian Media Directors' Council, "Media Cross-Ownership," *Media Digest 2014–2015*, 15.
6. Lara Mills, "Molson Overhauls Marketing Team," *Marketing*, September 20, 1999, 17.
7. Hannah Fleishman, "10 Businesses We Admire for Brilliant Global Marketing," *HubSpot Blogs*, November 30, 2012, **http://blog.hubspot.com**.
8. Patrick Bellerose, "BlueBlancRouge," *Marketing*, November 9, 2009, 16.
9. Jeromy Lloyd, "Juniper Loses Quaker North America," *Marketing*, March 14, 2012, **www.marketingmag.ca**.
10. Val Maloney, "OMD Is Top-Billing Agency Once Again," *Media in Canada*, July 30, 2014, www.mediaincanada.com.
11. Statistics Canada, *Projections of the Diversity of the Canadian Population: 2006 to 2031.* Catalogue no. 91-551-X. **www.statcan.gc.ca/pub/91-551-x/91-551-x2010001-eng.pdf**.
12. Megan Haynes, "BlueBand Opens up Ethnic Shop," *Strategy*, July 7, 2014, **www.strategyonline.ca**.
13. Eve Lazarus, "Getting to Know 123W in Five Easy Steps," *Marketing*, April 12, 2013, **www.marketingmag.ca**.
14. This information is from the Institute of Communication Agencies, **www.icacanada.com**.
15. Jeremy Mullman and Natalie Zmusa, "Coke Pushes for Pay-for-Performance Model," *Advertising Age*, April 27, 1009, pp. 1, 34.
16. Lucia Moses, "A Look at How Agency Compensation Has Changed," *AdWeek*, August 21, 2013, **www.adweek.com**.

PART 2 Marketing Communications Planning

Part 2 concentrates on the central theme of the text—planning the marketing communications effort.

Chapter 3 provides the foundation for marketing communications planning, presenting the important concepts of consumer behaviour, market segmentation and target marketing, and positioning.

Chapter 4 describes the elements of strategic planning and presents the content and structure of marketing plans and marketing communications plans. It establishes the relationships among these plans and provides an appreciation of the role and importance of planning in the development of all forms of marketing communications.

CHAPTER 3

Consumer Behaviour Concepts and Target Marketing

Learning Objectives

After studying this chapter, you will be able to

1. Explain how consumer behaviour concepts influence the development of marketing communications strategies
2. Assess the information needed to identify and select target markets
3. Distinguish between demographic, psychographic, geographic, behaviour-response, and direct segmentation variables
4. Explain the concept of positioning and its role in developing marketing communications strategies

This chapter discusses concepts that are important to the planning of advertising and marketing communications programs. The development of an effective advertising strategy relies heavily on an understanding of basic consumer behaviour. Uncovering what makes a particular customer group tick provides direction on what appeal techniques will grab an audience's attention. It may also provide insights into what media are best suited for reaching a group of customers. Organizations must identify profitable target markets by analyzing demographic trends, psychographic characteristics, and geographic or regional differences. The result of such an analysis is a clear description of a target market that is worth pursuing. The chapter ends with a discussion of a variety of product positioning strategies.

Consumer Buying Behaviour

Consumer buying behaviour refers to the study of how people buy, what they buy, and why they buy. It can be defined as the combined acts carried out by individuals when choosing and using goods and services, including the decision-making process that determines these acts. A firm understanding of how behavioural tendencies apply to purchase decisions is of significant benefit to the marketing organization. Consequently, leading marketing organizations spend a considerable amount of money on **marketing research** to learn as much as they can about their customers and perhaps get an edge on the competition in the process.

From a purely competitive perspective, marketers must have access to data concerning consumers' buying habits and which kinds of media consumers favour so that they can develop more convincing communications programs that stimulate response by the target market. The purpose of most research boils down to obtaining answers to a few key questions:

- Who makes the buying decision?
- Who influences the buying decision?
- What motivates the buyers and people of influence to take action?

Answers to these questions will provide valuable input for developing a marketing strategy and a marketing communications strategy. To illustrate, consider the time people now spend online researching product information. They gather considerable information, and when they arrive at a retail location, whether bricks and mortar or online, they know what they want to buy. Much of this information is gathered from the media. Marketers must consider the relative influence of various media that influence consumer buying behaviour. While findings vary from one study to another, one recent study on media influence revealed that all mass media have some influence, but to varying degrees. Newspapers ranked highest in influence among 25 percent of respondents (even though people are moving away from print media) followed by television (19 percent) and websites (19 percent).[1] While it is often assumed social media has considerable influence, some recent research refutes that notion. In a Gallup study, 62 percent of consumers said social media didn't influence their purchasing decisions at all, and a meager 5 percent said social media exerted a great deal of influence.[2] Let's consider the key influences on **consumer behaviour.**

NEEDS AND MOTIVES

Needs suggest a state of deprivation—the absence of something useful. **Motives** are the conditions that prompt the action that is taken to satisfy the need (the action elicited by marketing and advertising activity). The relationship between needs and motives is direct with respect to marketing and advertising activity. Such activity must sufficiently develop the target market's need—through an appealing presentation of appropriate benefits—so that the target is motivated to respond by purchasing the product or service.

Maslow's *hierarchy of needs* and *theory of motivation* have had a significant impact on marketing and advertising strategies. According to Maslow, needs are classified from lower level to higher level, as shown in Figure 3.1. His theory is based on two prevailing assumptions:

1. When lower-level needs are satisfied, a person moves up to higher-level needs.
2. Satisfied needs do not motivate. Instead, behaviour will be influenced by needs yet to be satisfied.[3]

Maslow states that individuals move through five levels of needs:

- ***Physiological needs***: hunger, thirst, sex, shelter
- ***Safety needs***: security, protection, comfort
- ***Social needs***: sense of belonging, love from family and friends
- ***Esteem needs***: recognition, achievement, status, to excel
- ***Self-actualization needs***: fulfillment, to realize potential (achieve what you believe you can achieve)

FIGURE 3.1

The hierarchy of needs

Source: Maslow, Abraham H., Frager, Robert D., Fadiman, James, *Motivation and Personality*, 3rd Edition, © 1987. Reprinted and electronically reproduced by permission of Pearson Education, Inc., Upper Saddle River, New Jersey.

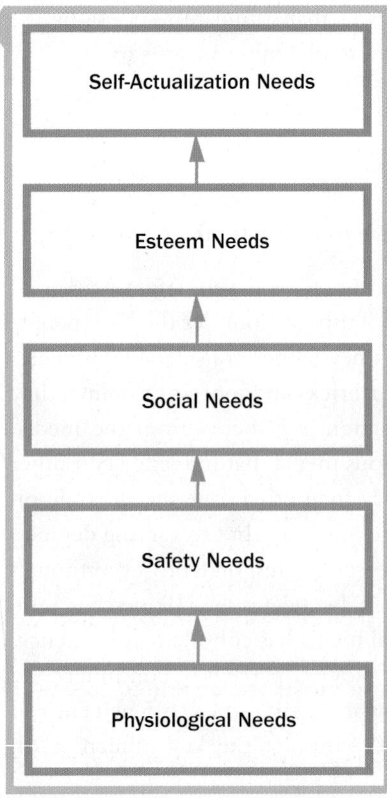

Numerous advertising examples can be cited to demonstrate advertising applications of Maslow's needs theory. Safety needs are used to motivate people to purchase life insurance, retirement savings plans, and cars. Allstate's famous advertising slogan "You're in good hands with Allstate" appeals to safety needs. Volkswagen once advertised its Jetta model as light, fuel efficient, and safe; headlines such as "Safe happens" and "Highest government side impact rating" delivered the message.

Beauty and personal care products are famous for appealing to social and esteem needs. Having softer skin, shinier hair, whiter teeth, and fresher breath are the hallmarks of brands in these product categories. Beauty brands such as Revlon and L'Oréal enhance the benefits of their products by using celebrities (influencers) in their advertisements. If you were to scan through any popular magazine targeted at women, you will see numerous advertisements extolling the virtues of skin care and hair care products. L'Oreal Excellence Age Perfect is a hair colouring product that promises full, natural-looking hair. Vaseline Intensive Care offers a serum that helps reverse dry skin damage. Products like these make women feel good about themselves—by making them look and feel younger. Refer to the image in Figure 3.2.

In the automotive industry, esteem needs are addressed in commercials that portray people in successful business roles and occupations; for example, an executive driving an automobile symbolic of success, such as a Cadillac, BMW, or Porsche.

PERSONALITY AND SELF-CONCEPT

Personality refers to a person's distinguishing psychological characteristics—those features that lead to relatively consistent and enduring responses to the environment in which that person lives. Personality is influenced by self-perceptions, which in turn are influenced by psychological needs, family, culture, and reference groups. Why do people buy designer-label clothing at high prices and in upscale boutiques when low-priced items performing the same functions are available? Such purchases are based on the images we desire to have of ourselves. To appreciate this principle, one must understand the self-concept theory.

Self-concept theory states that the self has four components: real self, self-image, looking-glass self, and ideal self.

- ***Real self*** is an objective evaluation of the individual. It is you as you really are.
- ***Self-image*** is how you see yourself. It may not be your real self, but a role you play with yourself.
- ***Looking-glass self*** is how you think others see you. This view can be different from how others actually see you.
- ***Ideal self*** is how you would like to be. It is what you aspire to.[4]

Marketers know that, human nature being what it is, many important decisions are based on the looking-glass self and the ideal self. In other words, many goods and services are bought on the basis of emotion: Goods that help us feel better, look better, and take us to the next level of fulfillment are very attractive to us. We may not achieve what we want, but there is some psychological satisfaction in having something that represents a higher level of achievement. Consequently, advertisers present messages that appeal to the next level of fulfillment.

As described in the previous section, grooming products are advertised to satisfy social and esteem needs. Such behaviour is influenced by a person's desire to achieve their ideal self—how they would like to be! What about urban males who buy big

Courtesy of Unilever

FIGURE 3.2

Personal care products appeal to the social and esteem needs of consumers.

trucks but never use them for their intended purpose—to haul things! There's more to a vehicle than getting from point A to point B. To own a truck like the Ram 1500, Ford F-150, or Chevrolet Silverado is an expression of how a person wants to be perceived, either his self-image or ideal self. It makes a statement! Refer to the image in Figure 3.3. For more insight into truck advertising and how it appeals to urban male consumers, read the Advertising in Action vignette **A Vehicle for the Real Man**.

ADVERTISING IN ACTION

A Vehicle for the Real Man

You've seen them—those guys driving shiny new trucks in cities. The question is: Why do they need a truck when they live and drive in such a congested environment? Well, it all has to do with image—or perceived image!

The pickup truck used to serve a basic purpose. It was the vehicle of choice for contractors and tradespeople, farmers and ranchers. It was a working vehicle. But now the pickup has gone mainstream—so mainstream in fact, that the Ford F-150 is Ford's biggest-selling vehicle in Canada. Urban buyers, or "urban dudes," as they are referred to, have vaulted truck sales to ever-increasing sales records each year.

For certain customers, a big truck says something. They may not need one, but they want one! Marketers classify some buyers as "fashion buyers." They are customers who lead an active lifestyle. They don't use the truck every day, but they may use it for towing a camper or boat. If they use it in the city, rarely does it leave a paved road. In their mind the truck projects the image of toughness they are after.

Even from an operational and design point of view trucks have changed. Many models drive more like a well-engineered cars and have all the trappings of a luxury automobile. And they are priced like a small mortgage! The good ol' truck has changed from a humble working vehicle to a high-priced lifestyle symbol.

In assessing the situation, analyst Dennis DesRosiers says, "It's a means of expression and a symbol of how you want to be perceived. And pickup trucks make a particular statement." Chris Kyle, author of *American Sniper*, puts it a different way: "The pickup is the ultimate male enhancement: behind the wheel you are converted from trodden-down schlub to Marlboro man."

The moral of the story is fairly simple: People buy vehicles that make them look and feel better. It's an emotional kind of buying decision. Urban males are buying trucks for that reason. The reality is that they are still the same person, but that's not how they want to be perceived. Marketers have truly capitalized on behaviour theory such as needs and motivation, personality, and the self-concept.

© David Cooper/ZUMA Press/Newscom

Adapted from Peter Cheney, "Urban Cowboy," *The Globe and Mail*, March 12, 2015, pp. D1, D10.

ATTITUDES AND PERCEPTIONS

Attitudes are an individual's feelings, favourable or unfavourable, toward an idea or object (the advertised product). Generally speaking, organizations present their products to consumers so that the products agree with the prevailing attitudes of the target audience. Product acceptance then comes more quickly. Companies have found that it is expensive to try to change attitudes.

For example, teens consider themselves to be on the edge of what their parents consider normal; thus, they are attracted to products whose advertising pushes the boundaries. Brands such as Mountain Dew (Do the Dew–style advertising) and Red Bull (Red Bull "gives you wings" advertising) present on-the-edge images that appeal strongly to the youth target market these brands are pursuing.

A more recent trend among advertisers is their pursuit of the lesbian, gay, bisexual, and transgendered (LGBT) market. Moving in this direction does present a risk for an organization. Such a move could alienate present customers who do not want to associate with a general shift in attitude about the LGBT market and LGBT marketing.

FIGURE 3.3

Advertisements for trucks appeal to urban males on the basis of how they want to be perceived.

However, organizations are seeking LGBT customers for a good reason—it's a huge and largely untapped market. In Canada, this group's total before-tax income amounts to roughly $98 billion, equal to approximately 7.2 percent of the GDP (gross domestic product). They have 22 percent more spending power than the average Canadian. That is significant, since the group comprises only about 6 percent of the population.[5] Such figures attract the attention of marketers. Among financial institutions,

TD Canada Trust is ahead of its rivals. In one TD commercial, a gay couple is seen advising a straight couple about the unforeseen costs of home ownership. Procter & Gamble's advertising is also reflecting the diversity of its customer base. A recent commercial for Tide shows a same-sex couple bickering over a classic household purchase decision—whether to buy the brand name or generic brand. Of course you know what the decision is! Refer to the image in Figure 3.4 for an example of advertising directed at gay consumers.

Perception refers to the manner in which individuals receive and interpret messages. From a marketing perspective, how individual consumers perceive the same product can vary considerably. It is safe to say that consumers accept messages that they perceive as being in line with their needs, personality, self-concept, and attitudes, and they reject messages they perceive as not being in line with them.

To demonstrate the importance of consumer perceptions, consider how perceptions held by consumers about food products, specifically healthy food products, affect sales. There has been a shift toward a more health-conscious lifestyle that has spawned all kinds of new food and beverage products. Kellogg's Special K has always been positioned as a healthy product and has benefited from the healthier living trend. The brand has launched many new products under the same positioning strategy. It seems that consumers wanting healthier products will quickly tune into messages that include phrases such as "lighter," "less," "all natural," and "no additives or preservatives," assuming these words signal it is a

Courtesy of TD Bank

FIGURE 3.4

Social changes have produced new targets: TD Canada Trust appeals to the LGBT community.

healthy product. It boils down to perception. Special K is firmly entrenched as a healthy product, but is a Special K Protein Meal Bar draped in chocolate and containing peanut butter healthy? The carryover image from Special K cereal will definitely help sell the protein bar. A common phrase applies here: "Perception is reality." And it is consumer perceptions that advertisers must deal with and capitalize on.

REFERENCE GROUPS

A **reference group**, or **peer group**, is a group, class, or category of people to which individuals believe they belong, whether or not they actually do. Their relationship to their reference group may influence their buying behaviour. Reference groups could include co-workers, sports teams, hobby clubs, fraternal organizations, and schoolmates. A member of a group experiences considerable pressure to conform to the standards of the group and thereby "fit in." The desire to fit in influences the type of products a member will purchase.

Peer influence is strongest among young people. For example, teens share a desire to own the latest electronic gadgets and shop at the trendiest stores. It's all part of their social scene and their desire to satisfy social needs. They turn to peers for information on what behaviour is desirable. With the right strategy, an advertiser need only associate its brand with a certain situation or lifestyle and the target will become interested in the brand. Beverage brands such as Mountain Dew, Red Bull, and Monster have carved out a significant niche with the youth market based on edgy advertising. In the snowboard market, a brand like Burton is popular; in the skateboard and clothing market, a brand like DC is popular. Such popularity is largely based on the image each brand projects in its advertising. See the illustration in Figure 3.5.

FAMILY

Members of a family influence the purchaser's buying decisions. The actual impact each member has on the decision depends on the type of product or service under consideration. Roles and responsibilities within families have changed with the times, and parental lines of responsibility have become blurred. Children seem to have more influence than ever before on what products their parents buy. Factors contributing to these role

FIGURE 3.5

Associating a brand with a situation or lifestyle has an influence on the target market. The youth market is influenced by brands perceived to be authentic in nature.

Shifting roles and responsibilities in the household have placed men in unfamiliar territory. Some 51 percent of males are now the primary shoppers for food and household items. Their purchase behaviour while in a store shopping is very different from women. Here are a few findings of a recent study:

- Men want to enter and exit a store as quickly as possible
- Men are less engaged, and therefore less interested, in brands, discounts, and promotions
- Men fill personal needs first; then they move to household and family needs
- Men are susceptible to self-oriented impulse purchases

Marketers may want to integrate this knowledge into their advertising strategies. For example, brand advertisers should rethink their message strategy to be less emotional and more rational.

Source: An Integer Study, as cited in Megan Haynes, "New Survey Highlights Shopping Habits of Men," *Strategy*, February 13, 2012, www.strategyonline.ca.

FIGURE 3.6

Shopping behaviour: Men shop differently than women.

changes are the increasing numbers of two-income families, the continued growth in the number of women working outside the home, as well as the growth of single-parent families.

No longer can an advertiser assume a woman is the primary shopper in a household. A recent study revealed that 51 percent of men were the primary grocery shoppers in their household.[6] Supermarkets and grocery product manufacturers are adjusting their merchandising and advertising strategies accordingly. For some interesting insight into how men shop, see the details in Figure 3.6. These details have implications for advertisers.

Companies that are tuned into changing responsibilities in households are **double targeting**, which means they are devising marketing strategies that reach both partners effectively. Financial institutions and automobile manufacturers recognize the influence of women in major buying decisions and are devising campaigns that reflect contemporary decision making. Recent data indicate that 31 percent of women earn more than their husbands and 20 percent earn about the same; therefore equality must be demonstrated in advertising, particularly for items classified as a major buying decision.[7]

© Kevin Van Paassen/*The Globe and Mail*/The Canadian Press

FIGURE 3.7

Mark's targets both genders effectively with its advertising.

Mark's (formerly Mark's Work Wearhouse) used to only advertise to men but came to realize that a good many women were in their stores shopping for their man. A decision was made to alter the product mix and target both genders with advertising. The company also shortened the name to Mark's to soften its image. The slogan "Clothes that work" appeals to both genders and aptly portrays the key benefit of what Mark's offers. See the illustration in Figure 3.7.

Identifying and Selecting Target Markets

The ability of a company to target specific customers is based on the concept of market segmentation. **Market segmentation** involves dividing a large market into smaller homogeneous markets (segments) based on common needs or similar lifestyles. Segmentation involves three steps: identifying market segments (e.g., describing the profile of the primary user), selecting the market segments that offer the most potential (typically, targets that offer the greatest profit potential), and positioning the product so that it appeals to the target market.

When an organization identifies a target market, it develops a profile of the customer it wants to pursue. That profile becomes the first cornerstone of all marketing and marketing communications strategies for the product. The second cornerstone is a sound positioning strategy. Positioning strategy is discussed later in the chapter.

A target market profile is the result of an organization's analysis of external variables that influence the direction of marketing strategy. These variables include demographic trends, social and lifestyle trends, geographic trends, and behaviour-response characteristics. Technology is having a significant impact on how marketers segment and target customers. We have actually reached the point where an organization can target individual customers directly with messages—a concept referred to as *direct segmentation*. These concepts are discussed in this section of the chapter.

DEMOGRAPHIC SEGMENTATION

With **demographic segmentation**, target markets are identified and pursued on the basis of variables such as *age, gender, income, occupation, education, marital status, household formation,* and *ethnic background*. In Canada, certain demographic trends are having a direct impact on the direction of marketing strategies and all forms of marketing communications.

For example, if an organization looked only at *age trends*, it would quickly understand that Canada's population is aging. By age, the population is divided into segments based on common characteristics. It is common to give various age groups labels, such as baby boomers, Generation Y, and Generation Z (among others). These segments are attractive to business organizations today, especially baby boomers, which are the largest market segment. Refer to Figure 3.8 for details on the various age segments.

The children of the baby boomers, referred to as Generation Y or millennials (people in their twenties and thirties), are another attractive target. Following them is a new cluster group called Generation Z, or digital natives, that includes people born between 1993 and 2011. Modern marketers seem obsessed with attracting younger buyers in the Generation Y and Generation Z groups. These targets are tech-savvy, so advertisers must recognize and use their communications tools. Interactive, social, and mobile communications will play a much larger role in the marketing communications mix. The dilemma that marketers face is fairly clear: They must adjust their strategies to stay in tune with the changing needs of older consumers while attracting younger consumers at the same time. Doing so successfully is the key to long-term growth.

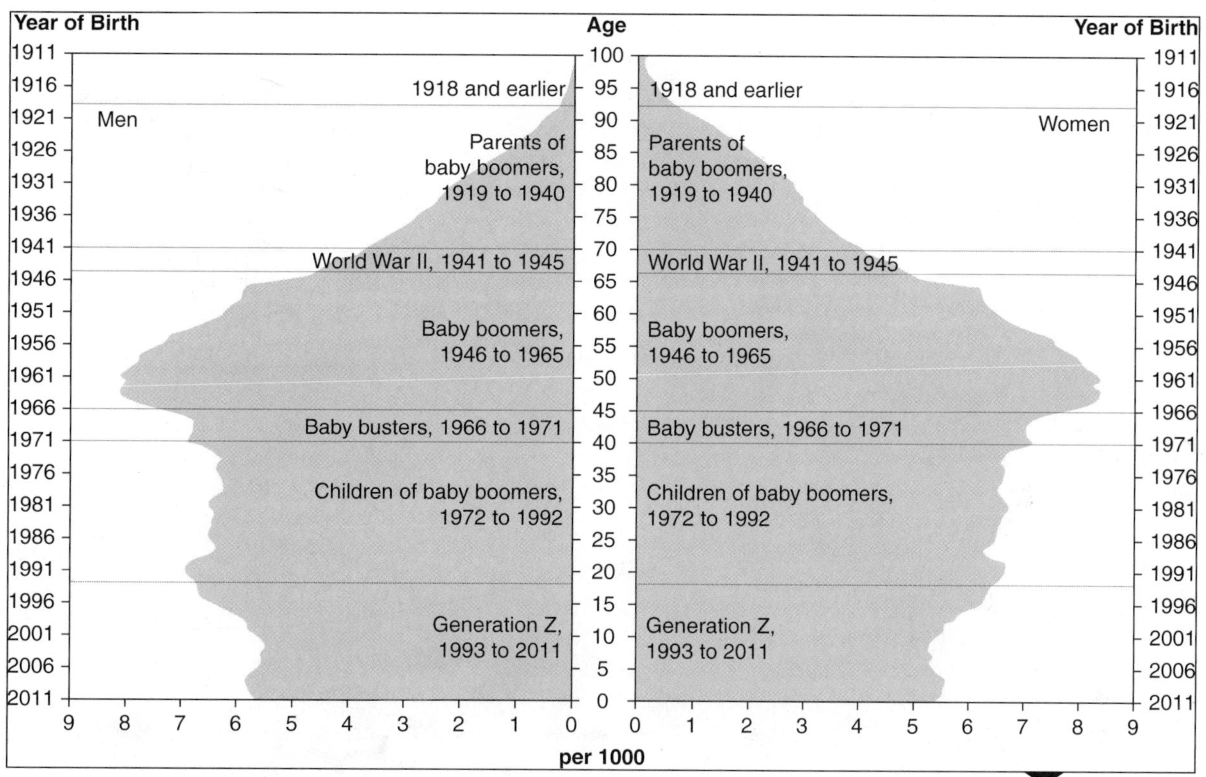

FIGURE 3.8

Canada's population by age

Source: Statistics Canada. (2011). Census of Population. Retrieved from http://www12.statcan.gc.ca/census-recensement/2011/as-sa/98-311-x/2011003/fig/fig3_2-2-eng.cfm.

To demonstrate the application of demographic segmentation, Mercedes-Benz, a maker of luxury automobiles, appeals directly to consumers in the 35- to 54-year-old age bracket—working professionals with higher education and healthy incomes. A Mercedes-Benz is not a young person's car, per se, but rather a car that appeals to someone slightly older who is moving up an organization—it is a vehicle that reflects success, a concept discussed earlier in the chapter. Refer to the image in Figure 3.9

Gender segmentation was introduced in the previous section during the discussion of double targeting. With more women than ever in the workforce, the lines of responsibility between men and women have blurred. Some recent data indicate that 92 percent of women are solely or jointly responsible for family finances. Therefore, if they don't make the buying decision, they certainly influence it. This position must be reflected in advertising. From a strategy perspective, it doesn't have to be about showing one gender or the other in an advertisement; showing both together seems to make sense. Prudent marketers recognize this change and are altering their communications strategies.

Financial institutions such as RBC, TD Canada Trust, and Scotiabank specifically target women in advertising their investment opportunities, insurance plans, and registered retirement savings plans. These companies recognize they are communicating with empowered women and are careful not to portray them in stereotypical situations. Advertising messages will have impact when they communicate to a woman based on how she sees herself or wants to see herself.

To further demonstrate the impact of gender knowledge on advertising, consider that males and females buy automobiles for different reasons: "Safety, comfort, practicality, and value are top priorities for women car buyers."[8] In contrast, men tend to be concerned with the look, style, and feel of the car—it's more of an emotional situation. Income permitting, they like flashier cars. No single advertising strategy will work on customers with such different needs.

Courtesy of Mercedes-Benz Canada Inc.

FIGURE 3.9

An automobile ad that appeals to middle-aged consumers with healthy incomes and progressive career aspirations

Ethnic diversity presents new marketing challenges and opportunities for Canadian advertisers. The population is quickly changing from one of a predominantly European background to an Asian background. In Canada, there are many cultural groups that have distinctive lifestyles based on religious, racial, and geographical differences. Canada's visible minority population presently accounts for 20 percent of the population and is expected to increase to about 30 percent by 2031.[9] In urban centres like Toronto,

Ad courtesy of TD Bank. Image by Tang Ming Tung/Flickr Select/Getty Images

FIGURE 3.10 Canadian advertisers recognize the importance of including visible minorities in their ads.

Vancouver, and Montreal, the visible minority population is also increasing rapidly. By 2031 Toronto's visible minority population will reach 63 percent; in Vancouver, 59 percent; and in Montreal, 31 percent.[10] Perhaps the term should be visible majority.

Companies that embrace ethnic markets with products and advertising campaigns will profit most in the future. The sheer size of this developing market and the fact that unique groups cluster in urban markets make them a reachable target for Canadian brands.

ADVERTISING IN ACTION

Ethnic Markets: Vital Customers Now and in the Future

The ethnic market is a big market in Canada. Statistics Canada reports that a vast majority of Canadians belonging to a visible minority group live in major cities. In Toronto they represent 63 percent of the population, in Vancouver 59 percent, and in Montreal 31 percent. Those numbers are significant! The largest visible minority group are people of South Asian descent, followed by Chinese, black, Filipino, and Hispanic.

Walmart grasped the significance of ethnic marketing quickly. It saw future growth coming from increases in spending by new population growth—immigrants entering the country. The number of new Canadians is growing at five times the rate of the overall population.

Walmart Canada developed a "store of the community" concept that caters to local needs and tastes. A store in the east end of a city carries different merchandise than one in the west end. The location of various ethnic groups in a city is a determining factor on what merchandise a store carries. The company advertises in many different languages and includes people from various ethnic groups in its ads.

Scotiabank holds similar views and is pursuing niche markets that competitors may be neglecting. Scotiabank recently focused on the Hispanic market in Toronto and Montreal. Fabiola Sicard, director of Latin markets at Scotiabank, says, "They are a smaller market than other immigrant communities, they are fragmented geographically, and no significant research has been done on their needs."

In demographic terms, the population of the Hispanic community is more than 600 000. They are highly educated—50 percent have at least a bachelor's degree and another 12 percent have a college diploma. Scotiabank sees Hispanic Canadians as a growth market for its StartRight bank accounts, which are tailored to the needs of newcomers.

In terms of marketing communications, Scotiabank stays away from mainstream media, preferring a more targeted, grassroots approach. The bank targets professional associations, street festivals, and blogs aimed at people living in Latin American countries who are mulling a move north. To reach recent arrivals, the bank gives seminars in Spanish—as many as 150 people show up. Scotiabank does not neglect the larger Chinese and South Asian communities, but the other banks are aggressively targeting them as well. Scotiabank is going into areas nobody else is targeting—a wise move on its part.

Courtesy of the Bank of Nova Scotia

Adapted from Marina Strauss, "Walmart Aims to Cater to a More Diverse Palate," *The Globe and Mail*, April 17, 2012, p. B7 and Simon Houpt, "Unknown, Ignored and Invisible," *The Globe and Mail*, November 18, 2011, p. B7.

Walmart is a leader in this area. It has identified the South Asian, Cantonese, Mandarin, Spanish, Portuguese, and Italian communities as priorities. Walmart adjusts its merchandising strategies to meet culture-based local market conditions and runs television commercials featuring people from these minorities.

Many other advertisers have followed suit by launching specifically targeted advertising campaigns and by including visible minorities in commercial and print advertisements; for an illustration, refer to Figure 3.10. In key urban markets, advertisers also have dedicated media alternatives to reach specific ethnic groups. Omni Television (owned by Rogers Communications), for example, provides programming, news, and information geared at people of specific ethnic origins (e.g., Chinese). This attracts local and national advertisers wanting to reach a specific population. For more insight into how Walmart and Scotiabank are reaching out to ethnic markets, read the Advertising in Action vignette **Ethnic Markets: Vital Customers Now and in the Future**.

PSYCHOGRAPHIC SEGMENTATION

Contemporary marketing organizations have added a more sophisticated variable referred to as *psychographics* to their marketing arsenal. The combination of demographic and psychographic information provides the marketer with a more complete understanding of its target market. Marketers know not only who buys, but also why they buy. Therefore, the hot buttons marketers identify about their targets are pressed when marketing communications are delivered.

Psychographic segmentation examines individual lifestyles in terms of *activities, interests,* and *opinions* (commonly referred to as AIOs). Many of the variables that contribute to a person's lifestyle were introduced earlier in the chapter. Variables such as needs and motivations, attitudes and perceptions, and personality and self-concept combine to influence a person's lifestyle. Therefore, when organizations target their products psychographically, advertising messages are associated with the lifestyle of the target market—the personality of the product matches the personality of the target.

Psychographic information shows how an individual's interest in a particular product depends on his or her lifestyle. Automakers produce and market a range of vehicles to satisfy the requirements of the various lifestyle groups. For example, trendy sports cars with European styling appeal to upscale and educated professionals who are motivated by status and prestige.

Marketers of fashion, personal care products, beer, and automobiles frequently develop advertising campaigns based on psychographic information about consumers. Marketing research companies such as Environics Analytics conduct annual attitudinal studies of Canadians; the results of these studies place people in various psychographic clusters. Unique labels describe the clusters. Environics groups Canadians into clusters and then into subgroups within clusters. Some of the Environics subgroup names include Cosmopolitan Elites, Electric Avenues, Les Chics, and Lunch at Tim's. This type of information is available to marketing organizations for a fee. See Figure 3.11 for more information about psychographic clusters.

Psychographics allows a company to position its products more effectively in the marketplace. Such intimate knowledge of consumers provides ammunition for compelling campaigns that focus on lifestyle associations. The combination of demographic and psychographic knowledge allows the marketing organization to better push the target's hot buttons. With sufficient motivation, consumers are more likely to make a purchase. With reference to the image in Figure 3.12, Subaru appeals to prospective car buyers on the basis of adventure—the advertisement is directed at people who like to get away on weekends and enjoy outdoor activities. The Subaru XV Crosstrek will get them there!

GEOGRAPHIC SEGMENTATION

Geographic segmentation refers to the division of a geographically expansive market (Canada) into smaller geographic units (Atlantic Canada, Quebec, Ontario,

FIGURE 3.11

A sampling of lifestyle clusters in Canada

Cluster Name	Description	Estimated Households 2006	% of total
URBAN ELITE			
Cosmopolitan Elite	Very affluent middle-aged and older city dwellers; incomes five times the national average	296 395	2.31
Urban Villagers	Wealthy middle-aged urban sophisticates; includes well-off immigrants	315 264	2.46
Money & Brains	Upscale and educated professionals and their families; high incomes and sophisticated tastes	292 366	2.28
Furs & Philanthropy	High-achieving cultured urban families; larger families, empty nesters, and widows	333 749	2.60
Suburban Elite			
Suburban Gentry	Well-off middle-aged suburban families; the up-and-coming business class; dual-income couples	161 402	1.26
Nouveaux Riches	Most affluent Francophone cluster; prosperous Quebec suburban families; successful professionals	178 326	1.39
Pets & PCs	Large upscale suburban families; active child-centred lifestyle; minivan and SUV crowd	115 832	0.90

Note: The clusters and descriptions represent a small cross-section of the segments identified in the Prizm C2 segmentation system. In total there are 18 clusters and 66 descriptions. For more information visit the Environics Analytics website at www.environicsanalytics.ca.

Source: Adapted from PRIZM C2 Segmentation System for Canada, Environics Analytics, 2013 **http://www.environics-analytics.ca/environics-analytics/data/consumer-segmentation/prizmc2**, Courtesy of Environics Analytics.

the Prairies, and British Columbia). The availability of psychographic information about target markets has complemented the use of geographic segmentation. Knowing more about targets in the various regions—their behaviour, attitudes, and interests—helps marketers and advertisers develop effective marketing and advertising plans.

The region with the most obvious differences from the rest of Canada is Quebec, whose language and cultural characteristics necessitate the use of different marketing and advertising strategies. Campaigns that are designed specifically with Quebecers in mind and presented in a manner that is culturally relevant will succeed; English-language

Courtesy of Subaru Canada, Inc.

FIGURE 3.12

Subaru appeals to prospective customers on the basis of outdoor adventure; it uses psychographic information about customers to its advantage.

campaigns adapted to Quebec in the form of a French-language voiceover are destined to fail. Quebecers see right through them.

Many advertising experts believe you can understand Quebecers only from the inside, so ad agencies with a foot in the door in Quebec have an advantage over agencies that make decisions about Quebec advertising from afar. "You've got to understand the sensibilities, the sense of humour," says David Yost, a former creative director at Marketel, a Quebec-based agency.[11]

To demonstrate what Yost is saying, consider a new campaign developed by advertising agency DentsuBos for Dr. Pepper. A television spot shows two guys moving a pinball machine down a staircase, when one of them is bothered by a sudden pain. A "doctor" arrives and offers a sip of Dr. Pepper, which he enjoys before being struck by pain once again. A voiceover in a thick Quebec accent says, "Dr. Pepper, c'est juste de la liqueur (It's only a soft drink)," poking fun at the brand's medical connotation. Bernard Young, brand manager at Canada Dry Mott's, says, "We know that Quebec, like Dr. Pepper, is one of a kind; that's why we wanted to have an original approach there, to make sure we would have immediate impact."[12]

More Canadians than ever before live in urban areas—81 percent, according to Statistics Canada.[13] Much of the population is concentrated in six census metropolitan areas. The combination of Toronto, Montreal, Vancouver, Calgary, Edmonton, and Ottawa-Gatineau comprise 42.4 percent of Canada's population. It's not surprising, then, that successful marketing and advertising strategies have an urban orientation and reflect contemporary households dealing with contemporary issues.

Geodemographic segmentation combines demographic characteristics with geographic characteristics and refers to the practice of isolating dwelling areas (e.g., areas within a city) based on the assumption that people seek out neighbourhoods that include their demographic peers. For example, younger, higher-income households may cluster in redeveloped downtown areas, and dual-income, traditional families may reside in suburbia. Sophisticated database marketing techniques give marketers an opportunity to target specific neighbourhoods if they so desire.

Many Canadian organizations are moving away from national marketing strategies and "one size fits all" advertising campaigns, and toward strategies based on regional considerations and opportunities. Other companies are proceeding in the opposite direction, developing universal strategies that are appropriate for all of North America, or even the global marketplace. Which direction an organization takes depends on the objectives of the organization and the financial resources available for marketing communications.

BEHAVIOUR-RESPONSE SEGMENTATION

Behaviour-response segmentation involves dividing buyers into groups according to their occasions for use of a product, the benefits they require in a product, the frequency with which they use the product, and their degree of brand loyalty.

Marketers using the *occasion-for-use* segmentation strategy show how the product can be used on various occasions; for example, breakfast cereal, orange juice, and milk being consumed at times other than traditional meal times. The Dairy Farmers of Canada designed an entire campaign presenting chocolate milk as a reenergizing beverage. Refer to the illustration in Figure 3.13.

Benefit segmentation is based on the premise that different consumers try to gratify different needs when they purchase a product. A shampoo buyer, for example, may be looking for shinier hair, fuller hair, wavier hair, and so on. To meet such a variety of benefits, a brand such as Garnier Fructis offers many variations under one brand name.

Frequency of use is another important segmentation variable. Some customers use and buy a product more frequently than others—they are called *heavy users*. Marketers often quote the 80/20 principle here: 80 percent of a product's sales volume comes from 20 percent of its users. Beer marketers know younger customers consume more beer than older customers, hence the concentration of advertising directed at the 19- to 25-year-olds. Who do you typically see in a commercial for Coors Light or Molson Canadian?

Courtesy of Dairy Farmers of Canada

FIGURE 3.13

Chocolate milk is advertised as a replenishing beverage suitable for active lifestyles.

Finally, the degree of *brand loyalty* influences segmentation strategy. Some customers are simply more brand loyal than others—they won't switch brands. Should marketers be able to identify the characteristics of brand loyal users and what motivates them to buy a particular brand, then strategies can be developed to attract users with similar characteristics and tendencies. For customers who may be less than loyal (they have a tendency to switch brands), marketers can devise strategies to keep less loyal customers in the fold. For example, an incentive such as a coupon distributed via the product (in-pack or on-pack) encourages a customer to buy the product again. For a summary of the various characteristics that may be included in a target market description, refer to Figure 3.14.

FIGURE 3.14

A summary and illustration of key target market concepts

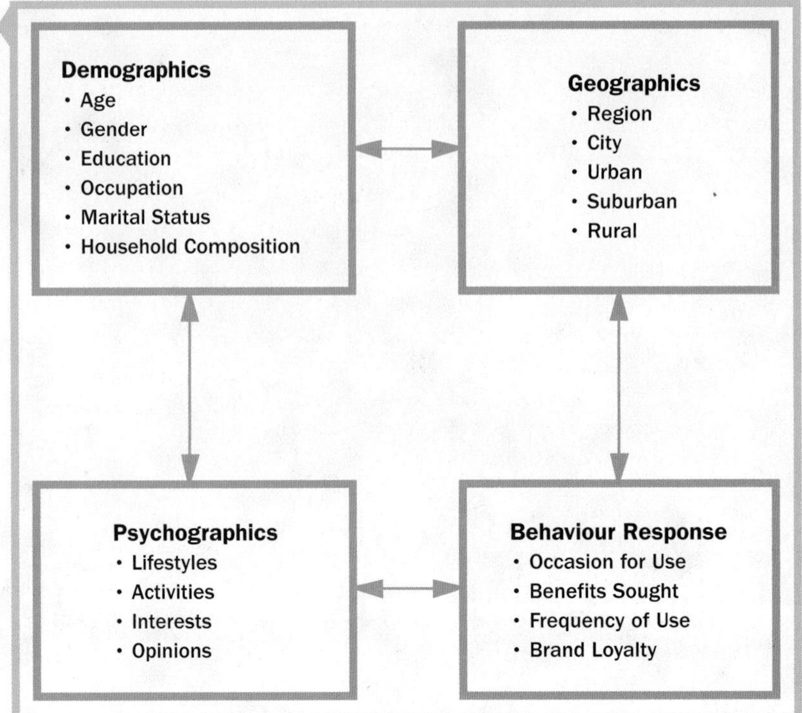

DIRECT SEGMENTATION

Direct segmentation (or *one-to-one marketing* or *individual marketing*) refers to a situation in which unique marketing programs are designed specifically to meet the needs and preferences of individual customers. Advancing technology encourages and enables such a definitive marketing practice. Marketers are empowered by more detailed consumer data that allow for a much higher degree of intimacy and frequency of contact with customers; the outcome of a good customer relationship management program.

Information captured about customers comes from many different sources: internal sales information, demographic and psychographic information (previously discussed in this chapter), media consumption information that is tracked by electronic meters in homes and other research studies, software in computers that monitors surfing behaviour, and electronic checkout counters that capture all kinds of purchase information (what, when, how much was spent, and so on). If you think Big Brother is watching you...he is!

In the digital media world, a concept referred to as *behavioural targeting* has taken hold. **Behavioural targeting** is a database-driven marketing system that tracks a consumer's behaviour to determine his or her interests and then serves ads to that person relevant to those interests. Armed with such knowledge, marketers are shifting away from mass media like television, radio, newspapers, and magazines and toward media that reaches consumers individually and more efficiently. The growth in media spending online and through mobile devices clearly reflects this change. This concept will be discussed in more detail in Chapter 12.

In summary, companies analyze and evaluate the trends and characteristics described in the foregoing sections to identify the most profitable targets to pursue. The result of the analysis is a profile of a prototype customer who is described in terms of demographic, psychographic, geographic, and behaviour-response characteristics. Alternatively, marketers have an opportunity to directly approach individual customers, assuming access to proper technology.

Market Positioning Concepts

Positioning can be defined as the selling concept that motivates purchase, or the image that marketers desire a brand or a company to have in the minds of consumers. Positioning is a strategy based on competition. It involves designing and marketing a product to meet the needs of a target market and creating the appropriate appeals to make the product stand out from the competition in the minds of the target market. Advertising and other forms of marketing communications play a key role in positioning a product in the customer's mind.

Positioning involves an assessment of consumer needs and competitive marketing activity to determine new marketing opportunities. It involves a thorough understanding of the product in relation to competing products. The result is a clearly worded positioning strategy statement that provides guidance for all marketing and marketing communications strategies. All forms of communication should send out the same message about a brand or company. The importance of positioning in the development of marketing strategy is presented in Figure 3.15.

The positioning strategy statement should be clear, concise, and uncomplicated while addressing the target market's need and the primary benefit to be offered. Many experts adopt the 4D-positioning rule when devising a strategy statement: The strategy statements must be *desirable* to consumers, *distinctive* from the competition, *deliverable* by the company, and *durable* over time.

Considered conceptually, a "position" is a mental space that a marketer can own with an idea that is compelling to the target audience. In that mental space, the product's benefit and the customer's most important needs meet and hopefully form a meaningful relationship. Here is a potential positioning strategy statement for Apple-branded products:

> *The core of Apple's brand is great innovation, beautiful design, and an ability to bring warmth and passion to those customers who may be averse to technical gadgetry, but need it nonetheless to survive in today's world.*

Now, think of the way Apple advertises its products: clear and simple images for innovative products that appeal to innovators and early adopters (think iPhone, iPad, and MacBook Pro). Refer to the images in Figure 3.16.

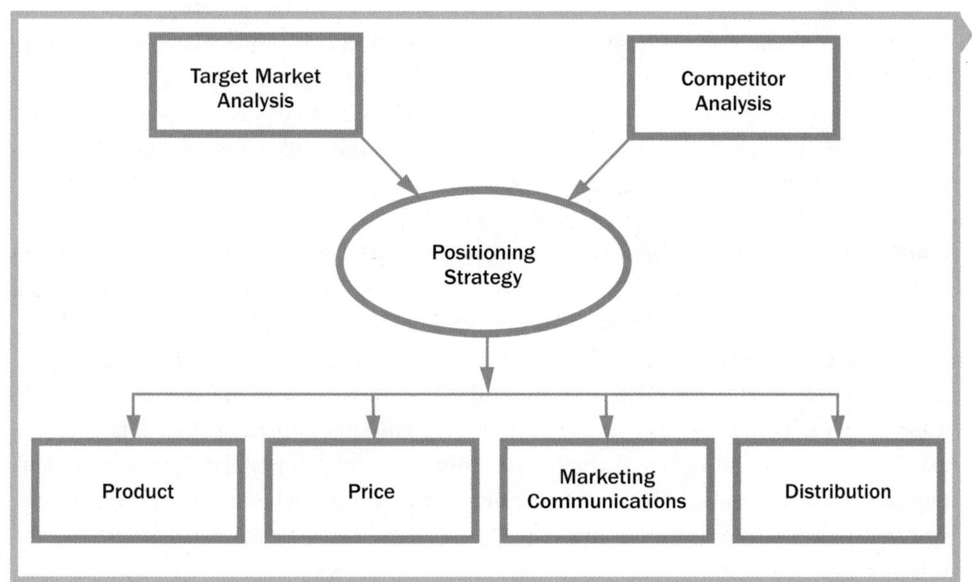

FIGURE 3.15
The importance of positioning in the development of marketing and marketing communications strategies

FIGURE 3.16

Innovation, design, and simplicity are core components of Apple's positioning strategy.

POSITIONING AND MARKETING COMMUNICATIONS

There are many ways a product can be positioned in the minds of customers, and advertising plays a key role in portraying the positioning strategy to customers. Let's discuss some of these positioning strategies.

HEAD-ON POSITIONING (COMPARATIVE POSITIONING) When a head-on positioning strategy is employed, a brand is presented as being equal to, or better than, another brand. The advertising message focuses on an attribute that is important to the target market. It is common to demonstrate how both brands perform. Bounty always shows how much moisture its paper towels pick up compared with other brands. Bounty is well positioned as the "quicker picker upper." Every now and then Pepsi-Cola dusts off its old "Pepsi Challenge" trick that shows Coke drinkers preferring the taste of Pepsi (some ads even show a Coca-Cola delivery man succumbing to the taste of Pepsi-Cola). In Canada, the Pepsi Challenge dates back as far as 1976. Some 9 million Canadians have actually participated in the taste test challenge.[14]

Challenger brands often adopt a head-on positioning strategy. Their goal is to instill "thought" leadership in the customer's mind. Such brands will spend considerable sums of money to deliver their message.

BRAND LEADERSHIP POSITIONING In their consumer communications, established brands often use icons or signatures that become highly recognized and synonymous with the brand. These devices then act as a simple and lasting reminder about the essence of the brand for consumers. Coca-Cola has successfully used this approach to build the world's most recognized brand. "Coke is it," "Can't beat the real thing," "Always Coca-Cola," and, more recently, "Open happiness" are examples of universally recognizable signatures that reinforce the brand's leadership position. The brand name, unique bottle, and popular slogans are a winning combination for Coca-Cola—they are instantly recognizable by consumers everywhere. Even the font used on cans and bottles has been adapted into other alphabets around the world.

Courtesy of Visa Canada

FIGURE 3.17

An advertisement portraying Visa's global positioning strategy

Brand leaders tend to have high levels of consumer awareness, products that are readily available, and significant marketing budgets to defend their position. In the debit and credit card market, Visa, another well-known advertiser, positions itself as a leader. Its most recent effort involves a global positioning strategy that is summed up in the tagline "Everywhere you want to be." Refer to the illustration in Figure 3.17.

PRODUCT DIFFERENTIATION POSITIONING Product differentiation is a strategy that focuses on the unique attribute of a product—a feature that distinguishes it from all other products. For example, the feature could be performance quality (it lasts longer), durability (it can withstand stress), reliability (it won't break down), or style (it looks attractive).

A new beverage called Rumble clearly differentiates itself from competitors—in fact, it is the first beverage to be classified as a "nourish drink" by the Canadian Food Inspection Agency. Its competitors are meal replacement drinks like Boost and Ensure, workout recovery drinks like Muscle Milk, as well as natural juices. Rumble is different; it's a milkshake-style drink that offers 3100 milligrams of omega-3s, 20 grams of protein, 400 milligrams of calcium, 8 grams of fibre, and natural fruits and vegetables. It combines the best elements of a meal replacement drink, energy drink, and smoothie in one beverage. The brand uses the slogan "Feed the good" to draw attention to all the goodness contained in the drink and its support of worthwhile causes. The company donates 1 percent of sales to charities that fight hunger. Refer to the image in Figure 3.18.

Tropicana juices launched a new variety called Trop50. The brand name is directly linked to the unique selling point—it offers 50 percent less sugar and calories than the leading orange juice. Consumers leading healthier lifestyles will be interested in this product.

INNOVATION POSITIONING Innovation is sometimes more important for a company as a whole than for individual products. The objective is to portray the company or brand as being, for example, leading edge, the first to market something, or ahead of its competitors. Apple serves as an example of an innovator. Just think of the innovative products the company has launched in recent years—many of which have been game changers—the iPod and iTunes, the iPhone and iPad. The prelaunch buzz alone, which is stimulated by effective public relations campaigns, creates high demand for the company's new products.

In the razor-blade market, the battle has traditionally been waged through advertising messages showing how various blades perform their functions (three blades, four blades, etc.). Gillette recently launched the new Fusion ProGlide razor with flexball technology, which promises men a smoother, closer shave. The image in Figure 3.19 demonstrates innovation positioning.

FIGURE 3.18
Rumble differentiates itself from competitors based on the nutritional benefits offered in its drink.

Courtesy of Rumble

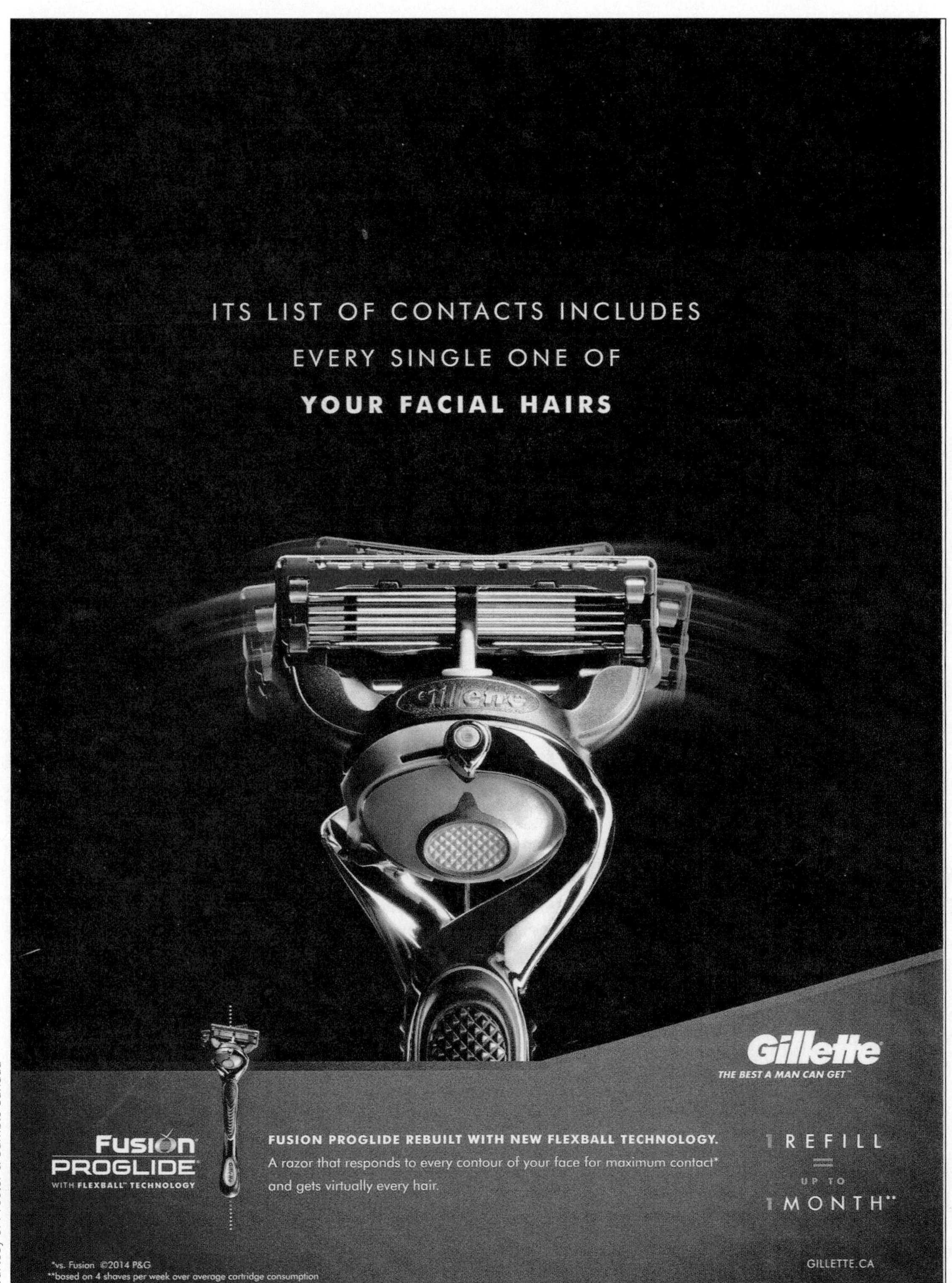

Courtesy of Procter & Gamble Canada

FIGURE 3.19

The technology built into a Gillette razor blade and the benefits it offers demonstrate innovation positioning.

LIFESTYLE POSITIONING In crowded markets where product attributes are perceived as similar by the target market, firms must identify alternative ways of positioning their products. The use of psychographic information has allowed advertisers to develop campaigns that are based on the lifestyle of the target market. Essentially, the product is positioned to "fit in with" or match the lifestyle of the user. Figures 3.3, 3.5, 3.9, and

3.12 are good illustrations of lifestyle positioning. In each advertisement, the product is shown as a natural part of a contemporary lifestyle.

Generally, lifestyle positioning through advertising uses emotional appeals such as love, fear, adventure, sex, and humour to elicit a response from the target. In the automobile industry, lifestyle imagery is effectively used to sell cars. It is common to see the rugged outdoors associated with sport utility vehicles and happy family situations associated with minivans. In the beer market, mainstream brands such as Molson Canadian and Coors Light rely heavily on lifestyle positioning. Young guys, beautiful girls, party situations, cottages, and sports (the desired lifestyle of the 20-something target audience) are common backdrops for their television commercials.

In the truck market, all major brands, such as the Ford F-150, Chevrolet Silverado, and Dodge Ram, appeal to the lifestyle of hardworking, adventurous males (even though many males outside this description buy these trucks). The message focuses on the strength and toughness of the vehicle. The message and image presented in Figure 3.3 demonstrates this notion. The Chevrolet Silverado, for example, uses phrases such as "Strong...for all the roads ahead" to establish the desired brand image.

REPOSITIONING

So far, we have discussed only the initial positioning of a product in the marketplace and in the minds of consumers. But the competitive market requires positioning strategies that can be readily changed if necessary. It is unrealistic to assume that the position a brand adopts initially will remain the same throughout its life cycle. Products will be repositioned according to the prevailing environment in the marketplace. **Repositioning** is defined as changing the place that a brand occupies in the consumer's mind in relation to competitive products. There are two primary reasons for repositioning: (1) The marketing activity of a direct competitor has changed, and (2) the preferences of the target market have changed. That said, there's an old expression: "If it ain't broke, don't fix it."

To demonstrate the principle of repositioning, consider the situation that Mountain Equipment Co-op faced. It was originally positioned as the store for back-country supplies and appealed to young adventurers who liked to tackle tough outdoor challenges such as mountaineering, rock climbing, ski touring, and hiking. The company was successful but understood that demographic changes would impact its future. Core customers were getting older and were shifting to more leisurely recreational pursuits. The population was also becoming less white and more urban. Mountain Equipment rebranded itself as MEC and reconfigured its product mix to include products for categories such as yoga, running, cycling, and fitness so that its appeal would be much broader. New marketing communications strategies presented the changes to the public.

SUMMARY

Market segmentation and knowledge of consumer behaviour are important factors in marketing and advertising planning. Both have a direct impact on product positioning, creative strategy, and media strategy. Marketers must also have good knowledge of how needs, motives, personality, self-concept theories, perceptions, attitudes, reference groups, and family influence behaviour. Understanding these concepts leads to more effective messages and media strategies.

In terms of market segmentation, organizations must identify their target markets as precisely as they can. Good use of information provided by demographic trends (the consumer's age, gender, income, occupation, education, marital status, household formation, and ethnic background), psychographic characteristics (the consumer's activities, interests, and opinions), and geographic variables (the consumer's location by region) allows for a precise definition of the consumer and enhances the quality of marketing and advertising plans. Other important segmentation variables are behavioural in nature and consider the occasions for and frequency of using a product, benefits sought by customers, and the degree of brand loyalty.

Technology now allows marketers to capture data from a variety of sources and accumulate it in a customer database. The outcome of a sound customer relationship management system is the development of unique marketing programs and the ability to reach customers directly with advertising messages, a concept referred to as *direct segmentation*. In the digital media world, the practice of behavioural targeting has taken hold. It is a data-driven marketing system that tracks consumers' behaviour online to determine their interests. Advertisements can be delivered to individuals based on those interests.

Positioning a product is an important part of pursuing target markets, and advertising plays a key role in positioning. Positioning involves designing a product or service to meet the needs of a target market, and then creating appropriate appeals to make the product stand out in the minds of the target market members. Common positioning strategies include head-on comparisons, brand leadership, product differentiation, innovation, and lifestyle techniques. Positioning strategies that are working should be retained for as long as possible. A marketer should resist any temptation to change something that is working well.

As a product matures, factors such as competitive activity and changing consumer preferences might dictate a reevaluation of positioning strategies. Under such a circumstance a marketer will make changes to a brand's marketing strategy and implement a communications strategy to present a new image for the brand. This activity is called *repositioning*.

KEY TERMS

REVIEW QUESTIONS

1. Explain the various levels of needs, and identify the two basic principles that needs and motivation theory are based on. Provide an advertising example for each level of needs.
2. Briefly explain each of the components of the self-concept. Provide a new example of an ad campaign that uses the looking-glass self or ideal self to its advantage.

3. Briefly explain how knowledge of attitudes and perceptions held by consumers influences the direction of advertising strategy.
4. What is double targeting? Provide a new example to demonstrate how it is applied.
5. What are the key elements of demographic segmentation, psychographic segmentation, and geographic segmentation? Briefly explain each.
6. Explain the concept of positioning in the context of marketing and advertising practice.
7. What is the difference between head-on positioning and brand leadership positioning? Provide a new example of each.
8. If a brand is using a product differentiation positioning strategy, what will the advertised message focus on? Provide two examples that show the application of this type of positioning.
9. What is repositioning, and why does it occur? Briefly explain.

DISCUSSION QUESTIONS

1. Provide some additional examples to show how advertisers use the following aspects of consumer behaviour theory:
   a) Social and esteem needs
   b) Self-image, looking-glass self, and ideal self
   c) Attitudes and perceptions
   d) Reference groups
2. "The economies of a national creative plan outweigh the need for numerous regional creative plans." Discuss this issue, choosing some products and ad campaigns as examples.
3. "To succeed in the future, products and services must be repositioned to appeal to older target markets." Comment on the implications of this statement.
4. "Companies are well behind in terms of recognizing the changes occurring in Canadian household formation, and this is reflected in the types of advertising they are showing." Is this statement true or false? Provide examples to support your opinion.

NOTES

1. Newspapers Canada, "Newspapers Drive Purchase Decisions," 2013, **www.newspaperscanada.ca**.
2. Marketing Land, "Survey: 62% of Consumers Say Social Media Doesn't Influence Their Purchase Decisions," **www.marketingland.com/survey-62-consumers-say-social-media-doesnt-at-all-influence-their-media-purchase-decisions**.
3. A. H. Maslow, *Motivation and Personality* (New York: Harper and Row Publishers, 1954), 370–396.
4. John Douglas, George Field, and Lawrence Tarpay, *Human Behavior in Marketing* (Columbus: Charles E. Merrill Publishing, 1987), 5.
5 Evra Taylor, "Is Canada's lesbian, gay, bisexual and transgender community worth pursuing?" *Marketing*, July 9, 2012, 70.
6. Megan Haynes, "New Survey Highlights Shopping Habits of Men," *Strategy*, February 13, 2012, **http://strategyonline.ca/2012/02/13/new-survey-highlights-shopping-habits-of-men**.
7. Karen Mazurkewicj, "The Pink Purse Strings," *Financial Post*, September 5, 2007.
8. Bengt Halvorson, "What Women Want: Her Favorite Vehicles," ForbesAutos.com on NBCNews.com, May 14, 2008.
9. Chris Daniels, "How the Multicultural Mosaic Spends," *Marketing*, March 12, 2012, **www.marketingmag.ca**.
10. "Projections of the Diversity of the Canadian Population," **www.outreach.ca/servingyouth/research/tabid/2304**.
11. Matt Semansky, "Plus ca change...," *Marketing*, September 27, 2008, p. 27.
12. Caroline Fortin, "Dr. Pepper Seeks Prescription for Growth in Quebec, *Marketing*, May 8, 2013, **www.marketingmag.ca/news.marketer-news/dr-pepper-seeks-prescription**.
13. Statistics Canada, 2011 Census of Population, **www.statcan.gc.ca/tables-tableaux/sum-som/101/cst01/demo62a**.
14. Susan Krashinsky, "To Catch Coke, Pepsi Dusts Off an Old Trick," *Globe and Mail*, May 17, 2012, B3.

CHAPTER 4

Strategic Planning Concepts for Marketing Communications

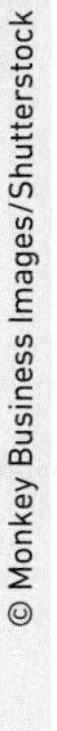

Learning Objectives

After studying this chapter, you will be able to

1. Identify the distinctions and relationships among the various types of planning
2. Describe the key variables that constitute a corporate plan
3. Outline the organization and content of a marketing plan and a marketing communications plan
4. Show how integrated marketing communications plans provide solutions to marketing problems

Business planning is an integrated process that involves planning at three levels of an organization: corporate planning, marketing planning, and marketing communications planning. Advertising is one aspect of marketing communications planning. It is important for students to understand the planning process and appreciate the interaction of the various plans. Marketing communications plans are not created independently; they are linked to plans at other levels of the organization. The corporate plan will influence the marketing plan, and the marketing plan will influence the marketing communications plan.

The nature and scope of marketing plans and advertising plans vary from one organization to another, and the structure of the plans depends on the needs and degree of marketing sophistication of the firm developing the plan. A well-thought-out plan should provide direction, outline key activities, and include a means of measuring its success. Students should be aware that there are no limits placed on the design, organization, or content of marketing or marketing communications plans.

Business Planning Process

Strategic business planning involves making decisions about three variables: objectives, strategies, and execution or tactics. Let's first define these planning variables:

1. **Objectives** are statements in the corporate, marketing, or advertising plans that outline what is to be accomplished.
2. **Strategies** are statements that outline how the objectives will be achieved and usually identify the resources necessary to achieve the objectives, such as funds, time, people, and types of activities.
3. **Execution (tactics)** refers to tactical action plans that outline specific details of implementation that collectively contribute to the achievement of objectives. Tactical plans usually provide details of an activity's cost and timing.

A diagram of the business planning process as it applies to marketing and advertising is provided in Figure 4.1.

Strategic Planning

When a company embarks on a plan, it anticipates the future business environment to determine the course of action it will take. For example, a firm will look at trends in the economy, population, culture, and technology, and then develop a plan that will provide growth. A typical plan considers the long-term (five years) and the short-term (one year) situations. Each year the plan is evaluated and changes are made where necessary.

Strategic planning is the process of determining objectives (setting goals) and identifying strategies (ways to achieve the goals) and tactics (specific action plans) to help achieve the objectives. A corporate plan originates at the top of the organization and is largely based on input from senior executives. Such plans are usually not elaborate documents, since their purpose is to identify the corporate objectives to be achieved over a specified period. The corporate plan acts as a guideline for planning in various operational areas of the company. Marketing and advertising are two of these operational areas.

In examining Figure 4.1, we find that business planning throughout the organization begins and ends at the corporate or senior management level. Senior management

FIGURE 4.1

PLANNING MODEL EXHIBIT

Strategic planning: The links between plans at various levels of an organization

The corporate plan provides guidance for the marketing plan, and the marketing plan provides guidance for the marketing communications plan. Corporate plans are strategic, while marketing plans and marketing communications plans are strategic and tactical.

formulates the overall strategic direction for the organization and establishes the financial objectives the company should aspire to (sales, profit, return on investment). Then, in accordance with the objectives and directions passed down from senior management, the marketing department develops marketing plans that embrace objectives, strategies, and tactics for individual products, divisions, or target markets.

Marketing plans consider such matters as the marketing mix (product, price, distribution, and marketing communications), target market characteristics, and control and evaluation mechanisms that determine the effectiveness of the strategies being implemented. Marketing plans are specific, and all activities related to product, price, distribution, and marketing communications are outlined in the plan. With reference to Figure 4.1, our primary concern is marketing communications, which is subdivided into advertising, direct response communications, online and interactive communications, sales promotion, personal selling, public relations, and experiential marketing. Advertising can be further subdivided into creative plans and media plans.

As this planning process indicates, each plan is related to the others. The saying "A chain is only as strong as its weakest link" is an appropriate description of these relationships. Strategic planning attempts to coordinate all activity so that elements from various areas work together harmoniously. In the case of marketing, advertising, and any other form of communications, all activity must present a consistent image of the company or its product to create a favourable impression in the minds of consumers. One weak link in the chain can create conflict or confuse the target market and be counterproductive to achieving objectives.

The Corporate Plan

A **mission statement** is the foundation of the corporate plan; it is a statement of the organization's purpose. It reflects the operating philosophy of the organization and the direction the organization is to take. Such statements are related to the opportunities the company identifies for itself. A good mission statement is customer and marketing oriented, considers the competition, and looks to the long term. Adequate resources (time and money) must be provided to carry it through.

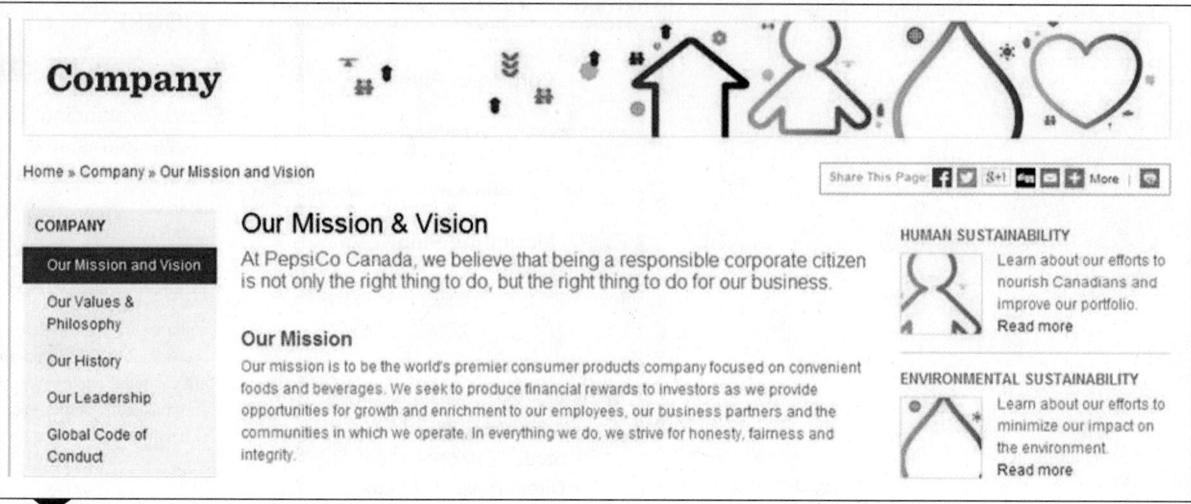

FIGURE 4.2
Mission statement of PepsiCo Canada

The format of a mission statement varies. Some organizations combine their mission with a longer-term vision of the direction the organization will take. PepsiCo's mission statement reads as follows:

> *Our mission is to be the world's premier consumer products company focused on convenient foods and beverages. We seek to produce financial rewards to investors as we provide opportunities for growth and enrichment to our employees, our business partners and the communities in which we operate. And in everything we do, we strive for honesty, fairness and integrity.*

PepsiCo's vision statement reads:

> *Pepsico's responsibility is to continually improve all aspects of the world in which we operate—environment, social, economic—creating a better tomorrow than today.*

Google's mission statement is short: "Google's mission is to organize the world's information and make it universally accessible and useful."[1] Sometimes a few words can say a great deal. Most companies publish their mission statement on their websites. Refer to Figure 4.2 for a PepsiCo illustration. PepsiCo is a global food and beverage company with annual sales revenue of $63.1 billion.[2]

CORPORATE OBJECTIVES

Corporate objectives are statements of a company's overall goals, and they take their direction from the mission statement. They may state what return on investment is desired, or what level of sales or market share is desired from a particular market segment. Social responsibility objectives now play a more prominent role in corporate planning than in the past. Good objective statements are written in quantifiable terms so that their success can be measured. They may also be qualitative, yet still provide direction, as indicated by the last of the following examples:

- To increase total company sales from $500 000 000 in 20XX to $600 000 000 in 20XX
- To increase market share from 25 percent in 20XX to 30 percent in 20XX
- To increase return on investment from 10 percent in 20XX to 13 percent in 20XX
- To financially support cause-related marketing programs that will benefit society

Objectives like these provide the framework for the development of detailed plans in the operational areas of the organization.

CORPORATE STRATEGIES

After the corporate objectives are confirmed, the organization must identify its **corporate strategies**, which are plans outlining how the objectives will be achieved. The factors considered when strategies are being developed are marketing strength, degree of competition in markets where the company operates, financial resources (e.g., the availability of investment capital or the ability to borrow required funds), research and development capabilities, and management commitment (i.e., the priority a company has placed on a particular goal).

Assuming growth (greater profits, market share, and return on investment) is the corporate objective, corporations could proceed in an endless range of strategic directions to achieve it. One option is to follow a **penetration strategy** that involves aggressively marketing current products. Arch rivals like PepsiCo and Coca-Cola are always looking for ways to grow in the food and beverage market. Both companies invest heavily in marketing to secure growth for their respective soft drinks, energy drinks, juice, and water products. Advertising plays a key role in the marketing plans of both companies. In the laundry detergent market, Tide leads in terms of market share and advertising spending, but it always faces pressure from other leading brands like Gain, All, and Arm & Hammer, which also advertise a lot to build market share. Refer to the illustration in Figure 4.3.

Another common corporate strategy to achieve growth is to invest in research and a **new product development strategy**. Beer is a rather mature market but one where new products are stimulating some growth. Alexander Keith's expanded beyond beer in 2012 when it introduced Alexander Keith's Original Cider, a beverage that would offer both taste and refreshment. The cider product was targeted at 25- to 34-year-olds who enjoy sharing a good drink with friends.[3] Refer to the image in Figure 4.4. A shift to healthier lifestyles forced Campbell Soup Company to introduce many new products. Like other processed food companies, Campbell was being squeezed by new competition

FIGURE 4.3

Investment in advertising and other forms of marketing communications plays a key role in achieving growth objectives.

FIGURE 4.4

New products are a means of generating revenue growth and profit for an organization.

© Hand-out/Alexander Keith's/Newscom

from smaller premium, organic, and natural food brands. The company recently introduced a new line of organic soups packaged in cartons as well as new V8 juices in flavours such as Carrot Mango and Sea Salt and Clam.[4]

Strategic alliances involve a relationship between two or more companies that decide to work cooperatively to achieve common goals and increase growth for both. Alliances are becoming popular because they offer a means of reducing costs and improving operating efficiency. CIBC and Tim Hortons recently formed an alliance with the introduction of the CIBC Double Double Visa card. The alliance links the bank to a loyal group of coffee drinkers across Canada, offering the company a means to grow its customer base. Cardholders can collect Tim cash as they make purchases. Through the alliance CIBC gained branding opportunities in 3500 Tim Hortons stores; 5.3 million customers visit these stores each day.[5]

Pursuing an **acquisition strategy** is another means of growing revenues and profits. Some recent examples include Loblaw's acquisition of Shoppers Drug Mart and Sobeys' acquisition of Safeway's Canadian operations. The latter acquisition made Sobeys the largest grocery chain in Western Canada. Under such a strategy it is common for large companies to simply merge together—the recent merger of Heinz and Kraft is a good example. With mergers of this scale, the new owners are looking for cost efficiencies to improve financial growth.

Rather than acquiring, some companies consolidate their operations by employing a **divestment strategy**—selling off parts of the company, such as operations that are not profitable or no longer fit with corporate goals. It seems bigger is not always better. Just recently, Procter & Gamble announced it would shed more than half of its brands—its new goal was to concentrate on the remaining brands, which together account for 90 percent of the company's sales and 95 percent of its profits. Among the brands sold off was Duracell—a $2-billion-a-year revenue producer globally.[6]

Marketing Planning

The marketing department operates within the guidelines established by senior management. The objectives, strategies, and action plans developed by the marketing department are designed to help achieve overall company objectives. Where planning is concerned, the major areas of marketing responsibility include the following:

1. Identifying and selecting target markets
2. Establishing marketing objectives, strategies, and tactics
3. Evaluating and controlling marketing activities

Marketing planning is the analysis, planning, implementation, evaluation, and control of marketing initiatives to satisfy market needs and achieve organizational objectives. It involves the analysis of relevant background information and historical trend data and the development of marketing objectives, strategies, and executions for all products and services within a company. The integration of various elements of the marketing mix is outlined in the marketing plan of each product. In contrast to corporate plans, marketing plans are short term in nature (usually one year), specific in scope (since they deal with one product and outline precise actions), and combine strategy and tactics (they are action oriented).

Although there is no typical format for a marketing plan, plans are usually subdivided into major sections based on background content and planning content. First, the company conducts a **situation analysis** (sometimes called an environmental analysis) in which data and information about external and internal influences are compiled. It is important to examine events that have an impact on the performance of a brand. External factors that are considered include economic trends, social and demographic trends, technology trends, and competitor activities. As well, information is compiled about the market and customers. In the marketing plan, the objectives, strategies, and tactics for the brand or company are clearly delineated. Figure 4.5 offers a description of the various elements of a marketing plan.

MARKET BACKGROUND—SITUATION ANALYSIS

As a preliminary step to marketing planning, a variety of information is compiled and analyzed. This information includes some or all of the following:

EXTERNAL INFLUENCES

- ***Economic trends*** Basic economic trends often dictate the nature of marketing activity (e.g., if the economy is healthy and growing, more resources are allocated to marketing activity; if the economy is in a recession, a more conservative approach is often adopted).

FIGURE 4.5

PLANNING MODEL EXHIBIT

Content of a marketing plan: a sample model

*Note: Including a SWOT analysis is optional. Many planners believe that you actually conduct a SWOT when the background information is compiled in the first four subsections of the background section of a plan. Other planners believe that such information must be analyzed further to determine priorities. The latter is the intention of a SWOT analysis.

Marketing Background—Situation Analysis	Marketing Plan
External Influences	**Positioning Strategy**
■ Economic trends	■ Positioning statement
■ Social and demographic trends	**Target Market Profile**
■ Technology trends	■ Demographic
Market Analysis	■ Psychographic
■ Market size and growth	■ Geographic
■ Regional market importance and trends	**Marketing Objectives**
■ Market segment analysis	■ Sales volume
■ Seasonal analysis	■ Market share
Target Market Analysis	■ Profit
■ Consumer data (target user)	■ Marketing communications
■ Consumer behaviour (loyalty)	■ Other
Product Analysis	**Marketing Strategies**
■ Sales volume trends	■ Product
■ Market share trends	■ Price
■ New product activity	■ Distribution
■ Distribution trends	■ Marketing communications
■ Marketing communications activities	■ Marketing research
Competitor Analysis	■ Budget (total available for brand)
■ Market share trends	**Marketing Execution**
■ Marketing activity assessment	(Action plans for each component)
SWOT Analysis*	■ Product
■ Strengths	■ Price
■ Weaknesses	■ Distribution
■ Opportunities	■ Marketing communications
■ Threats	■ Marketing research
	■ Profit improvement
	Budget and Financial Summary
	■ Budget allocation (by activity, time, area)
	■ Brand profit and loss statement
	Marketing Calendar
	■ Activity schedule by month

- ***Social and demographic trends*** Basic trends in age, income, immigration, and lifestyle influence decisions about which target markets to pursue. For example, the Canadian population is aging, and large cities are becoming more culturally diverse. New, younger generations such as Generation Y and Z are the next big group of consumers. These factors influence marketing strategy.

- ***Technology trends*** The rapid pace of change (e.g., in telecommunications and the delivery of content) influences the development of new products, shortens product life cycles, and influences the communications strategies used to reach customers.

MARKET ANALYSIS

- ***Market size and growth*** Trends in the marketplace over a period of time are reviewed. Is the market growing, remaining stable, or declining?
- ***Regional market importance*** Market trends and sales volume trends are analyzed by region to determine areas of strength or weakness and areas to concentrate on in the future.
- ***Market segment analysis*** The sales volumes of the total market and of segments within a market are reviewed. For example, markets such as hotels and automobiles are segmented based on a combination of price and quality, and descriptors such as economy, mid-market, and luxury are used to describe each segment. The marketer needs to know which segments are growing and which segments are declining.
- ***Seasonal analysis*** Seasonal or cyclical trends during the course of a year are examined. For example, traditions such as Christmas, Thanksgiving, and Halloween often have an impact on sales volume and affect the timing of marketing activities. The seasons of the year (spring, fall, summer, and winter) can also influence sales patterns.

TARGET MARKET ANALYSIS

- ***Consumer data*** Current users of a product are profiled according to factors such as age, gender, lifestyle, and location. The data may consider primary users as well as secondary users and indicate new areas of opportunity.
- ***Consumer behaviour*** The degree of customer loyalty to the market and individual brands within a market is assessed. Are customers loyal, or do they switch brands often? Other factors considered are frequency of use and the benefits sought in a product by the consumer. Such data indicate the need for strategies that will attract new customers or retain existing customers.

PRODUCT ANALYSIS A product's marketing mix strategy is assessed at this stage. In the assessment, relationships are drawn between the marketing activity that was implemented over the course of the year and the sales volume and market share that were achieved.

- ***Sales volume trends*** Historical sales trends are plotted to forecast future growth.
- ***Market share trends*** Market share success is the clearest indicator of how well a brand is performing. Market share results are recorded nationally and regionally, and areas of strength and weakness are identified.
- ***New product activity*** The success or failure of new products introduced in recent years is highlighted (e.g., new sizes, flavours, product formats).
- ***Distribution trends*** The availability of a product nationally and regionally is reviewed. Should a new marketing plan focus on areas where distribution is high or low?

- ***Marketing communications activities*** An assessment of current activities will determine if strategies are to be maintained or if new strategies are needed. Is the current creative working or not? A review of expenditures by medium, sales promotions, experiential marketing, social media, and any other activity is necessary to assess the impact of such spending on brand performance.

COMPETITOR ANALYSIS It is wise to know a competitor's products as well as your own. A review of marketing mix activities for key competitors provides essential input on how to revise marketing strategies.

- ***Market share trends*** It is common to evaluate market share trends of all competitors from year to year, nationally and regionally. Such analysis provides insight into which brands are moving forward and which brands are moving backward.
- ***Marketing strategy assessment*** An attempt is made to link known marketing strategies to competitor brand performance. What is the nature of competitor advertising, sales promotions, experiential marketing, and social media efforts? How much money do competitors invest in marketing? Have they launched any new products, and how successful have they been?

The combination of market analysis, product analysis, and competitor analysis helps provide direction to those managers responsible for developing a new marketing plan and presents senior managers with an overall perspective.

SWOT ANALYSIS

After the market information is assembled, it is appraised. While this may or may not be a formal part of the marketing plan itself, a manager should evaluate all information collected and then determine what the priorities are for the next year. This process is referred to as a **SWOT analysis**. The acronym SWOT stands for strengths, weaknesses, opportunities, and threats. A SWOT analysis examines the critical factors that have an impact on the nature and direction of a marketing strategy. Strengths and weaknesses are internal factors (e.g., resources available, research and development capability, management expertise), while opportunities and threats are external factors (e.g., economic trends, competitive activity, social and demographic trends).

The result of a SWOT analysis should be the matching of potential opportunities with resource capabilities. The goal is to capitalize on strengths while improving weaknesses. A SWOT analysis can be conducted at any level of an organization—product, division, or company.

THE MARKETING PLAN

POSITIONING STATEMENT **Positioning** refers to the desired image that a company wants to place in the minds of customers about the company as a whole or about individual products—it is the selling concept that helps motivate purchase. The concept of positioning was discussed in Chapter 3. Effective positioning statements are realistic, specific, and uncomplicated, and they clearly distinguish what a brand has to offer.

A **positioning strategy statement** is a working statement. It is the focal point from which relevant marketing and marketing communications strategies are developed. Further, it serves as the standard for considering which communications strategies to use and which not to use. Agency recommendations must fit with a brand's positioning strategy. For example, Nike's positioning strategy could be written as follows:

For serious athletes, Nike brings inspiration and innovation to every athlete in the world.

FIGURE 4.6

A positioning strategy guides the direction of a brand's marketing communications strategy.

This brief statement talks about the consumer (the brand promises inspiration and confidence) and the product (innovation implies Nike is the leader in shoe technology). Now think of Nike's famous advertising tagline: "Just do it!" The tagline aptly captures the essence of the positioning strategy. The images that appear in Nike ads show athletes excelling in their sport. Refer to the image in Figure 4.6.

TARGET MARKET PROFILE At this stage, the manager identifies, or targets, markets that represent the greatest profit potential for the firm. A **target market** is a group of customers with certain similar needs and characteristics. As discussed in Chapter 3, a target market description is devised based on demographic, psychographic, and geographic characteristics.

- ***Demographic profile*** Characteristics such as age, gender, income, education, and ethnic background are considered. Depending on the product and the extent of its appeal to the population, some characteristics will be more important than others.
- ***Psychographic profile*** The psychographic profile includes three essential characteristics: the target's activities, interests, and opinions. Such knowledge provides clues that will influence the direction of message strategies (how to appeal to the target) and media strategies (how to best reach the target). For example, the highly sought-after 18- to 25-year-old market watches much less television than previous generations did; current members of this demographic spend much more time online with social media and with their smartphones. This presents a challenge for marketers wanting to reach them.
- ***Geographic profile*** Much of Canada's population is urban, and certainly there are distinct regional differences that must be considered. Geography will influence decisions about regional versus national marketing strategies and will influence how a budget is allocated across the country.

For example, the following profile might represent a target market for an upscale automobile, watch, or someone interested in the services of a financial planning company:

- ***Age:*** 25 to 49 years old
- ***Gender:*** Male or female

- ***Income:*** \$120 000-plus annually
- ***Occupation:*** Business managers, owners, and professionals
- ***Education:*** College or university
- ***Location:*** Cities with a population of 500 000-plus
- ***Lifestyle:*** Progressive thinkers and risk-takers who like to experiment with new products; they are interested in the arts, entertainment, and vacation travel

This profile represents a good fit for a Rolex watch or a Mercedes-Benz. A sample of one company's advertising appears in Figure 4.7.

MARKETING OBJECTIVES **Marketing objectives** are statements identifying what a product will accomplish during one year. Typically marketing objectives concentrate on sales volume, market share, and profit (net profit or return on investment), all of which are quantitative (not qualitative) and measurable at the end of the period. Qualitative objectives might include new product introductions, new additions to current product lines, product improvements, and packaging innovations. To illustrate the concept of marketing objectives, consider the following sample statements:

- ***Sales volume*** To achieve sales of 200 000 units, an increase of 10 percent over current-year sales
- ***Market share*** To achieve a market share of 30 percent in 12 months, an increase of 4 share points over the current position
- ***Profit*** To generate an after-budget profit of \$600 000 in the next 12 months
- ***Marketing communications*** To launch a new advertising campaign in the second quarter that will increase brand awareness from 50 percent to 75 percent among the target audience

Objectives should be written in a manner that allows for measurement at the end of the period. Were the objectives achieved or not?

MARKETING STRATEGIES **Marketing strategies** are essentially the "master plans" for achieving marketing objectives. The importance of having a sound marketing strategy must be emphasized. All elements of the marketing mix and marketing communications mix must act in unison; collaboration is necessary to present a consistent and meaningful proposition to new and existing customers. The goal should be to have the right strategy and then work on improving the execution of it as time goes on.

At this stage of the planning process, the role and importance of each component of the **marketing mix** is identified. Priority may be given to certain components, depending on the nature of the market, the degree of competition, and knowledge of what motivates customers to buy. For example, brands like Coca-Cola and Pepsi-Cola rely heavily on media advertising, distribution strategies, and an online presence to build sales and market share. Walmart focuses on product and price—a combination that offers significant value to consumers across all income groups.

In the transportation market, the environment (a combination of product and additional services) is an important consideration among travellers. VIA Rail stresses the panoramic views (you can relax and enjoy them) and promises a good night's sleep (you can be comfortable). See the illustration in Figure 4.8.

Financial resources (the **budget**) will be laid out in the strategy section of the plan. Typically, the corporate plan has already identified a total marketing budget for the company.

Courtesy of Mercedes-Benz Canada, Inc.

FIGURE 4.7

Mercedes-Benz targets an upscale market with its SLK model.

That budget must be allocated across all company products based on the firm's analysis of current priorities or profit potential. Managers responsible for product planning must develop and justify a budget that allows enough funds to implement the strategies identified in their marketing plan and to achieve the financial objectives identified for the product. The final stage of the budgeting process is the allocation of funds among the activity areas in the plan (advertising, marketing research, consumer promotion, trade promotion, experiential marketing, and interactive communications, including social media).

Courtesy of Via Rail Canada

FIGURE 4.8
VIA Rail's advertising promises customers a relaxing and comfortable environment when travelling.

MARKETING EXECUTION **Marketing execution** (often called *marketing tactics*) focuses on specific details that stem directly from the strategy section of the plan. In general terms, a tactical plan outlines the activity, how much it will cost, what the timing will be, and who will be responsible for implementation. Detailed tactical plans for all marketing communications components included in the plan (e.g., media advertising, sales promotion, interactive communications, experiential marketing, etc.) are included here. It should be noted that the ad agency develops a detailed **advertising plan** in a separate document. If advertising is a key element in overall marketing strategy, then advertising strategy and tactics will be integrated into the marketing plan in summary form in the marketing communications section.

FINANCIAL SUMMARY AND BUDGET ALLOCATION A statistical presentation of key product performance indicators is commonly included as a summary of the entire marketing plan. Variables such as sales, market share, gross profit, marketing budget, and net profit are presented historically. Past performance and trends can be compared with the latest financial estimates in the new marketing plan. A detailed budget is included that indicates all activity areas in which funds will be spent. Major areas such as media, consumer promotion, trade promotion, and marketing research are often subdivided into more specific areas.

MARKETING CONTROL AND EVALUATION

Since clearly defined and measurable objectives have been established by the organization and by the marketing department, it is important that results be evaluated against the plans and against past performance. This evaluation indicates whether current strategies need to be modified or if new strategies should be considered.

Marketing control is the process of measuring and evaluating the results of marketing strategies and plans and taking corrective action to ensure that marketing objectives are attained. For example, if financial objectives are not being achieved, then new marketing strategies may have to be considered. This is also a good time to reevaluate the various marketing objectives. Perhaps some objectives were too aggressive and, considering the current dynamics of the market, should be adjusted accordingly. Any modifications to the marketing objectives will have an impact on the marketing activities as well. See Figure 4.9 for a diagram of the marketing planning and control process.

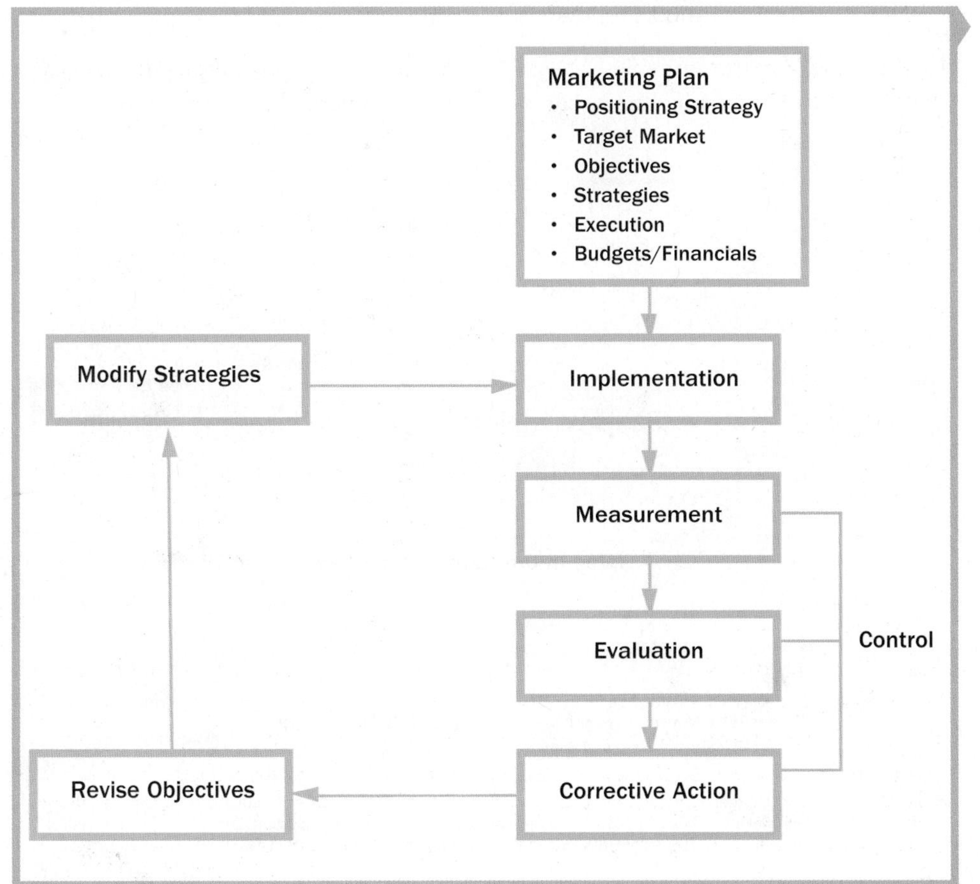

FIGURE 4.9

PLANNING MODEL EXHIBIT

The marketing planning and control process

Marketing Communications Planning

Prior to discussing marketing communications planning, it is imperative that you understand the nature of the communications process, particularly in the context of marketing communications. Refer to Figure 4.10 for a visual illustration of this process. Organizations and their agencies work together to devise a message that is transmitted via media (e.g., television, radio, magazines, newspapers, internet, smartphones, social media, video games) to a target audience. In this process the organization offers customers some kind of value (the benefits expressed in the message). If the message resonates with members of the target audience, it will grab their attention (a value exchange that benefits the advertiser).

How much attention a consumer gives to a message is affected by several factors: the quality of the message itself, the channel of communication employed, and the presence of competing messages. Competition for attention is referred to as **noise**. In the digital media environment, advertising must now entertain viewers. The emphasis on content has never been greater! From a planning perspective, the challenge is to create a message that will break through the clutter of competing messages and instill a positive impression in the receiver's mind (a positive value exchange). Should the desired action of making a purchase occur, so much the better! If the message does not break through the clutter or is not perceived as relevant to the individual receiving it, there is a negative value exchange. If the latter situation occurs, the very nature of the message strategy or the media strategy must be reevaluated.

When deciding what products to buy, a consumer passes through a series of behavioural stages, and marketing communications can influence each stage. One such model that refers to these various stages is AIDA. This acronym stands for *attention*, *interest*, *desire*, and *action*. Another model is ACCA—*awareness*, *comprehension*, *conviction*, and *action*. A description of the latter model follows:

- ***Awareness*** In the awareness stage, the customer *learns of something for the first time*. Obviously, this learning can occur only if the customer is exposed to a new advertisement.

FIGURE 4.10

Communications process in an advertising context

Source: Adapted from Jason Oke, "Op-Ed: Engagement Not Rocket Science—Leo Burnett, CanWest MediaWorks, Ideas Research Group," *Media in Canada*, October 5, 2006.

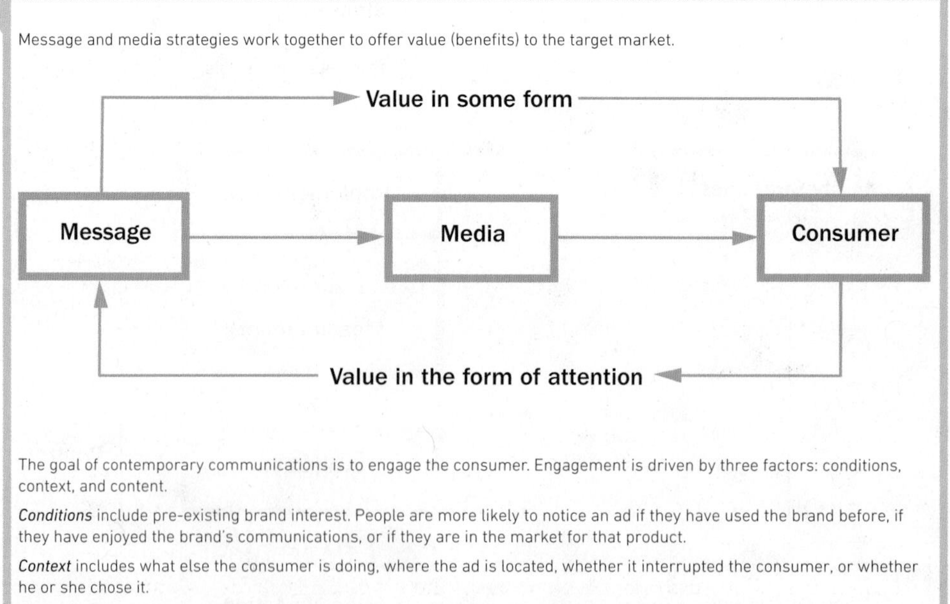

ADVERTISING IN ACTION

Engaging Millennials

Let's start with a few facts about the millennial market in Canada. Right now there are 9.5 million millennials roughly between the ages of 20 and 32. They account for 28 percent of the population—a target market well worth pursuing. Some recent research on this market revealed that nearly 6 in 10 millennials are loyal; they pay attention to brands that fit their personalities and offer self-expression. Further, millennials rely on brands that make their lives better and help them stand out from the crowd.

Kraft must have known this when it repositioned Crystal Light and introduced MiO to the market. Its strategies clearly demonstrated an understanding of millennial behaviour. For Crystal Light (a product that their mothers used to buy), the communications strategies focused on how young women are unique and special. Television commercials celebrated their being the "odd one out," and social media dwelled on what made them special. The tagline for the entire campaign was "weird, wonderful you."

Millennial women like to "connect," so social media played a key role. Personalized messages appeared on Vine (a video-sharing site). Each animated video offered a snapshot of a different customer. With such individualized flattery, the women were encouraged to share the videos with friends on other social media outlets.

For the launch of MiO, millennial men were the target. MiO is a flavouring additive that is mixed with water. Research on men revealed they appreciated authenticity, and rather than connecting on social media they wanted to be entertained. With this insight, MiO was launched with a quirky, off-the-wall style of advertising. It appealed to the target's off-beat sense of humour. Further, the product (a squirt bottle) allowed for some personalization each time they wanted a drink.

Each campaign was a success. Crystal Light has achieved an 8 percent market share in the mixed beverage market while MiO has reached market leadership status with 26 percent market share. MiO has exceeded all expectations the company had for the brand.

Is there a moral to the story? Yes! Wise marketers truly understand their target and build campaigns tailored to the target's needs and behaviour. Investment in research to gain such information is always wise. Approaching the millennial market is vital. Brands like Crystal Light and MiO hope that any brand loyalty that is achieved now will carry forward as these young people age.

© Rick Davis/Splash News/Newscom

Sources: Martha Beach, "Millennials Are Looking for Brands to Trust: Havas," *Marketing*, September 28, 2014, **www.marketingmag.ca** and Susan Krashinsky, "The Flavor of a Generation," *The Globe and Mail*," August 9, 2013, p. B5.

- ***Comprehension*** By the comprehension stage, *interest* has been created. The message is perceived as relevant, and the product, judged from the information presented, is considered useful. The product becomes part of the customer's frame of reference.
- ***Conviction*** The customer's evaluation of the product's benefits (as presented in the advertising) leads to a decision. The product is viewed as satisfactory and has gained *preference* in the customer's mind. The customer may be sufficiently motivated to buy the product.

- ***Action*** In this stage, the desired active *response* occurs. For example, a car advertisement may motivate a customer to visit a dealer's showroom or a website; a coupon may motivate a reader to clip it out for more information or for use in an initial purchase.

When trying to influence consumer behaviour that ultimately leads to the desired action, the marketer has to use the right message and the right combination of marketing communications components. The key to success is the integration of the various components to produce a unified approach to building the brand (or company). For insight into how Kraft attracted millennials to an existing product and new product, read the Advertising in Action vignette **Engaging Millennials**.

The Marketing Communications Plan

Similar to marketing planning, marketing communications planning involves the development of appropriate objectives, strategies, and tactics. The plan will also include objectives, strategies, and execution details for each of the marketing communications elements that are included in the plan. Students often get confused about objectives since there is a tendency for them to overlap. For example, an objective in the marketing communications plan (an objective for the entire plan) also appears as an advertising objective in the advertising plan (an objective for a portion of the overall plan).

To understand the difference, consider that each element of the marketing communications mix—advertising, interactive communications, sales promotion, public relations, experiential marketing, direct response communications, and personal selling—play a unique role in achieving overall marketing communications objectives. For example, advertising helps achieve awareness and preference objectives, interactive communications on social media achieve engagement objectives, and sales promotions help achieve trial and repeat purchase objectives. Given this conceptual perspective, you can start to see why overall objectives in a marketing communications plan will also appear in more specific communications plans. A sound marketing communications plan will include only those components that contribute to achieving the overall objectives. Refer to Figure 4.11 to see that marketing communications objectives and advertising objectives can be similar.

Usually a campaign is designed to resolve a specific problem or pursue an opportunity, so the primary objective or overall goal of marketing communications must be stated clearly. Depending on the situation, the overall goal could involve any one of the following:

- Creating or building awareness for a product or company
- Differentiating a product from competitive offerings
- Altering perceptions held by consumers about a product
- Fostering a strong public image of the product or company

The list could go on, but the point is that certain types of marketing communications are better than others at achieving certain objectives. Sometimes one form of communications, for example, advertising, may be enough to achieve the objective, while at other times a multidisciplinary approach is necessary. Which communications mix to use depends on the nature of the market, competitive activity, the target market to be reached, and the budget—some activities are much more expensive than others! The key to success is the integration of the various components to produce a unified approach to building the brand (or company).

FIGURE 4.11

PLANNING MODEL EXHIBIT

Marketing communications plan: A sample model*

Marketing Communications Objectives

(A selection of possibilities. Typically, a plan has a central focus and will include only one or a few overall objectives.)

- Awareness
- Preference
- Trial Purchase
- Altering Image
- Frequency and Variety of Use
- Promotional Incentives

Marketing Communications Strategies

- Positioning Statement
- Identification of the Role and Importance of Communications Mix Components
- Budget

Advertising Plan

Advertising Objectives

(A selection of possibilities; some could be the same as the marketing communications objectives)

- Awareness
- Product Differentiation
- Positioning or Repositioning of Product
- Trial Purchase
- Image Enhancement

Creative Plan

- Objectives (what message)
- Strategies (how to communicate message)
- Execution

Media Plan

- Objectives

  Who

  What

  When

  Where

  How
- Strategies

  Target Market Matching Strategies

  Rationale for Media Selection

  Rationale for Media Rejection
- Execution

  Cost Summaries (budget appropriation)

  Media Schedule (timing, coverage, usage)

Interactive Plan

- Objectives
- Strategies
- Tactics
- Budget

Direct Response Plan

- Objectives
- Strategies
- Tactics
- Budget

Sales Promotion Plan

- Objectives
- Strategies
- Tactics
- Budget

Public Relations Plan

- Objectives
- Strategies
- Tactics
- Budget

Experiential Marketing (Events and Sponsorships) Plan

- Objectives
- Strategies
- Tactics
- Budget

Personal Selling Plan

- Objectives
- Strategies
- Tactics
- Budget

**Assumes adequate input from the background section of the marketing plan.*

Note: More detailed discussion of objectives, strategies, and tactics occurs in chapters related to each element of the marketing communications mix.

To illustrate, the Bay of Quinte region in Ontario (two hours west of Toronto) wanted to attract people from Toronto to visit the region. The overall goal was to create awareness and encourage visits to the region, which could then lead to more people moving to or retiring to the region (it is already popular with retirees). The advertising campaign highlighted the region's natural beauty, numerous wineries, and affordable housing options. The media plan included social media, television, radio, digital, and print.[7]

A **marketing communications plan** is a document that is usually prepared by the company's marketing communications agency. Or it could be the result of a coordinated effort of several agencies that are doing specialized work. Agency specialists may be employed for creative and media planning, public relations, sales promotion, or experiential marketing. To develop the marketing communications plan, each agency must be informed about relevant marketing information. In the case of advertising, for example, the client will prepare a document that contains relevant information from the marketing plan. That document is commonly referred to as a **creative brief** (if message is the issue) or a **media brief** (if the issue is media related), or it may simply be called a communications brief. The creative brief is discussed in more detail in Chapter 5, and the media brief is discussed in more detail in Chapter 7.

As discussed earlier in the text, it is now common for all members of a client's agency team to meet and be briefed at the same time. Agency personnel may be positioned uniquely in their own organization, based on their area of expertise (e.g., art director—print and broadcast media, and art director—digital media; or media planner—broadcast media, and media planner—digital media). However, since all could potentially be involved in solving the client's advertising challenge, they must participate in the briefing and initial planning meetings.

MARKETING COMMUNICATIONS OBJECTIVES

Marketing communications objectives define the role that advertising and other forms of communications will play in selling the client's product or service and in achieving a stated marketing objective. For example, advertising usually plays a key role in creating brand awareness, sales promotions encourage trial purchases, public relations helps build and maintain brand image, and social media encourages people to engage with brands. The various plan components, therefore, work together to help achieve the marketing communications objectives.

In general terms, marketing communications objectives are diverse and tend to involve the following:

- Building awareness and interest in the product
- Changing perceptions held by consumers about a product
- Differentiating a product by presenting features and benefits
- Attracting new target markets
- Offering incentives to encourage people to buy the product
- Creating goodwill and fostering a good public image

A good objective statement makes it possible to quantify the success or failure of advertising by establishing the minimum levels of awareness and purchase motivation. Statements should also identify the target market.

To demonstrate communications objectives, assume you are the brand manager for Mountain Dew. Mountain Dew is a firmly established and well-known brand, so awareness objectives are not relevant. However, here are some examples that could apply to its market situation:

- To firmly position Mountain Dew as an "on-the-edge" brand in the minds of the primary target market
- To achieve a brand preference score of 40 percent among primary buyers (12- to 19-year-old males)
- To achieve a trial purchase rate for a new flavour of 25 percent among members of the primary target market

These objectives imply that marketing communications will embrace several components—advertising to firm up brand positioning and create brand preference, sales promotions and interactive communications to encourage trial purchase of the new flavour, and experiential marketing since Mountain Dew likes to sponsor extreme sports events. Refer to the image in Figure 4.12.

FIGURE 4.12

Mountain Dew is an "on-the-edge" brand that participates in extreme sports events.

MARKETING COMMUNICATIONS STRATEGIES

A **marketing communications strategy** includes a positioning strategy statement, identifies the various elements of the marketing communications mix that will be employed, and contains a budget for the plan. Refer to Figure 4.11 for an illustration.

If the marketing communications plan is a separate document from the marketing plan, then a positioning strategy statement should be included here even though it also appears in the marketing plan. (Positioning was discussed in the marketing planning section of this chapter and in Chapter 3.) The positioning strategy statement acts as a guideline for the development of all marketing communications strategies.

This section of the plan provides a basic outline of how the various components of the marketing communications mix will be used. The objectives (what is to be achieved) provide guidance on which components to include in the plan. Those components that are included may be ranked in terms of priority and what they are able to achieve. For example, advertising may be essential for generating awareness, sales promotion may be essential for generating trial purchases, and interactive communications may be essential for reaching mobile consumers.

The marketing communications section of the plan should identify the total budget available for marketing communications activities. It may even allocate the money among the various components of the mix that are included in the plan. What percentage of the budget will be allocated to areas such as advertising, interactive communications, sales promotion, and experiential marketing? More specific budget allocations (e.g., breakdowns for each component of the plan) should be left for the appropriate section of the plan.

Establishing the budget and allocating amounts to each of the components of marketing communications is a major decision area. There are various methods that can be used to develop a budget. Some methods estimate sales first and then base the advertising budget on sales. Other methods develop the budget first; these methods essentially presuppose that advertising and other forms of communications are an effective means of achieving sales objectives. Regardless of the method used, the budget must be carefully calculated and rationalized by the manager responsible for it so that the plan can be implemented as recommended.

The plan is usually subdivided at this stage, with objectives, strategies, and tactics identified for each component of the marketing communications mix that is recommended; these objectives correspond to the overall marketing communications objectives. For example, McCain Foods set out to alter consumer perceptions about its frozen potato products. To learn how message and media combined to do so, read the Advertising in Action vignette **McCain Is More Than French Fries.**

ADVERTISING OBJECTIVES

Advertising objectives outline specifically what the advertising effort will achieve. For example, when Pfizer Inc. launched the Schick Quattro four-blade razor, the product was positioned as superior to Gillette's three-blade razors. Gillette is the dominant brand leader. Schick's advertising objectives may have been stated as follows:

- To create a 75 percent awareness level for the Schick Quattro razor among 16- to 29-year-old males

ADVERTISING IN ACTION

McCain Is More Than French Fries

McCain Foods is a successful Canadian company. It is an international leader in the frozen food industry and employees around 18 000 people. Its products are sold in 160 countries generating sales revenue of $7 billion annually—nothing to sneeze at! But a company like this can't stand still. It must assess its environment and make adjustments to its marketing strategies to remain successful.

Recently, changing external factors have had an impact on McCain. Consumers' perceptions of the freshness and healthfulness of frozen foods is a concern, as is the trend of dining out more. Industry projections for at-home frozen food sales over the next three years vary from flat to marginal decline in revenue. Fortunately, McCain sells a large portion of its volume in the food service channel.

New strategies were needed to try and turn things around in the at-home market. Since everything starts with the product, the first step for McCain was to eliminate unfamiliar and unpronounceable ingredients from its products. The second step was to alter its packaging to present a completely new look, a contemporary feel that would have an impact on consumers as they scan the frozen food section.

The third step involved a new marketing communications strategy. From a strategic perspective, the message in the campaign would focus on showing consumers new occasions to enjoy potatoes and how McCain's products help create moments of connection with family and friends.

The creative execution featured different meal occasions and a wider variety of products, such as Superfries and Spicy Wedges. Visuals in the commercials showed people sharing food and good times together. The campaign showed how McCain products could be enjoyed beyond the dinner plate. For example, Spicy Wedges are a great snack to share with friends while watching the game. The entire theme of the campaign was wrapped up in the tagline "Share something good."

Source: Kristin Laird, "Warming Up A Brand," **Marketing**, August 2014, pp. 8, 9.

- To differentiate Schick from all other razors based on four-blade technology that offers the best possible shave
- To achieve a trial purchase rate of 20 percent among 16- to 29-year-old males

As stated before, objectives should be clearly stated and quantitative in nature where applicable.

CREATIVE PLAN

The **creative plan** documents what the nature of the message will be and what strategies and techniques will be used to communicate the message. As indicated by the advertising objectives above, Schick's message would focus on the benefits offered by the four-blade shaving system. The message usually revolves around a key benefit statement (a brand makes a promise of something) and a support claims statement (a statement that gives people a reason to buy the product).

Advertisers have a variety of appeal techniques they call upon to communicate the message. Among these appeal techniques are the use of sex, humour, celebrities, product comparisons, and lifestyle associations. As well, the message usually has a central theme so that all messages (print, broadcast, and interactive) are focused and say the same thing in the same way.

To demonstrate creative planning, Rethink (the ad agency for Molson Coors Canada) recently launched a new campaign for Coors Light that capitalized on the brand's strengths—something it had gotten away from. Coors Light is associated with mountains and young people having fun. The first commercial, titled "The Mountain Speech," targeted millennials and celebrated their natural ability to go for it and have fun. Mountains appear in the spot (the brand was born in the Rockies), but their inclusion was meant to be a symbol of endless possibilities. Molson Coors feels the commercial connects with the target's belief that the world around them is full of opportunities to seize. Action scenes and phrases such as "Take a chance," "You're on the right path," and "Don't hold it in" reinforce the message.[8] Refer to the image in Figure 4.13.

FIGURE 4.13

Coors Light encourages millennials to climb their personal mountain, go for it, and have fun (a 2-minute version of this ad is available on YouTube).

Courtesy of Molson Coors Canada

MEDIA PLAN

The **media plan** involves decisions about which media are best suited to reach the target audience in an effective and efficient manner. Since a lot of money is at stake, making the right decisions is crucial. The goal of the media plan is to provide maximum impact at minimum cost and to reach the target market at the right time. Therefore, numerous strategic decisions must be made. An advertiser must determine which media to use (television, radio, newspapers, magazines, outdoor, direct response, interactive); the best time to reach the target market and how often it must be reached; which markets to advertise in (geographically) and at what weight levels; and when and for how long the media campaign will run. To develop the media plan, an agency must be on top of media consumption trends and be able to blend together all media selected into a coordinated plan. The Coors Light campaign introduced in the previous section was targeted at millennials. The campaign used a combination of television, digital, social, and out-of-home media. All of this information would be summarized in a media plan. Media planning is discussed in detail in Chapter 7.

INTERACTIVE COMMUNICATIONS PLAN

The internet and other forms of interactive communications, such as mobile communications, social media, and video games, are now significant alternatives to consider when planning a marketing communications campaign. Company and product websites also play an integral role in communicating vital information to customers and other publics. When determining their use of online advertising, companies assess the value of search advertising, banner ads (ads in various sizes that viewers click on for more information), video content, sponsorship opportunities (advertising on other websites of interest to a brand's or company's target audience), and email opportunities. The rapid increase in smartphone penetration in Canada has moved a lot of online communications onto mobile devices such as smartphones and tablets. Advertisers are following along and increasing their investment in digital media. Interactive communications strategies are presented in greater detail in Chapter 12.

DIRECT RESPONSE PLAN

Due to advances in communications technologies, companies are now investing more heavily in direct response techniques to get their message out. Direct response includes direct mail, direct response television, catalogue marketing, and telemarketing activities. These types of activities can be measured for effectiveness more readily than mass advertising. Consequently, managers who are being held more accountable for producing results than ever before are investing in direct response advertising. Appropriate objectives and strategies are incorporated into the communications plan. Direct response communications are presented in detail in Chapter 11.

SALES PROMOTION PLAN

If promotion incentives are to be integrated with the advertising activities, a sales promotion section should be included in the marketing communications plan. Objectives of the promotions, such as securing trial purchase, repeat purchase, or multiple purchases, should be documented. A summary calendar outlining the activities, timing, and costs associated with the promotion must also be included. Refer to Chapter 13 for more insight into sales promotion planning.

PUBLIC RELATIONS PLAN

Public relations (unpaid publicity) can play a key role in launching a new product or generating interest about an existing product. A plan to secure media support for newsworthy information about a product should be developed. The value of such publicity can be worth much more than the value derived from paid advertising. Documentation about public relations activity should be included in the communications plan. It is now common for an organization to post all news releases, relevant photos, and video clips about the company or its products on its website. Social media also plays a key role in contemporary public relations practice. Refer to Chapter 14 for more insight into public relations.

EXPERIENTIAL MARKETING (EVENTS AND SPONSORSHIPS) PLAN

Getting people more involved with a brand—by having them experience the brand—is becoming more important to marketing organizations. When organizations participate in planned events hosted by others (a sponsorship opportunity) or when they create and implement a unique branded event, the target market gets more actively involved with a brand. Careful planning is needed if an organization is to achieve maximum value from an event. A variety of communications elements can be built into the plan to show how the event will be supported. Additional details about experiential marketing, including events and sponsorships, are included in Chapter 14.

PERSONAL SELLING PLAN

The job of an organization's salesforce is to communicate with members of the distribution channel. The role of the sales representative is to communicate the benefits of the products offered for sale in terms of how they will specifically resolve a potential customer's problem. As well, the sales representative communicates to the trade customer any support plans that will help the distributor resell the products (e.g., price discounts and allowances, advertising programs, sponsorships). Coordination of the personal selling effort with other marketing communications activities is crucial.

For some initial insight into what a communications plan looks like and how the various elements of the plan are linked together, refer to the plan that is included in Appendix I.

SUMMARY

The quality of marketing and marketing communications planning in an organization is influenced by the business planning process itself. Business planning is a problem-solving and decision-making effort that forces management to look at the future and set clear objectives and strategies.

In terms of marketing communications, three different but related plans are important: the corporate plan, the marketing plan, and the marketing communications plan. Each plan involves the development of appropriate objectives, strategies, and tactics, and, when one plan is complete, it provides direction for the next plan. The marketing plan, for example, directs the marketing communications plan, which in turn directs individual plans for various components of the marketing communications mix.

Corporate planning starts with the development of a mission statement followed by corporate objectives and strategies. Some of the more common corporate strategies include penetrating the market more aggressively, acquiring other companies, implementing new product development programs, forming strategic alliances with other companies, and selling off unprofitable divisions of a company to consolidate operations.

Strategic marketing planning involves the following steps: conducting a situation analysis, which is a procedure that reviews and analyzes relevant data and information; conducting a SWOT analysis, which highlights the general direction a brand or company should be heading in; establishing appropriate marketing objectives and strategies; identifying target markets; accessing budget support; and establishing measurement and control procedures. The evaluation and control procedure attempts to draw relationships between strategic activity and results. All of this information is included in a marketing plan.

The marketing communications plan identifies the various communications objectives to be accomplished and delineates strategy in several areas. The communications plan is subdivided into specific areas depending on what components of the mix are going to be used. The advertising plan is further subdivided into the creative plan and the media plan. The creative plan focuses on creative objectives and strategies (what message to communicate and how to communicate it). The media plan states the media objectives by answering who, what, when, where, and how. The media strategies rationalize the use of media alternatives and treat in more detail considerations of timing, market coverage, and scheduling of messages.

Finally, other elements of the integrated marketing communications mix may be included in the plan. The objectives a plan is trying to achieve influence decisions on whether to include interactive communications, direct response communications, sales promotions, public relations, experiential marketing (including events), or personal selling. All plans must work together to achieve the objectives stated in the marketing communications plan.

KEY TERMS

acquisition strategy 94
advertising objectives 110
advertising plan 102
budget 100
corporate objectives 92
corporate strategies 93
creative brief 108
creative plan 112
divestment strategy 95
execution (tactics) 90
marketing communications objectives 108
marketing communications plan 108
marketing communications strategies 110
marketing control 103
marketing execution 102
marketing mix 100
marketing objectives 100
marketing planning 95
marketing plans 91
marketing strategies 100
media brief 108
media plan 113
mission statement 91
new product development strategy 93
noise 104
objectives 90
penetration strategy 93
positioning 98
positioning strategy statement 98
situation analysis 95
strategic alliance 94
strategic planning 90
strategies 90
SWOT analysis 98
target market 99

REVIEW QUESTIONS

1. In planning, what is the basic difference between objectives, strategies, and tactics?
2. What is the relationship between a company's mission statement and a company's marketing activity?
3. What are the relationships among a corporate plan, marketing plan, and marketing communications plan?
4. What does the term *situation analysis* refer to? What are the key issues associated with such an analysis?
5. What role does a positioning strategy statement play in the development of marketing strategy and marketing communications strategy?
6. What are the essential components of a target market profile?

7. Briefly describe the key elements of the marketing strategy section of a marketing plan.
8. How will a precise target market profile affect the development of creative strategies and media strategies?
9. What is meant by *marketing control*? What are the three basic elements that constitute marketing control?
10. In the planning process, what role does a clearly worded marketing communications objective play?
11. What are the key decision areas of an advertising plan? In considering the key areas, identify the relationships between creative and media strategies.
12. What are the various components of the marketing communications mix? Briefly describe the potential role of each component in a marketing communications plan.

DISCUSSION QUESTIONS

1. "Good strategy, poor execution" or "Poor strategy, good execution"—which scenario will produce better results? Support your position with an appropriate rationale.
2. Evaluate the marketing situation for the following companies. What makes them unique, and what are their differential advantages compared to their primary competitors? Develop a positioning strategy statement for each company based on your assessment of the situation.
   a. Dairy Queen
   b. Gatorade
   c. Boston Pizza
   d. Häagen-Dazs
3. Compare and contrast the marketing communications strategies of two competing brands (e.g., a leader and a challenger). Do these brands have similar or different communications mixes? What conclusions can you draw from your analysis of each brand? Some brands to consider might include the following:
   a. Coca-Cola and Pepsi
   b. Nike and Adidas
   c. Canadian Tire and The Home Depot
4. Using a variety of online sources, conduct a market analysis for a branded product of your choosing. The market analysis should include the following information:
   a. Market size and growth rate
   b. Importance of regional markets
   c. Market segment analysis (which segments are growing, declining, etc.)
   d. Seasonal analysis

NOTES

1. **http://www.google.ca/about/company/**.
2. PepsiCo, *2015 Annual Report*, **www.pepsico.com**, 10.
3. Chris Powell, "Keith's Launches Ice Cider," *Marketing*, April 18, 2012, **www.marketingmag.ca**.
4. E. J. Schultz, "Campbell Plans 200 New Products," *Advertising Age*, July 28, 2014, 6.
5. Jacqueline Nelson, "CIBC Teams with Tims for Double Double," *Globe and Mail*, July 3, 2014, B3.
6. "P&G Splitting off Its Duracell Business," *Marketing*, October 24, 2014, **www.marketingmag.ca**.
7. Michelle Dipardo, "Bay of Quinte Campaign Pushes Wineries and Waterfront Living," *Marketing*, February 18, 2015, **www.marketingmag.ca**.
8. Rebecca Harris, "Coors Light Ad Calls Millennials to the Mountain," *Marketing*, March 11, 2015, **www.marketingmag.ca.**

PART 3 Creating the Message

© Mrs_ya/Shutterstock

In Part 2, the relationships between marketing and advertising were established and a detailed review of the planning process was presented. Clearly, the content of a marketing plan or advertising plan affects the direction of creative planning.

Part 3 describes the creative planning process in detail by differentiating among creative objectives, strategies, and execution.

In Chapter 5, the role of research in the creative evaluation process is examined along with the roles and responsibilities of the client and the agency in the message development process.

Chapter 6 presents the production considerations for print, broadcast, and interactive media.

CHAPTER 5

Creative Planning Essentials

© wavebreakmedia/Shutterstock

Learning Objectives

After studying this chapter, you will be able to

1. Identify the basic elements of the communications process
2. Distinguish between client responsibility and agency responsibility in the creative development process
3. Explain the stages in the creative development process
4. Explain the creative briefing process, and describe the content normally included in a creative brief
5. Clearly distinguish between creative objectives, creative strategies, and creative execution
6. Describe the various appeal techniques commonly used in advertising
7. Identify the various execution techniques used for presenting advertising messages
8. Explain the measurement techniques used for evaluating creative

An advertising plan is divided into two distinct yet connected sections: the creative plan and the media plan. Once the advertising objectives are clearly identified, it is the task of the agency to devise message and media strategies that will achieve the objectives.

As indicated in previous chapters, it is essential that creative planners and media planners work together in the initial stages to determine how best to engage consumers. Once the engagement decisions have been made (these usually involve media choices and decisions about other forms of marketing communications to be used), the creative planners can begin to develop the messages and the media planners can devise media strategies in more detail. The actual advertisements that we see, read, and listen to are simply the outcome of the planning process.

This chapter focuses on the creative planning process and the relationships between the client and the agency in that process. First the creative development process is examined, and topics such as the content of a creative brief are addressed. The concepts of creative objectives, creative strategies, and creative execution are examined in detail, and numerous advertisements and campaigns are included to illustrate these concepts. Since research plays a role in the creative development process, various evaluation techniques are also presented.

The Creative Development Process and Client–Agency Responsibilities

When creative is being developed, the roles and responsibilities of the client and agency are clearly defined. The client provides the necessary input (information) and evaluates agency recommendations; the agency takes the information and develops appropriate message strategies that will fit with other marketing communications strategies. The creative development process is subdivided into seven distinct stages. Refer to Figure 5.1 for a visual illustration of the stages.

CLIENT RESPONSIBILITY

Early in the process, the client must provide enough market, competitor, customer, and product information so that the agency understands the situation clearly. The client also plays a role in developing a list of creative objectives. The creative objectives identify the key benefits that are to be communicated to the target market.

Through consultation with the agency's creative team, the client will have some (limited) input in the development of creative strategy statements. The agency might gain general direction by noting the client's preference for emotional or humorous appeals, but strategy is largely the domain of the agency.

The last area of client responsibility is the client's involvement in the creative evaluation process. Since the client's money is on the line, the client has every right to apply qualitative and quantitative research assessments at any stage of creative development. Essentially, the client reviews creative recommendations to ensure they match the positioning strategy for the brand.

FIGURE 5.1

PLANNING MODEL EXHIBIT

Stages in the creative development process

Creative planners and media planners should work together when developing an ad plan.

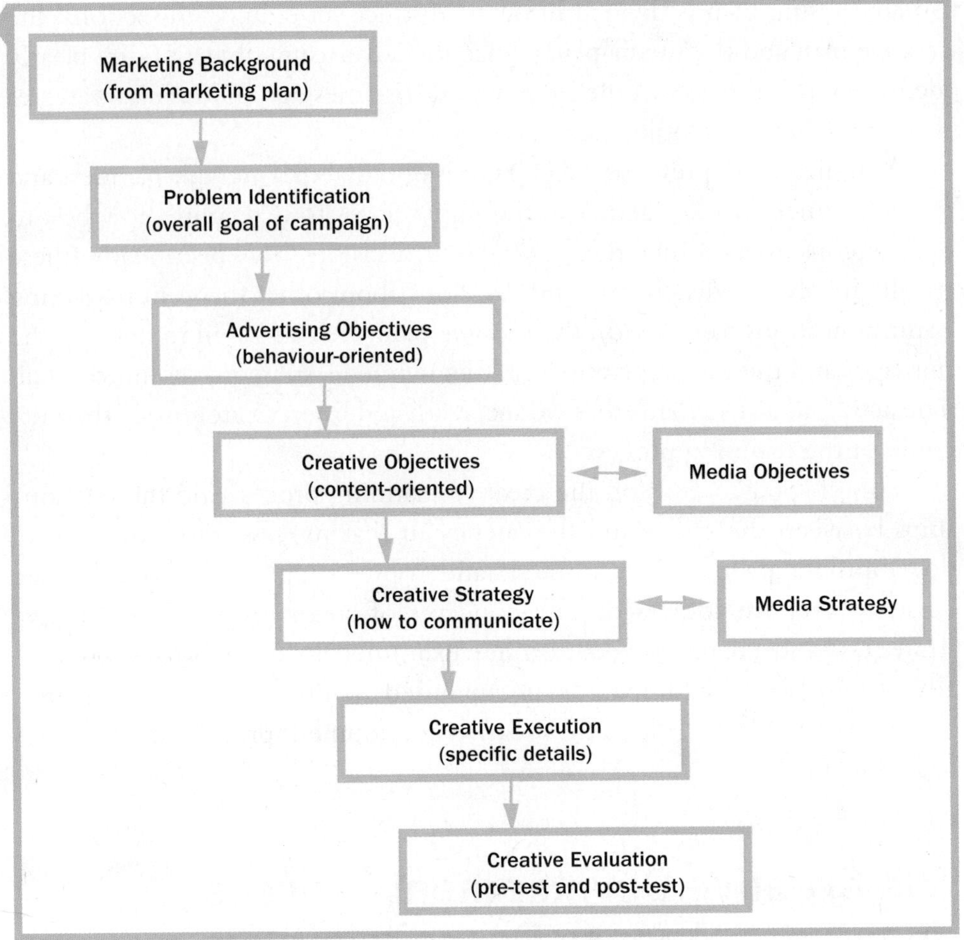

AGENCY RESPONSIBILITY

The agency first must familiarize itself, through consultation with the client, with the intricacies of the marketplace. Once the creative objectives have been decided, the agency must develop a more precise creative strategy. The creative team, comprising art directors and copywriters, works on numerous ideas and concepts and develops a short list of promising possibilities. The creative team also considers creative execution details to ensure the product will be presented in a convincing and believable manner. Agencies must recommend creative solutions that can be implemented in any or all media (broadcast, print, outdoor, and interactive).

Teamwork is an important component of the creative process because it provides consistency of thought and style to campaigns that stretch over extended periods. Therefore, it is essential that the copywriter and art director complement each other, appreciate each other's talents, and enjoy working together as a professional team.

When the creative team has completed the creative assignment, in the form of rough layouts for print or storyboards and scripts for television, for example, the ideas are submitted to senior agency personnel for internal approval and then to the client for approval. Depending on the outcome of the evaluation process, the agency either proceeds with creative execution or goes back to the drawing board to modify the concepts or develop new ideas. Often there are several meetings between agency and client before a campaign concept is finally approved.

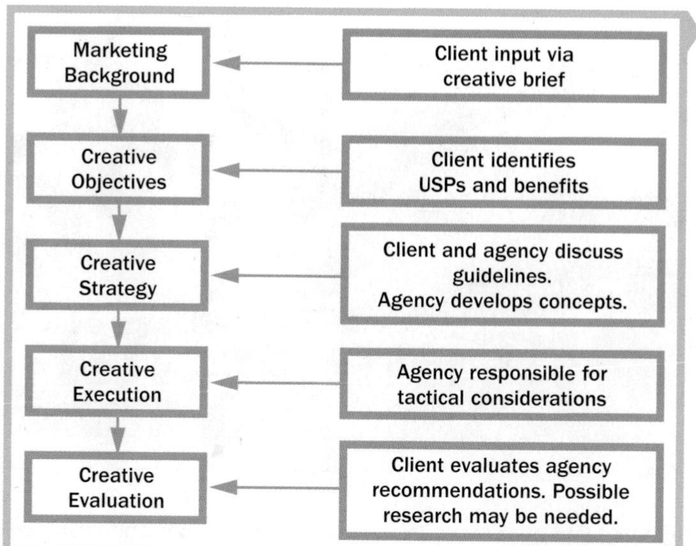

FIGURE 5.2

Client–agency responsibility in the creative development process

There isn't any magic formula for generating innovative advertising concepts. Each advertising agency has a unique perspective on how the development process should be handled. At TAXI Advertising, partner Paul Lavoie says, "We don't define creativity as visual or literary expression, but more as a way of thinking. Here, a small group of people—planner, writer, art director, and client—take responsibility for creative ideas rather than being caught up in the rigid hierarchy of differentiated roles, responsibilities, and job titles. We blend intuition with hard research. If we don't build our clients' business, we don't deserve to have it."[1]

At BBDO, Craig Cooper, vice-president and group creative director, says, "Great advertising has to have sound, solid strategic thinking behind it. Good creative has to touch and stimulate the consumer in an emotional way." Cooper says creative product is almost always the result of "gut-feel"—the skills of the writer and art director, combined with their instincts as consumers themselves.[2]

Regardless of the process, a common denominator is the working relationship between the agency and the client. Figure 5.2 summarizes the key roles of clients and agencies in the creative development process.

The Creative Brief

The starting point for any new advertising project is the creative brief. A **creative brief** is a document developed by the client that contains vital information about the advertising task at hand. The information contained in the brief is presented to and discussed with agency personnel so that copywriters and art directors fully understand the nature of the assignment. The brief is a discussion document; therefore, its content can change based on the discussion that takes place (e.g., the advertising agency may fine tune the brief after discussing all issues with the client). When briefing the agency, clients must resist the temptation to offer preferences for creative strategy—that is the expertise the client is seeking from its agency. Too much direction by a client sometimes has a negative influence on the creativity of copywriters and art directors.

To understand how client and agency come to agree on an advertising direction, you must first look at the information that both parties consider when determining what to say

FIGURE 5.3

"Be more human" became the creative concept in Reebok's new ad campaign.

Courtesy of Reebok Canada

in an ad and how to say it. The brief typically communicates essential background information, a problem statement or overall goal (sometimes referred to as a challenge statement), a list of advertising objectives, a positioning strategy statement, and a list of creative objectives.

Once the briefing process is complete, the creative team is in the spotlight. The team, comprising a copywriter, art director, and creative director from the traditional and digital sides of the agency (or separate agencies if that is the case), is charged with the task of developing the **creative concept** or "big idea" that will be the cornerstone of a campaign. To do so, the team considers information supplied by the client. To discover ways of solving a client's advertising problems, the creative team immerses itself in the product (company) and market (competitive environment) so the members fully understand the current situation.

To quickly demonstrate the "big idea" concept, consider a recent campaign from Reebok that was created by Venables Bell & Partners (the agency). The agency understood that while people traditionally worked out alone, a trend was emerging—working out was becoming an intense social experience (e.g., the CrossFit experience). People were pushing themselves harder. Such insight resulted in a campaign that challenged fitness buffs to "be more human." It would be a rallying cry for people to live up to their potential.[3] Refer to the illustration in Figure 5.3.

The next series of sections examine the content of a creative brief in more detail. Refer to Figure 5.4 for a summary of the information that is typically included in a creative brief. Students should understand that the content and structure of a creative brief vary from one organization to another. There is no standard or uniform way of presenting the information that is usually contained in the document. Also refer to Figure 5.5, a sample illustration of a creative brief.

MARKET INFORMATION

MARKET PROFILE Initially, agency personnel are briefed on happenings in the marketplace. Key issues include the size and rate of growth in the market, the existence of various market segments, the identification of major competitors and their market shares, and the notation of their strengths and weaknesses. It is important for the creative team to know the conditions that exist in the market and any influences affecting those conditions.

PRODUCT PROFILE The focus then shifts to the brand in question. The agency is briefed on the key benefits the brand offers—benefits that will entice consumers to buy. Typically,

MARKET INFORMATION

- Market profile
- Product profile
- Competitor profile
- Target market profile
- Budget

PROBLEM IDENTIFICATION OR CHALLENGE STATEMENT

- Clear identification of the problem or challenge advertising will resolve; or
- Overall goal of the campaign

ADVERTISING OBJECTIVES

(Include appropriate behavioural objectives based on problem or goal)

- Awareness
- Interest
- Preference
- Action
- New image
- New targets

POSITIONING STRATEGY STATEMENT

- Statement of the brand's benefits, personality, or desired image

CREATIVE OBJECTIVES

- List of message content objectives
- Key benefit statement
- Support claims statement

CREATIVE STRATEGY

- Buying motivation
- Theme
- Tone and style
- Appeal techniques

CREATIVE EXECUTION

- Tactical considerations
- Production considerations

FIGURE 5.4

PLANNING MODEL EXHIBIT

Content of a creative brief

Clients and advertising agencies are unique enterprises. Therefore, the style, structure, and content of this document will vary across the industry. This is a working model to highlight content that could be contained in a brief. The creative strategy section often isn't determined until the client and agency discuss the assignment.

the benefits offered are ranked by priority. For example, the key benefit could be economy, safety, variety, durability, reliability, or great taste for a food or beverage product. Once the primary benefit is identified, it should become the focal point of the advertising message. For example, Walmart differentiates itself by promising consumers they will save money on little things that help families live better. Nescafé Cappuccino Skinny promises the consumer a good, tasty beverage with less than half the fat, a compelling reason to buy the product. Refer to the image Figure 5.6.

FIGURE 5.5

An example of a creative brief

Source: This brief was prepared by the author for illustration purposes.

HARLEY-DAVIDSON

MARKET INFORMATION

- Market volume has been affected by the economic downturn and an aging rider population; unit sales for the industry dropped 20 percent this year versus one year ago
- Market divided into two segments: The heavyweight segment that Harley dominates caters to older buyers wanting style, quality, and status; the lightweight segment appeals to younger buyers seeking speed, agility, and affordability in a motorcycle
- Harley generates 70 percent of its sales in the United States and 30 percent internationally
- Canada accounts for 15 percent of Harley's international sales

MARKET SHARES

Harley-Davidson dominates the heavyweight segment. Current market shares are as follows:

Brand	2015 Share %	2014 Share %
Harley-Davidson	49.4	50.0
Honda	14.2	15.1
Suzuki	12.5	12.9
Yamaha	9.2	8.6
Kawasaki	7.2	6.8

BRAND PROFILE

- Harley competes on design and quality (intentionally unique-sounding engines)
- Harley's past growth and continued success is closely tied to its brand loyalty. (Harley owners have been known to tattoo the brand's trademark on their bodies and are members of H.O.G.—Harley Owners Group.)
- Harley has distinguished itself from other brands based on its heritage, image, and reputation—a "rebellious" image the company doesn't control
- Advertising messages portray the emotional connection between brand and rider

BRAND INSIGHT FROM LOYAL CUSTOMERS

"I love everything about a Harley. From the bike and clothing to the people you meet when riding, and the instant friends everywhere you go."

"When you ride a Harley, you feel a Harley. When you ride a [Honda] Gold Wing, you don't feel anything. The Harley engine has a soul. And a lot of Japanese bikes don't have soul."

COMPETITOR PROFILE

- Japanese competitors offer heavyweight models that appeal to price-conscious buyers more interested in the motorcycle's technology

TARGET MARKET PROFILE (CURRENT)

- Demographics: 45 to 59 years old; 88 percent male and 12 percent female; income $75 000 plus annually; reside in urban markets
- Psychographics: adventurous, like to travel, break away from routine on weekends, enjoy the freedom of the open road
- Behaviour: Current customers are extremely brand loyal and emotionally connected to the brand. "Weekend Warrior" is a nickname describing the customer

PROBLEM

The current customer is aging, and younger potential customers see a Harley as a bike that looks like their father's or grandfather's bike—it is the motorcycle of choice for aging baby boomers. Future growth depends on Harley's ability to attract new, younger customers. How does Harley-Davidson attract a younger customer?

COMMUNICATIONS OBJECTIVES

- Attract a younger customer in the 30- to 45-year-old age range
- Alter perceptions held by younger customers about the brand

POSITIONING STATEMENT

Harley-Davidson represents a sense of freedom, independence, even rebelliousness, and the chance to live on your own terms for a while. For individuals wanting a kindred spirit in a bike, Harley-Davidson is the brand for you.

CREATIVE OBJECTIVES

- To communicate an image or set of images more in line with younger lifestyles
- To portray the feeling of freedom and independence a younger rider will enjoy when riding a Harley
- To communicate an emotional connection between Harley-Davidson and the rider (younger rider)

CREATIVE STRATEGY

Strategy is left to the discretion of the agency, but it must be in line with the brand's overall positioning strategy. Emotional and lifestyle appeals that focus on freedom and independence have been successful in the past, but Harley-Davidson is open to new ideas. The recommended strategy must be suitable for print, broadcast, and digital media.

CREATIVE EXECUTION

- 4-colour print ads (magazine and outdoor executions)
- 30-second television spots
- Online video ads
- All images must portray the core positioning strategy of the brand

FIGURE 5.5

Continued

A brand's reputation can also influence the message. While creative direction often changes with time, quite often an important element from previous campaigns is retained in a new campaign. Such an element may have contributed positively to the image of the brand. For example, a good slogan can outlast numerous advertising campaigns, because the slogan is closely associated with the brand name and has high recall with consumers. Such is the case for the "I'm lovin' it" campaign from McDonald's. "I'm lovin' it" is "the company's most successful and longest-running campaign," and it is executed globally (117 countries and numerous languages).[4] To breathe new life into the campaign, however, agencies must develop new creative executions that fit with the existing creative strategy.

Here are a few other taglines that have stood the test of time:

- Mazda: "Zoom-Zoom"
- Nike: "Just do it."
- Campbell's: "M'm! M'm! Good!"
- Red Bull: "It gives you wings"

Also, a character, symbol, or spokesperson may be so closely associated with a product that their presence is expected in advertising. Here are a few examples:

- Kellogg's Frosted Flakes: Tony the Tiger
- Mr. Clean: Mr. Clean

© whiteboxmedia limited/Alamy

FIGURE 5.6
The primary benefits of Nescafé Cappuccino Skinny—taste and half the fat—are clearly communicated in this advertisement.

- TD Canada Trust: Cushy green chair
- Kraft Peanut Butter: Teddy bears

Elements such as these have longevity and therefore must be considered when a new creative direction is contemplated. Refer to the illustration in Figure 5.7.

COMPETITOR PROFILE A discussion of competitive creative strategies provides a more complete perspective on what is happening in the marketplace. The client should analyze the strengths and weaknesses of the competition and use the analysis as a guideline for creative direction. The creative team should know what competitor brands are saying and how they are saying it. The direction ultimately taken may be similar to or totally different from that of the competition. Competitive analysis can also have an impact on the tone, style, and appeal techniques used in advertising.

TARGET MARKET PROFILE The client must provide a complete profile of the target market, which includes all relevant demographic, psychographic, and geographic information. The better the knowledge of the target market, the easier the task of developing advertising messages. If adequate resources are allocated to the collection of research information—to identifying and understanding the motivations behind consumers'

Courtesy of TD Bank

FIGURE 5.7
TD Canada Trust's cushy green chair is a symbol of comfort in an industry many consumers find intimidating.

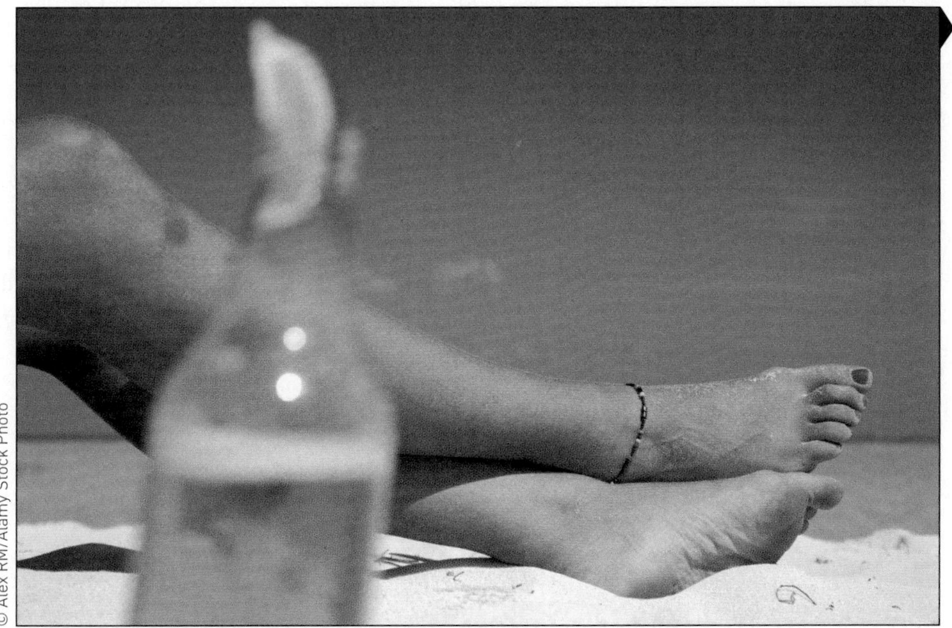

© Alex RM/Alamy Stock Photo

FIGURE 5.8

Corona encourages millennials to live life on their own terms. The brand frequently uses scenes of young people relaxing on the beach (getting away from it all) to deliver its message.

purchases—such information can be used to develop convincing messages. The ability to associate product benefits with buying motives or to present a product in a manner suited to a certain lifestyle is part of developing objective and strategy statements for the creative.

To illustrate the use of target profile information, consider the challenges an advertiser faces when trying to reach the millennial demographic, a unique target market. Ad agency Zulu Alpha Kilo recently developed a campaign for Corona beer directed at this target market. According to Mike Sutton, managing director at the agency, "They [millennials] really want to make a mark on the world, but it's very different from when I was in my twenties. It's really more about experiences now than possessions and things." He describes the target as confident, ambitious, and creative-minded. The campaign the agency recommended encourages today's youth to forget their troubles and "Live the finer life."[5] This slogan is about living life on your own terms rather than accepting the ordinary. Refer to the image in Figure 5.8.

As discussed in Chapter 3, target market profiles may comprise demographic, psychographic, geographic, and behavioural characteristics. Descriptive expressions, coined by demographers, such as baby boomers, Generation X, and Generation Y, have been used to describe targets. A firm understanding of the behaviours of these and other targets provides agency creative personnel valuable insights for developing a message strategy.

BUDGET At this stage of the planning process, the client should provide a budget guideline. The amount of money available will determine whether the use of certain media is restricted or eliminated. For example, a budget judged to be small eliminates the use of television. If the budget is large, a multimedia campaign is possible. Either way, the media under consideration influence the creative direction.

Problem Identification or Challenge Statement

Typically, advertising campaigns are designed to resolve a specific problem or pursue an opportunity. The client presents a challenge to its advertising agency. In other words, all of the analysis that has occurred so far points the campaign in a certain direction. Perhaps the problem or challenge is better described as the *overall goal* of the campaign. At this point, what the communications are expected to do is clearly identified. The following are a few generic examples of overall communications goals:

- To create or increase brand awareness (possibly for a new product)
- To position or reposition a product in the customer's mind
- To present a new image (re-image the brand)
- To attract a new target market

These examples suggest that a campaign must have focus. Attempting to accomplish too many goals at one time only creates confusion in the customer's mind. It is preferable to focus on one primary goal and ensure that it is achieved. For example, many consumers perceive gluten-free products to be less tasty and flavourful. When Quaker introduced gluten-free Crispy Minis (a light snack chip), it had to conquer that perception. Delicious-looking chips adorned the package, and the package itself was the featured element of the ad campaign. Body copy such as "same great taste" (as the original version) and "gluten-free and delicious" helped sell the taste promise.

Advertising Objectives

As indicated in the previous section, an advertising campaign typically has a central focus. Therefore, to facilitate the creative thinking process, the overall goal is subdivided into more specific advertising objectives. Advertising objectives usually focus on behavioural issues such as creating awareness and preference or altering the image and perceptions of a brand held by consumers, since these are the things that advertising is best at accomplishing. Objectives should be expressed in quantitative terms whenever possible, as the objectives are used to measure the effectiveness of the campaign at a later date.

The stage a product is at in its life cycle and the competitive environment of the marketplace often influence the advertising objectives. For example, at the introduction and growth stages of the life cycle, the emphasis is on awareness and preference and the message deals with **unique selling points (USPs)**. The goal is to differentiate one brand from another. In the mature stage, the message shifts to increasing frequency of use by consumers, expanding the variety of uses current customers have for the product, or attracting new users to the product.

To apply the concept of advertising objectives, consider the following examples that could apply when launching a new product:

- To achieve a brand awareness level of 60 percent among the defined target market within 12 months of launching the product
- To achieve a trial purchase rate of 25 percent among the defined target market

Since this is a new product, the objectives deal with awareness and trial purchase. Let's examine a few of these challenges in more detail and see how they influence the direction of the creative.

INCREASING AWARENESS AND PREFERENCE Thinking strictly in terms of consumer behaviour, advertising objectives are stated in terms of achieving certain levels of brand awareness and brand preference. Advertising that achieves the desired levels will produce a stronger likelihood of purchase among members of the target market. Achieving good levels of awareness and preference depends on a host of factors. For example, the impact of the message (how memorable it is) and the media (the impact of the medium itself) combine to influence consumer behaviour.

When trivago entered the North American market, its primary objective was to create brand awareness. An intensive television and digital campaign featured a character (now

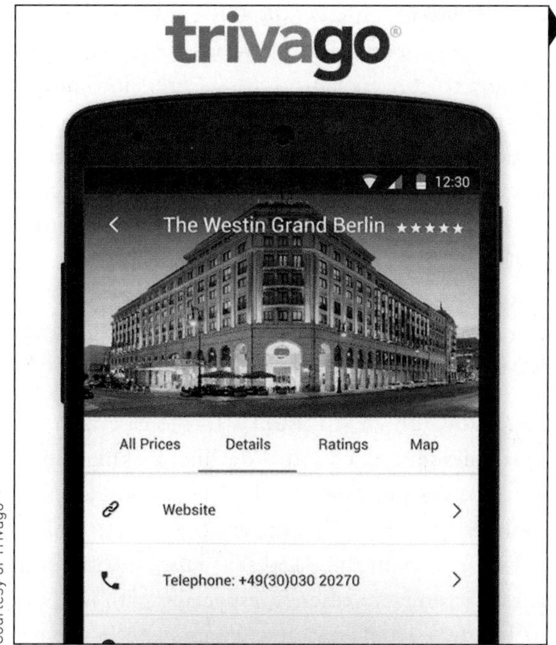

Courtesy of Trivago

FIGURE 5.9

Television commercials featuring a dishevelled-looking character presenting the message created high levels of awareness for trivago.

known as the "trivago guy") with a casual and laid-back demeanour, who some saw as an unconventional character and others saw as attractive. Regardless of the reaction, the guy inspired all kinds of buzz in social media.[6] The message emphasized the brand name while the presenter showed how easy it was to use the trivago hotel reservation website. The campaign was effective. trivago's awareness among travellers now ranks just below Priceline (the market leader) and ahead of Expedia and TripAdvisor. Refer to the image in Figure 5.9.

ENCOURAGING TRIAL PURCHASE When a product is in the introduction and growth stages of its life cycle, achieving high levels of awareness and trial purchase are key objectives. Sometimes incentives have to be offered to give consumers an extra nudge to buy. If that is the case, the ads will carry a coupon offer, refund offer, or some other incentive. The incentive provides an additional benefit for the customer.

Incentives help reduce the risk associated with purchasing something for the first time. For expensive goods, such as a car or household appliance, where the risk is high, incentives (cash discounts, 0 percent financing, etc.) encourage consumers to buy in a time frame that is desirable for the manufacturer.

The use of incentives does not preclude the idea that advertising alone will stimulate trial purchase. Good advertising can get people to buy! Axe, for example, a product aimed directly at 18- to 24-year-old males, is a market leader based solely on its advertising creativity. Messages that appealed directly to the mind-set of young males (the primary target), with images of young females fawning over them in television commercials, got the job done. That was incentive enough!

COMMUNICATING PROMOTION INCENTIVES Often an entire campaign revolves around a special offer from a manufacturer or retailer. In the previous section, some trial-oriented incentives were mentioned. Other promotional incentives include contests, premium offers, rebate offers, and loyalty programs. In these situations, advertising may temporarily depart from communicating USPs in order to focus on the brand name and promotion. For example, Tim Hortons runs an advertising campaign for its products all year round but shifts gears in early spring when it runs its annual "Roll Up the Rim" contest. Each March the promotion gets full attention in a multimedia campaign.

INCREASING FREQUENCY OR VARIETY OF USE When a product is firmly established in the market (mature stage of the product life cycle), the marketing objectives usually reflect an attempt to convert light or casual users into heavy users. Since users know the benefits of the product, the costs associated with increasing usage are often much less than those associated with attempting to attract new users. Advertising can play a role in building frequency of use or variety of use for a product.

To demonstrate, consider the recent campaign from Visa Canada with the tagline "Do you smallenfreuden?" Visa's objective was to convince consumers to use their credit cards for smaller purchases. Visa generates its revenue based on the number of transactions made on cards. Therefore, using cards more frequently is the key to growth.[7] An initial wave of advertising teased consumers by simply asking, "Do you smallenfreuden?"

TO ATTRACTING NEW TARGETS In the case of mature products that are experiencing marginal sales growth or actual decline, making the product appeal to different user segments represents opportunity. To illustrate, consider a recent creative campaign for Jaguar automobiles. Jaguar is a luxury car brand that traditionally targets 35- to 64-year-old males with incomes in the $150 000 range. With an aging population, Jaguar knows it must attract a younger audience, especially with its sportier-looking models. Refer to the image in Figure 5.10. To reach a younger, tech-savvy demographic, Jaguar launched a digital campaign that included interactive videos to engage viewers. In one instance, clicking on a digital banner ad took viewers to a video that showed how often Jaguar crash tests its cars to improve safety (not the typical Jaguar message). The video paused at key moments and prompted viewers to initiate action—such as crashing a car, for instance.[8]

COMMUNICATING PRODUCT IMPROVEMENTS In the late growth and early mature stages of the product's life cycle, marketing strategies often deal with product changes and improvements to keep the product competitive. This strategy is popular in the food industry (where advertisements often focus on a product's "new and improved" taste) and household products industry (where messages focus on improved product performance).

In this situation, advertising messages make the consumer aware of the improvement. Columbia improved its winter jacket performance by introducing "TurboDown"—natural down pumped with Omni-Heat insulation. Refer to the image in Figure 5.11. Gillette is always introducing new technology to promise men a cleaner, better shave. "FlexBall" technology is its latest innovation to improve the performance of its product.

© Michael Cole/Corbis/Getty Images

FIGURE 5.10

Jaguar launched an interactive campaign for its sportier-looking models to attract a younger, tech-savvy target market.

Courtesy of Columbia Sportswear Company

FIGURE 5.11

Columbia communicates how "TurboDown," a new insulation system, performs better.

COMMUNICATING A POSITIVE CORPORATE IMAGE In addition to product-oriented advertising, a company can implement advertising campaigns that benefit the company as a whole. These campaigns are typically part of an organization's social responsibility positioning. Energy companies are always facing the wrath of environmental groups and the public for the potential harm they are causing to the environment. Nonetheless, these

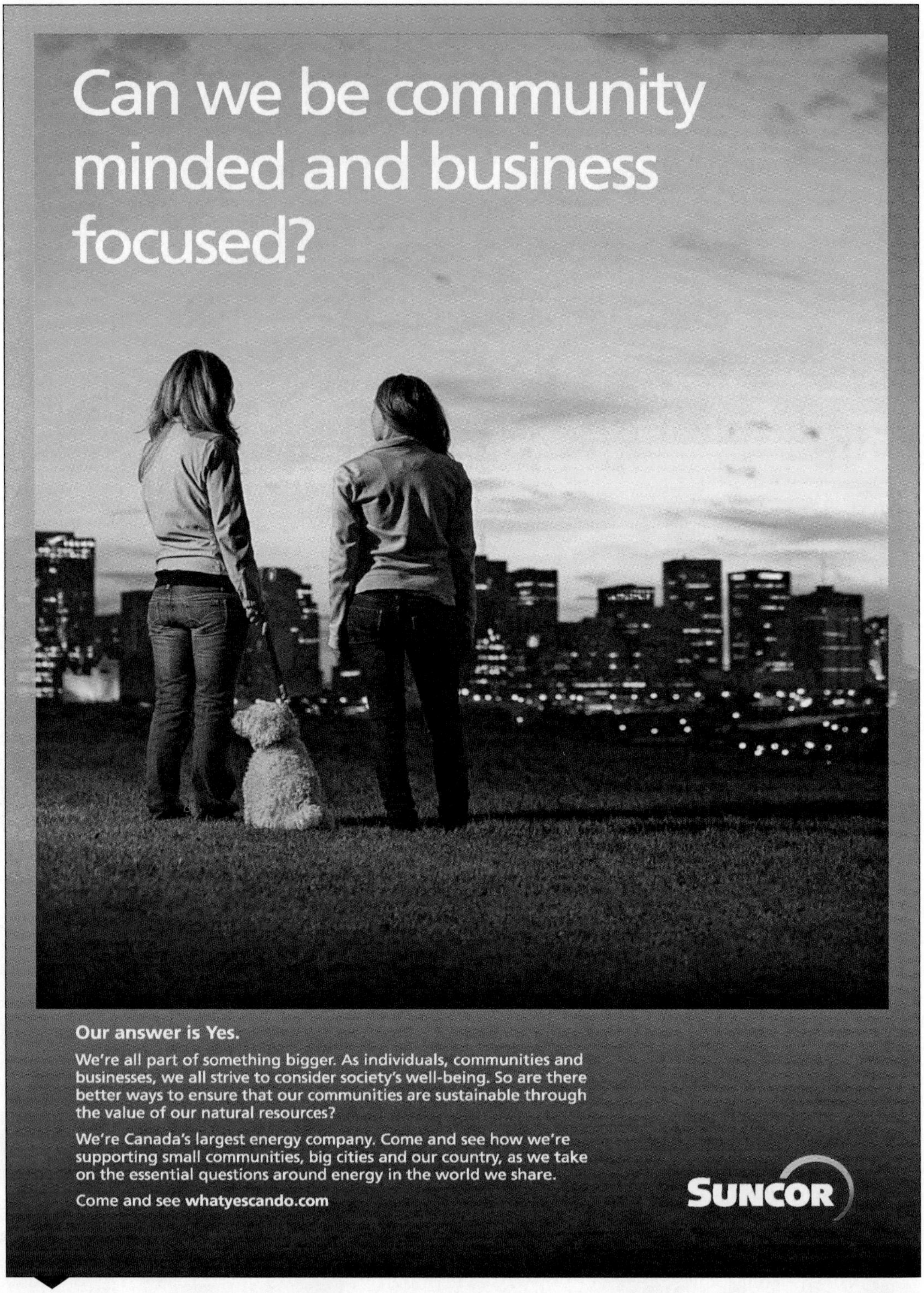

Courtesy of Suncor

FIGURE 5.12

An ad designed to build corporate reputation with the public

companies do good things as well. A recent Suncor campaign addressed sustainable development. Print ads invited consumers to visit a website (whatyescando.com) to find out how Suncor is creating opportunities for employment and economic prosperity in an era where environmental protection is paramount. Refer to the image in Figure 5.12.

ALTERING A PERCEPTION OR IMAGE Sometimes a company or a product has to deal with incorrect perceptions held by consumers—a challenging task for advertising to overcome.

Courtesy of Canada Bread Company, Limited

FIGURE 5.13

Canada Bread launched new products and an advertising campaign to dispel misconceptions people held about bread.

As an old saying goes, "Perception is reality." To illustrate, bread, particularly white bread, has taken a beating recently, and bread sales volume is declining across the industry. Consumers who Google "Can I eat bread?" see rather dismal results. Articles with titles like "6 Reasons Why You Should Not Eat Bread" may appear. How does a company like Canada Bread deal with that? The company introduced several new bread products that include new grains, such as quinoa and chia. Then, to dispel any myths and misconceptions about bread, Canada Bread launched a new advertising campaign that would take the guilt out of eating bread.[9] Refer to the image in Figure 5.13.

Positioning Strategy Statement

Positioning refers to the selling concept or message that motivates purchase of a particular brand of product or service. This concept was discussed in the previous two chapters. Therefore, comments here will focus on the impact a positioning strategy statement has on advertising. Agency creative people refer to the positioning statement when they are trying to discover the creative concept—that big idea for communicating the message effectively.

To illustrate how positioning strategy influences creative direction, consider the success of a brand like Secret deodorant. Secret has a familiar tagline: "Strong enough for a man, made for a woman." The tagline captures the essence of the positioning strategy for the brand—it is dependable, long lasting, and offers women the confidence to pursue activities they might otherwise avoid. This is a clever and compelling message that distinguished Secret from other brands.

When creatives (art directors and copywriters) are brainstorming ideas for a campaign, the creative concept or "big idea" often arises from the positioning strategy statement. (Ads have to fit with overall brand strategy.) The big idea must draw attention to and effectively communicate the key benefits. The slogan plays a key role by ingraining the essence of the positioning strategy in the customer's mind. Consider the following examples and how they relate to the brand's positioning strategy:

- Subway: "Eat fresh" (healthy, fast food for contemporary lifestyles)
- Tim Hortons: "Always fresh" (an obvious promise that drives the entire company)
- Nike: "Just do it" (an inspirational strategy to encourage people to participate or compete to the best of their ability)

For a look at a new positioning strategy and a new advertising campaign that stemmed from that strategy, read the Advertising in Action vignette **Hyundai's "H-Factor."**

ADVERTISING IN ACTION

Hyundai's "H-Factor"

For some time Hyundai has been designing and manufacturing superior quality vehicles and selling them at reasonable prices to car buyers. However, prospective consumers don't readily associate a reasonable price with quality, and that poses a problem for Hyundai. Hyundai is trying to position the brand as "modern premium," but what this means is misunderstood by many prospective car buyers.

Hyundai is implementing a four-pronged marketing strategy with the goal of elevating the Hyundai brand in the minds of Canadians. The marketing strategy includes the launch of all-new Sonata and Genesis models; modernized dealer facilities to improve the selling environment; a new training and certification program called Hyundai Signature Certification, which encourages dealers to continually strive to exceed customer expectations; and finally a new advertising campaign called "The H-Factor" to tell people about all the changes. The term "H-Factor" is used as a creative expression of the company's desire to deliver experiences that exceed expectations.

Previous advertising campaigns focused more on function, with ads highlighting various aspects of the vehicle and different engineering features. The new campaign brings better balance to the message by adding an emotional component. The H-Factor is the emotional response a consumer gets when interacting with Hyundai's products.

The initial television commercial takes the viewer on a journey from the inception of Hyundai's award-winning design to its advanced engineering, specialized manufacturing, durability testing, and finally the world-class driving experience that will surprise customers. The electrifying hit song "Radioactive" by Imagine Dragons is heard throughout the commercial.

Will the new campaign deliver? It's too early to tell, but Hyundai Canada CEO Don Romano has a positive outlook: "A new Hyundai is emerging. After years of developing award-winning, convention-shattering vehicles, we believe the new 'H-Factor' campaign will begin to give Hyundai the recognition it has long deserved."

© Xinhua/Photoshot

Source: "Hyundai Launches New Brand Positioning Campaign," press release, January 30, 2015, CNW Newswire, www.newswire.ca.

Creative Objectives

Whereas advertising objectives are behavioural in nature or are written to identify a certain task that advertising will achieve, **creative objectives** are statements that clearly indicate the content of the message to be communicated to a target audience. As indicated, positioning strategy statements have a direct influence on what will be said about a product or company. Although the formats for writing creative objectives vary, a common practice is to consolidate what has to be said about a product in a short list of objectives.

To demonstrate how creative objective statements are written, consider the situation Wrigley's Juicy Fruit gum once faced. Juicy Fruit was perceived by consumers as being old, stagnant, and boring, and half of its users were over 35 years of age. The brand had become irrelevant to teens. A new creative approach was needed to re-image the brand. Here are a few creative objective statements that could have applied to the campaign:

- To reposition Juicy Fruit gum to appeal to teenagers
- To communicate in a manner (with an edge) that will resonate with the teen market
- To communicate how "sweet" the gum is (sweet is cool with teens)

Wrigley recognized that a new creative approach could alienate its older target market but was willing to take the risk in order to start rebuilding the brand.

Another option is to present creative objectives in the form of a **key benefit statement** (what the most important information to communicate is) and a **support claims statement** (on what basis it can be stated). Let's examine each of these elements:

- ***Key benefit statement*** A statement of the basic selling idea, service, or benefit that the advertiser *promises* the consumer. This benefit is the primary reason for buying the product over any competitive product. For example, Colgate Enamel Health toothpaste promises consumers healthy, smooth enamel, which is a means of protecting your teeth.
- ***Support claims statement*** A statement describing the principal characteristics of the product or service—the characteristics that substantiate the promise made in the key benefit statement. It provides *proof* of promise based on consumer research or some criteria that measures the performance of the product. For Colgate Enamel Health, the unique, active fluoride formula transforms enamel from rough and weakened to smooth and strong. The advertisement in Figure 5.14 illustrates the point.

Creative Strategy

After confirming the message content, the next stage is to develop the creative strategy. In contrast to the first two stages, the agency's creative team plays a dominant role here. In essence, the client pays the agency primarily for the strategy (i.e., the ideas and concepts used in presenting the message). Sound strategies, in accordance with the positioning strategy and the creative objectives, are the foundation of successful advertising campaigns.

The **creative strategy** states how the message is to be communicated to the target audience. It is a statement of the character, personality, and image that the agency will strive to develop for the client's product or service. Strategy is reflected in the *central theme* that is developed along with the *tone, style,* and *appeal techniques* of the advertising. Tone and style, for example, can be informative, persuasive, entertaining, or warm in nature, to suggest just a few options. The creative team must determine which approach will have the most impact on the target audience. Information gleaned from the target's demographic and psychographic profile influences this kind of decision.

The **central theme** or **big idea** is the glue that binds the various creative elements together. It must work in all forms of media if it is to have impact. To demonstrate the role of the big idea, consider the campaign that Rethink created for Molson Canadian. Rethink had a lot of ideas that would rejuvenate interest in the brand, but the idea that caught fire was the "travelling beer fridge." It started as a sketch on a piece of paper. It was a simple idea with limitless possibilities. The commercials showed Canadian travellers interacting with the fridge during their travels abroad—their passport would open the fridge! The campaign created a new identity for Molson Canadian with a new generation of Canadians. The ads moved seamlessly across different media platforms and went viral

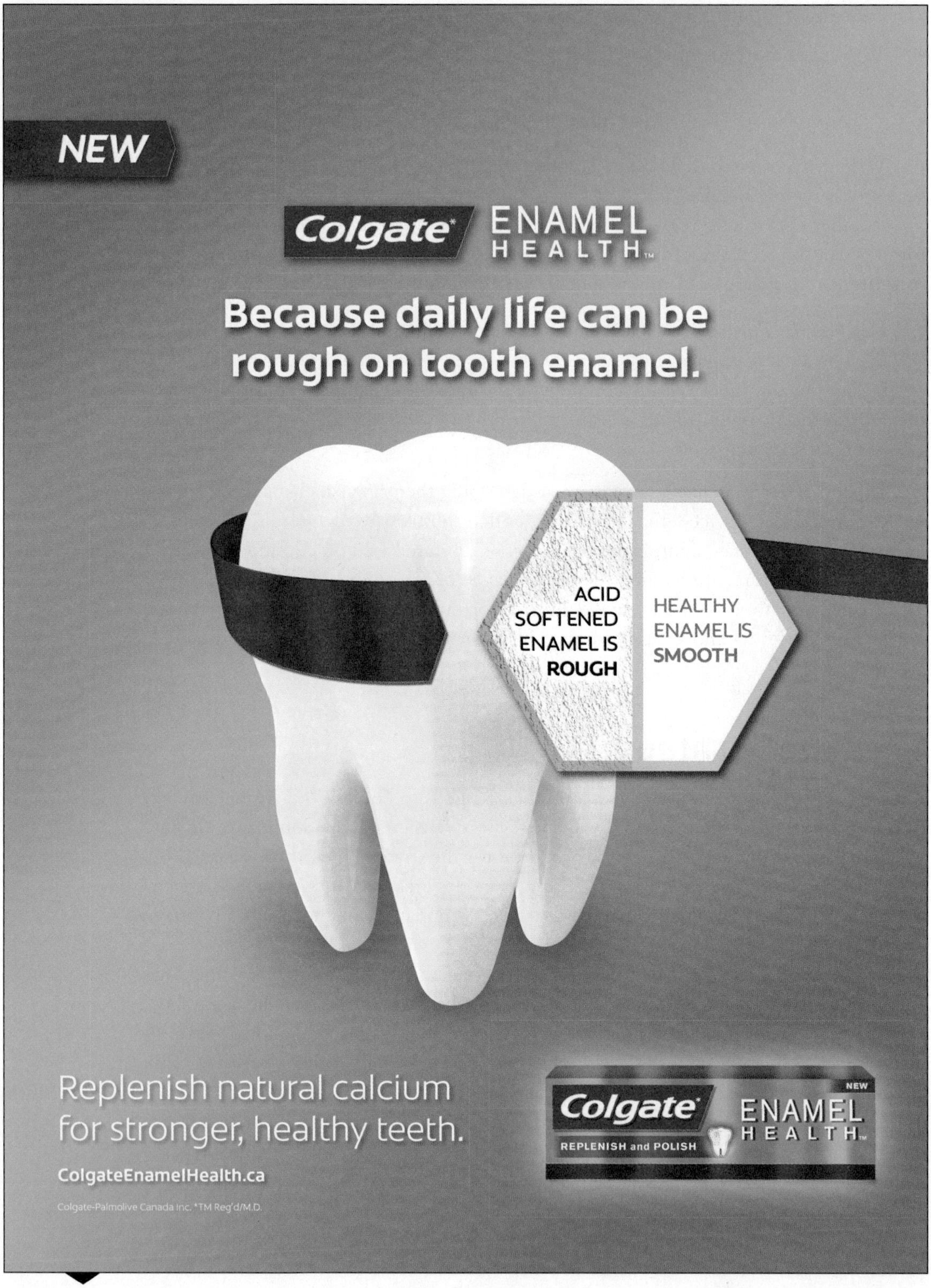

Courtesy of Colgate-Palmolive

FIGURE 5.14

Colgate's brand promise is "healthy and smooth tooth enamel"—a benefit many consumers are interested in.

online. Brand enthusiasts shared ads and images on social media.[10] Refer to the image in Figure 5.15.

These strategic characteristics of ads usually stem from the basic appeal technique that the creative team decides upon. A brand may appeal to a potential buyer on the basis of factual information, emotion, humour, or sex, to name only a few of the alternatives

© Neil Davidson/The Canadian Press

FIGURE 5.15

The "travelling beer fridge" campaign worked seamlessly across media platforms to create a new identity for Molson Canadian.

available. The following is a discussion of some of the more common creative appeal techniques.

POSITIVE APPEALS

When positive appeals are used in advertising, the product promise and benefits (i.e., the primary reason for buying the product) are presented as the basis of a positive, enjoyable experience for the consumer. The mood, tone, and style of the advertising are upbeat and are intended to leave the consumer with a favourable impression.

In the quick-serve restaurant market, the McDonald's "I'm lovin' it" campaign features a lot of music and happy people enjoying the McDonald's experience—fast food for people of all ages. McDonald's effectively uses positive appeals to entice customers to come to its restaurants. Subway's "Eat fresh" campaign positively portrays a healthy dining experience. Refer to the advertisement in Figure 5.16.

NEGATIVE APPEALS

In negative appeals, the product promise and benefits presented are based on an experience the potential buyer can *avoid* by purchasing the advertised product or service. In some cases, fear can be used to really grab people's attention. Insurance companies often use this technique by showing disastrous situations that homeowners may encounter; the message is clear: Make sure you have adequate financial protection through the insurance plans we offer.

"Tastes awful, but it works" is now a famous slogan coined by Buckley's cough mixture. Not many brands would want to say that about their product, but it works for Buckley's. Following a philosophy of "do what your momma says and you will get better," Buckley's has experienced new popularity and a positive increase in market share, based solely on its negative advertising style.

FACTUAL APPEALS

In this appeal technique, the promise and benefits are presented in a straightforward, no-nonsense manner. The benefits are stated in a factual way, and any visuals that are employed usually state the obvious. Products that appeal to the rational buying motives

© Carolyn Jenkins/Alamy Stock Photo

FIGURE 5.16

A positive appeal technique has been effective for Subway.

of consumers tend to employ a direct, here's-what-the-product-does approach. Such products include proprietary medicines—cough and cold remedies, nasal sprays, and liniments (which relieve the tension of aching muscles). In the pain relief market, Tylenol says, "Doctors recommend Tylenol more than all other brands combined to reduce fever and temporarily relieve minor aches and pains." The third-party endorsement by doctors has a definite impact, and its use aptly depicts the intent of factual appeals.

COMPARATIVE APPEALS

When comparative appeals are used, the benefits of the advertised product are presented through comparison of those attributes that the product shares with competitive brands—attributes that are important to the target market and are usually the primary reason why consumers buy the product. Comparative appeals can be indirect, in the form of a comparison with other unidentified leading brands, or direct, mentioning the other brand by name.

In recent years, comparative appeals have been common in the competitive telecommunications industry. Rogers, Bell, and TELUS all make claims that they are better than their competitors. Bell claims it is the "largest, fastest, and most reliable" network in Canada. Rogers claims that it is Canada's "most reliable" wireless network. Advertising claims can get messy, and they can also confuse consumers, negating any potential benefit of such claims.

Comparative campaigns are often undertaken by a "challenger" brand, a brand that ranks behind the leader in terms of market share. Showing comparisons where the challenger performs better than the market leader is a convincing presentation. It will make consumers think more about the brand they currently use. However, any claims a challenger brand makes must not mislead the public. If they do, the brand leader could instigate legal action, forcing the offending brand to offer proof of its claims.

HUMOROUS APPEALS

When an advertiser uses humorous appeals, the promise and benefits of the product are presented in a light-hearted manner. Humour is important in the age of social media: "Humour in advertising has always offered an incentive—a bit of pleasure in exchange for the audience's precious time . . . with social media, it provides an additional payoff." That payoff is the opportunity to be "funny by association": When someone passes along a humorous video to family and friends, he or she can also be seen as funny. As well, humour in social media enables an advertiser to break through the clutter.[11]

Volkswagen uses a "dry" style of humour in many of its television commercials. One recent commercial showed a young man behind the wheel of a parked Volkswagen in a parking garage. He glances to his right and spots a beautiful young woman in a short skirt carting a few grocery bags. Eager to see her legs as she passes by, he fiddles to turn on the backup camera. By the time he turns it on the woman has passed and a hairylegged male is in plain view. The driver's facial expression is priceless.

Advertisers must be aware of certain risks associated with humorous creative. Many campaigns suffer from premature wear-out after a few exposures. When the humour is familiar, it is no longer funny. Also, the use of humour allows for a great deal of creative latitude, and some advertisers argue that the humour gets more attention than the product. If brand name recall is low after research testing, the problem is often attributed to the excess use of humour in advertising.

EMOTIONAL APPEALS

Advertisers who use emotional appeals successfully do so by arousing the feelings of the audience or by showing the psychological satisfaction that can be gained by using the product. Tim Hortons effectively uses emotional appeals to demonstrate how its outlets and coffee are part of the Canadian experience.

For example, consider "Welcome to Canada," a now-famous commercial that initially aired during the Vancouver Winter Olympics: "An apparent African immigrant waits in anticipation at an airport, sporting bags of new winter coats. From the baggage area emerge his wife and two children. After an emotional reunion, he hands his wife a cup of fresh Tim Hortons coffee. 'Welcome to Canada,' he comments before gallantly escorting his family into what is presumably their first snowstorm."[12] The commercial brought a tear to the eye of a good many viewers. This emotional style of advertising has created a tight bond between Tim Hortons and Canadian consumers.

Campaigns that promote awareness of social causes also use emotional appeals. To illustrate, consider some of the images in television commercials for campaigns that discourage drinking and driving or encourage people to stop smoking. Recent research reveals that emotional advertising works. One British study showed that emotional ties to a brand have a higher long-term impact on profitability than rational messages do. According to the study, as time passed there was a higher correlation to profitability between emotional campaigns compared with rational campaigns.[13]

SEXUAL APPEALS

The use of sexual appeals is popular and appropriate in certain product categories. Categories such as cosmetics, colognes, perfumes, lingerie, and alcoholic beverages use sexual appeals as an effective motivator. Over the years, sexual appeals have played a large role in beer advertising. After all, sex is always on the mind of the 19- to 24-year-old males the beer brands are after, or so the marketers think.

Fashion brands such as Calvin Klein and Diesel use sexual imagery effectively to market jeans to 20-something males and females. Their ads typically show lots of

FIGURE 5.17

Sexual appeals are a popular means of attracting a younger target audience.

© Francis Dean/Dean Pictures/Newscom

skin and couples enjoying each other's company; the ads are provocative and tend to grab attention. You've heard the expression: Sex sells! Refer to Figure 5.17 for an illustration.

Advertising of this nature is risky, but it does reflect general trends in society. People are now more accustomed to seeing provocative imagery and language in television shows, movies, and music videos. These trends open up new doors for advertisers.

LIFESTYLE APPEALS

Advertisers who use lifestyle appeal techniques are attempting to associate their brand with the lifestyle (activities, interests, and opinions) of a certain target audience. The key to the success of this type of campaign is in the association. If an individual feels part of the lifestyle, then he or she is likely to view the product favourably. Lifestyle appeals are becoming increasingly popular owing to the greater availability of psychographic information on Canadian consumers.

Lifestyle appeals are common among automobile brands. In the sport utility segment, the need to experience adventure, for example, is effectively portrayed by placing a consumer and vehicle in an exciting situation. In the luxury segment, the need to experience recognition and status is portrayed by showing a young business executive behind the wheel of a luxury automobile. Images like these speak louder than words. Refer to the illustration in Figure 5.18.

Lifestyle advertising is problematic because little attempt is made to differentiate one brand from another. Usually, the advertisements focus on the lifestyles of the target market instead of the product benefits. Therefore, if such a technique is overused in a product category, a brand can expect to benefit only marginally from its use.

Once an advertising agency has its big idea in the bank, it has an array of appeal techniques to choose from when planning a campaign. In highly competitive markets, it is often the quality of advertising that separates success from failure. For more insight into how creative strategies are developed, read the Advertising in Action vignette **The Real Mr. Clean.**

porsche.ca

Rules the bends.

There are no rules that say a lighter chassis can't be more rigid and more nimble in the corners. No rules that say you can't improve fuel efficiency while still increasing horsepower. And no rules that say a balanced, performance-driven, mid-engine sports car can't still be within reach. The new Cayman turns a corner, without changing direction. Porsche. There is no substitute.

The new Cayman.

From $59,900.*

*Price is for a base model only and excludes upgrade options, freight, air tax, licence, fuel fill charge, insurance, PDI, PPSA, administration fees and other applicable fees and taxes which are all extra. Suggested retail price of model with options shown $64,555. Dealer may sell for less. See your local dealer for details.

FIGURE 5.18

Lifestyle appeal techniques will attract a segment of the population seeking a thrill in their ride.

ADVERTISING IN ACTION

The Real Mr. Clean

I'm certain everyone has heard of Mr. Clean, a tried-and-true cleaning product good for almost any job around the house. However, the brand had fallen on hard times—annual sales volume was down by 5 percent in a market where many other popular brands compete for consumers' attention. The problem the agency faced was clear: How to rekindle interest in an aging brand?

Presto! Insight from the brand's Facebook page revealed that consumers talked about Mr. Clean as a real guy—there was some kind of relationship there! The page adopted his voice and quickly grew to 500 000 fans, the highest ranking of all Procter & Gamble brands on Facebook. Social media started showcasing the man behind the myth to deepen women's connection through real-time, reactive content. It was Mr. Clean that responded on Facebook or Twitter.

With such an emotional attachment to the character, how could it work in traditional media communications? The agency's (Leo Burnett) creative recommendation was to make the character himself the star of the advertisements—he would be the "icon of clean," dedicated to helping people clean faster and easier. Suddenly, he is like a real guy!

Mr. Clean was relaunched by telling a story about how he came to be the king of clean. There were 60-second commercials running on television and in theatres. Outdoor, print, and online media were also incorporated into the media plan. Results were impressive. Nine months into the plan, sales volume had increased by 6 percent and there were 6.5 million views on YouTube—quite a reversal of fortune. With no change in media spending from the previous year it was clear the new creative strategy had impact!

Courtesy of the Procter & Gamble Company

Source: "Putting the Mr. Back in Mr. Clean," *Strategy*, February/March, 2015, p. 39.

Creative Execution

The **creative execution** stage of the creative development process is concerned with two main areas: tactical considerations regarding how to present the message (and generate impact on the audience) and production considerations regarding the media to be used.

TACTICAL CONSIDERATIONS

At this stage, the agency's creative team evaluates specific ideas on presenting the client's product or service. These ideas, often referred to as "tactics," are simply more precisely defined strategies. Tactics undertake to answer questions such as the following:

- What is the best or most convincing way to present a product so that the consumer will be motivated to take the desired action of purchasing the product?
- Does the advertisement use a demonstration, a product (brand) comparison, a testimonial, or a celebrity spokesperson?

PRODUCTION CONSIDERATIONS

As indicated earlier, the media budget has probably already restricted the use of certain media. Budget considerations may also affect the production of advertising messages. Considering the media to be used, the client must communicate to the agency any production restrictions. For example, if television is being used, what is the desired commercial length (15 seconds, 30 seconds, or longer)? How many commercials will be needed (one commercial, or a pool of commercials on the same theme)? Can the same message be used online and in the broadcast media, or are unique online ads necessary? If print is being used, what are the size specifications (one page or less)? Are there any restrictions on the use of colour (black and white, spot colour, or four-colour process)?

The creative team must decide how to best present the product so that the message will have maximum impact on the target market. Following are some of the more commonly used presentation tactics.

TESTIMONIALS In a **testimonial** ad, a typical real-world user of the product presents the message. Since real people are used, as opposed to professional models or celebrities, the message is usually perceived as believable even though the presenter works from a carefully prepared script. Walmart, for example, has developed a series of ads using people of various ethnic backgrounds to make the point that Walmart offers the value their respective families are looking for. Such a tactic broadens the reach of Walmart in cosmopolitan markets.

ENDORSEMENTS Essentially, there are two types of **endorsements**: those given by associations or other organizations, and those given by celebrities. Brands like Crest and Colgate have, for years, used the endorsement of the Canadian Dental Association in their advertising. Phrases such as "recommended by dental professionals" are common in these ads.

When a celebrity is used, the advertiser attempts to capitalize on the popularity of the star. Stars from television, movies, music, and sports form the nucleus of celebrity endorsers. For example, Calvin Klein employs Canadian superstar Justin Bieber. According to the company, his global recognition, expressed affinity for the brand, and powerful persona bring a compelling energy to the jeans and underwear brand.[14] Both Gatorade and Reebok employ Sidney Crosby to endorse their products. CCM, a division of Reebok, employs star goaltender Carey Price to endorse its goalie equipment. Having Canada's Olympic gold medal–winning goalie (2014 Olympics) as your primary spokesperson is a huge benefit to the brand.

Sport Chek recently launched a new campaign called "All sweat is equal." Developed by agency Sid Lee, the campaign features an ensemble cast of professional and amateur athletes, including NBA star Kyle Lowry (Toronto Raptors), NHL star Steven Stamkos (Tampa Bay Lightening), Christine Sinclair (Team Canada soccer star), and Rosie MacLennan (Olympic trampoline gold medalist). The athletes are shown in intense training sessions, building up to a sweat-covered conclusion that shows each panting in a resting stance. The intent is to show the grunt work involved in being successful, not the glory moments used by other brands in commercials.[15] Refer to the image in Figure 5.19.

A potential danger of celebrity endorsements is overexposure if the celebrity is associated with too many brands. How many brands a celebrity can endorse before any one brand gets lost in the mix is often debated. As well, if the image of the endorser takes a turn for the worse, any brand associated with the celebrity could incur negative publicity and potential damage to its reputation. Brands such as Nike and EA Sports, for example, quickly dropped Ray Rice (a star NFL running back) once his domestic abuse issues became public. Rice was seen on video punching his then-fiancée in an Atlantic City casino.

FIGURE 5.19

Advertisers benefit from an endorsement relationship with celebrities from the sports and entertainment world.

© Graham Hughes/The Canadian Press

PRODUCT DEMONSTRATION The use of a **product demonstration** is quite common in advertising focused on product performance. Several execution options are available to the advertiser. For example, a before-and-after scenario is a common strategy for diet-related products where the message implies usage by the presenter. Such a technique is suitable for both print and television media, although with television the technique is much more effective.

A second strategy is to simply show the product at work—a technique commonly used for advertising household products such as oven cleaners, tub and tile cleaners, and floor wax. Typically, such advertisements show how easy the product is to use or how well it works. In some advertisements the demonstration is exaggerated to dramatize the benefit the product offers. Pickup trucks like the Ford F-150 or the Dodge Ram are often shown performing stunts that no normal driver would undertake—but the ad drives home the toughness and dependability benefits of the vehicle.

PRODUCT-AS-HERO If the **product-as-hero** technique is employed, the advertiser presents a problem situation (e.g., using negative appeal strategy) that is quickly resolved when the product comes to the rescue. The advertisers of Glad garbage bags have used this technique effectively for many years. In many commercials, other garbage bags are shown ripping open, leaving a mess. The obvious message is that the use of Glad bags prevents such situations. In this example, the execution effectively dramatizes the durability of the Glad product.

PRODUCT COMPARISONS For product comparisons to be used successfully, the attribute singled out for comparison must be of value or highly interesting to the target market. So as not to mislead the consumer in the message, the competitor must be identified fairly and properly, and the advertiser must be able to substantiate its claims with independent, objective research. For example, which battery lasts longer? Is it Duracell, or is it Energizer? Each brand claims it lasts longer than the other. This can cause confusion in the customer's mind and can lead to lawsuits among marketing organizations. As cited in the creative strategy section, sometimes a brand will make a subtle comparison by simply mentioning "another leading brand" in the ad. This is a softer approach, but it does not have the same impact as mentioning the other brand directly.

PREPRODUCTION CREATIVE EXECUTION

With creative strategy and tactical details confirmed, attention shifts to the production requirements of the campaign. Production requirements are often determined by media usage. For example, storyboards must be prepared for television and online video ads, scripts for both radio and television, and layouts and designs for print advertisements.

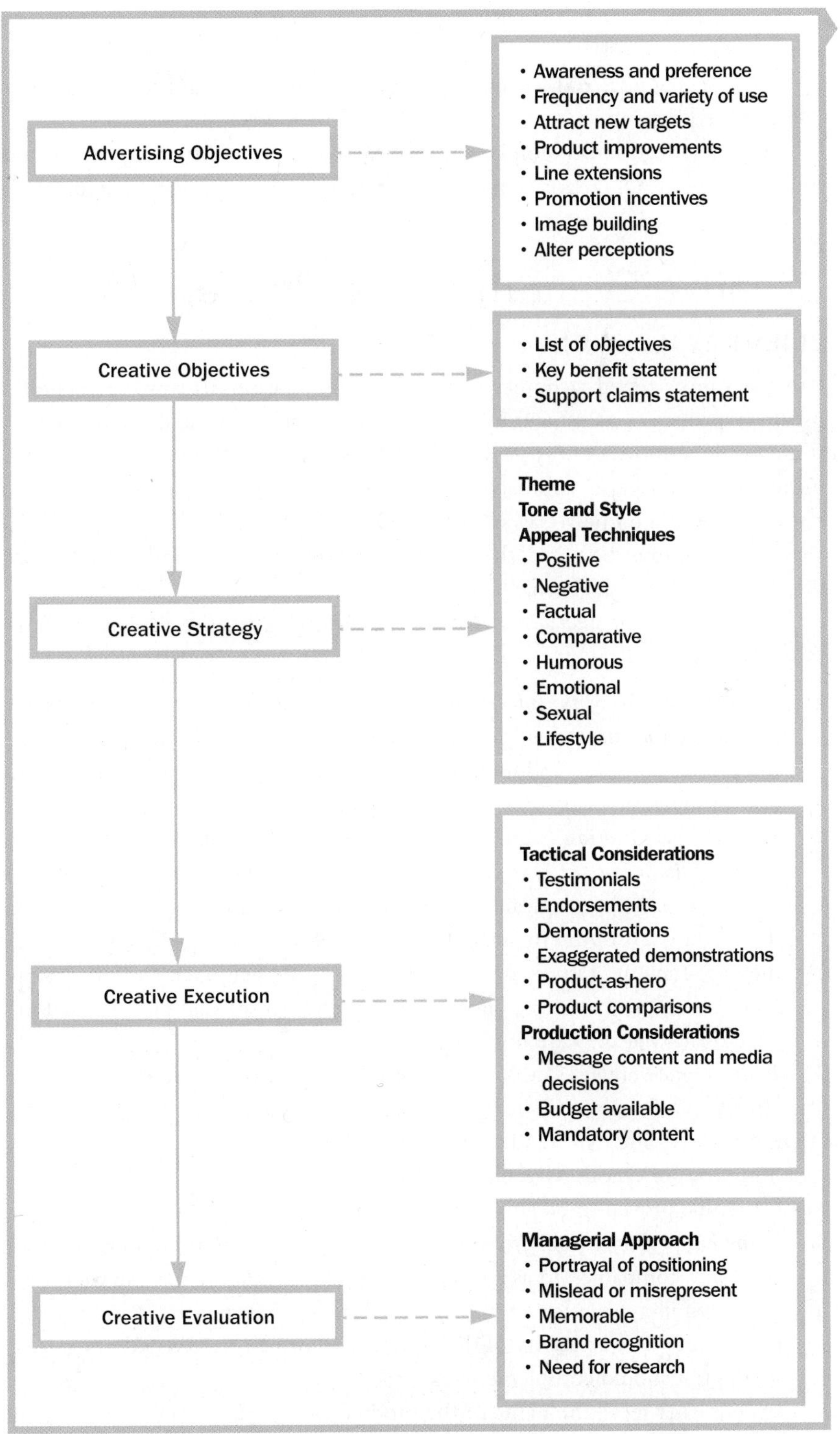

FIGURE 5.20

PLANNING MODEL EXHIBIT

A summary of the key elements and considerations of creative planning

Very often the content of the ad, if not the budget, restricts or makes necessary the use of certain media. For example, demonstrations are effective on television or online, while factual details are best left to magazines and newspapers. If sales promotion activity is to be part of the creative execution, a media mix may be required, with broadcast media used to build awareness and print media used to communicate details. Consideration must also be given to how effectively the message can be delivered in all media under consideration. A consistent look and theme should be common to all forms of media. Specific details about design, layout, and production are presented in Chapter 6.

Refer to Figure 5.20 for a summary of the key elements and considerations for effective creative planning.

For an applied illustration of advertising objectives, creative objectives, and creative strategies, refer to the marketing communications plan that is included in Appendix I.

Creative Evaluation and Research

CLIENT EVALUATION

Creative can be tested at numerous stages of the development process. The first step is usually a qualitative assessment by the client to determine if the message conforms to the strategic direction that was provided to the agency. This evaluation is conducted by means of a "managerial approach." In this evaluation, a client must resist the impulse to assess the creative on personal, subjective bases. However, if a "to proceed or not to proceed" decision must be made, the client reserves the right to conduct consumer research prior to making the decision.

Clients using the *managerial approach* for evaluating creative may apply some or all of the following criteria:

1. ***Does the content of the advertisement communicate the creative objectives and reflect the positioning strategy of the brand (company)?*** The client reviews the creative for the primary message and support claims outlined in the creative brief. If the ad is not on strategy, it won't be approved.
2. ***Does the presentation (strategy and execution) of the ad mislead or misrepresent the intent of the message? Is it presented in good taste?*** The client must be concerned about the actual message and any implied message, since the client is responsible for the truthfulness of the message. Legal counsel often has the final say regarding message content. Taste is always in the eyes of the beholder, and often consumers complain if an ad is too offensive. Sex and nudity, for example, are used in advertising, but they are hot buttons.
3. ***Is the ad memorable?*** Breaking through the clutter of competitive advertising is always a challenge, and a lot of advertising that is approved doesn't quite cut it. Is there something that stands out in the ad that customers will remember, say, a humorous or emotional scenario? The dishevelled-looking trivago guy mentioned earlier has proven to be a memorable character.
4. ***Is the brand recognition effective?*** There must be sufficient brand registration in the ad. Some companies go as far as to stipulate how many times the package should be shown in a television commercial or how many times the brand name should be mentioned. The creativity of the commercial or print ad should not outweigh the product; it should complement the product. For example, people often recall funny ads but can't recall the name of the product in the ad. So much for the laughs!

5. ***Should the advertisement be researched?*** When it comes to assessing the impact and effectiveness of the advertisement, subjective judgments by the client have the disadvantage of not being quantifiable. Prior to spending money on production or air time, the client may decide to conduct consumer research to seek quantifiable data that will help in the decision-making process. It is better to be safe than sorry.

The evaluation process can occur at virtually any stage of the creative execution process. A television commercial, for example, could be evaluated by consumers at the storyboard, rough-cut, or finished commercial stage. If the quality or effectiveness of the commercial is ever in question, the client should conduct research to avoid costly and embarrassing errors in judgment.

RESEARCH TECHNIQUES

Creative evaluation involves a variety of research techniques. The objective of most **creative research** is to measure the impact of a message on a target audience. Creative research is conducted based on the stage of creative development; it is either a pre-test or a post-test situation. **Pre-testing** is the process by which an advertisement, commercial, or campaign is evaluated before final production or media placement so that the strengths and weaknesses of a strategy and execution can be determined. **Post-testing** is the process of evaluating and measuring the effectiveness of an advertisement, commercial, or campaign during or after its placement. Post-testing provides information that can be used in future advertising planning.

Among the more common techniques used to measure the effectiveness of creative are recognition and recall testing, opinion-measure testing, and physiological response testing. Post-testing uses procedures such as inquiry tests and controlled experiments.

RECOGNITION AND RECALL TESTING In **recognition tests**, respondents are tested for *awareness*. They are asked if they can recall an advertisement for a specific brand. For example, consumers who have read a publication in which an ad has appeared are asked if they remember the ad and any of its content. Are they aware of the brand name that was advertised?

In **recall testing**, respondents are tested for *comprehension*, a measure of the impact of advertising. The test can be an **aided recall** situation (some information is provided to the respondent to stimulate his or her thinking) or an **unaided recall** situation (no information is provided). In either situation, respondents are asked to recall specific elements of an advertisement or commercial, such as its primary selling points, the characters used in it as presenters, or its slogan. Test scores are usually higher for tests where some aid is provided.

Two of the more common methods for collecting recognition and recall information are Starch readership tests and day-after recall tests. A **Starch readership test** is a post-test recognition procedure applied to both newspaper and magazine advertisements. The test measures how many readers saw the ad and what percentage of those who saw it actually read it. A consumer is shown a magazine, and once he or she has read it, an interviewer goes through the magazine ad by ad with the respondent. Each ad in the magazine is tested, and results are divided into three categories:

- ***Noted*** The percentage of readers who remember seeing the ad in this issue
- ***Associated*** The percentage of readers who saw any part of the ad that clearly indicated the brand or advertiser
- ***Read Most*** The percentage of readers who read half or more of the written material

The Starch readership test offers several benefits: The extent to which an ad is seen and read can be measured; by reviewing the results of other ads that were tested, the extent of clutter breakthrough can be determined; and by reviewing scores obtained by other products in previous tests, various layout and design options can be evaluated for effectiveness.

In the broadcast media, particularly television, the use of **day-after recall (DAR) testing** is common. As the name implies, research is conducted the day after an audience has been exposed to a commercial message for the first time. By means of a telephone survey technique, a sampling of the client's target market is recruited and asked a series of questions so that exposure to and recall of particular commercials can be determined. Specific information is sought about the primary selling message: likes and dislikes about the ad, areas of disbelief or confusion, and purchase motivation.

OPINION-MEASURE TESTING **Opinion-measure testing** exposes an audience to test commercial messages in the context of special television programs. A group of people are seated around television monitors, or they view commercials in a theatre environment, and respond to a series of questions. The test commercial is usually presented twice during the program in cluster situations, in which several ads are presented one after the other. In each cluster the test commercial is in a different position. Three key attributes are measured: the audience's awareness of the commercial based on brand name recall, the extent to which the main idea of the ad is communicated, and the effect the commercial could have on purchase motivation (i.e., the likelihood of the respondent buying the brand). This final measure is based on a comparison of pre-exposure brand purchase information and post-exposure brand preference data.

PHYSIOLOGICAL TESTING Advertisers also have access to a variety of physiological testing methods that measure involuntary responses to a specific element of an advertisement. In an **eye-movement camera test**, consumers read an advertisement while a hidden camera tracks their eye movements. Such a test gauges the point of immediate contact, the way a reader scans the various components of an ad, and the amount of time spent reading it. The **pupillometer test** measures a person's pupil dilation to determine the level of interest in the ad.

Testing procedures and the need for them are controversial issues in the industry, particularly among advertising agencies whose work is being tested. Many creative directors argue that too much testing defeats the creative process (it stifles creativity) and that what people say in research and do in the real world can be completely different. Nevertheless, clients like to know how customers will react to their messages, preferably before they spend money on them.

INQUIRY TESTS (SPLIT-RUN TESTS) Perhaps the most meaningful tests are those that measure an ad's actual influence on a target audience: Did the target actually purchase the product or take advantage of a special offer because of the ad? In an **inquiry test**, or **split-run test**, an advertiser can measure the effectiveness of two or more advertisements at once. For example, an advertiser can run two different ads with the same coupon offer (the coupon being precoded differently for each of the two ads). The number of coupons redeemed for each ad may be indicative of the relative strength of the overall ad. Small-scale tests of this nature are excellent for determining which advertisement should be more widely distributed.

CONTROLLED EXPERIMENTS To measure the potential impact of advertising activity on sales, an advertiser could set up a **controlled experiment** situation in which the advertising activity used in a test market differs from that used in a control market. To conduct this type of test, the advertiser selects two markets that are closely matched in demographics, shopping habits, and media consumption habits. In the control market, a given set of planned marketing activities are implemented. In the test market, the advertising variable is altered: Different media might be used, or the expenditure level or weight of advertising might vary. Sales are monitored closely in both markets so that test results are obtained and conclusions about advertising effectiveness reached.

SUMMARY

The creative development process begins with a creative brief, which is a discussion document prepared by the client. The brief includes the appropriate background information that creative personnel require prior to undertaking a new creative challenge. The content of a creative brief includes market background information, product information, competitor product and advertising information, a target market profile, a budget, a clear identification of the problem that advertising will resolve, advertising objectives, a positioning strategy statement, and a list of creative objectives.

Creative objectives are statements that clearly indicate the information to be communicated to a target audience. They include a key benefit statement and a support claims statement. The key benefit statement identifies the primary benefit and makes a promise to consumers about what the product will do. The support claims statement provides details that substantiate the promise made. The client is usually responsible for developing the creative objectives.

Creative strategy is the responsibility of the agency and is concerned with theme, tone, style, and appeal techniques. Some common appeal techniques include positive and negative approaches; the use of factual information; making comparisons with competitor products; and humorous, emotional, sexual, and lifestyle appeals.

At the creative execution stage, the primary concern is to make an impact on the target market. Considerations in this area include the use of testimonials, endorsements, demonstrations, and product-as-hero tactics. The final stage, creative evaluation, occurs when the client appraises and indicates approval (or disapproval) of the agency's creative recommendations. It may also involve conducting consumer research to evaluate the potential impact the advertisement or campaign will have on the target market.

Should research be necessary, a variety of pre-test and post-test techniques are available. If recognition and recall of the message are of concern, a Starch readership test, a day-after recall test, or an opinion-measure test can be implemented. These tests generate data regarding brand identification and message comprehension. In post-test situations, inquiry (split-run) tests and controlled experiments are undertaken.

KEY TERMS

REVIEW QUESTIONS

1. Briefly describe the key responsibilities of clients and agencies in the creative development process.
2. What is a creative brief, and how is it used by an advertising agency?
3. What are the stages in the creative development process? Briefly describe each stage.
4. In the context of creative development, what is the role of the positioning strategy statement?
5. What is the fundamental difference between advertising objectives and creative objectives?
6. What is the difference between creative strategy and creative execution?
7. Briefly describe the various appeal techniques commonly used in advertising.
8. Explain the differences between the following types of creative execution: demonstration, testimonial, and product-as-hero. Provide a new example of each.
9. What is meant by the "managerial approach" to evaluating creative output? Briefly describe the criteria that make up such an evaluation.
10. What is the difference between pre-testing and post-testing of creative?
11. What is the difference between recognition testing and recall testing?
12. What does a Starch readership test measure?

DISCUSSION QUESTIONS

1. "Humorous advertising campaigns are effective in the short term, but do little to achieve long-term objectives for a product or service." Agree or disagree with this statement, citing some specific examples to substantiate your position.
2. "Comparative advertising: Is it wise to acknowledge a competitor while you pay for the ad?" What is your opinion on this style of advertising?
3. Conduct some secondary research (online or otherwise) to compare and contrast the creative strategies being used by the following brands. Are the strategies similar or different?
   a) Coca-Cola and Pepsi-Cola
   b) GUESS jeans and Levi's jeans
   c) Home Hardware and The Home Depot
4. The "managerial approach" for evaluating creative was discussed in this chapter. Do you think this activity by the client impedes the creative process in the advertising agency? Discuss.

NOTES

1. Laura Pratt, "Cultivating Creativity," *Marketing*, November 28, 2005.
2. "Sponsored Supplement: Canada's Leading Creative Agencies: BBDO Seeks 'Creative Leverage'" Strategy, June 9, 1998.
3. Megan Haynes, "Welcome to Reebok's Freak Show," *Marketing*, January 28, 2015, **www.marketingmag.ca**.
4. Emily Brison York, "McDonald's Still 'Lovin it,'" *Marketing*, April 23, 2010, **www.marketingmag.ca**.
5. Carly Lewis, "Corona Targets Adventurous Millennials in New Campaign," *Marketing*, March 20, 2013, **www.marketingmag.ca**.
6. Dennis Schaal, "Trivago's Ad Pitch: Creepy, Handsome, or Just Effective?" *Skift*, August 11, 2014, **www.skift.com**.
7. Susan Krashinsky, "A Made-Up Word with a Serious Purpose," *Globe and Mail*, May 10, 2013, B4.
8. Matthew Chung, "Jaguar Ups Engagement with Interactive Ad," *Media in Canada*, February 9, 2015, **www.mediaincanada.com**.
9. Jennifer Hom, "Connie Morrison Breaks Bread with Skeptics," *Strategy*, December 17, 2014, **www.strategyonline.ca**.
10. "2015 Cassies Awards: Molson Canadian Beer Fridge," *Globe and Mail*, April 16, 2015, C1.
11. James Cowan, "Viral Ads that Smell as Good as this Guy," *Canadian Business*, April 7, 2011, **http://www.canadianbusiness.com/business-strategy/viral-ads-that-smell-as-good-as-this-guy/**.
12. Matthew McLearn, "Brands We Trust: On a First Name Basis," *Canadian Business*, May 10, 2010, p. 31.
13. Susan Krashinsky, "Getting Emotional," *Globe and Mail*, May 23, 2014, B7.
14. Leanne Delap, "Calvin Klein Keeps It Brief, Adds the Biebs to Its Ad Campaign," *Toronto Star*, January 7, 2015, E1, E3.
15. Russ Martin, "All Sweat Is Equal in Sport Chek's New Brand Campaign," *Marketing*, February 13, 2015, **www.marketingmag.ca**.

CHAPTER 6

Design, Layout, and Production

© Kzenon/Shutterstock

Learning Objectives

After studying this chapter, you will be able to

1. Explain the roles and functions of copywriters and art directors
2. Identify the design principles and creative considerations for developing print, broadcast, and interactive advertising
3. Explain the various types of print layout options
4. Explain the production stages of television and radio commercials

This chapter examines in greater detail the design, layout, and production considerations associated with the execution stage of the creative development process. Focusing on how the various media differ from each other, it examines the copywriting and art direction functions in more detail by presenting the techniques that are used to develop ads for the various media.

A significant portion of a client's advertising budget can be tied up in production expenses. In fact, the average cost of producing a 30-second TV commercial by an advertising agency for a national brand is in the range of $300 000–$320 000.[1] The combination of production expenses and the high cost of media time and space puts pressure on the agency to produce creative that sells the client's product or service effectively. The various elements of an advertisement or commercial must work together seamlessly to present a convincing message. In essence, the message must create a favourable impression in the mind of a consumer as quickly as possible. Further, in the context of integrated marketing communications, the message delivered should be the same in each medium—one sight, one sound, one sell!

The challenge for those who make their living developing advertising messages is to stop readers at a certain page, keep viewers in the room and mentally alert during commercial breaks, attract attention to a banner ad so that visitors click on it to obtain more information, or entertain people with a digital video posted on YouTube. To achieve this requires inspired copywriting and art direction and a desire to experiment with new approaches and techniques.

Some distinguished and successful advertising executives from the past have summarized the challenges faced by copywriters and art directors when it comes to developing good advertising—advertising that sells the product! Here's a few of their thoughts:[2]

> *"Make it simple. Make it memorable. Make it inviting to look at. Make it fun to read." (Leo Burnett)*
>
> *"The more informative your advertising, the more persuasive it will be." (David Ogilvy)*
>
> *"If it doesn't sell, it isn't creative." (David Ogilvy)*

When producing a print advertisement or broadcast commercial, the product must remain the focal point. Simply saying good things about a product in a persuasive manner will get the job done. Good creative is all about the art of persuasion.

Magazine and Newspaper Advertising

In print advertising, the central idea is conveyed primarily through the headline and visual illustration. The elements work together to produce a single message. As a unit, the headline and illustration must attract attention and create sufficient interest so that the reader moves on to the body copy that, in turn, must sufficiently expand on the promise made in the headline or illustration.

THE COPYWRITING FUNCTION

The major areas of concern for the copywriter are the headline and subheadlines, the body copy, and the signature elements of an advertisement. Each element will be discussed in the context of the influence it is intended to have on the reader.

HEADLINES The primary purpose of the **headline** is to command the reader's attention. According to legendary ad man David Ogilvy (co-founder of Ogilvy & Mather), "On the average, five times as many people read the headlines as read the body copy. It follows that, unless your headline sells your product, you have wasted 90 percent of your money."[3] There is no magic formula for distinguishing a good headline from a bad headline, but some research indicates that short headlines are more effective than long ones.

The *promise-of-benefit headline* makes an immediate promise to the reader. The promise is substantiated by body copy and illustrations. For example, a headline for CIL Golfgreen lawn fertilizer reads "Instant greenification." The illustration and supporting body copy reinforce the primary benefit. The tagline acts as a summary. Refer to the advertisement in Figure 6.1. Note that the headline meets the "sell" criteria described above by David Ogilvy.

A *curiosity headline* makes the reader inquisitive enough to seek more information (to look for an explanation). When Budweiser offered game-synced red lights to hockey

Courtesy of Premier Tech Home & Garden Inc.

FIGURE 6.1

An ad with a promise-of-benefit headline

fans, the headline of a magazine ad was "Hockey will never be the same." Why, you might ask? The advertisement created general awareness, but the reader had to visit a website to obtain more details about how to obtain the light. Refer to the illustration in Figure 6.2.

A *news headline* expresses a sense of urgency or announces something new to the reader. Words commonly used in news headlines are "new" or "introducing" or "finally." New technology, for example, is always news, as is a new automobile or a new beverage. When Canada Dry introduced a new lemon-lime flavour of club soda, it capitalized on its "club" name in a "finally it's here" type of headline. The combination of headline, visual illustration (of the product), and colour scheme work effectively to present a refreshing message.

A *command headline* politely requests the reader to do something. Most people know what Viagra is: a little blue pill that helps correct erectile dysfunction. Over the years Viagra has received lots of advertising support, so most men are well versed in the product's benefits. Some print ads say absolutely nothing about the product; they simply show a picture of a large blue pill with the headline "Talk to your doctor"—a great example of a command-style headline. See Figure 6.3.

SUBHEADLINES A **subheadline (subhead)** is a smaller headline that clarifies the main point of a headline, making it possible to keep the headline short; it also acts as a breaker between the headline and the body copy. Subheadlines are an optional component of a print ad. Many ads run without one. If there is to be a transition, it is from the headline to the body copy.

Courtesy of Labatt Breweries of Canada

FIGURE 6.2

A curiosity headline encourages the reader to take action to obtain more details.

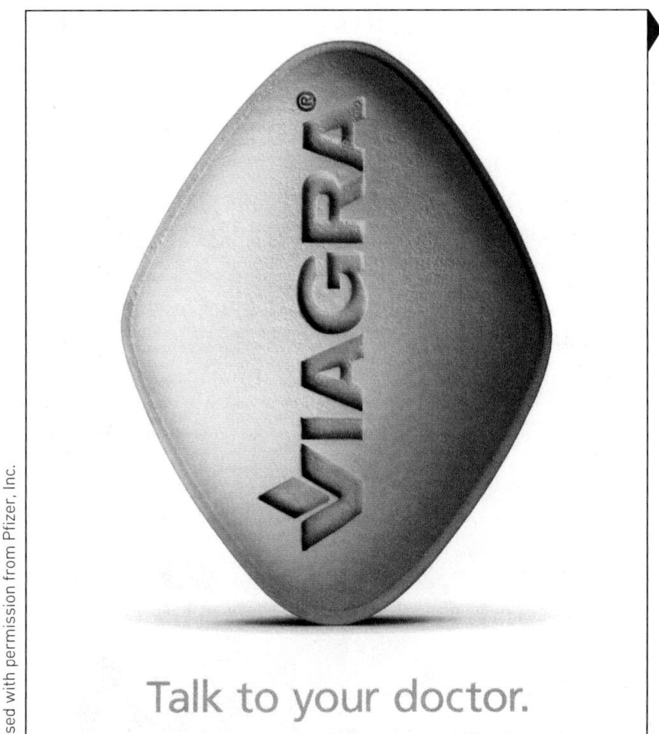

FIGURE 6.3

An example of an ad using a command-style headline. It also illustrates the one-line style of body copy

BODY COPY The **body copy** is the informative or persuasive prose that elaborates on the central theme of the advertisement. The body copy helps create preference by providing information the consumer needs to make a purchase decision. Body copy is the substantiation—the proof of promise or product claims. It is a device that integrates the headline with the illustration. The headline announces something new and the body copy and visual of the product provide proof. Body copy plays a key role in differentiating one brand from another and offers a means of presenting the multiple features and benefits of a product.

One of the key issues in print advertising is the length of the body copy. Should it be short or long? If an ad does have lots of body copy, there must be a compelling reason to read it. In the age of the multitasking consumer, time is a precious commodity; thus, a rule of thumb might be to include only body copy that is absolutely essential. If longer explanations are needed, it is better to refer the reader to a website.

There are several types of body copy commonly used in print advertising:

- ***Story*** A story approach involves a beginning, middle, and end. Within the framework of the ad, the body copy tells a story. The beginning helps establish the theme (the big idea for the ad), the middle gives readers a reason to buy the product, and the end offers a call to action. The story should flow smoothly from beginning to end.
- ***Bullet Point*** A bullet approach offers a means of highlighting key benefits quickly. Presenting key benefits in a list where the benefits are prioritized saves the reader time. The key is to keep the list as short as possible to avoid any confusion.
- ***One Line*** Many ads include only a headline and a visual illustration—message delivered. If an explanation isn't needed, why include body copy? Refer to the image in Figure 6.3. Again, the ad can direct readers to a website for more information.

Some creative experts believe the complete message should be communicated in the headline and visual. Their point is simple: The first thing people avoid is the body copy—they don't have enough time to read it. The illustrations in Figure 6.3 demonstrate this principle. Short copy is most appropriate for image advertising—a situation where a strong visual image and relatively few words communicate the message. In such a situation lengthy copy would detract from the image.

Other experts believe longer copy is necessary to fully explain key benefits—more like the story approach mentioned above. For instance, if the cost of a product or service is deemed expensive, consumers will seek information prior to making a buying decision. In this situation advertising is a source of information. Therefore, longer copy is necessary to explain things. Refer to Figure 6.4. This advertisement combines a softly worded command headline with long body copy to communicate the need for a business organization to offer benefit packages to its employees.

SIGNATURE The final copy element in a print advertisement is the **signature**. Often referred to as a **tagline** (or slogan), the signature can include a company or product logo

FIGURE 6.4

An illustration of an ad where the body copy fully explains the headline and why the reader should respond

Reckitt Benckiser (Canada) Inc.

FIGURE 6.5

Air Wick®'s brand logo and slogan aptly summarize the brand's positioning strategy.

and a brand or company slogan. A **logo** refers to the distinctive copy style that identifies the company or product. The purpose of the signature is to achieve the following:

1. ***To summarize the concept or central theme of the advertisement*** For example, the logo and slogan can reinforce a key benefit or reinforce a company or brand position. Essentially, the tagline should capture the essence of the brand's positioning strategy.
2. ***To position the product in the customer's mind*** For example, the logo and tagline will provide continuity for a campaign and may be the common component in a multimedia effort. The signature must leave a positive impression with the consumer. When you mention a brand name and someone else quotes the tagline, you know you have an effective signature.

Air Wick® is a brand leader in the household fragrance market. New scents are always being added to its product line to freshen peoples' homes. Air Wick® launched a range of fragrances called "Life Scents®." One of the fragrances, "Mom's Baking," comprises scents of vanilla, pie crust, and baked pear. With reference to Figure 6.5, the brand logo and tagline for Air Wick® appear as the signoff at the bottom of the ad. The tagline "Home is in the air™," reinforces the brand positioning strategy.

There is no magic formula for writing a good tagline, but a few basic guidelines offer some perspective. A good tagline should be short and simple—no more than six words, and three words are even better. A good tagline should also differentiate the brand from competitors. Visa uses the tagline "More people go with Visa" to imply that it is the card most used by consumers.[4]

Here are a few other good examples of brand signatures:

- "Have a break. Have a Kit Kat." (Kit Kat)
- "Just do it." (Nike)
- "Impossible is nothing." (Adidas)
- "Save money. Live better." (Walmart)

THE ART DIRECTION FUNCTION

The primary responsibility of the art director is to design the layout of the advertisement. **Layout** refers to the design and orderly formation of the various elements of an advertisement within specified dimensions (size specifications). The layout combines the illustration with the copy and offers an overall impression of what the final advertisement will look like.

Advancing technology has changed the nature of layout and design procedures as well as the way ads are prepared. A copywriter's words are now instantly transferred to an art director's layout. The art director chooses a font from a library of typefaces, sets it in position, imports images and logos from a library of images, and commissions artwork as needed. The art director can play with all of the parts until satisfied with a design, and then produce a colour printout for client approval. Computer-aided design allows art directors to quickly examine "what if" experiments with raw ideas. For the client, the technological changes mean shorter production times, lower costs, and more involvement in creative—the chance to see a more precise version of the final advertisement at an earlier stage.

Despite the technology, good art directors often revert to pencil and paper to get the creative juices flowing. Creating an ad involves ideas, and ideas are in people's heads, not on a computer. Good ideas are often jotted down on a napkin or the back of a file folder—who knows when creativity will strike! Art directors experiment with thumbnails until they strike the right design. **Thumbnail sketches** are small, experimental drawings of various ideas and design concepts. Their purpose is to identify a few options that can be used as a basis for more extensive design development. Once the right thumbnail has been devised, the art director may choose to draw the ad to actual size with all elements of the ad in place. Such an ad is referred to as **rough art**. Refer to the illustrations in Figure 6.6.

Once the big idea is fine tuned, a computer can be employed to advance the design concept to its final stage. Art directors must be familiar with software such as Adobe InDesign, Illustrator, and Photoshop, and online tools such as Flash and iMovie, among many other alternatives.

DESIGN PRINCIPLES AFFECTING LAYOUTS

The client and agency strive for distinctiveness in their ads to break through the clutter of competition. To achieve that distinctiveness, the art director considers factors such as balance, flow, unity, the use of colour, size alternatives, bleed pages, the use of artwork and photography, and the use of white space.

BALANCE **Balance** refers to the relationship between the left side and the right side of an advertising layout. *Formal* balance occurs when both sides are equal in weight. If different weights are assigned to the various elements of an ad, there is *informal* balance.

FIGURE 6.6

Thumbnail sketches are often the starting point for developing the layout of an ad. Rough art gives the client an impression of what the finished ad will look like.

FLOW **Flow** refers to the movement of the reader's eye—from left to right and top to bottom—when he or she is exposed to a print advertisement. When some people scan an advertisement, their eyes move diagonally, from upper left to lower right. Others follow a "Z" pattern, with eyes moving left to right across the top, then diagonally from upper right to lower left, and then across the lower portion of the page to the right corner. See Figure 6.7 for an illustration of these eye-movement patterns.

Such reading patterns suggest the ideal locations for various elements of a print ad. For example, headlines often appear at the top to attract attention and state the key point of the ad. The illustration is used as background to the entire page, or part of the page (say, in the middle) with body copy. The signature (brand logo and tagline) usually appear at the bottom of the page along with any purchase incentives to encourage action. Signatures are strategically located to make an impression on those who skip the body copy.

UNITY **Unity** refers to the blending of all elements of an ad to create a complete impression. The headline, visual, and body copy must work together to create an impression.

COLOUR, CONTRAST, AND WHITE SPACE Colour, or contrast in colour and style, can be an effective attention grabber. In a black-and-white medium, reverse printing (white letters on a black background) or spot colour may attract more attention. In a colour medium that uses photography, an ad can stand out by its use of black-and-white photos, line drawings, or spot colour.

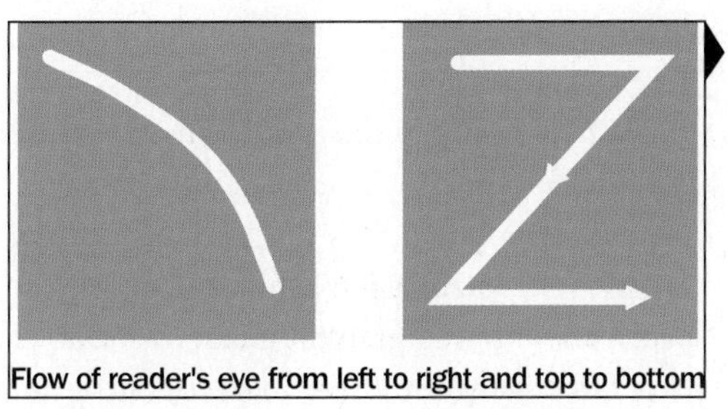

FIGURE 6.7

Reader's eye movement

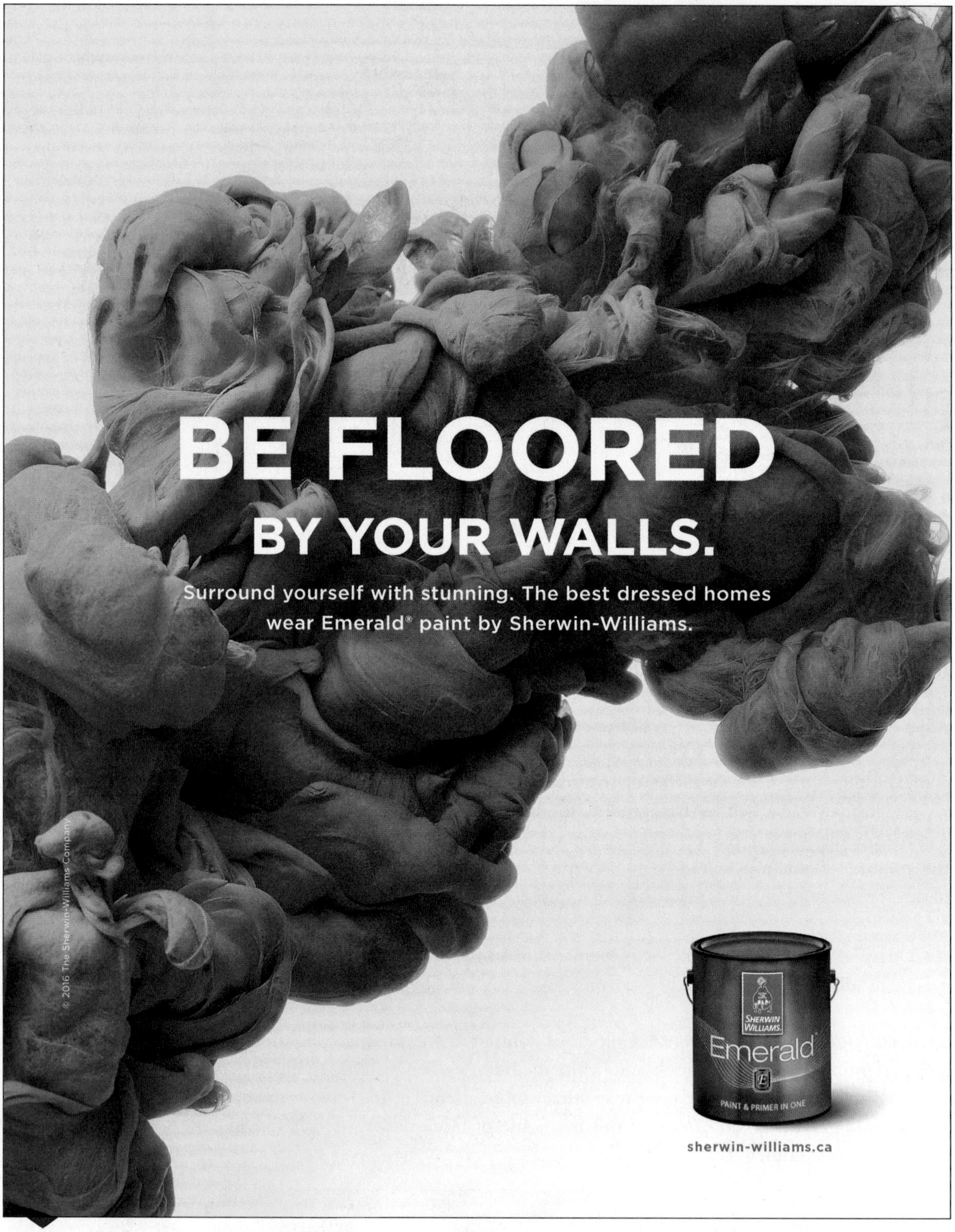

Courtesy of the Sherwin-Williams Company

FIGURE 6.8

An ad that effectively uses the principles of informal balance, unity, flow, and white space to deliver a complete message

White space is the part of an advertisement that is not occupied by other elements. The careful use of white space can provide effective contrast and focus attention on an isolated element, such as a beauty shot of the product.

Most magazines publish in full colour, so effective use of colour, contrast, and white space is essential to grab the reader's attention. A print ad for Sherwin-Williams Emerald paint effectively combines many design principles discussed thus far. The ad that appears in Figure 6.8 exemplifies good balance among the various elements of the ad: The design encourages eye movement from the top left to lower right corner, and there is good contrast between the vivid purple paint image and the lighter background colour.

SIZE The decision to use a full page, a double-page spread, or a fractional page (a half-page or a quarter-page) has an impact on how effectively an advertisement draws readers. Sometimes small ads can achieve the same result as larger ones (which is a boon to the client paying the bill). But, generally speaking, a double-page spread gets more readership than a full-page, and a full-page ad gets higher readership than a smaller ad.

BLEED PAGES In the case of a magazine, a **bleed page** is an advertisement in which the dark or coloured background extends to the edge of the page (often explained as an arrangement in which the colour appears to run off the page). The ads appearing in Figures 6.5 and 6.9 demonstrate bleed pages. A bleed page garners higher readership (15 percent more) than a non-bleed ad.[5] Typically, a majority of ads in magazines are bleeds, but some advertisers distinguish their ads by including framed borders or by surrounding the visual with white space.

PHOTOGRAPHY VERSUS ARTWORK The two basic illustrating devices are photography and drawn illustrations. Logic suggests that colour photography be used in magazines, but if it is the end product will, of course, be similar to numerous other ads in the same publication. An artist's drawing—something as simple as a black-and-white drawing—can command a higher level of attention through contrast. Research by the magazine industry shows that photographs garner higher attention scores (18 percent more) than drawings.[6]

However, there are benefits to using drawings. Drawings allow artists to create the desired impression in their own style. The final image can exaggerate or accentuate in ways a photograph often cannot match. A computer-generated character was created for Koodo from an original drawing or artist's vision. The character, named El Tabador, plays a role in all media advertising for Koodo. Refer to the advertisement in Figure 6.9.

CLARITY AND SIMPLICITY Any element that does not serve a specific function should be eliminated. Too much variety in type style, too many reverses or illustrations, and any unnecessary copy should be cut. To achieve the desired impact, the ad should be pleasant to the eye and easy to read.

All of the above factors are considered in the design of an ad, but there is no magic formula for success. The effect of advertising is in the eye of the beholder. Adhering to certain rules of design can negatively affect creativity. The objective is to be noticed and remembered—and that may mean breaking a few rules. The challenge for copywriters and art directors is to get the client to buy into such a philosophy.

TYPES OF LAYOUTS

The creative team considers the factors discussed in the preceding section when positioning the various elements in an ad. The creative team must develop a layout that blends all components together (headline, visual illustration, body copy, and signature) to create an overall look for an advertisement. Here are some common types of layouts.

POSTER The **poster** layout relies almost entirely on visual impression. The advertisement is picture dominant, with a minimum of copy. Refer to Figure 6.8 for an illustration.

FIGURE 6.9

A computer-generated character (El Tabador) plays a key role in Koodo advertising.

VERTICAL SPLIT In a **vertical split** layout, the copy dominates one side of the ad and the picture dominates the other side (left side versus right side). In a single-page ad, an imaginary line down the middle can divide the page.

HORIZONTAL SPLIT A **horizontal split** divides the page across the middle. A common format sees the copy on one half of the ad and the visual illustration on the other half. Refer to Figure 6.4 for an illustration.

MULTIPLE ILLUSTRATIONS In the **multiple illustration** layout, a series of illustrations is presented, either in sequence or showing a variety of related features and benefits. In Figure 6.10, Scion combines two illustrative components. Here, a poster layout is the primary image. Multiple illustrations are included to drive home the seasonal message in the headline.

Courtesy of Toyota Canada

FIGURE 6.10

An advertisement that combines a poster layout with a multiple illustration layout

LONG COPY The **long copy advertisement** is copy dominated, with limited or no use of illustrations. The body copy plays a key role in explaining the product's benefits.

INSERT LAYOUT In the **insert layout**, a smaller, secondary visual illustration appears as an "insert" on the page. Inserts are commonly used to emphasize the product, package, or special features.

For more insight into copy and design elements that produce better advertising, see the Advertising in Action vignette **Where Copy Meets Art.**

ADVERTISING IN ACTION

Where Copy Meets Art

Research reveals that the average ad has less than half a second to grab your attention. Having very little time to work with, the creative team must ensure that the relationship between copy and illustration is readily apparent.

A good ad has to effectively position the brand and what it stands for in the minds of consumers. Many experts believe that positioning is a word-oriented craft. Other experts believe that words are just words and that you need a good image to bring a brand's position to life. In her book *Visual Hammer*, Laura Ries reveals how words and images must work together to get the job done. She explains it as a nail (word) and hammer (image). She sees an abundance of slogans as the best way to grab the public's attention and secure a spot in their minds, but it's the visual image in an ad that makes an emotional connection with people.

Budweiser beer offers a good example of the nail and hammer concept. The nail is the authenticity expressed in the brand's "King of beers" slogan. The visual hammer is a team of Clydesdale horses pulling an old-fashioned beer wagon. More recently, the hammer is the images that portray an emotional relationship between a puppy, a horse, and their owner. That relationship has a big impact on people who view Budweiser commercials.

Award-winning Canadian creative director Brian Harrod had similar thoughts about the importance of visual images. He was a firm believer in strategic clarity, and to prove his point he frequently led his creative pitches with outdoor advertising (even if the client didn't want outdoor advertising). Harrod's explanation of clarity was about having the brand's "organizing idea" nailed down. What he said about the product, and how he said it, embraced a few good words and a resounding image to dramatize things. One of Harrod's most famous ads was an outdoor board for Milk-Bone dog biscuits. The organizing idea was canine oral care. The ad simply showed a Milk-Bone biscuit in the shape of a toothbrush. The message was delivered in seconds.

Adapted from Peter Nowlan, "Simple. Powerful. Outdoor," *Strategy*, October 2012, p. 48; and Harvey Schacter, "Hammering Home the Visual Image," *The Globe and Mail*, September 12, 2012, p. B19.

The greatest idea in the world will lose all its power when supported by uninspired writing and art direction. Consequently, copywriters and art directors like to present risky concepts to clients, believing that such messages stand out, make more noise, and are effective. Conservative-minded clients see things differently, and as a result there can be conflict between the two parties. Since good advertising resides in the eyes of the beholder, here are some final tips for budding copywriters and art directors to ponder when preparing print ads:[7]

- ***Focus on the most critical benefit*** When readers leaf through a publication, they don't spend much time on each page, so the ad needs to show the number-one benefit "prominently and persuasively."
- ***Offer visual magnetism*** An ad should be constructed so that a single component dominates the area—a picture, a headline, or text. The more pertinent the picture, the more arresting the headline, the more informative the copy, the better the ad will be.
- ***Select the right target*** There should be something in the ad that the reader can readily relate to. The ad should say to the reader, "Hey, this is for you."
- ***Promise a reward*** Readers must be given a reason to continue reading, for if they do, they will learn something of value. A promise must be specific. The headline "Less maintenance cost" is not as effective as "Cut maintenance costs by 25 percent."
- ***Back up the promise*** A promise is believable only if hard evidence is provided (e.g., comparisons with the competition can be convincing, as are third-party testimonials).
- ***Talk person to person*** Copy is more convincing when it talks to the reader as an individual. The writing style should be simple: short words and sentences.

As an exercise, you might wish to analyze some of the ads in this chapter and evaluate them against the tips described in this list.

Out-of-Home Advertising

Print media other than newspapers and magazines possess their own characteristics and present problems and opportunities for the creative team to explore. Out-of-home advertising embraces advertising formats such as outdoor posters, transit ads, outdoor digital displays, and mural ads. These formats usually function as supplemental media and seem to work best when introducing new products, building awareness, or adding reach to a campaign.

OUTDOOR POSTERS

A research study conducted by Perception Research Services (in the United States) indicated that 75 percent of all individuals who see an outdoor board are likely to be drawn to the name of the product advertised, so bold identification of the name is important. In addition, factors such as size and the creative use of space—sometimes beyond the frame of the board—affect the attention-getting ability of the board.

Other design factors important for **outdoor advertising** include the simplicity of the design and the use of colour. Since outdoor advertising is often used as a complementary medium (i.e., in conjunction with a primary medium such as television or online), the outdoor message should include creative concepts from the other media.

Here are some other fundamental guidelines for outdoor layout and design:

- ***Use bold colours and high contrast*** The objective is to attract attention, and bold colours achieve that. Even white space draws attention as long as it surrounds bold colour.
- ***Be telegraphic*** Use no more than nine words (some experts say six words). The viewer has only a few seconds to digest the copy. Include only essential components (e.g., headline and visual illustration or visual illustration and tagline).

FIGURE 6.11

Large visual, short copy, and strong brand identification are important factors in getting attention for an outdoor poster.

© Pierre Roussel/Agence Quebec Presse/Newscom

- ***Think big*** The image and typeface must be big since the viewer could be 200 metres away.
- ***Keep it simple*** Stick to one basic idea, and do a good job with it.
- ***Use the product and package instead of words*** Often the brand sells itself. If you are selling a Big Mac, show the product and the golden arches and you have delivered the message.

If simplicity is a key to good advertising, then telegraphic simplicity is the key to good outdoor advertising. Consider that people may drive by a street poster at 60 kilometres per hour or rapidly walk by it, arms loaded with packages. There is not a lot of time for the ad to communicate. The ad that appears in Figure 6.11 follows the guidelines mentioned and effectively communicates the brand's primary benefit.

One of the main strengths of outdoor boards is that they invoke our respect for the monumental. It is a medium that can inspire awe, so copywriters and art directors should take advantage of it. If they are not clear on what to say (with words or visuals), they are likely wasting the client's money.

TRANSIT ADVERTISING

Because the transit rider is sometimes moving and sometimes standing still, certain design considerations are particularly relevant to both interior and exterior transit advertising. With interior transit advertising, the advertiser can use time to its advantage. The average commuting time in Canadian markets larger than 1 million people is 40 minutes for bus riders, 44 minutes for subway riders, and 52 minutes for those taking light rail—ample time for copy and illustrations to be observed and read.[8] Alternatively, short and quick messages tend to be read and reread by idle passengers.

Exterior transit advertising reaches pedestrians and travellers in other vehicles. Since displays travelling on buses are often viewed from an angle and a distance, bold type, punchy copy lines, and absolute simplicity are preferable. The impact of a powerful visual must be respected in exterior transit advertising. The illustration in Figure 6.12 demonstrates this principle.

© Norman Pogson/Alamy

FIGURE 6.12

A strong visual is important in exterior transit advertising.

POINT-OF-PURCHASE ADVERTISING

Point of purchase is another form of "reminder" advertising that uses the design concepts of another medium; it may be similar in appearance to ads designed for newspapers or magazines. **Point-of-purchase (POP) advertising** encourages impulse buying and influences last-minute choices between comparable brands. When it comes to retail display materials, which include posters, shelf-talkers (small posters at shelf locations), ad pads (tear-off coupons, contests, and cash rebate offers at shelf level), and floor ads, the design must provide what the point-of-purchase industry refers to as the four *I*'s: impact, identification, information, and imagery. See Figure 6.13.

Photo by Keith J. Tuckwell

FIGURE 6.13

An illustration of point-of-purchase advertising that applies the four *I*'s concept: impact, identification, information, and imagery

- ***Impact*** The display must generate immediate impact. It must say, "Here I am, buy me."
- ***Identification*** The brand or business name must be boldly displayed. Identification must link the message to the source.
- ***Information*** In a brief format (i.e., in the copy and the illustration), the display must provide the consumer with a reason to buy.
- ***Imagery*** The overall impression must be relevant to the customer. As in a print ad, the various elements of a display must blend together to make a complete message.

Direct Response Print Advertising

Direct refers to a marketing situation in which the advertiser communicates offers directly to customers—it's a one-on-one type of communication. Direct response communication is usually designed to fulfill specific objectives. The objective may be to solicit a direct order, generate a lead, drive customers to a retail outlet, or initiate a long-term relationship between the advertiser and customer (customer relationship management). With **direct response print**, the message is communicated through magazines, newspapers, or mail. A response opportunity is provided for the customer through a toll-free telephone number, reply card, or web address. Direct response advertising aims to solicit a call for action quickly, either in the form of a purchase or a request for more information.

If mail is the medium of choice, there are three key components that will determine the success or failure of the campaign: the list of names to be used (the effort is only as good as the list), the offer (what incentives will be included to encourage action), and the creative (finding the right way to tell the story to attract attention, stimulate desire, and get people to act—now!).

Since direct mail remains the most widely used form of direct response advertising, let's focus on some copy and design characteristics of this medium.

1. ***Get the reader's attention*** Since so many people discard direct mail without opening it, there has to be some relevant copy or design element that gets the mail opened. The envelope must function like a headline in a print ad. It should grab the reader's attention through bright colours, unusual envelopes, and interesting graphics.
2. ***Personalize the mailing*** Direct mail is a targeted medium that relies on database marketing for success. Lists of names that match a brand's target market profile can be rented from list brokers so that the message can be personalized. Personalizing each mailing is integral to the one-on-one sales situation referred to earlier.
3. ***Include a complete presentation*** Direct mail advertising functions as a complete sales message. The copy must grab attention, stimulate interest and desire, provide ample proof of the promise, handle objections, and close the sale. The offer must be compelling and presented in a manner that makes it absolutely irresistible.
4. ***Include multiple pieces in the mailing*** A typical direct mail piece includes several items (e.g., letter, pamphlet, involvement device, offer of a free gift to encourage immediate action). Direct advertisers believe that many items working together to communicate the same message are more effective than one element alone. And, of course, it should be easy for the recipient to respond. Order cards must be easy to read and fill out. A postage-paid envelope, toll-free number, and web address should be included.

Television Advertising

The nature and content of a television commercial are derived from the same base of information as print advertising, but there are obvious differences. Print advertising uses space, whereas television advertising uses time. Since the message is delivered within a limited period of time (15, 30, or 60 seconds), the creative team is concerned with the flow of the commercial from beginning to end. A television commercial is typically divided into three distinct sections: an opening, middle, and closing. The *opening* must grab the viewer's attention and introduce the key benefit before the audience "disappears" physically or mentally. The *middle* section elaborates on the key benefits (offers proof of the promise) and clearly identifies the brand. The *closing* section, which is often the final few seconds, usually focuses on the brand's signature—the brand and package identification along with the tagline. It may also suggest some form of action (e.g., "Visit your dealer for a test drive today").

Figure 6.14 demonstrates the concept of opening, middle, and closing. In this ad, an unattended dog in a house leaps off a table (a place he shouldn't be) when he hears his owners return. These scenes demonstrate that Pine-Sol cleans the dirt you see and the dirt you don't know about. Examine the script and pictures to capture the flow of the ad.

"DOG TIRED"

Video: Open on a shot of a dog lying on a kitchen table. Camera stays on dog, still just lying on table.

Super: Pine-Sol cleans the dirt you know about.

Video: The dog then hears his owner returning home and jumps off the kitchen table.

SFX: Car pulling in, keys opening door.

Video: The dog settles into his same comfortable position, except now under the kitchen table.

Super: And the dirt you don't.

Video: Cut to a mid-shot of Pine-Sol Original bottle.

Super: The thorough clean.

FIGURE 6.14

A television spot with a well-defined opening, middle, and closing

DESIGNING TELEVISION COMMERCIALS

In designing a television commercial, the creative team first develops the **central theme** and then creates a story around it. For example, Molson Canadian effectively uses its proud Canadian heritage to advantage in its television advertising. Over the years many of its commercials have featured panoramic Canadian scenery and people enjoying the great outdoors. A recent campaign used the tagline "Made from Canada," a definitive and proud statement about the brand. One commercial in the campaign stated "Canada has more square feet of awesome per person than any other nation."[9] Molson Canadian also has close ties to hockey—Canada's national pastime—and often builds campaigns around a hockey theme. A recent commercial featured a hockey rink built on the top of a downtown Toronto office tower where some lucky Canadians had an opportunity to play a recreational game. Refer to the image in Figure 6.15.

When developing the commercial, the creative team is also concerned with creating the sequence of events. To do so, the team prepares a script and storyboard. A **script** is usually a two-column document that outlines the video elements in one column and the audio components in the other column. A **storyboard** is a set of graphic renderings (an artist's rough version of a finished commercial) in a television-frame format, with appropriate copy, showing what the commercial will look like. Clients approve advertising campaigns on the basis of the script and storyboard, so the combination of the two items must plant a good visual impression in their minds. Once approved, the script and storyboard act as the guideline for producing the commercial.

CREATIVE CONSIDERATIONS FOR TELEVISION

The creative team must consider several factors when trying to design a television commercial that will stand out from the competition. Given the context in which commercials appear (six or more in a cluster during a station break), the need for a commercial to break through a viewer's perceptual barriers is paramount.

UNITY Unity refers to the visual and aural flow of a broadcast commercial from the customer's perspective. Viewers perceive the ad as a continuum of action focused on a

FIGURE 6.15

Molson Canadian employs a patriotic theme in its advertising.

central idea. The commercial, therefore, must flow logically: It presents the problem or situation, and then provides an explanation and solution. In the case of the Pine-Sol commercial shown in Figure 6.14, the message flows quickly, but it clearly communicates in a humorous way how well Pine-Sol cleans the dirt you see and the dirt you *don't* see.

INTEGRATION OF AUDIO, VIDEO, AND SPECIAL EFFECTS In a commercial, the voiceover and action should be focused squarely on the product; if a benefit is depicted, it should be emphasized appropriately. The product should be the main element of the commercial; the creative team will consider using sound effects and music, where appropriate, but in so doing the team must recognize that the purpose of audio is to enhance the product message, not to overwhelm it.

Music can play a special role by grabbing the viewer's attention. It is common for advertisers to secure rights to use hit songs where appropriate (to fit with the target) or develop original music that will help establish the mood for a commercial.

Special effects that are usually done in the editing stage can manipulate graphics on the screen in many different ways, such as fades, zooms, and rotations. Special effects should only be used to enhance the commercial message.

PACE Using the 15-, 30-, or 60-second commercial time limit as a guideline, the creative team must produce a message that will communicate itself at a suitable **pace**. In recent years the 15-second commercial has become popular with advertisers, since it saves money in media time. However, scaled-down versions of 30-second commercials do not have the same impact. In any commercial the first few seconds are critical—they must be visually interesting.

The product and the appeal technique may also influence the pace of a commercial. For instance, the Budweiser "Lost Puppy" commercial that was discussed in the previous chapter used an emotional appeal technique and 60 seconds of time (a slower pace) to develop the relationship between the master, the puppy, and the horse. That can't happen in 15 or 30 seconds. In contrast, a commercial for a soft drink like Mountain Dew aimed at a youthful target market may use fast-paced rock music and action sequences to create the appropriate image for the product. It can be accomplished in a shorter commercial.

LIVE ACTION OR ANIMATION **Live action** involves using real-life situations and real people in a commercial. The real people may be amateur or professional actors. **Animation** is a technique whereby hand-drawn cartoons or stylized figures generated by design software on a computer are given movement and visual dimension. The animated television commercial for Koodo uses this technique. The animated figure is identical to the image that appears in the print ad featured in Figure 6.9.

KEEPING IT SIMPLE Finally, the best approach is to stick with one idea in a commercial. Cramming in too many selling points or too many scenes can be annoying to the viewer. The creative team's responsibility is to effectively communicate the brand's primary selling point in a convincing manner so that the viewer takes the intended action. The product should be front and centre in the ad, and if people are involved they should be involved with the product. As advertising icon Leo Burnett once said, "We want consumers to say, 'That's one hell of a product' instead of 'That's one hell of an ad.'"

STYLES OF COMMERCIALS

TV commercials tend to fall into certain categories based on the manner in which they are executed. Once the strategy for a commercial has been finalized, the creative team determines the best method to execute it. What is the best way to dramatize the key benefit?

1. ***Demonstrations*** In a demonstration, the objective is simply to demonstrate how the product works. There are several options: showing actual usage (e.g., the paper towel cleans up the entire spill), a comparison with a competitor (e.g., a household cleaner that cleans better than other cleaners do), or a before-and-after scenario (e.g., a shirt with a messy spill on it is stain free when removed from the laundry).
2. ***Slice of Life*** This option usually shows people enjoying the product. For example, beer commercials often show 20-somethings enjoying themselves at the beach or the cottage while holding bottles of a particular brand. The product is associated with a lifestyle. Alternatively, a problem situation is presented and the commercial goes on to show how the problem is remedied.
3. ***Testimonials*** Often referred to as "talking heads," testimonials have proven to be a durable technique in convincing customers about the merits of a product. Testimonials may come from a variety of sources, such as animated characters (e.g., the Pillsbury Doughboy), the common man or woman (e.g., the charming and lovable manager who appears in all A&W commercials), or real people (actual users of a product do have influence).
4. ***Celebrity Endorsements*** An endorsement by a famous sports figure or entertainer can bring attention and instant credibility to a brand. The key is to ensure the celebrity is a good fit for the brand and the target market. For example, Sidney Crosby appears in commercials for Reebok hockey equipment and clothing, Sport Chek stores, and Gatorade sports drinks. Crosby is a good fit in all cases. Using Brad Pitt to endorse Chanel N°5 perfume (the first male to ever endorse a perfume) seems like a questionable fit.

The casting of characters to appear in a commercial is a big decision for creative planners. The characters have to suit the product and the situation, and they have to have an immediate impact on the audience. Perhaps you have noticed that a particular actor appears in a lot of different ads and wondered why. It is usually because that person shows up on time and can land a joke; they are comedians by trade. The Second City comedy troupe based in Toronto is a fertile breeding ground for commercial actors.

Some advertisers will occasionally use consumer-generated content. Typically, the quality of these commercials is of a lower standard, but that is perceived as a positive. YouTube viewers aren't looking for professional commercials—they simply want to be entertained. An annual Doritos contest invites consumers to develop a commercial that will be aired during breaks in the Super Bowl broadcast as well as on YouTube. This is an example of an effort that generates buzz in the traditional media.

For more insight into strategy and execution decisions made by a creative team when developing a television commercial for Canadian Tire, read the Advertising in Action vignette **It's Cold as Ice**.

TELEVISION PRODUCTION STAGES

Once the client has approved the storyboard and script, the commercial goes into production. The production process involves four separate stages: cost quotations, pre-production, production, and post-production.

ADVERTISING IN ACTION

It's Cold as Ice

Canadian Tire capitalized on Canada's cold winters in an award-winning ad for its MotoMaster Eliminator AGM car batteries. When you think about buying a car battery . . . well, you don't really think about it. It's one of those purchases you tend to put off until your battery dies. Canadian Tire set out to change that mind-set.

The objective of the commercial was to make a battery purchase a proactive experience and increase sales by 10 percent. Canadian Tire was using a "Tested for life in Canada" platform to advertise its automotive parts products. Products are tested in unexpected ways under extreme conditions to prove how reliable they are. For the MotoMaster Eliminator battery, the advertising agency recommended what some in the industry would call an exaggerated demonstration—it was an idea that would demonstrate that the battery could withstand the harshest conditions and start no matter how cold it is. That idea was the Ice Truck!

Canadians often use the phrase "cold as ice" to describe our winters. That insight was the impetus for the ice truck idea. The battery would be tested in a truck built out of ice—11 000 pounds of it! From a commercial production viewpoint it would be a complicated, time-consuming process. To verify the truck's authenticity, a behind-the-scenes documentary-style video was created and posted on YouTube. The footage was an integral part of the campaign. A 30-second television commercial was the cornerstone of the campaign, and in it the battery started with absolutely no problem—it received the "Tested for life in Canada" stamp of approval.

The campaign was judged an overwhelming success. Media buzz created 80 million public relations impressions. There were 3.5 million YouTube views, and news outlets such as CBC, CTV, CNN, Fox News, and the *New York Times* carried stories about the commercial. In terms of advertising effectiveness, brand name recall was 63 percent above industry norms and brand link (the ice truck being linked with Canadian Tire) was 36 percent above the norm.

More to the point, there was a dramatic increase in sales of the battery—a 70 percent year-over-year increase—well above the objective set by the company. Proof again that good advertising works!

Source: "Cassies Gold: Canadian Tire Breaks Records from a Cold Start," *Strategy*, February 19, 2015, www.strategyonline.com.

COST QUOTATIONS The task of producing the commercial is the responsibility of a production house (i.e., a specialist in commercial production). Evaluating production cost estimates from various production houses is a critical assignment, as the cost of producing a 30-second live action commercial—without celebrity talent—averages between \$100 000 and \$300 000. If celebrities and distant locations for shooting the commercial are included, the costs go higher. Smaller advertisers in local markets can produce commercials for much less by using the production services offered by local television stations.

PRE-PRODUCTION At this stage, a meeting is held with representatives of the production house, the agency (i.e., the creative team), and the client. The storyboard and script are reviewed, and final decisions and arrangements are made. Prominent areas of discussion are casting; the use of secondary suppliers (e.g., music specialists, editors, mixers); and finding appropriate props, costumes, and film locations. If an announcer is required, who should it be? Announcers in a commercial do not appear on screen, but are heard as a **voiceover** that communicates a key point. Who does the voiceover is a big decision since the voice becomes associated with a brand over time. Think of a Ram truck commercial with Sam Elliott's voice saying "Guts, Glory, Ram."

PRODUCTION The actual shooting (production) of the commercial can be very long and tedious, but—since time is money—every effort is made to complete the task as quickly as possible. However, quality is also paramount. Therefore, when scenes are shot it is common to try several takes to get them right. However, scenes do not have to be shot in sequence. For example, scenes without sound, which therefore do not require a full crew, can be done last.

POST-PRODUCTION The post-production stage involves putting the commercial together and requires the coordinated effort of the director, film editor, and sound mixer. The normal procedure is to assemble the visuals and the sound separately, without extra effects such as dissolves or titles. Modern software technology makes the post-production stage easier than it used to be, but it does require time, talent, and experience to do a good job. No matter how good the editing is, though, it can't save a weak concept. Once all effects have been added and the commercial edited, the final version is presented to the client for approval.

Direct Response Television Advertising

Direct response television (DRTV) advertising has two distinct formats: the 30-, 60-, and 120-second spot or the 30-minute infomercial. An **infomercial** presents in more detail the benefits of a product or service and encourages immediate action through the use of toll-free telephone numbers. Some of the more common infomercials are for kitchen gadgets, health-oriented products (e.g., exercise equipment), and financial planning products. The objective of a direct response commercial is to initiate immediate action by the customer—think of Vince and the Slap Chop.

Mainstream advertisers are recognizing the benefits of direct response advertising. Companies and brands including Ford, Procter & Gamble, Rogers, Bell, Apple, and RBC Financial have entered the direct response arena. These organizations recognize that a closer relationship develops when the company allows the consumer to interact with the brand through toll-free numbers and other means. The customer is one step closer to the purchase decision.

Successful direct response commercials incorporate a strong offer that gives the viewer a reason to call. Stressing a sense of urgency, offering a discount, or providing free information or a bonus incentive such as a gift are some techniques that help create action. The following are some proven creative techniques used in infomercials:[10]

- Always focus on the product. Extol it, praise it, and sell it.
- Include a strong offer—one that is clear, compelling, and simple. The stronger the offer, the greater the response will be.

- Clearly demonstrate the product in a convincing manner, and establish and maintain credibility through testimonials, research statistics, and judicious use of the brand name.
- Present a problem and solve it. Present a situation the viewer can identify with or an old way of doing things. Solve it with a simple and immediate demonstration. Show the before and after, show results, and show benefits. Dramatize everything.
- Use an appropriate tone and style to communicate the message. The infomercial must consider the brand's image. For example, the tone and style of a Ford F-150 infomercial will be very different from one for the Slap Chop.
- Remember that longer is better. Sixty-second spots outperform 30-second spots, which makes the former a better investment. The additional time allows for a more thorough sales presentation.
- Guarantee the offer and have an urgent call to action. A guarantee lowers the doubts in the consumer's mind (e.g., an unconditional money back offer). Stress urgency—strongly suggest that the viewer doesn't want to lose out on this opportunity. An additional offer or free incentive will help stimulate the desired action.

The now-famous Slap Chop and Graty commercial featuring Vince adheres to the principles mentioned above. Refer to the illustration in Figure 6.16.

Courtesy of Square One Entertainment

FIGURE 6.16

A strong presenter and a clear focus on the product are the keys to successful direct response commercials.

Radio Advertising

As in television execution, radio execution focuses on the effective use of time and on making the commercial flow from beginning to end. The creative team develops the concept or central theme in script form, which indicates the words to be spoken and provides direction regarding the use of sound effects and music.

CREATIVE CONSIDERATIONS FOR RADIO COMMERCIALS

Radio commercials must grab the listener's attention immediately and hold it until the end. This is a challenging task; listeners tend to tune out quickly if they are not interested. Radio is often listened to when a person is doing something else (e.g., reading, driving, sunbathing). To command attention, therefore, the ad must be catchy and memorable. The most critical decision for a radio commercial is casting the voiceover. The person doing the voiceover is the star who pulls everything together. Some voices are authoritative while others are warm and friendly. The voice must match the situation being presented.

Some proven techniques in the creation of radio advertising include the following:

1. Mention the advertiser's name often. Many practitioners suggest that the brand or company should be mentioned three times during a 30-second commercial.
2. Be conversational, but use short words and sentences. There shouldn't be too many words; otherwise, the announcer may seem rushed.
3. Centre the message on one significant idea. Variations of the key message should be made repeatedly.
4. Use sound effects to create a visual image. Radio advertising, to be effective, must activate listeners' imaginations.
5. Make the tone of the radio commercial positive, cheerful, and upbeat.

To demonstrate how sound effects can stimulate a listener's imagination, consider the award-winning campaign created by Bleublancrouge for Bell Media. The commercials were promoting new crime shows on Séries+. In each commercial the announcer becomes a victim of a crime. In a commercial called "Shovel," the listener hears the announcer being hit by a shovel. She coughs and gets hit again. The sound of dirt being shovelled is heard followed by a body being dumped and a motorcycle revving up and driving away. In another commercial called "Gun," there is a sound of a gunshot, the announcer choking, and then a second gun shot. A body bag is zipped up and shoved in a vehicle, which drives away. The entire series of commercials won the Gold Award at the 2014 Marketing Awards. The award judges felt the commercials took full advantage of the theatre of the mind—they were simple and cleverly crafted.[11]

TYPES OF RADIO COMMERCIALS

Generally, radio commercials can be divided into four categories: musical commercials, slice-of-life commercials, straight announcements, and personality announcements.

MUSICAL COMMERCIALS For commercials in which music plays a major role, there are several ways of "deploying" music: a commercial may be all music, as in the case of many soft drink ads; music jingles may be interspersed with spoken words; or orchestral arrangements can be used.

SLICE-OF-LIFE COMMERCIALS Much like a slice-of-life television commercial, this type of radio ad involves the presentation of a problem and then of product benefits that will resolve the problem. Effective use of listeners' imaginations enhances slice-of-life commercials.

STRAIGHT ANNOUNCEMENTS With these commercials, the message simply states the facts. The message is relatively easy to prepare and deliver. Music may be used in the background.

PERSONALITY ANNOUNCEMENTS This method differs from the first three alternatives in that the advertiser gives up the control of commercial delivery. In a **personality announcement**, the radio host presents the message using his or her radio personality style. The radio station is provided a **feature sheet** that outlines the key benefits and the product slogan. The host develops the specific wording for the message.

The Internet

Organizations now use their own website, third-party websites, and social media sites such as Facebook, Twitter, and Instagram to communicate with consumers. It is common for an organization to develop meaningful and visually attractive content on its own website. On third-party websites and social media a variety of advertising options are available, including banner ads that direct users to a website when clicked on and video ads that deliver a message in TV-style format.

The internet is a desirable medium for several reasons. It is always on, so it provides information and entertainment 24/7. It is a personal medium that allows advertisers to interact directly with prospective customers. It is a dynamic medium that combines audio and video content at high speed and provides that content to people wherever they are located—at home, in a car, or in a restaurant, for example. Finally, it is a medium to which virtually everyone has access from somewhere (home, school, or work), allowing advertising messages to be delivered at the most opportune times.

As indicated earlier, it is important for digital media creative planners to meet with traditional media creative planners to discover the "big idea" that can be used across all media. All creative planners must understand the basic difference between online communications and traditional media communications. Traditional media are static, while the internet is dynamic. Traditional media target an audience; on the internet, consumers target the content they are interested in, and in the process they are exposed to messages that should be of interest.

From a creative design perspective, the primary internet options are banner ads, rich media ads, and video advertising. Establishing an interactive website is another option, though that is beyond the scope of copywriters and art directors at an advertising agency.

BANNER ADS

The most common form of advertising on the internet is the banner ad. A **banner ad** stretches across the screen in a narrow band, or appears in another shape such as a rectangular box or column down the side of a page (this style is known as a *skyscraper*). The content of the ad is minimal. Its purpose is to stir interest so that the viewer clicks the ad for more information. Refer to the illustration in Figure 6.17. Once the ad is clicked, the viewer sees the ad in its entirety or accesses additional information from the advertiser's

Courtesy of Scotiabank. Image Maximilian Stock Ltd./Photolibrary/Getty Images

FIGURE 6.17

Banner ads must attract attention quickly to encourage the desired action of clicking on the ad. Scotiabank uses the same colour scheme for its ads in all media.

website. The design characteristics of the banner ad are critical since the goal is to encourage clicking. Clicking is the first step in the conversation between the consumer and the marketer.

Rich media are banner ads that include animation, sound, video, and interactivity. There are several inside-the-banner options: An *expandable banner* employs multiple panels that are launched when the banner is clicked on; a *video strip* shows a strip of video in the banner space, but when clicked on expands to reveal the video and audio in a full-sized panel. Outside-the-banner options include a *floating ad* that moves over the page and plays within a certain area of the page, and a *window ad* downloads itself immediately and plays instantly when a page is loading.

Including features such as animations in a banner ad draws additional attention. Internet users perceive the internet to be a different medium than traditional mass media. When online, people expect to be entertained, and they want to receive information quickly. These expectations suggest that advertising must also entertain. Some proven techniques for the creation of online banner ads that encourage clicking include the following:[12]

1. ***Keep it simple*** You only have a few seconds to make impact. Therefore, the concept for the ad and the wording must be clear and concise so the viewer understands the message quickly. Using simple copy and an uncluttered image work best to encourage a click.
2. ***Ask for action*** A call to action is never out of place. It should be presented in a bright or contrasting colour. Phrases like "Click here," "Try it now," and "Shop now" encourage action by the viewer.
3. ***Provide design unity*** The banner and the website the viewer is directed to should be visually similar to improve the experience. Colours associated with the brand's image are appropriate. Refer to the image in Figure 6.17 for an example.

4. ***Emphasize a key benefit*** Focus on one benefit, and state it effectively. An ad for a tax service company, for example, might say "pay less taxes"—a tangible benefit a person can profit from.
5. ***Size matters*** Research has proven that bigger is better. The bigger ads get more attention and a higher clickthrough. Therefore, the use of rectangles and skyscrapers is preferable, even though they may cost more.

VIDEO ADVERTISING

Advertisers perceive **video advertising** to be similar to television commercials, so they are becoming more popular with business organizations. Video advertising is presently the fastest growing format for online advertising. Watching videos on YouTube, third-party websites such as news or sports sites, and social media is a favourite pastime for many people. With video content comes video advertising. Here are some tips to consider for creating online video ads:[13]

1. ***Choose short over long*** The online environment moves quickly, and a reworked 30-second TV ad will not appeal to internet users. One study found that most viewers would prefer shorter video ads, and that more 15-second ads are viewed in full than are 30-second ads.
2. ***Be consistent*** An online video has a different formula for success than a TV commercial does. For a multimedia campaign to work, ads should differ from medium to medium, but the message must be consistent.
3. ***Don't worry about production quality*** The quality of production (degree of sophistication) needn't be an issue for the advertiser. Online viewers see through slick ads that are designed for television. Viewers are entertained more by consumer-generated content that is produced by amateurs.

Online video advertising offers an advertiser the emotional impact of television with the accountability and interactivity of the internet—incredibly valuable benefits for any brand or company.

WEBSITES

Advertising communications typically encourage people to visit an organization's website or visit a Facebook page or Twitter feed. The objective of the ad is to get people to a site where more detailed information can be communicated. Internet users visit a website for a reason—they are interested in the content. Therefore, an organization must not let the user down when they visit its website; the experience must be enjoyable!

A website gives the organization an opportunity to tell a story and show more images at a much lower cost than would be the case in other media. Websites play a role in building brand awareness and preference, and they provide an opportunity for a company or brand to engage with its target audience.

Consumers like to visit websites for information, and they do so frequently when collecting information about particular products they are interested in purchasing. In general, they want a website to be easy to navigate, offer an enjoyable experience, and provide meaningful information. Much research has been done on how people view and read webpages. Eye-tracking studies reveal that people sweep their eyes over the text, stopping briefly when something of interest catches their eye. The sweeping occurs in a pattern roughly shaped like an F, starting in the upper left corner. There is a tendency to take two sweeps across the page, and then swipe vertically down the left side of the page.[14]

This viewing behaviour has implications for web design and layout. Content must be presented in a manner that can be grasped quickly by the reader. Here are some tips to improve the design of a website:

1. ***Capitalize on the "F-Pattern" scanning principle*** Place your value proposition at the top of the page or have a clear menu at the top that will quickly get the reader to where they want to go.
2. ***Use an informal writing style*** The web is an informative and immediate medium, so users appreciate a lighter style of writing combined with an element of humour.
3. ***Have a consistent look*** A corporate identity is important. Therefore, keep a consistent look and feel throughout the site by using the logo, graphics, and colours of the company's corporate identity. For example, a viewer would expect to see red on the Coca-Cola website.
4. ***Limit the use of graphics*** People like to navigate a site quickly. Too many full-page graphics take time to download and slow the navigation process considerably. Eye-tracking studies show large, crisp images work best.
5. ***Avoid scrolling*** Try to keep text in a visible window so readers don't have to scroll down. People spend 80 percent of their time looking at information above the fold (the part of the page that is visible when they land on the site). Important information should be above the fold.
6. ***Make graphics clear*** Don't use small fonts in graphics. Viewers may be visually impaired, so descriptions should always be available for graphics. A site should be tested with different fonts and font sizes.
7. ***Call out important words*** Use boldface or colour to highlight important words while still making the page easy to read.
8. ***Convert paragraphs to bullet points*** If you are communicating numerous key features and benefits, it is easier to read a list of points rather than a paragraph. Points should be listed from the most important to least important.

Web design is a combination of design features and emotional experiences. Good content clearly presented is the most important factor that leads to repeat visits. Remember, the web is a fluid medium; pages must be updated often to reflect the current situation. Burger King Canada recently redesigned its website to make it more engaging for visitors. The primary focus of the new design is on hunger-induced visuals of the products, special offers, and new features, such as an interactive menu and nutritional calculator. According to Burger King, the goal of the new design was to effectively combine the visuals with functionality, which would lead to better brand engagement.[15] Refer to the image in Figure 6.18.

VIRAL MARKETING

Any discussion of interactive creative brings up the subject of viral marketing. Let's clarify exactly what this type of marketing involves. **Viral marketing** encourages the receiver of a message to pass it along to others to generate additional exposure. It is nice when the receiver does this, but it cannot be planned. Who knows when a creative concept is going to suddenly become popular (a fad, if you will) and receive millions of views? The consumer alone determines whether this will happen. You can't ask an advertising agency to create a viral campaign.

Posting video content on YouTube or an advertisement on Facebook in the hopes of it being shared can lead to disappointment. If viewing and sharing does occur, and in big numbers, the advertiser will certainly benefit. It can result in unsolicited testimonials via

Courtesy of Burger King Canada

FIGURE 6.18

The visual presentation of the product is a key element of Burger King's new website design.

consumer-generated content. As discussed earlier in the textbook, word of mouth remains a very effective form of advertising.

Going viral does happen. A classic example involves Kmart in the United States. A campaign promoting a product delivery program appealed to the pre-teen humour in all of us. The campaign included a "Ship my pants" video that informed shoppers that out-of-stock store items would be shipped directly to them for free. In the video one shopper proclaims, "I shipped my pants." Another says, "I shipped my bed." Vulgar to some but funny to many, the video garnered 20 million YouTube views and one share for every nine views—proof that humour never goes out of style.[16]

More specific information on the strategic implications of interactive media and internet advertising is presented in Chapter 12.

SUMMARY

Numerous tools are used to penetrate customers' perceptual barriers. For example, the copywriter is responsible for the headline, body copy, and signature, and the art director is responsible for the illustration; the two join forces to create a complete message—an impression on the customer. In print advertising, the impression is affected by variables such as balance, flow, unity, use of colour and size, white space, clarity and simplicity, and use of artwork or photography in illustrations. Art directors also consider layout alternatives for delivering the message. Among the layouts commonly used are the poster, vertical split, horizontal split, multiple illustration, long copy, and insert layout.

Other print media have unique creative considerations. Out-of-home messages (outdoor posters, transit ads, and point-of-purchase ads) must be simple in design and use bold colours. In these media, strong visual imagery works to the advertiser's advantage. Point-of-purchase advertising must be brief, but also convincing enough to promote impulse purchasing. Transit ads have a more captive audience (often idle) and, therefore, their messages can be more detailed. In the case of direct response advertising, the advertiser must grab customers' attention quickly and use specific techniques that will hold their interest and encourage them to take the desired action.

The key considerations for television are the flow and pace of the commercial. Variables such as the integration of audio and video and the use of music and special effects are also significant in that they, too, have an impact on the viewer. Effective commercials keep things simple so as to not confuse the audience about what the key selling point is. Television commercials tend to use demonstrations, slice-of-life scenarios, testimonials, and celebrity endorsements to grab viewers' attention. In commercial production there are four stages: cost quotations, pre-production, production, and post-production.

Radio commercials are also concerned with flow. Effective commercials tend to be positive and upbeat in tone, conversational in nature, and focused on one central idea. Radio ads that involve the listener's imagination have proven to be successful. The production process is similar to that of television.

Online advertising presents unique challenges for copywriters and art directors. The most common forms of online advertising are banner ads, rich media ads, and video ads. If banner ads are employed they must be clear and concise and include a call to action. Rich media ads must be engaging and interactive and tell a story. Video ads appear much like television ads, but the rule of thumb online is to keep them short—15 seconds or less. Websites must be concise, have a consistent look, limit the necessity for scrolling, and include fonts of an appropriate size for good readability.

KEY TERMS

animation 171
balance 158
banner ad 177
bleed (bleed page or bleed ad) 161
body copy 155
central theme 170
direct response print 168
direct response television (DRTV) 174
feature sheet 177
flow 159
headline 153
horizontal split 162
infomercial 174
insert layout 163
layout 158
live action 171
logo 157
long copy advertisement 163
multiple illustration 162
outdoor advertising 165
pace 171
personality announcement 177
point-of-purchase (POP) advertising 167
poster 161
rich media 178
rough art 158
script 170
signature 156
storyboard 170
subheadline (subhead) 154

REVIEW QUESTIONS

1. Identify the basic elements of a typical print advertisement, and describe the primary purpose of each.
2. Briefly describe the various types of headlines.
3. What is the basic purpose of the signature in an advertisement?
4. Briefly describe the various types of body copy commonly used in print ads.
5. What is the basic difference between a thumbnail sketch and rough art?
6. Distinguish between the following:
   a) Balance versus flow versus unity (print advertising)
   b) Vertical split versus horizontal split (print advertising)
   c) Poster versus long copy (print advertising)
   d) Unity versus pace (television advertising)
   e) Live action versus animation (television advertising)
7. What are the design characteristics of an effective outdoor ad?
8. What are the four *I*'s of point-of-purchase advertising? Briefly explain each one.
9. In direct mail advertising, what copy and design characteristics are critical to success?
10. What are the various sections of a television commercial? Explain the role of each section.
11. Briefly describe the nature of a television script and storyboard.
12. Briefly describe the various styles of television commercials.
13. Identify and briefly explain each stage in the television production process.
14. Identify and briefly explain some of the proven techniques for producing effective infomercials.
15. What are the different types of radio advertising?
16. Identify and briefly explain any two copy and design elements for creating better banner ads and better video ads.

DISCUSSION QUESTIONS

1. Scan a magazine of your choosing, and select an ad you think is effective and one that is ineffective. Evaluate the impact of each ad based on some of the layout and design principles discussed in this chapter.
2. "Tell more, sell more." Discuss this statement in the context of print advertising (or web-based advertising).
3. What is your opinion of consumer-generated video content? Does this practice help or harm a brand? Conduct some secondary research on this activity, and present an opinion on it.
4. Visit a website of your choice. Analyze the site based on the design elements for websites included in this chapter.

NOTES

1. Estimate based on 2011 information, Steve McClellan, "Costs for TV Spots Rocket 7%," *Media Daily News*, January 29, 2013, **http://mediapost.com/publications/article/192213/costs-of-tv-spots-rocket**
2. "31 Creative Advertising Quotes," ThirtyOneCreative.com, **www.thirtyonecreative.com/blog31/31-creative-advertising-quotes**
3. David Ogilvy, *Ogilvy on Advertising* (Toronto: Wiley & Sons Ltd., 1983), p. 139.
4. Tom Alstiel and Jean Grow, *Advertising Strategy* (Thousand Oaks: Sage Publications Inc., 2006), 293.
5. "Magazine Essentials: Making the Most of Magazine Ads," *Magazines Canada*, 2012, 6.
6. Ibid., 66.
7. Alan Sneath, "If You Owned the Firm, Would You Run the Ad?" *Financial Post*, June 1, 2004, FP4.
8. "National Household Survey: GTA Commuting Times Are the Nation's Longest," *Toronto Star*, June 26, 2013, **www.thestar.com**
9. Courtesy of Molson Coors Canada

10. Based on Dean Rieck, "How to Write a Direct Response TV Commercial That Sells," *Pro Copy Tips*, December 9, 2009, **www.procopytips.com/wriote-tv-commercial**; and Ian French, "Trick of the Trade," *Marketing*, August 20, 2001, 18.
11. "The 2014 Marketing Awards," *Marketing*, special publication, 2014, 58.
12. Based on Emilie Futterman, "How to Design Banner Ads that People Actually Want to Click," *The Next Web*, January 7, 2014, **http://thenextweb.com/dd/2014/01/07/design-banner-ads-people-actually-want-to-click; and "Design Tips," AdDesigner.com, www.addesigner.com/tips.shtml**
13. "99 Designs," 99designs.ca, **http://99designs.com/designer-blog/2013/10/14/14-design-tips-for-more-clickable-banner-ads**
14. "How People Read on the Web," **http:/nichcy.org/dissemination/tools/tools/webwriting/reading**
15. Rebecca Harris, "Burger King Gets a Digital Revamp," *Marketing*, April 7, 2015, **www.marketingmag.ca**
16. "How the Top 10 Campaigns Became Viral Hits," *Entrepreneur*, April 23, 2014, **www.entrepreneur.com/article/233207**

PART 4 Communicating the Message: Planning Message Placement

© Mrs_ya/Shutterstock

Part 2 established the relationships between marketing planning and marketing communications planning. Part 3 described the creative planning process. Part 4 describes the media planning process and discusses each of the major media in detail.

Media planning involves identifying media objectives, strategies, and execution. Decisions in each area depend largely on budgets and media consumption trends—how people are consuming the media. Chapter 7 discusses media objectives and media strategies, along with budgetary issues. In Chapter 8, the print media are examined in detail, followed by the broadcast media in Chapter 9. Chapter 10 is devoted to out-of-home media. Chapter 11 examines the growing field of direct response communications, while Chapter 12 discusses online and other forms of interactive communications. Digital advertising is now the largest form of advertising in Canada in terms of dollars spent in the media.

Planning and buying media time and space varies from one medium to another. The unique considerations for the various media are presented in the appropriate chapters.

CHAPTER 7

Media Planning Essentials

© Sergey Nivens/Shutterstock

Learning Objectives

After studying this chapter, you will be able to

1. Identify key trends affecting media planning today
2. Assess the roles and responsibilities of both client and agency in media planning
3. Differentiate between media objectives, media strategies, and media execution
4. Use media planning terminology
5. Describe the steps involved in the media selection process
6. Identify the factors affecting the size of an advertising budget
7. Describe the methods of determining the size of an advertising budget

The process of developing a media plan is complex. The task of an agency's media planners is to reach the desired target market efficiently. Efficiency in media planning can be loosely defined as "gaining maximum impact or exposure at minimum cost to the client." The assignment is complicated by variables such as media reach information, the ways in which competitors use the media, and consumers' media habits. Technology and the on-demand media consumption patterns of consumers are changing the way planners look at the various media alternatives. In addition, the agency must develop and execute a plan that meets stated expectations within certain financial parameters.

Essentially, input from the client to the agency becomes the foundation of the media plan. The direction a media plan takes is largely based on the guidelines provided by the client's marketing plan. It is important to realize that the media plan is a subset of a broader marketing communications plan. Therefore, media strategies must be coordinated with other communications and marketing activities.

Key Trends Influencing Media Planning Today

So much of today's marketing activity is influenced by technology and changes in consumer behaviour that result from applications of technology. How information is collected, analyzed, interpreted, and applied has a huge impact on media decisions. Advanced software systems provide the means for making such decisions. As well, the increasing presence of mobile devices has resulted in high demand for video content, and as a consequence video advertising messages. Presently, 68 percent of Canadians own a smartphone device, and 76 percent of them watch videos on their devices.[1] Let's examine these issues in more detail.

INTELLIGENT APPLICATION OF DATA

In the past, media plans were devised well in advance of implementation—agencies prepared the plans, clients approved them, and agency buyers implemented them. Now that digital media are the largest advertising media in Canada, buying decisions are technology based and done in real time! Digital media has given rise to programmatic buying, a concept introduced in Chapter 1. In the programmatic system, advertisers bid on available advertising spots in real time—the highest bid gets the spot. Bids are based on the spots' ability to reach a certain target audience and the demand for the spot among advertisers. This buying process is in its early stages and is being used by early adopters, but it is poised for significant growth in the near future.

Consumer mobility presents another opportunity for advertisers. Mobile devices are being joined by other developing technologies, such as the connected car and the connected home. Being able to reach individuals in local markets is quite a change from targeting a large group of people with common characteristics and showing them a television commercial. The combination of mobile devices, GPS collection points including Wi-Fi hotspots, mobile search queries, and social media sites allows advertisers to target customers at the local level.[2] As a consequence, the mind-set of a media planner must change; the planner must think more in the now, as opposed to six months from now or a year from now. The key is to capture, analyze, and act upon data on the fly.

THE RISE OF VIDEO

The consumption of video content is escalating quickly, and as a result less time is spent with other media. What are the consequences? For television it means less potential reach if there are fewer viewers, less advertising revenue, and ultimately less program production. Further, Canadians are pulling the plug on cable and moving to video streaming services like Netflix. It is estimated that Netflix has 3.48 million subscribers in Canada (2015). Viewing behaviour on Netflix is different than conventional television. People will binge-watch an entire season of a program (e.g., *House of Cards* or *Breaking Bad*). For now these services are available on a subscription basis and are free of advertising. The internet was once free, but now it is the largest advertising medium in Canada. The growth of video streaming will eventually present new marketing and advertising opportunities—another option for media planners to evaluate.

Media Planning Process

Media carry a brand's selling message to a predetermined target market. The selling success of any advertising campaign, therefore, depends on the effectiveness of the media plan. **Media planning** involves developing a plan of action for communicating messages to the right people (the target market), at the right time, and with the right frequency.

Media planners must decide which media are best suited for delivering the message and choose among television, radio, newspapers, magazines, various out-of-home alternatives, direct response media, and digital media. Digital media embrace all forms of advertising on the internet, social media outlets, and mobile communications. Numerous strategic factors are evaluated when deciding which media to employ in a campaign. How people consume media is one of those strategic factors. For example, there was a time when we only watched television shows on the television. Now we watch shows on televisions, laptops, tablets, and mobile devices.

Complicating the situation is the fact that people are multitasking—consuming several media at the same time (e.g., watching television while browsing the web on a tablet). As well, people are consuming media on the go. Consequently, digital media now play a more prominent role in the **media mix**.

With media such as television, radio, magazines, newspapers, and outdoor advertising, the strategic emphasis has always been on reach and frequency—how many people receive the message and how often they receive it. It was the advertiser who controlled the timing of people's exposure to the message. With digital media it is more about consumer involvement and timing—specifically, the ability to reach a potential customer in real time. Further, consumers now control when they receive a commercial message. Television shows, news, and sports reports are now available online, which means consumers receive the message whenever they want to; it's random rather than predetermined.

Interactive media and devices such as tablets and smartphones are part of consumers' lifestyles. Consumers seamlessly switch between devices throughout the day to try and stay current on email, news, social media, and television viewing. Within that framework there is a definite shift to mobile platforms. Therefore, rather than stressing reach and frequency, digital media strategy focuses on timing and engagement. In the context of advertising, **engagement** refers to how involved an individual is with the media when the advertising message is delivered: The higher the degree of involvement, the greater the likelihood that the message will be noticed.

The creative plan and the media plan must flow from the marketing plan, and they are designed to work together to help achieve the overall advertising objectives. The client and ad agency both play a role in the media planning process. The client provides the agency's media personnel with background information, along with some basic direction for the media plan based on past experience and knowledge of the target audience.

Information typically provided to the agency is carefully outlined in a document called a **media brief**. The media brief includes some or all of the following information: a market profile, a product media profile, a competitor media profile, a target market profile (which includes media consumption habits), media objectives, and a media budget. Figure 7.1 illustrates a schematic diagram of the media planning process.

The client will brief the agency creative team and media team at the same time. Discussing the issues with all parties and inviting all people working on the project to participate in lively discussion allows the message and media strategies to evolve together. The result should be a stronger plan.

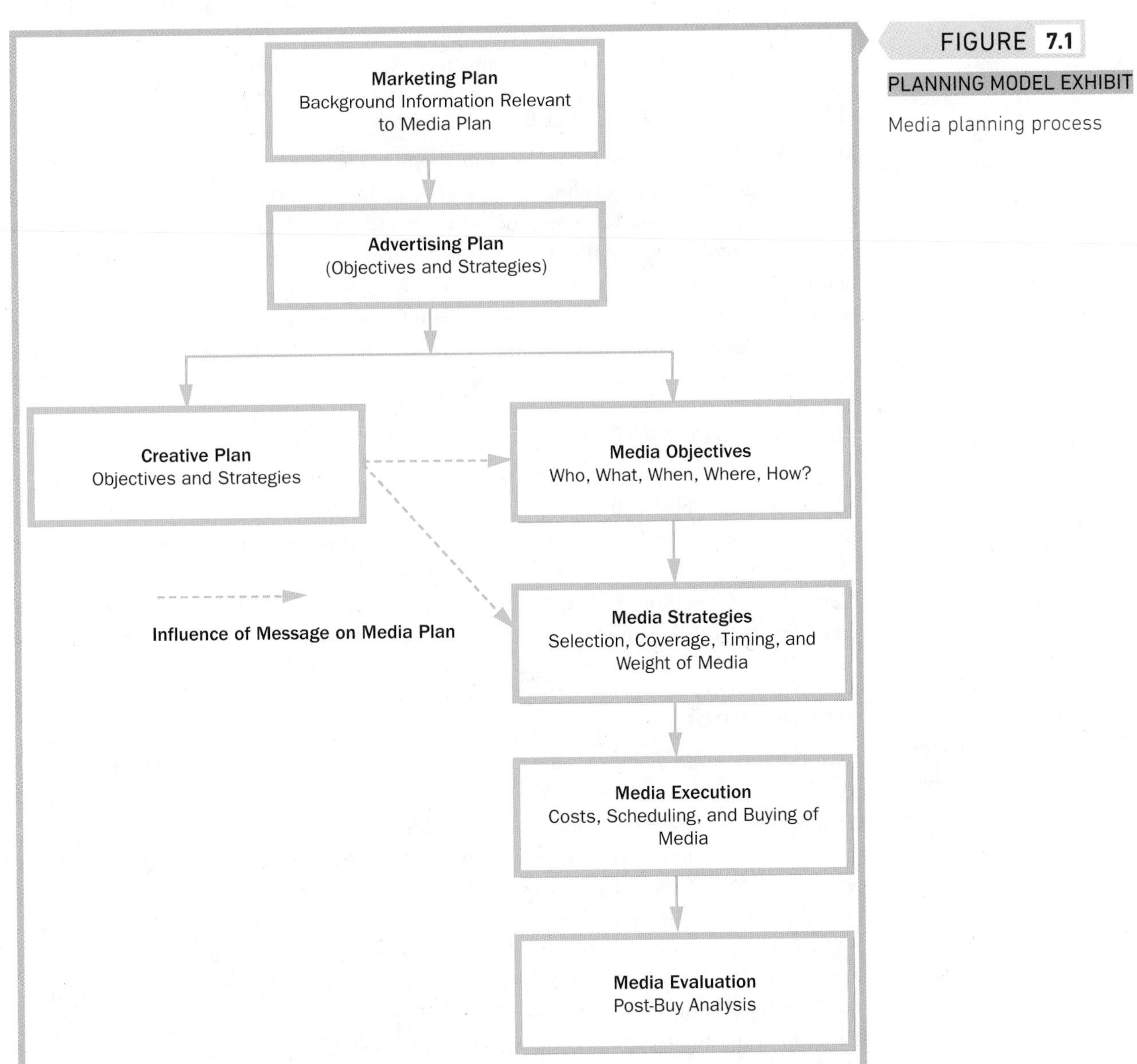

FIGURE 7.1

PLANNING MODEL EXHIBIT

Media planning process

MARKET PROFILE

The market profile reviews the market size and growth trends. It also includes current and historical market share trends, which give the media planner a perspective on what is happening in the market and the level of competition within it.

PRODUCT MEDIA PROFILE

Prior to developing a new media plan, it is wise to review and evaluate past media practices. Which media have been used, and how effective have they been? A qualitative and quantitative evaluation of the strengths and weaknesses of past media plans provides input for new plans. If little else, such a review should produce strong feelings about what worked and what did not. This information is particularly important if the client is briefing a new ad agency.

COMPETITORS' MEDIA PROFILE

A summary analysis of competitors' media usage and spending trends influences the strategic media direction chosen for the product. For example, which media do the competitors dominate? How much do they spend? Where do they spend it? Competitor information will influence a brand's media strategy. For example, should the brand use the same media or find alternative media to reach the same target market?

TARGET MARKET PROFILE

The media brief provides the media planner with a precise definition of the target market. Relevant demographic, psychographic, and geographic information will influence media strategy and execution. Knowing the activities and interests of the target market enables media planners to choose the best times and places in which to advertise. If information about the target's media consumption is known, it, too, should be communicated to the agency. For example, the medium the target refers to most and how frequently they refer to it is valuable information. Agency media planners are well versed in media consumption trends, and such information is combined with any information a client provides.

MEDIA OBJECTIVES

The provision of a precise description of the target market and a basic description of what the media plan will accomplish is the client's responsibility. Information regarding when, where, and how the message will be delivered is the responsibility of the agency. The client's intent is not to restrict the agency in its thinking; on the contrary, the detailed consideration of media objectives will be the responsibility of the agency media planners. Media objectives set priorities and establish guidelines for agency media planners. Media objectives are discussed in detail later in the chapter.

MEDIA BUDGET

Usually the amount allocated to the media budget has already been established by the time the client meets with the agency. At an earlier stage (the marketing plan or marketing communications plan) the budget is allocated among activities such as media advertising, sales promotion, experiential marketing, and public relations. The relative size of the budget provides the framework within which media planners must develop strategies and achieve stated goals.

Once the briefing process is completed, the agency media personnel take over. **Media planners** are specialists who put together the detailed media strategies and tactics. They assess all of the information provided and devise a media strategy and execution plan that will achieve the stated objectives. Media strategy is discussed in detail later in the chapter.

Once the media plan has been approved, **media buyers** purchase the time and space. They interpret the media plan and purchase the best deals available through the media representatives for the various media vehicles. A media buyer's task is to deliver the maximum amount of impact (on a target audience) at a minimum cost (client's budget). Computer technology enhances the ability of both media planners and buyers to generate more efficient media plans. Once the plan has been implemented, the agency is responsible for evaluating the plan through a post-buy analysis. A **post-buy analysis** is an analysis of actual audience deliveries (the actual number of audience members exposed to the ad) calculated after a specific spot or schedule of advertising has run.

The Media Plan

A **media plan** is a document that outlines all relevant details about how a client's budget will be spent: Objectives are clearly identified, strategies are carefully rationalized, and execution details are documented with precision.

Since a significant amount of the client's budget is at stake in an advertising campaign, communications between client and agency peak when media plans are presented. Media planners must present and defend their recommendations and be prepared to consider client input. Media plans have been known to undergo numerous revisions prior to final client approval. The structure and content of a media plan is discussed in this section. Refer to Figure 7.2 for a summary of the content.

Media Budget

- Total Budget Available for Media Advertising

Media Objectives

- Who (target market profile)
- What (nature of message)
- When (best time to reach)
- Where (market priorities)
- How (how many, how often, how long)

Note: Media objectives are usually clear, definitive statements.

Media Strategy

- Target Market Strategy (Shotgun, Profile Match, Rifle)
- Reach Considerations
- Frequency Considerations
- Continuity Considerations
- Engagement
- Market Coverage
- Timing
- Media Selection Rationale
- Media Rejection Rationale

Note: Media strategies usually expand upon the objective statements by providing details about how objectives will be achieved.

Media Execution

- Media Cost Summaries
  a. Spending by Media Classification
  b. Spending within Media Classification
  c. Spending by Time of Year
  d. Spending by Region or City
- Blocking Chart
  a. Calendar of Activities
  b. Media Used
  c. Market Coverage
  d. Gross Rating Points (GRPs)
  e. Timing

Note: For an applied illustration of these concepts, see the marketing communications plan for Schick Quattro in Appendix I.

FIGURE 7.2

PLANNING MODEL EXHIBIT

Content of a typical media plan

Media Objectives

Media objectives are clearly worded statements that outline what the media plan should accomplish. Within this framework, media objectives can be subdivided, and more precisely defined statements can be developed in response to questions concerning who, what, where, when, and how. Although answers to some of these questions are often judged to be strategic elements of the media plan, they are intended to provide broad guidelines for more detailed strategic considerations. Refer to Figure 7.3 for an illustration of these questions.

The components of media objective statements are as follows:

- ***Who?*** Who is the target market? The target market profile is described in terms of demographic, psychographic, and geographic characteristics. Media planners use this profile to match the target with a compatible media profile. For example, magazines know their readership profile, radio stations know their listener profile, and television networks know who watches specific shows. If there is a means to reach the target directly (as a group with special interests or as an individual), that, too, is considered.
- ***What?*** What is the message to be communicated? A brief summary of the selling message should be included in the objective statement. The message, and the manner in which it is presented, can have an influence on media selection. If media decisions are made first, such decisions could influence the direction of creative strategy and execution. Clients may prioritize differently from one another.
- ***Where?*** Where are the market priorities geographically? This question is critical, as most advertising campaigns are restricted by the size of the budget. Based on directives from the client regarding which regions or cities have priority, the media planner's goal is to work efficiently within the budget that is available. Does the client want a national plan, a key market plan, or some combination of both? The budget is usually the determining factor.
- ***When?*** When is the best time to reach the target market? Certain product and target market characteristics have a bearing on this question. For example, the fact that a product is sold on a seasonal basis will directly influence media timing. A heavier media schedule in the pre-usage season may be recommended as a way of building awareness prior to the purchase period of the seasonal product. Knowledge of the customer can also influence the timing of advertising messages. For example, is there a best time of the day, or better days of the week, to reach the target?

FIGURE 7.3

Questions from which media objectives are derived

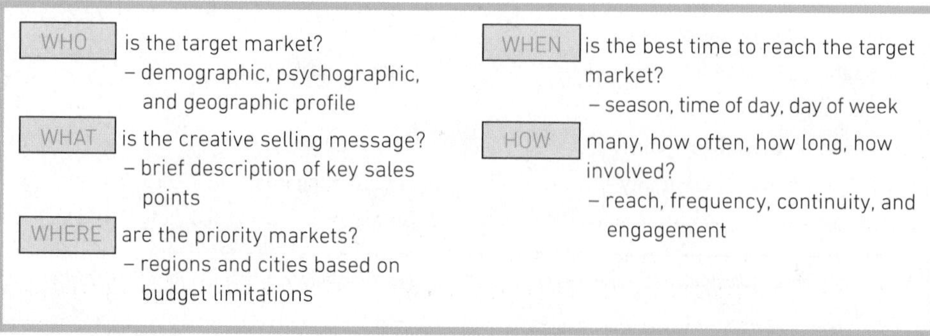

- ***How?*** How many? How often? How long? How involved? Several questions must be answered here. The client often determines which variable or variables should be given priority. These questions are strategic considerations regarding reach, frequency, continuity, and engagement. Strategy considerations will be discussed separately in this chapter.

Written media objectives should be clear, concise, and directional. In other words, they should give agency personnel just enough information for them to devise a sound media strategy. The following statements demonstrate how objective statements might be written in a media plan for a brand such as Degree deodorant (for women):

- To efficiently reach females, 25 to 54 years old, homemakers and career women, with post-secondary education, living in major urban markets
- To communicate that Degree is a reliable product—it will never let you down
- To reach a national audience with additional weight in the top five urban markets

Media Strategy

Media strategy focuses on *how* media objectives will be achieved—it results in a recommendation of which media to use, along with supporting rationale detailing why certain media were selected and others rejected. Consideration is given to a host of factors, and decisions must be made on each: which media to use, how often to advertise, for what length of time, and what markets to cover. The various factors that influence media strategy are discussed next.

TARGET MARKET

A well-defined customer profile must be provided to media planners. The more precise the target market definition is, the greater the likelihood that the planners will make an effective and efficient media recommendation. For example, a prototypical Lexus buyer is described as male or female, 35 to 49 years of age, earning $120 000 annually, and living in major urban markets. What media might a media planner recommend to reach the target? If print media is a consideration, a prominent business magazine such as *Canadian Business, Report on Business*, or the *Financial Post* would be suggested.

Essentially, the task of the media planner is to match the advertised product's target market profile to a compatible media profile, such as a magazine or newspaper's readership profile or a radio station's listener profile. Theoretically, the more compatible the match, the more efficient the media buy. The Lexus example demonstrates this principle. The same executive might watch television, but to place a television ad in prime time hours would reach people well beyond the target description. This would not be efficient. Consideration could also be given to reaching this individual directly by a mobile device—which is a more efficient opportunity.

There are three basic target market matching strategies: shotgun, profile matching, and rifle.

SHOTGUN STRATEGY The nature of the word *shotgun* suggests that the target market for which the **shotgun strategy** is best suited is more general than other target markets. For example, the target may be described as all adults 18 years of age and older. The product or service being advertised has widespread appeal. For target markets that are loosely defined, particularly demographically, the media selected to advertise the product can be more general in nature.

To illustrate the shotgun principle, members of a television audience watching a popular situation comedy or action/drama show during prime time (8:00 p.m. to 11:00 p.m.) will range in age, encompass both sexes, cover the entire range of income groups, and lead all kinds of lifestyles. Television is an effective means of reaching a broad target market, but it is costly. The cost of airing a 30-second commercial on a popular network show like *The Big Bang Theory* or *The Voice* could be in the $50 000 to $60 000 range. Less popular shows cost less, as would specialty channels that have smaller audiences. Other alternatives that reach a broad target in local markets include newspapers, outdoor, and transit media.

PROFILE-MATCHING STRATEGY In the case of a **profile-matching strategy**, the customer target market is carefully defined by demographic, psychographic, and geographic variables. When this strategy is used, the advertising message is placed in media whose readers, listeners, or viewers have a similar profile to that of the product's target market. The media planner looks for close matches.

Certain media types are characterized as general interest, while others are seen as special interest. Magazines such as *Canadian Living, Canadian Business*, and *Canadian Geographic* appeal to a more selective target market and may be suitable for a profile-matching strategy. *Canadian Living*, for example, appeals to female readers between the ages of 25 and 54 who are college or university educated, have a household income of $75 000+, own their own home, and reside in markets of 100 000-plus population. These females are independent and strive to balance career and family life. If that is the brand's target audience profile, then *Canadian Living* would be a wise media selection.[3]

On television, cable channels offer profile-matching capabilities. Cable networks such as HGTV, W, TSN, or Sportsnet appeal to a predominantly female or male audience. Radio is another medium suited to a profile-matching strategy. A radio station's format (e.g., adult contemporary, rock, soft rock, news, top 40) is designed to appeal to a particular demographic group. Advertisers wanting to reach a certain demographic group will select the appropriate stations in a local market.

Examine the profile presented in Figure 7.4. *Financial Post Magazine* (published by the *National Post*) reaches over 775 000 readers with each issue. The readers are 72 percent male and 28 percent female; are highly educated; possess high household incomes; and are classified as managers, owners, and professionals. The readership profile suggests that advertisers who appeal to a target that is more affluent and upscale should consider *Financial Post Magazine* as an appropriate advertising medium. *Financial Post Magazine* competes for advertisers with *Canadian Business* and *Report on Business Magazine*, a publication of the *Globe and Mail.*

RIFLE STRATEGY A **rifle strategy** is a matching strategy used in situations in which the target market can be precisely defined by some common characteristic, such as employment in a certain industry, having a certain occupation, or having a particular leisure-time interest or hobby. It is the common characteristic that makes this audience a target. In many situations, a specific medium can reach this target market.

A recreational interest such as gardening or golfing, for instance, could be the common characteristic of a group. The demographic profile of the group might be diverse, but the fact that all members of the group garden or golf is important to garden supply manufacturers and golf equipment manufacturers and golf destinations. A specific medium can be used to reach each target group. *Canadian Gardening* (magazine) would be an appropriate medium to select for a rifle strategy to reach gardeners, and *Golf Canada* (magazine) could be used to reach golfers. Advertisers should also consider the

DEMOGRAPHIC CHARACTERISTIC	Total Readers	Profile %	Index
Total Readers	775 000	100	100
GENDER			
Male	557 000	72	146
Female	218 000	28	55
AGE			
Adults 18–34	255 000	33	112
Adults 35–49	180 000	23	88
Adults 50+	340 000	44	99
Adults 18–49	436 000	56	101
Adults 25–54	399 000	51	100
HOUSEHOLD TENURE			
Own	601 000	78	102
Rent	175 000	23	94
EDUCATION STATUS			
University/Non-University Cert.	201 000	26	109
Bachelor's Degree	229 000	30	184
Post Graduate + Degree	118 000	15	181
EMPLOYMENT STATUS			
Employed Full Time	503 000	65	125
Self-Employed	107 000	14	122
Sr. Man./Owns/Man./Prof.	302 000	39	171
Business Purchase Influencers	300 000	39	145
HOUSEHOLD INCOME			
$75 000–$99 999	146 000	19	118
$100 000+	355 000	46	146
Average HH Income	105 928	—	129
PERSONAL INCOME			
$50 000–74 999	155 000	20	123
$75 000+	228 000	29	198
Average Personal Income	$65 750	—	146

Source: Article printed from National Post Media Kit: http://mediakit.nationalpost.com, URL to article: http://mediakit.nationalpost.com/magazine/reader-profile/, Copyright © National Post Media Kit. All rights reserved.

FIGURE 7.4

Readership profile of *Financial Post Magazine*

digital versions of these and similar magazines, which offer content on tablet and mobile platforms. Readership data show that about half of all magazine readers are accessing magazine content and advertising through tablets and smartphones—a factor that has to be considered when devising a media strategy. Placing ads online and on social media sites where a person's interests can be tracked offers another avenue for advertising gardening and golf products.

A summary of the various target market matching strategies appears in Figure 7.5.

FIGURE 7.5

Key aspects of target market matching strategies

Shotgun Strategy

Target market covers a wide cross-section of the population; therefore, media options that have a diverse reach are appropriate (e.g., conventional television networks, daily newspapers, outdoor advertising, transit advertising).

Profile-Matching Strategy

Target market is described by certain demographic, psychographic, and geographic variables. Media options with audience profiles that are a close match are selected (e.g., magazines, radio, business newspapers and journals, special interest television networks).

Rifle Strategy

Target market is precisely defined by a special characteristic such as a hobby, sport, or occupation. Media options that specifically reach the target are selected (e.g., special interest consumer and business magazines, special interest cable channels, direct mail, online and interactive communications).

NATURE OF ADVERTISING MESSAGE

The nature of the message, determined by the advertiser's needs, often influences the media selection process. If factual details such as technical data and performance ratings must be communicated, print media is a practical option, backed by a website. If an emotional connection between product and target is the objective, then television and interactive media options are good choices. If engagement with an audience is a concern, then the internet via laptops, tablets, and mobile devices presents opportunities for delivering the message. If sales promotion incentives are part of the message, a combination of media may be required—TV for awareness and print, online, and in-store communications for providing details.

For insight into a campaign that effectively links target market, message, and media, refer to the Advertising in Action vignette **Right Message, Right Media = Great Results for MiO!**

REACH/FREQUENCY/CONTINUITY

These strategic factors are grouped together because of their interaction in the media planning process.

REACH **Reach** is the total unduplicated audience (individuals or households) potentially exposed one or more times to an advertiser's schedule of messages during a given period (perhaps a week). It is expressed as a percentage of the target population in a geographically defined area (e.g., a television station and, by extension, the advertising messages on

ADVERTISING IN ACTION

Right Message, Right Media = Great Results for MiO!

Good communications plans call for effective collaboration between creative planners and media planners. Their goal is always to reach their target with the right message in the right medium, and when they do so good things happen. Here's a brief summary of a campaign that clicked for MiO.

Kraft Canada launched MiO, a first-of-its kind liquid water enhancer, in 2012. It is a unique beverage in which users determine how much or how little flavour they want. The target market was male millennials, a group highly sought after by many brands in other beverage categories. Kraft decided on this target because they like to try new things. Their acceptance of the product would produce new revenue for the company.

The communications objectives called for meeting aggressive sales targets, growing the beverage category, and building brand awareness by establishing a differentiated tone and personality for the brand. The budget was in the $2–3 million range.

What was known about the target was that they liked to make changes in their lives. MiO would be positioned as an agent of change. Creative would be rolled out in stages. The first stage would intrigue the target; the message would create a personality about something. The second stage would educate the target about product benefits. The third stage would leverage the message via sharing.

The creative team at TAXI (the ad agency) developed a series of TV spots. The first spot, called "Changes," used more than 100 visual changes to dramatize MiO's role as an agent of change. In it the male character instantly changed into all kinds of different costumes to reflect change. A second spot featured YouTube phenomenon Dude Perfect, a basketball trick-shot crew substituting quick squirts for trick shots. The spot created a unique branded content experience. A third spot, "Eye of the Squirter," took an irreverent shot at the juiced-up world of sports drink marketing. The male character was shown clumsily performing more than a dozen sports moves—sipping MiO along the way.

The media recommendation included television for awareness, digital media and pre-roll video for building a stronger relationship with the target, and YouTube content to heighten the brand experience and encourage sharing of content among friends on social networks. As the campaign progressed, more emphasis was placed on digital media.

Target, message, and medium all clicked. Each of the three spots garnered more than 1 million YouTube views. After one year on the market, brand awareness ratings (where the product is linked with the brand) were in the 70 percent range, and MiO attracted new users into the category. Sales revenue exceeded expectations by far—350 percent higher than what was originally forecast. Proof again that good advertising works!

Adapted from Cassies 2015, Packaged Goods Beverage (Gold), http://cassies.ca/entry/viewcase/12502.

that station might reach 30 percent of a metropolitan market). To explain the principle of reach, assume that a message on a particular station was seen by 40 000 households in a geographic area of 100 000 households. The commercial reached 40 percent of households in the area. Reach can be expressed as an absolute figure (40 000 households) or as a percentage of households reached (40 percent). Reach is calculated by the formula

$$\text{Reach} = \frac{\text{Number of households tuned in}}{\text{Number of households in area}}$$

So in this case,

$$\text{Reach} = \frac{40\,000 \text{ (tuned in)}}{100\,000 \text{ (in area)}}$$
$$= 40\%$$

The dynamics of reach apply to all media forms. The only variation is the timeframe for which reach is expressed. It may be weekly on television and radio, monthly in magazines, and daily in out-of-home media (outdoor and transit). Reach does not double-count people exposed multiple times if a media plan involves repeated ads in one media category.

FREQUENCY **Frequency** is the average number of times an advertising message has been exposed to a target audience (an individual or a household) over a period of time, usually a week. Reach and frequency variables are considered together in media planning. The media planner must delicately balance reach and frequency objectives within budget guidelines.

In any given market, households receive different numbers of exposures because of their different viewing habits. As a result, media planners think of frequency in terms of average frequency. The terms *frequency* and *average frequency* mean the same thing. Frequency is calculated by dividing the total possible audience by the audience that has been exposed to the message at least once (reach).

Therefore, average frequency is based on the formula

$$\text{Average frequency} = \frac{\text{Total exposures of all households}}{\text{Reach (households)}}$$

To illustrate this formula, let's assume that the total exposure of all households is 180 000, and the total number of households reached in one week is 50 000. The average frequency is as follows:

$$\frac{180\ 000}{50\ 000} = 3.6$$

A common dilemma faced by the media planner is whether to recommend more reach at the expense of frequency, or more frequency with less overall reach. The stage of the product life cycle a brand is in plus the size of the media budget often dictates which variable gets more attention. For example, a new product that has a high awareness objective may place greater emphasis on reach (and frequency, if the budget will accommodate it). A campaign with the objective of changing consumer attitudes will typically call for more frequency. A mature product that is trying to defend its position may opt for more frequency directed at a defined target audience.

IMPRESSIONS **Impressions**, or *total exposures*, refers to the total number of commercial occasions or advertisements scheduled multiplied by the total target audience (households or people) potentially exposed to each occasion. A media plan's impressions are usually referred to as gross impressions. You calculate the gross impressions by multiplying the actual number of people who receive a message (reach) by the number of times they receive it (frequency). To illustrate the concept of impressions, let's assume that a message on a television station reached 100 000 people and that the message was broadcast three times a week for eight weeks. The calculation for the number of impressions would be

$$\begin{aligned} \text{Impressions} &= \text{Reach} \times \text{Frequency} \\ &= 100\,000 \times 3 \\ &= 300\,000 \end{aligned}$$

Therefore, over the eight-week schedule, the gross impressions or exposures would be 2 400 000 (300 000 × 8).

GROSS RATING POINTS In television advertising the weight (amount) of advertising in a market is determined by a rating system. Media weight is expressed in terms of gross rating points. **Gross rating points (GRPs)** are an aggregate of total ratings in a schedule, usually in a weekly period, against a predetermined target audience. It is a description of audience delivery without regard to duplication or repeat exposure to the media vehicles, thus the word *gross*. Reach multiplied by frequency results in GRPs.

To explain the principle of GRPs, let's assume that an advertiser buys media time in Toronto at weight level of 200 GRPs. When calculating GRPs, a percentage figure for reach is used. The desired GRP level is achieved by manipulating both variables: reach and frequency. Therefore, if reach is 20 percent, the frequency would have to be 10 to achieve the 200 GRPs (10 × 20). If reach is 25 percent, the frequency would be 8 to achieve 200 GRPs (25 × 8).

To further illustrate this concept (GRPs = Reach × Frequency), let's assume that a message reaches 50 percent of the target households three times in one week. The GRP level would be 150 (50 × 3). If the message reaches 40 percent of the target households with an average frequency of 4.6 per week, the GRP level would be 184 (40 × 4.6).

The reach of a television program is also referred to as a *rating*. If, for example, *The Big Bang Theory* reaches 30 percent of households with televisions in its weekly time slot, the show has a 30 rating. Therefore, another way of calculating GRPs is to multiply a show's rating by the frequency of messages on that show. Here is an illustration:

Audience	Rating	Number of Spots	GRPs
18–49 years	30	2	60
18–49 years	25	3	75
18–49 years	20	2	40
Total		**7**	**175**

In this example, the advertiser scheduled seven spots over the period of a week on shows with various ratings. This resulted in a weight level of 175 GRPs for the week. Typically, an advertiser will vary the weight levels over the duration of the schedule and by geographic market. Markets that are given priority, for whatever marketing reason, will receive higher GRPs than less important markets.

Decisions about reach and frequency are difficult. Traditional wisdom suggests that frequency is the more important variable—you have to drive the message home before consumers will take action. But what is the reaction of consumers if they are exposed to the same message too many times? Will it hurt or help the brand? Some media traditionalists believe three ads get awareness, six ads get interest, and nine ads lead to possible action. At 12 ads, the consumer is tuning the message out. If the advertiser's goal is to maximize reach, a new medium should be added to a current one. This is an efficient solution compared with spending too much on one medium.[4]

Traditional buying models in the mass media are based on reaching as many eyeballs as possible, or on the weight of advertising (some combination of reach and frequency). Some media planners now give more credence to timing and have adopted a media concept referred to as *recency*. **Recency** is a model that suggests advertising works best by reminding consumers of a product when they are ready to buy.[5] The timing of the message is more important than the frequency of the message. According to Canadian media expert Lowell Lunden, "If recency is properly executed with creative that works, a single impression can influence behaviour if it is delivered at the right time. Powerful creative is memorable, linked to the brand, relevant and likeable, a combination that can cause the desired action to occur."[6]

The concept of recency is ideally suited to mobile communications. Advertisers now have the capability to reach consumers via their smartphones when they are on the go. Depending on a person's location and his or her interests, as determined by online tracking of behaviour, messages of interest can be distributed to consumers in real time. Behavioural targeting and its impact on media planning is discussed in more detail in Chapter 12.

CONTINUITY **Continuity** is the length of time required to ensure that a particular medium affects a target market. A single theme or selling proposition is delivered over that time period. For example, will the schedule be four weeks long, six weeks long, or eight weeks long? Media planners must juggle reach, frequency, and continuity factors to obtain maximum benefit for the dollars invested in media. Quite often continuity is the first of these variables to "give way" when budget (or a lack of budget) becomes a key factor.

Only an exceptional advertiser would purchase media time on an annual basis (52-week schedule). More moderate advertisers tend to stretch dollars over a one-year period by purchasing media time in **flights**. Flighting refers to the purchase of media time in periodic waves (usually expressed in weeks) separated by periods of inactivity, a tactic that stretches media dollars over an extended period of time. Refer to Figure 7.6 for an illustration of continuous spending versus flighting. The term **hiatus** refers to an inactive period between flights.

ENGAGEMENT

As described earlier, engagement is the degree of involvement a person has with the medium when using it. It is a response driven by emotion and is something that happens inside the consumer's mind. Both the message and the medium play a role in encouraging engagement.

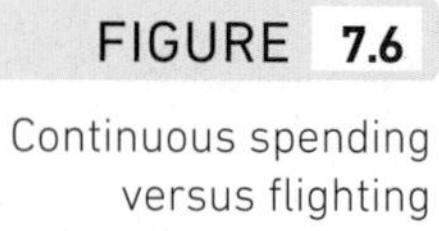

Continuous spending versus flighting

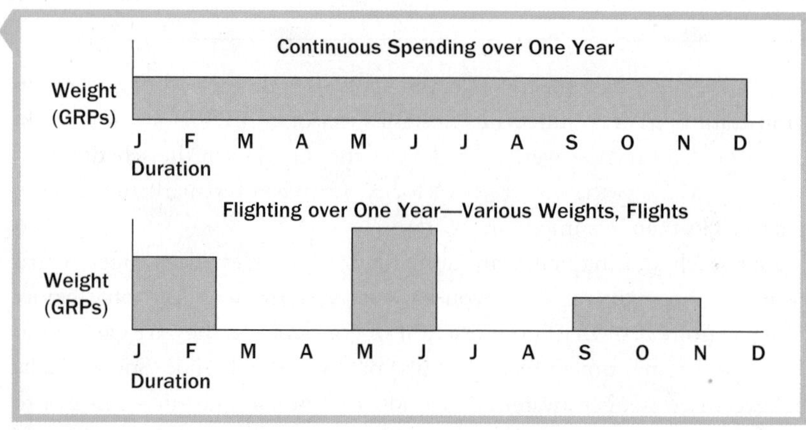

In a fragmented media universe (so much choice for consumers), media planners struggle to find ways of engaging consumers with advertising messages. People get distracted easily, or they multitask while viewing a particular medium. For example, a television viewer may avoid commercials by channel surfing during commercial breaks, or they may be doing something on their tablet while watching television. In contrast, an internet user, intent on what he or she is doing, or someone scrolling through their news feed on a social media outlet, could be more involved and consequently take more notice of advertising messages. A magazine reader might spend 30 minutes of uninterrupted time with a favourite magazine—that's engagement! The level of potential engagement varies from one medium to another.

From a strategic viewpoint, creative planners and media planners know that online and mobile communications must be entertaining if engagement is a strategic priority. As well, planners encourage engagement with the brand by using an ad in one medium (TV, radio, or print) to get consumers to go to a website or social network page for more information. Taking the time to go online suggests engagement. From a planning perspective, adopting an integrated strategy and execution will help achieve consumer engagement with a brand.

For a summary of issues relating to engagement, reach, frequency, and continuity, refer to Figure 7.7.

MARKET COVERAGE

Market coverage, or **coverage**, refers to the identity and number of markets in which advertising occurs over the course of the media plan's execution. Several coverage options are available to the advertiser. Market selection is often based on factors such as the level of distribution in a market (i.e., the availability of the product or service) and the importance of an area in terms of the sales volume generated there. Geographic areas that are designated as problems or opportunities are often identified for additional media spending. Several market coverage plans are available to an advertiser.

Reach	The total audience exposed one or more times to a message in a given period
Frequency	The average number of times a message has been exposed to a target audience over a period of time, usually a week
Continuity	The length of time required to ensure a particular medium affects a target market
Engagement	The degree of involvement an individual has with a medium when consuming it

Are these strategic variables equally important, or does any one variable take precedence over the others? Prior to the advent of the internet, media planners would wrestle with decisions regarding reach, frequency, and continuity. Any plan that included all three variables would be costly.

Now planners are seriously concerned about how engaged people are with the media. The more engaged they are with the media, the more likely they will be engaged with advertising messages. Therefore, planners must find the right media to engage consumers and then focus on strategic issues such as reach, frequency, and continuity.

One of the most difficult decisions for a media planner is frequency. How many times does the planner schedule a message to elicit action without overexposing the audience to the message? Too much exposure can turn off an audience.

FIGURE 7.7

Some key issues related to engagement, reach, frequency, and continuity

NATIONAL COVERAGE If a product is widely distributed and all geographic areas figure equitably in the success of the product, a national media strategy is an option. Funds can be allocated across media that reach the national market. Network television shows in prime time (e.g., *The Big Bang Theory, Survivor, NCIS*), national magazines such as *Maclean's* and *Reader's Digest*, and digital media including social media are good alternatives. Of course, target market profiles and the budget available would figure into such decisions. Prime time television and national magazines reach a broad cross-section of the population, and the cost in absolute terms is high.

If urgency is a criterion in the decision-making process (as it usually is when launching a new product or reacting to competitive activity), newspapers in major metropolitan areas, which collectively provide national coverage, are excellent vehicles to use. As well, online and mobile communications reach people anywhere, anytime—a 24/7 medium.

REGIONAL COVERAGE If an advertiser chooses to advertise regionally, there must be an equitable system of allocation so that all regions benefit from advertising. However, all regions do not require the same level of advertising weight; competitive advertising and promotion factors vary among regions, and this variance affects regional allocations and causes either upward or downward adjustments.

For example, assuming that Canada is divided geographically into five regions and that the regional sales volume importance (the contribution to total volume) shown in the table is accurate, an advertiser would allocate $1 million in media dollars, as shown in the third column of the table. Each region is treated fairly.

Geographic Regions	Regional Volume Importance (%)	Media Budget ($)
Atlantic	7	70 000
Quebec	23	230 000
Ontario	39	390 000
Prairies	18	180 000
British Columbia	13	130 000
Canada	100	1 000 000

Another way of allocating a budget to various regions is based on a brand development index. A **brand development index (BDI)** is a percentage of a brand's sales in a region in relation to the population of the region. For example, if a brand's sales in Ontario represent 34 percent of total sales but Ontario accounts for 39 percent of the total population, the BDI for the region would be 87.2 (34 divided by 39 multiplied by 100). This indicates that the brand is underdeveloped in Ontario. Therefore, if media advertising is a key influencer on purchase behaviour, additional media dollars may be needed there to correct the situation. Conversely, an overdeveloped region may require fewer advertising dollars.

When funds are being allocated and media are being purchased on a regional basis, media such as regional television networks, selective spot television, radio, regional editions of magazines, and newspapers are attractive alternatives.

KEY MARKET PLAN A **key market plan** is a media plan where time and space are purchased in urban markets that have been identified as priorities. Providing coverage in only key markets is often considered an option when budget constraints do not allow for much flexibility. In this situation, the advertiser uses a predetermined system to prioritize its key markets.

To illustrate, let's assume that a product had reasonably good national distribution but enough funds to advertise in only a selective list of markets. We know that Canada's population is largely urban. Therefore, urban areas could be ranked based on population. The top 10 cities in Canada, ranked by population, account for 54.6 percent of the total population (see the table that follows).[7] Advertising in those cities alone could have a positive impact on a brand's sales nationally.

Markets	Population (000)	Canadian Total (%)
Toronto	5 969.5	17.0
Montreal	3 981.8	11.3
Vancouver	2 443.3	6.9
Calgary	1 364.8	3.9
Ottawa-Gatineau	1 305.2	3.7
Edmonton	1 289.6	3.7
Quebec City	791.9	2.3
Winnipeg	771.2	2.2
Hamilton	558.1	2.2
Kitchener-Waterloo/Cambridge	504.2	1.4
Total	18 979.6	54.6

Source: Population data contained in the Canadian Media Directors' Council, *Media Digest*, 2014–15, p. 20.

The media planner would plan for adequate levels of reach, frequency, and continuity in all cities in which media advertising is recommended. Media time and space would be purchased from local television stations, daily newspapers, radio stations, and outdoor and transit advertising suppliers. Geographic targeting based on a person's location also makes mobile communications a good option.

While this system appears equitable, at least in this example, some cities and areas may never receive advertising support. Such decisions often create conflict between marketing/advertising managers and regional sales managers, who argue that they are being short-changed in the media allocation process. The illustration, for example, does not include any city in the Atlantic region or several larger cities in southern Ontario.

SELECTIVE COVERAGE PLAN In contrast to other market coverage plans, a selective plan does not consider factors such as level of distribution, population by area, or geographic product development. Instead, it attempts to reach a desired target market regardless of geographic location. Advertisers use a *selective coverage plan* with a *rifle* media strategy when a target market can be narrowly defined by a common characteristic.

A selective coverage plan works because of the nature of the advertised product, the common characteristic of the target market, and the availability of a specialized medium. For example, *Cottage Life* magazine and its website, www.cottagelife.com, would be an advertising vehicle appropriate for reaching people who own or aspire to own a cottage. *The Hockey News* and its online edition, www.thehockeynews.com, would certainly reach people interested in hockey.

Direct mail advertising remains a popular medium since organizations can develop unique offers for unique customers based on information contained in database management systems. Since customers chase after content they are interested in on the internet, the advertiser must follow the interests of its target audience and place ads on appropriate sites. Almost certainly, the cottagers and hockey enthusiasts mentioned above would visit websites dedicated to those interests.

BEST TIME TO REACH TARGET

Media strategy must consider the best time to reach the intended target market. The best time could refer to the best time of year, the best season, the best time of day, or the best day of the week. Placing an ad at the right time with the right message is a combination recommended by many media planners. But there are other considerations.

If a new product is to be launched into the market, should the advertiser intensify reach and frequency initially, or gradually build intensity over a longer period? These questions are addressed when decisions about scheduling media are being made. In most cases, the advertiser works within budget restrictions, so the money available must be allocated at optimal time periods during the media plan cycle. For example, there may be periods of the year when advertising is heavy, light, or nonexistent. Several scheduling options are available to advertisers. Refer to Figure 7.8 for a visual representation of each.

EVEN SCHEDULE According to the **even schedule**, media time and space are purchased in a uniform manner over a designated period. This schedule is best suited to large advertisers that need to sustain a certain level of advertising spending due to competitive pressures. Such a spending pattern is not very common since the goal should be to spend at a level necessary to achieve the desired action.

SKIP SCHEDULE In a **skip schedule**, media time and space are purchased on an alternating basis—every other week or month. In terms of media usage, skip can refer to alternating media—magazines one month, television another month. A skip schedule stretches media dollars over an extended period while maintaining the effect of advertising in the marketplace.

FIGURE 7.8

Media scheduling options

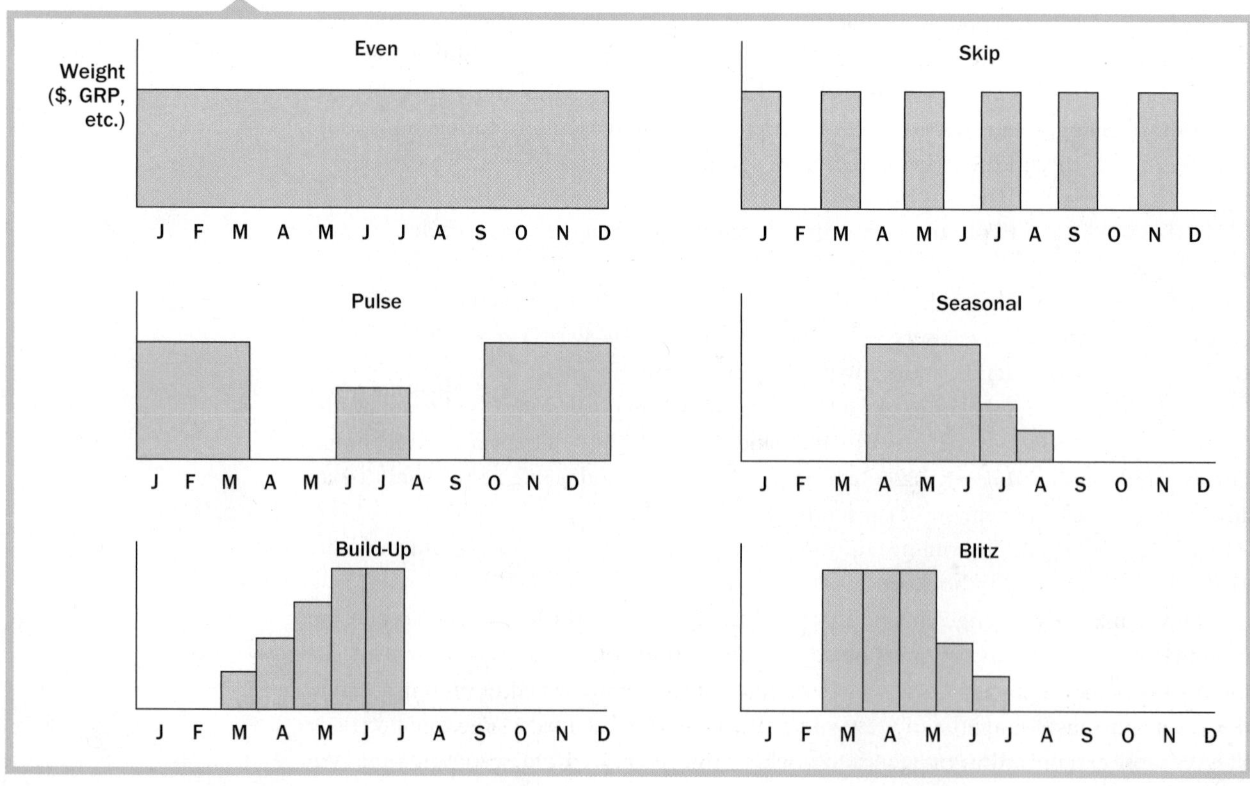

PULSE SCHEDULE A **pulse schedule** (or **pulsing**) involves scheduling advertising in flights but at different weights (a function of the amount of money invested in media and the reach and frequency) and duration (the length of time) over the course of a year. Such a schedule looks random when viewed visually, but the weight and duration of the spending pattern is carefully rationalized in the media plan. Flights, as mentioned earlier, are the periodic waves of time in which the product or service is advertised. In this case, a flight would be followed by a hiatus in a continuous cycle throughout the year. The grouping of advertisements in flights contributes to the synergistic effect desired.

SEASONAL SCHEDULE A **seasonal schedule** is used for products that are sold and purchased at traditional times of the year. Media advertising is usually heavy in the preseason and then tapers off in the purchase season. Advertisers of sun-related products such as lotions and sunblocks start advertising in late May and June (the preseason) to create the necessary awareness levels for July and August (the peak buying season). Retirement savings plans are advertised heavily in January and February—the deadline for contributions is usually the end of February.

BUILD-UP SCHEDULE A **build-up schedule** is characterized by low initial media weight, often due to selective use of media, that gradually builds to an intensive campaign in subsequent time periods, with an increase in media weight and the use of additional media. The build-up strategy is often associated with new product launches (e.g., new movies being released by Hollywood studios). Such a strategy is often called a *teaser campaign*.

BLITZ SCHEDULE The **blitz schedule** is often associated with the introduction of a new product, an event for which multimedia campaigns are implemented. To create high levels of awareness during the introductory period, advertising saturates the market then gradually tapers off. Another feature of this schedule is that certain media will be used less frequently, or eliminated, as time goes on.

So how do media planners determine which schedule to use? From the descriptions above, three factors generally influence the best approach to take: seasonality of product sales, the consumers' product purchase cycle, and the consumers' interval between decision making and consumption.

COMPETITIVE MEDIA STRATEGIES

Prior to committing to a plan, media planners should analyze competitors' media usage and expenditure patterns. What the competition does can help planners recommend a media direction for their own product. Should the media recommendation follow a similar pattern, or should a unique strategic direction be recommended?

Assume that a product has a large media budget and dominates other products because it is extensively advertised on television. Does a competitor attempt to compete at the same level in television (assuming adequate funds are available), or should its media planners choose another medium or media combination so that, by dominating the different media, the product can reach a similar target market? The media budget that is available influences such a decision.

FLEXIBILITY

Flexibility is the ability to modify media spending plans throughout the period that advertising is scheduled. Flexibility is not a variable that influences the media selection process. It is, however, important from the client's viewpoint, since rapidly changing conditions in the marketplace or within the company may require that media tactics be changed on short notice. For example, what happens when a client is forced to cut the budget in the midst of a media campaign? Cancellation policies must be known prior to committing to a plan. Typically, each medium stipulates a certain lead time for cancellation. On television, for example, major networks such as CTV, CBC, Global, and TVA have a noncancellation policy for 52-week contracts for the national level. Advertisers on regional networks must give four weeks' notice and be on the air for four weeks before they can cancel.

Conversely, an advertiser may decide to purchase additional media time. Competitive activity might dictate heavier-than-planned spending in a certain market. Often media time is sold well in advance of either air date or publication date, but the advertiser should be aware of the options that are available on short notice. Space in daily newspapers, time on the radio, and space in digital media can be purchased with fairly short lead times, assuming creative is available.

MEDIA ALTERNATIVES

Various media alternatives are available to advertisers—television, radio, interactive media (including social media and mobile), newspapers, magazines, out-of-home advertising, and direct response communications. Each medium has its own advantages and disadvantages, so selection is largely based on the nature of the product, the description of the target market, the media that this market refers to most often, and the budget available.

Typically, an advertiser will not rely solely on one medium but will select a combination of media to achieve the stated objectives of the campaign. An advertiser may identify a primary medium and support it with secondary media. As explained earlier, television may be ideal for creating awareness and for connecting with consumers emotionally, while print may be ideal for communicating details and appealing to consumers on a rational basis. Combinations of media, therefore, may be the best bet. Generally speaking, people are spending less time with television and newspapers and more time with online and mobile communications devices. This trend has a direct impact on a media planner's recommendations.

Detailed discussion about the various media options, and their advantages and disadvantages, are included in Chapters 8 through 12.

For more insight into an advertising campaign that effectively combined various strategic factors and media, read the Advertising in Action vignette **Right Message, Right Medium = Great Results for Tangerine**.

BUDGET

Essentially, all media strategy decisions are affected by the budget. For example, a small budget can restrict the use of media, extent of coverage, and reach and frequency levels; a sizable budget can provide considerable flexibility with respect to the same factors. A large budget allows flexibility in the media selection process, since a multimedia campaign can be considered. Media planners who face restrictions or smaller media budgets must be more selective in the evaluation process. The size of the budget (small or large) means that media planners face different challenges when trying to allocate funds efficiently.

To maximize the potential of scarce media dollars, media planners often recommend a primary medium that provides an effective and efficient means of reaching a target market. Such a plan is referred to as a **concentrated media strategy**, since most media dollars are allocated to a primary medium. The advantage of a concentrated strategy is potential media cost savings, since the purchase of one medium in larger quantities creates higher discounts. Then, after considering additional factors such as reach, frequency,

ADVERTISING IN ACTION

Right Message, Right Medium = Great Results for Tangerine

Good communications plans call for effective collaboration between creative planners and media planners. Their goal is always to place the right message in the right medium, and when they do good things happen. Here's a brief summary of a campaign that clicked for Tangerine.

What is Tangerine, one might ask? Well, that was the precise situation Scotiabank faced when it embarked upon a rebranding effort for ING Direct Canada. Scotiabank acquired ING Direct, and a legal requirement of the transition called for a new brand name and visual identity.

ING Direct was successfully positioned as a challenger to the big banks—it was a bank that did things differently and more simply. After 12 months of consumer research, the Tangerine name was decided upon. It stood for simple, unique, progressive banking.

The advertising objectives for the rebranding campaign were threefold:

1. To achieve an unaided brand awareness of 7 percent within six months
2. To drive customer acquisition based on the bank's value proposition
3. To ensure existing clients were aware of the name change and acclimatized to the transition before it occurred

Analysis of the situation by John St. (the ad agency) determined that simplicity would play a key role in messaging. The big banks are associated with complexity and doing things the old-fashioned way. Tangerine would stand for accessibility, innovation, and flexibility—money would be simpler to manage.

Strategically, timing would play an important role in message delivery, and transparency was crucial throughout the process. The bank maintained dialogue with employees and clients to ensure a smooth transition. Internal communications included live streaming of messages, events to help create buzz, and a microsite outlining how the name change was just another step in the history of the bank. A direct mail piece was sent to all clients informing them of the change and how they would be affected.

The initial launch took place in two phases. The first phase explained the transition of ING Direct to Tangerine. The message helped acclimatize Canadians to the name change and established Tangerine as a credible and trustworthy bank. The message was informative in nature; the focus was on the name and what wasn't changing: "We're changing our name, but we'll never change what we do."

The second phase was designed to make Canadians take notice. The message would encourage Canadians to stop and think about how they do their banking. Why were people with their existing bank when Tangerine was a simpler and superior alternative?

Media-wise, the first phase of the launch, was TV driven supported by print ads and a microsite. Ad placements were in media traditionally used for information: newspapers, digital banners, and news and information sites. In the second phase, the objectives focused on awareness, so a multimedia approach was recommended. In addition to 30- and 60-second TV spots, large-scale transit dominations, transit shelters, digital display ads, and pre-roll video were added to the media mix.

The transition campaign was a success. There was a sizable uptick in customer acquisition—a 90 percent increase in applications in the first two months of the campaign. Unaided brand awareness reached 15 percent within three months—well above target. News and media coverage achieved 81 million earned media impressions (free brand exposure), and there were 188 unique news stories about the name change transition. Proof again that good advertising works!

© Hand-out/Tangerine/Newscom

Adapted from Cassies 2015, "Off to a Good Start (Silver)," http://cassies.ca/entry/viewcase/17998.

FIGURE 7.9

Influence of budget on media strategy

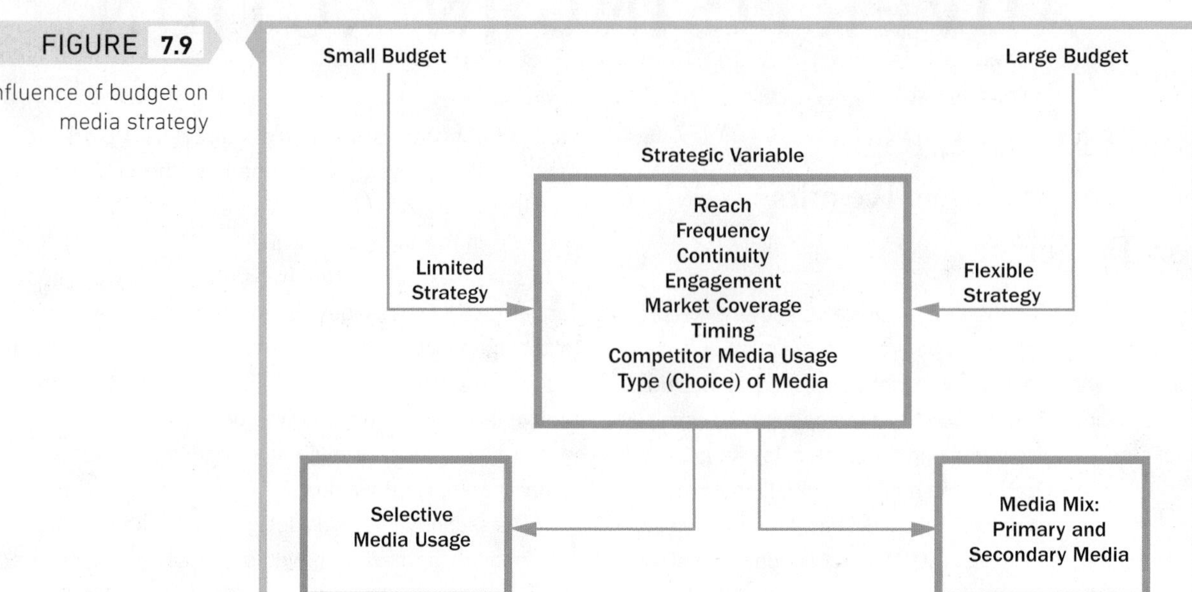

engagement, and market coverage, media planners will recommend secondary media. Secondary media are often used selectively and serve to complement the primary medium.

Alternatively, a media planner could recommend an **assortment media strategy** in which the media dollars are distributed more equitably among several media types. Such a strategy allows the advertiser to reach the same target market in different environments—if members of the target market are not watching television in their leisure time, they may be online or reading a magazine. Figure 7.9 summarizes the effect of budget size on media strategy.

Media Execution

The final stage in the media planning process is media execution. Essentially, *media execution* is the process of fine tuning the strategy and translating it into specific action plans. These action plans, or tactics, can be divided into the following areas: evaluating cost comparisons so that a particular medium may be chosen over another, scheduling specific media in a planning format (calendar or blocking chart), developing budget summaries that outline media spending details, and buying the media time when the client approves the plan.

MEDIA SELECTION PROCESS

Media selection can be viewed as a "funnelling" process, since the focus of the process is moving from the general types of media to a specific medium. The process is based on a three-stage decision system that involves selecting the general type of media to use (media strategy), selecting the class of media within the type, and selecting the particular medium. See Figure 7.10 for an illustration of the media selection process.

The first decision is selecting the *type of media* that will best allow the advertiser to meet the objectives for the product and to execute the advertising strategies devised for the product. In the selection process, the various media types are evaluated and compared on the basis of how effectively and efficiently they reach the target market.

The second decision involves comparing the *class options within the type of media* recommended. Such a decision often depends on the overall target market matching the

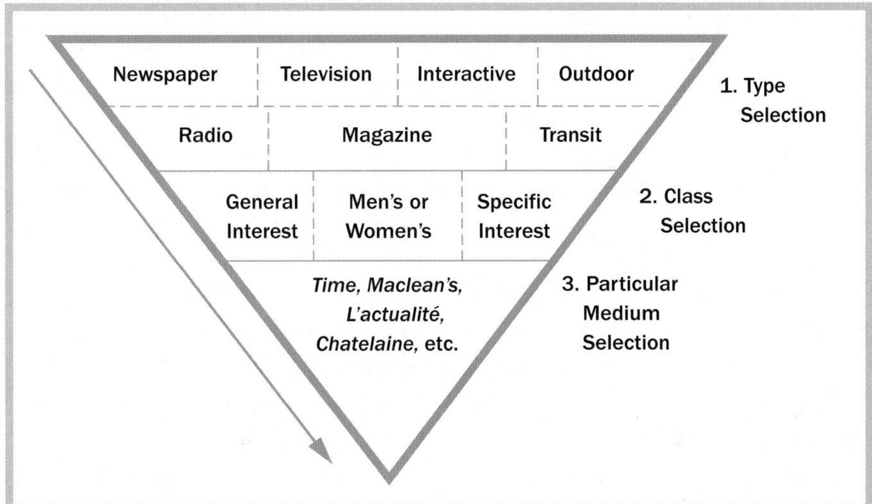

FIGURE 7.10

Media selection process

This figure assumes magazines are the selected medium. The second decision is the class of magazines (general interest) followed by the specific magazines in that class (*Time, Maclean's*, etc.).

strategy being employed: shotgun, profile matching, or rifle. For example, if magazines are recommended, what class of magazine should be used? Will it be general interest, specific interest, or a magazine tailored specifically to the needs of one gender? If television is recommended, will it be a conventional network such as the CBC or CTV, a specialty cable channel that has a specific theme (such as the Outdoor Life Network or Discovery), or a selective spot at a local market television station?

The third decision of the media planner is recommending which *particular medium* within a class provides the most cost-efficient means of delivering the advertiser's message. For example, if the female head of the household is the intended target market and magazines have been recommended, which publications are most cost efficient? The recommendation would have to consider magazines that have a high female readership. Some options include *Canadian Living, Chatelaine*, and *Style at Home.* Depending on funds available, one publication or all three might be recommended. If television is recommended, which network or which station or stations (to be purchased locally) should be part of the media buy? The decision is largely based on how cost efficient the medium is at reaching the intended target.

Cost **efficiency** is based on a mathematical model called CPM. **CPM (cost per thousand)** is defined as the cost incurred in delivering a message to 1000 individuals. In the case of magazines, the data required for the calculation are the cost of a comparable advertisement in each publication and the circulation figures. The CPM calculation allows for easy comparison of magazines that have different rate structures and circulations. Here is the formula for calculating CPM:

$$\text{CPM} = \frac{\text{Unit Cost of Message}}{\text{Circulation (in thousands)}}$$

The CPM comparison of three magazines is as follows:

Magazine (National Edition)	Cost ($) (1P, 4-colour)	English Circulation (in thousands)	CPM
Canadian Living	52 905	520.0	101.74
Chatelaine	53 480	524.0	102.06
Style at Home	18 955	238.0	79.64

Source: Rates obtained from each magazine's website (2015) and circulations obtained from Canadian Media Directors' Council, *Media Digest*, 2014–15, p. 81.

Each magazine competes for advertising revenue in the women's category. The figures reveal that *Canadian Living* and *Chatelaine* reach their respective audiences with a competitive CPM. Given their high circulation, both magazines would likely be recommended in a media plan. In contrast, *Style at Home* is more efficient at reaching the female target given its lower CPM. It, too, must be given consideration. An advertising agency could develop a plan that includes all three magazines by allocating a percentage of the budget to each one. To expand reach, ads could run in each magazine during different months of the year.

Other more qualitative factors are often considered in the decision-making process. Factors such as editorial content, quality of reproduction, and demographic selectivity can lead the media planner to prefer one magazine over another. For example, readers of *Style at Home* are interested in home decoration, furnishings, and renovation projects, and the content of the magazine reflects those interests. The other magazines offer more diverse content. Therefore, some advertisers (say a paint manufacturer or appliance manufacturer) would probably give more emphasis to *Style at Home*. Products such as perfumes, personal care, and food products might give more emphasis to *Chatelaine* and *Canadian Living*.

Similar calculations can be made for other media. In television, for example, the cost of the commercial divided by the size of the viewing audience (in thousands) produces a CPM figure. This calculation helps determine which show to advertise on. Generally, high-demand shows like *The Big Bang Theory* have high CPMs because television rates are determined based on the demand for time slots. For example, CTV may charge as much as \$65 000 for a 30-second spot on *The Big Bang Theory* (one of the most popular shows in Canada), but the show reaches an average national audience of about 2.8 million each week. The CPM is 23.21 (\$65 000 divided by 2800), a reasonable CPM compared with other media.

In deciding on the best media strategy and execution, a lot of variables must be considered. Companies and brands face unique situations, so the strategies they employ will certainly differ from one another. Certain media consumption trends also affect the decisions on which media to employ and how much money should be invested in them. More details about media consumption trends and media execution are included in Chapters 8 through 12.

MEDIA SCHEDULING AND BUDGETING

With the media selection process complete, planners proceed to the next stage in developing the media plan: formulating a media schedule and related budget summaries. This portion of the planning document outlines for the advertisers how, where, and when the media expenditures will occur. The media schedule is normally presented in a calendar format, often referred to as a blocking chart. A **blocking chart** outlines in one or two pages all of the details of the media execution (e.g., media usage, market coverage, weight levels, GRPs, reach, frequency, the timing of the campaign).

Budget allocation documents accompany the blocking chart. Typically, the media budget classifies spending allocations according to product (for multiproduct advertisers), medium, region, and time of year (months and quarters).

Detailed expenditure plans are important to the client for budget control purposes. As indicated in the strategy section of this chapter, flexibility in media planning is important because of the possibility of rapidly changing conditions throughout a planning cycle. Budget control documents are referred to often, particularly when cancellations are being considered.

For an applied illustration of the content of a media plan that includes media objectives, strategies, and execution, refer to the sample advertising plan in Appendix I.

MEDIA BUYING

The media buyer purchases the time and space according to the media plan, which requires the buyer to interpret the work of the media planners and to make decisions regarding actual buys. Buyers are also charged with the responsibility of making replacement buys if the original choice is unavailable.

Time is often a critical factor in the buying process. For example, in broadcast television the CBC, CTV, Global, and TVA networks are booked in late June to cover a 52-week period starting in September, with bookings being noncancellable. This buying pattern is referred to as **upfront buying**, or simply *upfront*. In a rather competitive situation, media agencies bid for time slots on popular shows, with the cost of any particular spot being dictated by the demand for the spot. Spots on popular weekly shows fetch high prices.

The system for upfront buying is gradually changing based on technology and changes in consumer behaviour. People now consume television differently. TV content is viewed on multiple screens when, where, and how people choose. They no longer have to make a date to watch their favourite program. These influences affect the demand factor cited above and ultimately the rates an advertiser pays for a television spot. During the upfront season agencies will buy ads for their clients covering all media platforms in which a program appears—online, tablet, or mobile. Other factors such as personal video recorders (PVRs), Netflix, online video, connected TVs, and social TV also have to be considered. Their presence has lowered the reach of conventional television and has affected rates for commercials accordingly. The immediate challenge for television media executives is how to transfer advertising dollars from television to other platforms where content is available to viewers.

The media buyer acts as a negotiator with media representatives. He or she must maximize the efficiency of the media budget by seeking favourable positions and negotiating the best rates possible in light of the guidelines in the media plan. In essence, the buyer fulfills the schedule by implementing the plan.

THE ROLE OF COMPUTERS IN MEDIA PLANNING

The process of media planning and buying has always been a complicated task, so it is not surprising that computers play a prominent role. User-friendly software developed by organizations such as Telmar HMS and Nielsen IMS Clear Decisions lets media planners and buyers alike make reasoned, detailed decisions. For instance, Nielsen offers media planning and analysis software for both industry and proprietary research. Their software uses data from PMB (Print Measurement Bureau), NADbank (newspaper data), and BBM RTS data (television consumption data).

Nielsen IMS Clear Decisions is a joint venture between the Nielsen Company and Interactive Market Systems. Clear Decisions software provides insight faster, creating a portfolio of analysis of media and marketing data. Agencies, media companies, and advertisers can mine data quickly to pinpoint markets and target groups. It helps organizations more accurately identify and profile key audiences—to make better media decisions and generate better return on investment.[8]

Nielsen captures conventional television viewing data electronically and video viewing across all screens: television, computers, and mobile devices. In mobile, Nielsen measures all ads, including video and display, for all iOS and Android platforms. On-device meter panels record every transaction users have with their mobile devices.[9] People are recruited and volunteer for these panels. Big brother will be watching!

Nielsen also compiles national and local TV ratings (e.g., which shows are most popular and how many people are watching) that help agencies and advertisers decide how to spend their media budgets. Ratings data is loaded into Media Advisor software that media planners can use for planning. Planners can "extract top rank[ed] shows, hours of tuning, station share, program profile . . . and comparison grids for standard demographics by programs and time periods."[10] Media Advisor lets a planner create custom demographics, such as women between the ages of 35 and 49 who are professionals and who have a household income of $70 000. The software identifies television programs that reach this demographic.

Telmar-Harris provides advertisers and agencies with a host of computer media planning and analysis services. Telmar offers Media 360 software that serves as a multimedia reach and frequency analysis system in which users can plan media simultaneously, including print, radio, TV, web, cinema, and beyond for cross-media delivery analysis. In television, for example, the software uses BBM data to generate exclusive reach and frequency distribution data for single stations, groups of stations, or specific programs. For print media the software can accumulate audience data across newspapers and magazines and their associated websites.

In the context of media planning, the software offered by Nielsen and Telmar gives planners the capability to maximize reach at the least cost. For more details visit the Nielsen website at www.nielsen.com or the Telmar website at www.telmar.com.

The Media Budget

How much to spend on advertising and how to allocate money across various media and other forms of marketing communications are always challenging questions for a manager to answer.

Senior executives like to know what their return on investment will be from their marketing communications expenditures, but the payback from advertising remains rather vague—a direct link to sales or profit just isn't there. Organizations must realize that investment in advertising requires a long-term commitment if a plan is to have a chance at success. To think otherwise is foolish, but chopping advertising budgets in midstream is a common phenomenon when advertisers try to protect short-term profit margins. Such decisions are questionable because they conflict with the long-term expectations of the brand, and they can accentuate a rough financial situation by further reducing revenues.

FACTORS AFFECTING BUDGET SIZE

To develop an advertising budget, the manager analyzes a host of factors that will influence the size of the budget. When these factors are examined collectively, they provide insight into the amount of money required for advertising. A discussion of each factor follows.

SIZE OF CUSTOMER BASE Organizations directing consumer products at mass target markets tend to rely more heavily on advertising, while organizations directing products at industrial markets, which represent a more selective and geographically centred audience, rely more on personal selling and online communications. Therefore, consumer products tend to have much higher advertising budgets than do business and industrial products.

DEGREE OF COMPETITION The amount of money spent on advertising by competitors may be the single most important influence on the size of a product's advertising budget. If nothing else, it is a useful indicator of how much money the company will have to spend to remain competitive. Planners like to refer to *share of voice* in advertising. **Share of voice** (or *share of advertising*) is the percentage of spending by one brand in a market category relative to the total spending of all brands in the category. Information on competitors' advertising spending is available to consumer goods advertisers through marketing research firms such as Nielsen Media Research. Historical spending patterns can be used to forecast future competitor spending and ultimately help justify a budget.

To demonstrate, consider the advertising battles that go on between brands like Coca-Cola and Pepsi-Cola. Even though they compete in a market that isn't growing (health and lifestyle trends are affecting the category), neither brand wants to blink for fear of losing market share. To protect their position, they keep their advertising budgets high.

STAGE IN THE PRODUCT LIFE CYCLE Advertising is more important in the introductory and growth stages of the product life cycle than in the mature and decline stages.

In the *introduction stage*, the advertiser is mainly concerned with creating a high level of awareness for the new product and achieving trial purchases. In relation to sales (which are low in this stage), the investment in advertising will be extremely high. Since the objective is brand development, it is quite common to have an advertising expenditure that exceeds the projected return in sales. Initial losses are offset by profits made in the longer term.

In the *growth stage*, competition is present, so the competitors' advertising budgets enter the picture. A manager is concerned about two objectives: continuing to build awareness and creating brand preference in the customer's mind. Accomplishing both objectives costs money. Improving market share in a competitive environment is a challenge and requires a budget that will attract users of competitive brands.

When the brand enters the *mature stage*, most advertisers shift the strategic focus from brand development to profit maximization. Rather than spending money on advertising, the company makes a conscious effort to preserve money wherever possible. However, there are exceptions to this principle, as demonstrated by the Coke/Pepsi situation already described. If life cycle extension strategies such as product modifications, new packaging, and new varieties occur, there may be a temporary need to invest in advertising to make consumers aware of these changes.

In the *decline stage*, profit motives take priority. Advertising budgets are generally cut significantly or withdrawn entirely. Profits that are generated from brands in this stage are allocated to brands that are in their developmental stages.

PRODUCT CHARACTERISTICS The nature of the product (the degree of its uniqueness) and its perceived value to potential customers can have an influence on the amount of money that is spent on advertising the product.

Assuming a *high-interest unique selling point* (USP) exists, an advertiser must invest heavily in advertising to establish the perceived value of the USP in consumers' minds. When Procter & Gamble launched Gain Flings, it had to communicate that the product was essentially three products in one—Gain detergent + Oxi Boost + Febreze. The multiple

FIGURE 7.11 To generate awareness and interest in new products, Procter & Gamble invests heavily in advertising.

benefits of Gain Flings were worthy of high-spend advertising support. Refer to Figure 7.11 for an illustration. Once the brand is established, or when adequate levels of brand loyalty have been achieved, the investment in advertising can be reduced.

For brands that have only *marginal unique selling points* (i.e., the unique selling points are easily duplicated), the amount spent on advertising is determined by the overall objectives for the brand and the degree of competition. For example, if a brand like Arm & Hammer liquid detergent (a follower in terms of market share and a brand without the high-interest USP of the market leaders) wants to be competitive with bigger brands such as Tide and Sunlight, it would have to spend at similar levels. That may not be possible. Arm & Hammer may choose a different strategic approach and focus on other areas of marketing or marketing communications (e.g., price incentives such as coupons and cash refunds) or simply market the product at a lower price.

MANAGEMENT PHILOSOPHY ABOUT ADVERTISING The size of a company and the attitude and perceptions of senior executives about the value of advertising often determine the financial resources available for marketing communications. For example, expense-oriented managers who consider only the short term may be reluctant to spend scarce dollars on advertising; investment-minded managers, however, are more willing to take budget risks to encourage long-term brand development. They will see a plan through to the finish before passing judgment on the investment. For a summary of the factors influencing the budget and of budgeting methods, refer to Figure 7.12.

BUDGETING METHODS

Annual sales and profit projections often become guidelines for developing potential advertising budgets. An advertising budget can be developed in a variety of ways, each with its own pros and cons. Since no one method is ideal for all situations, it may be wise to compare a variety of methods so that the budget is realistic, given the competitive situation in the marketplace. Discussion of the various methods follows.

PERCENTAGE OF SALES If a company uses the *percentage-of-sales* method, it usually forecasts the sales dollar volume for the forthcoming year and allocates a predetermined percentage amount of those sales to advertising. Management determines the percentage to be used. Percentages often used are past industry averages or simply the percentage the company has used in the past. This method of developing a budget has an obvious shortcoming. The philosophy underlying the method is that advertising *results from* sales, whereas the wiser manager prefers to believe that advertising *results in* sales. This method

FIGURE 7.12

Factors influencing size of budget and budget methods

Factors Influencing Budget Size	
Customer Base	Consumer goods require larger budgets than industrial goods, due to the size and location of the customer base.
Degree of Competition	Assuming growth is the objective, a brand must be at or above competitor advertising spending levels.
Stage in Product Life Cycle	Introduction and growth require significant budgets (awareness and trial); spending is reduced in maturity (retention) and nonexistent in decline.
Product Characteristics	High-interest USPs require high investment to promote benefits; marginal USPs should look at less costly alternatives.
Management	The perception of the value of advertising is questioned (short-term expense orientation versus long-term investment orientation).
Budgeting Methods	
Percentage of Sales	A predetermined percentage of forecast sales is allocated to advertising.
Fixed Sum/Unit	A predetermined dollar amount per unit sold is allocated to advertising.
Industry Average	The average amount spent on advertising by competitors (historical or forecast) is allocated to advertising.
Advertising Share/ Market Share	Invest at a level to retain share (ad share equals market share); invest at a level to build market share (ad share is greater than market share).
Task (Objective)	Define the task; determine the activities to achieve the task; associate a cost with the activities.

is popular largely because of its simplicity and because it relates advertising expenditures directly to sales.

Note: Depending on the competitive situation, the stage the product has reached in the life cycle, and other factors, the actual percentage allocated to advertising may vary as time passes. For example, a company may allocate a very high percentage of the sales to a new brand, perhaps 200 percent (two dollars in advertising for every one dollar in sales), to establish the brand's position (thus sacrificing short-term profit). Conversely, a mature brand with a high level of annual sales will be allocated a reduced percentage (perhaps 5 to 10 percent) since maximizing profit is the motivation at this stage.

FIXED SUM PER UNIT SOLD The *fixed sum per unit sold* method of budgeting is similar to the percentage-of-sales method in that the volume of product sold has a direct influence on the size of the brand's advertising budget. According to this method, the company allocates a predetermined amount to advertising for each unit sold. For example, an automobile company like Toyota Motor Corporation may spend $500 on media advertising for every car it sells. That figure could vary from year to year depending on the market situation and degree of competition.

This method is suitable for products with a high unit price (appliances, automobiles). Similar to the percentage-of-sales method, the major weakness of this method is that the budget fluctuates with changes in sales volume.

INDUSTRY AVERAGE (COMPETITOR SPENDING) Advertisers using the *industry average* approach base their advertising budgets on what competitors are spending. Depending on the performance objectives established for a product, the advertiser could choose to lag behind, to be equal to, or to exceed the spending of the competition. Using competitors' past expenditures as a starting point, advertisers attempt to forecast competitive advertising expenditures for the next year, and then position their own budgets accordingly. To demonstrate, consider the following levels of advertising spending:

Brand A	$400 000
Brand B	200 000
Brand C	300 000
Industry Average	**$300 000**

Using this method, we see that Brand B falls behind its competitors. Assuming advertising is equally important to all brands, the company that produces Brand B would not anticipate much in the way of improved brand performance if the budget remains at $200 000.

An advertiser may also review historical industry averages as a starting point. For example, if the cosmetic industry historically spends 20 to 25 percent of revenues on advertising, then this is the range a company must adhere to if it wishes to remain competitive. Share of voice is important!

TASK (OBJECTIVE) METHOD Which comes first, the chicken or the egg? In contrast to other methods, the *task* or *objective* method shows how advertising can influence sales instead of being dependent upon sales. The task method involves a few basic steps: defining the task, determining the type and quantity of advertising needed, and determining the cost of the advertising recommendation.

- ***Defining the task*** The task of advertising is often expressed in communications terms; for example, "to increase brand awareness for Brand X from 60 to 75 percent in the next year."
- ***Determining the type and quantity of advertising*** The difficult part of the task method is determining the most efficient and effective ways of achieving the desired objectives. A detailed understanding of the strategic variables discussed earlier in the chapter—reach, frequency, continuity, impressions, GRPs, and engagement—is essential for determining reasonable and reliable budget estimates.
- ***Determining the cost of the advertising recommendation*** This last step in the process is more mechanical. Presuming there is agreement as to objectives and the type and quantity of advertising required (i.e., the first two stages), the costs are calculated mathematically according to media. Production costs are estimated, and the sum of all media and production variables becomes the advertising budget.

Since many variables are considered in the task method, it is often viewed as the most scientific of the various methods. Once a budget figure is arrived at, the company must decide if it can afford to spend that much on advertising. If it can't, the objectives of the plan must be reevaluated and the plan altered accordingly.

SHARE OF ADVERTISING (OR VOICE)/SHARE OF MARKET Share of advertising, or **advertising share**, refers to the amount invested in advertising by one brand expressed as a percentage of the total category investment in advertising. This method is based on the premise that advertising plays a key role in motivating consumers. A brand that spends at a level where advertising share equals market share can reasonably expect to retain its market share position. Brands that want to grow in a market and increase market share will have to increase spending so that advertising share is greater than market share. Consider the example in the table that follows and the consequences it presents:

Brand	Market Share (%)	Projected Advertising Budget ($)	Advertising Share (%)	Consequences
A	40	5 000 000	50	Share increase
B	30	2 500 000	25	Decrease
C	20	1 500 000	15	Decrease
D	10	1 000 000	10	Maintenance
	100	10 000 000	100	

If Brand A spending is 50 percent share of advertising, it follows that a market share increase will occur. Conversely, Brands B and C share of advertising fell below market share, which could result in a decrease in market share.

The use of this method requires an advertiser to review competitors' media spending. It produces a good starting point (guideline) for developing a budget. However, it does not consider profit objectives. A preoccupation with what competitors are spending may force a company to spend more than it can afford.

This chapter has presented the various components of a media plan and demonstrated how the budget influences the nature and direction of a plan. For an applied illustration of how the budget and the media objectives influence media strategy and the selection of specific media, refer to the advertising plan that appears in Appendix I.

SUMMARY

In the media planning process, the client is responsible for providing the agency with adequate background information, which is usually contained in the marketing plan. Using this information, the agency develops a detailed media plan and assumes responsibility for selecting, scheduling, and buying media time and space.

The media plan flows logically from the overall marketing strategy and marketing communications strategy. The media plan is divided into three basic sections: media objectives, media strategies, and media execution.

Media objectives are statements that outline who (who the target market is), what (what the selling message is), where (where the markets in which to advertise are located), when (when the best time to reach the target market is), and how (how often and for how long one should need to reach the target market). These objectives act as the framework for more detailed strategies and tactics.

Media strategy deals with the selection of appropriate media to accomplish media objectives. Strategies are affected by variables such as the characteristics of the target market; the nature of the message; reach, frequency, and continuity; the degree of engagement; the flexibility of the plan; the degree of market coverage desired; the best time to reach the target; competitive influences; the pros and cons of the various media alternatives; and the budget.

Media execution is the section of the media plan that outlines the specific tactics for achieving the media objectives. Within these detailed action plans are the specific media usage recommendations and summaries of how media funds will be allocated. Once the client approves the media plan, the agency media buyers negotiate the best possible prices with media representatives.

Whether the budget devised is appropriate for a media plan depends largely on the marketing sophistication of the organization. A variety of factors influence the potential size of an advertising budget, including the size of the customer base, the degree of competition in the market, the stage the product has reached in the product life cycle, the product's characteristics, and management's commitment to advertising.

There are a variety of methods for determining an advertising budget. Commonly used methods include percentage of sales, fixed sum per unit of sales, industry average, and the task (or objective) method. Since each method offers benefits and drawbacks, it is recommended that a company use several methods and compare the results of each before committing to a final budget.

KEY TERMS

advertising share 217
assortment media strategy 208
blitz schedule 205
blocking chart 210
brand development index (BDI) 202
build-up schedule 205
concentrated media strategy 206
continuity 200
CPM (cost per thousand) 209
efficiency 209
engagement 188
even schedule 204
flexibility 205
flight (flighting) 200
frequency 198
gross rating points (GRPs) 199
hiatus 200
impressions 198
key market plan 202
market coverage or coverage 201
media brief 189
media buyer 190
media mix 188
media objectives 192
media plan 191
media planner 190
media planning 188
media strategy 193
post-buy analysis 191
profile-matching strategy 194
pulse schedule (pulsing) 205
reach 196
recency 200
rifle strategy 194
seasonal schedule 205
share of voice 213
shotgun strategy 193
skip schedule 204
upfront buying 211

REVIEW QUESTIONS

1. Identify and briefly explain the basic roles and responsibilities of the client and the agency in the media planning process.
2. What are the basic differences between media objectives, strategies, and execution?
3. Identify and briefly describe the components of media objective statements.
4. Describe the differences between the following:
   a) Profile-matching strategy
   b) Shotgun strategy
   c) Rifle strategy
5. Briefly explain the impact that reach, frequency, and continuity have on strategic media planning.
6. What are gross rating points (GRPs), and how are they calculated?
7. Briefly explain how the degree of engagement affects decisions regarding which media to recommend.
8. What is the difference between a key market media plan and a selective market plan?
9. What is a pulse media schedule? What strategic variables combine to create the pulsing effect?
10. Briefly explain the difference between a build-up media schedule and a blitz media schedule.
11. What is the difference between a concentrated media strategy and an assortment media strategy?
12. What are the stages in the media selection process?
13. What is CPM? How is it calculated? What purpose does it serve?
14. Identify and briefly describe the factors that influence the size of an advertising budget.
15. Contrast the strengths and weaknesses of the percentage-of-sales budgeting method with those of the task (objective) budgeting method.
16. How does the product life cycle influence the amount of money a company or brand invests in advertising?

DISCUSSION QUESTIONS

1. "Media planning is an activity that should be in the hands of specialists." Discuss in the context of clients doing their own media planning, using a full-service agency, and using a media buying service (a specialist).
2. "The client is at the mercy of the agency's media recommendations." Is this a problem? Discuss.
3. "The budget should be based on the media plan, not the media plan based on the budget." Discuss from the perspectives of both the client and the agency.

NOTES

1. "Nielsen Adds New Mobile Metric," *Media in Canada,* April 21, 2015, **www.mediaincanada.com**
2. "Trends + Issues," Canadian Media Directors' Council, *Media Digest*, 2014–2015, 11.
3. *Canadian Living* (information from 2015 Media Kit), **www.canadianliving.com**
4. Tom Hespos, "Reach and the Law of Diminishing Returns," *Media Post*, January 6, 2004, **www.mediapost.com**
5. Chris Daniels, "Media Buying Gets Scientific," *Marketing*, July 31, 2000, 11, 12.
6. Lowell Lunden, "LLunden & Associates Limited", 2003.
7. Calculation based on data included in Canadian Media Directors' Council, *Media Digest*, 2014–2015.
8. "Nielsen and Interactive Market Systems Launch New Media Planning Software Platform," press release, Nielsen Company, May 28, 2008.
9. Nielsen Company, **www.nielsen.com**
10. Nielsen Media Research, **http://www.nielsenmedia.ca/English/services_en.html**.

CHAPTER 8

Print Media: Newspapers and Magazines

Learning Objectives

After studying this chapter, you will be able to

1. Identify the classifications of newspapers and magazines available to Canadian advertisers
2. Explain the advantages and disadvantages of newspapers and magazines as advertising media
3. Assess the considerations and procedures involved in buying newspaper and magazine space
4. Understand the basic terminology used in newspaper and magazine advertising
5. Assess the influence of technology on print media

Newspapers in Canada

In Canada, there are currently 110 daily newspapers with a total daily circulation of 5.6 million copies. The largest daily is the *Toronto Star,* which has an average Monday–Friday circulation of 360 515 per day and a readership of 2.2 million across its print and digital platforms.[1] Circulation and readership are important factors to consider when formulating a media plan. Included in these figures are 19 free daily tabloids that are distributed in major urban markets. The term *circulation* in newspapers and other print media refers to the number of issues sold. **Circulation** is defined as the average number of copies per issue of a publication that are sold by subscription, distributed free to predetermined recipients, carried within other publications, or made available through retail distributors.

Despite the shift to digital information sources, newspapers remain a viable advertising medium for reaching Canadian adults. The most recent Newspaper Audience Databank (NADbank) study reveals that newspapers reach 70 percent of Canadians in a typical week. As well, 40 percent of newspaper readers are accessing content via digital editions.[2] How Canadians read newspapers is changing—there is a definite trend toward digital versions that are being read on laptops, tablets, or mobile devices. The consumption trend is another factor to consider when devising a media plan.

Community newspapers are generally smaller-circulation newspapers published once a week and directed at a local target audience. These papers are ideal for local retail advertisers and are used extensively by national retailers for distributing weekly flyers. There are just over 1000 English- and French-language community newspapers in Canada. Advertisers can also choose from the many newspapers aimed at Canada's diverse ethnic population. Due to the local nature of community newspapers, readership is high—61 percent of adults read their community newspaper.[3]

Newspaper Formats

Canadian newspapers are published in two basic formats: tabloids and broadsheets. **Tabloids** are flat and resemble an unbound magazine. The tabloid page is 10 to 10 ¾ inches wide by 11 to 14 inches deep. The highest circulation tabloids in Canada are *Le Journal de Montréal* (279 000), the *Toronto Sun* (153 800), and the *Vancouver Province* (140 000).

Broadsheets are much larger newspapers with a horizontal centre fold. A broadsheet page is 10 to 12 inches wide by 20 to 22 inches deep. The majority (67) of Canadian daily newspapers are published in broadsheet format, those with the highest circulation being the *Toronto Star*, the *Globe and Mail*, and *La Presse*. The Canadian daily newspapers with the highest circulations are listed in Figure 8.1.

Newspaper Readership Highlights

Readership data about newspapers is compiled by an industry-sponsored measurement organization called Vividata. Vividata is the result of a merger between NADbank Inc. (an independent newspaper source) and PMB (the Print Measurement Bureau, which was a magazine measurement source) in 2014. This organization provides advertisers, advertising agencies, and daily newspapers with accurate and credible information on newspaper readership, retail data, and consumer behaviour. Newspaper data is updated annually by conducting a detailed survey of Canadian adults. The information collected includes weekday and weekend readership, demographic profiles of readers, and media habits (e.g., other media referred to).

FIGURE 8.1

Canada's top 10 daily newspapers by paid circulation

Source: Adapted from Canadian Media Directors' Council, *Media Digest*, 2014-15, p. 53.

Market	Newspaper	Circulation (000s)
Toronto	*Toronto Star*	360.5
Toronto	*Globe and Mail*	356.5
Montreal	*Le Journal de Montréal*	279.1
Montreal	*La Presse*	250.0
Toronto	*National Post*	163.7
Vancouver	*Vancouver Sun*	161.8
Toronto	*Toronto Sun*	153.8
Vancouver	*Vancouver Province*	140.0
Calgary	*Calgary Herald*	118.0
Ottawa	*Ottawa Citizen*	110.2

There are several daily newspapers that are distributed for free that also have high circulation figures:

Market	Newspaper	Circulation (000s)
Toronto	*24 Hours*	233.0
Toronto	*Metro Toronto*	258.0
Montreal	*Journal Metro*	172.0
Montreal	*24 heures (Fr.)*	145.6

Newspaper circulation and readership is declining. The availability of "news" information online from so many different sources plays a large factor in this decline. The news is not all bad, however, as the industry is making a concerted effort to transfer readers to its digital editions. There's a real shift in how Canadians are accessing newspaper content. Digital readership has increased more than 40 percent since 2010, and now 4 in 10 Canadians access content via digital platforms. At the same time, mobile readership in the top 18 markets reaches more than 1.7 million readers a day.[4]

From a strategic advertising perspective, newspapers are an engaging medium. Data regarding time spent with newspapers reveal that Canadians spend 46 minutes a day with hard copy editions and 30 to 40 minutes a day with digital editions. Moving forward, newspapers will protect their market position by being proactive in building their digital editions. Refer to the image in Figure 8.2 for details. The combination of hard copy and digital reaches a mass audience that makes them attractive to advertisers.

By the numbers, daily newspapers reach 40 percent of Canadian adults daily (weekdays). By region (Atlantic Canada, Quebec, Ontario, Prairies, and British Columbia) and by age in each region, readership does not vary significantly. There is, however, a tendency for readership to increase as a person's level of education and income increases. For example, readership is higher in households with post-secondary education.[5]

The trend toward digital consumption will continue, and ultimately the breadth of choices will have a negative impact on newspaper readership. The immediate challenge for the newspaper industry is to adjust their advertising revenue model so that new revenues from digital editions compensate for lost revenues on the hard copy side of the business.

For a summary of newspaper readership by key demographic variables, refer to Figure 8.3.

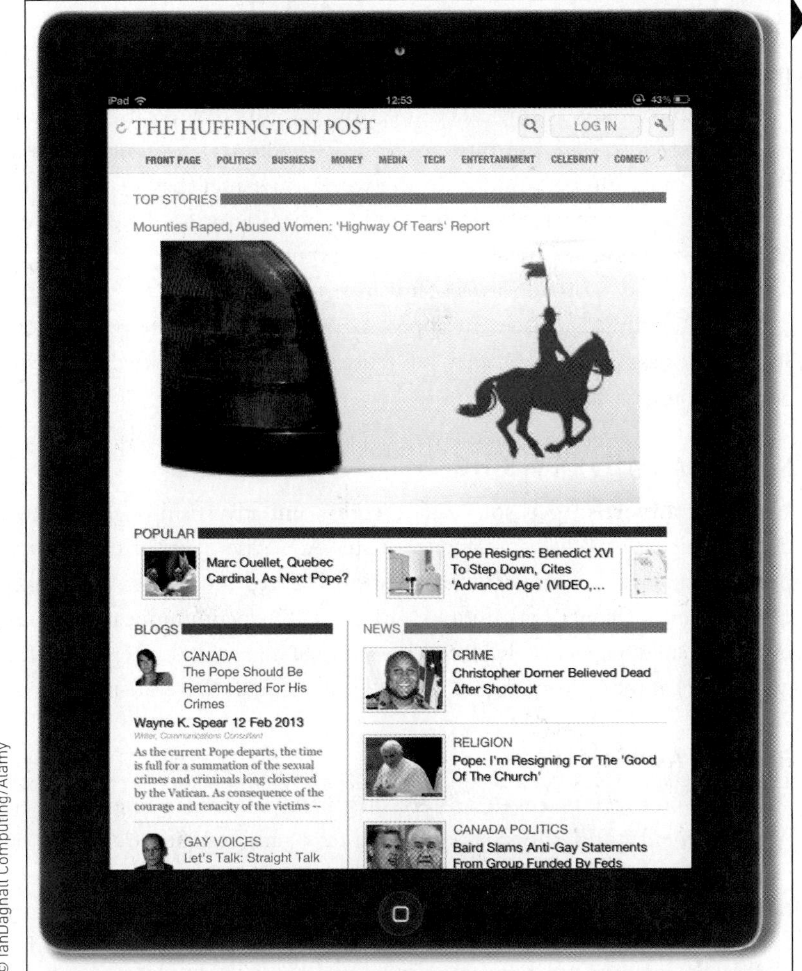

FIGURE 8.2

HUFFINGTON POST IN IPAD

More and more Canadians are accessing newspaper content through a variety of electronic devices.

FIGURE 8.3

Readership of daily newspapers by demographic characteristics: income and education

Source: 2013 NADbank Study. Digital includes PDF, APP and Website. Canadian Media Directors' Council *Media Digest*, 2014 – 15, p. 68.

	Print (Monday–Friday)		Digital (Weekly)	
Annual Household Income $	**%**	**Index to Population**	**%**	**Index to Population**
75 000+	50	104	63	133
50 000–75 000	23	98	20	83
30000–50 000	14	101	9	68
20 000–30 000	8	96	5	64
Under 20 000	6	79	3	42
Education—Highest Level				
University Grad+	37	108	53	152
Some Post-Secondary	35	97	33	91
High School Grad	18	99	10	57
Some High School	9	90	3	29

Types of Newspaper Advertising

Revenue generated by advertising has a significant impact on the viability of a newspaper. Consequently, advertising accounts for roughly 60 percent of newspaper space. Advertising layouts are put into position first; editorial content is then arranged around the advertising. On certain days of the week, the paper may be much thicker because of the addition of preprinted flyers inserted in the publication. Flyers and sponsored content (native advertising) are another source of revenue.

There are two broad forms of advertising: *display and classified*. **Display advertising** is defined as any advertisement appearing in any part of the publication, excluding the section of classified ads. Display advertising can be subdivided into two types: *national advertising* and *retail advertising*.

NATIONAL ADVERTISING

National advertising is sold to advertisers and advertising agencies by a national sales department or a media representative firm. Advertisements of this kind normally feature products or services marketed on a national or regional basis. For example, automotive manufacturers, financial institutions, airlines, and telecommunications companies advertise heavily in newspapers. Ads placed by national advertisers often include a **hooker** (also called a *tag*) at the bottom that identifies local retailers where the product can be purchased.

RETAIL ADVERTISING

As the name suggests, **retail advertising** involves advertisements placed in newspapers by department stores, supermarkets, drugstores, and restaurants, among others. Retail ads usually stress sale items and specials, or they re-advertise national brands that are carried by the retailer. Another important function of retail ads is the communication of store locations and hours of operation. Most daily newspapers have a sales department that is responsible for selling retail ad space.

CLASSIFIED ADVERTISING

Classified ads provide readers with opportunities to buy, sell, lease, rent, or obtain a variety of products and services such as jobs, houses, apartments, cars, recreational vehicles, and furniture. Publishers have shifted much of their classified advertising from the printed edition to the digital edition.

PREPRINTED INSERTS

Preprinted inserts, often referred to as **free-standing inserts** or *flyers*, are inserted into the fold of the newspaper and look like a separate, smaller section. Large users of inserts include supermarkets, department store chains, and automotive and hardware chains, to name a few.

While many advertisers do not perceive flyers to be a glamorous medium, Canadians rate flyers as their top source of local shopping information. A recent study revealed that 84 percent of Canadian adults check grocery store flyers before they shop, and 56 percent read digital flyers. The main driver for flyer consumption is value: 92 percent of adults look for sales in flyers.[6]

SPONSORED CONTENT

The increasingly fragmented media landscape has forced newspapers to introduce new methods for advertisers to deliver their message. The concept of *native advertising*

Photo by Keith J. Tuckwell

FIGURE 8.4

An illustration of sponsored content (on the right page), where advertising content looks similar to editorial content.

was introduced earlier in the text—newspapers have embraced this concept and now devote space to sponsored content. Typically, the content looks much like editorial content. While it is not intended to trick the reader in any way (it is clearly designated as "sponsored"), it is possible that readers do not know they are reading advertising material. Regardless, it is proving to be an effective way for advertisers to get their message delivered. An illustration of sponsored content appears in Figure 8.4.

Newspapers as an Advertising Medium

An advertiser must assess the use of newspapers in the context of the problem that advertising has to resolve and the objectives of a campaign. This section presents the case for selecting or rejecting newspapers for advertising purposes.

ADVANTAGES OF NEWSPAPERS

GEOGRAPHIC SELECTIVITY Newspapers serve a well-defined geographic area (town, city, trading zone), so they are attractive to local merchants. For the national advertiser, newspapers offer placement on a market-by-market basis. The advertiser can select specific newspaper markets or all the markets in a region. Therefore, newspaper advertising is useful for national advertisers following a key market media strategy.

Although predominantly local, Canada's largest daily illustrates how newspapers can expand coverage into regional markets. The *Toronto Star* has excellent penetration in trading zones surrounding metropolitan Toronto. Over the course of an entire week, the *Toronto Star* and thestar.com reach over 2.2 million people, or about 40 percent of the Toronto CMA (census metropolitan area). The digital edition of the *Star* reaches 957 000 readers.[7]

COVERAGE AND REACH Newspapers reach a broad cross-section of the adult population effectively. Current readership statistics show that newspapers reach 49 percent of men and 51 percent of women 18 years of age and over. The medium also offers high reach among all household income, occupation, and education groups. Readership increases proportionately with higher income, more education, and a more professional occupational status. For advertisers with loosely defined target market profiles, newspapers represent significant reach opportunity.

ENGAGEMENT Newspapers are an engaging medium—people devote a considerable amount of time to reading the paper, and they tend to consume it more carefully than other media such as radio or television. A study conducted by the Canadian Newspaper Association reveals that readers are distracted less while reading the newspaper. Although readership patterns (how a newspaper is read) vary among individuals, readers do tend to go through the entire paper. Such reading tendencies suggest a high possibility of exposure for products and services advertised there.[8]

FLEXIBILITY Newspapers provide several forms of flexibility. The newspaper is a medium in which ads can be placed with short lead times, say, two to three days. Therefore, it is a useful medium for reacting to unforeseen competitive activity. In terms of creative execution, an advertiser can take advantage of flexform advertising. **Flexform advertising** refers to an advertisement that does not conform to normal shapes. Editorial can intertwine with the ad in a variety of ways. Oddly shaped advertisements stand out from the clutter surrounding them.

CREATIVE AND MERCHANDISING CONSIDERATIONS Since newspapers are a closely read medium, and since there are many size options for ads, advertisers are able to present messages that include long copy or factual information (not the case with broadcast media). Also, newspapers offer merchandise tie-in opportunities, such as cooperative advertising with local distributors or ads containing coupons or other promotional incentives geared toward trial purchase or building loyalty. Newspapers are often referred to as the "sales action" medium since many ads carry incentive-oriented promotions that encourage purchase.

EDITORIAL SUPPORT Newspaper content can offer positive benefits to advertisers. For example, a luxury automobile ad that is targeted at business executives can be placed in an appropriate section of the newspaper—the business section. Similarly, an ad for a sports and recreation product could be seen by readers of the sports section. It should be noted, however, that requests for specific positions in the newspaper add to the costs of advertising. An advertiser must pay a position charge for specific page or location requests. Position charges are discussed in the media buying section of this chapter.

SUITABILITY FOR SMALL ADVERTISERS To retail advertisers, particularly local market independents, newspapers offer high reach and flexibility at relatively low cost compared to other media. Also, retailers lacking advertising expertise can draw upon the creative services of the newspaper, usually at no extra cost. Retailers and automobile dealers are among the largest local investors in newspaper advertising across Canada.

For insight into the effectiveness of newspapers as an advertising medium, read the Advertising in Action vignette **Newspapers Effective for Automobile Advertisers**.

ADVERTISING IN ACTION

Newspapers Effective for Automobile Advertisers

Newspapers have always been a "go to" medium for automobile manufacturers like General Motors, Ford, Chrysler, Toyota, and Honda. As well, their local market dealers use newspapers to announce sales and special offers on new and used cars. Now the combination of print editions and digital editions has combined to make the relationship between automobile advertisers and potential customers more significant.

Recent independent research conducted on behalf of Newspapers Canada among 2500 English and French Canadians, including 500 recent car buyers, tells a good tale about the impact of newspapers on the automobile buying decision process. Most importantly, it should be acknowledged that newspapers remain a primary medium for baby boomers, a target audience that remains the largest customer segment of car buyers.

The research concluded that newspapers' print and web properties are the "most impactful" media at each stage of the typical two-and-a-half month buying process—a process that includes research, website visits, dealer visits, and test drives. Eleven different media were measured in the study. Here are some key findings:

- 48 percent of new car buyers said they consulted print and web editions of newspapers, ahead of auto websites (28 percent), TV (24 percent), and magazines (23 percent).
- 36 percent of respondents said they used print and digital editions in the research process compared to websites (32 percent) and magazines (20 percent).
- 32 percent of respondents said newspapers triggered visits to manufacturer websites compared to magazines (24 percent) and TV (22 percent).
- Newspapers ranked first in triggering visits to a dealership.

Many automobile manufacturers are shifting advertising funds away from newspapers, following the consumer trends to digital media and social media. Based on this research, they may wish to reconsider. It seems an old standby—the print edition of a newspaper combined with the digital edition is an impactful combination. To further dramatize the point, 75 percent of people in the study said they read vehicle ads in print newspapers, compared to only 14 percent who read ads in social media. Food for thought!

Photo by Keith J. Tuckwell

Adapted from Chris Powell, "Newspapers Still Key in Automotive Path to Purchase," *Marketing*, January 21, 2015, www.marketingmag.ca.

DISADVANTAGES OF NEWSPAPERS

SHORT LIFESPAN "There is nothing as stale as yesterday's news." This phrase sums up any newspaper's biggest drawback—a short lifespan. A daily newspaper is around for only one day or less, so the likelihood for an advertisement to receive exposure is drastically reduced if the newspaper is not read on the day of distribution. To reach the audience, an ad may have to be placed several times during the week. In a digital environment, the situation is different. Readers tend to go back several times throughout the day, so there is an opportunity for multiple exposures to an advertisement.

LACK OF TARGET MARKET ORIENTATION Excluding newspapers like the *Globe and Mail* and the *National Post,* which have a more selective target market reach (a reach determined by demographics), newspapers in general reach a very broad cross-section of the population. Newspapers serve a purpose for advertisers using a shotgun strategy (mass reach). But advertisers wishing to reach a target market that is upscale in income, occupation, or education must recognize that newspaper advertising will reach many who are not in the target market, resulting in wasteful spending of an advertising budget.

CLUTTER **Clutter** is the extent to which a publication's pages are fragmented into small blocks of advertising or editorial. Therefore, making an ad stand out to make an impression on the reader is a challenging creative task. The inclusion of advertising inserts on certain days compounds the clutter problem, as does the hasty manner in which some people read newspapers. Colour will increase an ad's attention-grabbing ability, but colour is an added cost.

POOR REPRODUCTION QUALITY Advertisers can compare newspapers with magazines on any number of points. With respect to quality of print reproduction, however, newspapers compare very poorly. Detracting from the quality of the print production in newspapers are the speed of the printing presses and the poor quality of newsprint. Newer, technically advanced offset presses are improving the quality of reproduction, particularly for colour ads, but it is not magazine-standard quality.

HIGH COST Placing newspaper ads in local markets is relatively inexpensive for local market advertisers, but for national advertisers that want to advertise in a lengthy list of daily newspaper markets, the costs can escalate quickly. Advertisers wanting to expand their reach nationally by using daily newspapers in key urban markets need to be selective in the number of markets where they advertise. The budget available dictates the extent of complementary key market coverage.

Buying Newspaper Space

Historically, newspaper space has always been sold on the basis of agate lines. **Agate line** is the standard measurement unit for most newspapers; there are 14 agate lines per inch of depth. Width is generally measured in columns, which vary by newspaper. The combination of agates, depth, and width is used to calculate the actual size of a newspaper ad.

The basic procedure for buying newspaper space is to determine the size of the ad in agate lines. The cost is calculated by multiplying the width of the ad (number of columns) by the depth of the ad (inches of depth). Other factors that influence costs include the number of insertions, creative considerations such as the use of colour, and position charges, if applicable. The following section includes some examples of how to calculate the costs of newspaper advertising.

Some newspapers have moved away from the agate line system and are selling ads by standardized sizes (e.g., half-page vertical, one-third page, quarter-page horizontal). Refer to Figure 8.5 for a visual illustration of some size options. A dollar cost is associated with the various sizes of ads a newspaper offers. From a cost calculation perspective, this system is easier to work with. The *Toronto Star*, *National Post*, *Edmonton Journal*, and many other newspapers have moved to this system.

The *Globe and Mail* now offers some very creative formats for advertisers wanting to get noticed in a cluttered environment. Such unique names as centre pillar, bookends, and upside down T-spread suggest the format an ad will appear in. Ads like these require uniquely designed creative.

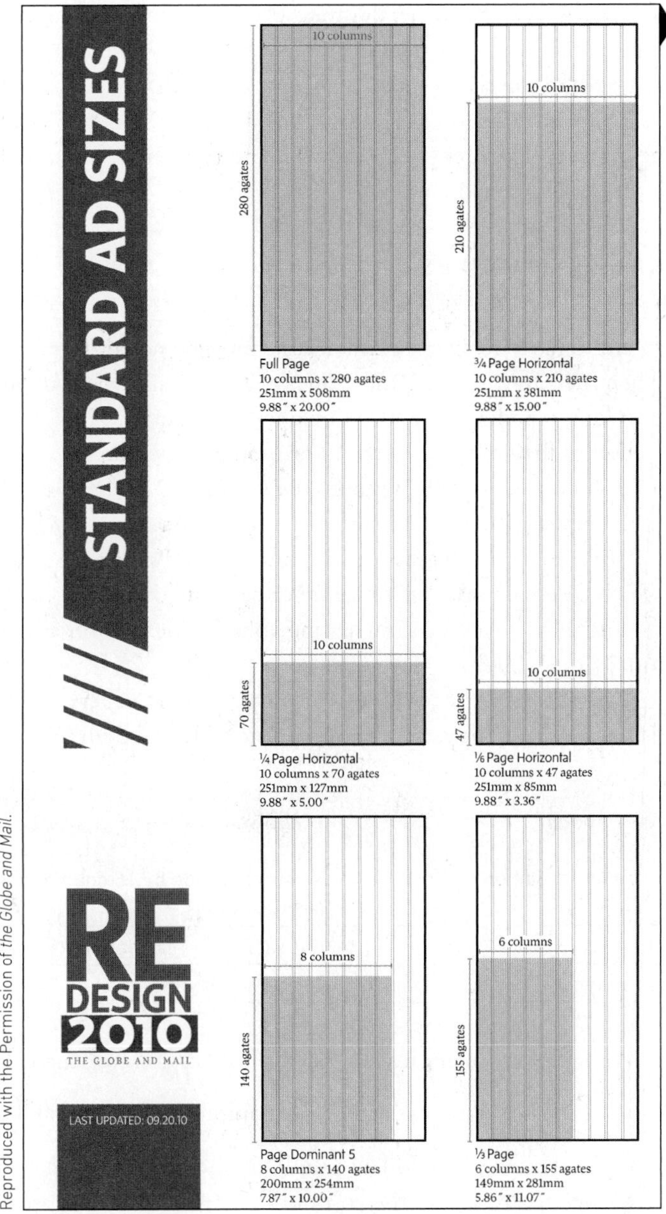

FIGURE 8.5

A selection of standard ad sizes available in newspapers. There are many others for an advertiser to consider.

DETERMINING SPACE SIZE

For the sake of example, let's assume that space is being purchased in agate lines. The size of the ad is 6 columns wide by 8 column inches deep. Considering that each column inch of depth equals 14 agate lines, the size of the ad would be calculated with the following formula:

$$\text{Number of columns wide} \times \text{inches of depth} \times 14$$
$$6 \times 8 \times 14 = 672 \text{ agate lines}$$

If the size of the advertisement were 4 columns wide by 12 inches deep, the size of the ad in agate lines would be:

$$4 \times 12 \times 14 = 672 \text{ lines}$$

These two examples illustrate that different configurations of ads (combinations of width and depth) can produce the same size of ad in terms of space occupied and rates charged for the space.

If an advertiser were to place the ad with the newspaper 12 times, it would actually be buying 8064 lines (672 × 12). The newspaper would likely have a discounted line rate (cost per line) for such a buy.

RATE SCHEDULES

Line rate is defined as the advertising rate charged by newspapers for one agate line. With regard to rate schedules, several factors must be noted. First, rates charged by line go down when the advertiser buys more lines over a specified period. Second, costs for the addition of colour or preferred positions are quoted separately. Third, the line rates can vary from one section of the paper to another. For example, the line rates for advertisers in the *Globe and Mail*'s News, Report on Business, and Globe T.O. sections are higher than for other sections of the newspaper. More highly read sections command a higher price for advertising.

In the chart in Figure 8.6, the rates quoted start with a **transient rate** (or *casual rate*), which is defined as a one-time rate or base rate that applies to casual advertisers. Discounts are offered to advertisers purchasing volume lineage over a more extended period of time, usually one year.

To illustrate how costs are calculated in newspapers, let's develop a hypothetical plan using the agate line rates for the *Globe and Mail* shown in Figure 8.6.

Newspaper	*Globe and Mail*—News Section
Size of Ad/Edition	4 columns wide by 10 column inches deep, News Section of Metro edition
Rate	Casual Rate—Transient Rate
Frequency	Once (Monday)

The first calculation would determine, as follows, the total number of agate lines:

4 columns wide × 10 column inches deep × 14 = 560 lines

The next step would be to multiply the number of agate lines by the line rate by the frequency to determine the cost of the insertion. In this case, the casual rate would apply because there are not enough lines to earn a discount:

560 × $25.18 × 1 = $14 100.80

Advertisers earn discounted line rates when they commit to an annual dollar volume with the newspaper. For example, assume an advertiser commits to $150 000. At that level, the line rate for the Metro edition of the *Globe and Mail* drops to $19.52 if the ads are placed in the News, Business, or T.O. sections. Therefore, if the dollar commitment is divided by the line rate ($150 000/$19.52), the advertiser can place ads in various sizes totalling about 7684 lines. From the previous example, the total line space was 560 lines for one ad, which means that the ad could run 14 times for a total of 7840 lines. This lineage earns the discounted line rate and on a dollar basis is just over the $150 000 discount plateau. The revised calculation would be as follows:

560 × 14 × $19.52 = $153 036.80

National Rates

2015 GLOBE MEDIA KIT **NEWSPAPER | NATIONAL**

APRIL 8, 2015

FULL PAGE = 2,800 LINES (10 COLUMNS X 280 LINES)

ALL RATES ARE GROSS

NEWS, REPORT ON BUSINESS, GLOBE T.O.

	MONDAY TO FRIDAY			SATURDAY		
	NATIONAL	CENTRAL (ON/PQ)	METRO	NATIONAL	CENTRAL (ON/PQ)	METRO
Transient	$31.88	$27.42	$25.18	$35.06	$30.16	$27.71
$15,000	27.91	24.00	22.04	30.69	26.38	24.24
$25,000	27.09	23.32	21.40	29.81	25.63	23.54
$50,000	26.30	22.62	20.78	28.94	24.88	22.85
$100,000	25.51	21.93	20.16	28.06	24.13	22.15
$150,000	24.70	21.26	19.52	27.18	23.38	21.48
$250,000	23.91	20.56	18.89	26.30	22.62	20.78
$350,000	22.96	19.75	18.14	25.26	21.72	19.94
$500,000	21.99	18.92	17.37	24.18	20.81	19.13
$750,000	21.03	18.09	16.61	23.14	19.91	18.29
$1,000,000	20.08	17.27	15.87	22.09	19.00	17.45
$1,500,000	19.14	16.46	15.12	21.03	18.09	16.61
$2,000,000	18.17	15.63	14.37	19.97	17.19	15.80
$2,500,000	17.22	14.80	13.61	18.94	16.29	14.95

NEWS
Daily All editions

ROB
Daily National

GLOBE T.O.
Saturday Metro

COLOUR

MONDAY TO SATURDAY	NATIONAL	CENTRAL	METRO
HALF PAGE PLUS	$10,697	$9,727	$8,950
LESS THAN HALF PAGE	$8,557	$7,782	$6,846

REAL ESTATE, TRAVEL, DRIVE

	MONDAY TO FRIDAY			SATURDAY		
	NATIONAL	CENTRAL (ON/PQ)	METRO	NATIONAL	CENTRAL (ON/PQ)	METRO
Transient	$19.77	$17.00	$15.62	$21.73	$18.70	$17.18
$15,000	17.29	14.86	13.75	19.02	16.36	15.03
$25,000	16.80	14.44	13.27	18.48	15.89	14.60
$50,000	16.31	14.04	12.88	17.94	15.42	14.17
$100,000	15.81	13.61	12.50	17.39	14.95	13.74
$150,000	15.32	13.18	12.11	16.85	14.48	13.31
$250,000	14.82	12.74	11.70	16.31	14.04	12.88
$350,000	14.23	12.74	11.24	15.65	13.45	12.36
$500,000	13.64	11.74	10.78	15.00	12.90	11.85
$750,000	13.05	11.22	10.30	14.36	12.34	11.33
$1,000,000	12.46	10.71	9.83	13.69	11.79	10.82
$1,500,000	11.86	10.20	9.36	13.05	11.22	10.30
$2,000,000	11.26	9.69	8.90	12.38	10.66	9.80
$2,500,000	10.69	9.17	8.44	11.75	10.10	9.27

REAL ESTATE
Friday Metro

TRAVEL
Tuesday in Life & Arts, National and Metro
Saturday National, Central and Metro

DRIVE
Thursday Metro

COLOUR

MONDAY TO SATURDAY	NATIONAL	CENTRAL (ON/PQ)	METRO
HALF PAGE PLUS	$8,557	$7,782	$6,846
LESS THAN HALF PAGE	$6,846	$6,846	$5,477

THE GLOBE AND MAIL Media Group

tel 1.800.387.9012 email advertising@globeandmail.com or globelink.ca/newspaper 4

FIGURE 8.6

Globe and Mail rate card

Advertising Information

2015 GLOBE MEDIA KIT **NEWSPAPER | NATIONAL**
APRIL 8, 2015

COLOUR MANDITORY POSITIONS

Certain positions are colour mandatory. Please contact your Globe and Mail representative for more details.

PREMIUM STOCK SURCHARGE

$5,000 net per page except for Globe Style.

- The Front News section is wrapped in semi-gloss premium stock Monday through Saturday.
- These pages feature our front banner, page 2, inside back cover (IBC) and outside back cover (OBC) advertising positions.
- The Globe Style (Saturday) section is printed on our semi-gloss premium stock.

ADDITIONAL INFORMATION

- Double Trucks: Gutter is charged as full column.
- Regional material changes: $579 per split. Not available in Report on Business, Style, Books or Careers.
- Position charge: +25 per cent.
- Front News Banner: +50 per cent.
- Page 3, News: +40 per cent.
- Front Report on Business banner: +25 per cent.
- Pages 2 & 3, Report on Business: +40 per cent.
- Floating Banners: +50 per cent.
- Charge for Globe and Mail box number: $100.
- Charge for affidavits: $100.
- Cancellation charge: 50 per cent for ads cancelled after deadline. No cancellations accepted the day prior to publication.
- The Publisher shall not be liable for errors in advertisements beyond the actual space paid. No liability for non-insertions of any advertisement.
- There is a $100 production charge for ads under 50 MAL that are not camera-ready.

ADVERTISING SPECIFICATIONS

10 Columns, 9.88" wide x 20" deep

Column depth: 280 modular agate lines for full page ads (2,800 lines per 10 column page)

For complete layout, mechanical and digital specifications, please visit **globelink.ca/adformats**

PLEASE NOTE: Before booking any advertising, please review our terms and conditions available from **globelink.ca/mediakits**

CONTACT INFORMATION

TORONTO ONTARIO & MANITOBA
advertising@globeandmail.com
TOLL FREE 1.800.387.9012

WESTERN CANADA
advertisingwesternca@globeandmail.com
ALBERTA & SASKATCHEWAN
1.403.245.4987 or 1.403.774.8024
BRITISH COLUMBIA 1.800.663.1311
NORTHWEST TERRITORIES & NUNAVUT
1.604.685.0308

EASTERN CANADA
OTTAWA REGION, QUÉBEC & ATLANTIC CANADA
advertisingeasternca@globeandmail.com
TOLL FREE 1.800.363.7526

UNITED STATES, INTERNATIONAL
globeandmail@publicitas.com
TOLL FREE 1.212.946.0219

GLOBELINK.CA/NEWSPAPER
CONTACT DIRECTORY globelink.ca/contactdirectory

tel 1.800.387.9012 email advertising@globeandmail.com or globelink.ca/newspaper 9

FIGURE 8.6

Continued

FIGURE 8.7

Illustrations of calculating newspaper advertising rates

Refer to the rate card in Figure 8.6. The transient line rate was used in each calculation. The following illustrations consider two aspects of newspaper buying: the addition of colour and requesting specific locations.

ILLUSTRATION 1—ADDITION OF COLOUR

Newspaper:	*Globe and Mail* Metro Edition, News section
Size of Ad:	6 columns wide by 8 column inches deep
Colour:	All ads are full colour
Frequency:	4 insertions (Monday–Friday)

The cost calculation would be:

Total Number of Lines

$(6 \times 8 \times 14) \times 4 = 2688$ lines

Cost of the Ad (in black and white)

$2688 \times \$25.18 = \$67\ 683.84$

Additional Cost for Colour

$\$8950 \times 4 = \$35\ 800$

Total Cost

$\$67\ 683.84 + \$35\ 800 = \$103\ 483.84$

ILLUSTRATION 2—POSITION REQUEST

Newspaper:	*Globe and Mail* National Edition
Size of Ad:	3 columns wide by 8 column inches deep
Colour:	Black and white
Frequency:	6 insertions (Monday–Friday)
Location Request:	Page 3, News section

The cost calculation would be as follows:

Total Number of Lines

$(3 \times 8 \times 14) \times 6 = 2016$ lines

Cost of Ad

$2016 \times \$31.88 = \$64\ 270.08$

Position Charge (add 40%)

$\$64\ 270.08 \times 1.40 = \$89\ 978.11$

If the advertiser has only $150 000 to spend, one option would be to marginally reduce the size of the ad so there are fewer total lines. For additional illustrations of how to calculate costs, refer to Figure 8.7.

Advertisers who commit to a certain dollar figure are billed at the corresponding line rate during the year. If the advertiser does not meet that dollar volume by the end of the contract period, the line rates would be adjusted appropriately. The advertiser would actually owe the newspaper some money.

RATES BASED ON DESCRIPTIVE SIZES

Advertising rates for some newspapers are quoted based on size and are described by such terms as double-page spread, full page, ½ double page, ½ half-page horizontal, and so on. The rate cards establish a cost for each size. With reference to the rate card in Figure 8.8, the cost of a black-and-white ½ double page ad, Monday to Thursday, is $25 000.

FIGURE 8.8

Newspaper rate card based on standard ad sizes

This rate card has been created to demonstrate to the reader the key factors that influence a newspaper media buy in newspapers that sell space based on standard-sized ad spaces.

Newspaper Rate Card Standard Advertising Units		
Ad Size	**Black-and-White Transient Rates Monday–Friday**	**Colour Net Rates**
Double-Page Spread	$50 000	$7500
Full Page	$23 500	$3750
½ Double Page	$25 000	$6000
¾ Page	$18 100	$3750
½ Page H or V	$11 750	$2625
¼ page H or V	$ 5875	$2250
⅛ Page	$ 2950	$1875
Volume Discount Schedule		
Net Contract Level		**Discount**
$ 25 000		25%
$ 50 000		27%
$100 000		30%
$300 000		32%
$500 000		35%

Additional Information

- Rates are based on standard ad sizes. Other sizes may be available
- Discounts only apply to black-and-white rates
- Weekend rates are quoted separately and will vary based on circulation increases or decreases

A ½ half-page horizontal ad costs $11 750. Therefore, if an advertiser ran two ads in each size, the cost calculation would be as follows:

½ double page: $25 000 × 2 = $50 000
½ page horizontal: $11 750 × 2 = $23 500
Total Cost = $73 500

The rate card shows volume discounts based on the dollar value of the space purchased. In the example above, the advertiser would qualify for a 27 percent discount. Therefore, the net cost calculation would be:

Gross Cost = $73 500
Less Discount: $73 500 × .27 = $19 845
Net Cost = $53 655

POSITION CHARGES

Since a disadvantage of newspaper advertising is clutter, advertisers and agencies normally request positions in the newspaper that are deemed to be favourable. The request may be for a particular section, or it could be for the first few pages of the newspaper. To keep advertisers satisfied, a newspaper will do its best to accommodate requests, but there are no guarantees that requests will be honoured.

The privilege of having a preferred position in a newspaper comes at a higher cost—that cost is referred to as a **position charge**. The position charge is normally quoted as a percentage increase over the insertion cost. Referring to the *Globe and Mail's* rate card (the second page of the rate card in Figure 8.6), we see that position requests start with a 25 percent additional charge, and specific page requests can add 40 to 50 percent to the cost of the insertion. The advertiser usually justifies the additional expense of a position request by referring to the improved recognition and recall that will result from the better position.

Newspaper publishers reserve the right to place advertisements at their discretion, unless a preferred position charge is paid. The placing of advertisements anywhere within the regular printed pages of a newspaper is referred to as **ROP (run of press** or **run of paper)**.

COLOUR CHARGES

Although newspapers are often referred to as the black-and-white medium, colour is available to advertisers willing to pay for it. Colour charges are normally quoted on the basis of spot colour or full colour. With reference to the *Globe and Mail*'s rate schedule in Figure 8.6, the addition of full colour in the national edition for an ad larger than ½ page will add $10 697 to the cost of the ad. If the ad is less than ½ page, the additional cost is $8557. Usually there is a minimum size requirement for ads appearing in full colour. Refer to Figure 8.7 for cost examples that include colour and position charges.

When deciding to use colour or not, the advertiser must weigh the potential impact of colour on the reader against the additional cost. Much research has been done on the impact of colour in newspaper advertising. The research finds that full colour draws readers to ads (noted scores are higher) and keeps them more involved in the message. Colour has more of an impact on readers than does the size of the ad.[9]

PREPRINTED INSERTS

Preprinted **inserts**, such as advertising flyers for supermarkets and department stores, are inserted into and distributed by most newspapers. Costs are usually quoted on a CPM (cost per thousand) basis, with rates increasing as pages are added. For example, an 8-page insert in the *Toronto Star* has a CPM of $56.50, while a 24-page insert has a CPM of $67.00.[10] The CPM is multiplied by the circulation (in thousands) to arrive at total cost. Assuming the circulation of the *Toronto Star* is 360 500, the cost of an 8-page insert would be $20 368.25 ($56.50 × 360.5).

DIGITAL NEWSPAPER ADVERTISING

The digital editions of newspapers also offer numerous advertising alternatives. Banner ads are the most commonly used type of advertising. Banners are available in a variety of sizes and different degrees of animation and motion. Video-style ads are also available. The costs of banner ads are quoted on a CPM (cost per thousand) basis and consider the number of impressions (or exposures) the advertiser commits to. Sponsored content opportunities are also available. Clicking on a sponsored banner ad will lead the reader to a feature article by a sponsor organization. The cost calculations for digital advertising are explained in detail in Chapter 12.

INSERTION ORDERS

Details of a newspaper ad are communicated via an insertion order. The **insertion order** specifies pertinent details, including the size of the ad, the dates of its insertion, use of colour, position requests, and the line rate to be charged. Closing dates and cancellation dates may also be included.

To verify that an advertisement actually ran, the agency or the advertiser receives a tear sheet from the newspaper. As the name implies, a **tear sheet** is an ad that the newspaper personnel extract from the newspaper to illustrate to the advertiser how it actually appeared. Should there be any problems with the ad, such as poor production quality, the advertiser or agency might request a **make good**, a rerun of an ad at the publisher's expense.

COMPARING NEWSPAPERS FOR EFFICIENCY

In larger metropolitan markets, where several newspapers compete for advertising revenue, advertisers must decide which papers to place advertising with. If using a shotgun strategy, the advertiser may use all newspapers. Conversely, if budgets are limited and target markets are more precisely defined, the advertiser may be more selective in the decision-making process.

Since the circulations and the costs of advertising (line rates) vary among newspapers, the advertiser must have a way of comparing the alternatives. To make this comparison, the advertiser may use a standard figure called the CPM. **CPM** is the actual cost of reaching 1000 readers in a market. The formula for calculating CPM is as follows:

$$\text{CPM} = \frac{\text{Unit Cost of Message}}{\text{Circulation (in thousands)}}$$

To illustrate the concept of CPM, consider that advertisers wanting to reach adults in the Edmonton market would choose between two daily newspapers. See Figure 8.9 for specific details of how the newspapers are compared.

As shown in Figure 8.9, the newspaper CPM is strictly a quantitative figure and the results vary considerably. If the advertiser's decision regarding which newspaper to use were based solely on this principle, the decision would be an easy one—the *Ottawa Sun* has the lower CPM of the two newspapers. However, its reach among adult readers is much lower than that of the *Ottawa Citizen*. Not shown in a CPM calculation is the demographic profile of the readers of the two newspapers. The *Ottawa Citizen* reader and the *Ottawa Sun* reader are different. Since both of these newspapers offer mass appeal to a broad cross-section of the Ottawa population, an advertiser would be wise to include both in the media mix.

In summary, CPM is a quantitative figure that fluctuates with changes in the line rate or circulation: the higher the circulation, the lower the CPM. Advertisers can use it as a base guideline for comparing the varying cost efficiencies of specific newspapers that reach a mass target market.

FIGURE 8.9

Comparison of newspapers based on CPM: cost of reaching 1000 people

Specifications	*Ottawa Citizen*	*Ottawa Sun*
Ad Size (lines)	900	900
Line Cost	$9.09	$2.65
Ad Cost (rate × lines)	$8181	$2385
Circulation	110 173	41 297
CPM	$74.23	$57.75

Analysis: The CPM for the *Ottawa Sun* is lower than the *Ottawa Citizen*, so it is a cost-efficient choice. However, the absolute reach of the *Ottawa Sun* is low compared to the *Ottawa Citizen*. To expand reach among adults in the Ottawa market, both newspapers would likely be used.

Source: Line rates obtained from the 2015 display rate cards for each newspaper. Circulation data from Canadian Media Directors' Council *Media Digest*, 2014–15. p. 69.

Magazines in Canada

Currently, almost 1300 consumer magazines are published and distributed in Canada. It seems there is a publication for every conceivable interest. As well, some 700 business magazines are in circulation covering a wide variety of industries and business interests. Magazines are classified in many ways—by content and audience reached, by circulation, by frequency of publication, and by size and format.

CONTENT AND AUDIENCE REACHED

In terms of content and audience reached, publications fall into two major categories: consumer magazines and business magazines. Both categories include general interest and special interest publications. In both consumer and business magazines, the content is such that it has high interest among a precisely defined target market.

CONSUMER MAGAZINES *Canadian Advertising Rates & Data* indexes 50 subclassifications of consumer magazines, with the classification based on the publication's content and audience. There is a strong base of general interest magazines, as well as a host of specialized classifications such as art and antiques, children's, entertainment, hobbies, sports and recreation, and women's. Popular, high-circulation magazines in their respective categories include *Reader's Digest* (general interest), *Maclean's* (news and current events), *Chatelaine* (women's), *Flare* (fashion), and *Canadian House & Home* (decor).

BUSINESS MAGAZINES Business magazines can be broadly subdivided into subject areas such as trade, industry, professional, and institutional. Subclassifications of these general areas include broadcasting, engineering, construction, food and food processing, hardware trade, hotels and restaurants, photography, and telecommunications. Business publications tend to be very specialized, their content appealing to a particular industry, trade, or professional group. With a very well-defined target audience, such specialized publications allow an efficient use of media dollars by advertisers.

Business magazines can also be classified as horizontal or vertical. A **horizontal publication** appeals to people who occupy the same level of responsibility in a business—the senior management level, for example. Horizontal publications tend to be more general in content, dealing with subjects such as business issues and trends, finance and marketing, and effective business management principles. Examples of horizontal business publications are *Canadian Business*, *Report on Business Magazine*, and *Financial Post Magazine.* Also classified as horizontal are those publications aimed at people who have functions in their companies similar to those discussed in the magazine. A magazine such as *Modern Purchasing* would be directed at the purchasing managers and agents in any number of industries.

Vertical publications appeal to all levels of people in the same industry. All specialized classifications and corresponding magazines fall into this category. *Canadian Grocer*, for example, appeals to those people employed in the food processing and food distribution business in Canada, while *Foodservice and Hospitality* appeals to those employed in the restaurant, hotel, or food service industry.

CIRCULATION BASE (DISTRIBUTION)

Some Canadian magazines are distributed on the basis of **paid circulation**, which refers to subscriptions and newsstand sales. Magazines such as *Maclean's*, *Chatelaine*, *Flare*, and *Canadian Business* are paid-circulation magazines and rely on subscriptions, newsstand sales, and advertising space to generate revenue.

Some magazines are distributed on the basis of **controlled circulation**. In this case the magazine is distributed free to a predetermined target market (e.g., a target defined by demographic segment, geographic area, or job function). A controlled-circulation magazine generates revenue from advertising space only. Typically, receivers of the magazine are in a unique position to influence sales, so they are attractive to advertisers. *CAA Magazine* is an example of a controlled-circulation magazine. It is mailed to 1.6 million members of the Canadian Automobile Association (CAA) four times a year.

FREQUENCY OF PUBLICATION AND REGIONAL EDITIONS

The frequency of publication varies considerably from one magazine to another. The most common frequencies are monthly and weekly. To illustrate, *Chatelaine* and *Canadian Living* publish monthly, and *Maclean's* publishes weekly. Many popular magazines offer regional editions to meet an advertiser's geographic needs. *Maclean's* publishes 10 regional editions, and *Chatelaine* offers seven regional editions, including one edition that reaches only five key urban markets: Toronto, Montreal, Vancouver, Edmonton, and Calgary. French editions of many publications serve the Quebec market. *L'actualité* and *Châtelaine* are good examples.

SIZE AND FORMAT

Canadian magazines are published in three distinct sizes: digest, standard, and larger size. Owing to the rising costs of production, mailing, and distribution, there is currently a trend toward smaller publications.

A *digest-size* magazine's approximate dimensions are 5 ½ inches × 7 ¼ inches (14 cm × 18.4 cm) with a two-column printing format. *Reader's Digest/Sélection du Reader's Digest* is a good example of this type of format. The dimensions of a *standard-size* magazine are 8 inches × 11 inches (20.3 cm × 27.9 cm) with a three-column format. Among the popular magazines that appear in this size and format are *Maclean's*, *Chatelaine*, *Canadian Business*, and *Canadian Geographic.*

MAGAZINE CIRCULATION AND READERSHIP HIGHLIGHTS

As with newspapers, the consumer shift to online reading has affected the circulation and readership of hardcopy magazines. Magazine space is sold to advertisers on the basis of circulation and readership. The drop in circulation has had a negative impact on revenue. Despite a drop in circulation, though, readership remains healthy.

Vividata collects data over a two-year period that tracks readership information, which is cross-referenced with other information such as product and brand usage and lifestyle information. Advertisers use this information to select the right magazines to advertise in. The latest data from Vividata reveal that three-quarters of Canadians read a magazine in the past three months, each magazine issue is read by an average of five people, and readers spend an average of 49 minutes with a magazine.[11]

Wise managers will look at both circulation and readership when making decisions. It is possible that a magazine with a lower circulation has more readers per copy than a magazine with higher circulation, resulting in a higher readership level. **Readers per copy** is the average number of people who read a single issue of a publication. For example, *Reader's Digest* has a circulation of 480 000 and 10.1 readers per copy, for a total monthly readership of 4 869 000. It has more readers than any other magazine in Canada.[12]

The circulation of magazines in Canada is audited by the Alliance for Audited Media (AAM). AAM issues standardized statements, referred to as *publisher's statements*, verifying circulation statistics for paid-circulation magazines and some daily newspapers in Canada.

FIGURE 8.10

Circulation and readership of selected magazines

In their respective classifications, each of these magazines competes for advertisers. Advertisers use circulation and readership data to determine which magazines to select and with what frequency. Readers per copy data are compiled from an annual research study conducted by the Print Measurement Bureau.

Classification/ Magazine	Average Circulation	Readers per Copy	Total Readership
BUSINESS			
Canadian Business	64 000	11.6	757 000
Financial Post Magazine	159 000	5.8	924 000
Report on Business Magazine	265 000	4.0	1 056 000
WOMEN'S			
Canadian Living	520 000	7.0	3 621 000
Chatelaine	524 000	5.6	2 945 000
Châtelaine (Fr.)	170 000	5.0	849 000
Elle Canada	132 000	11.7	1 538 000

Analysis: Although the circulation of *Canadian Business* is much lower than that of the other two business magazines, the number of readers per copy is much higher. *Canadian Business* compares favourably with *Report on Business Magazine* and *Financial Post Magazine* in readers reached. *Canadian Living*'s circulation is marginally lower than *Chatelaine*'s, but it has more readers per copy, resulting in a higher readership. Both magazines are viable options for advertisers. Similar comparisons can be made in other classifications of magazines.

Source: Adapted from data reported in Canadian Media Directors' Council, *Media Digest*, 2014–15, pp. 80–81

A **publisher's statement** includes the average paid circulation for the past six months, new and renewal subscriptions, and a geographic analysis of **total paid circulation**. The audited statements show a decline in hardcopy circulation; magazine readers now seek content online. Most magazines now offer digital editions available on websites, tablets, and mobile devices.

Digital magazine readership is increasing and now accounts for about 10 percent of circulation. To lessen the impact of dwindling print readership, Rogers Communications offers a service called Texture (formerly Next Issue) that bundles all of its publications' digital editions into one subscription. Each download of a magazine title counts toward its single-copy sales number, resulting in significant increases in single-copy sales.

For a summary of circulation and readership data for a selection of magazines, refer to Figure 8.10. In each of the classifications in Figure 8.10, the magazines listed compete with each other for advertisers. How efficient they are at reaching the target is an important influence on which magazines an advertiser chooses.

Magazines as an Advertising Medium

Magazines offer advertisers a unique set of advantages and disadvantages. This section presents some of the strategic considerations for using or rejecting magazines for advertising purposes.

ADVANTAGES OF MAGAZINES

TARGET MARKET SELECTIVITY Magazines are often referred to as being a "class" medium rather than a "mass" medium. Both consumer magazines and business magazines have target audiences that are well defined by some combination of demographic and psychographic variables. Therefore, advertisers with well-defined target markets can select specific magazines by using a profile-matching strategy (i.e., by selecting magazines whose audience closely matches the product's target market).

GEOGRAPHIC FLEXIBILITY Numerous high-circulation consumer magazines offer regional editions. An advertiser wishing to advertise in a certain area, such as the Prairies or the Atlantic provinces, can make use of the flexibility offered by regional editions—provided, of course, that the regional readership is similar to the advertiser's target market. Regional editions also provide advertisers with the opportunity to increase spending in certain geographic areas on an as-needed basis. Canada's more popular magazines, such as *Maclean's, Canadian Living, Chatelaine*, and *Reader's Digest,* offer regional editions.

LIFESPAN Because of the relative infrequency (in comparison to newspapers) of magazine publication (weekly, biweekly, monthly), the advertiser gets the benefit of longevity. Magazines remain in the home and are read intermittently over a period of time; hence, readers are exposed to an advertisement several times during the lifespan of the magazine (which means that the product gets repeat exposure at no extra cost).

ENGAGEMENT Magazines are purchased and read because the editorial content interests the reader. Some research studies show an overwhelming percentage of readers pay full or complete attention when reading magazines. Magazine readers demonstrate the lowest level of multitasking when compared with multitasking rates for other media. An advertiser will benefit from the prestige of the magazine and the quality it represents, and from the attention shown by readers while reading.

QUALITY OF REPRODUCTION Magazines are printed on high-quality paper by means of a four-colour process that creates a high-calibre, attractive presentation of both editorial and advertising content. Recent innovations, such as bright metallic inks that create a striking visual effect, have added to the quality of reproduction. Ads always look good in a magazine.

CREATIVE CONSIDERATIONS Magazines offer some flexibility in creative strategy and execution. For example, most magazines offer gatefolds (multiple-page fold outs), double-page spreads, and French doors on covers (an ad that folds out from the middle of the cover). Other unique options include fragrance strips, scratch and sniff, and tip-ins and glue-ons (for distributing product samples). Although the use of such options may increase the cost of advertising, the resulting distinction and potential impact on the reader may justify the additional expense. See Figure 8.11 for an illustration.

PASS-ALONG READERSHIP Magazine space is sold to advertisers at costs that are based not only on the magazine's circulation but also on the number of readers it reaches. As well as being exposed to its primary readers, a magazine may be exposed to other readers. A **primary reader** is a person who qualifies as a reader because he or she lives (works) in the household (office) where the publication is initially received. Additional readers, called **pass-along readers**, are those who do not live (work) in the household (office) where the publication is originally received. The combination of primary readers and pass-along readers equals *total readership.*

The Canadian Tourism Commission (now known as Destination Canada) launched a multimedia campaign in 2010 to stimulate foreign travel to Canada as well as domestic travel. A magazine component played a key role in raising interest in little-known local

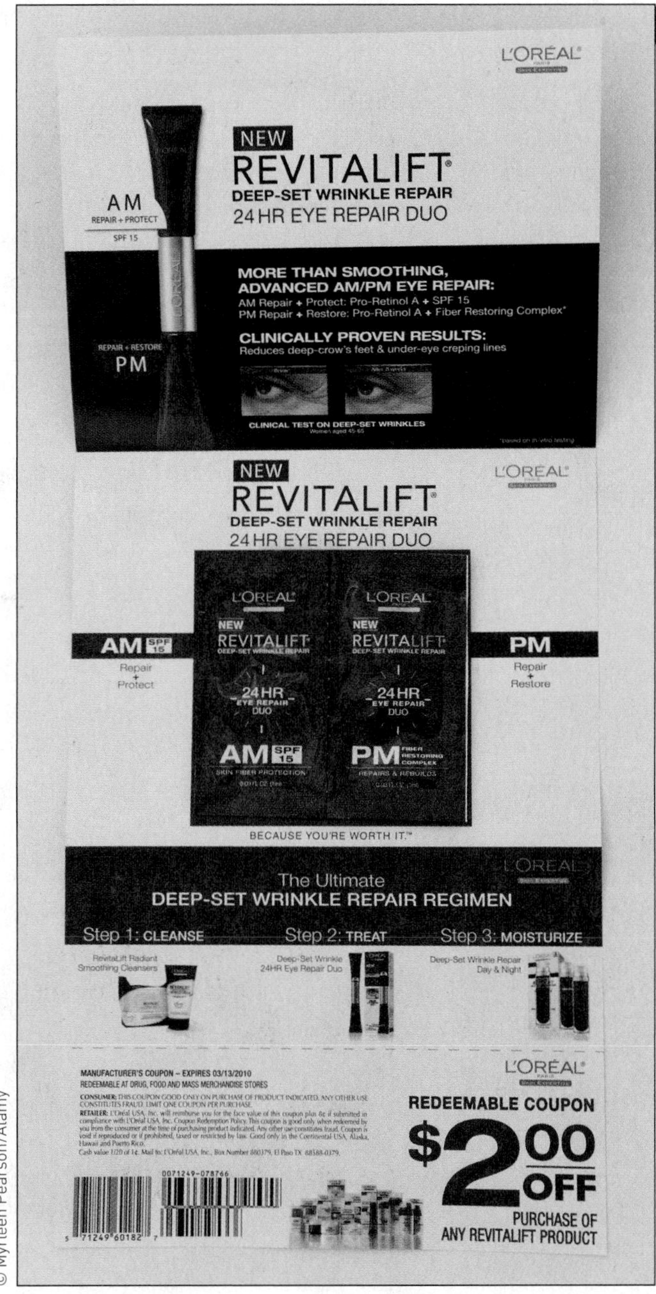

FIGURE 8.11

An insert (tip-in) in a magazine that includes a sample of the product

tourist attractions. The ads tempted people to figure out where the attraction was located. For insight into this campaign, see the Advertising in Action vignette **Discovering Canada**.

DISADVANTAGES OF MAGAZINES

LEAD TIME The layout of a monthly magazine is planned well in advance of the issue date, so an advertiser must prepare the advertisement long before the magazine goes to press. For a weekly magazine, an average of four weeks is required. Long lead times do not allow advertisers the flexibility of changing advertising content should market conditions so warrant; nor can advertisers increase advertising weight on short notice.

ADVERTISING IN ACTION

Discovering Canada

The Canadian Tourism Commission set lofty goals for a new marketing communications campaign designed to stimulate domestic travel in Canada. The Tourism Commission wanted the 240 000 (4.26 percent) of Canadians who were planning to travel abroad to switch plans and vacation in Canada in 2009.

The magazine effort was unique. Colourful visual images of many local tourist attractions were shown in the ad along with the headline "Where is this?" According to Nora Ahern, vice-president of business development at DDB Canada, "The campaign was edgy and not without risk. It was a leap of faith to show a picture of a location and an experience and just have it say, 'Where is this?' Fortunately, the Canadian Tourism Commission was open to innovation and anxious to do new things to make them stand out and have the audience talk about them."

The Tourism Commission invested $10 million in the effort. The commission was motivated by the fact that Canadians love to travel outside the country and don't always feel that Canada offers much in the way of exciting and undiscovered travel experiences. The campaign was designed to alter that perception.

Canadians were urged to take a "staycation." The "Locals know" campaign featured ads showing "little-known destinations such as rolling sands in Saskatchewan, horseback riders on a volcano in B.C., and people swimming in the blue waters of Georgian Bay. "Where is this?" asked the headline in each ad. Ads were also run on television (15-second spots) and online.

The campaign encouraged people to visit www.localsknow.ca, where they could share their stories and upload their own images. Many Canadian celebrities posted their favourite destinations at the website. The website attracted over 450 000 visitors and had 2.2 million page views.

PR buzz generated 39 million media impressions valued at over $1.1 million and *Forbes* magazine ranked the campaign as one of the top 10 travel campaigns in the world. The tangible result was that the Tourism Commission estimated 200 000 Canadians stayed home for their vacation—a great start to a rather creative effort.

Courtesy of Destination Canada

Source: Adapted from Eve Lazarus, "The best of 09 marketers: Canadian Tourism Commission," *Marketing*, November 23, 2009, p. 10; Eve Lazarus, "Marketer of the Year," *Marketing*, December 11, 2009, www.marketingmag.ca

CLUTTER Clutter in magazine advertising refers to the clustering of ads near the front and back of the magazine. Advertisers can partially overcome the problem by ordering preferred positions (covers), assuming such positions are available. Although covers are available at higher cost, the resulting impact may justify the additional expense. Other position requests, such as being on the right side (as opposed to the left side), are available at no additional cost, but the publisher will not guarantee the position.

COST Magazine production costs, particularly for four-colour advertisements, are significantly higher than newspaper production costs. The combination of production costs and space costs makes magazines less efficient for local and regional advertisers, particularly if their target is small. Although many magazines offer regional editions, the absolute cost of advertising does not decline proportionately with the decline in circulation. In fact, the cost of reaching the regional reader is actually higher. National advertisers, with their larger budgets, can consider regional editions and the higher costs associated with them when market conditions warrant such activity.

FREQUENCY Although mass-circulation magazines offer high reach to the advertiser, and specialized magazines offer selective reach, magazines do not offer the advertiser much opportunity to reach the audience *frequently*, because the distribution frequency of magazines is low. Building frequency using one publication is extremely difficult for advertisers.

Courtesy of Canadian Tourism Commission

FIGURE 8.12
An example of a bleed ad

They can overcome this problem by adding magazines that reach similar target markets, but such a solution is expensive.

Magazines are often a medium of choice among consumer goods advertisers that want to reach fairly specific targets with a message. Generally speaking, magazines are useful when a profile-matching media strategy or a rifle media strategy is in place.

ADVERTISING FEATURES OFFERED BY MAGAZINES

Magazines have some special features that make the medium attractive to potential advertisers. The use of these features adds to the cost of advertising, however, so advertisers must carefully weigh the additional cost of these features against the potential impact their use will have on readers. These features include bleeds, gatefolds, preferred positions, and inserts and reply cards.

BLEEDS The term **bleed** refers to a situation in which the coloured background of an ad extends to the edge of the page (there are no margins). An ad can bleed on some or all sides of the page, depending on creative strategy and execution. Most magazines offer bleeds, and either build bleed charges into published four-colour rates or quote the additional costs separately. An example of a bleed ad is shown in Figure 8.12.

GATEFOLDS A **gatefold** is an advertisement that folds out of a magazine, spanning two, three, or four pages. Gatefolds are usually used on special occasions. For example, a car manufacturer might use gatefolds when launching a new model. The most common position for a gatefold is the inside front cover. Since gatefolds are not used very frequently and require significant lead times, most magazine rate cards state that rates are available on request. An example of a gatefold appears in Figure 8.13.

PREFERRED POSITIONS Obtaining a **preferred position** in a magazine involves requesting a specific position for an ad to be placed within the magazine. Since the potential for an advertisement to be seen is great if it is positioned on the inside front or back cover, such

FIGURE 8.13

Unique formats such as gatefolds (a cover foldout) garner higher attention in magazines.

Photo by Keith J. Tuckwell

positions command a higher price than others. While the cost of cover positions varies from one magazine to another, an increase of 15 to 20 percent above a normal page is common. Position charges are discussed in the magazine media buying section of this chapter.

INSERTS AND REPLY CARDS Practically any size of **reply card**, small multiple-page insert, or booklet can be bound into a magazine. Business reply cards are common in business publications, as are **pop-up coupons** and small recipe booklets in consumer publications. **Tipping** (gluing) items such as recipe booklets or small samples of products into magazines is now very popular. The illustration in Figure 8.11 is an example of a tip-in. Advertisers usually must contact the publisher for rates and availability information.

Buying Magazine Space

The procedure for buying magazine space begins with deciding on the size of the ad, which involves choosing from among the variety of page options sold by the magazines under consideration. The rates quoted are based on the size of page requested. Other factors that could influence the cost of advertising in magazines include the frequency of insertions and appropriate discounts, the use of colour, guaranteed-position charges, and the use of regional editions.

SIZE OF AN ADVERTISEMENT AND RATE SCHEDULES

Magazines offer a variety of page options or page combinations. For example, *Canadian Geographic* sells space in the following formats: double-page spread, one page, two-thirds page, one-half page, and one-third page. See Figure 8.14 for illustrations of various magazine ad sizes.

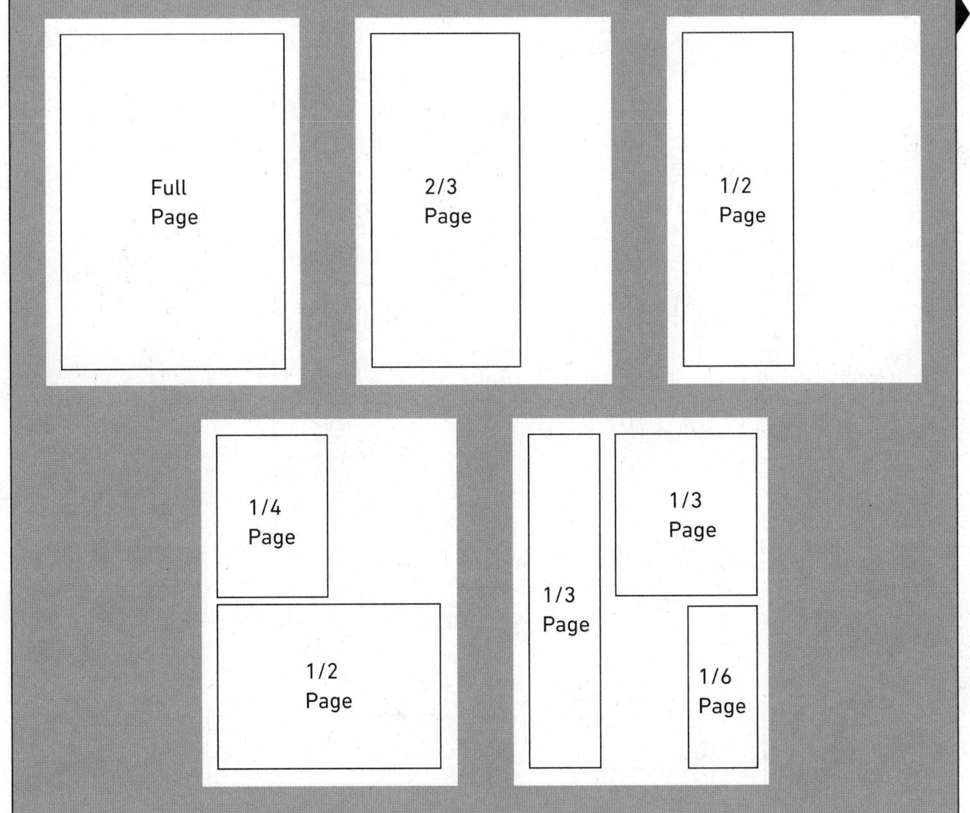

FIGURE 8.14

Various sizes of magazine ads

dates and rates

Material deadlines and rates

CANADIAN GEOGRAPHIC PUBLISHING SCHEDULE 2015

6 ISSUES ANNUALLY	EDITORIAL FEATURE	CLOSES	IN MARKET
January/February 2015	Wildlife issue	December 3, 2014	December 22, 2014
April 2015	Expeditions	February 25, 2015	March 18, 2015
June 2015	Raising *Erebus*	April 22, 2015	May 13, 2015
July/August 2015	Earthquakes	June 10, 2015	July 2, 2015
October 2015	Ultimate Canadian Geography Quiz	August 19, 2015	September 9, 2015
December 2015	Wildlife issue	October 28, 2015	November 18, 2015

NATIONAL ADVERTISING RATES 2015

NATIONAL	1X	3X	6X	9X	12X
Full page	$17,290	$16,770	$16,250	$15,730	$15,210
Double-page spread	$32,845	$31,855	$30,875	$29,885	$28,910
2/3 page	$13,830	$13,415	$12,995	$12,585	$12,170
1/2 page	$12,965	$12,575	$12,190	$11,790	$11,405
1/3 page	$8,640	$8,385	$8,120	$7,865	$7,595
IFC spread	$38,035	$36,895	$35,750	$34,610	$33,465
OBC	$22,470	$21,795	$21,125	$20,450	$19,780
IBC	$20,745	$20,015	$19,415	$18,840	$18,265
EAST/WEST SPLIT RUNS	**1X**	**3X**	**6X**	**9X**	**12X**
Double-page spread	$24,685	$23,950	$23,215	$22,530	$21,880
Full page	$12,995	$12,610	$12,220	$11,865	$11,515

*GROSS CANADIAN DOLLARS

FIGURE 8.15

Canadian Geographic rate card

The size selected for the advertisement determines the rate to be charged. Magazine rates are typically quoted for all page combinations sold on the basis of full colour. Rates may also be quoted for black-and-white ads and black-and-white ads with one colour added.

To illustrate how costs are calculated, let's consider a simple example. Assume an advertiser would like to purchase a one-page, four-colour ad in *Canadian Geographic* for the January/February and April issues (see Figure 8.15). Since the frequency of the advertising does not reach the first discount level (three insertions), the advertiser would pay the one-time rate. The cost calculation would be as follows:

One-page rate × Number of Insertions = Total cost
$17 290 × 2 = $34 580

DISCOUNTS

Advertisers that purchase space in specific magazines with greater frequency will qualify for a variety of discounts. The nature of these discounts may vary from one publication to another. Some of the more common discounts offered by magazines include frequency, continuity, and corporate discounts.

In magazines, a **frequency discount** refers to a discounted page rate, with the discount based on the number of times an advertisement is run. The more often the ad is run, the lower the unit cost for each ad. In the *Canadian Geographic* rate card, the unit rate is reduced when the ad is run 3 times, 6 times, 9 times, and 12 times.

A **continuity discount** is an additional discount offered to advertisers that agree to purchase space in consecutive issues of a magazine (such as buying space in 12 issues of a monthly magazine). When continuity discounts are combined with frequency discounts, lower unit costs per page of advertising result.

Large advertisers that use the same magazine to advertise a variety of products may qualify for corporate discounts. Procter & Gamble, for example, will buy a sizable number of pages in *Canadian Living* each month since many of its products target the same consumer. A **corporate discount** involves consideration of the total number of pages purchased by the company (all product lines combined), resulting in a lower page rate for each product.

POSITION CHARGES

Additional costs for a **guaranteed position** are quoted separately on the rate card. For a guaranteed position, such as the back cover or the inside front or inside back cover, the additional costs are usually in the 15 to 20 percent range when compared with the cost of a regular page. Rates for guaranteed positions are usually quoted as a percentage or a dollar amount increase over the normal four-colour page rate. As for any regular page, the unit rate for a cover decreases as the frequency increases.

MAGAZINE BUYING ILLUSTRATIONS

To illustrate the cost calculations of buying magazine space, let's develop two examples based on the *Canadian Geographic* rate card (Figure 8.15) and on the following information:

Example 1:
Size of ad: One-page, four-colour ad, national edition
Number of insertions: Ad to run in four consecutive issues

The calculation for this buying plan will be as follows:

Costs for one-page, four-colour:
Base rate = the 4 times rate
$16 770 × 4 = $67 080

Example 2:
Size of ad: Double-page spread (DPS), four-colour ad, national edition
Number of insertions: six issues

The calculation for this buying plan will be as follows:

Costs for DPS, four-colour:
Base rate = the 6 times rate
$30 875 × 6 = $185 250

SPACE CONTRACTS AND THE MAGAZINE SHORT RATE To facilitate the use of discount scales offered by magazines, larger advertisers usually enter into a space contract with magazines they use frequently. The space contract provides an estimate of the advertising space required for a one-year period. At the end of the year, adjustments are made (whether positive or negative) when actual usage of space is known. Should advertisers not meet their estimates, a **short rate** would be due the publisher. To illustrate, let's assume the advertiser estimated that 12 ad pages would be purchased in *Canadian Geographic,* but by the end of the contract period only 8 pages had been purchased. The advertiser would be billed as follows:

Ran 8 times but paid the 12 times rate:
8 × $15 210 = $121 680

Earned only the 6 - 8 times rate of $16 250:
8 × $16 250 = $130 000

In this example, the advertiser owes the magazine $8320, according to the terms of the space contract. Conversely, if the advertiser purchased more than the estimated amount, to the point where another frequency discount plateau was reached, the magazine would rebate the difference to the advertiser.

MAGAZINE INSERTION ORDERS Depending on the extent of an advertising campaign with any particular magazine, the advertiser may decide to enter into a space contract with the magazine or place an insertion order on an as-needed basis. To obtain the best possible rate, large advertisers will opt for the space contract. The space contract is not an order for a specific amount of space; rather, it protects the advertiser's right to buy space at a certain rate. Publishers retain the right to announce increases in rates at predetermined levels.

When the advertiser is ready to run an ad, an insertion order is sent to the magazine. The insertion order specifies the date of issue, the size of the ad, any applicable position requests, and the contracted rate. The advertiser must be aware of the closing date for placing ads. The **closing date** usually refers to the deadline for the insertion order and material due at the publication. In some cases, however, the insertion order date is a few weeks in advance of the material date. The insertion order date is the last date for ordering space, and the **material date** is the last date for having production material at the publication.

COMPARING MAGAZINES FOR EFFICIENCY

Assuming that a decision has been made to use magazines, with the understanding that magazines usually have a well-defined target audience based on demographic variables, advertisers must choose particular magazines in which to advertise. Since costs and circulation figures vary, the advertiser must have a way of comparing alternatives. As with newspapers, CPM is an effective quantitative means of comparing competing magazines.

	Chatelaine	Canadian Living	LouLou
1 page, 4-colour	$53 480	$52 905	$19 175
Circulation	524 000	520 000	120 000
CPM	$102.06	$101.74	$159.79

CPM is calculated by dividing the cost of the ad by the circulation in thousands. For *Chatelaine* the calculation would be $53 480 divided by 524.0. That results in a CPM of $102.06. On a purely quantitative basis, both *Canadian Living* and *Chatelaine* appear to be efficient magazines for reaching the target audience; their CPMs are comparable.

Source: Adapted from Canadian Media Directors' Council, *Media Digest*, 2014–15, p. 81

FIGURE 8.16

Comparative statistics used for making magazine buying decisions

In most magazine classifications, there is usually a group of publications competing for the same market. For example, *Chatelaine*, *Canadian Living*, and *LouLou* compete against each other in the women's classification. Although the editorial content varies from one magazine to another, they do reach a similar target, so advertisers must look at the efficiencies of each.

Figure 8.16 contains the comparative calculations for these three magazines. As a purely quantitative measure, *Chatelaine* and *Canadian Living* reach women with the same target profile with competitive CPMs. Therefore, advertisers are likely to include both magazines in a media plan and expand their reach.

Technology and the Print Media

The information age and the digital revolution together have changed the very nature of newspaper and magazine publishing. While the printed format remains the dominant form, major daily newspapers and national magazines have launched websites and digital editions that are available in computer, tablet, and mobile formats. Refer to the illustration in Figure 8.17.

For advertisers using newspapers or magazines, the digital editions offer a means of reaching the same audience profile in a different way. Ads in the form of banners, rich media (ads that include animation or motion), video ads, and sponsorship opportunities are available in the digital formats. Since readers are migrating to digital editions of newspapers and magazines, publishers must follow suit and convince their advertisers to place

Courtesy of Chatelaine, Rogers Media

FIGURE 8.17

Magazines are now available in different digital formats, offering a convenient way for subscribers to access content.

FIGURE 8.18

Canadian House & Home magazine has expanded into a variety of media.

ads in the online version of the publication. More details about digital advertising opportunities are included in Chapter 12.

Magazines are also expanding into television. *Cottage Life* magazine operates a cable channel of the same name that features design, renovation, and real estate shows of interest to cottagers and potential cottagers. *Canadian House & Home* magazine produces a television show called *House & Home with Lynda Reeves* that reaches an audience of 768 000. Videos and TV shows are also available on its website. Refer to the image in Figure 8.18. *Canadian House & Home* magazine has a circulation of 228 000 and readership of 2.1 million monthly. The combination of magazine, television, and online television offers advertisers a means of increasing reach and frequency against a fairly specific target audience.

There is acknowledgement within the industry that the revenue model for newspapers and magazines must change. While people are accustomed to viewing online information for free, such a system is not sustainable for publishers. The logical solution is a pay (subscription) model similar to how television cable channels operate. For their part, television cable channels are keenly interested in the idea of magazines expanding into television shows. The cost of producing the show is a cost for the magazine, not the television channel.

SUMMARY

With respect to print media, the primary options for an advertiser are newspapers and magazines.

Newspaper advertising is divided between daily and weekly publications. Dailies and community newspapers attract both national and local advertisers, though they are more suited to local market advertisers. A newspaper is published in one of two formats: the broadsheet, which is the larger, folded newspaper; and the tabloid, which is the smaller, flat newspaper. Newspapers receive revenues from different types of advertising: national advertising, retail advertising, classified advertising, preprinted inserts (flyers distributed via a newspaper), and sponsored content.

As an advertising medium, newspapers offer the advertiser geographic selectivity, local market coverage, and flexibility. Major disadvantages include the short lifespan, the lack of target market orientation (demographic distinctions), and clutter. The rates charged to an advertiser decrease as the volume of lines purchased increases, and rates are increased by position requests and requests for the use of colour.

Magazines are classified according to factors such as size and format, frequency of publication, circulation base, and content and audience reached. As an advertising medium, magazines offer target market selectivity, quality in reproduction and editorial environment, and a longer lifespan than other media. On the negative side, significant lead times are required for materials, the use of colour raises costs, and clutter remains a problem.

Additional features of magazines that make them an attractive advertising medium include the use of gatefolds, insert and reply cards, fragrance strips, tip-ins, and glue-ons. Magazine advertising rates depend on the size of the ad, the frequency of insertion, and the use of colour. A variety of discounts are available to advertisers that choose magazine advertising, with frequency and continuity being the most important factors reducing the cost of advertising.

In the wake of the digital revolution, newspapers and magazines have expanded their content availability to websites and digital editions for computers, tablets, and mobile devices. The availability of content in hardcopy and digital formats presents new opportunities for advertisers to reach their target market.

KEY TERMS

REVIEW QUESTIONS

1. What is the difference between a tabloid and a broadsheet?
2. What are the differences between national advertising, retail advertising, and classified advertising?
3. What are the advantages and disadvantages of using newspapers as an advertising medium?
4. In a city where more than one daily newspaper dominates the market, how would you determine which

newspaper to advertise in, assuming you could select only one? What factors would enter into your decision?

5. Provide an explanation for the following newspaper terms:
   a) Hooker
   b) Transient rate
   c) Make good
   d) ROP
   e) Tear sheet
   f) Flexform advertising
   g) Position charge
6. Calculate the total cost of the following newspaper campaigns based on the information provided in Figure 8.6. Use the transient rates for each calculation.

   Campaign 1

   Newspaper: *Globe and Mail* Sports Section, National Edition
   Size of Ad: 4 columns wide by 8 column inches deep
   Colour: Black and white
   Frequency: 10 ads (2 ads each week—Tuesday and Thursday)

   Campaign 2

   Newspaper: *Globe and Mail* National Edition
   Size of Ad: 6 columns wide by 6 column inches deep
   Colour: Black and white
   Position Request: Page 2 ROB section
   Frequency: 8 ads (2 ads each week—Wednesday and Friday)
7. What are the advantages and disadvantages of using magazines as an advertising medium?
8. What is the difference between the following pairs of magazine terms:
   a) Paid-circulation magazine versus controlled-circulation magazine
   b) Vertical publication versus horizontal publication
   c) Primary reader versus pass-along reader
9. Provide a brief explanation of the following magazine terms:
   a) Bleed ad
   b) Gatefold
   c) Tipping (tip-in)
   d) Reply cards
   e) Insertion order date
   f) Material date
   g) Space contract
   h) Preferred position
10. Calculate the cost of the following magazine campaigns using the information provided in Figure 8.15.

    Campaign 1

    Magazine: *Canadian Geographic*
    Size: 1/2 page
    Frequency: 4 ads
    Colour: Full colour
    Edition: National

    Campaign 2

    Magazine: *Canadian Geographic*
    Size: 1/3 page
    Frequency: 8 ads
    Colour: Full colour
    Edition: National
11. Identify and briefly describe the various discounts frequently offered by magazines.
12. How does the magazine short rate work?
13. Explain the CPM concept as it applies to the purchase of advertising space in magazines.

DISCUSSION QUESTIONS

1. Newspapers like the *Toronto Star*, the *Vancouver Sun*, and the *Globe and Mail* charge higher rates to advertisers requesting specific sections and specific pages for their ads. In some cases, the additional charge is as much as 40 to 50 percent more. Do the benefits gained outweigh the costs involved? What is your opinion?
2. "Paying a premium price for a cover position (inside front, inside back, or outside back) in a magazine is always a wise investment." Discuss this statement.
3. "The location of an advertisement in a newspaper is the key factor in determining the success of the ad." Discuss this statement in the context of other variables you judge to be important.

NOTES

1. Matthew Chung, "NADbank: Newspaper Readers Still Prefer Print," *Media in Canada*, October 27, 2014, **www.mediaincanada.com**
2. Chris Powell, "PMB/NADbank Release Final Readership Studies," *Marketing*, April 22, 2015, **www.marketingmag.ca**
3. Canadian Media Directors' Council, *Media Digest*, 2014-2015, 73.
4. Powell, "PMB/NADbank Release Final Readership Studies."
5. Canadian Media Directors' Council, *Media Digest*, 2014-2015, 68.
6. Josh Kolm, "When It Comes to Flyers, Print Still Has Pull," *Media in Canada*, November 18, 2014, **www.mediaincanada.com**
7. Chung, "NADbank: Newspaper Readers Still Prefer Print."
8. Canadian Newspaper Association, "The Scoop on Daily Newspapers in Canada," 2008.
9. Canadian Newspaper Association, *Outstanding Newspaper Advertising—Thirteen Creative Principles*, n.d., 12.
10. *Toronto Star* Media Kit, 2014, Insert Program.
11. "NADbank and PMB Release Spring 2015 Readership Studies," press release, Newspapers Canada, April 22, 2015.
12. Data obtained from Canadian Media Directors' Council, *Media Digest*, 2014–2015, 81.

CHAPTER 9

Broadcast Media: Television and Radio

© Goodluz/Shutterstock

Learning Objectives

After studying this chapter, you will be able to

1. Identify the organizations involved in the Canadian broadcasting industry
2. Identify key trends affecting television and radio broadcasting and television and radio advertising
3. Assess the advantages and disadvantages of television and radio as advertising media
4. Explain the factors considered in, and procedures used for, buying television and radio time
5. Identify recent technologies affecting commercial television and radio in Canada

The latest statistics available reveal that 98 percent of Canadian households are reached by both television and radio. Further, 90 percent of households are equipped with satellite or cable TV, and 40 percent subscribe to streaming services like Netflix. The result is endless viewing alternatives. Television reaches 98 percent of Canadians on a weekly basis, and Canadians spend an average of 27 hours per week viewing television. Radio offers impressive numbers as well. The medium reaches 89 percent of adults in a week, and people listen for an average of 17 hours.[1] These figures suggest that the potential impact of broadcast media on their audience is enormous, and from an advertising perspective the placement of messages in broadcast media offers the same high reach and high impact potential.

While these facts are impressive, the television and radio industries are in a state of transition because new technologies are affecting the way people watch television and listen to the radio. For instance, watching television through portable electronic devices such as laptops, tablets, and mobile devices is common now, a situation that advertisers must react to if they want to reach their target audience. On the radio side, people can listen to digital radio stations through SiriusXM Radio, a subscription-based satellite service.

Perhaps the biggest change of all is that consumers now control when, where, and how they receive broadcast shows and advertising messages. Consumers have more control over their consumption of media than ever before. Consequently, the broadcast industry is offering different advertising models. Placing 30-second spots on prime time television shows is no longer the answer—just part of the answer. The competition for eyeballs and ears is intense.

The Canadian Television Market

Television remains one of the largest sources of media advertising in Canada, just recently eclipsed by online media. In 2014, Canadian advertisers spent $3.5 billion on television advertising. The television market is divided among conventional *national networks* and stations, regional networks and stations, specialty networks, digital networks, and pay TV. The conventional English-language networks include the CBC, CTV (a division of Bell Media), Global (a division of Shaw Media), and City (a division of Rogers Media). French-language networks include Radio-Canada and TVA.

A multitude of *specialty networks* are available to viewers. Some of the more popular specialty networks are TSN, Sportsnet, Showcase, Discovery, HGTV, CBC Newsworld, and The Weather Network. For additional fees a large group of digital networks are also available. This group includes ESPN Classic, FX Canada, Leafs TV, NHL Network, TVA Sports (French), Teletoon Retro (French), and many more. Pay TV options such as HBO Canada and The Movie Network are also available to cable and satellite subscribers.

Trends Affecting Television and Television Advertising

The landscape of the Canadian television industry is changing. Several trends are converging on the industry. Consumers' fascination with the internet and the availability of programs online has fragmented the viewing audience; technologies in the form of the PVR allow viewers to record shows and edit out commercials automatically; and mobile devices such as tablets and smartphones provide nontraditional viewing opportunities. As a result of these trends, fewer Canadians are watching conventional television, and those who do are spending less time doing so. The reduced reach of the medium is a concern for broadcasters and advertisers.

AUDIENCE FRAGMENTATION

The combination of conventional networks and stations, specialty channels, digital channels, and pay TV services gives Canadians unprecedented choice of what to watch. With so much choice, the problem of **audience fragmentation** is affecting networks. A popular show today in prime time does not draw the same numbers of people that it did, say, five years ago. Audience size is a key determinant of advertising rates charged by networks. The irony is that the costs of television advertising are increasing while the audience size is decreasing. How long will advertisers pay more for less?

On the positive side, the specialty channels do offer some targeting capability, though the audience that the advertiser reaches is usually smaller than on conventional networks. Advertising rates are lower on specialty channels, and because of the targeting capability, advertisers are moving their dollars in that direction. Stations such as TSN (sports) and HGTV (home and garden) are examples of channels that are attractive to advertisers wanting to reach specific demographic and lifestyle targets.

Adding to the fragmentation issue is the increasing presence of streaming services such as Netflix. Netflix has seen tremendous growth in Canada since its launch in 2010. Presently, 40 percent of households subscribe to Netflix but it only accounts for about 5 percent of all television viewing. Netflix hasn't been much of a negative influence—its subscribers watch significantly more television programming, so it has become a supplement for TV enthusiasts.[2]

COMMERCIAL AVOIDANCE AND PERSONAL VIDEO RECORDERS

A personal video recorder (PVR) allows consumers to digitally record and store their favourite shows for later viewing—a phenomenon referred to as *video on demand*. Commercials can be skipped in the recording process, which is a frightening thought for the networks and advertisers.

PVR penetration in Canada has reached 50 percent, but despite such a high presence, most Canadians still spend most of their time watching live television. Playback of a show occurs quickly—70 percent playback within one day, according to Numeris meter data. Research studies from the United States reveal that viewers skip 90 percent of the ads in recorded programs—a frightening statistic! From an advertiser's perspective, any form of commercial avoidance is a potential issue. To compensate, advertisers are looking at options such as product placement in shows, branded content, and sponsorship opportunities. These strategies are discussed later in the chapter.

ALTERNATIVE VIEWING BEHAVIOUR AND VIDEO VIEWING

Television consumption habits are changing, particularly among younger age groups. The younger the audience, the more likely the consumption will be on a device other than a television; tablets and smartphones are the preferred options. Presently, one in six Canadians has abandoned their television set and now watches all of their programs on a digital device. In lay terms, many people are cutting the cord; they prefer the convenience and interactivity of online video content, which can be consumed anytime, anywhere. In the 18- to 24-year-old age group, one in four people are cord cutters, compared to one in five in the 24- to 35-year-old age group. Consumers aged 45 and older are more likely to only watch TV.[3]

Advertisers must be mindful of this trend if they want their campaigns to keep reaching their intended audience. If a target audience is migrating to different platforms, the advertiser must follow. From a planning perspective, an advertiser must consider a program's availability on conventional television and online, and allocate its budget accordingly.

Broadcasters like CTV and others are offering more and more of their shows online to meet viewers' current expectations and to protect the network's audience for advertisers. The networks stream prime time shows online, and these shows can carry the same advertisements that appear in live broadcasts. Therefore, exposure to online advertisements compensate for lower exposure on live broadcasts.

Bell Media (CTV) also offers a subscription streaming service called CraveTV. The service is commercial free and includes full seasons of popular television shows, both present and past, for a monthly fee. Rogers Communications and Shaw Media offer a similar service called shomi, which offers feature movies and television shows.

Despite the presence of television shows online, a majority of the content viewed is unrelated to what the networks offer. YouTube (owned by Google) dominates online video in terms of reach and video streams viewed. A recent study among people who stream online content revealed that YouTube content topped the list with a 69 percent response rate. That was followed by TV shows and clips (39 percent), full-length movies (34 percent), newscasts (32 percent), and sports highlights (29 percent).[4]

MOBILE MEDIA

The screen is small, the audience's attention span is short, and the environment is busy—not exactly the best conditions for delivering an advertising message, yet the possibilities for reaching consumers at a critical time (when they are ready to buy) makes this medium very attractive to advertisers. At the start of 2015, 68 percent of Canadians owned a smartphone. Usage is highest among 18- to 34-year-olds, the next big generation of customers.[5] Refer to the illustration in Figure 9.1.

Smartphones are now the hub of the internet universe. Google and Facebook now find that a majority of their interaction with users is through a smartphone instead of a computer. Moving forward there is little doubt about the impact mobile technology will have on marketing. It presents an anytime, anywhere opportunity for marketers. Canadians use their phones to search for products—it is a tool for comparative shopping whether in a store, standing in line somewhere, or when you are eating. Phones have a ubiquitous presence; we don't leave home without it! For brands that want to succeed in digital in the future, mobile advertising will be a key ingredient of a media strategy.

The challenge for marketers revolves around how best to present advertising messages in a mobile format. Duplicating television messages has become common practice, but their length (30 seconds) is bothersome to time-pressed consumers. They want information

FIGURE 9.1

Television viewing on mobile devices could be the next big thing for advertisers to consider.

© Hand-out/Bell Canada/Newscom

quickly. Some research has determined that 10-second messages (maximum length) are acceptable. That presents a creative challenge for advertising agencies.

MEDIA CONVERGENCE

Media convergence refers to a concentration of ownership of a variety of media outlets by one company. For example, Bell Media owns 2 TV networks, 20 conventional stations, 35 specialty/digital stations, 106 radio stations, 9500+ outdoor faces, and 200+ digital properties. Rogers owns 12 conventional stations, 13 specialty networks, 42 cable channels, 57 magazine titles, 51 radio stations, and 90+ digital properties. Quebecor owns 1 TV network, 10 conventional stations, 8 specialty channels, 38 daily newspapers, 70+ magazine titles, 200 digital sites, and 2700 outdoor faces.[6]

The premise of convergence is simple: If the advertiser doesn't generate sufficient reach in one medium (e.g., television), additional reach is possible by advertising on other media outlets controlled by the company. Packaged deals embracing a number of media outlets produce economies of scale when buying the media time and space.

Several trends have been discussed in this section. Collectively, they point to a more complex television market in Canada. Advertisers will have to look beyond the 30-second spot if they are to reach their target audience. Change is occurring rapidly so advertisers will have to adapt to change . . . quickly!

Television Viewing Highlights

Media-viewing data are collected by Numeris Canada. Numeris measures TV audiences two ways: paper diaries and portable people meters. Diaries collect data on single weeks of viewing in 40 markets across Canada from a recruited panel. Viewing is recorded in 15-minute increments from 6:00 a.m. to 2:00 a.m. Diary information is captured by an electronic scanning system, which is validated and processed.

A **people meter** is a portable device that is carried by a television viewer panel member. It automatically detects inaudible codes that broadcasters embed in their programming. At the end of each day, the device is attached to a base unit and the codes are downloaded to Numeris for tabulation. The tabulations determine the popularity (audience size) of television shows. People meter devices are in 50 000 homes across Canada.[7]

Each week Numeris publishes the top 30 programs nationally and by selected key markets. This information is a valuable resource for advertisers and agencies to assess the value of their advertising expenditure and for networks to identify which programs are popular or unpopular. An illustration of Numeris data appears in Figure 9.2.

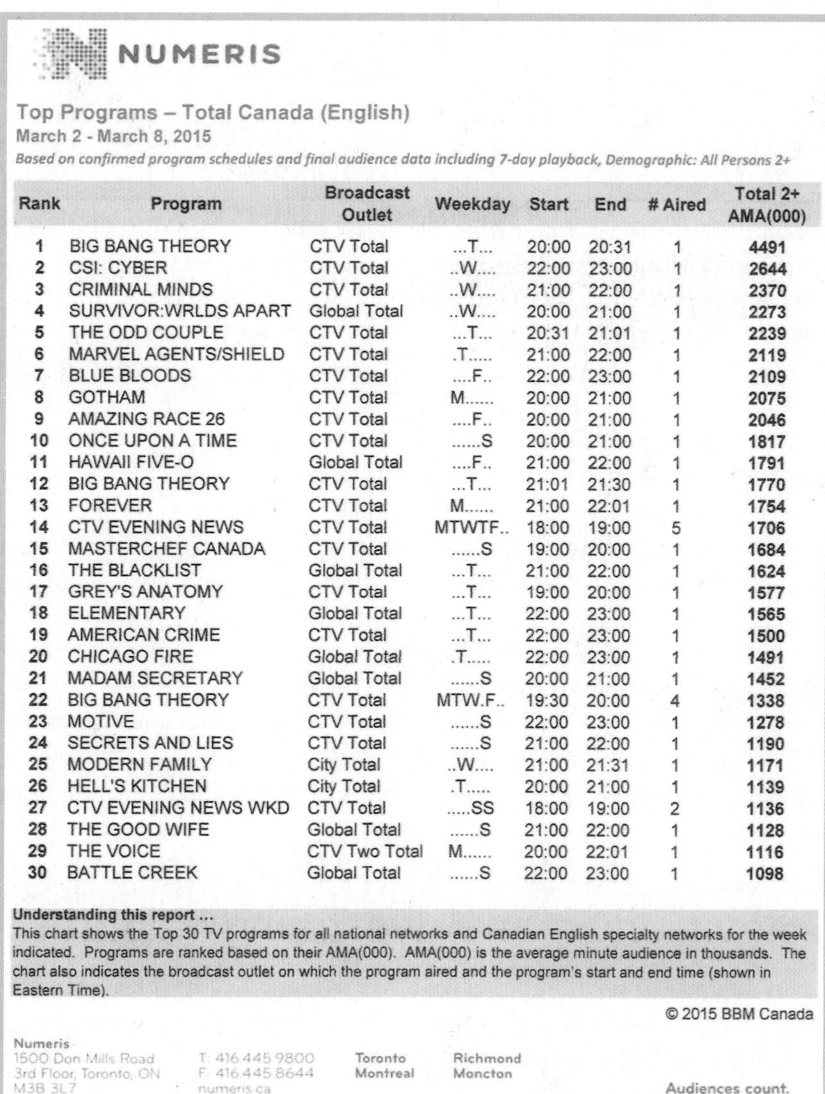

NUMERIS

Top Programs – Total Canada (English)
March 2 - March 8, 2015
Based on confirmed program schedules and final audience data including 7-day playback, Demographic: All Persons 2+

Rank	Program	Broadcast Outlet	Weekday	Start	End	# Aired	Total 2+ AMA(000)
1	BIG BANG THEORY	CTV Total	...T...	20:00	20:31	1	4491
2	CSI: CYBER	CTV Total	..W....	22:00	23:00	1	2644
3	CRIMINAL MINDS	CTV Total	..W....	21:00	22:00	1	2370
4	SURVIVOR:WRLDS APART	Global Total	..W....	20:00	21:00	1	2273
5	THE ODD COUPLE	CTV Total	...T...	20:31	21:01	1	2239
6	MARVEL AGENTS/SHIELD	CTV Total	.T.....	21:00	22:00	1	2119
7	BLUE BLOODS	CTV Total	....F..	22:00	23:00	1	2109
8	GOTHAM	CTV Total	M......	20:00	21:00	1	2075
9	AMAZING RACE 26	CTV Total	....F..	20:00	21:00	1	2046
10	ONCE UPON A TIME	CTV Total	......S	20:00	21:00	1	1817
11	HAWAII FIVE-O	Global Total	....F..	21:00	22:00	1	1791
12	BIG BANG THEORY	CTV Total	...T...	21:01	21:30	1	1770
13	FOREVER	CTV Total	M......	21:00	22:01	1	1754
14	CTV EVENING NEWS	CTV Total	MTWTF..	18:00	19:00	5	1706
15	MASTERCHEF CANADA	CTV Total	......S	19:00	20:00	1	1684
16	THE BLACKLIST	Global Total	...T...	21:00	22:00	1	1624
17	GREY'S ANATOMY	CTV Total	...T...	19:00	20:00	1	1577
18	ELEMENTARY	Global Total	...T...	22:00	23:00	1	1565
19	AMERICAN CRIME	CTV Total	...T...	22:00	23:00	1	1500
20	CHICAGO FIRE	Global Total	.T.....	22:00	23:00	1	1491
21	MADAM SECRETARY	Global Total	......S	20:00	21:00	1	1452
22	BIG BANG THEORY	CTV Total	MTW.F..	19:30	20:00	4	1338
23	MOTIVE	CTV Total	......S	22:00	23:00	1	1278
24	SECRETS AND LIES	CTV Total	......S	21:00	22:00	1	1190
25	MODERN FAMILY	City Total	..W....	21:00	21:31	1	1171
26	HELL'S KITCHEN	City Total	.T.....	20:00	21:00	1	1139
27	CTV EVENING NEWS WKD	CTV Total	.....SS	18:00	19:00	2	1136
28	THE GOOD WIFE	Global Total	......S	21:00	22:00	1	1128
29	THE VOICE	CTV Two Total	M......	20:00	22:01	1	1116
30	BATTLE CREEK	Global Total	......S	22:00	23:00	1	1098

Understanding this report ...
This chart shows the Top 30 TV programs for all national networks and Canadian English specialty networks for the week indicated. Programs are ranked based on their AMA(000). AMA(000) is the average minute audience in thousands. The chart also indicates the broadcast outlet on which the program aired and the program's start and end time (shown in Eastern Time).

Numeris
1500 Don Mills Road
3rd Floor, Toronto, ON
M3B 3L7
T: 416.445.9800
F: 416.445.8644
numeris.ca
Toronto
Montreal
Richmond
Moncton
Audiences count.

FIGURE 9.2

The top 30 English-language shows on Canadian television by audience size

FIGURE 9.3

Time spent with television and various other media

Weekly Hours of Television Viewing in Canada by Age Group

Age	Hours of Viewing
Adults 18+	24.0
Adults 18–34	15.3
Adults 25–54	20.3
Adults 55+	33.4

Source: Adapted from TVB Canada, *TV Basics 2014–2015*, 26.

Time Spent Weekly with TV and Other Media

Adults 18+	Hours per Week
Television	24.0
Radio	17.3
Internet	21.4
Daily Newspaper	1.9
Local (Weekly Newspaper)	0.3

Source: Adapted from TVB Canada, *TV Basics 2014–15*, p. 27

The data collected from the people meter panel are used to determine the rating of a program. **Ratings** are audience estimates expressed as a percentage of a population in a defined geographic area. For example, if a show has a rating of 20, it reaches 20 percent of that market's population.

Generally speaking, Canadians spend more time with television than with any other medium. On average, adults watch for 24 hours each week. Teens spend only 20 hours watching TV, while those over 55 watch 33 hours weekly.[8]

The data collected by Numeris reveal other key trends. By **daypart**, a block of time in a programming schedule (e.g., a half-hour or one-hour period), prime time (7:00 to 11:00 p.m., Monday to Sunday) attracts the most viewers. While accounting for only 20 percent of viewing hours, prime time generates 41 percent of total viewing time.

Seasonally, there is a dropoff in viewing in the summer, a reflection of consumers changing their patterns when the weather is warmer. After all, why watch reruns when you can enjoy the outdoors? Generally speaking, viewing drops by about 20 percent in the summer. Advertising rates charged for summer shows are lower, reflecting the viewer dropoff. For additional information about television viewing, see Figure 9.3.

Television as an Advertising Medium

As an advertising medium, television offers numerous benefits—but there are also some drawbacks. The advertiser must assess the merits of using television in the context of the problem that advertising is trying to resolve and the target market the advertiser is trying to reach.

ADVANTAGES OF TELEVISION

IMPACT AND EFFECTIVENESS OF MESSAGES Compared with all other media, television stands out as a multi-sense medium. Advertisers can use the combination of sight and sound that television offers to create maximum impact on the viewing audience. It is a medium that is ideally suited for delivering an exciting and emotional message. However, viewers are easily distracted during commercials. A recent research study revealed that 59 percent of watchers always or often use another device while watching television.[9]

Even though viewers may be distracted, a research study by Numeris revealed that Canadians are most receptive to advertising delivered on television. Respondents in the survey claimed television is the "most influential, most effective and most persuasive advertising medium" among adults 18 and older.[10]

HIGH REACH Television's reach is astounding, particularly during prime time. As Figure 9.2 indicates, a commercial shown on any of the top 30 shows in Canada has the potential to reach more than 1 million viewers. Further, television reaches a broad demographic range, and in many cases mirrors the Canadian population on specific demographics, making it an extremely attractive medium for advertisers targeting fairly general audiences. The variety of programming in prime time (comedy, reality, and drama shows) is equally attractive to adult males and females.

FREQUENCY POTENTIAL Television is an expensive medium in absolute-dollar terms, but advertisers with large budgets can use television effectively to build frequency. For example, an advertiser may purchase more than one spot within a certain program or during a certain time of day. Alternatively, an advertiser could build **frequency** by purchasing the same time slot in a program over a continuous period—perhaps 13, 26, or 52 weeks. In either case, owing to viewers' loyalty to a certain program or to the appeal a certain time period has for a particular target market, the target audience will be exposed to the same commercial message over an extended period. Strategically, the advertiser wants just enough frequency to prompt action—too much repetition could have a negative impact on the viewer.

SOME DEMOGRAPHIC SELECTIVITY Television is primarily a mass-reach medium, but it can target demographic groups based on the nature of the programming. Programs such as *Hockey Night in Canada* and *Blue Jays Baseball* are sold to advertisers on the strength of their potential to reach males of all ages. Specialty networks offer demographic targeting potential as well. TSN reaches 5.4 million people weekly (a predominantly male audience), HGTV reaches 2.6 million people (predominantly female), and The Family Channel reaches a mixed audience of 2.1 million people weekly.[11] Viewers of specialty channels like those just mentioned migrate to these channels because they offer the program content these viewers like.

COVERAGE FLEXIBILITY Network advertisers receive good national coverage on national networks (CBC, CTV, and Global). However, smaller-budget advertisers that want to use television can purchase commercial time from individual stations rather than from a national network. Thus, advertisers can be selective about where they advertise. Consideration of variables such as competition and opportunity markets helps advertisers determine which markets to purchase. For network advertisers, additional advertising on selected stations can be used to increase the weight of advertising in a particular market when needed, perhaps to counter competitive spending.

DEMONSTRATION CAPABILITY Television offers creative flexibility. It is the appropriate medium for verifying a product's claims because it can show the product being used, which provides proof. Convincing demonstrations provide potential customers with a reason to buy the product. In addition, television is an effective medium for building consumers' awareness of and ability to identify the packages of products, particularly the packages of new products.

DISADVANTAGES OF TELEVISION

HIGH COST Television offers high reach potential and relatively low CPMs, but in real spending terms it is very expensive. The cost of a prime time 30-second commercial on the CBC can be as high as $52 000 (e.g., during a Stanley Cup playoff game); on the CTV network it can be as high as $65 000 (e.g., during a leading show such as *The Big Bang Theory*), although the average costs are not nearly that high. Costs of television ads are determined by supply and demand—a concept discussed in the media buying section of this chapter. In addition to the cost of media time, television advertising involves high production costs; the cost for a finished 30-second commercial ranges between $150 000 and $250 000. To counter the high costs of television advertising, many advertisers are choosing 15-second commercials that deliver quick brand messages.

CLUTTER Television **clutter** refers to the clustering of too many commercials during a program break or the scheduling of too many breaks during a program. The level of clutter has a direct bearing on both viewing patterns and message recall. Viewers are likely to reach for the remote control when a program pauses for a commercial break, focus more intently on another device in their possession, or leave the room temporarily. Network promos at every break that plug upcoming shows add to the clutter. Too much clutter negates much of the reach potential of television. Due to the clutter situation, many advertisers feel that particular placement within a **cluster** is important. Generally, the first and last positions in the cluster are preferable.

LACK OF TARGET MARKET SELECTIVITY As indicated by the list of advantages, television offers high reach to mass audiences, with some potential for reaching target markets that are defined by age and sex. However, for advertisers with target markets precisely defined by a combination of demographic, psychographic, and geographic variables, television advertising is wasteful since the message reaches many people outside the target definition. Wasted reach means a reduction in cost efficiency. Consequently, advertisers should consider other media that reach their target markets more efficiently.

AUDIENCE FRAGMENTATION While the number of channels and alternate viewing options has increased dramatically over the past decade, the total number of viewers hasn't grown. The viewing audience is fragmented in such a manner that the size of the potential audience reached is lower while the cost of placing the ads is higher. The efficiency of television is becoming an issue.

COMMERCIAL AVOIDANCE Viewers watch the shows, but do they watch the commercials? If viewers leave the room, fast-forward through commercials, or simply pay less attention during commercial breaks, then the size of the audience is reduced. New technologies are available to track the number of people watching commercials. Once those technologies are fully implemented, the model for buying television ads, along with the cost structure, will change. Rates will have to be pegged to the lower number of people watching the commercials.

LACK OF PLANNING FLEXIBILITY To plan and buy television advertising space requires significant lead time. For example, network buys are negotiated in June for a complete broadcasting year that commences with the new fall program schedule in mid-September. Network contracts are usually noncancellable, and spot advertising can be cancelled only on the basis of a minimum run and a specified notice period (e.g., advertising must run for four weeks, and four weeks' notice must be given prior to cancellation). Facing this contract, advertisers must be prepared to make an investment in television advertising.

CREATIVE LIMITATIONS Television is a multi-sense medium offering significant impact capabilities, but a television commercial is very short—the normal length is 30 seconds. Considering the viewer behaviours discussed earlier in this section, advertisers are using even shorter commercials in an attempt to break through the clutter. From a creative perspective, it is questionable whether a 15-second spot can achieve the same communications results as a 30-second spot. Other experts argue that shorter commercials that grab attention are more likely to be viewed in their entirety.

Considered strategically, television advertisements must focus on one major benefit of a product if communications are to be effective. If a more complete story is needed, a commercial should direct viewers to a website or social media site where more detailed information is available. Television is frequently the medium of choice when an advertiser wants to reach a large audience quickly, say, in the case of a new product launch. For an applied illustration of recommending television as part of a media plan, refer to the advertising plan in Appendix I.

Television Advertising Alternatives

When buying television time, advertisers choose between network advertising (either national or regional), selective spot advertising, sponsorship opportunities, and local market spot advertising. In addition, advertisers now look at product placement and branded content opportunities (the concept of native advertising presented earlier in the text).

NETWORK ADVERTISING

Network advertising is suitable for advertisers whose products and services are widely distributed and who have relatively large media budgets. All stations within a network carry a set of programs at a certain time—usually prime time, with some daytime. The network sells the commercial time. The advertiser must supply one commercial to a central source, and the message is broadcast across the entire network. Network advertising offers an advertiser substantial reach at relatively low cost. Popular prime time shows such as *The Big Bang Theory*, *Criminal Minds*, *The Amazing Race*, and *NCIS* can reach between 2.0 million and 3.5 million people each week.

NATIONAL SPOT OR SELECTIVE SPOT ADVERTISING

At the regional or local station level, stations fill in the balance of programming time with non-network programs and sell commercial time directly to clients wanting to advertise in that market. Alternatively, the local station that carries network programs may have the

© Lenscap/Alamy Stock Photo

FIGURE 9.4

Budweiser sponsors the "Coach's Corner" segment on *Hockey Night in Canada.*

© Montreal Gazette/The Canadian Press

opportunity to sell some advertising time directly to advertisers during the network program. For example, in network shows such as *Marketplace*, *the fifth estate*, and *Hockey Night in Canada,* a certain portion of the commercial time available is allocated to local stations for selective spot sales. In either case, the advertiser buys spots on a station-by-station basis, such as CBLT Toronto, CBOT Ottawa, or CBUT Vancouver.

Selective spot advertising offers two advantages to advertisers. First, it provides a network advertiser with the opportunity for incremental coverage in key markets where more frequency is desired. Second, advertisers with smaller budgets or advertisers following a key market media strategy can choose only markets that are important to their situation (e.g., markets where they have good distribution).

LOCAL ADVERTISING

Local advertising is similar to selective spot sales. The local television station sells the time to local market advertisers (such as retailers, restaurants, and entertainment facilities). In contrast to network and selective spot advertising, however, local advertising is noncommissionable. Since local market advertisers do not usually work with an advertising agency, the individual television stations provide assistance in the development and production of commercials for local clients.

SPONSORSHIP OPPORTUNITIES

In response to changing client needs, the major networks actively market sponsorship opportunities that will integrate television advertising with other marketing and promotion efforts. Television **sponsorship** allows advertisers to take "ownership" of television properties that are targeted at their consumer audience. If the fit is right, the advertiser can leverage the sponsorship by extending the package to include consumer and trade promotions and alternative media exposure. On HGTV, IKEA sponsors *Open House Overhaul*, a show where designer Samantha Pynn and her crew overhaul homes to fetch top dollar on the real estate market. IKEA has category exclusivity for the show, brand mentions within the show, and 15-second spots driving viewers online to IKEA-sponsored webisodes featuring Pynn giving design tips.[12]

ADVERTISING IN ACTION

No Better Place to Bring Your Brand to Life

Beer wars between Labatt and Molson are nothing new. Each company tries to get an edge on the other by getting involved in unique advertising opportunities. Advertising plays a major role in building brands in the beer category. Therefore, both companies aggressively pursue advertising opportunities on *Hockey Night in Canada*, which is now owned by Rogers Communications but broadcast by the CBC on Saturday nights.

Hockey Night in Canada is the longest-running and most influential program in Canadian television history. The broadcast offers an advertiser excellent reach among 25- to 54-year-old males and females across Canada, and while the cost of 30-second spots can be pricey, being associated with the broadcast brings a certain element of prestige. Prominent beer, automotive, hardware, and financial institutions are among the advertisers.

For the 2013–2014 season and beyond, Labatt's Budweiser brand will be the exclusive sponsor of the well-known and very popular (if not controversial) "Coach's Corner" segment featuring Don Cherry and Ron McLean. The multiyear agreement also includes advertising spots during the game and digital ads on tablets and mobile devices.

Molson also advertises during the games, but Labatt feels strongly that the association with "Coach's Corner" will clearly give Budweiser an advantage in terms of brand recognition and recall among viewers. Labatt views the "Coach's Corner" sponsorship as a tactical means of muscling into the sport without paying huge sponsorship fees to the league. Guerrilla marketing in play, perhaps?

What are the true benefits of Budweiser's relationship with *Hockey Night in Canada* and "Coach's Corner"? According to Budweiser marketing director Kyle Norrington, "There's no better place to bring your brand to life than Saturday night hockey! We are, and have been, committed to hockey for a long time." Apparently Don Cherry also loves the beer, so the partnership is a natural one.

© Food Drink and Diet/Mark Sykes/Alamy Stock Photo

Source: Adapted from Susan Krashinsky, "Labatt Strikes Back against Molson with *Hockey Night* deal," *The Globe and Mail*, January 17, 2013, www.globeandmail.com.

A prominent and ongoing sponsorship in Canada is *Hockey Night in Canada* (*HNIC*), a Saturday night institution. Currently, Labatt's Budweiser brand has a multiyear deal to sponsor the "Coach's Corner" segment featuring the ever-popular Don Cherry. Budweiser also appears in two other parts of the broadcast and is a sponsor of a package of digital extras the network offers on computers and mobile devices.[13] Refer to the image in Figure 9.4.

For additional insight into Budweiser's decision to associate with *Hockey Night in Canada*, read the Advertising in Action vignette **No Better Place to Bring Your Brand to Life**.

PRODUCT PLACEMENT AND BRANDED CONTENT

Product placement refers to the visible placement of branded merchandise in television shows, movies, and video games. In any given show, numerous products are given exposure; such exposure has more credibility with the audience than regular advertising. Coca-Cola was a prominent brand on *American Idol*, one of the most watched programs every year for 13 years. Coca-Cola just recently (2014) ended its relationship with the show, acknowledging that reality shows are less popular now. Product placement is a growing form of marketing communications; the value of placements in all media (TV, film, online, mobile, and music) in North America was $4.7 billion in 2012.[14] Advertisers are shifting dollars to product placement for a good reason—viewing of programs on conventional TV is declining in favour of time-shifted video consumption and viewing on alternative media platforms. Product placement is a natural next best option for brand messages.

Branded content (sometimes called brand integration or branded entertainment) takes placement a step further and integrates the brand into the script of the show. Sometimes an advertiser can benefit from both of these opportunities at the same time. The hit series *The Big Bang Theory* was the perfect prime time opportunity for Microsoft to use to build excitement with its core audience. In one episode, Xbox One was featured throughout the show as Sheldon spoke to its key differentiating features while obsessing over which new gaming system to buy. The episode had 16.5 million viewers in the United States and over 3 million viewers in Canada.[15]

Petro-Canada and Scotiabank partnered with *The Amazing Race Canada*, a show broadcast on CTV. Carl Reader, director of brand communications at Suncor Energy, sees the deal as a great fit. "As Canada's gas station, we know about keeping Canadians moving across our great country." One of the prizes on the show is free gas for life from Petro-Canada. Scotiabank sponsors "pit-stop" prizes, and its American Express travel rewards credit card is used by contestants to purchase plane tickets in the show. Jeff Marshall, vice-president of marketing at Scotiabank, says, "Travel is a key pillar of our sponsor strategy. Being featured in vignettes and challenges in the show give us a platform to intertwine ourselves in viewer's minds." The true benefit of the partnership is high reach: The show attracts a family audience and reaches an average of 3.3 million viewers per episode.[16]

Television Advertising Rates and Buying Procedures

INFLUENCES ON TELEVISION ADVERTISING RATES

Numerous factors converge to influence advertising rates on television. Generally speaking, popular programs with large audiences command higher advertising rates. What follows is a discussion of the major factors that influence advertising rates.

SUPPLY AND DEMAND For the CBC, CTV, and Global networks, advertising costs are based on fundamental economic principles—mainly the availability of supply and the demand exerted on that supply by competing advertisers. Under such conditions, prospective advertisers outline their advertising needs in terms of desired reach levels, frequencies, seasonal implications, the ratio of prime time to fringe time, and the budget. The network assembles a package and then the price of the advertising is negotiated between the agency's media buyer and the network sales representative. This system places added pressure on media buyers, since the rate that their clients pay depends largely on the buyer's ability to negotiate.

NATURE OF THE ADVERTISING PURCHASE This negotiation process occurs well in advance of a media schedule, usually in late spring for the following broadcast year. Major networks such as CBC, CTV, and Global operate in a similar manner: They book time in mid- to late June to cover a 52-week period starting in September. Once the new season's program schedules are announced, the networks establish a *declaration date* (referred to as D-Day), at which time most advertisers place their orders for the coming broadcast year.

Every effort is made to accommodate each order as placed. If overbooking should occur as a result of the volume of orders, preference is allocated according to the following priorities: (1) incumbency position, (2) length of contract, (3) volume of contract, and (4) start date. Large-budget advertisers that have advertised on network programs in the past (incumbents) are given priority in this system. This procedure for buying air time is referred to as **upfront buying**. Part of the current buying process involves gambling on what new shows will be popular. As indicated earlier in the chapter, there is a possibility that commercial ratings (instead of a show's ratings) will be more of a factor in establishing the cost of TV advertising in the future.

TYPES OF PROGRAMS Network and selective spot advertising is sold on the basis of a regular program schedule that is established for the entire year. Examples of such programs embrace sitcoms such as *The Big Bang Theory*, dramas such as *Criminal Minds*, variety shows such as *Dancing with the Stars*, and sports broadcasts such as *NFL Football*. A sample program schedule for the CTV network appears in Figure 9.5.

In the case of sports programs, hockey and baseball broadcasts appeal largely to a particular viewing audience (i.e., males aged 18 to 49) and, as a result, are attractive to a particular type of advertiser. Since the network is seeking sponsors willing to make long-term commitments over the entire season, separate rates and discount schedules apply to those that make such commitments. For example, Scotiabank is the title sponsor of *Wednesday Night Hockey* on Sportsnet and *Hockey Day in Canada,* as well as the presenting sponsor of *Sunday Night Hockey* on City.

DAYPARTS (TIME OF DAY) Television can be divided into three broad time categories: *prime time, fringe time,* and *daytime.* Since the type of audience and size of audience vary according to daypart, so must the rates for commercials within the dayparts.

Prime time is usually designated as the viewing hours between 7:00 and 11:00 p.m. Most network shows are scheduled during prime time, and the shows with the largest audiences are usually scheduled between 8:00 and 11:00 p.m. (shows such as *Hawaii Five-O, Criminal Minds, Survivor,* and *Blue Bloods*). Prime time accounts for approximately 40 percent of all viewing. Advertising rates in prime time vary from show to show based on popularity and reach potential. As discussed in Chapter 7, each show has a rating and the rating places advertising rates within a certain dollar range. As mentioned, estimating the ratings for new shows is difficult. For advertising purposes, it is safer to buy time on established shows where audience estimates are based on past experience.

Fringe time is usually defined as the time preceding and following prime time. For example, early fringe would be 4:00 to 7:00 p.m., and late fringe would be 11:00 to 1:00 a.m. or sign-off. In early fringe time, viewing is somewhat lower among the adult population but is high among kids returning home from school. Fringe time accounts for approximately 12 percent of all viewing. Early fringe rates are lower than prime time rates. Program content in this time period usually consists of comedy reruns, music videos, and talk shows. Late fringe includes talk shows and

FIGURE 9.5

Sample program schedule for the CTV network

CTV Summer 2015

	Monday	Tuesday	Wednesday	Thursday	Friday	Saturday	Sunday	
6:00	Canada AM					Juicebox	Canada AM Weekend	6:00
6:30								6:30
7:00							The Marilyn Denis Show	7:00
7:30								7:30
8:00						Canada AM Weekend	Corner Gas	8:00
8:30							PAID	8:30
9:00	Live! With Kelly and Michael (s-ABC)					The Marilyn Denis Show		9:00
9:30								9:30
10:00	The Marilyn Denis Show					PAID		10:00
10:30								10:30
11:00	The View (s-ABC)						Canada's Worst Handyman	11:00
11:30						etalk		11:30
12:00	CTV News					SPORTSCENTRE		12:00
12:30								12:30
1:00	The Social					Corner Gas	W5	1:00
1:30						Corner Gas		1:30
2:00	The Dr. Oz Show					Canada's Worst Driver	CTV Movie	2:00
2:30								2:30
3:00	Dr. Phil (s-NBC)					Cash Cab		3:00
3:30						Cash Cab		3:30
4:00	The Ellen DeGeneres Show (s-NBC)					The Marilyn Denis Show	The Social	4:00
4:30							etalk	4:30
5:00	Hot in Cleveland					The Social	The Amazing Race Canada	5:00
5:30	Hot in Cleveland					etalk		5:30
6:00	CTV News							6:00
6:30								6:30
7:00	etalk					W5	The Big Bang Theory (s-WPCH)	7:00
7:30	The Big Bang Theory (s-WSBK/WPCH)						The Big Bang Theory (s-WPCH)	7:30
8:00	So You Think You Can Dance (s-FOX)	Spun Out	MasterChef (s-FOX)	The Big Bang Theory (s-CBS)	Shark Tank (s-ABC)	The Amazing Race Canada	The Goldbergs	8:00
8:30		Hot in Cleveland		The Odd Couple			Various Comedies	8:30
9:00		Zoo (s-CBS)	The Amazing Race Canada	Mistresses (s-ABC)	Motive	Orphan Black	19-2	9:00
9:30								9:30
10:00	Castle (pre-ABC)	Hollywood Game Night (s-CBS)	Criminal Minds (s-CBS)	Saving Hope	Blue Bloods (s-CBS)	Bitten	CSI : Cyber (s-CBS)	10:00
10:30								10:30
11:00	CTV National News with Lisa LaFlamme					CTV National News with Sandie Rinaldo		11:00
11:30	CTV News							11:30
12:00	The Daily Show with Jon Stewart				The Big Bang Theory	CTV Movie	Castle	12:00
12:30	Late Night with Seth Meyers (s-NBC)							12:30
1:00							Criminal Minds	1:00
1:30	Conan				Castle			1:30
2:00						Criminal Minds	Infomercials	2:00
2:30	etalk							2:30

movies. Viewing is also lower in the late fringe period, so advertising rates are adjusted accordingly.

Daytime television runs from early morning (sign-on) to 4:00 p.m. The reach potential of television is relatively low in the morning, except for the potential to reach young children. Daytime accounts for approximately 22 percent of all viewing. Television rates are lowest during the day. However, audiences increase during the day, and the rates are increased accordingly. The types of programs scheduled during the daytime range from news and information in the early morning, to kids' shows in the morning, to soap operas and talk shows in the afternoon.

LENGTH OF COMMERCIAL Most advertising rate schedules are based on the purchase of 30-second units. Commercials that are longer—60, 90, and 120 seconds—are usually sold at two, three, and four times the 30-second rate. Commercials that are shorter—15, 10, and 5 seconds—cost less. A 15-second commercial, for example, typically costs 65 percent of the 30-second ad rate—it isn't half price.

Split 30s (the scheduling of two 15-second commercials by the same advertiser during a commercial cluster) may be accepted at the 30-second rate or range as high as 120 percent of the 30-second rate, depending on the network. Some experimentation is now occurring with 5- and 10-second commercials, but presently they account for only about 3 percent of all commercial time. The standard 30-second spot accounts for just over half of all commercials shown on television.

BUYING TELEVISION TIME

In recent years, dramatic changes have occurred in television advertising. Factors such as audience fragmentation, budget cutbacks due to economic circumstances, the impact of digital media on television viewing, the introduction of optimizers, and demographic and lifestyle influences have created a need for new approaches to buying and selling television time.

Media buying in television is a complicated process that requires a high level of expertise on both sides of the negotiating table (i.e., among media buyers who represent clients and among sales representatives who represent the networks and individual stations). In a textbook of this nature it is not possible to illustrate the negotiation process, as there is so much variation among the networks. Instead, a brief overview of some of the key points for the major networks is presented below. An illustration of a specific media buy is also included in this section. The concept of media optimizers will be discussed in more detail later in the chapter.

NATIONAL AND REGIONAL NETWORK RATES The supply and demand system is based on a standard **grid card** with varying price levels. The highest level on the CBC is in the $52 000 range and at CTV is as high as $70 000 for the highest-demand 30-second spot in prime time. Average rates in prime time are much lower. In this type of system, rates are adjusted periodically and are affected by factors such as inventory of time available, projected audiences, continuity, and seasonality. When the agency and the network negotiate the rates, client-oriented factors, such as competition for time, budget available, the ratio of prime time to fringe time required, and the program mix desired, come into play. Canadian media directors estimate the average rates of buying 30-second spots on all Canadian networks based on these factors.

The three major English-language networks offer regional packages. On the CBC, for example, spots can be purchased from CBC Maritimes, which covers New Brunswick, Prince Edward Island, and Nova Scotia; CBC Ontario, which covers the entire province; and CBC Pacific, which covers all of British Columbia.

LOCAL MARKET TELEVISION RATES In the case of **spot sales**, advertisers purchase broadcast time on a station-by-station basis (i.e., non-network time) from the stations that constitute the CBC or CTV networks. Agencies can negotiate rates with member stations individually. Commercial material must be supplied to each station where time is purchased. Spot announcement rates established by local stations also depend on the daypart (time classification) in which the commercial is scheduled to appear, projected audience size, and the time of year.

Similar to the networks, the local market station offers a continuity discount to advertisers booking a 52-week contract. In addition, some television stations may offer a seven-day reach plan. The reach plan is an interesting concept for television; it is more commonly used in radio as a way of selling off nonpeak time. Commercials are rotated vertically throughout the day and horizontally during the week. Since the demographics of the audience change throughout the day, the number of people reached in a particular target group will vary with the schedule. However, with respect to the entire viewing audience, reach will be maximized and the plan is purchased at a discounted rate, a trade-off that must be considered against daypart scheduling.

GROSS RATING POINTS The concept of gross rating points (GRPs) was introduced in Chapter 7. When purchasing commercial time on networks or specific television stations, media buyers request a certain level of GRPs, basing their request on the reach and frequency objectives of the advertiser. The GRP concept offers a way of measuring the advertising weight levels in a market in terms of reach and frequency variables; it is based on the formula

$$\text{GRPs} = \text{Reach} \times \text{Frequency}$$

Assume, for example, that a commercial message reaches 20 percent of target households in a market, and the commercial is scheduled five times in a week. The GRPs (weight) would be 100 [Reach (20) × Frequency (5) = 100]. In another week, the reach may be 25 percent and the frequency 4; in that case, the GRP level would remain at 100. Consequently, from week to week in a television advertising flight, the actual number of commercials varies depending on the estimated reach of the programs the ads appear on.

To demonstrate a television media buy at a local market CBC station, refer to the information in Figure 9.6. This is a fictitious plan that was created to reach an adult target 25 to 54 years old in Nova Scotia. Thirty-second spots were placed on a variety of prime time shows, all with different ratings. The media buy was scheduled over a three-week period. The unit price per spot shown in the schedule is the price for a local market spot (in this case on the Halifax station) during a network broadcast. Depending on the show, the number of spots purchased varies from week to week, as do the ratings for each show.

DISCOUNTS OFFERED BY TELEVISION

A variety of discounts are available to television advertisers, depending on the extent of their advertising commitment. In general terms, discounts are based on the amount of advertising time purchased, seasonal factors, and other factors important to the network or station.

FREQUENCY, VOLUME, AND CONTINUITY DISCOUNTS A **frequency discount** is usually earned through the purchase of a minimum number of spots over a specified period of time. Offered on a percentage basis, the discount increases with the number of spots purchased in the stated period of time. For example, the purchase of 5 to 10 spots per week may earn a 5 percent discount, and 11 to 15 spots per week may earn a 10 percent discount.

A **volume discount** is linked to the dollar volume purchased by the advertiser over a 52-week period. The greater the volume purchased, the greater the discount. A network such as the CBC or CTV would typically offer a volume discount in the range of 2 to 10 percent.

A **continuity discount** is earned when advertisers purchase a minimum number of designated spots over an extended period (usually 52 weeks, but the period can be shorter). The value of the continuity discount may increase with the number of spots purchased. For example, purchasing a minimum number of prime time spots, perhaps

FIGURE 9.6

Sample media buy on CBHT, Halifax

CHANNEL: CBHT - Halifax

CBC

Purchaser: Time and Space Media
Attn: ANGIE REID

Plan ID: 9568472 Rev. #: 0
From: Mar-18-2013 To: Apr-07-2013
Target Grp: A 25-54 / Primary demo
Source: BBM
Advertiser: Quest Vitamins
Phone:
Fax:
PO/Product:

Submitted on:
Booked on:
Revised on:

GENERAL AVAILS CHART

Line #	Selling Component	Commercial Type	F/M	Unit	MTWTFSS	Time	*	Brk	Pos	# Week	Unit Price	By spot GRPs	By spot AUD	CPP $	CPM $	Mar 18	Mar 25	Apr 01
4	Ron James Series	Regular	L	30	..W....	20:30-21:00			N	3	49.33	1.1	14.0	46.98	3.52	X	X	X
5	Cracked	Regular	L	30	.T.....	21:00-22:00			N	2	78.33	1.6	12.0	50.21	6.53		X	X
6	Murdoch Mysteries	Regular	L	30	M......	21:00-22:00			N	3	103.33	1.8	13.6	58.38	7.60	X	X	X
8	Coronation St - Prime	Regular	L	30	MTWTF..	19:30-20:00			N	1	223.67	3.2	25.0	71.01	8.95			X
9	Dragons' Den	Regular	L	30	......S	20:00-21:00			N	2	168.00	2.7	31.3	61.31	5.36		X	X
11	HNIC Prime West	Regular	L	30	.....S.	23:00-26:00			N	3	80.67	1.2	10.5	67.23	7.68	X	X	X
12	CBC News: @ Six	Regular	L	30	MTWTF..	18:00-18:30			N	1	240.00	3.8	16.5	63.16	14.55	X		
14	Disney	Regular	L	30	......S	17:00-19:00			N	1	28.33	0.8	8.5	37.77	3.33	X		
15	Republic Of Doyle	Regular	L	30	......S	21:00-22:00			N	1	120.67	1.5	18.0	80.45	6.70			X
16	CBC Evening News	Regular	L	30	MTWTF..	17:00-18:00			N	3	79.67	2.4	14.5	33.90	5.49	X	X	X
17	Cdn Reflections - Sun	Regular	L	30	......S	24:00-24:30			N	3	1.00	0.1	1.0	10.00	1.00	X	X	X
18	Fifth Estate - Sun	Regular	L	30	......S	23:30-24:30			N	3	1.00	0.1	1.5	10.00	0.67	X	X	X
19	Dragons' Den Rotation	Regular	L	30	MTWTF..	16:00-17:00			N	2	8.00	0.2	1.5	40.00	5.33	X		X
23	HNIC Afternoon	Regular	L	30	.....SS	15:00-19:00			N	1	44.33	1.4	9.8	31.22	4.54			X

Accepted on behalf of Purchaser | Sales Rep.: Wilson, Alexandra | (902) 420-4315 / | Email: | GST/HST: 10076 0909 RT0001
X - Date: | Sales Admin.: Veysey, Catherine | (506) 451-4132 / | Email: VEYSEYC@Fredericton.cbc.ca | QST: 1006030706 TQ0005

Rates protected for 5 working days from the date submitted

CBHT-Halifax Purchase © 2013. Courtesy of CBC-Halifax

FIGURE 9.6

(Contunued)

CBC

PROPOSAL

CHANNEL: CBHT - Halifax

Purchaser: Time and Space Media
Attn: ANGIE REID

Plan ID:	9568472		**Rev. #:**	0
From:	Mar-18-2013	**To:**	Apr-07-2013	
Target Grp:	A 25-54 / Primary demo			
Source:	BBM			
Advertiser:	Quest Vitamins			
Phone:				
Fax:				
PO/Product:				

Submitted on:	February 14, 2013
Booked on:	-
Revised on:	February 14, 2013

RATING SUMMARY

Line#	Selling Component		By spot AUD
	ProRata	%	
	Total Cost (000's)	$	
	Avg Weekly Cost (000's) $	$	
	Total AUD/GRP		
	CPM/CPR	$	
	Avg Weekly AUD/GRP		

WEEKLY MARKET RATINGS

	Week Of	Occasions	By Week AUD
		Total Delivery	

CBHT-Halifax Purchase © 2013. Courtesy of CBC-Halifax

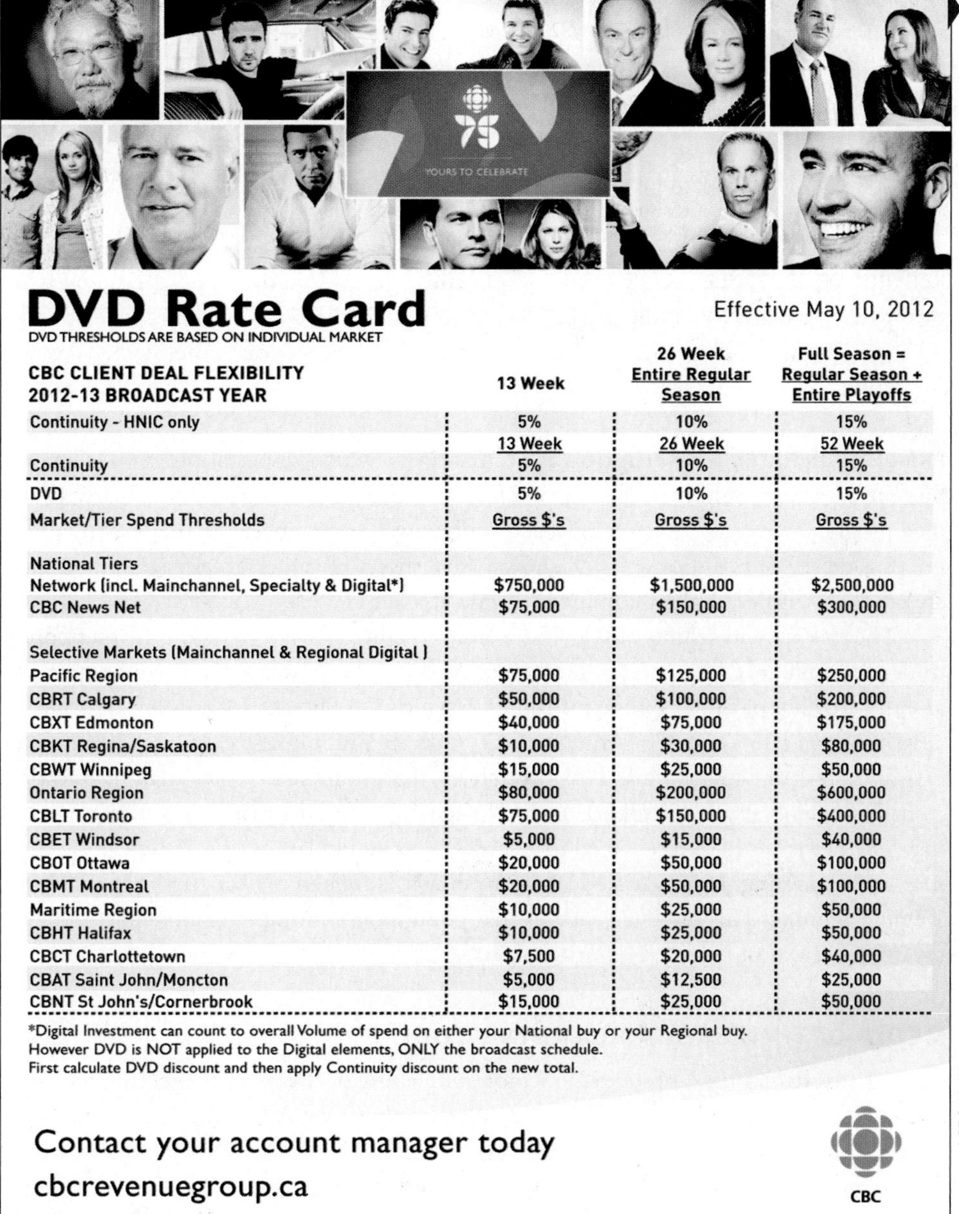

DVD Rate Card

Effective May 10, 2012

DVD THRESHOLDS ARE BASED ON INDIVIDUAL MARKET

CBC CLIENT DEAL FLEXIBILITY 2012-13 BROADCAST YEAR	13 Week	26 Week Entire Regular Season	Full Season = Regular Season + Entire Playoffs
Continuity - HNIC only	5%	10%	15%
	13 Week	26 Week	52 Week
Continuity	5%	10%	15%
DVD	5%	10%	15%
Market/Tier Spend Thresholds	Gross $'s	Gross $'s	Gross $'s
National Tiers			
Network (incl. Mainchannel, Specialty & Digital*)	$750,000	$1,500,000	$2,500,000
CBC News Net	$75,000	$150,000	$300,000
Selective Markets (Mainchannel & Regional Digital)			
Pacific Region	$75,000	$125,000	$250,000
CBRT Calgary	$50,000	$100,000	$200,000
CBXT Edmonton	$40,000	$75,000	$175,000
CBKT Regina/Saskatoon	$10,000	$30,000	$80,000
CBWT Winnipeg	$15,000	$25,000	$50,000
Ontario Region	$80,000	$200,000	$600,000
CBLT Toronto	$75,000	$150,000	$400,000
CBET Windsor	$5,000	$15,000	$40,000
CBOT Ottawa	$20,000	$50,000	$100,000
CBMT Montreal	$20,000	$50,000	$100,000
Maritime Region	$10,000	$25,000	$50,000
CBHT Halifax	$10,000	$25,000	$50,000
CBCT Charlottetown	$7,500	$20,000	$40,000
CBAT Saint John/Moncton	$5,000	$12,500	$25,000
CBNT St John's/Cornerbrook	$15,000	$25,000	$50,000

*Digital Investment can count to overall Volume of spend on either your National buy or your Regional buy.
However DVD is NOT applied to the Digital elements, ONLY the broadcast schedule.
First calculate DVD discount and then apply Continuity discount on the new total.

Contact your account manager today
cbcrevenuegroup.ca

CBC

Courtesy of CBC-Halifax

FIGURE 9.7

CBC Television (network and local stations) offers volume and continuity discounts to advertisers.

two per week over 52 weeks, may earn the advertiser a 4 percent discount. If the number increases to three spots, the discount may move to 6 percent. In the CBC discount schedule that appears in Figure 9.7, dollar volume discounts and continuity discounts are calculated based on 13-, 26-, and 52-week intervals.

SEASONAL DISCOUNTS The time of year has an effect on potential reach and the size of the television viewing audience. Traditionally, television viewing drops off in the summer; it is lightest from mid-June to mid-September. Consequently, **seasonal discounts** are available to advertisers wishing to purchase commercial time in non-peak seasons. Networks and stations usually offer summer discounts in the 15 to 20 percent range.

PACKAGE PLANS Networks and stations offer **package plans** to sell off fringe or daytime spots at a discount, sometimes in combination with the purchase of prime time. The nature of such plans varies considerably. For example, an advertiser who purchases two prime time spots per week in a popular American series may be required to purchase equivalent time in a prime time Canadian series or equivalent time in daytime periods. Essentially, advertisers who demand the premium time spots must be prepared to make sacrifices through the purchase of less desirable time as well.

ROS (RUN OF SCHEDULE) **ROS (run of schedule)** refers to a discount offered by a station to an advertiser that allows the station to schedule a commercial at its discretion during any time in the programming day. The ads run in various time blocks, days, or programs.

PRE-EMPTION RATES **Pre-emption** is a situation in which a special program, such as a miniseries, an entertainment special, or a hockey playoff game, replaces a regularly scheduled program. Advertisers are usually determined well in advance, and they pay premium prices for the right to sponsor such shows. Advertisers of the originally scheduled show are credited with equivalent commercial time at a later date.

The buying and selling of television time is evolving with changing market conditions. It is influenced by economic conditions that force advertisers to reduce spending and the viewing of shows online instead of TV screens. The net result is less demand for advertising on television. Consequently, networks are rethinking the upfront buying process and are launching new shows throughout the entire year rather than at one time (usually September and October). Such changes affect media planning and media buying. The networks have discovered that shows launched in late spring and even the summer are garnering larger audiences than shows launched in the traditional heavier viewing months. This discovery proves that good programming will attract an audience regardless of season.

MEDIA OPTIMIZERS: A PLANNING TOOL

Buying advertising time on television more efficiently is always the objective, and software technology plays a big role in achieving that objective. An **optimizer** is a software program that searches a ratings database (e.g., Numeris or Nielsen TV ratings) for daypart or program combinations that increase target reach (or reduce the cost of buying it). According to Bill Harvey, a marketing expert, "all media optimization models require the input of media audience and cost data . . . and the input of the brand's requirements in terms of budget, target audience, reach/frequency, types of programs. The model is a complex set of equations which considers all of this input and [generates] one or more 'best schedules' within the budget constraint."[17]

Telmar HMS and Nielsen IMS Clear Decisions are media research organizations that offer media optimization software. Telmar's system uses all the factors just mentioned and reports ratings for time period, programs, and custom dayparts; it also provides station reach and frequency analysis of any schedule.

Procter & Gamble is one company that is advancing the use of optimizers. P&G's objective was to reduce the amount of time bought at expensive dayparts while still maintaining reach. With optimizers, agency media planners can "investigate complex viewer targets . . . examine co-viewing and circumstance of viewing . . . study the viewer and duplication patterns of programs, dayparts and networks and determine how many targeted rating points in a venue is enough for a brand."[18]

The Canadian Radio Market

As of 2015, there were 707 commercial radio stations in Canada: 574 FM and 133 AM. FM stations reach far more Canadians 12 years and older than do AM. Because AM stations tend to offer "all news" or "all sports" programming, this type of radio reaches more men than it does women. In an average week, radio reaches 89 percent of Canadians 12 and older, and the average adult listener spends about 17 hours a week listening to the radio when all locations for listening are included (e.g., home, work, automobile).[19]

Radio broadcasting in Canada is divided between the CBC, which is funded by the government (or, more precisely, by the taxpayers of Canada), and independently owned and operated stations that survive on advertising revenues. All AM and FM stations are self-regulating, with no restrictions on the number of commercial minutes they can air. The 30-second spot is the most commonly aired spot length. The radio airwaves in Canada are controlled by several large media companies, including Rogers Media, Corus Entertainment, and Bell Media.

Trends Influencing the Radio Industry

Much like television, the radio industry is in transition. New technologies are bringing radio signals to people in different ways, resulting in a gradual migration of listeners away from traditional stations. That said, conventional radio's place in the lives of Canadians has remained relatively constant despite the advent of the internet and satellite radio.

INTERNET AND DIGITAL RADIO

Online radio offers listeners incredible sound quality. Music content is available from a variety of streaming services. As online radio grows, it will take advertising revenue away from traditional radio. True internet radio through services such as Spotify and Pandora are in their infancy as only 4 percent of Canadians access internet stations each day. Their impact on terrestrial radio listening is yet to be determined.

Most stations broadcast in both digital and analogue formats. Both formats are needed because the industry's projected growth of digital radio did not materialize. Consumers rejected the notion of having to buy new receivers and instead gravitated to online listening where digital signals were available at little or no cost. Consequently, the industry has shifted its focus to websites where music is streamed over a variety of platforms (laptop, tablets, and mobile devices) and additional content is offered (e.g., in-depth interviews and podcasts).

A **podcast** is "an audio recording posted online, much like a short radio show . . . 'Podcasting' is a pun on 'broadcasting,' implying, of course, that you listen to it on your iPod or another portable device." A podcast can be accessed at the listener's convenience and is generally free.[20] For example, on TSN's website several podcasts are available for the sports-minded listener. There's the *NHL Insider* featuring Bob McKenzie, the network's resident expert on all rumours and happenings in the NHL, as well as *The Reporters* with Dave Hodge, a weekly no-holds-barred live roundtable sports debate show.

Websites offer another revenue stream for radio stations, assuming they can show advertisers the benefit of advertising in both media.

SATELLITE RADIO

Satellite radio offers commercial-free programming and is available through one supplier in Canada: SiriusXM Radio. The service is available on a subscription basis. Subscribers access programming through integrated satellite radios installed in vehicles or through tablet and smartphone apps. There are currently 2.2 million subscriptions in Canada.[21] Satellite radio offers commercial-free, coast-to-coast coverage with digital quality sound and content not found on terrestrial stations, including live sports, news, and talk and entertainment programming.

Radio Listening Highlights

Numeris Canada compiles listening data using two methods: paper diaries and portable people meters. Diaries are used to collect data on single weeks of listening by individuals 12 years and older. Tuning is recorded in 15-minute intervals. Over 100 markets are measured for eight weeks each fall. Portable people meters are an electronic methodology that provides audience data in the top five markets across Canada. The data are recorded on a minute-by-minute basis, allowing media planners to gain greater insight into consumer tuning patterns. Both methodologies collect additional data that include market share, audience profiles, and listening locations.

AM VERSUS FM

Conventional radio signals are transmitted two ways: **AM (amplitude modulation)** and **FM (frequency modulation)**. Amplitude refers to the height at which radio waves are transmitted; AM stations transmit waves by varying amplitude. Frequency refers to how fast waves travel in thousands of cycles per second (kilohertz); FM transmits waves by varying frequency. FM frequencies are above the static and noise level of AM. This results in clearer reception and better sound on FM stations. FM radio is more effective than AM in reaching all age categories and accounts for 79 percent of all tuning. AM stations tend to target male listeners with "all sports" or "all news" formats. Refer to Figure 9.8 for AM and FM audience share data by age classification.

TUNING HOURS: HOW MUCH, WHEN, AND WHERE

The average listener spends anywhere from 13 to 20 hours a week with radio, depending on age category. Teens spend much less time with radio, averaging only about seven hours a week. Other entertainment options such as the internet, iPods, and video games are more attractive to teens. Older age groups spend more time with radio. Adults 18 to 49 years old average 17 hours per week, and the 50+ year age group average 19.5 hours per week.

By time of day, radio is the inverse of television: Radio is much more popular in the morning, but as the day progresses listening tapers off. The use of Radio during the day

FIGURE 9.8

AM and FM share of tuning by age classification

	Reach		Share	
Canada	AM%	FM%	AM%	FM%
12+	26	79	17	80
Women 18+	25	81	17	82
Men 18+	31	79	19	78
Teens 12–17	9	71	5	94

Source: © Copyright Numeris.

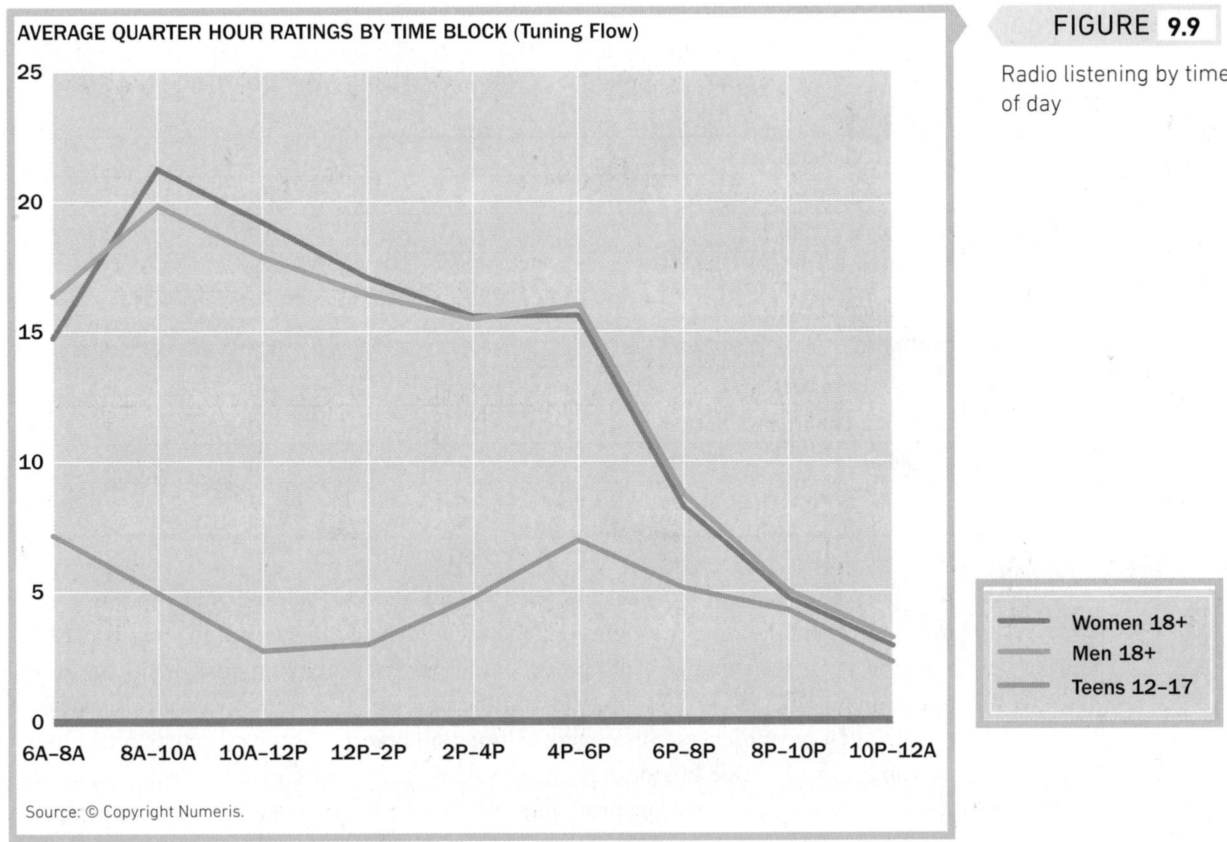

Source: © Copyright Numeris.

FIGURE 9.9

Radio listening by time of day

is high because people tune in when they wake up, while they travel to work, and while they are at work. Refer to Figure 9.9 for details.

One of radio's advantages is its mobility. Listeners can be reached in a variety of contexts. For listeners aged 12 and up, listening from home accounts for 45 percent of listening time, automobiles account for 32 percent, and listening from work accounts for 21 percent of listening time.[22] Advertising messages can be delivered anytime, anywhere.

Radio Station Formats

One of the major advantages of radio is its ability to reach selective target audiences. The audience reached depends on the format of the station. **Format** refers to the type and nature of the programming offered by an individual station. Basically, the content is designed to appeal to a particular target group, usually defined by age and interests. The most popular station formats in Canada are country, adult contemporary, and album-oriented rock. Refer to Figure 9.10 for details.

Country music appeals to a cross-section of ages and varies in popularity by region (it is more popular in Atlantic Canada and the Prairies). *Adult contemporary* stations play popular and easy-listening music, current and past, and generally appeal to an audience in the 25- to 54-year-old range. *News/talk* stations focus on frequent news reporting and listener call-ins to discuss current newsworthy issues. Some stations focus specifically on news niches such as sports. The Fan 590 in Toronto and Team 1040 in Vancouver, for example, are sports stations popular with males 25 to 54 years old. *Top 40* stations are popular in urban markets.

FIGURE 9.10

Radio format and listening share for the more popular formats (all diary-measured Canadian markets)

Format	Share
Country	17.0
Adult Contemporary	12.0
Hot Adult Contemporary	11.0
News and Talk	8.0
Classic Hit Radio	8.0
Album-Oriented Rock	8.0
Top 40	7.0
Classic Rock	4.0
Modern Alternative Rock	2.0
Oldies	1.0

Source: Adapted from CRTC Communications Monitoring Report 2014

The variety of radio formats in urban markets reflects each individual station's desire to be successful. Finding the right niche (a niche that is underserved in a market) makes a station attractive to a particular group of advertisers. The main considerations are the age demographics of the local market and the number of competitive stations appealing to similar target audiences. Since radio stations are being consolidated corporately under the umbrella of major broadcasters like Bell, Rogers, and Corus, station formats and music are trending to the more profitable and popular formats of adult contemporary, hot adult contemporary, and top 40.

Radio as an Advertising Medium

Radio offers advertisers several advantages and disadvantages. The decision to select radio as an advertising medium depends on the problem that the advertiser is trying to resolve.

ADVANTAGES OF RADIO

TARGET MARKET SELECTIVITY Because they tend to adopt a specific music format (e.g., adult contemporary, country, news/talk, oldies), radio stations appeal to more precisely defined demographic groups than television stations do. Consequently, advertisers can use a profile-matching strategy and select stations with audience profiles that closely match their target market. Even in smaller markets, where music formats change within a single station and the **audience flow** varies by daypart, the advertiser can schedule radio commercials at the appropriate time of day so that dollars will not be wasted reaching people outside the target. For example, advertisers for beverages and snack foods aimed at a youthful target would concentrate their advertisements in the evening time block, when the youthful target market is most likely to be listening.

REACH POTENTIAL Since radios are almost everywhere—with multiple receivers in the home, in the car, and at the beach—radio has the potential to reach large audiences, particularly if advertisers place ads on several stations in an urban market. Since morning is the most popular listening time, reach is highest in this time period. Other factors that

PPM Top-line Radio Statistics

Toronto CTRL

Survey period: Radio Meter 2014/15 – December 1, 2014 - March 1, 2015
Demographic: A2+
Daypart: Monday to Sunday 2am-2am
Geography: Toronto CTRL
Data type: Respondent

December 1, 2014 - March 1, 2015
Average Daily Universe: 6,030,000

Station	Market	Share (%)	Cume (000)	Daily Cume (000)
CBL FM	Toronto CTRL	2.2	1,447.0	143.0
CBLAFM	Toronto CTRL	9.0	1,727.0	429.0
CFMJ	Toronto CTRL	2.7	882.0	129.0
CFMZF+	Toronto CTRL	7.7	2,283.0	318.0
CFNYFM	Toronto CTRL	2.7	2,694.0	345.0
CFRB	Toronto CTRL	7.2	1,132.0	261.0
CFTR	Toronto CTRL	6.1	3,155.0	609.0
CFXJFM	Toronto CTRL	2.0	2,466.0	311.0
CFZM	Toronto CTRL	3.7	1,143.0	168.0
CHBMFM	Toronto CTRL	6.5	4,475.0	567.0
CHFIFM	Toronto CTRL	13.6	5,652.0	1,052.0
CHKXFM*	Toronto CTRL/Hamilton	0.8	841.0	75.0
CHUM	Toronto CTRL	0.9	1,063.0	103.0
CHUMFM	Toronto CTRL	10.1	5,092.0	795.0
CIDCFM	Toronto CTRL	2.5	2,848.0	381.0
CILQFM	Toronto CTRL	3.9	2,939.0	390.0
CINA	Toronto CTRL	0.7	284.0	57.0
CINDFM	Toronto CTRL	1.3	1,557.0	164.0
CINGFM*	Toronto CTRL/Hamilton	0.5	1,587.0	99.0
CJCL	Toronto CTRL	2.5	1,148.0	187.0
CJRTFM	Toronto CTRL	1.2	1,274.0	102.0
CKDXFM	Toronto CTRL	1.6	819.0	87.0
CKFGFM	Toronto CTRL	1.7	1,010.0	88.0
CKFMFM	Toronto CTRL	5.2	5,138.0	766.0
CKISFM	Toronto CTRL	3.5	3,651.0	555.0

** = spill station*

TERMS

Share: Within a central market area, the estimated total hours tuned to that station expressed as a percentage of total hours tuned to Total Encoded Radio.

Cume (000): Expressed in thousands, this is the total number of people who were exposed to the stations for at least one minute during the analyzed period.

Average Daily Universe: The average daily universe for the analyzed period. The universe is expressed as daily averages because it changes slightly daily as the intab changes.

FIGURE 9.11

Market share and audience reached for radio stations in Toronto

influence reach include mobility (e.g., 32 percent of listening occurs while driving) and portability (a radio can be played outside and as background music while listeners are doing other tasks). Refer to Figure 9.11 for details about the reach potential of radio stations in the Toronto market.

FREQUENCY Radio is usually referred to as a *frequency medium*, a name that suggests radio's probable foremost advantage. If target market selectivity is used, an audience can be reached on several occasions throughout the day or week (vertical and horizontal rotation plans) at a relatively low cost. For local advertisers wanting to advertise sales, radio is a preferable medium; numerous announcements can be scheduled before and during the sale to stimulate immediate response from consumers. For national advertisers, the radio can boost frequency in key markets as needed. Because radio offers frequency at a reasonable cost, advertisers can use it to supplement the reach of other media in a campaign.

COST The low cost of radio advertising attracts local clients for whom advertising would otherwise not be affordable. Radio advertising is cost favourable in two areas. First, production costs are much less than they are for television, and changes to copy can be made on short notice. Second, the basic cost for each spot is relatively low (making radio an efficient means of reaching selective audiences), and numerous discounts are available for larger volume advertisers. The combination of reasonable cost and frequency potential makes radio a good medium to supplement other media in a total campaign.

FLEXIBILITY Radio offers flexibility in three areas: creative, time scheduling, and market scheduling. As stated, copy changes can be made on short notice to meet the needs of changing competitive situations as well as the needs of local markets. With respect to scheduling, the lead time required is short (two weeks or less); however, demand for popular stations in urban markets is quite high. Nonetheless, schedules can be "heavied up" (i.e., advertising can be increased) on short notice if the competitive situation so dictates.

Strategically, radio is an ideal medium for advertisers who are following a key market plan. Because stations are local and reach a specific demographic, an advertiser can select popular stations in each urban market it has designated as a priority. Consequently, the advertiser is not paying for any wasted reach.

For more insight into the benefits of radio advertising, read the Advertising in Action vignette **Apps Add Value to Local Radio Advertising.**

DISADVANTAGES OF RADIO

AUDIENCE FRAGMENTATION While reach potential is high, the variety of station formats means the radio audience is fragmented by the demographic groups appealed to by competing stations. An advertiser wishing to reach the teen audience in urban markets may have to purchase time at several rock stations to achieve adequate reach levels. Listener loyalty to a certain station contributes to the fragmentation problem. The net effect of fragmentation is that radio is recognized as a low-reach/high-frequency medium.

MESSAGE RETENTION Several factors restrict the ability of listeners to retain radio messages. First, radio messages are short; there is limited opportunity for the communication of details in 30 seconds. Sixty-second commercials offer more creative flexibility, but they are less popular because of costs. Second, radio is a background medium; therefore, the attention levels of listeners are potentially lower. Third, clutter is a problem, particularly on AM stations. Fourth, radio is only a sound medium; as a result, there is no chance for the customer's mind to register the way a package looks (an important consideration for a new product), and there can be no product demonstration.

MEDIA PLANNING CONSIDERATIONS For local market advertisers, the advantages of radio outweigh the disadvantages. For national advertisers purchasing time in a large number of

ADVERTISING IN ACTION

Apps Add Value to Local Radio Advertising

The radio industry is in transition, moving from analogue to digital signals, but the transition has been slower than expected. Some recent research conducted by Media Technology Monitoring reveals that 66 percent of Canadians still only listen to the radio through traditional receivers—online streaming is not that popular, yet!

Corus Radio (a network of stations across Canada) observes a slightly different trend. Some 74 percent of its listeners go online to stream content through mobile devices. To take fuller advantage of the online transition, Corus is introducing a set of apps designed specifically to serve listener needs in local markets. The content will offer customized features tailored to a particular station's audience (e.g., Rock 101 in Vancouver and News Talk 770 in Calgary).

The local apps are different from the more general apps like Spotify, which serve broader demographics. The Corus apps allow music listeners to view artist profiles, pictures, videos, concert listings, and competitions. News/talk apps will offer the latest news, weather, and real-time traffic information. According to Chris Duncombe, director of new media at Corus Radio, "It allows us to have a conversation with the audience in a way we couldn't in the past."[23]

More to the point, the apps will produce advertising revenue. Reaching a local market audience in a unique and interactive way should be of high interest to local advertisers, and national advertisers following a key market plan. The apps provide for display and preroll advertising opportunities.

© Hand-out/Corus Entertainment Inc./PR Gr/Newscom

Source: Adapted from Jordan Pinto, "Corus Launches a Slew of Radio Apps," *Media in Canada*, February 18, 2015, www.mediaincanada.com and Jordan Pinto, "Traditional Radio Listeners Won't Tune Out," *Media in Canada*, April 23, 2015, www.mediaincanada.com.

radio markets, other media factors must be considered. Generally speaking, radio time is in high demand, particularly among leading stations in urban markets. This demand makes it difficult for media buyers to purchase the specific times desired by their clients. In fact, the high demand for time has precipitated a demand-driven rate card at top-ranked stations in major markets. Lead time is an important issue for advertisers wanting to maintain costs and access preferred inventory.

The industry has consolidated in recent years, producing larger radio networks (Bell and Rogers). These networks can offer packaged media buys for all of their stations coast to coast. This helps alleviate some of the problems associated with planning and buying media time.

Radio Advertising Rates and Buying Procedures

The rates paid by radio advertisers are affected by several factors: the season or time of year in which commercials are placed, the daypart or time of day for which the commercials are scheduled, the use of reach plans, and the availability of discounts offered by individual stations. The type of advertiser (national or local) also has an impact on the basic rate charged to advertisers.

INFLUENCES ON RADIO ADVERTISING RATES

SEASONAL RATE STRUCTURES The rates charged by radio stations are often influenced by seasonal fluctuations in listening. Generally, radio rates fluctuate with the seasons, as follows:

Time Period	Rate
May–August (summer) and December	Higher
September–November	Mid-range
March–April	Mid-range
January–February	Lower

DAYPARTS Since the size and nature of the audience varies according to the daypart, different rates are charged for each. Generally, the dayparts are classified as follows:

Classification	Time
Breakfast	6:00 a.m. to 10:00 a.m.
Midday	10:00 a.m. to 4:00 p.m.
Drive	4:00 p.m. to 7:00 p.m.
Evening	7:00 p.m. to midnight
Nighttime	Midnight to 6:00 a.m.

Dayparts vary from one station to another, with some stations having more or fewer classifications than those listed above. In addition, weekend classifications are often different from weekday ones, as the listening patterns of the audience change on weekends.

REACH PLANS Radio advertisers can purchase specific time slots and schedule a particular rotation plan during the length of the media buy, or they can purchase a reach plan. For the first option, a **rotation plan**, the advertiser specifies the time slots and pays the corresponding rate associated with them. Two types of rotation plans are available:

- **Vertical rotation** is the placement of commercials based on the time of day (within various dayparts).
- **Horizontal rotation** is the placement of commercials based on the day of the week (same daypart on different days).

Earlier in the chapter, potential reach was identified as an advantage of radio. However, since listening levels and the type of audience vary with the daypart, radio stations have developed reach plans to maximize reach. In a **reach plan (total audience plan)**, commercials are rotated through the various dayparts in accordance with a predetermined frequency to reach different people with the same message.

With reference to Figure 9.12, reach plan spots are equally divided among breakfast, daytime, drive time, and evening/weekend dayparts. The benefit of the reach plan for the advertiser is twofold. First, the reach potential is extended, and second, the rates charged for the reach plan collectively are lower (because of the discounts) than those that would

FIGURE 9.12

CKET Radio rate card

This rate card has been created to demonstrate to the reader the key factors that influence a radio media buy: spot rates, reach plan rates, volume discounts, and continuity discounts. Discounts are not usually published in *Canadian Advertising Rates and Data.*

CKET Radio

640 AM

All Talk! 24/7

NEWS ON THE HOUR EVERY HOUR

30-sec spot rates

Daypart / Grid	1	2	3	4	5
Breakfast 6:00 to 10:00 am	109.00	98.00	88.00	79.00	72.00
Daytime 10:00 am to 3:00 pm	92.00	82.00	73.00	64.00	58.00
Drive 3:00 to 7:00 pm	98.00	88.00	79.00	70.00	63.00
Evening and Sunday	76.00	68.00	65.00	57.00	49.00

Reach Plan - 30-sec. spots					
Breakfast 25% Daytime 25% Drive 25% Evening and Sunday 25%	88.00	79.00	71.00	62.00	54.00

Discount Schedule			
Contract Buy (Continuity)		*Volume (Spots)*	
14 to 26 weeks	Grid 3	250	Grid 3
27 to 39 weeks	Grid 4	450	Grid 4
40 to 52 weeks	Grid 5	700	Grid 5

result from the individual purchase of similar time slots. Reach plans do require a minimum spot purchase on a weekly basis.

TYPE OF ADVERTISER Radio advertising rates vary with the nature of the advertiser. National advertisers are charged the general (national) rate that is generally higher than rates charged to local advertisers (such as retail establishments and restaurants). Rates for national advertisers are commissionable to recognized advertising agencies at the rate of 15 percent. Retail rates, being lower, are noncommissionable, but owing to their importance in the local radio station's revenue mix, stations offer production assistance either at no cost or at reasonable cost to encourage retailers to advertise. On average, local advertisers contribute 75 percent of a radio station's revenue.

DISCOUNTS OFFERED BY RADIO

Advertisers that purchase frequently from specific stations qualify for a variety of discounts. While the criteria for earning discounts vary, the discounts are similar in nature.

A *frequency discount* is a discounted rate earned through the purchase of a minimum number of spots over a specified period of time, usually a week. Having earned such a discount, advertisers are referred to a lower-rate grid schedule, or they could be quoted a percentage discount, such as 5 percent for 15 to 20 spots per week, 8 percent for 21 to 30 spots per week, or 10 percent for more than 31 spots.

With a *volume discount*, the advertiser is charged a lower rate for buying a large number of spots; the discount might be 5 percent for 260 spots, for example, or 10 percent for 520 spots.

With a *continuity discount,* the advertiser is charged a lower rate for making a contract buy that covers a specified period of time. At intervals of 26, 39, and 52 weeks, advertisers are charged according to a discounted grid schedule, or the percentage discount offered increases with the length of the contract.

As discussed earlier in the chapter, radio can increase advertising reach; it can gain access to a different audience by rotating commercials through the various dayparts. To increase reach, stations offer reach plans or total audience plans that require advertisers to purchase a minimum weekly number of spots in return for a packaged discount rate, such as 16 spots per week divided equally among four dayparts. A station may offer additional discounts to advertisers if allowed to vertically and horizontally rotate commercials through a schedule at its own discretion. This is referred to as a *run-of-schedule* rate.

BUYING RADIO TIME

Similar to television rates, rates for many radio stations are now based on supply and demand rather than a rate card with specific prices. The ability of an advertiser or an advertising agency to negotiate with a radio station plays a key role in determining the actual rates paid. In order to get the best possible rate from a station or network of stations, all details of the plan must be known by the radio station. Factors such as frequency (the total number of spots in the buy), the timing of the schedule (time of day or season in which the plan is scheduled), and continuity (the length of the plan) collectively have an impact on the rate that is charged to the advertiser.

Where rate cards are published, these factors will place an advertiser on a particular grid with the station. Advertisers that purchase large amounts of time usually benefit from the discounts just described.

To illustrate some basic cost calculations used in buying radio time, let's develop some examples based on the rate card shown in Figure 9.12.

EXAMPLE ONE: BUYING INFORMATION

30-second spots	15 drive spots per week
10 breakfast spots per week	12-week schedule

Based on the length of the schedule (12 weeks), the advertiser does not qualify for a continuity discount. Therefore, the first calculation is to determine the total number of spots in the buy, to see if the advertiser qualifies for a volume discount:

Total Number of Spots	= spots per week × number of weeks
Breakfast	= 10 per week × 12 weeks = 120
Drive	= 15 per week × 12 weeks = 180
Total Spots	**= 300**

Based on the total number of spots (300), the rate charged will be from Grid 3. In this case, the 30-second rate is $88 for breakfast and $79 for drive time. The cost calculations are as follows:

Total Cost	= number of spots × earned rate
Breakfast	= 120 spots × $88 = $10 560
Drive	= 180 spots × $79 = $14 220
Total Cost	**= $24 780**

EXAMPLE TWO The advertiser would like to evaluate a reach plan, involving 16 commercials per week, against a specific buying plan. Details of each plan are as follows:

Plan A—Reach Plan (30-second spots) Information
Involves 16 spots per week
Rotated among breakfast, drive, day, and evening/weekend
Runs for 16 weeks, June through September

Plan B—Specific Plan (30-second spots) Information
8 breakfast spots per week
8 drive spots per week
16-week schedule

COST CALCULATIONS FOR PLAN A In this case, the advertiser qualifies for a continuity discount because of the 16-week schedule. Based on the rate card, the earned rate would be under Grid 3 in the reach plan. The earned rate is $71 per spot. Therefore, the cost of the reach plan is

Total Cost	= total number of spots × earned rate
	= (16 weeks × 16 spots/wk) × $71
	= **$18 176**

COST CALCULATIONS FOR PLAN B The total number of spots in the buy are

Breakfast	= 8 spots per week × 16 weeks = 128 spots
Drive	= 8 spots per week × 16 weeks = 128 spots
Total Spots	**= 256**

Based on this calculation, the advertiser is charged the Grid 3 rate, based on the volume discount (256 spots) or the continuity discount, since the contract runs for 16 weeks. Therefore, the total costs for Plan B are as follows:

Breakfast	= 128 spots × $88 = $11 264
Drive	= 128 spots × $79 = $10 112
Total Cost	= **$21 376**

In conducting a comparative evaluation of Plan A and Plan B, the advertiser must weigh the more selective reach potential of Plan B against the savings of Plan A. Perhaps the advertiser wants to reach business commuters in drive time to and from work. With Plan A, the advertiser can reach a somewhat different audience by means of a daypart rotation of spots. The net result is a cost difference of $3200 in favour of Plan A. Should the advertiser decide to go with the cost savings of Plan A, or with the more selective reach of Plan B at greater cost? Would you like to make the decision?

SUMMARY

The Canadian television market comprises conventional national networks and stations, regional networks and stations, specialty networks, digital networks, and pay TV. How people view television varies according to the time of day and the season. Television viewing tends to be lowest in the morning, somewhat higher in the afternoon, and highest in the evening. Viewership is much lower in the summer.

A trend in the industry is the gradual movement away from conventional mass-market television toward specialty channels that appeal to niche targets (e.g., YTV, HGTV, TSN), and streaming services such as Netflix. Of great concern are issues such as audience fragmentation, technologies contributing to commercial avoidance, the shift to alternative viewing options such as tablets and smartphones, and mobile technology that allows for anywhere and anytime consumption of shows. Less conventional viewing has an impact on audience size and advertising rates.

As an advertising medium, the primary advantages of television are high reach, message impact, and effectiveness; frequency (for large advertisers); some demographic selectivity; demonstration capability; and coverage flexibility. Disadvantages include high cost, audience fragmentation, clutter, commercial avoidance, and the lead time required to plan and implement a media buy.

Depending on the degree of coverage they desire, advertisers can purchase television time from the national networks for national or selective spots, or from local stations. To compensate for clutter and commercial avoidance, advertisers are taking advantage of sponsorship opportunities, product placement, and branded content opportunities. These strategies offer product exposure during the programs. The rates an advertiser pays are affected by supply and demand, type of program purchased, daypart, and the length of the commercial. The cost of television time is highest in prime time (7:00 to 11:00 p.m.). Discounts are generally offered on the basis of frequency, volume, continuity, and season.

Computer software now plays a key role in planning and buying television commercial time. Referred to as optimizers, the software programs allow planners to search media databases for the best program combinations to increase target reach.

The radio industry is also in transition as radio listening levels are influenced by new technologies such as internet and digital radio, and satellite radio. Traditional stations have reacted to these influences and offer interactive websites where listeners can access music and other information.

In contrast to television viewing, radio listening peaks in the morning (6:00 to 10:00 a.m.) and tapers off as the day progresses. Radio signals are transmitted in three ways: AM, FM, and digitally. FM is currently the most popular form of transmission, but digital audio broadcasting will grow in the next decade, stealing market share from traditional stations.

As an advertising medium, radio offers target market selectivity, reach and frequency potential (based on its relatively low cost), and coverage flexibility. Radio's ability to reach selective targets is based on the format of the station.

Currently, country, adult contemporary, the combination of oldies and rock, and news/talk are among the most popular station formats. The disadvantages of radio as an advertising medium include audience fragmentation, problems associated with message retention, and clutter.

Radio rates are affected by several factors: season, daypart, reach plans, and the type of advertiser (local advertisers pay lower rates). Advertisers are offered discounts based on frequency, volume, continuity, and the use of package plans (reach plans).

KEY TERMS

AM (amplitude modulation) 276
audience flow 278
audience fragmentation 256
branded content 266
cluster 262
clutter 262
continuity discount 270
daypart 260
daytime 268
FM (frequency modulation) 276
format 277
frequency 261
frequency discount 270
fringe time 267
grid card 269
horizontal rotation 282
media convergence 258
network advertising 263
optimizer 274
package plans 274
people meter 259
podcast 275
pre-emption 274
prime time 267
product placement 266
ratings 260
reach plan (total audience plan) 282
ROS (run of schedule) 274
rotation plans 282
seasonal discounts 273
selective spot sales 264
split 30s 269
sponsorship (TV) 264
spot sales 269
upfront buying 267
vertical rotation 282
volume discount 270

REVIEW QUESTIONS

1. What is the purpose of the various time classifications in television and radio?
2. Identify and briefly explain the key issues confronting the television industry (and TV advertisers) today.
3. What are the primary advantages and disadvantages of television advertising for the national advertiser? For the local advertiser?
4. Explain the difference between network advertising and national or selective spot advertising.
5. Identify and briefly explain any three factors that influence the cost of television advertising.
6. Identify and briefly explain the television discounts that are based on the amount of time purchased by advertisers.
7. Explain the following television terms:
   a) Branded content
   b) Audience fragmentation
   c) Sponsorship
   d) Daypart
   e) Clutter
   f) Upfront buying
   g) Prime time versus fringe time
   h) Package plans
   i) Pre-emption rates
   j) GRPs
8. Identify and briefly discuss the key issues confronting the radio industry (and radio advertisers) today.
9. What does "station format" refer to in radio broadcasting?
10. What are the major advantages and disadvantages of radio advertising for the national advertiser? For the local advertiser?

11. Identify and briefly explain any three factors that influence the cost of radio advertising.
12. What is a reach plan, and what benefits does it provide the advertiser?
13. Calculate the cost of the following radio campaign. Use the rate card in Figure 9.12 to do your calculations.

CKET Radio

30-second spots as follows:

Breakfast:	4 spots per week; Mon–Fri; 28 weeks
Drive:	4 spots per week; Mon–Fri; 28 weeks
Daytime:	8 spots per week; Mon–Fri; 28 weeks

Calculate the cost of a 16-spot reach plan for 28 weeks. How much money is saved compared with the original calculation? Is the reach plan a better deal?

14. If you made the decision to use radio in a city such as Toronto, Ottawa, or Vancouver, on what basis would you select specific stations? Discuss your reasons.
15. Briefly explain the following radio terms:
    a) Vertical rotation
    b) Horizontal rotation
    c) Reach plan
    d) Frequency discount
    e) Volume discount
    f) Continuity discount

DISCUSSION QUESTIONS

1. "Influences such as video on demand and commercial avoidance will be the demise of television advertising as we know it." Is this statement true or false? Conduct some secondary research on the issues and present a viewpoint.
2. What impact will mobile technology have on the future of television viewing and television advertising? Will people be satisfied watching television shows on small screens? Discuss.
3. Identify some additional strategies advertisers should be using to counter the problem of commercial avoidance (either viewers leaving the viewing area or viewers using PVRs to avoid messages). Should funds be reallocated to other media? Present a position on this issue.
4. Are product placement and branded content viable means of advertising? Will too much placement and branded content harm the credibility of television programs and the advertiser's reputation? Evaluate the issues surrounding this form of advertising, and present a point of view.
5. Target market selectivity is the key benefit of radio advertising. On what basis can the radio industry exploit this advantage? Discuss appropriate strategies the industry might use to attract advertisers.
6. Are internet radio and satellite radio a threat to conventional radio broadcasters? If so, what strategies should conventional broadcasters be implementing now or in the near future to protect their position? Discuss.

NOTES

1. Canadian Media Directors' Council *Media Digest*, 2014 - 15, p. 54.
2. Ibid., 51.
3. "Number of Cord Cutters Is Growing, 16% of Canadians No Longer Watch TV," *Marketing*, July 11, 2013, **www.marketingmag.ca**
4. "Streaming Continues to Gain Steam: MTM," *Media in Canada*, April 13, 2015, **www.mediaincanada.com**
5. Catalyst Canada, "With Growth Comes Change: The Evolving Mobile Landscape in 2015," **www.catalyst.ca/2015-canadian-smartphone-penetration**
6. Canadian Media Directors' Council, *Media Digest*, 2014-2015, 15.
7. Numeris Canada, **www.numeris.ca**
8. TVB Canada, *TV Basics 2014-2015*, 26.
9. Canadian Media Directors' Council, *Media Digest*, 2012-2013, 11.
10. TVB Canada, *TV Basics 2014-2015*, TVB Canada, p. 27
11. Ibid., 41, 42.
12. "IKEA Brings the Kitchen Sink to HGTV Show," *Media in Canada*, March 3, 2015, **www.mediaincanada.com**
13. Susan Krashinsky, "Labatt Strikes Back against Molson with *Hockey Night* Deal," *Globe and Mail*, January 27, 2013, **www.theglobeandmail.com**
14. "New PQ Media Data: Global Product Placement up 12% to 8.3B in 2012," *PR Web*, May 1, 2013, **www.prweb.com**
15. Corbis Entertainment, **www.corbisentertainment.com/casestudy**
16. Josh Kolm, "*The Amazing Race Canada* Adds Petro-Canada, Scotiabank," *Media in Canada*, June 18, 2014, **www.mediaincanada.com.**
17. Bill Harvey, "A Brief Personal History of Media Optimization," Bill Harvey Consulting, **www.billharveyconsulting.com**
18. Erwin Ephron, "Where's Robobuyer?," *Advertising Age*, May 1, 2000, p. 45.
19. Canadian Media Directors' Council, *Media Digest*, 2014-2015, 55, 57.
20. David Pogue, "In One Stroke Podcasting hits Mainstream," *The New York Times*, July 28, 2005, **www.nytimes.com**
21. Canadian Media Directors' Council, *Media Digest*, 2014-2015, 57.
22. Ibid., 58.
23. Jordan Pinto, "Corus launches a slew of radio apps," *Media in Canada*, February 18, 2015, **www.mediaincanada.com**

CHAPTER 10 Out-of-Home Media

© Design Pics Inc./Alamy Stock Photo

Learning Objectives

After studying this chapter, you will be able to

1. Differentiate among the various forms of out-of-home media
2. Explain the advantages and disadvantages of the key types of out-of-home media
3. Describe the factors considered and procedures used for buying various forms of out-of-home media

Out-of-home media include various forms of outdoor advertising, transit advertising, and in-store and at-retail advertising. This chapter presents the basic types of out-of-home advertising alternatives, the advantages and disadvantages of each alternative, and the procedures for buying media space for each.

Out-of-home advertising and the variety of alternatives included in its domain represent a highly visible and effective alternative for advertisers. Think about it. If you drive a car, travel by transit, or stroll through shopping malls, you are constantly exposed to out-of-home advertising messages. Out-of-home advertising messages reach a massive cross-section of a city's population 24 hours a day, 7 days a week. The latest data available (2013) show that spending on out-of-home advertising amounts to $514 million annually in Canada, and it is a growing segment of the advertising industry—online advertising is the only medium growing at a faster rate.[1]

Several factors are contributing to the popularity of outdoor advertising. The specialization and fragmentation that has occurred in other media, especially television and magazines, has caused advertisers to shift dollars toward outdoor. Many planners now pay more attention to "when and why consumers come in contact with media and advertising messages." These planners believe that "the proximity and timing of an advertising exposure" are important.[2] Outdoor ads can reach people when they are ready to buy. As well, new technologies have created new and innovative formats that have transformed outdoor boards from a static medium to a dynamic and interactive medium—newer digital boards can actually entertain people who pass by. On digital outdoor boards the message can be changed quickly based on demographic considerations or events that may occur. Finally, mobile devices such as smartphones and tablets are transforming the content of out-of-home creative, allowing for unprecedented interaction.

Outdoor Media Research

The Canadian Out-of-Home Measurement Bureau (COMB) is responsible for compiling reliable circulation data and information about outdoor advertising. COMB audits the circulation of outdoor media, which is based on municipal or provincial traffic counts, and that of indoor media, which is based on empirical data and statistical methods. For example, mall posters are measured based on head counts conducted by independent research organizations in each market location.

Sellers of outdoor media also rely on research data that are integrated with sophisticated software programs to help plan campaigns. For example, Mediacom uses a system called SMART—Strategic Mapping and Response Tool—that uses data from Statistics Canada. These data, which are constantly added to SMART, include "traffic flow and traffic volume information." Referred to as *geodemographic mapping*, the data have helped outdoor advertisers to "effectively stage campaigns that target specific ethnic neighbourhoods with advertising in the appropriate language."[3] Outdoor has never been considered a targeted medium, but the combination of information and technology is changing things.

To facilitate accurate planning for their clients, agency media planners can access COMBNavigator. COMBNavigator "provides comparative reach and frequency schedules by market, operator, and product for multiple demographic breaks in Canadian markets."[4]

Outdoor Advertising

POSTERS

The **poster** is the most commonly used form of outdoor advertising. Posters are either horizontal or vertical and are commonly referred to as **billboards**. The poster is composed of stripped sheets of special paper designed to withstand the wear and tear of outdoor conditions. To maximize reach potential, posters are strategically located on major routes within, or leading to, the business and shopping districts of a community. To maximize the frequency of the message, and to extend the daily viewing by consumers, posters are often illuminated. Advertisers can purchase poster space either in single panels or as a "showing." A **showing** refers to the buying of multiple panels to achieve a desired level of reach and frequency in a market. See Figure 10.1 for an illustration of an outdoor poster.

BACKLIT POSTERS

A **backlit poster** (often called a *backlight*) is a luminous sign containing advertising graphics printed on translucent vinyl material. Colour reproduction and impact are among the advantages offered by a backlit poster. At night, the lighted display takes on a three-dimensional effect. Backlit posters are strategically located at major intersections and high-volume traffic routes. The primary advantage of backlit posters is the image enhancement they offer; there is strong visual impact during the day and at night. The cost of producing backlit posters is quite high, but the opportunities for exposure are estimated to be twice that of a standard poster. Refer to the illustration in Figure 10.2.

FIGURE 10.1
An outdoor poster

© Francis Vachon/Alamy Stock Photo

FIGURE 10.2
An illustration of a backlit poster

© Joe Fairs/Alamy Stock Photo

Some backlights in high traffic locations have a scrolling feature. The messages are timed to change with the flow of traffic so that everyone gets a chance to see messages from three advertisers.

SUPERBOARDS

A **superboard** is an oversized display unit (as long as 60 feet horizontally) positioned at high-traffic locations. These boards may include elaborate extensions that further increase the size. A superboard with an extension is referred to as a **spectacular**. For instance, imagine a KFC bucket of chicken rotating above a board advertising KFC. A spectacular is created to meet a specific advertiser's needs.

Depending on production values, spectaculars can either be made of paper or vinyl materials. A recent innovation is the computer-designed 3-D billboard that produces a product replica as large as 16 metres high. The "trivision" board is a three-sided board that rotates. Each rotation has louvres that rotate to change the ads.

Superboards and spectaculars are usually one-of-a-kind structures fabricated at great expense. They also require a long-term commitment from the advertiser. Spectaculars are beyond the budgets of most advertisers. Refer to the image in Figure 10.3.

TRANSIT SHELTERS

A *transit shelter unit* consists of two street-level backlit posters that are incorporated into the design of glass-and-steel transit shelters. Each shelter has two faces that are backlit from dusk until dawn. Transit shelter units are located on busy public transit routes and offer advertisers high levels of potential exposure to motorists, pedestrians, and transit riders.

Transit shelter advertising offers the advertiser strong visual impact, since the colour reproduction is of superior quality. These units are sold to advertisers on the basis of site-selection flexibility. That is, advertisers can select sites that reach certain age, income, or

FIGURE 10.3

Superboards are attention-getters in urban high-traffic areas.

© Nick Ut/AP Photo/The Canadian Press

ethnic groups, or they can concentrate on a geographic trading zone, depending on the target they would like to reach. Transit shelters offer high reach and heavy frequency.

DIGITAL SIGNS

Digital sign units display advertising messages electronically, with ads from numerous advertisers displayed on a rotating basis around the clock. Ads are typically 10 to 15 seconds in length. These signs offer tremendous flexibility, since an advertiser can change the message quickly if necessary. They are generally located in high-traffic areas within large urban centres across Canada. Prime location means heavy weekly frequency can be achieved.

DIGITAL VIDEO DISPLAYS

In key urban markets, large-format **digital video screens** are available. The high-resolution screens are remotely programmable, which, as with digital signs, provides advertisers with the flexibility to change creative quickly. Digital video screens have rejuvenated interest in outdoor advertising. The new boards can display multiple messages at the same time (e.g., a manufacturer could rotate ads for several of its brands), or ads can be integrated with news and weather information. Coca-Cola recently ran a campaign for its Simply Lemonade beverage. The ads only appeared when the temperature reached 25 degrees Celsius.

Advertisers are finding many applications for outdoor video ads. Messages can be customized based on location, weather, changing market conditions, and other influences. From a media planning perspective, digital boards add flexibility to a campaign and allow advertisers to reach consumers with real-time communications. The ability to be responsive gives a creative team much latitude for developing new ideas. An illustration of a digital video display appears in Figure 10.4.

STREET-LEVEL ADVERTISING

Street-level units are illuminated from behind and are positioned adjacent to high-traffic streets in the downtown cores of major markets. Many of these signs are now popping up along sidewalks and in public squares. Their presence gives advertisers an opportunity to reach people in hard-to-target urban areas where there is a good deal of pedestrian foot traffic in the daytime. The signs are visible to vehicle traffic as well.

FIGURE 10.4

Digital video boards offer high-impact communications and are capable of displaying multiple messages.

The ads appear much as they do on a transit shelter except the street-level unit is a stand-alone structure that contains only the advertising message. An example of this form of advertising appears in Figure 10.5.

A recent innovation in this category is the mega-column. The mega-column is a tall structure that contains a combination of brand advertising and municipal information on three-sided or four-sided units.

FIGURE 10.5

This Apple iPad ad is an example of street-level advertising.

FIGURE 10.6

Banners mounted inside a building

WALL BANNERS AND MURALS

Banners are large vinyl sheets usually framed and mounted on the inside or outside wall of a building. They can be moved and reused. Refer to the illustration in Figure 10.6.

Mural banner advertisements are hand-painted outdoor extravaganzas on the sides of buildings. They are very large, often the entire height of the building. They can be three dimensional, which adds to their attention-grabbing capability. See Figure 10.7 for an example of a mural advertisement.

FIGURE 10.7

An example of outdoor mural advertising

MALL POSTERS

Unlike all other forms of outdoor advertising, **mall posters** do not rely on vehicular traffic. Typically located inside shopping malls, these backlit posters are seen at eye level by passing pedestrians as they walk through the mall. These posters reach consumers at a crucial time—a time when they are making buying decisions—so the posters are a good outlet for retailers and branded products available right in the mall. The very presence of a message on a mall poster may encourage impulse buying. As a medium, mall posters are a good secondary vehicle in a multimedia campaign. They are ideal for reinforcing a brand's primary selling message.

The quality and impact of mall posters is advancing. Some malls hang oversized wall murals from various structures so that the advertising message is clearly visible to passersby.

Outdoor as an Advertising Medium

Many advertisers overlook or ignore the benefits of outdoor advertising, yet it is a medium that is excellent at reinforcing a message communicated in another medium, such as television, the internet, and magazines. This section presents the benefits and drawbacks of outdoor advertising.

ADVANTAGES OF OUTDOOR ADVERTISING

TARGET REACH AND FREQUENCY Outdoor advertising provides advertisers with the opportunity to reach a very large cross-section of a market's population in a short period of time. Depending on the weight level purchased (gross rating points, GRPs) and on the strategic location of outdoor boards on busy thoroughfares, outdoor advertising has the potential for multiple exposures. Some research data indicate that as much as 90 percent of a city's traffic is concentrated on 10 percent of the streets (streets where outdoor boards are located).[5]

TARGETING FLEXIBILITY Advertisers that want to advertise in only certain areas have the flexibility to do so with outdoor advertising. Outdoor units are typically purchased on a market-by-market basis. Within major metropolitan markets, advertisers can also use outdoor posters to target neighbourhoods based on a combination of demographic and geographic characteristics. Advertisers that want to increase weight levels in selected markets can use outdoor advertising to supplement a national campaign in another medium. Outdoor is an ideal medium for a key market media strategy.

SIZE AND QUALITY OF MESSAGE Backlit posters, spectaculars, and transit shelter advertising units all offer advertisers high reproduction quality. Although the messages communicated by outdoor advertising must be short, a strong visual impression can attract the attention of people passing by. As the old saying goes, "A picture is worth a thousand words." If the goal is to create a monumental impression on consumers, outdoor boards have the capability.

COMPATIBILITY WITH OTHER MEDIA Outdoor advertising can reinforce the message of other media in two ways. First, it can extend the total reach and frequency of a campaign beyond what a single medium can do. Therefore, it is a good complementary medium—a good means of reinforcing important sales messages. Second, outdoor advertising can increase the total number of impressions made on a target market that may be only light consumers of other media. For example, a light viewer of television, who is hard to reach regardless of the weight level purchased, may be easier to reach via outdoor advertising.

CREATING PRODUCT AWARENESS Traditionally regarded as a complementary medium, outdoor advertising can also be effective in generating product awareness when used as a primary medium, particularly if a shotgun media strategy is used (e.g., if an advertiser wanted to reach all adults aged 18 to 49 in specified markets). As an example, watchmaker TAG Heuer used outdoor posters to make a quick impression on upscale consumers in key urban markets in Canada. The outdoor ads reached busy executives and professionals who commute to downtown each day. The outdoor component of TAG Heuer's advertising campaign complemented its more targeted magazine campaign. In magazines, more product information is communicated.

COST When the absolute cost of outdoor advertising is evaluated in terms of reach potential—the opportunities for exposing consumers to outdoor messages—the medium begins to seem like a fairly efficient media buy. Using Toronto as an example and assuming an advertiser purchased standard outdoor posters sold by Outfront Media for a four-week period at a 50-GRP level, we would calculate the CPM (cost of reaching a thousand people) as follows:

$$\begin{aligned} \text{CPM} &= \frac{\text{Cost}}{\text{Population}} \\ &= \frac{\$265\,845}{5\,959.5} \\ &= \$44.61 \end{aligned}$$

This represents the cost of reaching a thousand people once. Therefore, when the daily travel patterns of people are considered (and thus the potential for multiple exposure), the cost efficiencies of outdoor advertising improve.

CONTENT FLEXIBILITY Due to advancing technology, an additional advantage of outdoor media is content flexibility. Unique to digital signs and digital video displays is the fact that content can be changed quickly, based on market conditions, competitive activity, or the advertiser's desire to simply display a different message. It is the advertiser's space to use as it sees fit. A fast-food restaurant, for example, could deliver a breakfast or lunch message in the morning and a dinner message in the afternoon and evening. A television network could advertise upcoming shows or specials, a situation in which the content would be constantly changing.

DISADVANTAGES OF OUTDOOR ADVERTISING

CREATIVE LIMITATIONS The nature of the outdoor advertising medium (as seen by people passing by either in a vehicle or on foot) is such that it must rely on instant visual impact to get attention. The message itself must be short and simple to read, and it must quickly draw attention to the brand name. However, creative limitations are a bit of a myth to Brian Harrod, a former creative director at several prominent Canadian ad agencies. According to Harrod, "If you can't present an advertising idea on an outdoor board, it isn't simple and focused enough to be an effective advertising idea."[6] Examine the ad in Figure 10.8.

LACK OF TARGET MARKET SELECTIVITY The broad reach potential of outdoor advertising (it reaches all adults and children) makes it impossible for an advertiser to focus on a target market. Therefore, due to wasted circulation, the CPM figures that show efficiency

FIGURE 10.8

This milk campaign was executed in magazines and various forms of outdoor advertising.

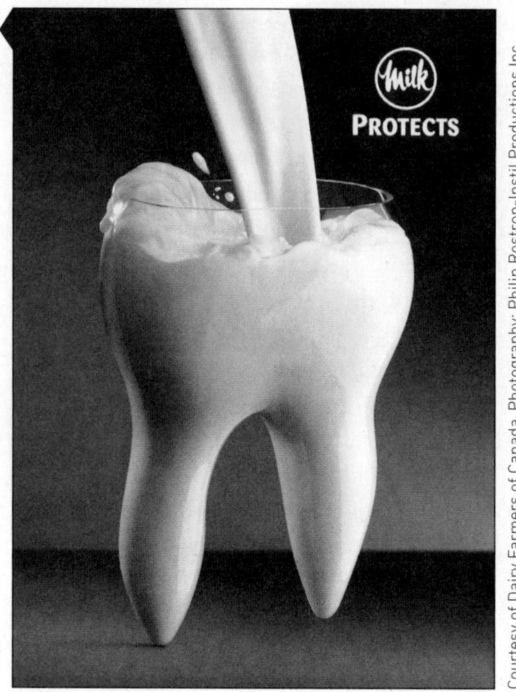

Courtesy of Dairy Farmers of Canada. Photography: Philip Rostron-Instil Productions Inc.

may be deceptively low (since the medium reaches many people who would never purchase the product).

COSTS Costs of outdoor advertising are high in two areas. First, the costs of producing finished materials for units such as backlit posters, mall posters, and transit shelters are high (printing on a plastic vinyl material is expensive). Second, the absolute cost of buying media space is high. A four-week showing of horizontal outdoor posters in the Toronto census metropolitan area at a 25-GRP level costs $139 569. At a 100-GRP level the cost rises to $478 521. Corresponding figures for the same GRP levels in Edmonton and Calgary are $28 500 and $97 700, respectively. Costs can add up quickly and account for a sizable portion of an advertising budget.

LACK OF PRESTIGE Outdoor advertising does not always enhance the image of the product, whereas advertising in a quality magazine can rely on the surrounding editorial content to aid in image development. Also, the association of the product with a medium that clutters the landscape may produce a negative impact. Many critics of outdoor advertising refer to it as "pollution on a stick." With due respect to these critics, digital outdoor advertising in the form of digital video, along with new and more extravagant outdoor alternatives, has added an element of quality to the medium.

UNOBTRUSIVE MEDIUM Despite the reach and frequency potential of the medium, people who pass by may not notice outdoor ads. Unless the message catches the attention of passersby, the outdoor board will blend into the background and not break through the consumer's perceptual barriers. In urban downtown locations, the clustering of outdoor advertising may prevent any single message from being noticed.

For more insight into the potential role out-of-home advertising can play in a media campaign, read the Advertising in Action vignette **Big, Bold, and Branded**.

ADVERTISING IN ACTION

Big, Bold, and Branded

There's one really good thing to be said about out-of-home advertising: It's a medium that can make a big impression on people! Superboards and spectaculars, backlit posters at night, and digital video displays present a bold and vivid advertising message. From a strategic planning perspective, including outdoor advertising in the mix helps create brand awareness and recognition. If used properly, it can also capture the essence of the message that is presented in more detail in other media.

Honda discovered these benefits with the launch of the 2015 Honda Fit. The vehicle was launched with a national media campaign that embraced television spots, digital ads (internet), and outdoor. The creative for the campaign emphasized how much space there was in a subcompact vehicle—consumers would be surprised by how much could be packed into the car.

The creative was based on an "inside/outside" idea. Using superboards that were divided in half, the left side showed a photo of a fully packed Fit; the right side showed a real layout (in a 2D format) of all the items that are inside. David Crichton, creative partner at Grip (Honda's ad agency), says, "We took the tactic of going into key markets and created spectacles that people will notice." It was a great way to demonstrate the space available in such a small car.

Mediawise, these boards couldn't run everywhere due to cost, so placement was restricted to 20 boards in key locations in Vancouver, Toronto, Montreal, and Quebec City. The combination of creative and media worked in unison. While boldly demonstrating how much space there was in the car, the actual creative could change based on location and who was likely to see the boards. For instance, in Leaside, an urban family-oriented area of Toronto, the ad featured camping equipment. On the Gardiner Expressway, a major traffic artery for commuters and shoppers going to IKEA, the ad showed how much furniture can fit inside.

From a media planning perspective, the boards helped achieve awareness objectives by capitalizing on the reach and frequency benefits of the medium. The ads were only placed on very busy routes where travel patterns tend to be habitual in nature—the same person sees the outdoor board travelling to and from work each day. Outdoor advertising significantly increased brand awareness and prompted the audience to take action, be it to visit a website for more information or visit a dealer to learn more about the car.

Courtesy of Grip Limited.

Source: Adapted from Josh Kolm, "Honda Finds the Right Fit for Out-of-Home," *Media in Canada*, October 6, 2014, www.mediaincanada.com.

Buying Outdoor Media Space

Regardless of the outdoor advertising format under consideration, there are similarities in the media buying process. Outdoor space is sold in four-week periods and is available on a market-by-market basis. Advertisers can purchase a single market, a group of markets, or a national buy, if strategy demands it and budget permits it.

Media space is purchased on the basis of the advertising weight level desired by the advertiser, expressed in terms of GRPs (gross rating points). As indicated in Chapter 7, GRP is a weighting factor that combines reach and frequency variables. In the case of outdoor advertising, GRP is defined as the total circulation of a specific outdoor advertisement expressed as a percentage of the market's population. With reference to Figure 10.9 (an Outfront Media poster rate card), on a weekly basis a weight level of

100 GRPs delivers exposure opportunities equal to the population of a market. A weight level of 50 GRPs offers one-half the exposure opportunities.

OUTDOOR ADVERTISING—RATES AND DISCOUNTS

Outdoor advertising rates are quoted on a four-week basis. To illustrate outdoor cost calculations, let's consider a few media buying examples. Rates and data from Figures 10.9 and 10.10 are used to calculate costs.

Outdoor Buying Plan: Example 1	
Medium:	Outdoor Horizontal Backlights (CBS Outdoor)
Markets:	Toronto (CMA), Edmonton (CMA), Vancouver (CMA), and Winnipeg (CMA)
Weight:	Toronto and Vancouver at 25 GRPs; Edmonton and Winnipeg at 50 GRPs
Contract Length:	8 weeks

Using the data from Figure 10.10, we would calculate the appropriate costs for each market over a four-week period as follows:

Toronto	$139 569 × 2	= $279 138
Vancouver	46 601 × 2	= 93 202
Edmonton	54 250 × 2	= 108 500
Winnipeg	16 830 × 2	= 33 660
Total Cost		= **$514 500**

The length of the contract is eight weeks. Therefore, the cost for each market is multiplied by a factor of two (eight weeks divided by a four-week rate). Should volume and continuity discounts apply, they would be deducted from the gross amount shown in this illustration.

Outdoor Buying Plan: Example 2	
Medium:	Transit Shelters (CBS Outdoor)
Markets:	Hamilton (CMA), London (CMA), Calgary (CMA), and Halifax (CMA)
Weight:	50 GRPs weekly
Contract Length:	16 weeks

According to Figure 10.10, the costs for a four-week period for each market would be as follows:

Hamilton	$19 277
London	8 474
Calgary	56 430
Halifax	8 925
Total Cost	**$93 106**

2013 CBS Outdoor RATEBOOK: Horizontal Posters (10' X 20')

				2013 Est.	Avg. Daily Circ. In-Market Oct '12 CDR	Single Panel Rate $ Net	*Average # of Panels to deliver GRPs*				*4 week net rate*			
											(+5%)	flat	(-5%)	(-10%)
Province	**Code**	**Market**	**Operator**	**Population**	**Circ In-Market**	**$ Rate**	**25**	**50**	**75**	**100**	**@25**	**@50**	**@75**	**@100**
Quebec	090	**Montreal CMA**	CBS	3,744,300	36,635	$ **4,418**	26	52	78	103	$ **80,399**	$ **153,140**	$ **218,225**	$ **275,652**
Ontario	182	**Toronto CMA**	CBS	5,572,700	24,964	$ **4,191**	56	111	166	222	$ **139,569**	$ **265,845**	$ **378,829**	$ **478,521**
Manitoba	318	**Winnipeg CMA**	CBS	722,800	21,614	$ **1,733**	9	17	26	34	$ **8,836**	$ **16,830**	$ **23,983**	$ **30,294**
Alberta	395	**Edmonton CMA**	CBS	1,165,500	16,923	$ **1,938**	18	35	52	69	$ **28,481**	$ **54,250**	$ **77,306**	$ **97,650**
British Columbia	425	**Vancouver CMA**	CBS	2,338,000	30,720	$ **3,000**	19	37	55		$ **46,601**	$ **88,763**	$ **126,487**	

Printed with permission from Outfront Media

FIGURE **10.9**

Rate card for outdoor posters (actual rate card includes many other markets)

2013 CBS Outdoor RATEBOOK: Street Furniture - Transit Shelters, APTs, Mapstands, Kiosks, Mediacolumns (68 1/4" x 47 1/4")

				2013 Est.	Avg. Daily Circ. In-Market Oct '12 CDR	Single Panel Rate $ Net	*Average # of Panels to deliver GRPs*				*4 week net rate*			
											25 GRPs (+5%)	50 GRPs flat	75 GRPs (-5%)	100 GRPs (-10%)
Province	**Code**	**Market**	**Operator**	**Population**	**Column2**	**$ Rate**	**25**	**50**	**75**	**100**	**@25**	**@50**	**@75**	**@100**
Nova Scotia	019	**Halifax CMA**	CBS	393,600	9,451	$ **750**	11	21	32	42	$ **4,686**	$ **8,925**	$ **12,718**	$ **16,065**
Ontario	199	**Hamilton CMA** (+ 10% discount with Toronto)	CBS	705,700	9,320	$ **912**	19	37	56	74	$ **10,120**	$ **19,277**	$ **27,470**	$ **34,699**
Ontario	224	**London CMA**	CBS	462,800	12,538	$ **781**	10	19	28	38	$ **4,449**	$ **8,474**	$ **12,075**	$ **15,253**
Alberta	362	**Calgary CMA**	CBS	1,218,200	9,199	$ **1,500**	33	66	99	131	$ **29,626**	$ **56,430**	$ **80,413**	$ **101,574**

Printed with permission from Outfront Media

FIGURE **10.10**

Rate card for street-level advertising (actual rate card includes many other markets)

Since the length of the contract is 16 weeks, the cost of the markets above would be multiplied by a factor of four (16 weeks divided by four-week rates). The gross cost would be calculated as follows:

$$\$93\,106 \times 4 = \$372\,424$$

Outdoor media usually offer advertisers volume discounts (a reduced rate based on dollar volume purchased) and continuity discounts (a reduced rate for extended buys such as 12 weeks, 16 weeks, etc.).

Transit Advertising

Every week 5.7 million Canadians take an average nine trips on public transit.[7] Further, daily commuters using public transit spend 40 minutes on a bus, 44 minutes on a subway, and 52 minutes on a light rail vehicle getting to work.[8] What a great opportunity for advertisers to reach and interact with people! Transit riders represent a captive audience that often has a need for visual stimulation. Bored with travelling on buses and subway cars, riders frequently read advertising messages. In fact, they may read the same message over and over again. If they are habitual transit users, there is potential for the message to be seen repeatedly. Recent studies show riders use their smartphones while in transit. The smartphone provides immediate interaction with active consumers, turning bus stops, vehicles, and stations into points of sale.

The major forms of transit advertising include interior transit cards, exterior bus posters, vinyl transit wraps, station posters, subway digital screens, and station domination.

INTERIOR CARDS

Interior cards are print advertisements contained in racks above the windows of public transit vehicles (i.e., in buses, streetcars, subway cars, and light rail cars). The cards are available in a variety of sizes depending on the needs of the advertiser. Interior cards located above windows have a horizontal orientation. Given that the audience is captive and that the average travel time in a transit vehicle in major markets is estimated to be 40 minutes, the advertiser has the flexibility to include longer copy, which is not an option with other out-of-home media.

EXTERIOR BUS POSTERS

Two options are available in the **exterior bus poster** format. The first is a *king poster* (larger format) located on the side of surface transit vehicles only. The second option is called a *seventy poster* (smaller format) that is located on either the side or the tail of surface transit vehicles. The unique characteristic of exterior bus posters is their mobility. They move through every area of a city and are seen by motorists, transit riders, and pedestrians. A relatively new option is the tail poster. *Tail posters* appear in the back window of surface vehicles. An illustration of an exterior bus poster is shown in Figure 10.11.

VINYL TRANSIT WRAPS

The **vinyl wrap** allows an advertiser to "own" a whole bus or part of a bus or streetcar. Wraps are described as full wraps, full backs, or murals. The advertising is printed onto a vinyl product that is applied to the vehicle. A **full wrap** would cover the entire bus excluding the front; a **full back** would cover the back end of the bus; and a **mural** would cover one side of the bus. See Figure 10.12 for an illustration.

© Francis Vachon/The Canadian Press

FIGURE 10.11

An exterior transit ad

© Francis Vachon/The Canadian Press

FIGURE 10.12

An example of a vinyl wrap advertisement on a bus

Advertising rates for wraps are quoted differently than other forms of transit ads. Typically, the wrap rates are quoted on a cost-per-bus or cost-per-car (subway car) basis. Rate cards also include the production costs, which can be quite high.

STATION POSTERS AND BACKLITS

Station posters are advertisements located on platforms and at the entrances and exits of the subway and light rail transit systems in Canada. They are available in a variety of sizes, and the most common of these is called the *station poster*. The station poster is the same size as a transit shelter or mall poster (standard size specifications encourage cross-usage of various out-of-home media). Station posters fall into two broad categories: platform

FIGURE 10.13 Subway platform poster advertising

posters and subway backlits. **Platform posters** are located on the subway wall opposite the rider waiting on the platform. In the Toronto subway system, posters are also attached to steel pillars in the area between rail lines. In the Montreal Métro, with no pillars between the rails, the posters are attached to the walls of the platforms and are large enough to be seen by passengers on the opposite platform. Passengers waiting on both platforms are exposed to these messages. See Figure 10.13 for an example of this type of advertisement.

The second option is the subway backlit. The backlit poster is a vinyl poster with rear illumination. Backlits are usually located along station walls and above and below escalator stairwells throughout the Toronto and Montreal subway systems and the GO Transit system in southern Ontario. Light rail transit systems in Vancouver, Edmonton, and Calgary also offer a variety of backlit and poster options.

SUBWAY—DIGITAL SCREENS

The Toronto and Montreal subway systems offer digital communications capability through LCD screens mounted above subway platforms. Idle, waiting passengers can easily see the screens. Smaller screens will eventually be installed in subway cars. The screens feature news, sports, business news, and weather, along with video advertisements and sponsorship opportunities.

INNOVATION AND STATION DOMINATION

Much innovation is occurring with transit advertising. It now seems that any space is available for advertising purposes. An advertiser can adorn walls, add floor graphics, wrap entry and exit turnstiles, and place ads on train platforms. As well, interactive digital elements with face-recognition technology and prop installations are an option that will keep commuters engaged. An illustration of some innovative transit advertising appears in Figure 10.14.

One of these innovative concepts is **station domination**, an opportunity that gives a single advertiser control of every advertising space in a subway station. Station domination is available on the Toronto and Montreal transit systems. For advertisers looking for inventive ways of breaking through the clutter, station domination will certainly do it.

FIGURE 10.14

Innovative spaces are being employed to grab attention of riders in subway stations.

Included in the mix are innovative concepts such as ceiling decals, extended wall ads, super-sized floor ads, and digital video.

Transit as an Advertising Medium

ADVANTAGES OF TRANSIT

CONTINUOUS EXPOSURE AND CREATIVITY Commuters tend to be creatures of routine, so they are exposed to the same messages on a daily basis. This provides some creative opportunity, as longer copy can be used and riders can become more involved. In this regard, transit advertisements are a good vehicle for reinforcing the messages of in-home media.

REACH AND FREQUENCY Transit advertising reaches a mass audience quickly. Transit riders cut across all demographics, with the heaviest concentration in the adult category. In fact, transit use is highest among young adults who have a university degree and are employed in MOPE positions (manager, owner, professional, executive).[9] Consumers generally encounter the message more than once because of daily riding patterns, and the combination of high reach and frequency translates into an extremely high number of impressions on the target market.

FLEXIBILITY Certain transit media are flexible because the message can be changed easily. For example, the message can be easily changed in any form of digital communications depending on advertising need or circumstance (i.e., a change in creative direction or competitor activity). Transit markets can be purchased on a geographic basis, so it is a good complementary medium to add reach and frequency in a total advertising campaign.

MARKET COVERAGE In any given market, transit advertising covers all sections of the community—residential, urban, and suburban; industrial; and commercial—where other forms of out-of-home media may not be available.

COST On a market-by-market basis, the dollar outlay for transit media space is relatively low, and considering the number of consumers reached the cost per thousand is low. Essentially, transit is a cost-efficient medium that reaches a mass audience. As a result, it is attractive to smaller-budget advertisers and to larger-budget advertisers needing a complementary medium to reach urban customers.

DISADVANTAGES OF TRANSIT

LACK OF TARGET MARKET SELECTIVITY In large urban markets, transit use reflects the general, nonspecific demographic and socioeconomic characteristics of those markets.

Therefore, the use of transit results in wasted circulation for an advertiser attempting to reach a precisely defined target. Consequently, the cost-per-thousand efficiencies, which are based on high reach of a mass audience, may be artificially low.

MEDIA ENVIRONMENT The environment in which transit advertising operates is often a hectic one—people coming and going quickly, particularly during the morning and evening rush hours. In such an environment, advertising messages are easy to avoid. In the case of interior transit, the environment is often cluttered and crowded (particularly during peak-usage periods such as rush hour), a circumstance that makes the messages both less visible and less attractive. This environment may detract from the prestige of the product.

CREATIVE LIMITATIONS While transit advertising offers good colour reproduction, the actual amount of space it provides advertisers to work with is quite small. In the case of exterior bus posters, platform posters, and digital video, there is more creative flexibility. As indicated in the previous section, some new and innovative concepts that take advantage of the available space in a subway station present greater creative potential.

Both outdoor advertising and transit advertising are often the choice of media planners when the target market description is fairly broad in scope (e.g., age, income, occupation, lifestyle) or if specific geographic markets (e.g., cities) are important. As mentioned earlier in the chapter, planners now perceive outdoor and transit as a timely medium. That also factors into media recommendations.

Buying Transit Advertising

Transit advertising rates are affected by variables such as the number of markets being covered, the length of the showing (which affects discounts), the desired weight level in any given market, and the size of the space required. Transit space is generally sold on the basis of four-week minimums and is available on a market-by-market basis. Advertisers can purchase space in a group of cities in a region to qualify for greater discounts; major Canadian cities might constitute a group; cities within a geographic region might also constitute a group. Outfront Media, Pattison Outdoor, and Lamar Advertising are among the largest sellers of transit advertising space in Canada.

The first thing to consider when purchasing transit space is the weight level desired in each market. As in outdoor advertising, transit weight is expressed in terms of gross rating points, with GRP referring to the total circulation of a showing expressed as a percentage of a market's population.

As indicated earlier, all rates are based on the purchase of a four-week period, starting with a base rate for each market purchased. Usually, a *continuity discount* is available to advertisers that meet predetermined time commitments (e.g., 12-, 24-, and 52-week periods), with the percentage of the discount increasing with the time commitment.

MEDIA BUYING ILLUSTRATIONS

Let's consider a media buying example, using the rates and data in Figure 10.15 as a basis for calculating the costs. Please note that all rates are quoted for a *four-week period*.

This rate card has been created to demonstrate to the reader the key factors that influence a transit media buy: the number of units available in a market, the daily reach expressed in GRPs, and the cost for each four-week period.

UltraTrans Media—King Posters						
	50 Daily GRPs		75 Daily GRPs		100 Daily GRPs	
Market	Units	$ Rate	Units	$ Rate	Units	$ Rate
Halifax	16	7200	24	9600	32	11800
Montreal Central	225	81000	340	117000	450	148000
Quebec City	60	17100	85	29200	120	37500
Ottawa	53	21500	80	32400	105	42600
Thunder Bay	10	4200	15	6000	20	8000
Calgary	65	35100	100	52600	135	70300
Edmonton	65	33500	100	48500	130	63050

- Rates quoted are for four weeks
- All rates subject to applicable taxes
- Discounts may apply. Consult UltraTrans for more details

FIGURE 10.15

UltraTrans media rate card—King posters

Transit Buying Plan: Example 1	
Medium:	Exterior King Bus Posters
Markets:	Montreal Central, Ottawa, and Calgary
Weight:	50 GRPs in all markets
Contract Length:	12 weeks

According to Figure 10.15, the costs for these markets for four weeks at the specified GRP levels would be

Montreal Central	$ 81 000
Ottawa	$ 21 500
Calgary	$ 35 100
Total Cost (4 weeks)	**$137 600**

Therefore, the total cost for the 12-week contract would be

$$\$137\,600 \times 3 = \$412\,800$$

Transit Buying Plan: Example 2	
Medium:	King Bus Posters
Markets, Weight, and Continuity:	Halifax, 50 GRPs, 8 weeks; Quebec City, 75 GRPs, 12 weeks; Edmonton, 75 GRPs, 8 weeks

According to Figure 10.15 the cost would be

Halifax	$ 9 600 × 2 = $ 19 200
Quebec City	$ 29 200 × 3 = $ 87 600
Edmonton	$ 48 500 × 2 = $ 97 000
Total Cost	**$203 800**

Other Forms of Out-of-Home Advertising

Outdoor advertising is everywhere! There always seems to be a unique means of reaching consumers when they least expect it. Some of the more unique and innovative vehicles for sending messages include elevator advertising, arena and stadium advertising, taxicab advertising, and theatre-screen advertising. The stream of new advertising vehicles continues to grow.

AIRPORT DISPLAY ADVERTISING

Essentially, this is outdoor advertising located at major airports. Included in the range of options are outdoor posters and spectaculars on roads leading to and from the airport, and backlights inside the terminals. Backlights are offered in a variety of shapes and sizes, and a scrolling option is available (i.e., the poster scrolls to reveal a new advertising message). Clear Channel Communications is a major supplier of airport advertising in North America. Airport advertising presents a good opportunity to reach business travellers. Refer to the image in Figure 10.16.

FIGURE 10.16

Airport display ads reach a captive audience in arrival and departure areas of airports.

Photo by Keith J. Tuckwell

WASHROOM ADVERTISING

Washroom advertising involves the placement of mini-posters in public washrooms, usually above men's urinals and on the back of stall doors. The posters are located in colleges and universities, sporting facilities, hospitals, restaurants, and bars. Levi's and Budweiser are two brands that use this form of advertising. Ads in washrooms offer a certain degree of targeting. For a beer brand such as Budweiser, the advertisement reaches the target audience in a location where the purchase decisions are made.

ELEVATOR ADVERTISING

This sort of advertising uses glass display cases on side panels adjacent to the control panels in high-rise elevators. The Elevator Network and the Captivate Network are two suppliers in this advertising category. The Elevator Network places ads in 1500 high-rises in major cities. Ads in elevators are perceived as a welcome distraction that effectively engage a captive audience. Pizza Pizza has used elevator advertising and achieved good response to it. Over a six-week period in a variety of buildings, ads produced sales increases ranging from 2 percent in a seniors' building to 24 percent in a downtown apartment building filled with younger people.[10] Clorets gum has also used elevator ads to advantage. The elevator is an environment where people are close together—there is a definite need for fresh breath![11]

SPORTS AND ARENA ADVERTISING

Advertising in a sports environment can reach a more targeted audience. Some alternatives include tee-off sign boards on golf courses, signs affixed to arena boards, backboard signs placed on backstops and outfield fences, and poster advertising on ski-lift towers. Where sporting events occur, an ad is not far behind.

Within arenas and stadiums, there are numerous advertising opportunities. Advertising starts right at the front door, with companies paying megabucks to have an arena adorned with their name. Rogers Arena in Vancouver, the Air Canada Centre in Toronto, and the Bell Centre in Montreal are just a few examples. See the illustration in Figure 10.17. In hockey

© Darren Maginley

FIGURE 10.17

Arena advertising starts right at the front door.

arenas, ads can be on the ice, behind the player's benches, and in the penalty box. At ballparks, rotating signs behind home plate are popular, and there are courtside signs on basketball courts. These signs receive additional exposure when a game is broadcast on television.

CINEMA ADVERTISING

Cineplex theatres have recently introduced a fast-paced 20-minute preshow package that blends ads with entertainment. The new package places commercials between entertainment news, interviews with Hollywood stars, and music videos. As well, Cineplex offers full-motion advertising just prior to the presentation of movie trailers or the feature film. Cinema advertising is becoming a big hit with companies seeking to reach younger consumers. The big screen offers a larger-than-life impression. Good sound and good visuals get attention. Refer to the image in Figure 10.18.

Other cinema advertising opportunities include digital lobby signs, digital backlits, and ads printed on movie tickets. The benefits of cinema advertising must be weighed against the costs. There is a clear benefit to cinema advertising: Unlike most other media, in which ads can be avoided, the captive audience in a theatre cannot avoid the ads. The cost of a 30-second commercial in Cineplex theatres nationally (2364 screens in 310 theatres) over a four-week period is $274 200. The average weekly audience is 1 860 000.[12]

WILD POSTINGS

Wild postings are ads that are slapped on the hoarding at construction sites. Once the domain of concert promoters and sports promoters, they are now a strategic element of many mainstream advertisers' media plans. Wild postings give a brand a hip, urban feel. Unfortunately, they can be torn down easily and to date there is no means of measuring their effectiveness. In most cases the owners of the construction site are paid by the advertisers for the privilege of putting up the signs. Much like an oversized outdoor poster, the advertising message appears on the boards that surround the construction site.

FIGURE 10.18

An advertiser can make a larger-than-life impression with big-screen cinema commercials.

Photo courtesy of Cineplex Entertainment Corporation. Used with permission of the Bank of Nova Scotia.

Students are advised to check the out-of-home section of *Canadian Advertising Rates & Data* for more information about the diverse range of out-of-home media alternatives. It seems that out-of-home advertising is everywhere—and entrepreneurs keep pushing the boundaries.

At-Retail Media

The term "at-retail media" is suggestive of retail communications that go well beyond traditional point-of-purchase activities. **At-retail media** embrace various communication opportunities. For example, shelf-talkers, pads of tear-off coupons, smart shopping carts, store window signs and displays, and digital screens are tactics employed by advertisers. Setting up displays and erecting signs to draw attention to sale items is one thing, but planning and implementing a coordinated marketing communications campaign to make the shopping experience more delightful is quite another. Retail media can play a key planning role in both the brand and trade marketing mix. It is the final opportunity to communicate with customers before they make their purchase decision.

A good marketing communications strategy at point of purchase will achieve several objectives. For example, it can remind consumers of a product just before they make a purchase decision. Ongoing research studies conducted by Point-Of-Purchase Advertising International (POPAI) in the United States generally reveal that 76 percent of all purchase decisions are made in store. That represents a lot of opportunity for a brand, but also for competition.[13] The in-store decision rate has been gradually increasing yearly, mainly due to the influence of smartphones, shopping apps, and mobile coupons. Therefore, a compelling advertising message at just the right time in the right place could lead to an immediate purchase.

Some of the more common types of at-retail media include in-store video displays, exterior signs, display shippers, and display cards.

DIGITAL DISPLAYS

Digital point-of-purchase advertising has advanced in recent years. Messages can be tailored to specific stores (e.g., they can vary from one location to another), and a good video presentation can stimulate purchases. In the restaurant industry, both Tim Hortons and McDonald's do an excellent job of visually presenting their products in a digital format. Large plasma screens can advertise the right product at the right time: in the morning, breakfast sandwiches and coffee; at noon, lunch specials; on hot days the emphasis can be on cold beverages and ice cream treats. Good visuals make the meal combos look very tempting! See the illustration in Figure 10.19.

Large department stores and national chain stores such as Best Buy, Canadian Tire, and Home Hardware are integrating digital communications into their in-store media strategies. Home Hardware uses something it calls a *demomercial* to highlight the benefit of products unique to the company. The demomercial effectively demonstrates a flaw in an existing product and then introduces a solution in the form of a nifty Home Hardware item; it's a clincher in the decision-making process!

Best Buy goes a step further to satisfy the requirements of today's mobile-oriented shopper. With so many shoppers doing prepurchase research while on the go, Best Buy developed an application that allows shoppers to seek information without having to speak with a sales associate. The application allows a shopper to check for product availability, track products that are on sale, and secure directions to the nearest store.[14]

FIGURE 10.19
Tempting in-store video presentations stimulate purchases.

Photo by Keith J. Tuckwell

FIGURE 10.20
Store signs and logos play a key role in retailer message strategy

© Larry W. Smith/EPA//The Canadian Press

EXTERIOR SIGNS

The primary function of a store sign is to identify the business. The style and lettering of the sign (i.e., the store logo) becomes familiar to customers in the market area and helps draw them to the business. The logo style of the business sign is integrated with other forms of store advertising. The golden arches of McDonald's; Tim Hortons "Always Fresh" sign; and Best Buy's yellow tag sign are very familiar and can be seen and identified from a great distance by motorists or pedestrian traffic. For most retailers, store signs and logos play a prominent role in message strategy and execution. Refer to the illustration in Figure 10.20.

DISPLAY SHIPPERS

A **display shipper** is a cardboard shipping carton that converts into a temporary in-store display when opened and assembled. Designed to encourage impulse purchases, display shippers are often used to merchandise seasonal products. Display shippers for Halloween candies and for the summer barbecue season (exhibiting barbecue-related products such as

Photo by Keith J. Tuckwell

FIGURE 10.21

An example of a display shipper: A shipping carton unfolds to form a temporary display. Separate displays stimulate impulse purchases.

spices and sauces) are quite common. The displays are used at the discretion of store management and can be assembled by store personnel or the manufacturer's field sales representative.

Displays do influence purchases. Recent data from POPAI reveal that one in six purchases are made when a display for a brand is present in store. Floor stands such as a display shipper now account for 50 percent of all displays in stores. Retailers have embraced the notion that displays that are totally separate from a product's regular location have a positive impact on sales.[15] Refer to the illustration in Figure 10.21.

DISPLAY CARDS

Display cards include paper or paperboard posters, shelf-talkers (small posters that hang from the store shelves where the product is located), and tear-off ad pads that often include coupons or other purchase incentives. Designed to encourage impulse purchases, these forms of advertising can be used with display shippers or on displays that are set up at the ends of aisles or other store locations. Their primary role is to draw the customer's attention to something special and prompt a decision to buy. Manufacturers commonly use tear-off ad pads to promote contests, refunds, and other sales promotion activity.

OTHER AT-RETAIL MEDIA

Supermarket chains and convenience store chains have been particularly innovative regarding new forms of in-store advertising and merchandising concepts. These concepts are often developed by independent media advertising companies, and the merits of the concepts are sold to potential advertisers.

Among the options are grocery cart advertising and floor ads. **Grocery cart advertising** uses full-colour posters that are attached to the front of shopping carts. Shoppers facing an approaching shopping cart are exposed to the message, while the shopper pushing the cart also sees a message from inside the cart. **Floor ads** are portable floor decals (often called *ad tiles*) that carry advertising messages. They will not scuff or peel. These ads appear in convenience stores and help stimulate impulse purchases. Floor ads cut through the clutter of other forms of in-store advertising. All of these options provide advertisers with last-minute exposure right at the point of purchase.

At-Retail Media as an Advertising Medium

There are numerous pros and cons to the various at-retail media alternatives. Advertisers who use this medium do so because it is the last opportunity to reach a target audience before an actual purchase decision is made. In this section, some of the benefits and drawbacks are presented.

ADVANTAGES OF AT-RETAIL MEDIA

IMPULSE PURCHASING In the case of frequently purchased products such as candies, snack foods, toiletries, and beverages, at-retail media advertising stimulates impulse purchasing. Furthermore, research studies indicate that close to three-quarters of all purchase decisions are made right in the store. Such behaviour creates ample opportunity for point-of-purchase advertising to influence last-minute decisions. It is often referred to as the "last chance" medium.

MESSAGE REINFORCEMENT While the display or presentation itself stimulates action, the incidence of consumer action increases when the display visuals are used to supplement the advertising done in other media. Point of purchase reinforces prior messages, finalizing sales to consumers who have been preconditioned by other forms of advertising.

MESSAGE RECEPTIVENESS The message is communicated when consumers are shopping (i.e., it appeals to the right audience, in the right place, at the right time). Since consumers generally shop in stores that contain merchandise they can afford, the selling message is visible to the desired target audience.

LAST CHANCE (DECIDING FACTOR) IN SALE For product categories in which impulse buying is not a factor (such as expensive durable goods), point-of-purchase material can be used to inform and educate consumers. Shopper influence studies conducted by POPAI reveal a high level of recall of in-store marketing materials. In one recent study, 65 percent of shoppers recalled and interacted with displays, signage, merchandising, or media for products they had purchased the same day.[16]

MERCHANDISE TIE-INS In-store communications promote the trial of new products, new packaging, and new sizes and flavours. These communications draw attention to warranties, rebate programs, contests, and other forms of promotional activity. They are also an effective vehicle for developing cross-promotions with related products sold in the same store (soup and crackers, potato chips and dips, and bandages and antiseptics, for example, are product lines that could be displayed together to encourage additional purchases).

DISADVANTAGES OF AT-RETAIL MEDIA

PLACEMENT The most eye-catching display will be ineffective if it is not located in the appropriate position in the store. The problem facing the retailer is the limited area in which to place the abundant display material available from manufacturers. If good placements are not found, the displays will not achieve sales objectives.

CLUTTER Consider the number of displays you are exposed to while walking through a drugstore, grocery store, or hardware store. Assuming a retailer grants a manufacturer permission to erect a display or poster material, the manufacturer's display will face considerable competition from other products in commanding consumers' attention. Due to clutter, some displays will be relegated to poor locations (where they may as well not be there at all). The same principle applies to video presentations. New research about in-store consumer behaviour indicates that the location of a video presentation is important and that too many presentations will reduce the potential impact.

WASTE Some displays and other point-of-purchase materials never get erected in the store. Manufacturers generally require permission from the retail store's head office to erect display units in corporate-owned retail stores. Even if permission is granted, if and how the display units will be used is often left to the discretion of store managers. Securing cooperation from retail managers is the responsibility of the field salesforce. This task can sometimes be difficult.

SUMMARY

Out-of-home media is the second-fastest-growing medium in Canada. New technologies and new formats such as digital video displays have attracted new advertisers—advertisers that have shifted dollars away from television and print.

Out-of-home media comprise a variety of outdoor poster options, transit advertising, and at-retail advertising. The various forms of outdoor advertising are posters, backlit posters, superboards and spectaculars, mall posters, transit shelters, digital signs, street-level advertising, digital video screens, wall banners, and murals.

Outdoor advertising offers high target reach and frequency and geographic flexibility. It is an effective medium because it can reinforce a message that appears in other media, and, in the case of digital signs and video screens, the message can be changed quickly if need be. Among the weaknesses of outdoor advertising are the lack of target market selectivity and the creative limitations related to the speed at which people pass by.

There are various forms of transit advertising, including interior and exterior cards, bus wraps and murals, a variety of station posters, and station domination. Digital screens mounted on station platforms that feature content and advertising are a more engaging way to communicate with people. Some new and innovative use of subway space for advertising purposes (floors, walls, ceilings, and pillars) is creating new interest in transit as a medium.

Transit advertising offers continuous exposure (a result of transit users' consistent travel patterns) and high reach and frequency against a general target market. The major weaknesses of the medium are the lack of target market selectivity and the creative limitations owing to space restrictions.

Some unique forms of out-of-home advertising media include airport display advertising, washroom advertising, elevator advertising, sports and arena advertising, cinema advertising, and wild postings. Each option captures a unique target audience.

At-retail media (point-of-purchase) advertising is effective in stimulating impulse purchases and reinforcing a message delivered by another medium. Advertising on digital screens is now a popular option used by retailers. A drawback of at-retail media advertising is the lack of use by retailers because of the abundance of display materials they receive from suppliers. As well, having too many displays in a store reduces the impact of any individual display. Point-of-purchase advertising is often referred to as "last chance" advertising. It reaches consumers at a critical moment—that point in time when brand decisions are made and wallets are about to be opened.

KEY TERMS

at-retail media 311
backlit poster 291
banners 293
billboards 291
digital sign 293
digital video screens 293
display cards 313
display shipper 312
exterior bus poster 302
floor ads 313
full back (bus) 302
full wrap (bus) 302
grocery cart advertising 313
interior cards 302
mall poster 296
mural banner 293
mural (transit) 302
platform poster 304
poster 291
showing 291
spectacular 292
station domination 304
station posters 303
street-level units 293
superboard 292
vinyl wrap (bus) 302
wild posting 310

REVIEW QUESTIONS

1. Briefly explain the differences among an outdoor poster, a backlit poster, a spectacular, and a full-motion video screen.
2. Identify and explain two advantages and two disadvantages of outdoor advertising.
3. Using the rate card in Figure 10.9, calculate the cost of the following outdoor campaign:

   Medium: Horizontal Posters
   Markets and Weight: Montreal and Toronto 25 GRPs; Vancouver 50 GRPs
   Time: Montreal and Toronto 8 weeks; Vancouver 12 weeks
4. Using the rate card in Figure 10.10, calculate the cost of the following advertising campaign:

   Medium: Transit Shelters
   Markets and Weight: Halifax and London 50 GRPs; Calgary 25 GRPs
   Time: 16 weeks in all markets
5. What is the difference between an exterior king poster and an exterior seventy poster?
6. Explain briefly the nature of the following transit advertising vehicles: interior cards, station posters, and station domination.
7. What are the major types of transit advertising?
8. What types of products or services are suitable for transit advertising?
9. Identify and briefly explain two advantages and two disadvantages of transit as an advertising medium.
10. Using the rate card in Figure 10.15, calculate the cost of the following campaign:

    Medium: King Bus Posters
    Markets and Weight: Halifax and Ottawa 75 GRPs; Calgary and Edmonton 50 GRPs
    Time: 12 weeks in all markets
11. Identify and briefly describe the major types of at-retail media.
12. Explain the following terms in the context of the term in parentheses:
    a) Superboard (outdoor)
    b) Mural ads (outdoor)
    c) 75 GRPs (outdoor)
    d) Backlit poster (outdoor)
    e) Digital video display (outdoor)
    f) Display shipper (at-retail media)
    g) Floor ads (at-retail media)
13. Identify and briefly explain two advantages and two disadvantages of at-retail media (point-of-purchase) advertising.

DISCUSSION QUESTIONS

1. "Out-of-home media are primarily recognized as a means of complementing other media forms." Is this statement true or false? Discuss this statement, assuming the role of a marketing manager—first for a packaged goods company and then for an automotive manufacturer.
2. Assume you are developing a media plan to launch a new luxury automobile model (e.g., BMW, Lexus, Infiniti). The target market is male and female, 35 to 49 years old, professionals or executives. Would outdoor advertising be part of your marketing communications mix? Justify the selection or rejection of outdoor advertising. What other media would you include in the mix?
3. There is statistical evidence showing point-of-purchase advertising to be effective in prompting purchase response, at least in the short term. Should advertisers be spending more or less on this form of advertising in the future? Should investment in this form of advertising come at the expense of traditional brand advertising in the mass media? Discuss these issues, using examples of your choice.
4. Naming rights to arenas and advertising inside arenas such as the Air Canada Centre and Rogers Arena are popular. What potential benefits do you see for advertisers that pursue this media strategy? Do you think arena advertising is effective? Explain your position.

NOTES

1. Canadian Media Directors' Council, *Media Digest*, 2014–2015, 8.
2. Joe Mandese, "New Outdoor Media Options Challenge Conventional Media Planning Wisdom," *Media Post*, August 13, 2003, **www.mediapost.com**.
3. Patti Summerfield, "The Last Mass Medium Goes Niche," Strategy, September 24, 2001, p. 25.
4. Canadian Out-of-Home Measurement Bureau, **www.comb.org**.
5. CBS Outdoor Media, **www.cbsoutdoor.ca**.
6. Brian Harrod, "The Truest Test of a Great Idea," *Marketing*, April 12, 1999, p. 42.
7. OMAC Canada, **www.omaccanada.ca**.
8. "National Household Survey: Slight Increase in Transit Ridership," *Toronto Star*, June 26, 2013, **www.thestar.com**.
9. OMAC Canada, **www.omaccanada.ca**.
10. The Elevator Network, **www.metromediacanada.ca**.
11. Mary Klonizakas, "The View on the Way to the Top," *Marketing*, April 12, 1999, 36.
12. Cineplex Media, http://media.cineplex.com/ratecard.aspx.
13. POPAI, *2012 Shopper Engagement Study*, **www.popai.com/** docs/12SES-MemRep.pdf.
14. Alicia Andrioch, "Around and around We Go," *Marketing*, June 4, 2012, 45.
15. POPAI, *2012 Shopper Engagement Study*, **www.popai.com/** docs/12SES-MemRep.pdf.
16. POPAI, *Shopper Influence Study*, n.d.

CHAPTER 11

Direct Response Media

Learning Objectives

After studying this chapter, you will be able to

1. Describe the various types of direct response advertising
2. Explain the advantages and disadvantages of various forms of direct response advertising
3. Assess the factors considered in and procedures used for buying direct mail
4. Assess the strategies for delivering effective messages via direct response techniques

Dozens of good reasons to give your feet a vacation from socks

What's your favourite type of beach?
An endless stretch of white sun-kissed sand;
the perfect place
for you and that new paperback?
A low-tide shore
filled with tell-tale clam holes?
A warm-water beach
where you can wade in shallows forever?
Our Island is surrounded by shores
that beg you to go barefootin'.
No wonder *Travel + Leisure* magazine
voted us one of the world's best islands.

Take the first step today
and get your FREE Visitors Guide,
call *1-888-PEI-PLAY* and ask for *ALANNA*
or visit *www.peiplay.com/alanna*

Courtesy of the Province of Prince Edward Island

Direct response advertising is a form of media advertising that communicates messages directly to prospective customers. Among the options available, direct mail is the most common means of delivering these messages. However, other forms of direct communication, such as direct response television, direct response print, direct response interactive, and telemarketing, also play a significant role. These forms of communication are discussed in this chapter.

Direct Response Advertising

Direct response advertising is one segment of the direct marketing industry, and it now plays a major role in influencing consumer purchase patterns. Thanks to a convergence of trends, including the diverting of ad dollars from traditional TV and print media and the rise of social media sites such as Facebook, Twitter, and YouTube, direct response techniques are popular with advertisers.

Direct response advertising is big business. The latest revenue figures available indicate that direct mail generates $1.24 billion in net advertising revenues in Canada. As an advertising medium, direct mail ranks fifth, just behind online, television, newspapers, and radio.[1] Over the past three years, direct mail revenue growth has been flat. Similar to other media, direct mail revenue has been affected by advertisers moving more dollars into online advertising.

Direct response techniques allow marketers to engage the consumer more effectively and to market products with more in-depth sales messages. Some of Canada's largest companies have integrated direct response communications into their mix. They see value in managing customer relationships—one of the benefits of direct response. Among these companies are Bell Canada, Rogers Communications, Shoppers Drug Mart, Mountain Equipment Co-op, and most major financial institutions. These organizations are attracted to direct response advertising because of its targeting capabilities, its sophisticated measurement devices, and its ability to account for all dollars spent.

The shift to direct response advertising follows on the heels of companies adopting software technology that encourages database management techniques and the implementation of customer relationship management programs. Firms can now design and develop programs that reach customers individually and efficiently. Such capability offers significant competitive advantage. And the ability to reach customers directly with a message is a lot cheaper than delivering messages through the traditional mass media.

Direct response advertising is advertising through any medium designed to generate a response by any means that is measurable (such as mail, television, a print ad, telephone, or the internet). If traditional mass media are used, the message includes a toll-free telephone number, mailing address, or website address where more information can be secured. Trish Wheaton, former president of Wunderman Direct, a large direct marketing agency, feels that a relationship with the internet is helping direct response advertising grow. She uses direct mail as the door opener, which then drives the consumer online to learn more.[2] Consumers today spend a lot more time doing research online than reading something they receive in the mail. For many advertisers, the role of direct mail has changed—it's more about getting one's attention with useful information. Other means may be required to generate the purchase.

The major forms of direct response advertising are direct mail, direct response print, direct response television (DRTV), direct response interactive, telemarketing, and catalogues.

The role of the internet and mobile communications in direct response communications is discussed in more detail in Chapter 12.

- **Direct mail** is a form of advertising communicated to prospects via the postal service or independent delivery agents.
- **Direct response print** is a response-oriented message delivered to prospects by magazine or newspaper advertisements.
- **Direct response television (DRTV)** is a form of advertising communicated to prospects via television commercials (e.g., 30-minute infomercials or messages seen on cable channels, or 60-second commercials seen on conventional television stations that encourage people to buy something immediately).
- **Direct response interactive** involves placing ads on the internet that include a call to action. When people click on a banner ad (the desired action), they are transferred to a site where additional information is provided.
- **Telemarketing** involves the use of telecommunications to promote the products and services of a business.
- **Catalogues** are important communications vehicles for retail organizations. Catalogues promote the sale of goods or motivate consumers to visit stores.

Direct Mail

The use of direct mail is widespread because the medium enables the sender to personalize the message with the prospect's name, send lengthy messages (e.g., copy-oriented sales messages along with reply cards and contracts that are returned by prospects), and obtain a high degree of geographic coverage economically (the mailing can be distributed to designated postal codes anywhere in Canada). There are numerous options available to companies wishing to use direct mail, and these can be combined to form a compelling package of information. A typical direct mailing has several components, each designed to serve a specific purpose.

ENVELOPE

The envelope is a critical component of a mailing. Since direct mail is usually unsolicited, the envelope has to suggest strongly why the recipient should read the contents. There should be a sense of urgency for the recipient to open the envelope.

SALES LETTER

The letter introduces the prospect to the product or service and encourages the receiver to read more about the offer in other pieces included with the mailing. The letter may be unaddressed (delivered to the householder) or addressed (with the person's name on it). Addressed mail offers some degree of personalization and garners a higher response rate. Typically, the language used in the letter is persuasive, since the goal is to generate interest and desire, and ultimately get the receiver to respond to the offer.

LEAFLETS AND FOLDERS

A **leaflet** is usually a one-page document, printed front and back, containing vital information about the offer: Here's what the product is, and here's why you should buy it. Again, the copy is persuasive, and a strong visual usually supports the copy. A *folder* can vary in size from half a page to a multipage foldout. Typically, folders and leaflets are printed on heavier stock to suggest their importance and to draw attention to an incentive, which is usually included with the offer. An *incentive* is designed to solicit an immediate response.

ORDER FORM

A well-designed order form is essential. It must be easy to read and communicate all details regarding price, additional costs such as shipping and handling charges, and means of payment (usually by credit card). The receiver must be able to place the order effortlessly.

POSTAGE-PAID RETURN ENVELOPE

Eliminating the need for a postage stamp is another means of encouraging action by the recipient. The combination of a clear and concise order form with a prepaid return envelope or an offer on a prepaid return leaflet makes the ordering process hassle free from start to finish.

STATEMENT STUFFERS

A **statement stuffer** or **bounce back** is an additional offer that rides along with the delivery of another offer or with the delivery of a monthly statement. Capitalizing on the ease of purchasing by credit, such mailings make it convenient for the prospect to take action. In this case, one order leads to another, and the prospect is reached at very low cost. Usually, the credit card number is the only information the seller requires.

DVDs

Organizations now send serious prospects information by more sophisticated means. DVDs are a popular means for demonstrating how a product works, how nice a vacation resort is, or how well an automobile performs. In business-to-business markets, a DVD offers a way of demonstrating the product at a time convenient for the prospect. DVDs are more commonly included with more expensive products and services.

Direct Mail Strategy

Since you are just learning about direct response advertising and direct mail, you may be somewhat skeptical of its effectiveness, perhaps because of your own personal behaviour when dealing with advertising mail that comes your way. To alter any possible negative perceptions, consider some basic facts that demonstrate why marketers believe in direct mail. For example, some 72 percent of Canadians use direct mail to buy products and services—it is an acceptable way to learn about products and to place orders should you be so inclined.

The use of direct mail in marketing communications campaigns has been negatively affected by the shift to digital communications. But that shift is questioned by many in the industry. While email communications and offers have exploded in recent years (see the discussion in Chapter 12), wise marketers will use both mail and email (an integrated approach) to garner better results.

When looked at individually, direct mail outperforms email. The Direct Marketing Association in the United States reports that direct mail boasts a 4.4 percent response rate compared to the average response rate of emails of 0.12 percent. The response rates for direct mail have been declining modestly over the past 10 years, but the medium remains a solid channel for generating return on investment. Direct mail remains strong because consumers are continually bombarded with digital messages they don't want. Consider how you personally respond to advertising emails to verify this thought. The proliferation

FIGURE 11.1

Some facts and figures about direct mail advertising

Source: Adapted from "Direct Mail by the Numbers," *Sorted* (Canada Post Publications, 2012) and Direct Response Marketing Group Inc., www.drmg.ca/why-direct-mail.

They say numbers don't lie, but they are open to interpretation. The numbers below clearly indicate the potential usefulness of direct mail advertising as part of a marketing communications strategy. You be the judge:

- 72.5% of consumers use direct mail to buy products and services
- 9 out of 10 people are likely to open direct mail if it looks interesting
- 87% of potential customers open direct mail that is addressed to them personally
- 75% of customers pay greater attention to direct mail compared to other advertising mediums
- 83% of households actively clip and use coupons
- 43% of Canadians will read most mail promotions just in case something catches their eye

It's important to note that the message is just as important as the medium. The direct mail piece should be compelling, interesting, and unique—it must stand out from the clutter!

of emails and online display ads everywhere makes direct mail look like a more viable option.[3] For more facts and figures about direct mail advertising, refer to Figure 11.1.

Essentially, an organization has the option of delivering a mail piece by itself or delivering an offer as part of a package that includes offers from other companies. This is the difference between solo direct mail and cooperative direct mail.

Solo direct mail, also known as *selective direct mail*, refers to specialized or individually prepared direct mail offers sent directly to prospects. With this strategy, the marketing organization absorbs all of the costs. Solo direct mail pieces are commonly employed in business-to-business communications, supplementing the messages frequently communicated via traditional business publications. The growth of database marketing by consumer goods organizations has led to greater usage of solo direct mail by these organizations.

Solo direct mail can be personally addressed to an individual or organization, or it can be delivered as unaddressed mail. Refer to the illustration in Figure 11.2. The more

FIGURE 11.2

An illustration of addressed and unaddressed solo direct mail offers

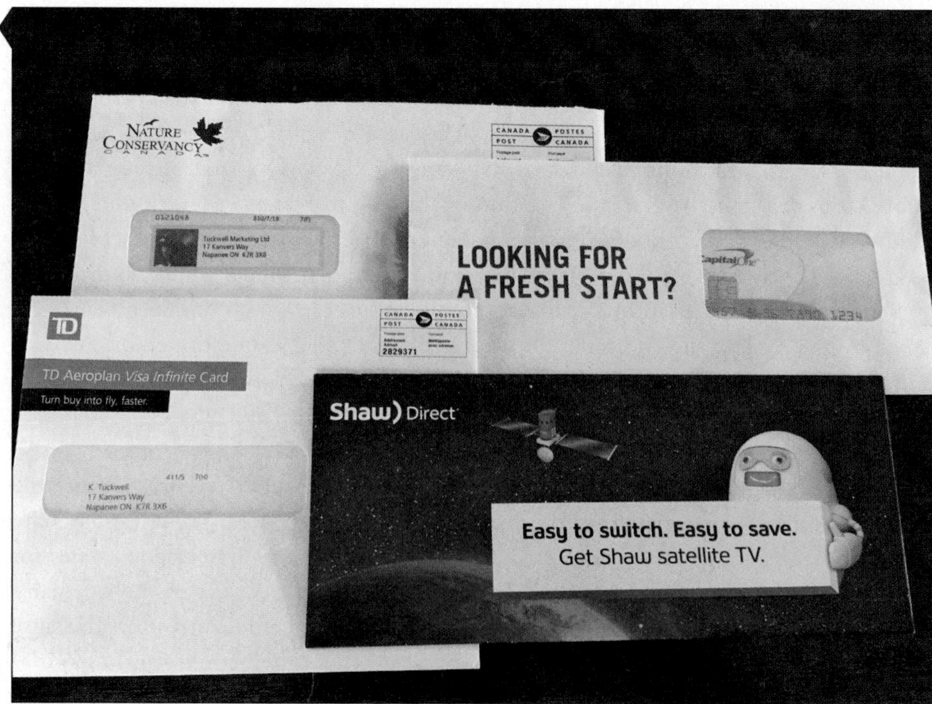

Photo by Keith J. Tuckwell

personalized the mailing is, the higher the response rate. People are generally more responsive to information that has their name on it. Response rates to personalized mail offers are much higher than for cooperative mail offers.

In local markets, retailers and service companies often use solo direct mail to target potential customers in their immediate trading area. Using a shotgun approach, the mailing increases awareness for the business and often includes an incentive to encourage action by prospective customers. Quiznos, a quick-serve restaurant, has used unaddressed admail to send coupons to prospective customers. Direct marketing plays a key role in Quiznos's marketing mix. According to Kyle Holmes, senior director of marketing at Quiznos, "Each coupon campaign translates into instant sales results. One recent direct mail coupon resulted in an 8 percent increase in sales."[4]

Another type of direct mail that attracts more attention and gets higher response rates is dimensional mail. **Dimensional mail** can take any form other than the typical flat piece of mail. An object may be in the envelope, for example, or a unique box or package contains the mail offer. Dimensional mail stands out from standard-looking direct mail pieces.

Cooperative direct mail refers to envelopes containing special offers from non-competing products. Refer to the illustration in Figure 11.3. Since many companies can be involved in the mailing, the costs are shared among participants. Consumer goods marketers commonly employ this method. A typical mailing contains coupons for a variety of grocery, drug, and household products; magazine subscription offers; or discount coupons for more expensive goods such as eyewear. Cooperative direct mailing has proven to be one of the most effective forms of print media for generating trial purchase.

Both solo direct mail and cooperative direct mail generate good response rates. Mail can be used to achieve different marketing objectives: It can secure direct orders, generate leads, and build traffic in both business-to-business and business-to-consumer markets.

Direct Mail as an Advertising Medium

Many leading organizations operating in a variety of industries are moving a portion of their marketing communications budgets into direct mail advertising. These companies have learned that potential and current customers take notice of direct mail if the mailing

FIGURE 11.3
An illustration of cooperative direct mail advertising

© Don Denton/The Canadian Press

is executed effectively. Research studies conducted by Canada Post help justify a marketer's investment in direct mail: 89 percent of people will open a direct mail piece if it comes from a company they know; 86 percent will open it if it looks intriguing; and 79 percent will open it if it has their name and address on it.[5]

Direct mail is a medium that fits nicely between traditional mass media and online media. TV, radio, and print interrupt media consumption (ads are pushed upon viewers) while online media force consumers to search for information (users pull out the information they want). Direct mail is neither. Consumers receive the message among their bills and letter mail and decide if and when they will read it.[6] Canada Post reports that 68 percent of Canadians open their mail right away, and 95 percent read their mail the same day it arrives.[7] Therefore, direct mail can be a timely call-to-action medium within an integrated campaign and an ideal medium for building a relationship with current customers. Clearly, the advantages of direct mail are attractive to companies that want to deliver messages to customers one on one.

ADVANTAGES OF DIRECT MAIL

AUDIENCE SELECTIVITY Using direct mail, advertisers can pinpoint and reach targets that are precisely defined in terms of demographics—assuming that the organization acquires lists identifying the primary prospects. A good list results in minimal circulation waste. As well, a company's own customer list is a good starting point for any direct mail campaign. Additional discussion of lists appears in the media buying section of this chapter.

HIGH REACH Solo direct mailings reach everyone the advertiser would like to reach—unlike other media, which reach only a portion of the target. For example, a life insurance or credit card organization that wants to reach all university graduates may be able to obtain access to a list of alumni. The national reach potential of cooperative direct mailings (i.e., mass distribution to selected Canadian households) is very high. In this case, there is much circulation waste, but the response rates are usually adequate to cover the costs of mass mailings.

GEOGRAPHIC FLEXIBILITY A proper mailing list offers an advertiser not only demographic selectivity but also the opportunity to deliver direct mail messages to specific geographic locations. This advantage appeals to retailers and other local businesses that want to confine mailings to certain areas. National advertisers can also use direct mail to isolate geographic areas where they would like to concentrate, say, an area where sales are lower than average.

CREATIVE FLEXIBILITY Like advertising in business publications, direct mail offers the flexibility to include long copy in advertisements (the longer the better, according to some practitioners). Since various pieces are often included in a single mailing, there is also flexibility in style, length, and format. Generally speaking, a combination of formats in a single medium is effective. In this area, only imagination, budget, and applicable postal regulations limit the advertiser.

DISTRIBUTION OF INCENTIVES Direct mail provides the opportunity to include items that will reach desired targets. It is a good medium for distributing coupons, free samples, and trial offers.

EXCLUSIVITY Another advantage of direct mail is that mailings delivered to the household do not compete with other media when they are received, although they do compete for attention with other mail. This exclusivity contrasts with the clutter of newspaper and magazine advertising in which ads compete with each other and with editorial content. Online and television advertising may also suffer from clutter, which gives rise to avoidance of advertising messages.

MEASURABILITY The success of a direct mail campaign is measured in one way—the sales generated by the mailing. As a general rule, business-oriented direct mail receives 15 percent of the responses within the first week of the mailing. Early responses, used in conjunction with historical conversion patterns, can be used to project sales for a longer period of time. In this regard, the success of a direct mail campaign can be determined in a short period. Similar calculations cannot be made when using traditional forms of advertising.

DISADVANTAGES OF DIRECT MAIL

HIGH COST PER EXPOSURE When the absolute costs of production, renting or purchasing lists, fulfillment (stuffing and sealing envelopes), and mailing are tallied, the total can be higher than it is for other print alternatives. Remember, though, that the selectivity of the medium reduces waste circulation.

ABSENCE OF EDITORIAL SUPPORT In comparison to magazines, where there is editorial support that encourages people to read, direct mail stands alone. It must grab attention without assistance; therefore, it is imperative that the message be designed in a format that combines verbal and illustrative elements attractively. In other words, the envelope itself must be attractive or the message may be quickly discarded. Refer to Figure 11.4.

IMAGE AND LIFESPAN Direct mail is not a prestigious medium. Many consumers perceive direct mailings to be "junk mail," and pieces are promptly discarded when they reach the household. Many consumers do not perceive the special offers to be all that special. Direct mailings to businesses can suffer the same fate (i.e., they may be discarded), particularly if several mailings from different suppliers are received at the same time. However, the physical form of direct mail enables consumers to retain it for future reference.

For more insight into the benefits of direct mail communications, read the Advertising in Action vignette **Boston Pizza's Direct Mail Yields Good Results.**

Buying Direct Mail

Three basic steps are involved in buying direct mail: obtaining a proper prospect list, conceiving and producing the mailing piece, and distributing the final version.

OBTAINING DIRECT MAIL LISTS

The direct mail list is the backbone of the entire campaign. Both the accuracy and definition of the list can have a significant bearing on the success or failure of a campaign. It is estimated that as much as 60 percent of the success or failure of any mail campaign hinges on the list that is used.[8] Companies recognize that it costs more to acquire a new customer than it does to keep an existing one. Marketing now exists in a data-driven era, and companies are constantly collecting and analyzing information about their customers to devise effective communications programs. Direct mail

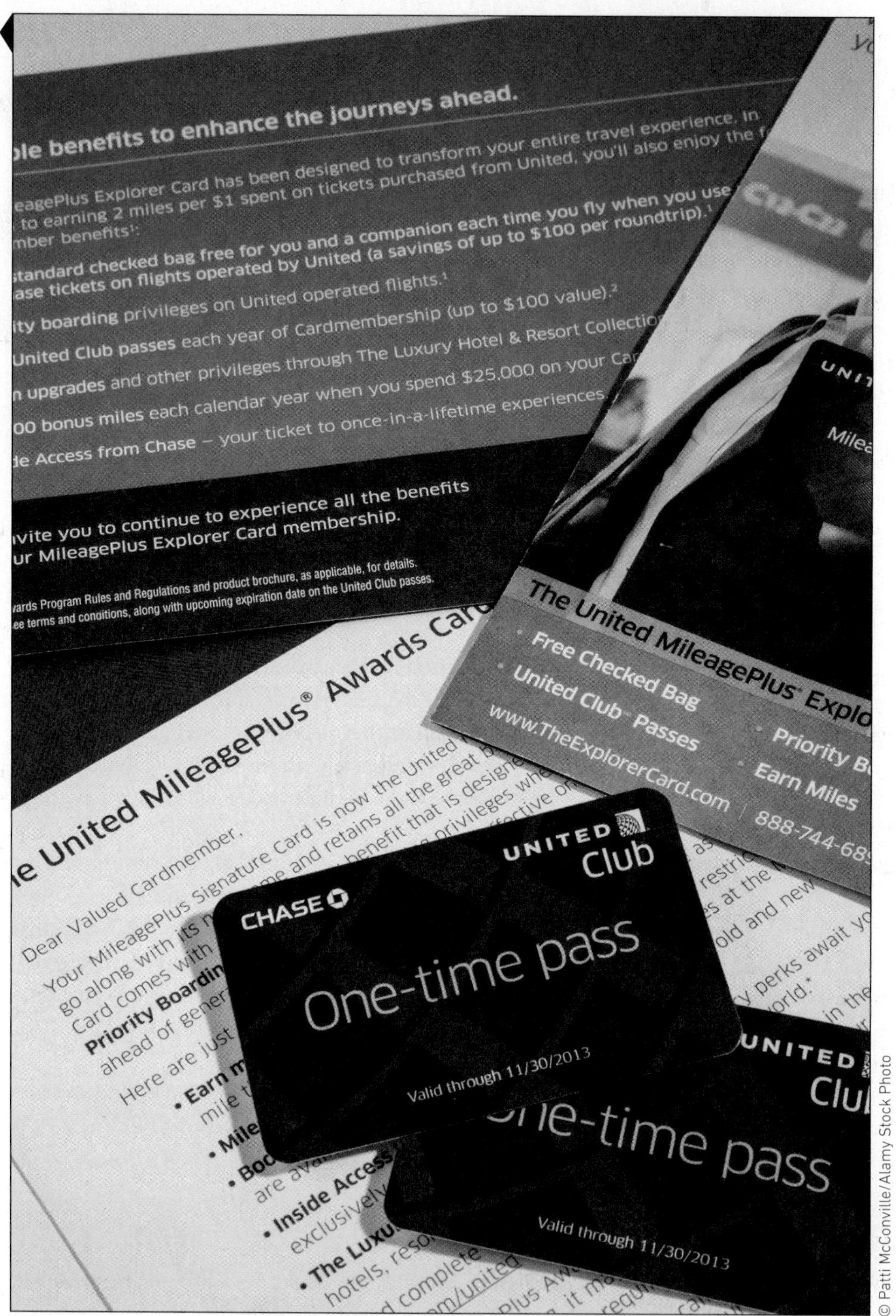

© Patti McConville/Alamy Stock Photo

FIGURE 11.4

To grab a reader's attention, a direct mail piece must combine copy and visual images effectively. The copy invites the reader to open the direct mail piece.

remains an effective means to deliver the communications. Direct mail lists are secured from internal and external sources.

INTERNAL SOURCES There is no better prospect than a current customer. Consequently, companies now implement customer relationship management programs that are based on the data they collect about their customers.[9] **Customer relationship management (CRM)** refers to strategies designed to optimize profitability, revenue, customer retention, and customer satisfaction. CRM is concerned with developing relationships with

ADVERTISING IN ACTION

Boston Pizza's Direct Mail Yields Good Results

Boston Pizza effectively combines the mass reach of television and online advertising with the highly targeted reach of direct mail. Each component plays a key role in building Boston Pizza's business in Canada.

According to Andrew Borsk of Boston Pizza, "Direct mail is a more tactile and permanent way to get into guests' homes." Delivering a menu to area homes, for example, provides the stimulus for delivery and takeout orders—a growing portion of Boston Pizza's business.

A recent national campaign using the theme "The Joy of Finger Cooking" used direct mail as the anchor medium. Key elements of the campaign were based on selective use of geographic, demographic, and psychographic data provided by Statistics Canada and Canada Post. Boston Pizza targeted mid- to high-income households with children located within two kilometres of each of its 315 restaurants across Canada.

In "The Joy of Finger Cooking" campaign, direct mail enabled Boston Pizza to deliver large amounts of information—something you cannot do in a 30-second TV spot. In planning the direct mail piece, Boston Pizza recognized the creative had to be entertaining to get people to read it and respond to it. Humour was integrated into the copy. Scattered throughout the piece were "Finger Tips," such as "One of the joys of finger cooking is the food preparation stage. This is because there is no food preparation stage."

With direct mail, standing out from the crowd is important. The mailing piece must be unique and noticeable. Says Borsk, "If it doesn't stand out, you might as well have delivered it straight to the local recycling centre."

Direct mail has produced good results for Boston Pizza, and as a result it remains a key component of the marketing communications mix. The direct mail for "The Joy of Finger Cooking" campaign produced volume growth in the high teens for the takeout and delivery business compared to the same period a year earlier.

© Helen Sessions/Alamy Stock Photo

Source: Adapted from "The Joy of Finger Cooking," *Sorted*, (Canada Post Publications, 2013), pp. 12–14.

customers over the long term. To capitalize on the potential of CRM programs, an organization must make a considerable investment in software technology. The technology ensures an organization's customer database is updated and monitored routinely.

Shoppers Drug Mart, for example, accumulates considerable data about customers who have a Shoppers Optimum rewards card. Refer to the image in Figure 11.5. Over time it has amassed information about its customers' demographics and shopping patterns so it can pinpoint what people are likely to buy. Through its Optimum card, Shoppers has one of the largest databases in the country (10 million members and counting). The Optimum program has been successful—cardholders apparently spend 60 percent more on their purchases than nonmembers.[10]

FIGURE 11.5

The Shoppers Optimum database provides information that produces offers of interest that are sent to Shoppers Drug Mart customers.

Direct mail remains a viable and efficient means of delivering messages to current customers. From internal data, customized mail offers can be sent directly to current customers who have consented to receive such offers. Getting current customers to buy more is a much easier challenge than trying to attract new customers. In direct mail terms, an internal customer list is referred to as a **house list**.

EXTERNAL SOURCES People who have a history of responding to mail offers tend to be attractive prospects for new offers; buying by mail is part of their behaviour. Therefore, the challenge is to find prospects who have a demographic profile—and perhaps a psychographic profile—that mirrors the profile of current customers. A **list broker** can assist in finding these prospects. The buyer provides the broker with the profile of the target customer, and the broker supplies a list of possible prospects. Generally, a high-quality list is developed through a **merge/purge** process whereby numerous lists are purchased, combined, and stripped of duplicate names. Names are purchased (actually, rented) on a cost-per-thousand basis. List brokers charge a base rate for names, and charge more if additional requests are made. Additional requests, called *selects*, are usually demographic variables, interest or lifestyle variables, or geographic variables.

The Cornerstone Group of Companies is a database company that classifies names by behaviours and interests. Cornerstone's database is derived from information voluntarily provided by consumers. For instance, the cost of Cornerstone's pet ownership list starts at $100 per thousand ($100/M).

TC Transcontinental, a Canadian publishing and database management company, uses a technique called geomapping to assist its clients with direct mail campaigns. **Geomapping** targets an audience based on demographic, psychographic, and behavioural data. All the target information is overlaid on a special map to hone in on a specific group of potential customers.

Canada Post is very active in providing direct mail services to advertisers. It offers a service called Precision Targeter. If employed properly, the service will deliver messages to an organization's ideal customer. Precision Targeter is a free online tool that helps an advertiser plan the best delivery routes for a direct mail campaign. The software tool, which combines consumer data (e.g., age, income, presence of children) with interactive maps, allows advertisers to select from 14 demographic categories and maps that visualize areas of interest, then it adjusts routes based on budget considerations and offers pricing estimates for a potential campaign.[11]

A few types of external lists are available: response lists, circulation lists, and compiled lists.

RESPONSE LISTS A **response list** is a list of proven mail-order buyers. Such lists include people who buy from the Book of the Month Club, for example, and those who order from cooperative direct mailing firms. Because these lists are made up of proven mail-order buyers, they tend to cost more. TargetSource, a list broker, charges an additional $20/M for proven mail-order buyers in Canada.

CIRCULATION LISTS **Circulation lists** are magazine subscription lists that target potential customers by an interest or activity. A publishing company, for example, rents its list of subscribers to other reputable, noncompetitive businesses that are interested in a similar target. Cornerstone (mentioned above) is a leading provider of prospecting, database management, and data integration solutions. It also provides circulation lists to prospective advertisers. Should an organization wish to reach people interested in outdoor activities and travel, for example, Cornerstone offers a list of subscribers to *Canadian Geographic* magazine at a base cost of $130/M. Requesting additional demographic variables (age, gender, income, etc.) involves an additional charge. For insight into lists and list costs, see Figure 11.6.

COMPILED LISTS **Compiled lists** are prepared from government, census, and other public information, or from surveys conducted by marketing organizations such as Epsilon TargetSource Canada. TargetSource's consumer survey captures a wide range of data points on purchase behaviours and intentions, lifestyles, life stage, hobbies and interests, product ownership, and demographics. From a total universe of over 2 million Canadian households, marketers can target specific segments. For example, there are 16 000 expectant mothers in the TargetSource database, available at a cost of $225/M.[12] That list would be of interest to marketers of baby foods and other baby needs.

In the business-to-business market, names of business prospects are compiled from print sources such as the Standard Industrial Classification, *Fraser's Canadian Trade Directory*, and *Scott's Industrial Index*. Provincial and national associations like the Canadian Medical Association provide lists of their members, as do other associations, for example, those for accountants, engineers, or purchasing managers.

PRODUCTION

When designing a direct mail package, the advertiser usually engages the services of a specialist organization. In Canada, numerous full-service direct marketing and direct response agencies meet the needs of clients. Among them are Wunderman Direct and Rapp Canada. With direct and digital marketing playing a more important role in the communications mix, most large agency networks mentioned earlier in the book have either started or acquired direct response agencies. For instance, Rapp Canada is now a subsidiary of DDB Canada (a full-service agency network). Other direct agencies include Digitari (part of the JWT Group), OgilvyOne (part of Ogilvy & Mather), Proximity Canada (part of BBDO), and Tribal DDB (part of DDB Canada).

Once the mailing package is designed, it is ready for printing. Various factors such as size, shape, number of pieces to be included, and use of colour influence the cost. Costs are usually quoted on a per-thousand basis, with larger runs incurring lower unit costs. Once printed, the mailing pieces are turned over to a letter shop that specializes in stuffing and sealing envelopes; affixing labels; and sorting, binding, and stacking the mailers. Once this task is complete, the mailing units are sent to the post office or a private carrier for distribution.

DISTRIBUTION

The most common means of delivery for direct mail is Canada Post. A number of options are available through the postal system based on the nature of the mailing: Is it addressed

20 Eglinton Avenue West, 4th Floor, Toronto, Ontario M4R 1K8
Tel: (416) 932-9555 Fax: (416) 932-9566
www.cstonecanada.com

List Name: LIFESTYLE SELECTOR CANADA: PETS

CLASSIFICATION	TYPE	LIST SIZE	MIN ORDER	BASE COST/M
PRODUCTS	CONSUMER PETS	3,00,785	5,000	$100.00 US

This is a compiled list of buyers of consumer products who voluntarily completed and mailed detailed customer questionnaires that are packed with the products. These buyers have provided information about their individual and household lifestyles, hobbies and demographics.

This affinity interest sub-set includes the following topics: Household Pets, Own a Dog, Own a Cat. A Fundraiser Rate of $90/M is available.

Sample counts available for selection include:
Income: <$15K; $15–$19.9K; $25–$29.9K; $30–$39.9K; $40–$49.9K; $50–$59.9K; $60–$74.9K; $75–$99.9K; $100–$149.9K; $150–$174.9K; $175–$199.9K; $200–$249.9K; $250K+
Occupation: Professional/Technical; Management; Sales/Marketing; Clerical; Blue Collar; Student; Homemaker; Retired; Self Employed.
Education: Completed High School; Completed College; Completed Graduate School; Attended Vocation/Technical School.
Credit Cards: Travel/Entertainment; Bank; Other (Gas/Dept. Store).
Home Ownership: Owner; Renter.

This list is updated monthly.

Also available are the following affinity lists: Blue Chip, Charitable, Cultural, Do-It-Yourself, Domestic, Fitness, Family, Good Life, Older & Wiser, Outdoors, Pets and Technology (Please see datacards).

TERMS: Any order placed will incur a set up fee of $25.00. In addition a $100.00 fee will apply to all cancelled orders. Pricing will vary based on the stage of the order.
Orders cancelled after mail date must be paid in full.
* A minimum of 1,000 names applies to all re-use orders.

SELECTS	COSTS
FSA	$10.00/M
Province	$10.00/M
Nth	$0.00/M
Key Records	$2.00/M
Gender	$10.00/M
Age	$10.00/M
Behaviour	$10.00/M
Credit Card	$10.00/M
Education-Responder	$10.00/M
Education-Spouse	$10.00/M
Home Ownership	$10.00/M
Income	$10.00/M
Marital Status	$10.00/M
Multibuyer	$10.00/M
Number of Children	$10.00/M
Occupation-Responder	$10.00/M
Occupation-Spouse	$10.00/M
Radius	$10.00/M
Recency	$10.00/M

FORMATS	COSTS
E-mail	$60.00 F
Secure File Transfer	$60.00 F
FTP	$60.00 F

SORTING	COSTS
Postal	$0.00/M

PROVINCIAL BREAKDOWN

NL 1.77%	NB 3.03%	MB 4.24%	BC 13.18%
NS 4.23%	QC 16.41%	SK 4.16%	YK 0.15%
PE 0.56%	ON 40.20%	AB 11.93%	NT 0.13%
NU 0.00%			

Call for a quote for the following services:
- Merge/Purge
- Data Cleansing and Appending
- Do Not Call Management solutions

Contact Jennifer Grant at:
416-932-9555 ext. 2380 or
jgrant@cstonecanada.com

List Owner asserts that this list is subject to and compliant with the Personal Information Protection and Electronic Documents Act (PIPEDA).
Status Recorded: March 07, 2002

Cornerstone makes its best efforts to ensure the accuracy of its media profiles. However, we receive information from third-parties and cannot guarantee our profiles' accuracy or completeness.

Our research shows this list was last updated: October 25, 2013
Print Date: November 22, 2013 **CLB Profile Updated: November 09, 2013**

FIGURE 11.6

An illustration of the costs associated with renting a direct mail list

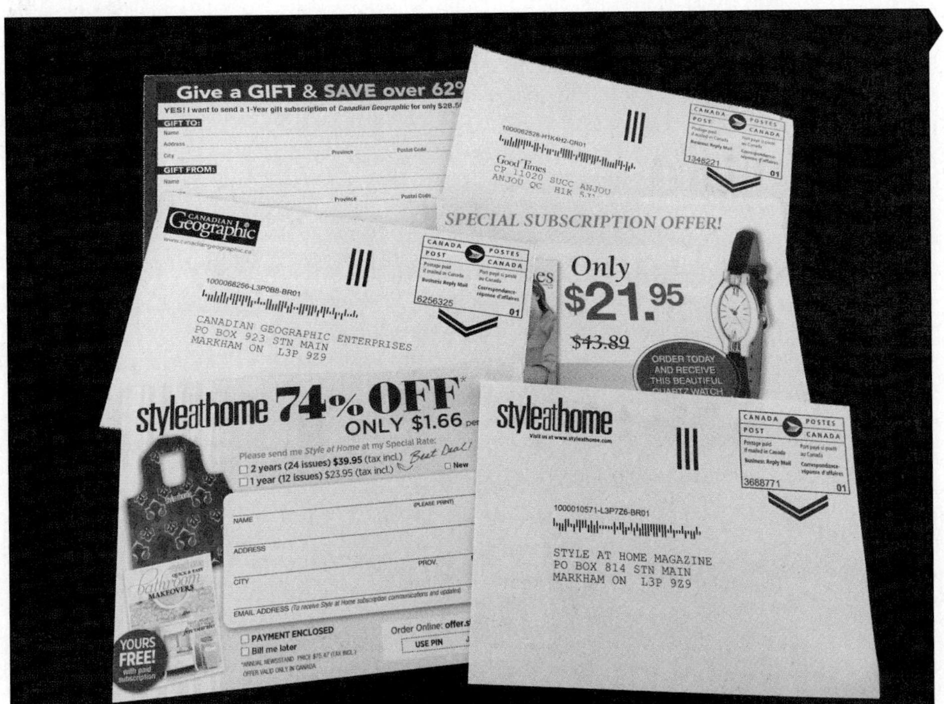

Photo by Keith J. Tuckwell

FIGURE 11.7

A postage-paid reply card makes it easier for consumers to respond.

mail, unaddressed mail, or business reply mail, or is it a bulky item like a catalogue? Size and weight are factors that affect the cost of a mailing.

A standard sized *addressed mailing* piece under 50 grams costs 45 cents; up to 100 grams the cost is 55 cents. Costs get more complicated as the size and weight increase. *Unaddressed admail* (e.g., restaurant flyers and leaflets) under 50 grams costs 15.8 cents; up to 100 grams the cost is 18.1 cents. Oversized unaddressed mail costs slightly more. *Business reply mail* (e.g., a leaflet with a postage-paid return order form) has a round trip cost of 84 cents for a domestic mailing. Business reply mail that is oversized and weighs more than 50 grams costs significantly more. Refer to Figure 11.7 for an illustration of business reply mail.

The cost of mailing a small catalogue or other type of multiple-page publication is affected by many factors, including size, weight, whether the publication can be sorted by machine or not, and the extent of the delivery (city, region, or national). The base cost for a small publication up to 50 grams is 65 cents. National delivery of a 500 gram publication costs $2.09.[13]

An alternative option for distribution is to use a private delivery service, which will have a completely different rate structure.

Media Buying: Cooperative Direct Mail—An Example

The procedures for estimating the costs of solo direct mail and cooperative direct mail are similar. Taken into consideration are factors such as the distribution, printing, and mailing costs, and the costs associated with fulfillment. As indicated previously, an advertiser can either undertake all of these costs or share the costs with others in a cooperative mailing program. For this example, we will assume that a cooperative direct mail program will be undertaken in the Valassis Canada Inc. mail envelope. Refer to the rate card in Figure 11.8 for details about the distribution cost.

FIGURE 11.8

Rate card for a cooperative direct mailing

The forgoing material is extracted from CARDonline™, reciting Valassis Canada Inc. listing and rate card information as owned by and used with permission of Rogers Publishing Limited.

VALASSIS CANADA INC.

GENERAL INFORMATION

Valassis Canada Inc., 47 Jutland Rd., Toronto, ON M8Z 2G6

Phone: 416-259-3600

Website: www.valassis.ca

Edward Cassidy, Vice-President of Print Media Sales (email: cassidye@valassis.ca)

Member: Coupon Industry Association of Canada

PROFILE

Valassis is a full-range media and marketing services company. We deliver value to consumers how, when, and where they want, achieved through exceptional targeting insights, results analysis, and diverse media portfolio.

COMMISSION AND CASH DISCOUNTS

None

GENERAL ADVERTISING

Rates confirmed January 1, 2013

Rates are net

Rates based on 1 side of page & exclusivity for 1 product category only. Additional categories extra. Multiple-page, volume, or frequency discounts available on request. Regional buys subject to 10% surcharge with min. $500 in each market purchased.

Size	Rate Per M
1 Page	$8.00
½ Page	5.20
Front Cover	12.50
Back Cover	11.50
Front Tab	9.50
Back Tab	9.00

ADDITIONAL MARKETING OPPORTUNITIES

Offers Redplum free-standing inserts delivered in newspapers, polybags, targeted preprinted inserts, door-hang cards; product sampling; and digital marketing.

Data from CARDonline, www.cardonline.com

INFORMATION: VALASSIS CANADA INC. COOPERATIVE MAILING

The Offer:	1 Page Folded That Includes a $1.50 Coupon
Redemption rate:	3 percent
Distribution:	2 million households

COST CALCULATIONS

Distribution Cost (Cost to Insert an Offer into an Envelope) 1 Page Folded That Includes a $1.50 Coupon	
2 000 000 × $8.00/M	= $ 16 000
Printing cost (estimated cost) 2 000 000 × $6/M	= $ 12 000
Redemption cost (estimated at 3 percent of total coupons distributed) 2 000 000 × 0.03 × $1.50	= $ 90 000
Total Cost	**= $118 000**

Direct Response Television

There are two types of direct response television advertising: short form and long form. **Short-form DRTV** commercials vary in length and may be 15, 30, 60, 90, or 120 seconds long; they typically appear on cable channels. **Long-form DRTV** commercials, commonly referred to as **infomercials**, can last 30 or 60 minutes. Infomercials tend to be much like a television program. They include characters and follow a script. The benefits of the product are presented in great detail. These commercials encourage consumers to move closer to a buying decision or to actually make the buying decision. The effectiveness of direct response ads is measured by responses such as cost per order, cost per lead, or cost per call.

Infomercials are now presented in an entertaining manner; there is less hard sell than in years past. Consumers can simply evaluate the message and take action if they so desire. Unlike regular television ads, direct response commercials ask consumers to take action immediately—think of Vince and the Slap Chop or Schticky! Refer to the image in Figure 11.9. The effectiveness of the ad can be measured immediately. In the case of a short-form ad, the phones at the call centre should start ringing immediately. The advertiser can quickly assess the revenues generated from the offer against the cost of the infomercial—the return on investment is measurable. In an age in which managers are more accountable for their marketing investments, this benefit is very attractive.

Serious mainstream marketers now employ well-produced and highly informative infomercials. Among them are automobile marketers like Ford and General Motors; financial institutions such as TD Canada Trust, RBC Royal Bank, and Manulife; and packaged goods companies like Procter & Gamble and Unilever.

Courtesy of Square One Entertainment, Inc.

FIGURE 11.9

Direct response commercials encourage immediate action; the effectiveness of the ad is measured immediately by the response rate.

Manulife Financial recently aired three 120-second commercials to more clearly articulate the types of life circumstances that people could be in that lend themselves to insurance. For example, one commercial depicted a family facing mounting child healthcare costs that aren't covered by government insurance—a compelling reason to have insurance protection.[14]

Direct response commercials do not always have to sell something. In fact, a good commercial will meet other objectives, such as generating leads, driving traffic to retail stores, creating awareness for new products, and protecting or enhancing a brand's image. Procter & Gamble does not sell directly to consumers but finds direct response commercials effective for promoting its products that are sold by retailers. Essentially, advertisers are pursuing a dual benefit—they are combining a brand message with a DRTV technique of encouraging action. DRTV's ability to do both excites advertisers!

Getting into DRTV isn't cheap. Experts say it costs as much as $250 000 to produce a 30-minute infomercial, and if celebrities are included the costs can go much higher. By comparison the average cost of a 30-second national TV commercial can exceed $300 000—so the comparison is for 30 minutes of airtime versus 30 seconds of airtime.[15]

To keep media placement costs reasonable, shorter commercials (up to 60 seconds) usually employ the run-of-schedule option rather than buy time on specific programs. Advertisers may also buy **remnant time**, which is unsold inventory available on short notice at a lower cost.

Direct response television may not be for every marketing organization, but for those that understand how overwhelmed consumers are with information will see that DRTV cuts through the clutter and explains clearly the benefits of a product. It is a medium that can drive sales on air, on a website (if the consumer is directed there), and in retail stores. For more insight into direct response television, read the Advertising in Action vignette **DRTV: Impactful and Measurable**. Refer to Figure 11.10 for a summary of some advantages and disadvantages of direct response television advertising.

Direct home shopping is a service provided by cable television channel TSC (The Shopping Channel). Messages to prospects are shown in the form of close-up shots of the product or, in the case of clothing and accessories, by models wearing the goods. Many popular brands, such as Sony, KitchenAid, and Bose, are promoted on this channel. Details about how to order are broadcast frequently, and a 1-800 number is usually shown on the screen along with a description of the product. Goods are also available through the website. The Shopping Channel offers Canadians a broad and deep assortment of products. Home shopping offers the shopper a great deal of convenience.

FIGURE 11.10

Advantages and disadvantages of direct response television advertising

ADVANTAGES

- *Message Content*—numerous benefits can be communicated in detail
- *Demonstration*—added time allows for lengthier and more dramatic demonstrations
- *Cost*—production and media costs of short commercials are less than traditional TV ads
- *Flexibility*—message can be altered if necessary

DISADVANTAGES

- *Time*—even a 60-second commercial faces time constraints
- *Lifespan*—commercials are fleeting; frequency is necessary
- *Image*—consumers are often skeptical about the message; are the claims believable?

ADVERTISING IN ACTION

DRTV: Impactful and Measurable

There are those who believe television is dead. They claim it's an old medium—it's out of touch with on-demand consumers who want to watch programs when they want to watch, not when the station wants them to watch. Not so fast, say many direct response industry experts! What about those direct response commercials? Tacky to some, impactful to others, these commercials can certainly move the merchandise.

Stop and think about those infomercials that have grabbed your attention late at night or on weekend mornings: the FlavorWave Oven, the Ab Rocket Twister, or the Bowflex Max Trainer. The Bowflex Max Trainer boasts "The ultimate 14-minute workout!" Don't snicker . . . these ads work! A study conducted by the Electronic Retailing Association reveals that 63 perent of the population watches some form of DRTV advertising. The viewers are both female and male, are more affluent than the rest of the population, and are younger rather than older—a desirable target to pursue.

The television universe is becoming fragmented. There are too many stations—too much choice for viewers. Regular television spots can get lost amidst the clutter. With direct response it is possible to target consumers in a more accurate manner and at lower cost. Further, with conventional television or radio commercials, or a print ad, it is difficult to link the ad to sales since so many other variables come into play.

With an infomercial, the phones start to ring right away, so the impact of the ad and the resulting sales are known almost immediately. For advertisers concerned about financial accountability, direct response television is an ideal fit.

So what makes a consumer pick up the phone to place an order? Experts in the industry say the message must be clear and concise; it must resolve a problem a consumer is experiencing; it must provide instant gratification; and it must be offered at a price point where the value is recognizable. Above all, the benefits of the product must be easy to demonstrate!

You may be too young to recall the George Foreman Grill, but the DRTV campaign for the product met all of these criteria. George Foreman was a heavyweight boxing champion of his era. Foreman estimates he made $200 million from the sale of grills bearing his name, which he neither invented nor initially wanted anything to do with. The success of the direct response campaign paved the way for retail distribution of the grill. The grill was produced and marketed by Salton, Inc., an appliance maker that didn't expect the grill to be much of a hit. For Foreman and Salton, it was like money falling from heaven. Proof that good direct response advertising serves a real business purpose.

© Roy Letkey/EXNEW/AP Photo

Adapted from Simon Houpt, "Call Now to Take Advantage of This Special TV Advertising Offer," *The Globe and Mail*, December 16, 2011, p. B5 and Jon Nathanson, "The Lucrative Secret Behind Infomercials," *The Week*, www.theweek.com.

Direct Response Print Media

It is common for advertisers to communicate direct response offers through newspapers and magazines. Both options are good for fielding leads for future marketing programs, for channelling prospects to a website, and for getting prospects to take action immediately. Since newspapers are a local market medium, an organization that has adopted a key market media strategy can target prospects geographically. Local market retailers that want to employ direct response strategies can do so through their local daily or weekly newspaper.

Magazines are a good alternative for advertisers targeting specific audiences based on demographic or geographic characteristics. For example, a company such as Intrawest, which markets year-round travel destinations (including Whistler Blackcomb, Mont Tremblant, and Blue Mountain), will place direct response ads in travel magazines or in general interest magazines that reach higher-income households. Such ads always include a 1-800 telephone number and a website address so that prospects can obtain more information or book a vacation. Provincial governments follow a similar strategy with their tourism marketing campaigns. The print media are ideal for showing colourful pictures of local tourist attractions. Inquiring minds will get in touch for more specific information. See the ad for Prince Edward Island in Figure 11.11 for an illustration.

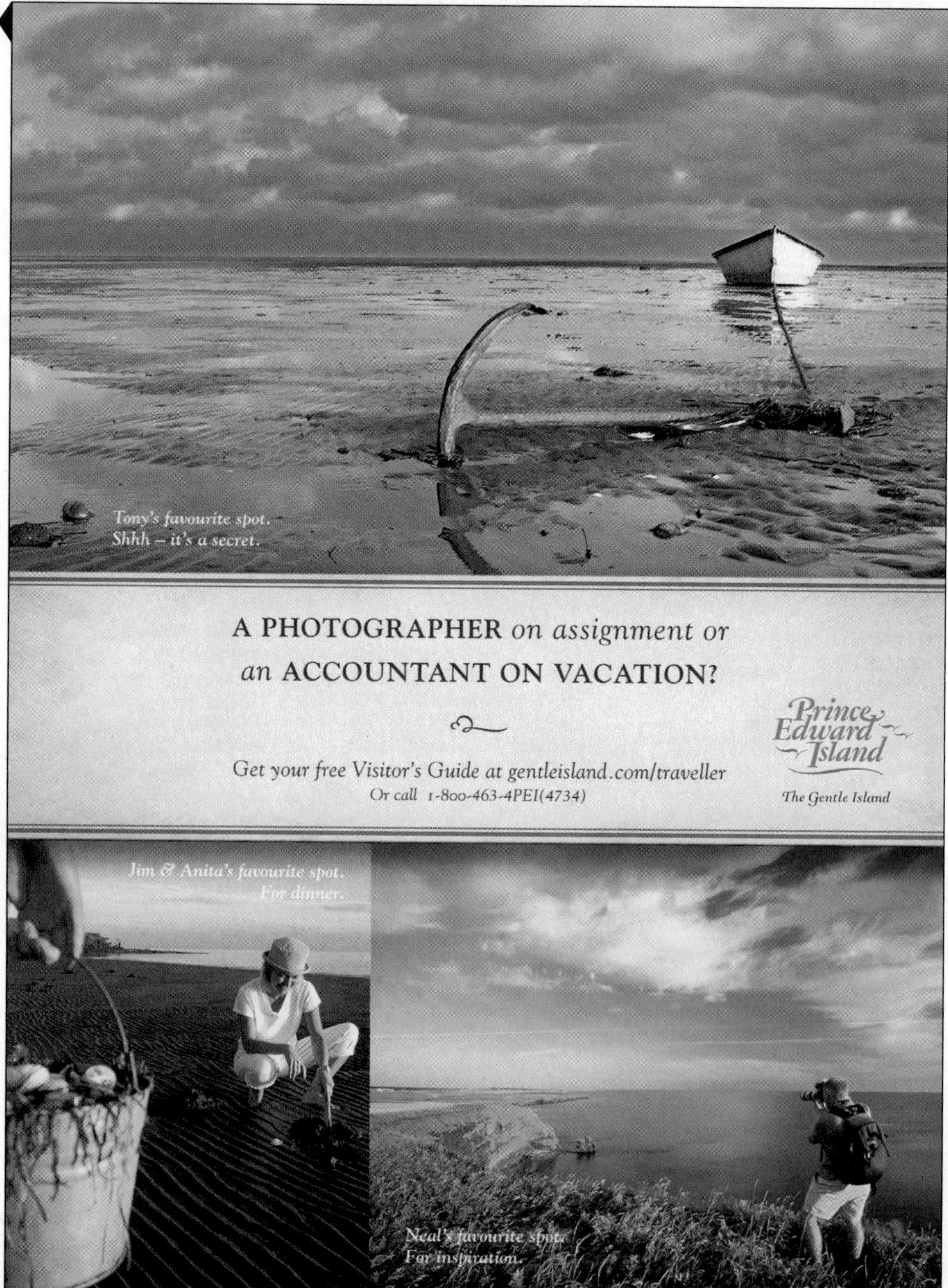

FIGURE 11.11
An illustration of direct response print advertising

Courtesy of the Province of Prince Edward Island

FIGURE 11.12

An illustration of a direct response insert that was distributed with a magazine ad

Courtesy of the Province of Prince Edward Island

Another print media alternative is the insert. An **insert** is a single- or multiple-page document inserted loosely or stitched directly into a publication. Sometimes an insert is strip glued (a gum-like glue) directly onto a page. In these cases an advertiser usually places an ad and then attaches the insert on top of the ad. This type of insert is referred to as a **tip-in**. See Figure 11.12 for an illustration of an insert. This Prince Edward Island insert was stitched into the magazine so that it appeared on top of the print ad that is included in Figure 11.11. Note that the government of Prince Edward Island is collecting valuable database information that can be used in future marketing efforts.

Another direct response print option is the flyer. There are more than 16 billion print flyers distributed annually in Canada at an investment of more than $3.3 billion. Media is about 30 percent of the costs with the balance composed of print design and production and transportation to the media.[16] Flyers are typically distributed by daily and community newspapers, special delivery service companies, and Canada Post.

Direct Response Interactive

Many advertisers include interactive advertising in their marketing communications mix. Most websites include various forms of advertising, with display ads (banner ads) being among the most popular. Display ads do not communicate much information. Their primary purpose is to provide just enough information to tempt the viewer to click on the ad. Once clicked, the viewer is transferred to another web location where more information is provided.

Given the procedure just described, it could be said that all display ads are a form of direct response advertising. But that is not the case. True direct response interactive ads will include a call to action similar to those in other media. For example, a call to action may be something as direct as "Buy now," a phrase that certainly communicates the desired action. More subtle phrases such as "Explore now" or "Find out more" will encourage action without commanding such a strong commitment. Refer to the illustration in Figure 11.13. Regardless of the call to action used, the objective remains the same—click the ad! More insight into interactive advertising is presented in Chapter 12.

© Ian Dagnall/Alamy Stock Photo

FIGURE 11.13

The call to action is a key element of a direct response interactive ad.

Telemarketing

Telemarketing is a booming business in North America. Much telemarketing activity is conducted through call centres. A **call centre** is a central operation from which a company operates its inbound and outbound telemarketing programs.

According to the Canadian Marketing Association (CMA), there is more money spent on telemarketing in Canada in a one-year period than there is on conventional television advertising. That may be difficult to comprehend, but consider that we do not see telemarketing in practice (so we don't think about it), whereas we do see a considerable amount of television advertising. The latest statistics available in Canada (2008) reveal that \$4.1 billion was spent on telemarketing, and it produced \$26.1 billion in sales.[17]

There are two types of telemarketing: inbound and outbound. **Inbound telemarketing** refers to the reception of calls by the order desk, or customer inquiries and direct response calls often generated through the use of toll-free numbers. **Outbound telemarketing**, on the other hand, refers to calls a company makes to customers to develop new accounts, generate sales leads, and even close a sale. Effective telemarketing programs often involve a two-or-more call process: the first call (or series of calls) determines the needs of a prospect or existing customer. The second call (or series of calls) motivates the prospect or existing customer to make a purchase.

Many consumers voice displeasure with outbound telemarketing practices, citing aggressive and sometimes abusive behaviour by callers. In fact, the CMA reports that the number one source of marketing-related complaints is telemarketing.[18] Negative consumer attitudes about telemarketing persist even though legitimate organizations are trying to contact consumers in a highly professional manner.

Marketing organizations do recognize the consumer's right to privacy and have taken steps to ensure that all government-legislated guidelines and policies are followed. The federal government passed "do-not-call" legislation (in 2005) to further protect consumers from unwanted phone calls. The CMA supports the legislation, stating that "without reasonable laws regulating organizations that use the telephone to market their goods and services, the industry risks losing its rights to use this valuable marketing channel to acquire new customers."[19] Organizations that disregard the do-not-call legislation are subject to fines of "up to $15 000 per call"—a stiff penalty to pay.

In addition to the do-not-call legislation that organizations must abide by, the CMA has self-regulating policies that organizations follow in all forms of direct marketing practice. Refer to Figure 11.14 for more details about the CMA's privacy code.

There is also legislation in place that protects personal privacy. Individuals are protected by the federal Personal Information Protection and Electronic Documents Act, which sets out ground rules for how private sector organizations may collect, use, or disclose personal information in the course of commercial activities. The law recognizes the right of consumers to protect their personal information and provides flexibility for organizations to use consumer data to grow their business.[20]

Given that the practice of telemarketing is not well liked by consumers, perhaps the future success of telemarketing lies in inbound telemarketing. Organizations will have to integrate 1-800 telephone numbers into their other forms of advertising, encouraging consumers to make an inbound call. Alternatively, as many companies are now doing, the creation and implementation of customer relationship management programs allow for communications with customers in a variety of formats. In communicating through a mixture of telephone, mail, and the internet, there is less reliance on the telephone alone.

The primary advantage of telemarketing is cost. Compared with traditional forms of mass advertising and the cost of sending a salesperson to make a business call, telemarketing offers considerable savings. In comparison to direct mail, the response rate for telemarketing is about 100 times higher, so even though direct mail may appear to be cheaper than telephone solicitation, it is actually more costly in the long run.

The Canadian Marketing Association has been at the forefront of Canadian privacy issues for over a decade and has been actively involved in various national and international forums discussing privacy issues and the protection of personal information.

The CMA's privacy code gives every Canadian the right to

- Consent before your personal information is transferred to a third party
- Access information held about you
- Obtain the source of your name on marketing lists
- Correct erroneous information
- Have your name removed from telephone and direct mail marketing lists

Each year members of the CMA sign a commitment to follow the code.

FIGURE 11.14

Members of the Canadian Marketing Association are committed to ethical guidelines governing marketing practice.

Source: Adapted from the Canadian Marketing Association, www.the-cma.org.

FIGURE 11.15

Some tips for more effective telemarketing campaigns

Organizations that want to move into the telemarketing arena must take steps to ensure that they do it right. In this regard, some tried and true principles of telemarketing communications should be considered. Here are some of the elements of successful scripting:

- ***Focus on the relationship*** Selecting people with whom you have a relationship will produce higher campaign results (e.g., current customers). It is far less costly to generate sales from existing customers than it is to attract new customers.
- ***Adjust the script approach to your audience*** A well-tested verbatim script works well for marketing a simple or low-cost product. A guided or outline script is more suited to a business product environment, where numerous unplanned objections may occur.
- ***Empathize with the receivers*** Approach each prospect as an individual with unique needs.
- ***Establish rapport and gain attention quickly*** Clear identification of the caller, the company, the relationship, and the reason for the call should occur in the first sentence. Every phrase should reflect honesty and sincerity to put the recipient at ease.
- ***Keep it short and simple*** Use short words and sentences. Write the script in the same way as you speak.
- ***Be prepared*** Practise and role play are important before making a call. Receive feedback to fine tune the presentation.
- ***Make it easy to say yes*** Structure the offer to reduce risk. Show the savings, or offer a free trial, discount, or return option. Test various offers to make sure that the one selected produces the best results.

For telemarketing to be effective, the call must be carefully planned but remain flexible to allow for recipient feedback. There must be proper training and preparation for telemarketing representatives, just as there is for field sales representatives. Planning the message is as important as the medium itself. Refer to Figure 11.15 for details.

Distinctions must also be made between business-to-consumer telemarketing and business-to-business telemarketing. Business-to-business telemarketing is firmly grounded in customer relationship marketing practices, and the marketing strategies follow a very professional approach. In many business organizations, telemarketing is often referred to as inside sales. Highly trained inside salespeople contact or receive calls from customers (i.e., other businesses) and then process sales orders accordingly.

Catalogues and Magazines

Catalogues are reference publications, often annual, distributed by large retail chains and other direct marketing organizations. Catalogue marketing involves the merchandising of products through catalogue sales. When someone thinks of catalogues, the Sears catalogue comes to mind immediately, and for good reason. The Sears catalogue is the largest in Canada and is distributed to more than 4 million households. Sears publishes two semi-annual catalogues (Fall & Winter and Spring & Summer) as well as numerous seasonal catalogues, such as the Christmas Wish Book and sale catalogues.

Sears is a fully integrated marketing communications organization that generates $3.55 billion in revenues in Canada annually. Much of its business is generated from catalogue sales. The Sears catalogue reaches Canadians in the largest urban centres and smallest rural and northern communities. It is Canada's most extensive general merchandise catalogue. The combination of retail stores, catalogue, and online ordering at the Sears website are an effective combination for marketing and distributing products to customers. There are 1300 pickup locations across Canada, which are operated by catalogue agents.[21]

Other prominent catalogue retailers in Canada include Canadian Tire, Home Hardware, Mountain Equipment Co-op, and IKEA. These retailers are merging their retail operations with online buying. The catalogues they distribute drive traffic to their respective websites or to their retail stores. These retailers see real value in catalogue and online marketing activities. Sales through catalogues definitely take away from store sales, but companies are responding to their customers' demand for convenience. Customers today are into multichannel shopping. These companies effectively combine media advertising (television, print, and flyers) with nontraditional marketing communications (online, direct mail, email, and catalogues).

Rather than distribute catalogues, some companies have taken the concept a step further and are publishing their own magazines for distribution to current customers. The purpose is to stay in touch with customers after the sale. Harry Rosen, a prominent upscale menswear store, distributes *Harry* magazine in hardcopy and online to customers and prospective customers. The magazine keeps customers informed about fashion, health, and lifestyle trends and offers stories of interest. The magazine provides a means of building a sound relationship with customers and is part of Harry Rosen's customer relationship management program. Refer to the image in Figure 11.16. In the automotive market, Mazda publishes *Zoom Zoom*, a magazine dedicated to keeping current customers up to date on the latest happenings at Mazda. A digital edition is emailed to customers in the Mazda database.

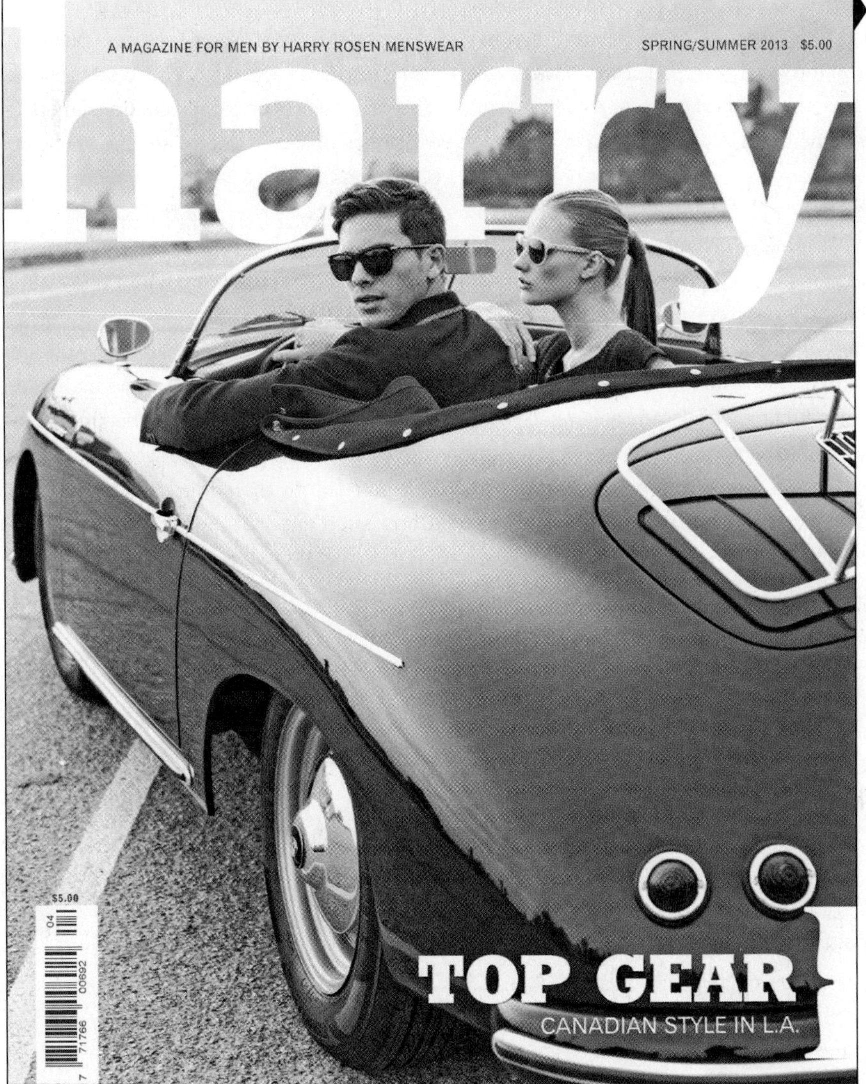

FIGURE 11.16

Harry Rosen builds a relationship with customers through *Harry* magazine.

SUMMARY

Direct response advertising is one of the largest advertising media in Canada. Its purpose is to generate a response by any means (through any medium) that is measurable. The major forms of direct response advertising are direct mail, direct response television, direct response print, direct response interactive, telemarketing, and catalogues.

Direct mail is the most prominent form of direct response advertising. A direct mailing usually includes an attention-grabbing envelope, sales letter, leaflet or folder, and possibly a statement stuffer. Advertisers choose between solo direct mail and cooperative direct mail. Solo distribution is much more expensive than cooperative distribution but more effective in generating the desired response. With cooperative direct mail, the costs are shared among participating organizations.

The primary advantages of direct mail for advertisers are its audience selectivity (which makes it an excellent medium for the business advertiser), high reach potential, and geographic flexibility. Disadvantages include poor image and the absence of editorial support. The success of any direct mail campaign largely depends on the quality of the list the advertiser uses. The best list is an internal list of customers, which should be readily available in the organization's database.

Lists are also available externally from list suppliers and other secondary sources such as directories and trade indexes. Lists provided by list brokers are rented on a cost-per-thousand basis.

Advancing technology has spurred growth in direct response television and telemarketing. There are two forms of direct response television: short form and long form. Short-form commercials are 30-second or longer commercials on cable channels. Long-form commercials, or infomercials, are 30- or 60-minute commercials that look much like a television show. Infomercials are becoming more popular with traditional advertisers and are used to establish leads, build image, and launch new products. They are effective in communicating information that involves a lot of detail or in situations in which the advertiser wants to expose an audience to a lengthy list of product benefits.

Direct response print (ads in newspapers and magazines) is another option for advertisers. Print ads typically include a call to action, and customers can easily respond through the 1-800 telephone number or website address included in the ad. Direct response inserts are another print media alternative. Inserts are placed loosely in the newspaper or magazine or stitched directly into the magazine, much like a normal page. It is also common for an advertiser to place an ad and an insert in a publication at the same time. The ad creates awareness and interest while the insert stimulates action.

There are two types of telemarketing. Inbound telemarketing refers to the reception of calls by an order desk, usually through a toll-free number. Outbound telemarketing refers to calls made by a company to customers to generate leads and even close a sale. Companies are attracted to telemarketing because of the relatively low cost. Quite simply, telemarketing is far less expensive than face-to-face communications or mass advertising. A drawback is the negative perceptions people have about this communication technique. Consumers tend to dislike the persistence of telemarketers and the timing of their calls.

Catalogues are popular with retail organizations. Time-pressed consumers appreciate the convenience of catalogue shopping, and catalogues help direct consumers toward offline purchases (at retail locations) and online purchases (at a website).

The primary advantages of all forms of direct response advertising are targeting capability and measurability. From a marketing planning perspective, the impact of any direct response offer can be measured while the communication is in progress or shortly thereafter. No form of traditional mass media has such capability. The advance of computer and communications technologies will continue to encourage much greater use of direct response communications.

KEY TERMS

long-form DRTV 333
merge/purge 328
outbound telemarketing 338
remnant time 334
response list 329
short-form DRTV 333
solo direct mail 322
statement stuffer 321
telemarketing 320
tip-in 337

REVIEW QUESTIONS

1. What are the major forms of direct response advertising?
2. Identify and briefly explain the components of a direct mail package.
3. What is the difference between a solo direct mail campaign and a cooperative direct mail campaign?
4. What are the advantages and disadvantages of direct mail advertising for a business product advertiser (e.g., a manufacturer of business equipment)?
5. How important is the mailing list in a direct mail campaign? Briefly explain.
6. Explain the differences between a response list, a circulation list, and a compiled list.
7. What is a list broker, and what functions does a list broker perform?
8. Explain the following terms as they relate to direct response advertising:
   a) Bounce backs
   b) House list
   c) Insert
   d) Merge/purge
   e) Infomercial
   f) Inbound telemarketing versus outbound telemarketing
   g) Call centre
9. What are some of the advantages and disadvantages of telemarketing for selling products and services?

DISCUSSION QUESTIONS

1. "The dollars an advertiser invests in direct mail advertising are wasted, owing to the poor image of the medium." Discuss.
2. "Persistent invasion of consumer privacy will be the undoing of the direct response advertising industry." Is this statement true or false, and does it depend on the type of direct response an advertiser uses? Discuss.
3. "Direct response television will play a more prominent role in future television advertising campaigns for traditional advertisers such as banks, automobile manufacturers, and insurance companies." Is this statement true or false? Discuss.
4. Conduct some secondary research to find a company that has successfully used direct response advertising as part of an integrated marketing communications campaign. What role did direct response play? Describe the success that resulted from the direct response effort.

NOTES

1. Canadian Media Directors' Council, *Media Digest* 2014–2015, 9.
2. "A Winning Combination," *Sorted*, Spring 2006, S48.
3. Allison Schiff, "DMA: Direct Mail Response Rates Beat Digital," *Direct Marketing News*, **www.dmnews.com/dma-direct-mail-response-rates-beat-digital**.
4. "Direct Impact: As Part of an Integrated Campaign, Direct Mail Still Drives Business Results," *Financial Post*, October 23, 2013, **http://business.financialpost.com**.
5. "How to Get the Most out of Your Direct Mail: Direct Marketing Resource Guide," *Marketing*, November 14, 2005, 4.
6. "Why Would Anyone Use Direct Mail?" *CR Marketer*, November 13, 2012, **www.thecrmarketer.com**.
7. "Direct Impact," *Financial Post*.
8. "Target Your Audience," *Direct Mail: What Works?* Supplement to *Strategy*, 2006, S48.
9. AMA Dictionary of Marketing Terms, **www.marketingpower.com**.
10. Chris Daniels, "It's in the Cards," Loyalty + Incentives Report, *Marketing*, August 30, 2010, L12.
11. Canada Post, **www.canadapost.com**.
12. Epsilon TargetSource Canada, "Expecting a Baby Mailing List," **http://lists.nextmark.com/market?page=order/online/datacard&id=224021**.
13. Rates obtained from Canada Post, **www.canadapost.ca**.
14. Matt Semansky, "Manulife Financial Flexes DRTV Muscle," *Marketing*, January 9, 2008, **www.marketingmag.ca**.
15. "The Economics of Informercials," *The Week*, November 14, 2013, **http://priceonomics.com/the-economics-of-infomercials**.
16. Canadian Media Directors' Council, *Media Digest*, 2015–2016, 158.
17. "Do-Not-Call-List," *CBC News*, September 30, 2008, **www.cbcnews.ca**.
18. Ibid.
19. "Canada's Largest Marketing Organization Welcomes National Do-Not-Call-List," press release, Canadian Marketing Association, November 28, 2005.
20. Canadian Marketing Association, **www.the-cma.org/consumers/protecting-privacy**.
21. Sears Canada, **www.sears.ca**.

CHAPTER 12

Interactive Media

Learning Objectives

After studying this chapter, you will be able to

1. Describe the various elements of interactive communications
2. Evaluate the various interactive advertising models available to marketing organizations
3. Identify key aspects of online audience measurement systems
4. Assess the potential of the internet, social media, mobile communications, and video games as advertising media
5. Describe and apply various models for pricing and buying online advertising

Technology is changing how marketers and marketing communications practitioners think about media. Specifically, online communications have turned the nature of marketing communications from a one-way process (disruptive messaging) to a two-way process (participative messaging). Interactive media allow an organization to listen to customers, learn from them, and deliver content and services tailored to their responses and actions.

In the digital universe, control has shifted from the advertiser to the customer—this is a change that marketers are adapting to. It's no longer about delivering a message, but rather allowing customers to participate in developing messages and interacting with brands—a concept referred to as *engagement*. Viewers now have unprecedented choice regarding how they engage with advertisers, and with the recent invasion of smart TVs we now live in the four-screen universe—computers, smartphones, tablets, and televisions.

Advertising on the internet has grown significantly in recent years and now leads the pack in terms of advertising revenue. Internet advertising now totals $3.8 billion per year (2014 data). Television advertising has slipped into second place at $3.3 billion. While online revenue growth is slowing down, revenues generated by mobile devices are increasing at a rapid rate. Mobile advertising now generates $903 million in revenue (as of 2014).[1] Mobile advertising is driving the expansion of internet advertising and will continue to do so in the future.

There has been a clear shift in how advertisers allocate their advertising budgets in the wake of changing consumer behaviour. Knowing that consumers are so attached to their electronic devices, advertisers can now reach customers any time of day anywhere. Procter & Gamble clearly recognizes the value of online advertising and now allocates 35 percent of its marketing budget to it. The growing interest in digital media is based on advertisers' desire to be where consumers are and to spend their advertising dollars effectively.[2]

All age groups are online, so agency planners must give greater consideration to the opportunities the medium offers. In making media recommendations, however, one thing hasn't changed much: Budgets have remained relatively stable, making the media choices more difficult. Advertising on the internet is an expensive proposition, so the funds to support such an investment must come from other media an advertiser has traditionally used. The challenge for media planners remains the same: Find the best combination of media to effectively and efficiently reach the target audience. This chapter will discuss the opportunities presented by the various interactive media.

Internet Advertising in Canada

The internet is revolutionizing how companies look at advertising. The irony, however, is that there is still a gap between how much advertisers spend online and how much they should be spending online. Internet advertising presently accounts for 34 percent of all advertising revenue in Canada, but not many companies are allocating that much of their budget to the medium.

Canada's **online advertising** market has reached $3.8 billion, with almost one-quarter of that revenue generated via mobile communications. Smartphones are becoming a crucial device for consumers to access information, hence the need for advertisers to consider a mobile advertising investment. Presently, four industries account for about half of the internet advertising revenue in Canada: consumer packaged goods, automotive, retail, and financial. Companies in these industries, such as Unilever and Procter & Gamble, General Motors and Ford, Canadian Tire and Walmart, and RBC Financial and CIBC, lead the way.

Canada is one of the few countries where internet revenue exceeds television revenue. The rapid growth of internet advertising revenue has had a significant impact on other media. Out-of-home media is the only other category experiencing revenue growth, mainly because of the addition of digital screens. Television has encountered a marginal decline in revenue, while the print media (newspapers and magazines) have suffered double-digit negative growth in recent years.[3] These trends are expected to continue in the foreseeable future.

The latest data available about consumer participation on the internet reveals that 86 percent (29.7 million people) of Canadians are internet users. Canadian participation ranks second in the world, just behind the United Kingdom. The amount of time Canadians spend online is a factor considered by media planners—more time equates to greater opportunities to reach a target audience. The average time Canadians are online using a computer is close to five hours a day. Mobile device users are connected for an average of just under two hours.[4] Figures like these clearly justify the need for a good balance of advertising spending between digital media and traditional media such as television, newspapers, magazines, and radio.

Such high internet participation is having an impact on time spent with other media, but it seems that Canadians have seamlessly adopted digital media technologies while maintaining a strong appetite for traditional media. The amount of time spent online does vary be age category, and younger age groups are leading the charge. Whereas television once ruled the roost, the internet leads the way in the 18- to 24-year-old category and ranks second with the 35- to 54-year-old category. Not surprisingly, the internet falls to third place in the 55+ age group. Among older people, television remains the dominant medium. This information has clear implications for media planners. For additional insight into how much time Canadians spend with the various media, refer to Figure 12.1.

The internet is an ideal medium for reaching younger Canadians, and it is a reasonable medium for reaching older Canadians. If income is a targeting consideration, the

FIGURE 12.1

Time spent with media by Canadians

Medium	18–24 Years	35–54 Years	55+ Years
TV	1 218	1 572	2 382
Internet	1 384	1 243	470
Radio	675	1 135	1 202
Newspaper	100	151	266
Magazine	26	34	39

Note: All figures are weekly minutes per capita.

Source: "2014: Internet in the Media Garden," *The 2014 CMUST Report*, IAB Canada.

internet is somewhat of a puzzle. The distribution of internet users in Canada by household income reveals that all income groups have access to the internet, but some more than others. The $100 000+ income group comprise 35 percent of internet users, while the $40 000 to $75 000 group comprise 29 percent of users. Individuals earning less than $40 000 only comprise 18 percent of internet users. Therefore, advertisers wishing to target middle- to upper-income households must consider the internet a viable option.

Moving forward, the smartphone will be the preferred method for accessing the internet, hence the need for advertisers to reevaluate how budgets are allocated. Smartphones enable advertisers to reach consumers anywhere and anytime—a significant advantage over any other medium. Additional data about trends in mobile communications are presented later in this chapter.

While advertising is taking hold on the internet, its effectiveness is much debated. Advertisers who are accustomed to metric measures, such as circulation and audience reached by the print and broadcast media, are adapting to different measures online. Online it is not necessarily about the number of impressions made, but about the amount of time a consumer spends with a brand—how engaged he or she is with a brand. Marketers are trying to figure out if engagement translates into consumer purchases, and if so to what degree.

To be effective with online communications, the advertiser must respect some essential differences between the internet and traditional media. The internet is a true source of information and entertainment for consumers and is a "participative" medium. For example, fans of a brand are known to produce their own commercials for the brand and post them on YouTube for others to view. In contrast, mass advertising through traditional media, such as television, radio, magazines, and newspapers, is "interruptive" and the communications are one way—advertiser to consumer. Therefore, an advertiser must adapt and produce advertising that is suitable for the online arena. A host of digital advertising agencies have emerged ready to meet the challenge of online advertising.

A few key issues related to the placement of ads online and how they are measured are factors that make advertisers reluctant to invest in the medium. The key issues focus on whether or not ads are actually viewed and whether or not real people are clicking on the ads. *Viewability* is a hot issue among marketers. Since companies are pouring more money into online advertising, they want assurances that their ads actually appear in front of humans. While this concern may appear odd, recent data show that less than 50 percent of ads appearing "in view" were actually seen. *In view* means that at least half of the ad was visible on a webpage for one second or more. Such a brief view counts as an impression, which advertisers pay for. Advertisers question the value of this kind of impression.

Advertisers are also concerned about **click fraud**, a situation where bots that look like human web users click on advertisements. A click is a click, and advertisers must pay for ads that are seen by this nonhuman traffic. The fraud that the bots enable is a major problem. The various means by which advertisers pay for online advertising are discussed later in the chapter.

The issues of viewavility and click fraud need to be addressed by the industry. It is not unreasonable for advertisers to demand that their ads have the opportunity to be seen the way they are in other media. Further, ads that are not seen by a human are a wasteful use of an advertiser's scarcest resource—money!

From a media planning perspective, the rapid growth in internet consumption strongly suggests the inclusion of interactive media in a marketing communications strategy. The challenge facing marketers and media planners is twofold. First, they must devise a plan that effectively integrates online advertising with other forms of advertising. In doing so, they must understand certain differences in consumer behaviour that people exhibit when using digital media. Second, they must determine how much to invest (share of budget) in online advertising. From an industry perspective, greater transparency is needed for issues related to viewability and click fraud to ensure continued revenue growth.

Interactive Communications Planning

When an interactive communications plan is being devised, decisions about which medium to use are based on the target market the advertiser wishes to reach, the communications objectives, and the budget. Once these elements have been determined, the next step is to evaluate various interactive media options from a strategic viewpoint. Among the options are various forms of internet advertising that include search, display, rich media, video, sponsorships, and permission-based email. As well, an advertiser must consider social media, mobile options (smartphones and tablets), and video games.

TARGETING ONLINE

On the internet, consumers voluntarily visit websites they prefer. It is much like television, where people select the shows they want to watch. Therefore, audiences can be targeted based on demographic and geographic variables, by time of day, day of week, and behaviour. All websites accumulate data on who visits and how long they visit. Such data aid a media planner when planning audience reach and frequency scenarios.

To demonstrate demographic targeting, consider that a website like TSN.ca attracts a male audience and is a favourite destination for males between 18 and 24 years of age. On a monthly basis, TSN.ca attracts 1.7 million visitors who average 14.3 visits.[5] Dodge advertises its Ram trucks on the site and sponsors a daily contest called "1V1," which pits a challenging highlight (e.g., a spectacular catch by a baseball player or a great goal by a hockey player) against the reigning champion highlight. Visitors vote to determine the winner. Dodge is reaching its primary target audience on this website.

Programs and video content that are shown on the cable channel HGTV have a strong female reach, particularly in the 25 to 49 age range. This is an attractive advertising opportunity for companies in the furniture, appliance, decorating, and renovation business. Refer to the illustration in Figure 12.2.

Once a target is identified demographically, geographic refinement is also possible. Advertisers can place ads in specific regions, cities, or postal codes. From the TSN example above, an advertiser may want to reach young males in Toronto only. Such a request is possible based on data TSN.ca collects about its visitors.

Daypart targeting is another planning option. Prime time for online communications is during the day when people are at work or at play. The at-work audience is vast and comprised of a demographically attractive group of individuals who have higher-than-average incomes and education and who tend to research and buy online. To demonstrate the impact of daypart targeting, Best Buy ran a three-week campaign on Yahoo! Its ads ran Monday to Friday between 5:00 and 11:00 a.m. in Ontario and Quebec. The campaign generated a 200 percent conversion lift (consumers who took action based on the advertising) over previous campaigns.[6]

Unlike other media, the internet is a medium where advertisers can target customers based on their online behaviour. **Behavioural targeting** involves the delivery of ads to individuals based on previous surfing patterns (you are being watched!). Surfing behaviour

FIGURE 12.2

HGTV.ca effectively reaches females in the 25 to 49 age range.

is tracked by uploading a **cookie**, which is a small text file, to a consumer's web browser and sometimes stored on that person's hard drive. If the system works properly, ads delivered to an individual should be relevant to their interests. For example, if someone spent considerable time on a website such as Style at Home or HGTV, they would be expressing an interest in home decorating and renovation projects. A retailer such as The Home Depot, who sells many products related to home improvement, would be interested in placing ads on the site. Refer to the image in Figure 12.3.

To test the impact of behavioural targeting in generating leads, an automotive advertiser targeted consumers who recently visited automotive sites. Two plans were used: demographic targeting and behavioural targeting. The demographic plan produced 183 million impressions and 47 leads per 1 million impressions. An **impression** is defined as

FIGURE 12.3

The HGTV website is an ideal fit for any brand wanting to reach people interested in decorating and home renovation projects.

a measurement of responses from a web server to a page request from a user's browser. The behavioural plan only had 6 million impressions (at much lower cost), but those impressions generated 116 leads per 1 million impressions. Behavioural targeting produced almost three times the number of leads per million as did demographic targeting. This experiment verifies that a well-planned online communications strategy can reach far fewer people yet produce better business results.

Mobile communications is also shaping individual targeting practices. With such a high penetration of smartphones in Canada, it is now possible to reach people while they are on the move—a concept referred to as location-based targeting. **Location-based targeting** is an effort to integrate consumers' location information into the marketing or advertising strategy. Essentially, a person's location information (available through GPS chips built into smartphones) can work to an advertiser's advantage.

INTERACTIVE COMMUNICATIONS OBJECTIVES

Online media communications will help an advertiser achieve its marketing and marketing communications objectives. In any marketing communications plan, the first step is to identify the objectives; the second step is to evaluate the various media options strategically. This section examines how interactive communications help achieve marketing and marketing communications objectives.

CREATING BRAND AWARENESS

If creating brand awareness across a wide demographic is the mission, the internet does a great job! Portal sites such as Google and Facebook offer great reach and therefore great potential for brand awareness. A **portal** is a website featuring several commonly used services, such as news or searching, and serves as a gateway to other services such as shopping, discussion groups, and links to other sites. These sites are the most visited sites on the web and include Google (1.1 billion unique visitors per day), YouTube (1.0 billion), Facebook (900 million), Yahoo! (750 million), and Amazon (500 million).[7] In Canada the most visited sites are almost the same: Google, Facebook, YouTube, Yahoo!, and Wikipedia. Presently, 19 million Canadians (54 percent of the population) have a Facebook profile. Statistics like these demonstrate the potential value of advertising online.

Placing ads on popular sites or more targeted sites that reach a more specific audience will contribute to achieving awareness objectives. Another means of achieving awareness is looking at the number of video ads shared on social media. For instance, one ad for Activia yogurt in Brazil, titled "La La La," achieved 1.4 million shares in a one-month period.[8] This number can be added to the number of impressions achieved elsewhere.

Recent research indicates that internet advertising works best when used as part of a media mix. To illustrate, when Dove (a popular Unilever brand) launched a new line of skin care products, a mix of magazine, outdoor, television, and online media was used. Dove discovered that the addition of online and outdoor advertising lifted awareness scores by 33 percent. These data suggest the importance of online communications in an integrated marketing communications plan.

BUILDING AND ENHANCING BRAND IMAGE

A common objective is to have consumers perceive a brand in a positive and consistent manner. Companies in the telecommunications, automotive, and financial services industries are masters at matching message strategies across all media outlets. Automotive companies in particular do an excellent job of creating and building an image for new car models.

When a tempted car buyer first sees a new model advertised on television or in a magazine, he or she often migrates to the internet for more information. Placing similar ads on appropriate websites (e.g., an automobile magazine website) and developing an effective microsite for the new vehicle will play a key role in creating a favourable and consistent image for the vehicle. Posting fresh and newsworthy information on a Facebook page can also enhance a brand's image.

OFFERING INCENTIVES

The internet is now the most popular means of delivering information about sales promotion offers (contests, coupons, and other special incentives) that act as immediate motivation to buy a product. It is common for an organization to use television, print media, and outdoor advertising to create awareness for a promotion offer (e.g., the annual "Roll Up the Rim to Win" contest at Tim Hortons). Tims uses online advertising to help create awareness, but online information also communicates the finer details of the contest to consumers. Many other brands follow a similar strategy.

GENERATING LEADS

In business-to-business and business-to-consumer marketing situations, the internet is a useful medium for generating leads. In the online world, people seem more willing to disclose personal information when entering a contest or searching for information. Businesspeople will leave the same vital information when doing their searches (e.g., company name, position held, size of company). It's the way of doing business online. Any information collected can be analyzed and mined (**data mining**) to identify potential targets (one-to-one marketing) and to customize messages and products that are suited to that target. The internet plays a central role in collecting data for future marketing endeavours.

CONDUCTING TRANSACTIONS

Online shopping is becoming a bigger factor in the consumer and business purchase cycle. The presence of online retailers such as Amazon and eBay has had a negative impact on bricks-and-mortar retailers. Some have gone out of business (Mexx, Jacob, Smart Set, and Future Shop) while others have streamlined operations and closed under-performing stores to cut costs (Sears and Best Buy). In today's marketplace it is necessary to have a website, but surprisingly less than half of Canadian companies have one (as of 2012). Ecommerce transactions are growing at a rate of about 10 percent a year and reached $22.3 billion in consumer sales in 2012. That year 50 percent of online Canadians used the internet to order a good or a service.[9] Customers in the 25- to 34-year-old category are the most prolific online shoppers; they have money, good credit ratings, and a high degree of comfort with buying online.[10]

An organization's **website** plays a key role in the communications process. Companies such as Canadian Tire and Chapters Indigo use the internet to communicate effectively with shoppers, and these companies have combined emarketing with traditional methods of conducting business. To remain competitive, more businesses must do the same.

In terms of strategic planning, organizations must carefully select the right mix of media to achieve their marketing and marketing communications objectives. Within that mix, ads placed in traditional media should refer people to the advertiser's website or a social media site where more details are available. This tactic encourages people to engage more with their favourite brands.

Online Advertising Strategies

Today's media planners are technologically savvy; they recognize the value of the various forms of interactive communications and make appropriate recommendations when devising an advertising strategy. Planners understand that interactive communications can achieve high reach and frequency, though advertisers must be careful about budgets when the various cost models are evaluated (models are discussed later in the chapter). At portal sites such as Google or Yahoo!, the number of daily unique visitors is incredibly high. In contrast, niche sites, which focus on a special interest, hobby, or activity, reach smaller numbers of people but are more targeted. Both types of sites can be considered when devising an online advertising strategy.

There are a variety of creative opportunities available to online advertisers. These options include search advertising, display advertising (banner ads), video ads, sponsorships, and email advertising. Search and display advertising currently account for the largest portion of this advertising investment, but video ads are the fastest-growing form of online advertising. Video is popular with advertisers because of its similarity to television ads—sight, sound, and motion. For additional insight into the options, refer to Figure 12.4.

Prior to examining the various advertising alternatives, some basic terminology should be understood. All terms relate to how internet ads are measured for strategic variables such as reach, frequency, and engagement:

- ***Impressions (Ad Views)*** An ad request that was successfully sent to a visitor. This is the standard way of determining exposure for an ad on the web.
- ***Frequency (online)*** **Frequency (online)** is the number of times an ad is delivered to the same browser in a single session or time period. A site can use cookies to manage frequency.
- ***Clicks (Clickthroughs)*** **Clickthrough** refers to the number of times users click on a banner ad. Such a measurement allows an advertiser to judge the response to an ad. When viewers click the ad, they are transferred to the advertiser's website or to a special page where they are encouraged to respond in some way to the ad.
- ***Click Rate (Clickthrough Rate)*** **Click rate** is the ratio of ad clicks to ad impressions. It is calculated by dividing the total number of clicks by the total number of impressions. For example, if during 1 million impressions there are 20 000 clicks on the banner, the click rate is 2 percent. A high click rate indicates the banner ad was effective in its purpose.

FIGURE 12.4

Internet advertising spending in Canada by type of ad

Ad Type	2013 $ in Millions	2014 $ in Millions	% Change
Search	1802	2052	+14
Display	1091	1274	+17
Classifieds	289	171	-41
Video	208	266	+28
Email	18	19	+8
Video Gaming	11	11	+/-0

Search and advertising lead all forms of online advertising.

Source: Printed with permission of Interactive Advertising Bureau of Canada.

- ***Unique Visitor*** The number of unduplicated (counted only once) visitors to a website over a course of a specified time period. Visitors are determined by cookies, a small text file stored in a user's browser.
- ***Visit*** A **visit** is a sequence of page requests made by one user at one website. A visit is also referred to as a *session* or *browsing period.*

SEARCH ADVERTISING

With **search advertising**, an advertiser's listing is placed within or alongside search results in exchange for paying a fee each time someone clicks on the listing in those search results. This is also known as *pay-per-click advertising*. Most search engines, such as Google and Yahoo!, set advertisers against one another in auction-style bidding for the highest positions on search results pages. For example, Google offers a service called AdWords, which allows companies, for a small fee, to have a link to their website featured when a user searches for a particular word that the company has specified. For example, if a user types in the term "mutual funds" and RBC Financial has bought that term, an advertisement for RBC Financial appears on the screen. Other bidders may also appear on the same list, but the highest bidder for the word or term is at the top of the list. When a consumer clicks on the sponsored link, he or she is immediately directed to the advertiser's webpage, where detailed information is provided.

DISPLAY ADVERTISING

Display advertising includes **banner ads** in a variety of sizes. Advertisers place banner ads on websites of interest to the target audience (users target content). The Interactive Advertising Bureau has established standard sizes for banner ads based on width and height in pixels to make the planning and buying of online ads more efficient. For example, the **leaderboard** banner ad that stretches across the top of a webpage is 728 × 90 pixels. A large leaderboard that offers even more width and height is 900 × 150 pixels. A **big box** is almost square with slightly more width than height (300 × 250 pixels). A **skyscraper** is a tall, slim, oblong ad that appears at the side of a webpage (160 × 600 pixels). The larger the ad is, the greater the opportunity for an advertiser to deliver a more complete message, even if the user doesn't click on it. An illustration of a leaderboard banner ad appears in Figure 12.5.

Research does indicate that larger ads achieve higher scores for brand awareness and message association. Larger ads provide an opportunity to deliver a more complete message and are more difficult for users to avoid. Because of their size and better performance, they command a higher price. The average click rate for a banner ad is now 0.09 percent, meaning only one person in a thousand actually clicks on an ad, even though the ad, by its presence on the page, made an impression on the person viewing the page.

Rich media are banner ads that include animation, sound, video, and interactivity. Often referred to as **animated banners**, these banners have higher click rates than

FIGURE 12.5

Enbridge reaches potential customers using a leaderboard banner ad on House & Home Media's website.

Switching to natural gas has its rewards.

Visit naturalswitch.com today and learn how to start saving.

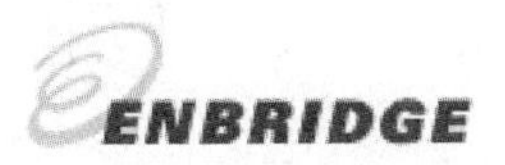

Courtesy of Enbridge Inc.

static banners. The average click rate is 0.27 percent, meaning that almost three people click on the ad for every 1000 impressions.[11] There are also several inside-the-banner options. An **expandable banner** employs multiple panels that are launched when the banner is clicked on. A **videostrip** shows a strip of video in the banner space but when clicked on expands to reveal the video and accompanying audio in a full-sized panel. A **push-down banner** slides advertising out of the way to reveal additional content rather than covering it up.

Outside-the-banner options include the **floating ad**, which moves within a transparent layer over the page and plays within a specific area of the page. A **window ad** downloads itself and plays instantly or when a new page is loading. A **wallpaper ad** is a large image that replaces the web background. So many styles can grab the viewer's attention in different ways—or irritate the viewer if they are too intrusive.

VIDEO ADS

The massive influx of video content on the web (e.g., news, sports, amateur video content) has had a profound impact on advertising. Video advertising is attractive to advertisers because it is similar to television advertising—something they are familiar with. As well, video ads offer more emotional impact than other forms of online advertising.

Television networks now stream their prime time shows online. The CTV network offers many of its popular shows and shows from its cable channels, including TSN, Comedy Network, MTV, Discovery, and Bravo, among others. Production companies such as House & Home Media also stream their shows online. Refer to the image in Figure 12.6. Streamed shows present advertising opportunities. Having shows available online reflects the on-demand nature of the present television market.

The online shows include video ads before, during, and after the show. **Pre-roll** ads refer to ads at the start of the video, **mid-roll** ads are placed during the video, and **post-roll** ads appear after the video. Embedding an ad within the show ensures that the ad will be viewed. To watch the desired content, the viewer has no choice.

FIGURE 12.6

Popular TV shows are now streamed online and include short video commercials.

Courtesy of House & Home Media, houseandhome.com

With regard to the creative, advertisers have the option of creating unique commercials for the internet or running the same commercials they show on television. There was a time when the unique commercial was the preferred option, but since consumers now recognize the internet as another mass medium, they are more accepting of commercials that resemble those appearing on television. Molson Canadian will advertise on a TSN hockey broadcast and show the same commercial as part of a highlight package on TSN.ca. Delivering the same message in all media offers greater impact and reflects a well-planned, integrated advertising effort.

SPONSORSHIPS

With a **sponsorship**, an advertiser commits to an extended relationship with another website. Advertisers are attracted to sponsorships on the basis of web content. If the content is of particular interest to an advertiser's target market, visitors are apt to visit the site frequently. People interested in business and finance news visit financial sites. Sports junkies visit TSN.ca and Sportsnet.ca. TSN runs various contests during the year, all of which are sponsored by national brands.

Kraft Canada sponsors the annual Kraft Celebration Tour on TSN and TSN.ca. The partnership between Kraft and TSN promotes healthy and active lifestyles across Canada through an annual showcase that rewards communities who have shown their commitment to the spirit of sport and play. Each year Kraft and TSN go on the road to visit 10 towns in 10 days. A TSN live sportscast and numerous community events occur in each town. The winning communities, as voted by the public, each receive $25 000 to upgrade local sports facilities. The TSN network, its broadcast personalities, and the website actively promote the sponsorship. TSN.ca is one of Canada's busiest websites, so Kraft benefits from its popularity and the traffic it draws (high reach and frequency). Refer to the image in Figure 12.7.

FIGURE 12.7

Kraft and TSN are partners in the Kraft Celebration Tour, which rewards communities who show commitment to the spirit of sport and play.

FIGURE 12.8

Email advertising is an effective method of delivering financial incentives to current customers.

® Registered trademarks of Cara Operations Limited

EMAIL ADVERTISING

One of the most promising applications in online advertising doesn't use flashy graphics or oversized banners. **Permission-based email**, in which a user chooses to receive messages from a particular advertiser, is growing quickly. This form of advertising is relatively inexpensive, response rates are easy to measure, and it is targeted at people who want information about certain goods and services. Email is an efficient method of delivering new product information and information about promotional offers. A company that is active in the practice of customer relationship marketing will use its own database to deliver financial incentives to current customers by email—a strategy that encourages brand loyalty. Refer to the image in Figure 12.8.

The success of an email ad campaign depends on the quality of the list. There are two kinds of lists: a rented email list and an in-house list. The *rented list* is usually obtained from a list broker. Typically, these lists include "opt-in" names and addresses. *Opt-in* means the people on the list have agreed to receive direct email. Generally, email advertising results in higher response rates than direct mail because receivers of email messages agree to accept them. Receivers may unsubscribe if they no longer deem the content relevant. How often an advertiser communicates with customers by email is an issue. "Many experts say there is a fine line between sending emails to customers on a consistent basis and crossing into annoyance-marketing territory."[12] Old Navy sends out an email to its Canadian database five times a week—that's irritating!

Unsolicited email messages, referred to as **spam**, were a problem in the past. Canada's Anti-Spam Legislation is now in effect to protect consumers from receiving unsolicited email. According to the legislation, it is prohibited to send a commercial electronic message to an electronic address unless the person to whom the message is sent has consented to receiving it; further, the message must comply with prescribed form and content requirements. This is the concept of permission-based email described above. With regard to the prescribed form, the email must clearly identify the sender of the message, provide information regarding who a person can respond to, and offer an unsubscribe mechanism. The legislation includes a few exceptions. For example, the consent requirement does not apply to email that solely provides requested product or service quotes, completes an ongoing commercial transaction, involves product warranty or recall notices, or deals with ongoing subscriptions, memberships, or similar relationships. It should be noted that consent is implied if there is an existing business relationship or nonbusiness relationship.[13]

In the age of database marketing, the compilation of an in-house list is essential. Since all forms of advertising should invite people to visit a website, the site should include a section where people can sign up for email newsletters or email updates that could announce the introduction of new products. In other words, the list should comply with anti-spam legislation. Online promotions such as contests provide another opportunity to secure email addresses. Sending email to customers and prospects who specifically request the mail will almost always work better than using a rented list.

CONTENT MARKETING: WEBSITES AND SOCIAL MEDIA

Traditional forms of advertising can tell a story, but not necessarily the complete story. Therefore, traditional media combined with effective web content give an advertiser ample opportunity to tell the whole story. In any form of traditional advertising (broadcast or print), part of the message should encourage the viewer or reader to visit a website or follow a brand (company) on a social media network. The common phrase is "Follow us on Facebook, Twitter, Instagram, Google+, and LinkedIn."

Companies are creating unique video content about their products and services and posting it on their own website or their YouTube channel and Facebook page, a process called **content marketing**. Unlike a television commercial, where time restrictions apply, a video can be longer, offer more entertainment value, and be more creative to engage viewers. It is also tends to be less "sales driven."

While the number of potential viewers of video content is much lower than for a conventional television ad, the fact that viewers choose to watch it indicates the benefit of producing video content. People behave differently on the web and will watch advertising content as long as it is enjoyable and engaging.

Video content is ideally suited for inclusion at a company website. To illustrate, consider how much more meaningful content a manufacturer of cars can present about a new car model in a five-minute video compared to a 30-second television commercial. On television or in print, the message focuses on image but does little in terms of telling buyers about design and technical specifications. If a potential buyer visits an automobile manufacturer's website, he or she wants detailed information and demonstrations—information that will influence a buying decision.

To further show the importance of having informative and engaging content on a website, consider the amount of research people routinely do online before they make a buying decision. Recent research reveals that some 57 percent of consumers felt product videos made them more confident in a purchase. Further, 41 percent of consumers are more likely to share product videos than other product content.[14] In an era of marketing where consumer recommendations (word of mouth on Facebook and Twitter) are important, marketers must react accordingly and produce content that consumers are willing to share.

Organizations also establish microsites that serve unique purposes. A **microsite** is an individual webpage or series of pages that functions as a supplement to a primary website. For example, Unilever has a corporate website in which all brands have a page. However, some of its more high-profile brands have their own site. For example, Axe, a popular men's grooming product line, has its own site that encourages young males to look their best. All it takes is a visit to the Axe.ca website. When Axe launched a new line of dry spray antiperspirant, a short video appeared on the website and the brand's YouTube channel. For a brand like Axe that appeals to a youthful target, web communications are a critical component of the communications mix.

ADVERTISING IN ACTION

BMW Reestablishes Its High Performance Image with Video

Should an upscale automaker use online videos to promote its brand? Is advertising online in keeping with the brand image? Is it a medium that luxury car buyers would respond to? These were questions on the mind of Marc Belcourt, communications manager at BMW Canada, prior to making the decision to jump into the world of YouTube video.

To get some answers BMW launched a video titled "Walls" in 2011. In the video a roaring BMW M1 Coupe, with brakes screeching, hurtled toward a concrete wall only to narrowly slide through a cut-out hole in the wall—an exciting and dramatic portrayal of how the vehicle handles! The video got 4 million views on YouTube, and sales of the Series M vehicles increased 12 percent that year. Always in a battle with Mercedes-Benz, the videos helped BMW outpace its rival in sales volume.

In 2012 BMW launched another video for its M5 series, and it, too, achieved 4 million views on YouTube. From an advertising strategy perspective, BMW learned a lot from the video effort. The perception that only young, tech-savvy consumers watch videos quickly vanished. Older and more affluent consumers are watching as well! The M5 is targeted at men 45 to 64 years old with household incomes of $300 000+ with an interest in architecture and design. Research indicated online video could reach that target.

Executives who may question the use of online video need only look to BMW's success for guidance. The old way of doing things has changed forever. People of all ages and incomes are active online—searching for information and watching videos. While television and print remain "must haves" in the media mix for luxury car campaigns, digital media will play a more dominant role in the future.

© Brian Kersey/UPI/Newscom

Source: Adapted from Susan Krashinsky, "Online video ads get revved up," *The Globe and Mail*, September 21, 2012, p. B5.

BMW has been actively involved in producing video content for consumption on YouTube. For more insight into the potential impact of online video content, read the Advertising in Action vignette **BMW Reestablishes Its High Performance Image with Video**.

The Internet as an Advertising Medium

As with any medium, advertising on the internet has some advantages and disadvantages. Media planners must assess the advantages and disadvantages of this medium in the context of the target market the advertiser is trying to reach and how cost effective the medium is.

ADVANTAGES OF ONLINE ADVERTISING

TARGETING CAPABILITY Since the internet is based on technology, advertisers have a new range of targeting capabilities. As discussed earlier, consumers can be targeted demographically, geographically, or by their behaviour (by a person's browsing behaviour and personal preferences). Once a consumer's preferences are known, an advertiser can target the individual with ads that are of potential interest.

BROAD REACH The size of the internet continues to grow. Because advertisers buy online ads by the impression (see the next section of this chapter for buying details), an advertiser can buy as much or as little of that audience as desired.

DEPTH OF CONTENT Unlike a television commercial or print ad, a banner ad or video ad is simply the beginning of the process of transferring information. More detailed information is only a click away. Once a person arrives at an advertiser's website or Facebook page, he or she can access as much information as wished—a true benefit to the company or brand.

TIMING The internet doesn't sleep—messages can be delivered 24 hours a day, 7 days a week, 365 days a year. As well, the content of a campaign can be changed at a moment's notice. Technology allows for constant monitoring of a campaign for success or failure, so changes, updates, or cancellations can be made much more quickly than in any other medium.

INTERACTIVITY AND ACTION Internet users like to be entertained along the way. Therefore, companies have an opportunity to interact with prospects and customers and develop more meaningful relationships with them. Messages encourage interaction by asking people to perform a task, enter a contest (where valuable information is transferred), or play a game.

TRACKING AND MEASUREMENT Advertisers can get timely, detailed reports on the success of their campaign. Banner ads can be tracked the next day—with specific numbers of impressions and click rates. Many websites that sell advertising provide these detailed reports to clients online. Such measurements gauge the effectiveness of the advertising investment and allow an advertiser to alter the online message strategy if need be. These measurements are difficult—if not impossible—to generate for traditional media.

DISADVANTAGES OF ONLINE ADVERTISING

LOW CLICK RATES Some click rates are very low (in the 1 percent or less range), which means that only a small audience visits a website for more information. Better creative executions are needed to stimulate higher click rates.

ADVERTISING OVERLOAD Many popular websites are cluttered with advertising, meaning that no particular ad commands a high degree of attention. Consequently, consumers avoid the ads, causing low rates of return for the advertising investment.

CONSUMER FRUSTRATION Consumers are starting to feel frustrated, even harassed, by the constant barrage of banner ads that suddenly appear or by being subjected to the same ad over and over again when searching for information. A recent survey revealed that 56 percent of online Canadians now avoid certain companies or brands because their messaging annoys them.[15]

PRIVACY CONCERNS Consumers perceive a loss of privacy because access to a website can involve complex registration procedures. With registration, customers give up information about themselves that can be used for marketing purposes at a later date. The transfer of personal and credit card information to other parties is a serious issue among internet users.

TOO MEASURABLE A marketer can be overburdened with data from an online advertising campaign.

Internet Advertising Rates and Media Buying

Several advertising models are available. Since marketers and advertising agencies are accustomed to cost-per-thousand (CPM) comparisons before making critical media decisions, the CPM model is the most popular on the internet. Other pricing models include *pay for performance* and *flat fees.*

CPM MODEL

CPM is the price charged for displaying an ad 1000 times. The calculation for CPM is cost multiplied by impressions (number of impressions divided by 1000). For online advertising, an organization pays a rate for every 1000 impressions made. Therefore, if the total number of impressions was 1 000 000 and the CPM was $40.00, the total cost of the advertising campaign would be $40 000 (1 000 000 impressions/1000 × $40.00). CPM rates vary based on the level of targeting desired by the advertiser. As the degree of targeting increases, so does the CPM.

With reference to the rate card for the *Globe and Mail* digital edition shown in Figure 12.9, observe that rates are based on location (e.g., section of the newspaper) and the size of the ad unit. The rates also vary by format (e.g., desktop rates are different than tablet and smartphone rates). For example, a run-of-section placement in the News section costs $28/M. In the Business section, the rate is $30/M. With reference to size, observe that a half-page ad (300 × 600 pixels) in the News section is $38/M, increasing to $40/M in the Business section. While not shown on this rate card, volume discounts may also be available from a publisher based on the total dollar value of advertising purchased.

To further demonstrate how to calculate the cost of advertising, consider the following examples:

EXAMPLE 1

Type of Ad and Location:	**Canvas Unit (1000 × 700 pixels), *Globe and Mail* Digital Edition; Business Section**
Impressions Desired:	2 000 000
CPM:	$60.00
Cost Calculation:	**(2 000 000/1000) × $60 = $120 000**

EXAMPLE 2

Type of Ad and Location:	**Mobile/Web Smartphone; Standard Unit (300 × 250); *Globe and Mail* Digital Edition; News Section**
Impressions Desired:	1 500 000
CPM:	$28.00
Cost Calculation:	**(1 500 000/1000) × $28 = $42 000**

Globe Digital and Alliance Rates

2015 GLOBE MEDIA KIT **DIGITAL**
APRIL 8, 2015

HOMEPAGE SPONSORSHIP PRODUCTS			ALL RATES ARE NET
Premium Globe and Mail Homepage Sponsorship	Billboard	$35,000	Single ad
Standard Globe and Mail Homepage Package	IAB Std	$30,000	3 Std IAB ad units/page
Standard Globe Alliance Homepage Package	IAB Std	$45,000	Std IAB ad units/page

	CORE CHANNELS			NICHE CHANNELS		
GLOBE AND MAIL DIGITAL PRODUCTS	**NEWS**	**BUSINESS**	**LIFESTYLE**	**ADVISOR**	**AUTO**	**SMALL BUSINESS**
DESKTOP DISPLAY						
GLOBE AND MAIL AND ALLIANCE PARTNER* NETWORK (STANDARD IAB FORMAT)						
Section Sponsorship	$32	$34	$30	$45	$36	$40
Run of Section/Run of Channel	$28	$30	$26	$40	$32	$35
Run of Site/Run of Network	$22	$22	$22	$22	$22	$22
Alliance partners: The Globe and Mail, Forbes, ABC News, Reuters, The Guardian, Washington Post, US Weekly, Rolling Stone, Elite Daily						
WALL STREET JOURNAL DIGITAL NETWORK						
WSJ Homepage	Flat fee: 300 x 250 = $5000/day, half pager = $7500/day (100,000 daily impressions)					
Run of Section	$35	$37	$33	——	——	——
Run of WSJDN	$32	$32	$32	——	——	——
CULTURAL DIVERSITY NETWORK						
South East Asia channel	$20	$20	$20	$20	$20	$20
SPECIAL AD FORMATS						
Half page unit (300 x 600) Available on all sites	$38	$40	$36	$50	$42	$45
IAB rising star units (portrait/filmstrip) Available on Globe and Mail only	$43	$45	$41	$55	$47	$50
Canvas unit (1000 x 700) Available on Globe and Mail only	$58	$60	$56	$70	$62	$65
SMALL AD FORMATS						
Tile (120 x 240)	Sponsorship $13.00; Std CPM $10.00					
VIDEO PRE-ROLL	$50	$50	$50	$50	$50	$50
TABLET AND SMARTPHONE (INCLUDES ALLIANCE PARTNERS)						
Tablet interstitial/Smartphone Interstitial	$45	$45	$45	$45	$45	$45
Tablet (Custom)	$35	$35	$35	$35	$35	$35
Tablet (Standard IAB)	$26	$28	$24	$35	$35	$35
Mobile Web/Smartphone (Standard 300 x 250, 300 x 450)	$28	$30	$26	——	$32	$35
Smartphone (Standard 300 x 50)	$18	$20	$16	——	$18	$18
Mobile Website (300 x 50)	$14	$15	$13	——	$18	$18
TARGETING PRODUCTS (INCLUDES ALLIANCE PARTNERS)						
Audience re-targeting based on behaviour – 1st party data	$25					
Custom audience segments – 3rd Party data	Prices available upon request					
EMAIL NEWSLETTER						
Editorial e-newsletters	$27	$27	$25	$35	$30	$30
Advertising exclusive e-blast (per 1000 sent)	$125	$125	$125	$125	$125	$125
PERFORMANCE PRODUCTS (ACROSS TGAM AND ALLIANCE SITES)						
Private exchange (RTB/Programmatic)	Prices subject to market for RTB and/or negotiation for direct programmatic deals					
Direct response campaigns	Varies based on program					

Rates effective Jan 1, 2015

tel 1.800.387.9012 email advertising@globeandmail.com or globelink.ca/digital 5

FIGURE **12.9**

Rate card for the *Globe and Mail* digital edition

CPM rate cards vary from site to site, but high-traffic sites of course charge a higher CPM. Although standard rates are quoted, the reality of the situation is quite similar to offline advertising. CPM rates are negotiable and depend on factors such as length of the campaign, season, and relationship between client and vendor. Effective negotiation skills in the media buying process could result in lower CPM rates. Rates are also influenced by a relatively new concept called *programmatic buying* and *real-time bidding*. That topic is discussed at the end of this section.

PAY-FOR-PERFORMANCE MODEL

Advertisers must remember that the purpose of the banner is to stir initial interest so that the viewer clicks the ad for more information. Once the ad is clicked, the viewer sees it in its entirety. Since clicking is the desired action, many websites use a **CPC (cost per click)** pricing model. The degree of clicking achieved by an ad indicates the effectiveness of the ad.

If the success of an ad is based on the click rate, many current campaigns are not doing very well. For years click rates have been shrinking across all web destinations. As responsiveness declines, ad targeting is becoming more attractive to online advertisers. The ability to target based on location and behaviour does have a positive impact on click rates. Pricing models based on CPC are becoming more popular, but, as mentioned earlier, are plagued with click fraud. Click fraud is the practice of artificially inflating traffic statistics by repeatedly clicking on an advertisement. This practice makes a campaign look better than it really is and inflates the cost of the campaign for the advertiser. Tighter restrictions and controls are needed if the pay–or-performance model is to succeed.

FLAT-FEE MODEL

Some websites charge a flat fee for advertising—typically, a set amount for the length of time the ad appears on the site. For example, an advertiser will pay a daily rate irrespective of impressions served or clicks. This practice is also common for sponsorships of contests or other special activities on a website. For example, a site such as TSN.ca might offer a flat-rate sponsorship opportunity to an advertiser in combination with a CPM or pay-for-performance advertising package. At TSN, advertisers who opt for a sponsorship package will receive preferred positions for their banner ads.

PROGRAMMATIC MEDIA BUYING

The various advertising buying models described above are inefficient in nature. For instance, in the CPM model the advertiser is buying impressions in bulk at the same price, even though each impression may have a different value to a campaign. As well, any inventory left unsold at a publisher's website could be sold at a much lower price to another advertiser. In the cost-per-click model, click fraud can occur, a situation that ultimately drives up the cost of advertising. Advertisers are very concerned about both issues.

Programmatic media buying starts to address these issues. It is an automated system that considers an advertiser's budget, objectives, and audience data. The system rapidly adjusts dozens of variables in real time (milliseconds) based on performance to determine the right campaign settings to achieve a desired return on investment. It sounds complicated, but be assured that it is based on mathematical algorithms that filter impressions based on behavioural data. The result is the impressions achieved will have greater value to the advertiser.

Within the programmatic media buying system is a process called real-time bidding. **Real-time bidding** is an auction system in which advertisers bid against each other over individual ad impressions as those impressions are shown to online users. Ad buyers seek out and bid on auctions that match their campaign criteria (budget, objectives, and audience). When the auction is complete, the winning bidder's ad is delivered to the user.

Programmatic media buying offers advertisers and their media agencies several benefits. From an advertiser's perspective it enhances targeting capabilities, offers cost-effective reach, and eliminates wasted ad dollars. From an agency's perspective it offers better control over campaign performance and improves spending efficiencies.[16] Programmatic media buying only accounts for a small portion of online media buying presently, but given the benefits it offers it will play a much greater role in the coming years. Large online advertisers such as Procter & Gamble and Kellogg are spending 70 percent of their digital budgets on programmatic buying. According to Kellogg, programmatic buying results in measurably better performance.[17]

Social Media Networks

A **social media network** connects people with different types of interests at one website. At the website, people become friends and form communities—in effect the community could be viewed as a potential target market. Refer to the illustration in Figure 12.10.

Recent research indicates that Canadians are married to the social web. In fact, Canada has the highest social media network penetration in the world. Presently, 82 percent of Canadians use a social network, and 91 percent of Canadian internet users have a social media account. In terms of popularity, Facebook is the undisputed leader, followed by Twitter, Google+, LinkedIn, and Pinterest.[18] In the context of media planning, time spent with a medium is a factor, and Canadians spend a considerable amount of time on social media—an average of 1.7 hours per day (2014 data).[19] Who's online is

FIGURE 12.10

Facebook is a popular social network destination for Canadians.

FIGURE 12.11

Demographic profile of social media users in Canada

	% Respondents in Each Group			
	Facebook	**LinkedIn**	**Twitter**	**Instagram**
GENDER				
Female	60	25	22	18
Male	59	37	27	14
AGE				
18–34	75	30	36	32
35–44	68	37	31	19
45–54	63	41	23	11
55–64	47	31	15	4
65+	32	12	9	2
LANGUAGE				
French	65	23	19	16
English	58	33	26	16
TOTAL	59	30	25	16

Note: Social networks on which Canadians have a profile as of January 2015.

Source: Forum Research, "The Forum Poll," January 6, 2015, as published by *eMarketer*, **www.eMarketer.com**. Used with permission of Forum Research Inc.

another planning factor, and social media now reaches all age groups. Refer to the data in Figure 12.11.

ADVERTISERS MUST ADAPT TO THE SOCIAL MEDIA ENVIRONMENT

Organizations are operating in an era where consumers have more control over marketing communications. In previous eras, the marketer would push its communications on to consumers. In the social media era, the communications process is more participative—the goal is to get consumers talking about brands and promoting brands on behalf of the organization. This shift in control is often referred to as *brand democratization*.

Advertisers that adapt to this shift in control see the benefit of consumer involvement in brand content. For example, an organization could put out a call for consumer-produced content (e.g., as part of a contest promotion) to potentially be used in a subsequent marketing campaign. Much of the content on social media networks is created by amateurs. **Consumer-generated content** refers to content created by consumers for consumers. People will create brand-oriented content without being asked, and in many cases they present the brand effectively. People who do this are often called *brand advocates*—those who will do anything to promote their favourite brand. For many people, this type of content carries more weight than marketer-generated content.

When a company invites the public to participate in the marketing of its brands, it is employing a technique referred to as crowdsourcing. **Crowdsourcing** uses public sources to complete tasks that a company would normally assign to a third-party provider (e.g., an advertising agency or production company). Essentially, this approach takes advantage of the creativity and enthusiasm that people have for a brand. Typically, the task can be completed more quickly and at much lower cost.

To demonstrate the principle of crowdsourcing and the power of social media, nobody does it better than Doritos. Each year Doritos invites the public to submit video content for its "Crash the Super Bowl" contest. The winning video, as judged by public voting on the finalists, is shown during the Super Bowl game. It has produced some of the most effective advertising on the game despite the fact the ads compete for attention against professionally produced ads from other brands. All of the ads from the group of finalists are posted on the Doritos website and on YouTube.[20]

There's an expression: "Any publicity is good publicity." Whether that is true or not is debatable, but if consumers create and upload content and it is viewed by millions of people, there must be some benefit for the brand. Marketers must embrace this phenomenon and add social media to their communications arsenal. It sounds almost frightening to let consumers take charge, but consumer control is the ultimate form of engagement that marketers are searching for.

Types of Social Network Advertising and Marketing Communications

The advertising opportunities on social media vary from one network to another (e.g., size, shape, format). This section will examine some of the more common types of social media advertising along with some other forms of marketing communications an organization may employ.

DISPLAY ADVERTISING

As in other online advertising, the placement of banner ads is available on some social networks. Given the abundance of information that social networks collect about users, there is a significant targeting advantage available to advertisers. Sites such as Facebook and Twitter offer a sophisticated demographic filtering process that can be combined with collected behavioural data about individual users. For example, should an advertiser want to reach females, 21 to 35 years old, married, and interested in fashion, that target request would be entered in the Facebook or Twitter database. The advertiser would then know the approximate number of women fitting that profile and plan a campaign to reach them.

Click rates are low on a site such as Facebook. One recent study observed an average click rate for display ads at 0.04 percent on Facebook, about half that for display ads across the web.[21] Low click rates are causing advertisers and social network publishers to look for other, more effective options to advertise in this medium.

SUGGESTED POSTS AND SPONSORED POSTS IN A NEWSFEED

Appearing much like news from friends, these ads appear within an individual's newsfeed. Typically, these ads include a small amount of copy and a visual image to attract attention. People receive these ads as "suggestions" based on their online behaviour (e.g., expressed interests) or because they fit the target profile a particular advertiser wants to reach. These ads are available in a variety of sizes. To attract attention, ads with bold images and a larger size fair better than smaller ads. Refer to the image in

FIGURE 12.12

An illustration of a sponsored post advertisement

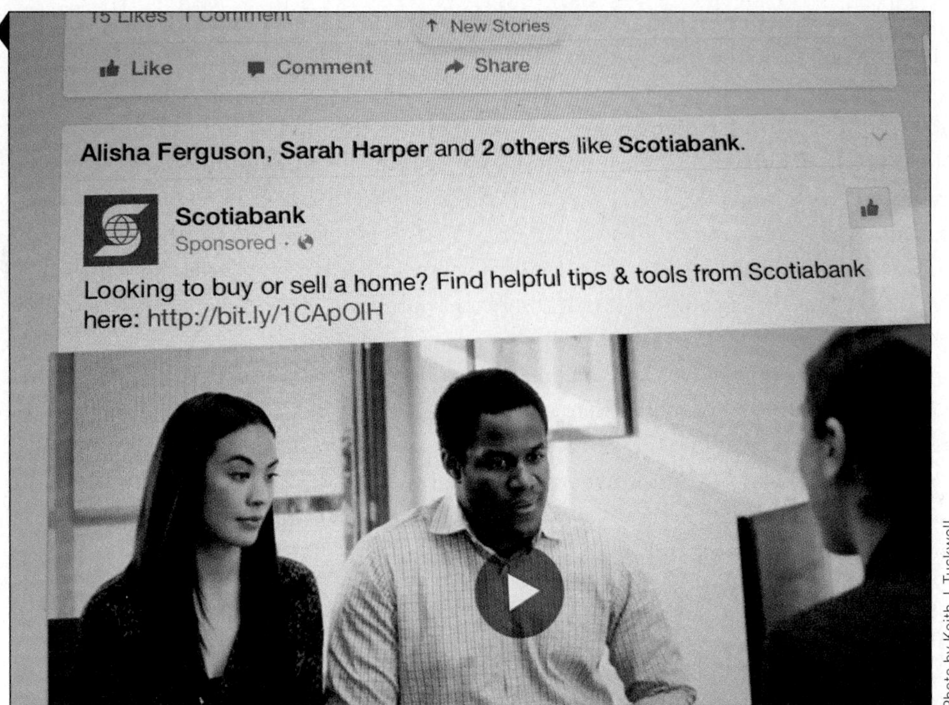

Photo by Keith J. Tuckwell

Figure 12.12. The average click rate for a sponsored post in a Facebook newsfeed is 2.09 percent, considerably better than display ads. In the Facebook environment, a person will share sponsored posts that they like with their friends. Sharing expands the reach of the advertiser's message.

Sponsored posts on Twitter are called *promoted tweets*. They, too, are available in a variety of sizes and typically include body copy (to a prescribed limit) and a small visual image (square or rectangular shape). For advertisers, a popular option is the product card, which allows users to share information, product photos, and video content directly through tweets. The visual images will help an ad stand out in a sea of text on a Twitter stream and also increase the likelihood that customers will click on and retweet an advertiser's post.

Mazda Canada recently used targeted promoted tweets to encourage potential car buyers to take a test drive. The brand launched two lead generation campaigns (a trial campaign and a follow-up) that took advantage of the many conversations on Twitter revolving around automobiles. Promoted tweets targeted users talking about comparable vehicles. Mazda's message focused on the superior capabilities of its vehicles and offered a strong call to action to encourage a test drive. The targeting and tracking capabilities on Twitter allowed Mazda to trace leads from the corporate level right down to the showroom floor.[22] Its message was delivered with precision and accuracy. Refer to the image in Figure 12.13.

On both Facebook and Twitter, sponsored posts and promoted tweets do not seem to interfere with how people engage with a feed.

VIDEO ADS (AUTOPLAY)

Video ads are the fastest-growing form of online and social media advertising. Facebook recently introduced a new ad unit called *premium video*, a 15-second ad that starts playing automatically as a user scrolls by it in their newsfeed. These video ads play automatically without sound until a consumer pauses on the ad. If the consumer taps on the ad, it will fill the full screen. These ads are another means of improving the viewability of online ads. Advertisers will now be able to evaluate new metrics, such as unique video views,

Courtesy of Mazda Canada, Inc.

FIGURE 12.13

Mazda successfully used promoted tweets on Twitter to encourage people to take test drives.

audience retention, and average duration of a video view, as a means of determining the success or failure of a campaign.[23]

BRAND PAGE (FAN PAGE)

Marketers can create their own page on Facebook that users choose to join. Users who click on a brand's "Like" button become members of the brand's fan page. Contests or other incentives motivate fans to visit the page, resulting in an expanded base that can be used for future marketing programs.

The value of a "like" is often questioned by advertisers. Presently, many marketers equate social media success to the number of likes they have, and they implement programs to build their number of likes. But the value of a like remains elusive, since only 5 percent of people who "like" a brand go back to that brand page.[24] Such limited engagement needs to be evaluated by advertisers if an adequate return on investment is desired. A prudent marketer must shift his or her way of thinking and devise strategies that give "engagement" a priority over "likes."

Getting people to revisit a brand's fan page is a challenge. Certain motivation (e.g., incentives and deals communicated via sponsored posts) may be required as well as the constant updating of the content on the fan page. Updating the fan page requires commitment in time and financial resources—a proper budget is required. Simply put, if marketers want consumers to be engaged with their brand, the marketer must also be more engaged—it's a two-way participative form of communication.

COMPANY BLOGS

A **blog** is a website where journal entries are posted on a regular basis and displayed in reverse chronological order. Blogs provide commentary on news or particular subjects of interest such as politics, business, food, and fashion. A typical blog includes text, images, and links to other blogs.

A company blog is proving to be an effective means of presenting relevant information in a positive manner. It gives an organization the opportunity to be part of the discussion on matters that are important to customers. People access blogs because they want to read the content. With a blog, an organization can communicate with customers in a more relaxed environment. A brand has an opportunity to develop an online personality that goes beyond what can be accomplished in traditional media communications.

Although most company blogs are not written mainly to sell products or services, providing useful information in the blog can indirectly influence customers to make a purchase.

YOUTUBE CHANNELS

Everyone views video content on YouTube, don't they? With that in mind, doesn't it make sense for an organization to have its own YouTube channel, where it can show some exciting videos about its brands? On YouTube, a *channel* is the word used for a user's profile. Other users can access a channel/profile to find out what videos have been uploaded. You can also subscribe to a user's profile and be notified when that user uploads new videos to the site.[25]

The principle just described can certainly apply to a company and its brands. Axe is all over social media and recently launched a dedicated channel on YouTube: **www.youtube.com/AXECanada**. Similar to Axe communications in other media, the YouTube channel offers a provocative perspective on topics of male interest. According to Shelley Brown, president and CEO of CP+B (Axe's ad agency), "Axe is a brand that, as it moves through social space, needs to stay very relevant, very fresh. It needs to be in a state of continual renewal."[26]

VIRAL MARKETING AND COMMUNICATIONS

Successful campaigns in social media can be measured based on how people engage with a brand and share information with friends. Sharing information introduces the concept of viral marketing. **Viral marketing** involves a strategy that encourages individuals to pass on marketing messages to others, creating the potential for exponential growth in the message's exposure and influence.

An organization can't really plan a viral campaign—it is up to the receivers of the message to determine if a campaign goes viral, so the receiver of the message is in control. One of the most talked-about campaigns that went viral was Old Spice's "The Man Your Man Could Smell Like" campaign. The videos featured the rather handsome actor Isaiah Mustafa. The original videos were viewed 36 million times. The final video in the series was viewed 23 million times in 36 hours—that's viral! Viral campaigns take off fast and have a short life cycle. Why this video campaign took off remains a mystery, but the entertainment value did break through the clutter of competitive advertising. Offline the campaign also garnered much publicity, all of which benefited the brand. This campaign demonstrates that "brands don't make viral videos, users make videos go viral."[27]

BUYING SOCIAL MEDIA ADVERTISING

The models for buying advertising space on social media involve the CPM (cost per thousand) and CPC (cost per click) options that were presented earlier in the chapter. To demonstrate their application, we will use Facebook and Google for illustration purposes. Which model to use is based on the primary objective of the campaign. For example, if awareness is the objective, the CPM model is chosen since the advertiser will want to maximize the number of impressions. If some kind of action is the objective, the CPC option is chosen.

Facebook gives an advertiser the option of reaching a broad audience, if so desired, or a targeted audience according to various criteria, therefore ensuring an optimum return on investment. There is a set procedure at its website that any advertiser can use to purchase space. It is a step-by-step process. Let's assume a sponsored post is being purchased. The initial step involves the composition of the advertisement. The ad is composed with a title (25 characters or less), body copy (maximum of 135 characters), and a visual illustration.

The advertiser then selects the target audience. On Facebook an advertiser can target an audience based on demographic variables such as location, gender, age, education, language, and relationship status. Interest-based targeting is also possible by choosing keywords. For example, if an advertiser chooses "soccer," it will have access to all people that have liked or shown interest in topics around that sport.[28] The advertiser then establishes a daily budget (the maximum an advertiser is willing to spend) and decides which pricing model is preferred (CPM or CPC). The price of the CPC model will be higher than the CPM model, but the advertiser will only pay for the actual traffic the click generates.

Google offers a service called AdWords, an auction-style system that determines the ads that appear on its search results page. The advertising cost is based on what the advertiser is seeking (e.g., awareness, website traffic, conversion). If awareness is the objective, costs are based on a CPM (cost-per-thousand impressions) basis. If web traffic is the objective, costs are based on a CPC basis. Each time a person clicks on the ad, the advertiser pays a fee. For more seasoned advertisers, a CPA (cost per acquisition) system is available. In this system an advertiser pays a fee once the person takes specific action at the advertiser's website. The CPC system is the most widely used option on Google.[29]

BENEFITS AND DRAWBACKS OF SOCIAL MEDIA ADVERTISING

There are several key benefits available for a marketing organization that engages in social media communications. From a ***targeting*** perspective, all age groups are engaged with social networks. Some 91 percent of internet users have a social media account, and those users encompass all age groups. Therefore, social media is an ideal complementary medium in the marketing communications mix.

One of the most potent forms of influence on brand decisions is ***word of mouth***, a situation that marketers have no control over. As mentioned earlier in the chapter, a significant amount of information sharing occurs among friends on social networks—an intangible benefit that is part of the relationship-building process between a brand and consumers.

A survey of US marketing executives reveals that ***customer engagement*** with the brand is the single most important benefit of advertising on a social network site. Engagement is an essential element of the relationship-building process that will indirectly have an impact on sales. Other benefits include direct contact with potential customers (a situation that allows the marketer to listen to customers and gain insights into how they feel about the company or brand) and the quickness of feedback (actual results of initiatives).[30]

Despite these benefits, many companies are reluctant to invest in social media communications. The ***absence of sound metrics*** (beyond click rates) to determine return on investment are a stumbling block. Despite the abundance of analytical information that is available (e.g., reach, clicks, time spent) marketers are looking for something more tangible—a link to sales performance. Embarking on a social media program requires ***time and financial commitment***. Information must be constantly refreshed if an organization expects a consumer to engage with a brand for an extended period. Out-of-date information could ultimately have a negative impact on how consumers perceive a brand.

Staying abreast of social media trends poses a challenge for executives. Erich Marx, director of interactive and social media at Nissan, effectively puts social media communications into perspective for modern-day advertisers: "From an ROI standpoint, are we selling hundreds of cars through social? No. But, you have to be there. It's not about ROI, it's about COI—cost of ignoring. It's too big to ignore."[31]

Social media is and will continue to be a strategic component of future brand communications. Simply stated, advertisers must be where their customers are. If time spent

ADVERTISING IN ACTION

Social Media Boosts Ticket Sales for Stratford Festival

For any annual event like the Stratford Festival, one of the keys to success is attracting former patrons back to the theatre. It is the combination of current patrons and new patrons who fill the seats. Many people attend a play or two, enjoy the experience tremendously, but don't return. The Festival needed a new marketing communications strategy to reach out to lapsed and new patrons.

The Festival had never used the targeting capabilities of Facebook before, so a plan was hatched to enter social media. Facebook's audience insight tools allow advertisers to target sponsored posts to users based on interests, liked pages, and attended events. Being able to target people who like theatre productions was a real attraction.

The impact of the campaign was easy to measure since the budget did not change from the previous year—the only change was the addition of social media. The results were significant: a threefold increase in the number of tickets sold and revenue generated, specifically in sales to new and lapsed patrons. Anita Gaffney, the executive director of the Festival, commented that it was a bigger return on its dollar than ever before and attributed the success to the targeted advertising.

Direct mail has always been the backbone of the Festival's marketing effort. The inclusion of targeted social media was a natural extension of the direct mail effort. Stratford had a lot of insight into the interests and habits of its audience and provided very accurate profiles to the audience insight tool at Facebook. Stratford also has a Facebook page to generate discussion about the Festival's productions and answer questions from patrons.

The plan for the future is to include more targeted social media communications in a bigger way. Both direct mail and social media allow Stratford to measure results and evaluate its return on investment—a key benefit of both media.

© Performance Image/Alamy Stock Photo

Adapted from Josh Kolm, "The Verdict: Much Ado About Facebook Targeting," *Media in Canada*, August 21, 2014, www.mediaincanada.com/2014/08/21/the-verdict-much-ado-about-facebook-targeting.

with a medium is important to advertisers, then social media trumps everything but television. In the end, the right combination of media will vary from one brand to another depending on the situation a brand faces. It is the combination of owned, earned, shared, and paid media connections that creates marketplace impact, consumer engagement, and brand value.

Social media advertising played a key role in improving ticket sales for the Stratford Festival. For insight into its campaign, read the Advertising in Action vignette **Social Media Boosts Ticket Sales for Stratford Festival**.

Measuring the Impact of Social Media Communications

People don't visit social media sites to view advertising; they visit to socialize. Very low click rates verify this notion. In a social media campaign, advertisers must look at a softer set of measurement tools to judge whether a communications effort was successful. It's more about engagement and conversation than it is about selling a product.

Essentially, there are two ways of measure a social media campaign: ongoing analytics and campaign-focused metrics. Ongoing analytics deals with tracking activity over time. For example, how much buzz did a campaign generate and what was the nature of the conversation? In contrast, campaign-focused analytics involve hard and fast numbers that help justify the investment. Numeric indicators involving reach, engagement, and conversions are evaluated. *Reach* figures are a reflection of how impactful the social content is—remember that the quality of the creative plays a role in attracting attention and conversation. Reach indicators include the number of likes on Facebook, followers on Twitter, views and subscribers on a YouTube channel, and LinkedIn connections.

Engagement is measured by determining how many people actually interacted with a message. Therefore, if a campaign includes several different messages (different creative), an advertiser can determine what type of message its followers like the most. A follower engages with a brand message and cares enough to do something about it. The extent of engagement is determined by the number of clicks, shares, and comments on Facebook; retweets and mentions on Twitter; and ratings for videos on YouTube.

Conversion is a measure of how many people actually took the desired action after exposure to a message. Conversion metrics include actions such as email subscriptions, content subscriptions, registration for content downloads, and online sales. Obtaining figures like these typically require the services of Google Analytics. This service can track which visitors arrive at an organization's website from the links an advertiser provides on social media.

The viral nature of social media can be another means of measuring success. For example, Dove (a Unilever brand) created a video titled "Dove Beauty Sketches." The video featured an FBI-trained forensic artist sketching women to show them how their self-image differed from how others see them. In one month the video reached more than 100 million views across different channels.[32] The video also earned Dove much free publicity.

Marketers who realize the difference between offline and online communities reap the benefits of online communications. To members of the online community, the Dove message was highly acceptable. It caught their attention, was innovative, and was discussed by millions of viewers—that's success!

Mobile Communications

The screen is small, the audience's attention span is short, and the environment (possibly a busy and noisy street) is variable. Yet the possibilities of mobile marketing are capturing the attention of advertisers. **Mobile marketing** is defined as "a set of practices that enables organizations to communicate and engage with their audience in an interactive and relevant manner through any mobile device or network."[33]

The latest data (2013) indicate there are 28.4 million wireless phone subscribers in Canada and that smartphone penetration has reached 73 percent. Further, 6 in 10 Canadians access the internet via a mobile device.[34] Generally speaking, Canadians are emotionally attached to their mobile phone (check your own behaviour)—79 percent of people don't leave home without it![35] Data and behaviour like this strongly suggest the need for including mobile in the marketing communications mix—it is an ideal medium for reaching consumers on the go with advertising messages. For some other interesting facts and figures about mobile phone behaviour, refer to Figure 12.14.

FIGURE 12.14

Mobile communications: Some facts and figures

© Andresr/Shutterstock

As a communications medium, mobile phones offer great potential for advertisers.

- 97% of mobile users use their phone at home; 83% while on the go
- 80% of mobile users use a smartphone
- 77% use mobile phones in stores (looking at reviews, price comparisons, and competitive retailers)
- 86% of smartphone users notice mobile ads
- 79% of smartphone users won't leave home without their phone

Canadian consumers are ahead of the game when it comes to anything digital. Canadians are embracing social media and are using their smartphones virtually everywhere they go.

Source: Adapted from "The State of Canadian Connectedness: Internet Usage, Mobile, Search, and Social Media," 6S Marketing, **www.6smarketing.com/blob/infographic-canadia-internet-usage**

In the past few years, mobile advertising revenue has surged in Canada—in 2014, it amounted to $903 million and accounted for 24 percent of internet advertising revenue. Four years earlier (2011) mobile only generated $82 million in advertising revenue.[36] Factors such as the penetration of smartphones, the ability to offer location-specific messages, and consumers' willingness to make online transactions have attracted mobile-minded advertisers. Leading the way are packaged goods companies, retailers, telecommunications companies, restaurants, and automotive companies.

Earlier in the chapter the issue of time spent with the media was discussed. It is a critical factor to consider when developing a media plan. Recent data show that Canadians are spending 2.5 hours a day with their mobile device (phone or tablet) and 80 percent of their mobile time is within an app.[37] These data confirm the need for an advertiser to consider advertising in social media applications such as Facebook, Twitter, YouTube, and so on. Facebook recently reported that mobile ads now account for 62 percent of its revenue.[38]

MOBILE COMMUNICATIONS OPPORTUNITIES

Advertising on mobile devices is similar to internet advertising except the ads are smaller. Many advertising options are available, including text, graphical banners, and video. Each of these formats is deliverable directly to a smartphone or tablet. The ads will appear when a person visits a website or when using an application (e.g., a social media site like Facebook or Instagram). Advertising within video games is also a popular option. Similar to internet advertising, mobile messages can be delivered to consumers in a highly targeted manner.

Mobile media allow an advertiser to reach targets where they are located at any point in time—a concept referred to as *location-based targeting*. Essentially, a person's location information (available through GPS chips in smartphones) is factored into a marketing communications effort. Let's assume that a fast-food restaurant such as McDonald's or Wendy's knows where you are; the company can send you an incentive (coupon) instantly to encourage you to visit a nearby location. It's an unexpected incentive you just might take advantage of. Refer to the image in Figure 12.15.

Let's examine the primary means of communicating with consumers through mobile media.

TEXT ADS

Text messaging refers to the transmission of text-only messages. The popularity of mobile devices such as the Apple iPhone, Samsung Galaxy, and Google Android has allowed text messaging to emerge as a popular communications tool. Believe it or not, Canadians send 270 million text messages a day.[39] Texting is popular because of its speed, portability, and low cost.

Marketers interested in reaching younger targets can use text messaging and run promotions that include "call to action" short codes. Codes are usually mentioned in other media to create awareness for the promotion. Scotiabank entered the text messaging arena successfully. Its initial effort was a contest in support of the bank's

© iPhone/Alamy Stock Photo

FIGURE 12.15

Through mobile communications, offers can be sent to consumers in real time.

sponsorship of the Canadian Football League. Contest entrants earned the chance to win a VIP Grey Cup Experience and a selection of secondary prizes. The objectives of the promotion were to encourage participation, broaden reach beyond that of traditional media channels, and drive the brand's association with the sponsorship among consumers. The campaign was a multimedia effort with web, email, online media, TV, stadium advertising, and mobile components. A full 20 percent of all entries were made through the text short code "Scotia" (726842). The mobile component helped make the contest a success.[40]

BANNERS AND GRAPHICAL BANNERS

A standard banner ad (320 × 50 pixels) typically appears at the top or bottom of a mobile screen. Due to the size of the ad and the absence of meaningful content, click rates for them are quite low. For strong brands that simply want to leave a brand impression (e.g., a brand such as Nike or RBC Financial,) the standard banner will work, because the brand doesn't require any context or additional information.

A graphical banner can appear in a variety of settings on a website. For example, it can appear in the middle of a news article a person is reading—a box-like format is most common. A person can scroll by the ad (it counts as an impression) or click on the ad for more information. A graphical banner can also take up an entire screen. Such an ad allows for more content, clearer call to action, and more sophisticated creative—it can also include animation or video content. Refer to the image in Figure 12.16.

Photo by Keith J. Tuckwell

FIGURE 12.16

Banners and graphical banners that include animation or video are a popular option used by mobile advertisers.

VIDEO ADS

Videos are the fastest-growing form of mobile advertising—and for good reason. People are watching long-form video content on their mobile phones—in fact, some 41 percent of all video viewing (e.g., television shows, sports events, YouTube videos) occurs on a smartphone or tablet.[41] These same viewers want the largest flat-screen television in their living room. This is behaviour irony at its best.

Advertisers who are interested in the next generation of consumers are taking advantage of mobile video communications. Teens and young adults have grown up with technology, and mobile phones are ubiquitous among them. These consumers will carry their mobile behaviour forward, and it will have a dramatic impact on how they learn about and buy products. Some current research reveals that consumers are receptive to video advertising; they are willing to sit through ads to access the content they want if it means saving a few dollars. The IAB (Interactive Advertising Bureau) found that 78 percent of respondents in a survey would rather watch free mobile videos with ads versus 15 percent who would rather pay a monthly mobile video subscription fee with no ads.[42]

It is very costly to produce a 15- or 30-second video advertisement. To save money, brands that advertise on television will often show the same commercial on a mobile device. This tactic is questionable, since mobile users prefer shorter messages. A recent Canadian study concluded that people are more attentive to shorter ads and exhibit a 98 percent completion rate for messages that are 7 to 10 seconds long. The completion rate plummets to 37 percent for 15-second messages.[43] Advertisers should consider shorter, snappier ads to deliver their message.

Are mobile ads effective? Recent research indicates that mobile ads are outperforming standard banners on the internet. MediaMind, an organization that tracks the performance of online and mobile campaigns, reports that the clickthrough rate for mobile banners is 0.61 percent, almost eight times as high as the clickthrough rate for standard online banners in campaigns that had at least one mobile ad.

MOBILE APPLICATIONS

All smartphone suppliers, such as Google and Apple, offer applications that encourage in-application advertising. Within an application, an advertiser can have a full-screen video ad or select from less intrusive forms of advertising. The number of applications available on the market is mind boggling: Google has over 1 500 000 and Apple has over 1 400 000.[44] While placing ads on popular social media sites such as Facebook, Twitter, and Instagram may be easy decisions, with so much choice, how does an advertiser select which apps to place ads in?

There's a common complaint about applications among consumers, however: "There's so much choice, but nothing I really want." Finding apps that fit with one's lifestyle is challenging. Well, here's one that Canadians will love: At Tim Hortons you can combine the convenience of paying with a TimCard with the TimmyMe app. This new mobile feature allows a person to use his or her phone to make payment once a TimCard is registered. Another useful feature of the TimmyMe app is TimmyRun, which allows users to take orders for a group of people. The volunteer who initiates a run collects orders from members of a group. The runner can pay for the order with his or her mobile device. Refer to the image in Figure 12.17.

Among media companies, Rogers-owned City offers a video application that allows iPhone and iPad users to view live and on-demand content on their mobile devices. Regular scheduled programs are available to mobile users. The application gives advertisers the ability to reach consumers on a greater variety of platforms—online, tablet, and mobile. Pre-roll and mid-roll video ads are sold to advertisers.[45]

FIGURE 12.17

A unique online and mobile application from Tim Hortons

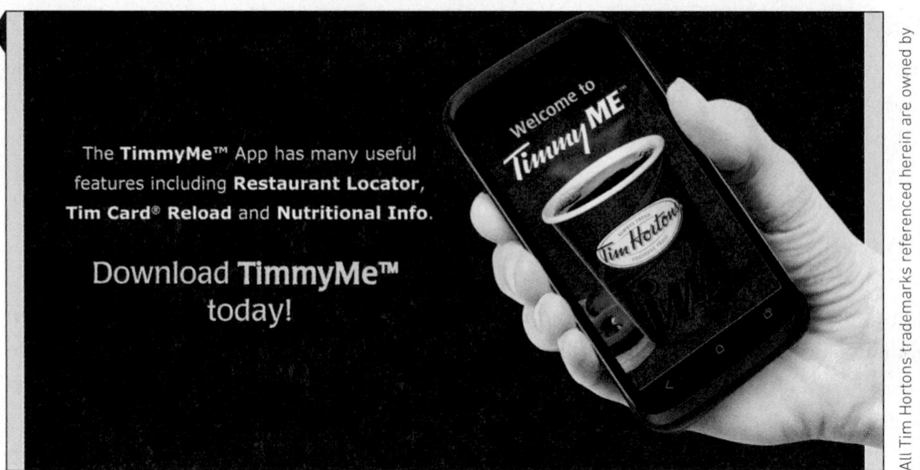

QR CODES

A **QR (quick response) code** is a two-dimensional barcode that can be scanned and read by smartphones. Made up of small squares with black-and-white patterns, the code allows for sharing of text and data. To read the code, a person needs to download a QR code reader, available at various app stores (e.g., Tag Reader for an iPhone).

To secure information, a user takes a picture of a code and is then linked to a website, a phone number, or perhaps a YouTube video that offers more information about a product or service. While this process sounds simple, consumers are reluctant to use QR codes. One American study revealed that only 21 percent of smartphone owners ever scanned a code. Many industry people believe that the lack of use stems from poor communication with consumers about what these codes are and how to use them. Marketers have a different view. In fact, marketers who have used them see them as an effective mobile marketing tactic. From a recent survey among marketing executives, 29 percent of respondents said they were very effective, and 66 percent said they were effective.[46]

Thus far, Canadian advertisers have enjoyed mixed results using the codes; their effectiveness in stimulating interest and ultimately a desired action is yet to be determined. The gap between consumers' acceptance of the technology and marketers' belief that the codes are a useful tactic has to be narrowed before any significant results can be achieved. Assuming the gap can be narrowed, QR codes offer several benefits: They can communicate additional information to the customer in a cost-efficient manner, and when customers snap the picture they are instantly engaged with the brand.

Video Game Advertising (Advergaming)

Advertising in video games, or **advergaming**, refers to the placement of ads in commercially sold games or in games played online or on mobile devices. The notion that video games are a male (young male) dominated activity initially restricted the level of interest in the medium by advertisers. However, new data suggest that video games are growing in popularity across both genders and all age categories. According to statistics from the Entertainment Software Association, 59 percent of all Americans play video games, the audience is split evenly between males and females, and the average age of a gamer is 31.

Integrating a brand into games helps achieve several objectives: It can generate positive brand awareness and higher brand preference ratings, as well as help stimulate purchases. The tactic is seen as being more effective than product placements in TV shows, mainly due to the intensity of the behaviour while gamers are playing—they see and recall the brand messages.

© Chris Ratcliffe/Bloomberg/Getty Images

FIGURE 12.18

Ads in video games offer a sense of reality to game players.

Gamers do not seem to mind the presence of ads. In fact, they expect to see ads and are receptive to their presence. A study conducted by IGA Worldwide (a game vendor) discovered 70 percent of respondents felt that the ads made them feel better about the brands. Further, brands running ads in games experienced an average 44 percent increase in brand recall among consumers when compared to awareness prior to seeing the brand in the game.[47]

With video games, an organization can go in two directions: create its own branded game or place ads in commercially produced games. Many brands have developed their own games for visitors to play at their website. Such games promote interactivity and offer good entertainment value—things people are looking for when they visit a website. These games often feature the company's products and get people to spend more time on the website—more time means greater opportunity to communicate useful information to prospective customers.

In commercially sold games, there is a diverse range of possibilities, including fully integrated opportunities (having a game designed around a brand or brands), interactive product placements, outdoor-style billboards, and 30-second video spots. Refer to the image in Figure 12.18. In EA Sports's NHL games, rinkboard advertising is present to make the game simulate the environment of a real hockey game. Advertisers that appear in the games include the same brands that advertise on televised games: Tim Hortons, Reebok, Bauer, and CCM.

SUMMARY

Companies are moving away from traditional advertising media such as television and newspapers and toward interactive communications, and for good reason. Canadians are leaders in internet consumption, and as a medium it has surpassed all other media in terms of revenue. People in all age categories are spending time online, so advertisers are adjusting their budgets accordingly. Money formerly spent in print media is going to digital media.

While high internet penetration is attractive to advertisers, there is concern about how advertisements are viewed (how long an ad appears on a screen and what counts as an impression) and click fraud (nonhuman clicking on ads). In terms of message, advertisers have to adapt to the participative nature of online advertising. Messages must be short yet informative and entertaining to encourage engagement with the audience.

Interactive communications strategies can be tailored more directly to consumer preferences, a concept referred to as *behavioural targeting*. When this concept is applied, the ads that appear on screen are related to the consumer's previous browsing behaviour. Ads can also be targeted based on demographic and geographic profiles.

Advertising on the internet helps achieve several marketing objectives: It is ideal for achieving brand awareness, building and enhancing image, offering incentives, generating leads, and conducting business transactions. Strategically, there are numerous advertising options available, including search advertising, display advertising (which includes static and animated banners), video ads, sponsorships, email, and posting content on websites and social media sites. Video ads are growing in popularity due to their similarity to television ads.

As an advertising medium, the internet offers targeting capability, depth of content, broad reach, and tracking capabilities that measure the effectiveness of campaigns in a variety of ways (clicks, leads, and conversions). As well, the interactive nature of the medium provides an environment that fosters building solid relationships with customers. Some drawbacks of the internet include consumers' frustration with unwanted email and the barrage of banner ads that are on some sites, and the perception among users that advertisers are invading their privacy.

Interactive media advertising rates are typically quoted on a cost-per-thousand-impressions basis. Other options include cost per click and flat fees. The media buying process is transitioning to an automated process called *programmatic buying*. The process is based on advertiser's objectives, target audience, and budget and makes instantaneous decisions (based on algorithms) regarding where to place ads.

Social media such as Facebook, Twitter, Instagram, and YouTube represent unique advertising opportunities. These sites feature user-generated content, some of which is commercials generated by amateurs. Companies are placing their own commercials on social network sites and establishing fan pages, hoping for positive word of mouth (buzz) about their brands. The more common types of ads include display (banners), sponsored posts, video ads, brand pages (fan page), company blogs, and posting video content on YouTube.

The advantages of social media advertising include the medium's targeting capabilities, its potential for positive word of mouth among friends, and the extent of consumer engagement with a brand that can occur. Some disadvantages include the absence of reliable metrics to measure the impact of a campaign and the time and financial commitment required to keep content fresh. Campaigns are measured for success based on reach, engagement (including likes and shares), and conversions (action taken).

Mobile advertising is the fastest-growing form of online advertising. Factors such as smartphone penetration, location-based targeting capability, and the amount of time people spend with their phones have attracted advertisers to this medium. The various advertising options available include text messages, banners and graphical banners, video ads, ads in mobile applications, QR codes, and video game ads. Marketers are attracted to mobile media because of the immediacy and intimacy they offer. Video games are proving to be an effective means of reaching all age groups. People are now spending a lot of time playing games instead of watching television. Advertisers must capitalize on this trend and adjust their media budgets accordingly.

KEY TERMS

advergaming 376
animated banner 353
banner ad 353
behavioural targeting 348
big box 348
blog 367
click fraud 347
click rate 352
clickthrough 352
consumer-generated content 364
content marketing 357
conversion 371
cookie 349
CPC (cost per click) 362
CPM (cost per thousand) 360
crowdsourcing 364
database mining 351
daypart targeting 348
display advertising 353
engagement 371
expandable banner 354
floating ad 354
frequency (online) 352
impression 349

leaderboard 353
location-based targeting 350
microsite 357
mid-roll 354
mobile marketing 371
online advertising 346
permission-based email 356
portal 350
post-roll 354
pre-roll 354
programmatic media buying 362
push-down banner 354
QR (quick response) code 376
real-time bidding 363
rich media 353
search advertising 353
skyscraper 353
social media network 363
spam 356
sponsorship 355
text messaging 373
videostrip 354
viral marketing 368
visit 353
wallpaper ad 354
website 351
window ad 354

REVIEW QUESTIONS

1. What characteristics make the internet different from traditional media?
2. Explain the concept of behavioural targeting as it applies to online communications.
3. Explain the following terms as they relate to advertising on the internet:
   a. Clickthrough
   b. Click rate
   c. Frequency
   d. Impression
4. What is search advertising, and how does it work?
5. What is display advertising, and how does it work?
6. Briefly explain the following interactive communications terms:
   a. Permission-based email
   b. Opt-in
   c. Pre-roll and post-roll
   d. Consumer-generated content
   e. Crowdsourcing
7. Explain the concept referred to as *brand democratization*.
8. Identify and briefly explain two advantages and two disadvantages of online advertising.
9. Briefly describe the various advertising opportunities available on social media networks.
10. What is the CPM pricing model, and how does it work? What factors influence the price charged in the CPM model?
11. If the CPM is $30.00 and the banner ad campaign achieves 1.5 million impressions, what is the total cost of the campaign?
12. If the total cost for a banner campaign was $30 000 and the impressions generated a total of 1.2 million, what is the CPM for the campaign?
13. How is the CPC advertising model different from the CPM model?
14. What does the term *advergaming* refer to?
15. Briefly explain two key benefits of social media advertising.
16. In mobile communications, what does *location-based targeting* refer to? Briefly explain.

DISCUSSION QUESTIONS

1. "Persistent invasions of consumer privacy will be the undoing of internet-based advertising." Is this statement true or false? Conduct some secondary research online to update the status of this issue. Report on your findings.
2. How important will mobile communications be in the future? Will consumers be accepting of advertising messages in this medium, or will they perceive them to be a nuisance? Describe and defend your opinion on this issue.
3. Review how the pay-for-performance model for advertising on the internet works. What is your opinion of this model? Examine the situation from both the advertiser's and the website's perspectives.

NOTES

1. IAB Canada, *Canadian Internet Advertising Revenue Survey 2014*, June 29, 2015, **www.iabcanada.com**.
2. Serena Ng and Suzanne Vranica, "P&G Shifts Marketing Dollars to Online, Mobile," *Wall Street Journal*, August 1, 2013, **www.wsj.com**.
3. IAB Canada, *Canadian Internet Advertising Revenue Survey 2014*.
4. Melody McKinnon, "Canadian Digital, Social and Mobile Statistics on a Global Scale, 2014," January 23, 2014, **http://canadiansinternet.com/canadians-digital-social-mobile-statistics**.
5. **TSN.ca**, **http://adsalescdn.bellmedia.ca/Press%20Releases/TSN/TSN_Network_Overview_2013.pdf**.
6. IAB Canada, "Interactive Marketing + Online Advertising," May 20, 2009, 145.
7. "Top 15 Most Popular Websites, July 2015," eBiz/MBA Guide, **www.ebizmba.com/articles/most-popular-websites**.
8. Tim Nichols, "Video Advertising Builds Brand Awareness," ExactDrive, June 4, 2014, **www.exactdrive.com/news/video-advertising-builds-brand-awareness**.
9. Canadian Internet Registry Authority, *Factbook 2014*, **http://cira.ca/factbook/2014/the-canadian-internet.html**.
10. "Online Shopping Becomes Mainstream in Canada," *Marketing*, November 8, 2008, **www.marketingmag.ca**.
11. David Chaffey, "Display Advertising Clickthrough Rates," *Smart Insights*, **www.smartinsights.com/internet-advertising/internet-advertising-analytics/display-advertising-clickthrough-rates/**.
12. Maureen Morrison, "Consumers Balance on Verge of 'Offer Anarchy,'" *Advertising Age*, February 13, 2012.
13. "Overview of Canada's Anti-Spam Legislation," Information + Privacy Law Blog, Alexander Holburn Beaudin + Lang LLP, **http://informationandprivacylawblog.ahbl.ca/2014/03/20/overview-of-Canadas-anti-spam-legislation**.
14. Daisy Whitney, "57% of Consumers Rely on Product Videos," *Online Video Insider*, Media Post Publications, March 28, 2013.
15. Rebecca Harris, "Irrelevant Messages Drive Rise of 'Deletist' Consumers," *Marketing*, April 21, 2015, **www.marketingmag.ca**.
16. "Real Time Bidding Explained," Acuity, **www.acuityads.com/real-time-bidding**.
17. Jeff Fraser, "We Use Programmatic Because Market Research Tells Us To: Kellogg's Smilanich," *Marketing*, November 11, 2014, **www.marketingmag.ca**.
18. Melody McKinnon, "Canadian Digital, Social and Mobile Statistics on a Global Scale 2014," **Dotster.com**, **http://canadiansinternet.com/canadian-digital-social-mobile-statistics**.
19. Shea Bennett, "28% of Time Spent Online Is Social Networking," *AdWeek*, January 27, 2015, **www.adweek.com/socialtimes/time-spent-online-613474**.
20. E. J. Shultz, "Why 'Crash the Super Bowl' Burned out for Doritos," *Advertising Age*, January 24, 2013, **www.adage.com**.
21. "Facebook Ad CTR Study—Newsfeed v. Display," Wolfgang Lab, Wolfgang Digital, **www.wolfgangdigital.com/blog/digital-marketing/facebook-ad-ctr-study-newsfeed-display-wolfgang-lab**.
22. "Mazda Canada: How Can an Automotive Company Drive Qualified Leads with a Simple Tweet?" Twitter, **https://biztwitter.com/success-stories/maxda-canada**
23. Russ Martin, "Facebook Launches Video Autoplay Ads in Canada," *Marketing*, May 20, 2014, **www.marketingmag.ca**.
24. Mark Walsh, "Engagement: Brands Should Drive Traffic to Facebook Page," *Online Media Daily*, June 4, 2012, **www.mediapost.com/publications/article/176841/engagement-brands-should-drive-traffic-to-facebook.html**.
25. Michael Miller, "Joining the YouTube Community—and Creating Your Own Channel," May 4, 2007, **www.quepublishing.com**.
26. Chris Powell, "Axe Launches Its Own Web Channel," *Marketing*, August 25, 2011, **www.marketingmag.ca/news/marketer-news/axe-launches-its-own-web-channel-34902**.
27. Brenna Ehrlich, "The Old Spice Social Media Campaign by the Numbers," *Mashable*, July 15, 2010, **http://mashable.com/2010/01/15/pld-spice-stats**.
28. Alicia Andrioch, "Facebook Rolling out New Targeting Options for Marketers," *Marketing*, February 21, 2014, **www.marketingmag.ca**.
29. Google, "AdWords: Advertise Your Business on Google," **https://support.google.com/adwords/answer/1704424?hl=en**.
30. "Data: What Are the Benefits of Social Media Marketing?" Mashable, December 29, 2008, **www.mashable.com**.
31. Rich Thomaselli, "Nissan Looks to Facebook to Help Launch Five New Models," *Advertising Age*, June 25, 2012, **www.adage.com/article/digital/Nissan-facebook-launch-models/235616**.
32. Susan Krashinsky, "Marketing at the Speed of Social Media," *Globe and Mail*, May 20, 2013, B9.
33. "MMA Updates Definition of Mobile Marketing," Mobile Marketing Association, November 17, 2009, **www.mediapost.com**.
34. Canadian Wireless Telecommunications Association, **www.cwta.ca/facts-figures**.
35. "The State of Canadian Connectedness: Internet Usage, Mobile, Search, and Social Media," 6S Marketing, **http://6smarketing.com/blog/infographic-canadiian-internet-usage**.
36. IAB Canada, *Canadian Internet Advertising Revenue Survey 2014*.
37. Michael Oliveira, "Video and Mobile Use Doubles Canadians' Time Spent Online, Research Says," *Globe and Mail*, November 12, 2014, **www.theglobeandmail.com**.
38. Susan Krashinsky, "Mobile Ads Fuel Facebook Revenue Surge," *Globe and Mail*, July 24, 2014, **www.theglobeandmail.com**.
39. "CWTA: Canadians Love for Text Messaging Is Declining," **MobileSyrup.com**, December 2, 2013, **http://mobilesyrup.com**.
40. "Take Possession," Mobile Marketing Supplement to *Strategy*, August 2008, S32.
41. "Mobile Phones Strengthen Lead for Mobile Video Viewing," *eMarketer*, July 2, 2015, **www.emarketer.com/Article/Mobile-Phones-Strengthen-Lead-Mobile-Video-Viewing/1012683**.
42. Ibid.
43. Jordan Pinto, "Canada Likes Its Mobile Ads Short and to the Point," *Media in Canada*, April 24, 2014, **http://mediaincanada.com/2015/04/24/Canada-likes-its-mobile-ads**.
44. "Number of Apps Available in Leading App Stores in May 2015," The Statistics Portal, **www.statistica.com/statistics/276623**.
45. Matt Semansky, "Citytv Goes Mobile with Video App," *Marketing*, December 8, 2011, **www.marketingmag.ca/news/media-news/citytv-goes-mobile-with-video-app-41991**.
46. Lindsay Kolowich, "Are QR Codes Dead?" **Hubspot.com**, August 14, 2014, **http://blog.hubspot.com/marketing/qr-codes-dead**.
47. Mike Shields, "IGA: Most Gamers Cool with In-Game Ads," *AdWeek*, June 17, 2008, **www.adweek.com**.

PART 5 Communicating the Message: Integrated Media Choices

© Mrs_ya/Shutterstock

Part 5 looks at the various marketing and promotional choices that enhance the communications plan.

Chapter 13 introduces various sales promotion alternatives that are frequently used in an integrated marketing communications campaign. Discussion is divided between consumer promotions and trade promotions, with each area examined for its ability to achieve marketing and marketing communications objectives.

Chapter 14 describes the role of public relations and experiential marketing in the integrated marketing communications mix. Various public relations techniques are introduced along with some principles for planning a public relations campaign. Experiential marketing, which involves event marketing and sponsorships, now plays a more prominent role in an organization's marketing communications mix. The strategic considerations for participating in these activities, and the various benefits and drawbacks of such participation, are discussed in this chapter.

CHAPTER 13

Sales Promotion

Learning Objectives

After studying this chapter, you will be able to

1. Identify the roles of various consumer and trade promotion activities in the marketing communications process
2. Outline the nature of various consumer and trade promotion activities
3. Assess strategies for integrating sales promotions into the marketing communications mix

This chapter examines the various sales promotion activities that are often integrated into a marketing communications program or marketing program. In the context of marketing communications planning, the manager must evaluate the contribution that sales promotion activity will make to the achievement of overall objectives. Assuming sales promotions are a worthwhile strategy, decisions are made regarding the types of promotions to implement. For example, some promotions are good at achieving trial purchase, while other promotions are good at achieving multiple purchases or for building brand loyalty. Organizations now use promotions, particularly contests, as a means of engaging consumers. Entering a contest, for example, typically involves a visit to a company or brand website.

Our initial discussion reviews the nature and intent of promotion activity in general. The various types of consumer promotion and trade promotion activities are presented, followed by a discussion of how sales promotions are integrated with other marketing communications strategies.

Sales Promotion

Sales promotion can be defined as activity that provides special incentives to bring about immediate response from an organization's salesforce, consumers, and distributors; in other words, it encourages the decision to buy. Sales promotion plans are developed with three groups in mind. The *consumer*, or final user, must be motivated to take advantage of the promotion offer. The *distributor* must actively support the promotion to achieve its goals, such as greater volume of sales, higher profit margins, or inventory movement. Finally, the *salesforce* must be motivated to sell the promotion at the wholesale and retail levels to make the promotion work successfully for the firm.

Sales promotion activities can be subdivided into two broad categories: consumer promotions and trade promotions. **Consumer promotions** refer to those activities that are designed to stimulate consumer purchase, in effect, to help pull the product through the distribution channel. Common types of consumer promotion activities include coupons, free sample offers, contests, premiums, cash-back offers, and a variety of frequent-buyer (loyalty) programs.

Trade promotions refer to those activities designed to encourage distributors to purchase additional volume and provide additional marketing support to stimulate consumer purchase. In effect, trade promotions help push the product through the distribution channel. Common types of trade promotion activities include price discounts and allowances, cooperative advertising funds, and point-of-purchase display materials.

Branded promotion merchandise or giveaway items that carry brand logos are a form of promotion that fits with either consumer promotion or trade promotion plans. Trade shows can also be a key component of an organization's consumer promotion or trade promotion plans.

Sales Promotion Planning

Promotion planning relies on input from the overall marketing plan—specifically, the marketing objectives and strategies. The sales promotion plan can be developed by the advertising agency, but more often a specialist agency does it. Regardless of who develops the plan, there is a direct relationship between advertising and sales promotion. Traditional thinking meant that the advertising agency created a national advertising campaign to position the product or service in the marketplace, while the promotion plan complemented the advertising: The plan helped create demand for the product, encouraged trial purchase, or built loyalty through repeat purchase incentives. In today's environment, where planners consider an integrated marketing approach, sales promotions are not viewed as separate entities. They are planned at the same time as the advertising plan to ensure that synergy is achieved across all forms of communications.

PROMOTION OBJECTIVES

Like other elements of the marketing mix, promotional activity must complement the total marketing effort. Thus, each element of the mix is assigned a goal based on what it is capable of contributing to the overall plans. As with other plans, promotion objectives should be realistically achievable, quantitative (for measurement purposes), directed at a carefully defined target, and capable of being evaluated and modified when necessary.

It should be noted that the objectives for consumer promotions and trade promotions are quite different, but they complement each other when implemented. Objectives of consumer promotions focus on achieving *trial purchase* and *repeat or multiple purchases* and *building brand loyalty*. Trade promotions focus on *selling more volume* of merchandise and encouraging *merchandising support* among channel members that buy and resell products. These objectives are examined in detail in appropriate sections of this chapter.

PROMOTION STRATEGY

Promotion strategy focuses on the selection of the best promotion activity to meet the objectives. There are two basic types of promotion strategy: *pull* and *push*.

In a **pull strategy**, the organization creates demand by directing promotional efforts at consumers or final users of a product. Pull strategies tend to rely on a mixture of media advertising, social media (paid and shared), and consumer promotion activities. These activities cause consumers to search for the product in stores; by asking for the product, they can put pressure on the retailer to carry it. The promotion activities considered include coupons, samples, contests, and premiums.

In a **push strategy**, the organization creates demand for a product by directing promotional efforts at intermediaries, who in turn promote the product among consumers. Push strategies tend to rely on a mixture of personal selling and trade promotion techniques to create demand. These trade promotions include a variety of financial incentives referred to as trade allowances, performance allowances, and cooperative advertising allowances. For a visual impression of the concept of pull and push promotion strategies, refer to Figure 13.1.

FIGURE 13.1

The flow of pull and push promotion strategies

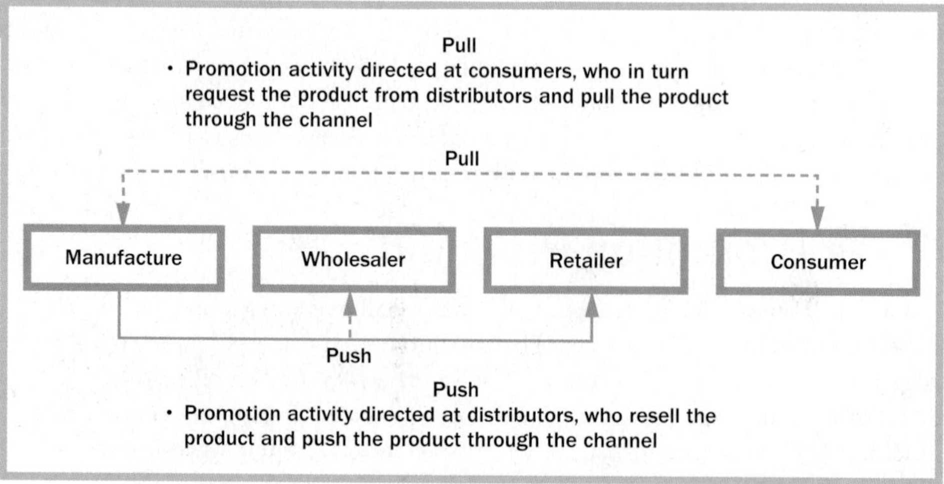

Most firms feel that attention must be given to both final users and channel members; thus, it is common for firms to combine push and pull promotion strategies. Companies such as Kraft, Colgate-Palmolive, and Apple advertise their products heavily to end users while their salesforce uses a combination of trade promotion and personal selling to sell the products to business customers or channel members. Successful promotions are promotions that are effectively integrated with brand advertising. Brand advertising builds a brand's image over the long term, while promotions, which tend to be short term, encourage purchases along the way. Having a great promotional concept is just the start of a promotion plan.

Consumer Promotion Planning

Consumer promotion is any activity that promotes extra brand sales by offering the consumer an incentive over and above the product's inherent benefits. It is designed to pull the product through the channel by encouraging consumers to take immediate purchase action. The most common objective of consumer promotion activity is to have the consumer make a *trial purchase*. In the case of a new product, the marketer is concerned that the initial trial and consumer acceptance of the product occur quickly. Even when a product is firmly established on the market, marketers will still attempt to secure trial purchase by nonusers. See Figure 13.2 for an illustration of a trial purchase incentive.

© Helen Sessions/Alamy Stock Photo

FIGURE 13.2

A consumer promotion that encourages trial purchase of a product

A second objective of consumer promotion activity is to *protect loyalty* by offering incentives that encourage repeat purchase. For example, a coupon distributed via the product itself is a good vehicle for maintaining customer loyalty—a reward for patronage. Current customers are also very likely to use media-delivered coupons for products they normally purchase to save money. Since the purchasers are already "sold" on the product's benefits alone, they view the coupon as an added bonus.

A third objective of consumer promotion activity is to encourage *multiple purchases*. Promotions fulfilling this objective are designed to "load up the customer" or "take customers out of the market" for a time. For example, a cash refund offer could increase in value with the number of purchases made. A coupon offer could stipulate a specific number of purchases that must be made to receive the discount.

Types of Consumer Promotion Activity

The major types of consumer promotion activities implemented in Canada include coupons, free sample distribution, contests such as sweepstakes or instant-wins, cash rebates, premiums, frequent-buyer or loyalty programs, and delayed payment incentives. Financial incentives are very attractive to consumers contemplating purchases—an incentive could be the final nudge that causes consumers to take action. A survey conducted by NCH Promotional Services among packaged goods companies (i.e., food, household goods, personal care products, and pet food manufacturers) revealed that 77 percent of the manufacturers viewed coupons as their most important form of consumer promotion activity. Following, in order of importance, are sampling, contests, cash refunds, and premiums.

COUPONS

Coupons are price-saving incentives offered to consumers to stimulate quicker purchase of a designated product. The array of products and services that use coupons is endless. Coupons are used to discount the price of movie and theatre tickets, to lower the price of restaurant meals, and to encourage purchase of a brand of breakfast cereal. Among packaged goods marketing organizations, coupons are frequently used to encourage purchases of household products, personal care products, and food products.

In 2012, the latest year for which statistics are available, companies in the packaged goods industry alone distributed 6.8 billion coupons to Canadian households. Of these, 86 million coupons were redeemed—a response rate of 1.3 percent. On an annual basis, coupons save Canadians over $100 million in redeemed value.[1] The typical household likely to use a packaged goods coupon includes a male or female head of household with children under 18 years of age.[2] Households with high incomes ($100 000+) are twice as likely to use coupons compared to lower income households (less than $40 000). Apparently, "it's cool to be frugal today." Coupons are attractive to value-conscious shoppers.[3]

Coupons are an excellent medium for achieving several marketing objectives at various stages of the product life cycle. Coupons can encourage *trial purchase* among new users (and encourage competitive brand users to switch brands), and they can encourage *repeat purchases* by current users. In the latter situation, the coupon is a means of building brand loyalty.

The method by which the coupons are distributed to consumers is based on the objectives of the coupon offer. When a product is new or relatively new, trial purchase is the marketer's primary objective, so **media-delivered coupons** are popular. Options for delivery include newspapers (through **free-standing inserts [FSI]**), magazines, direct mail, in-store distribution, online (including social media), and mobile devices. Several websites distribute coupons on behalf of manufacturers. Among them are save.ca, smartcanucks.ca, and savealoonie.com. Refer to the image in Figure 13.3.

Photo by Keith J. Tuckwell

FIGURE 13.3

Media-delivered coupons help achieve a variety of marketing objectives.

Consumers are now very receptive to coupons distributed digitally. Similar to the shift in advertising dollars toward digital media, coupon distribution is moving toward greater digital distribution. Now, mobile apps, digital coupons, and text message discounts provide shoppers with an array of money-saving opportunities they can access from their mobile device. According to Nielsen's *Digital Consumer Report*, 87 percent of US smartphone and tablet owners use their devices to shop, and nearly half have used mobile coupons.[4] Refer to the illustration in Figure 13.4. Digital coupons save the consumer time—no need to clip anything—and they can be redeemed quickly at the cash register of a store. Retailers who distribute digital coupons see them as a means of improving the customer's shopping experience. Smartphones also let people access deals on the go and are capable of delivering coupons that are relevant based on location, behaviour, and timeliness.

Once a product moves into the late growth and early mature stages of its life cycle, a marketer's attention shifts from trial purchase to *repeat purchase*. By now there are many competing brands, all of which have a certain degree of consumer loyalty. As a defensive measure, rewarding current customers in one form or another is important. The package itself becomes an important medium for distributing coupons. The insertion of a coupon in or on a package, for example, is an incentive for a customer to keep buying the product.

Coupons contained inside a package are called *in-pack self-coupons*, because they are redeemable on the next purchase. Usually the face panel of the package makes mention of the coupon contained inside. A coupon that appears on the side panel or back panel is called an *on-pack self-coupon*. Another option is the *instantly redeemable coupon*, which is attached to the package in some fashion and can be removed immediately and used on the purchase of the product. Sometimes two different products collaborate on a coupon offer. For example, Kellogg's Corn Flakes includes an in-pack coupon for Tropicana Orange Juice, and Tropicana places a Kellogg's coupon on its side panel; the relationship between the two brands is obvious. Each brand capitalizes on the other's consumer franchise in its effort to attract users. This type of coupon is called a **cross-coupon** or **cross-ruff**.

The category of *in-store-delivered coupons* includes coupons distributed by in-store display centres and dispensing machines that are usually located near the store entrance,

FIGURE 13.4

Coupons distributed by mobile devices can deliver offers to people based on location and behaviour.

© Sarah-Maria Vischer/The Image Works

on the shelves via shelf pads (the consumer tears off a coupon that can be redeemed instantly), or by handout as the customer enters the store or samples a product in the store.

The success or failure of a coupon offer is often determined by the redemption rate that is achieved. The **redemption rate** refers to the number of coupons returned to the manufacturer expressed as a percentage of the total coupons in distribution. If, for example, 1.5 million coupons were distributed and 75 000 were returned, the redemption rate would be 5 percent (75 000 ÷ 1 500 000 × 100).

For budgeting purposes, it is important to know the average redemption rates for the various methods of delivering coupons. For starters, the Nielsen *2014 Coupon Trends Report* reveals that print coupons have an average redemption rate of 1 percent. That may seem low, but the redemption rate will vary based on the method of distribution. Coupons in magazines, for example, have a range of 1 to 7 percent, and addressed direct mail coupons have an average redemption rate of 6.5 percent. Nielsen reports that digital coupons have a much higher

FIGURE 13.5

Evaluating the financial impact of a coupon offer

Coupon Promotion Plan			
Face Value of Coupon		$1.20	
Handling Charge for Retailer		$0.15	
Handling Charge for Clearinghouse		$0.05	
Distribution Cost (direct mail)		$16.00/M	
Distribution		3 million households	
Printing Cost (digest-size ad with coupon)		$8.00/M	
Redemption Rate		2.5%	
Retail Price of Product (Manufacturer receives 65% of retail price when distributors' markups are deducted.)		$4.49	
The cost and revenue calculations are as follows:			
Costs	**Cost Calculation**	**Total**	**Grand Total**
Distribution	3 000 000 × $16/M	$48 000	
Printing	3 000 000 × $8/M	$24 000	
Coupon Redemption	3 000 000 × 0.025 × $1.20	$90 000	
Total Cost		**$162 000**	**$162 000**
Revenues	**Revenue Calculation**	**Total**	**Grand Total**
Per Unit of Revenue	$4.49 × 0.65	$2.92	
Total Revenue	3 000 000 × 0.025 × 0.80 × $2.92	**$175 200**	**$175 200**
Return on Investment			**$ 13 200**

Note: A misredemption rate of 20% is included above, hence the 0.80 factor in the revenue calculation.

average redemption rate—14 percent! Clearly, people are enticed to take action when they receive a digital coupon.[5] The perceived value of the offer in relation to the regular price will also influence the redemption rate. If it is not a worthwhile incentive, it won't be acted upon.

The costs of a coupon promotion should be monitored closely by the marketing organization. A variety of factors have an impact on the total costs of a coupon promotion: the method of distribution, which affects delivery costs and redemption costs; the printing costs; the handling costs for the retailer and clearinghouse (the latter being the agent responsible for redeeming coupons, paying retailers, and reporting redemption and cost information to the marketing organization); and the coupon's face value. The marketer should weigh the costs of a coupon promotion against the potential revenues to ensure that a positive financial payout will result from the activity. The difference between revenues and costs is the return on investment. Revenues can be estimated based on the value of the product sold by the manufacturer multiplied by the number of purchases generated by the coupon offer. Figure 13.5 illustrates in detail how to evaluate the financial payout of a coupon offer.

The revenue calculation also considers the misredemption of coupons. A coupon is misredeemed if it was not used to purchase the product but was sent to the clearinghouse anyway—this is a common occurrence in the industry. The illustration in Figure 13.5 considers a misredemption rate of 20 percent (80 percent are redeemed on an actual purchase).

FREE SAMPLES

A free **sample** is a free product distributed to potential users either in a small trial size or in its regular size. Sampling is considered the most effective method of generating trial purchase since it eliminates a consumer's initial financial risk. Therefore, it is commonly practised when a company is introducing a new product or a line extension of an existing product (e.g., a new flavour of a food product). Unlike any other type of promotion, sampling is the only alternative that can convert a trial user to a regular user solely on the basis of product satisfaction.

The most frequently used method of sample distribution is in-store. There are several variations on in-store sampling: product demonstrations and sampling in stores, saleable sample sizes (small replica pack sizes of the actual product), and cross-sampling. **Cross-sampling** refers to an arrangement whereby one product carries a sample of another product (e.g., a regular-sized box of Cheerios cereal carries a small sample package of Lucky Charms cereal). The popularity of one brand is used to secure the trial usage of another brand.

In-store sampling is a tried and true approach, particularly for food products. Costco uses this approach extensively by setting up sample stations at the ends of food aisles. A smart shopper can practically have a free lunch while shopping at Costco on a Saturday. When packaged goods companies do sample testing in local supermarkets, they usually outsource the promotion to an independent company that specializes in this activity. Booths are strategically placed in stores to intercept customers as they shop. See Figure 13.6 for an illustration of in-store sampling.

Other alternatives for delivering free samples include cooperative direct mail (provided the sample is small and light enough to be accommodated by the mailing envelope), home delivery by private organizations, event sampling, and sample packs that are distributed to specific target markets. Several companies specialize in the distribution of samples in Canada.

FIGURE 13.6

In-store sampling encourages trial purchases.

Sampling programs tend to be an expensive proposition for the marketing organization because of the product, packaging, and distribution costs. In spite of these costs, sample promotions rank second in popularity among marketers, so clearly the potential long-term benefits outweigh the short-term costs. Further, sampling combined with a coupon is the best way to gain trial and convert these trials to immediate purchase. On the downside, a sample is the fastest and surest way to kill an inferior product.

Companies are discovering new ways of delivering samples while at the same time generating positive publicity for the brand involved in the promotion. Some refer to it as *on-site sampling*; others call it *experiential marketing*. Regardless of what it is called, it involves potential customers interacting directly with the product. True experiential marketing goes beyond distributing samples. A more thorough discussion of this topic is included in Chapter 14.

Carefully planned sampling programs can make a product stand out in the clutter of advertising messages a consumer receives each day. Research supports this point of view. According to the Promotion Marketing Association's Sampling and Demonstration Council, 83 percent of consumers agreed that experiencing a product (a sample) or seeing it demonstrated live increases their comfort level when purchasing.[6]

Speaking of well-thought-out sampling programs, McDonald's has offered consumers free coffee as part of its business-building strategies. For details, read the Advertising in Action vignette **Sample Promotion Helps Build McDonald's Coffee Business in Canada**.

CONTESTS

Contests are designed and implemented to create temporary excitement about a product. The structure of a contest usually entails incentives for consumers to purchase. Entrance often requires, for example, submission of a label or product symbol (or facsimile) and an entry form. To enter a contest, consumers are often directed to a website where they must enter a PIN code that appeared on a package or container. Consumers are encouraged to enter as often as possible, resulting in many consumers making multiple purchases.

As a marketing vehicle, contests tend to attract the current users of a product but are less effective in inducing trial purchases than are coupons and samples. Consequently, contests are most appropriate in the mature stage of the product life cycle, when the aim is to retain current market share. Sweepstakes and instant-wins are two major types of contests.

A **sweepstakes** contest is a chance promotion involving a giveaway of products and services of value to randomly selected participants who have submitted qualified entries. Prizes such as cash, cars, homes, and vacations are given away. Consumers enter contests by filling in an entry form, usually available at point of purchase or through print advertising, and submitting it along with a proof of purchase to a central location where a draw is held to determine winners. The odds of winning depend on the number of entries received. Usually an independent organization selects the winners on behalf of the sponsor company.

Sweepstakes contests are now a popular vehicle to engage consumers with brands. Brands execute the contests online. While entering the contest, the consumer might be asked to submit some personal information. This information is accumulated in a database for later use. In other words, the contest is a building block for developing a customer relationship management program.

Many companies and brands run contests in partnership with TSN. TSN actively promotes the contests. Some big contests from the past include Wendy's "Kick for a Million"

ADVERTISING IN ACTION

Sample Promotion Helps Build McDonald's Coffee Business in Canada

Coffee is the beverage of choice among Canadians, and 35 percent of all coffee is consumed in restaurants. It's a huge market, and one that McDonald's Canada wanted a piece of. But the competition would be fierce. How does McDonald's Canada (with a 2 percent market share in the restaurant coffee market) attract customers away from Tim Hortons, Starbucks, Second Cup, Coffee Time, and a host of independent coffee shops?

As in any market, the right combination starts with a good-quality product supported by media advertising for awareness and impactful sales promotions to encourage trial. Aimed at attracting new customers away from competitors, McDonald's Canada implemented a free coffee promotion in April 2009 to reintroduce its Premium Roast coffee, a medium dark blend, to Canadians. In subsequent years, similar free coffee promotions have been executed, and the promotions have been successful. Not only was the coffee good, but the cup was superior to any competitor—a nifty double-walled cup with a lid that could be easily opened!

The key objective for McDonald's Canada in conducting the free coffee promotion was to get people to try the coffee. According to president and CEO John Betts, "We needed to do something bold to disrupt the market and get people talking—and nothing works like free." Over a four-year period starting in April 2009, 113 million cups of coffee were given away, and during that time McDonald's Canada's market share of the brewed coffee business grew to 11 percent. A very good return on investment! The market share increase suggests customers altered their routines and now visit McDonald's for their coffee. The free coffee promotion has exceeded the company's expectations.

Another important change at McDonald's started in 2011, when the company began remodelling its restaurants in Canada. Some of the changes included flat-screen televisions, fireplaces, long communal tables, and arm chairs. The remodelling created a more relaxed environment where patrons could linger over their coffee and food while chatting with friends.

© Chih-Chung Johnny Chang/Alamy Stock Photo

Source: Adapted from Hollie Shaw, "McDonald's making gains in Canadian coffee Wars, as U.S. Sales Decline Deepens," *Financial Post*, December 10, 2014, http://business.financialpost.com and James Cowan, "McDonald's in Trouble. Meet the Canadians Engineering its Comeback," *Canadian Business*, April 28, 2014, http://www.canadianbusiness.com.

contest, which generated an unprecedented numbers of entries, and General Motors's "Million Dollar Shootout": Successfully kicking a football through uprights or shooting a puck into a tiny hole from a considerable distance in front of a live audience wins someone $1 million. Contests like these generate excitement for the sponsoring brand.

Kraft Canada in partnership with TSN and RDS recently launched a contest called "Kraft Project Play." With a social responsibility theme, the contest helps communities build better places to play—the emphasis is on soccer, basketball, and tennis facilities. The contest is rooted in research evidence that suggests Canadians perceive recreation services make a significant contribution to improved health (93 percent) and boost social cohesion (89 percent). Communities across Canada are invited to submit video clips that showcase their unique contribution to sports. Four finalists will be determined by a judging panel, with Canadians at large then voting to see who wins the grand prize ($250 000) and secondary prizes ($25 000). Former Toronto Raptor basketball star Mo Peterson is the face of the contest in media advertising and promotion materials. Kraft has a long-standing commitment to improving places for Canadians to play. Over the last nine years, Kraft has contributed $4 million across 138 communities to refurbish recreation facilities.[7] Refer to the illustration in Figure 13.7.

A **game** (or **instant win**) contest is a promotion vehicle that includes a number of predetermined, pre-seeded winning tickets in the overall fixed universe of tickets. Packages containing winning certificates are redeemed for prizes. Variations of this type of contest include collect-and-wins, match-and-wins, and small instant-wins combined with a grand prize contest. Tim Hortons uses the instant win vehicle with its "Roll Up the Rim to Win" contest that runs annually each spring. The contest does have an impact on sales, but the company does not measure its success that way. The company sees the contest as a way of saying "thank you" to its customers for their loyalty. Simply by enjoying a cup of coffee,

FIGURE 13.7

The "Kraft Project Play" contest encourages community and consumer engagement with Kraft and helps build corporate image.

customers get a chance to win a prize. Further, the contest is accessible to virtually every Canadian, a situation that gives Tim Hortons a huge advantage over its competitors.[8]

Contests are governed by laws and regulations, and any company that runs one must publish the following information: how, where, and when to enter; who is eligible to enter the contest; the prize structure, value, and number of prizes; the odds of winning and the selection procedure; and conditions that must be met before a prize can be accepted (e.g., a skill-testing question must be answered).

A contest requires a significant investment in media advertising. In effect, the focal point of a brand's advertising switches temporarily from the product to the contest in an attempt to build excitement for the brand. To create awareness for the contest, a multimedia mix is frequently used. Broadcast media generates excitement; print media and online communications (e.g., a microsite) communicate necessary details; and social media, both paid and shared, engages consumers with the contest and brand. In-store communications is vital to draw attention to the contest at point-of-sale. Contests are usually well received and supported by the retail trade—indeed, they are often launched with trade promotion programs to encourage feature pricing and maximize display activity at retail. Refer to the image in Figure 13.8.

The success of a contest depends on the consumer's perception of the value and number of prizes to be awarded, and of the odds of winning. Contest prizes should also match the image of the product (e.g., a quality product must offer quality prizes). In terms of attracting participation, prizes of automobiles generate the highest number of contest entries, but vacations and trips are the prizes most offered by sponsoring companies. When designing a contest, the marketer must consider these factors and must either develop a high-value grand prize that will attract attention and create excitement or have prizes of less value awarded frequently to compensate for the disappointment factor associated with most contests ("I'll enter, but who ever wins?"). Many online contests now adopt the latter approach. In some cases, prizes are awarded on an hourly or daily basis. Frequent prizes keep people visiting the website.

FIGURE 13.8

In-store communications play a key role in creating awareness for a contest.

Photo by Keith J. Tuckwell

CASH REFUNDS (REBATES)

A **cash refund**, or **rebate**, as it is often called, is a predetermined amount of money returned directly to the consumer by the manufacturer after the purchase has been made. It is a reward for buying a product within the promotion period. Cash refunds are a useful promotion technique for packaged goods companies in the mature stage of the product life cycle. They reinforce loyalty effectively by tempting consumers to make multiple purchases.

The most common type of refund is the single-purchase refund, in which a consumer receives a portion of his or her money back for the purchase of a specified product. However, refunds are designed to achieve several objectives; hence, they can be offered in different formats. Refunds encourage consumers to make multiple purchases and stock their pantries. For example, the value of a refund may escalate with the number of items purchased. An offer could be structured as follows: buy one and get $1.00 back; buy two and get $2.00 back; buy three and get $5.00 back.

In refund offers in which multiple purchases are necessary, slippage can occur. **Slippage** happens when a consumer purchases a product intending to redeem a coupon, request a rebate, or send in for a premium but fails to do so. Time-pressed consumers often forget about the rebate offer.

Strategically, refund offers for packaged goods items should be advertised at point of purchase since it is when consumers are at point of purchase that they make brand buying decisions. A common technique is to use **ad pads**, which are shelf pads with tear-away sheets containing details of the promotion offer. Prominent display cards in a retail environment can also communicate details of a rebate offer. Refer to Figure 13.9.

Rebates are now popular among a variety of durable goods. For example, automobile companies entice consumers with "cash-back" offers as high as $5000 on cars and $8000 on trucks. These offers were created out of necessity (to keep the companies operating), but consumers are adapting to rebate offers so well it seems they now won't buy a new car unless some kind of incentive is offered. Car buyers are doing a lot of comparative shopping. This tactic is not in the best long-term interests of the automobile industry.

For inexpensive packaged goods products, rebate offers are best offered in the mature stage of the product life cycle. Encouraging multiple purchases or increasing the frequency

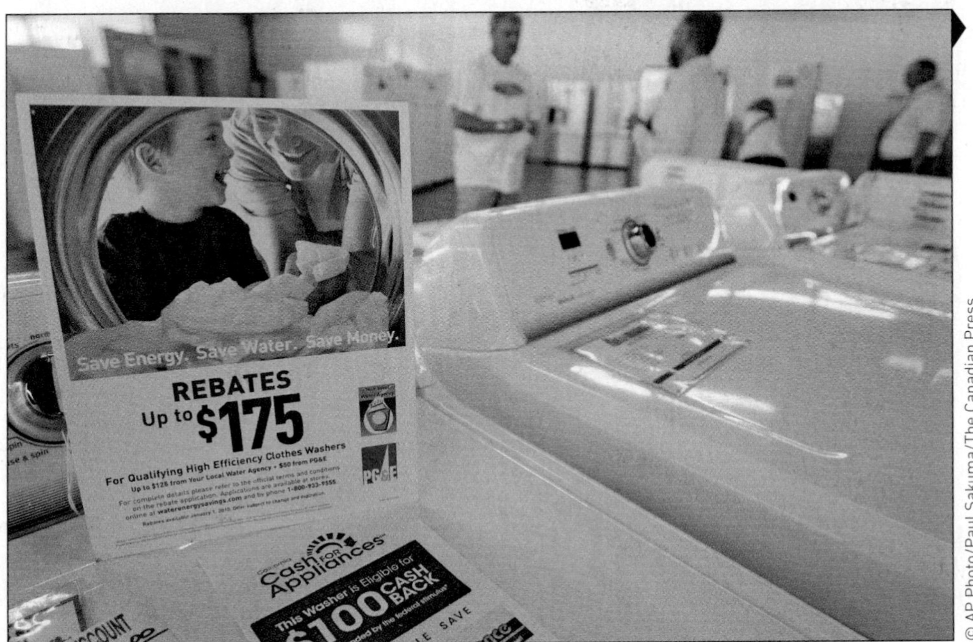

FIGURE 13.9

Cash rebate incentives are popular among appliance manufacturers.

© AP Photo/Paul Sakuma/The Canadian Press

of purchase is a common objective for mature products, and maintaining customer loyalty is critical. Apart from the automobile rebates just mentioned, the cost of a rebate offer isn't that expensive. Since those who take advantage of rebate offers tend to be current users, advertising support can be confined to the package and various in-store opportunities, such as shelf cards and product displays.

PREMIUM OFFERS

A **premium** is an item offered free or at a bargain price to encourage consumers to buy a specific product. The goal of a premium offer is to provide added value to new and repeat purchasers. McDonald's and other fast-food restaurants consistently use premiums (e.g., free toys with kids' meals) because they are effective with the primary target (families) and they reinforce the company's goal of offering value to consumers.

Premiums are usually offered to consumers in three ways: either as a mail-in (send in proofs of purchase and the item will be returned by mail), as an in-pack or on-pack promotion (an item is placed inside a package or attached to a package), or by a coupon offer distributed by in-store shelf-talkers (small posters that hang from store shelves). Distributing premiums with a product is popular because it provides instant gratification. Cereal manufacturers are very active in premium promotion offers. Premiums with a high perceived value have a direct impact at point of purchase because they encourage brand switching—attractive offers attract new customers, even if only on a temporary basis. Refer to the image in Figure 13.10.

Beer manufacturers see premium offers as a vital tool for building business in the critical summer months. Labatt and Molson Coors frequently battle over which company offers the best value-added proposition to customers. They will offer branded T-shirts, ball caps, and golf balls in cases of beer, or offer larger cases (extra bottles of beer) to entice consumers to buy. Both companies realize these offers are expensive but necessary in such a competitive market. However, rather than create loyalty, they simply encourage drinkers to switch brands constantly.

An offshoot to a premium offer is the bonus pack. The bonus pack offers the consumer more for less. For example, a brand offers a package size that gives the consumer

FIGURE 13.10 In-pack premium offers are popular among cereal manufacturers; a good premium offer encourages brand switching.

Photo by Keith J. Tuckwell

25 percent more product for the regular price. Another option is to offer a related item free with the purchase of the product. Offers like these, if implemented properly, will attract new users and reward current users.

A well-thought-out premium offer helps achieve several marketing objectives. The premium can increase the quantity of brand purchases made by consumers, help retain current users, attract competitive users (as in the beer offer mentioned above), and provide a merchandising tool to encourage display activity in stores. A good premium offer enhances differentiation between competing products. Typically, premium offers rely on the package and in-store display cards to advertise the offer.

FREQUENT-BUYER (LOYALTY) PROGRAMS

Canadian retailers and various service industries such as airlines, credit cards, and hotels have made frequent-buyer or loyalty programs popular. A **frequent-buyer (loyalty) program** offers consumers a small bonus, such as points or "play money," when they make a purchase. The bonus accumulates with each new purchase. Air Miles and Shoppers Optimum are loyalty programs that are popular with consumers.

The Shoppers Optimum loyalty program encourages loyalty among Shoppers Drug Mart customers. In this program, customers accumulate points that are redeemable on future purchases. The Shoppers Optimum card is an integral component of Shoppers's customer relationship management program. Refer to the illustration in Figure 13.11. The company can electronically cross-reference transaction data and work with its product suppliers to tailor offers to specific customers. Technology and the desire to manage customer relationships better are the fuel that drives loyalty programs.

Canadian Tire's program is, perhaps, the best-known and longest-running (over 58 years) frequent-buyer program in Canada. It rewards regular shoppers who pay for merchandise with cash or a Canadian Tire credit card with Canadian Tire "money." Canadian Tire money is collected digitally (virtual currency) on the company's house

FIGURE 13.11

The Shoppers Optimum loyalty program encourages current customers to remain loyal to Shoppers Drug Mart.

Courtesy of Shoppers Drug Mart

ADVERTISING IN ACTION

Loyalty Programs Help Sway Purchase Decisions

How many rewards cards do you have in your wallet? Count them. You might be surprised by the number you have. There is little doubt that rewards programs are popular with consumers. A recent survey in Canada reveals that loyalty programs definitely sway purchase decisions. Here are a few facts from the survey:

- 56 percent of respondents make an effort to visit retailers where they have a loyalty card.
- 47 percent of cardholders say loyalty programs impact how much they spend.
- 33 percent of respondents say they buy more products and services to accumulate more points.
- 52 percent of respondents said they would shop on a particular day if they could earn more points.

The survey looked at all categories where loyalty cards are present—retail, coalition, entertainment, gasoline, and travel—and discovered that 90 percent of Canadians have a loyalty card, and on average each person carries four cards. Not surprisingly, Air Miles is the leading loyalty card—it's been around the longest of the more popular cards. Others in the top five include Shoppers Optimum, Canadian Tire Rewards/Money, Aeroplan, and HBC Rewards.

Organizations contemplating offering a rewards program must consider how consumers react to such programs. Several common themes emerge when consumers are asked about loyalty programs. First, consumers want value—the incentives offered must be tangible and easily recognized. They don't want to collect a massive number of points for an incentive not perceived as meaningful. Second, they want simplicity. The program must be easy to understand, and the rewards must be easy to secure. On those issues nobody does it better than Canadian Tire. At the cash register, the first question asked is: "Do you want to redeem your points?" Or McDonald's: Buy seven cups of coffee and get one free cup (regular or espresso variety). What could be more tangible and simple than that?

A good loyalty program offers an organization many benefits. Foremost is the information the card collects about customer shopping behaviour. The information can be used to tailor offers of interest to individual customers. Loblaw's recent launch of PC Plus, a digital loyalty program, does just that. The program will actually draw up grocery lists for customers and send them recipes for meals based on what they like and what's on sale. Consumers collect points (20 000 points equals $20 in savings) and redeem them at the cash register.

There is another rather unique benefit to PC Plus rewards: The program targets the most valuable customers rather than spreading the rewards over every customer on every transaction. Essentially, it rewards loyal customers over "cherry pickers," who scoop up sale items only. Another benefit is that the offers are invisible to competitors and are based on local markets, right down to the individual store locations. Communications with customers occurs by email, all behind the scenes, so to speak. Access to the program is also available through a mobile application.

© Fernando Morales/The Globe and Mail/The Canadian Press

Source: Adapted from Rebecca Harris, "Loyalty Programs: What's in It for Marketers?," *Marketing*, March 31, 2015, www.marketingmag.ca and Francine Kopun, "Loblaw Launches Smart-Phone Based Loyalty Program," *The Toronto Star*, May 2, 2013, www.thestar.com.

credit card, its website, and its affiliate MasterCard. Canadian Tire money captures the essence of a rewards program because customers can purchase something for "free."

Loyalty programs are popular with customers. In fact, a recent study revealed that 90 percent of Canadians have a loyalty card and, on average, Canadians have four loyalty cards in their wallet. The presence of loyalty cards indicates Canadian consumers are certainly looking for value when they shop; they also show a preference for cards with no annual fees.[9]

Free rewards are a real incentive, but people don't realize they may be paying for the privilege. The true benefit for the organization is the information it is collecting about customer purchase behaviour. The ability to mine such data is useful as organizations move toward individualized marketing programs.

For more insight into rewards and loyalty programs, read the Advertising in Action vignette **Loyalty Programs Help Sway Purchase Decisions**.

DELAYED PAYMENT INCENTIVES

In a **delayed payment incentive** promotion, a consumer is granted a grace period during which he or she pays no interest or principal for the item purchased. Once the purchase is made from the retailer, a finance company assumes the agreement and charges interest if full payment is not made by the agreed-upon date. Leon's Furniture pioneered the delayed payment concept in Canada with promotions called "Don't Pay a Cent Event" and the "No Money Miracle."

This type of promotion has spread to other retail markets. The Home Depot now provides numerous delayed payment incentives. The company offers an array of household repair and renovation services to its customers: interior and exterior renovations, electrical and plumbing upgrades, and shingle and window replacements, to name just a few. These types of services are expensive undertakings for consumers. To attract potential customers, The Home Depot will offer six-month and one-year interest-free financing packages. Such an offer gives The Home Depot a competitive edge over independent contractors, who demand payment when such jobs are completed.

COMBINATION OFFERS

To maximize the effectiveness of a promotion, marketers often combine the consumer promotion techniques discussed in this chapter. For example, it is quite common to combine a trial coupon offer with a premium or contest promotion. The coupon will get the initial purchase, and the premium or contest will encourage repeat or multiple purchases.

Trade Promotion Planning

Trade promotion is promotional activity directed at distributors to push a product through the channel of distribution; it is designed to increase the volume purchased and encourage merchandising support for a manufacturer's product. For any new product, the objective of trade promotion activity is to secure a listing with distributors (wholesale and retail). A ***listing*** is defined as an agreement made by a wholesaler to distribute a manufacturer's product to the retailers it supplies. If, for example, the head office of Sobeys or Provigo agrees to purchase a specific product, then that product is available to all Sobeys and Provigo retail stores. To secure a listing, manufacturers will offer distributors a combination of trade allowances and cooperative advertising allowances that will cover the costs of securing the listing, obtaining distribution, and possibly selling the product at a special introductory price.

A second objective of trade promotions is to *build volume*, either on a seasonal basis or on a preplanned cyclical basis throughout the year. For example, it is quite common for a company to offer trade allowances and other merchandising programs quarterly for key products. The availability of trade allowances encourages retailers to purchase heavily during the promotion period to support the manufacturer's promotion and to "load up" on inventory at the end of the promotion. These goods can be sold at regular price, thus improving the profit margins of the distributor.

In the case of seasonal products, allowance programs are essential means of encouraging wholesalers and retailers to stock up before the season and promote the product during the season. For example, sunscreen will be promoted in the spring, canning and preserving supplies in the late summer, baking supplies in the late fall before the holidays, and school supplies in the late summer.

A third objective is to *secure merchandising support* from distributors. For many products sold through drug, grocery, hardware, or department stores, manufacturers will offer complete promotion programs to encourage display activity, feature pricing, and retail advertising support. Programs of this nature are often agreed to in a signed contract or promotion agreement, and the distributor is reimbursed only when the performance requirements of the agreement are met.

Types of Trade Promotion Activity

The most commonly used types of trade promotion activity are trade and performance allowances, cooperative advertising, retail in-ad coupons, dealer premiums, collateral material, dealer-display material, and trade shows.

TRADE ALLOWANCE

A **trade allowance** is a temporary price reduction designed to encourage larger purchases by distributors (wholesalers and retailers). Such price reductions may be offered in the form of a percentage reduction from list price, a predetermined dollar amount off list price, or as a free-goods offer (e.g., buy 10 cases, get 1 free). These allowances can be deducted from the invoice immediately, and in such cases they are called *off-invoice allowances*. Or they can be offered on the basis of a *bill-back*, in which case the manufacturer keeps a record of the amount of merchandise shipped to distributors and, when the deal period is over, issues a cheque to reimburse the retailers for the allowances they have earned.

PERFORMANCE ALLOWANCE

A **performance allowance** is an additional discount (over and above a trade allowance) offered by manufacturers to encourage retailers to perform a specific merchandising function (e.g., display the product at retail, provide an advertising mention in a retail flyer, or offer a lower price at retail for a short period). Before paying the allowance, the manufacturer requires proof of performance from the retailer. Performance allowances are a useful tactic if the marketing objective is to increase sales in the short term.

COOPERATIVE ADVERTISING ALLOWANCE

Cooperative advertising allowances are funds allocated to pay for a portion of a retailer's advertising. The weekly specials advertised by major supermarket chains, for example, are partially sponsored by the manufacturers whose products are part of the ads in any given week. In some cases, a manufacturer may agree to pay half of the retailer's cost of advertising (media and creative) if the retailer agrees to feature the manufacturer's product for a specified period. Frequently, the manufacturer provides advertising material that can be integrated into the retailer's own advertising.

It is a common strategy to offer trade allowances, performance allowances, and cooperative advertising funds as an integrated offer to maximize the impact of a trade promotion. Such plans are attractive to retailers because the financial rewards are much greater and the offer facilitates efficient use of advertising dollars to support the retailer's advertising and merchandising activities.

Considering the information provided in this section, you can now appreciate that many of the in-store merchandising activities implemented by retailers are actually subsidized by the manufacturers whose brands are involved in the promotions. The costs of trade promotions are significant and take a considerable portion of a brand's marketing budget. For this investment to be successful, a coordinated effort with consumer promotions and brand advertising is essential.

RETAIL IN-AD COUPONS

A **retail in-ad coupon** is a coupon printed in a retailer's weekly advertising material, either in run-of-press newspaper advertising or in supplements inserted into a newspaper. These coupons are redeemable on national brands and are paid for by the manufacturers, not by the retailer. Such programs are the result of an agreement struck between the manufacturer's sales representative and the retailer's buyers. Usually, the funds to cover the cost of these coupons come out of the trade promotion budget, hence their inclusion as a trade promotion activity even though they are designed to encourage consumer response. Being able to offer branded products at lower prices is an attractive stimulus for retailers to buy more and sell more of the advertised item.

DEALER PREMIUMS

A **dealer premium** is an additional incentive offered to a distributor by a manufacturer to encourage special purchase or to secure additional merchandising support from a retailer. Premiums are usually offered in the form of merchandise (e.g., a set of golf clubs, or other forms of sports- or leisure-oriented equipment and clothing); the value of the premium increases with the amount of product purchased by the retailer.

Their use is often controversial. Some distributors forbid their buyers to accept premiums because they feel only the individual buyer, rather than the organization, benefits. Such a situation, often referred to as *payola*, might lead a buyer to make unnecessary purchases. These practices are perceived by many as unethical, and they should not occur. Nonetheless, some dealings do happen under the table, so students should be aware of it.

COLLATERAL MATERIAL

To facilitate the selling process, the salesforce must provide considerable data in the form of **collateral materials** to customers (e.g., dealers, wholesalers, retailers, industrial companies). These materials include price lists, catalogues, sales brochures, pamphlets, specification sheets, product manuals, and digital sales aids prepared by the manufacturer. Having access to digital information is important for communicating lengthy and complex information.

DEALER-DISPLAY MATERIAL (POINT OF PURCHASE)

Dealer-display advertising, or **point-of-purchase advertising**, consists of self-contained, custom-designed merchandising units, either permanent or temporary, that display a manufacturer's product. It includes posters, shelf-talkers, channel strips (narrow strips containing a brief message attached to the channel face of a shelf), advertising pads

Photo by Keith J. Tuckwell

FIGURE 13.12

Product displays with advertising materials have a positive impact on brand sales at point of purchase.

or tear pads (tear-off sheets that explain the details of the promotion), and display shippers (shipping cases that convert to display bins or stands when opened).

The use of such displays and materials is at the discretion of the retailers whose space they occupy. The role of the manufacturer's sales representative is to convince the retailer of the merits of using the display. Retailers usually have an abundance of manufacturer's display material to choose from, so they can be selective. A good display, properly positioned in a high-traffic area, will have a positive impact on the sale of the brand. Refer to the illustration in Figure 13.12.

TRADE SHOWS

Manufacturers often introduce new products or advertising campaigns to their dealer network and the public at trade shows. **Trade shows** are exhibitions organized so that companies in a specific industry can showcase and demonstrate their latest products and services. There are, for example, toy shows, automobile shows, home shows, and boat shows, among many others.

The unique benefit of a trade show is that it allows buyers and other decision makers to come to a central location to secure the most recent product information from suppliers. For retailers and manufacturers, it is an important opportunity to develop a prospect list that the salesforce can follow up on. Thus, participants compete for visitors' attention at the show and usually invest considerable sums to build unique and enticing display exhibits.

The Home Depot sees great value in trade shows. According to Pat Wilkinson, director of marketing for the company, "Trade shows are a key piece of a larger integrated marketing program. It is an interactive way of talking to customers outside the store." Enhancing the home in the age of cocooning is a trend that The Home Depot is tapping into. The Home Depot is also a large sponsor and advertiser on various decorating and home renovation shows on the HGTV network. Such shows are now quite popular, and they reach The Home Depot's customers.[10]

BRANDED PROMOTION MERCHANDISE

The branded promotion merchandise industry is big business; in Canada it is a $3.5 billion industry.[11] **Branded promotion merchandise** is defined as useful or decorative products featuring an organization's logo or brand mark that are distributed to existing customers and prospects in appreciation for their business and their loyalty. As a promotional vehicle, branded promotion merchandise can be used in both consumer and trade programs. There are limitless ways to use this merchandise; some popular uses include business gifts, free goods at orientation programs, components of a corporate communications program or incentive program, and giveaways at trade shows.[12] In Canada, the most widely used promotional item is apparel, followed by writing instruments, drink containers, and calendars. Refer to the image in Figure 13.13.

The value of branded promotion merchandise escalates when properly integrated into a marketing communications plan. Such merchandise is effective in building brand awareness and loyalty among trade customers. Promotional product advertising has proven to be effective because of its unobtrusive, targeted, and personalized approach. Promotional products tend to be kept and used, leading to voluntary repeat exposure, recognition, and retention of the advertiser's name or message. Buyers in business-to-business markets and business-to-consumer markets like to receive branded merchandise. Marketers see the value in branded promotion. Offering such merchandise creates a brand experience that can be more effective than advertising, particularly if the objective deals with building a brand's image.

FIGURE 13.13

Branded merchandise is effective for achieving awareness and loyalty objectives.

Sales Promotions and Media Strategy

Commitment to a sales promotion plan requires commitment to media advertising support. For any consumer promotion to have a chance, the target market must be made aware of the activity and the specific details of the promotion offer. Usually, a media mix is required to achieve the communications objectives of a promotion plan, and the budget is spent in a concentrated period to generate high levels of awareness for the promotion. For complex promotions such as contests, a well-balanced media mix is required. For example, think of all the ads you see for Tim Hortons's "Roll Up the Rim" promotion each year. For a short period they're everywhere! For a premium offer, free sample, or coupon, the marketer can be more selective.

BROADCAST MEDIA

To create awareness and encourage consumers to respond quickly is largely the responsibility of television and radio. High-impact advertising in a short period (a blitz campaign) is quite common. In the case of a contest promotion, television and radio can create excitement and convey a sense of urgency (to get consumers to take advantage of the offer—*now!*). As well, television and radio can direct consumers to websites where more detailed information about the promotion is available.

PRINT MEDIA

Various combinations of print media are used to create awareness and, more importantly, to communicate essential details of the promotion offer. Consumers are conditioned to look for details at point of purchase, so this medium is a must for contests and other offers.

ONLINE MEDIA

More and more brands promote online contests as a means of driving traffic to their websites. As well, broadcast and print media encourage potential participants to visit the website for contest details and to register in the contest. Online communications help create excitement for a contest and provide a convenient means of communicating complex details such as contest rules and regulations.

Social media also plays a key role in building awareness and interest in a promotion. Sponsored posts on Facebook, mentions on Twitter, and visual images on Instagram encourage sharing among friends and additional exposure for the promotion.

To demonstrate how a promotion may be integrated into a larger marketing campaign, consider a recent effort by Campbell's Soup. Campbell's revamped its ready-to-serve soup lines with new packaging, reformulations of long-standing brands, and the introduction of new varieties; refer to the illustration in Figure 13.14. A multimedia campaign introduced all of the changes to consumers. To encourage immediate purchases, a contest promotion was added to the mix with prizes appealing to family interests—vacations were the main prize. To create awareness and excitement for the contest a combination of media advertising, in-store display materials, coupons, and social media were used. The promotion was called "Look Under the Lid."

Marketers must also take appropriate action to notify the trade customer. As discussed earlier in this chapter, consumer promotion and trade promotion activity (the combination of pull and push) is often integrated into a complete plan to maximize impact on and response from both customer groups—consumers and distributors. Therefore, sales representatives must have proper sales aids (literature and display material) so that more effective presentations can be made to distributors. These presentations should provide promotion details and encourage retailers to build inventories and participate in display activities to derive maximum benefit from the promotion.

Photo by Keith Tuckwell

FIGURE 13.14

Campbell's relaunched its ready-to-serve soup lines with new packaging, reformulated products, and a multimedia and sales promotion campaign.

Sales Promotion Integration with Marketing Communications

Sales promotion activity is not usually the focal point of a brand's marketing strategy. In most cases, it is used to supplement regular brand advertising. Regardless of the promotional direction the company or brand takes, it must ensure that the strategies employed are integrated with other marketing communications strategies so that synergy is created and objectives are achieved. Strategic decisions must be made on the frequency of promotions, the impact the promotion will have on brand image, and the way the promotion will build brand equity.

FREQUENCY OF PROMOTION ACTIVITY

How frequently an activity should be used depends on the type of activity and the consumer purchase cycle for that particular product. Once a year is usually adequate to generate excitement for a brand (a contest might be used in peak season to counter competitive activity or during a traditionally low season to stimulate incremental volume). In general, coupon activity can be implemented much more frequently than cash refunds, premium offers, and contests and is less disruptive to the regular sales message.

BRAND IMAGE AND PROMOTIONS

Much of the discussion about promotion strategies in this chapter mentioned lowering prices so that consumers get a better deal. In the short run, such a strategy brings positive results. However, if this practice becomes frequent, consumers will perceive the sale price to be more of a regular price. In the long term, such a practice will hurt the brand's image and will lower profit margins. Domestic automobile manufacturers are facing this dilemma right now. Advertising is so focused on rebates and low financing packages that much less time is devoted to building an image, the former priority of these companies.

BUILDING BRAND EQUITY

The cumulative force of all marketing communications is a key factor in building brand equity. Marketers must be aware that sales promotions are a rather chaotic sequence of deals and events that create noise in the marketplace. They are not a sustainable message. It is preferable to adopt a view about promotions that will pay attention to long-term brand values and a consistent approach that will build good relationships with trade partners and consumers. A few of the promotions mentioned in this chapter do just that. Among them are Tim Hortons's "Roll Up the Rim to Win" and Canadian Tire's reward money. Promotions like these become a positive part of the brand's heritage and reinforce relationships with customers.

The overall objective of sales promotion is to increase a product's sales in the short term. Numerous examples have been provided in the chapter to show how various promotions have an impact on sales. To be successful, a promotion plan must be integrated—consumer and trade promotions must work together to achieve common objectives. As well, various forms of advertising must be considered to raise awareness and interest in the sales promotion activity.

For an applied illustration that integrates consumer and trade promotion strategies with other communications strategies, see the marketing communications plan that appears in Appendix I.

SUMMARY

The advertising manager must consider the impact that sales promotion activity will have on the achievement of marketing objectives, so a sales promotion plan is often developed concurrently with the advertising plan. Sales promotion activities are designed to encourage immediate purchase response by consumers and distributors. In comparison to media advertising, where the objective is to build an image, sales promotion encourages action immediately. There are two categories of sales promotion activity: consumer promotions and trade promotions.

Consumer promotions are designed to pull the product through the channel of distribution. Specific objectives are to achieve trial purchase by new users and to achieve repeat and multiple purchases by current users. The types of activities commonly used to achieve these objectives include coupons, cash refunds, samples, contests, premium offers, loyalty (frequent-buyer) promotions, and delayed payment incentives.

Each type of promotion is suited for certain objectives. Coupons, for example, are good at encouraging trial and repeat purchases, depending on the method of distribution. Samples are effective for trial purchase and are appropriate for use when launching a new product. Refunds, premiums, and contests are better suited for maintaining loyalty and are more commonly used by brands in the mature stage of the product life cycle.

Trade promotions are designed to help push the product through the channel of distribution. Specific marketing objectives are to secure listings and distribution, build volume on a preplanned cyclical basis, and achieve merchandising support from distributors. Trade promotion activities that help achieve these objectives include trade allowances, performance allowances, cooperative advertising, retail in-ad coupons, dealer premiums, point-of-purchase display materials, collateral materials, and trade shows. Branded promotion merchandise is a type of promotion that straddles both consumer and trade promotion. Small items emblazoned with brand logos are given away and are popular with recipients.

Sales promotion has traditionally been regarded as a supplemental activity that supports regular product advertising, but the results are more effective when activities are planned and implemented as part of an integrated marketing communications effort. When planning promotions, the manager must guard against running them too frequently so as not to harm the image of the product. Promotions that are implemented should complement the existing image of the product. From a media strategy perspective, a combination of broadcast, print, online advertising, and social media communications are recommended as the means of creating awareness and communicating the details of the promotion offer.

KEY TERMS

ad pad 395
branded promotion merchandise 403
cash refund 395
collateral material 401
consumer promotion 383
contest 391
cooperative advertising allowance 400
coupon 386
cross-coupon (cross-ruff) 387
cross-sampling 390
dealer-display advertising 401
dealer premium 401
delayed payment incentive 399
free-standing insert (FSI) 386
frequent-buyer (loyalty) program 397
game (instant win) 393
media-delivered coupon 386
performance allowance 400
point-of-purchase advertising 401
premium 396
pull strategy 384
push strategy 384
rebate 395
redemption rate 388
retail in-ad coupon 401
sales promotion 383
sample 389
slippage 395
sweepstakes 391
trade allowance 400
trade promotion 383
trade show 402

REVIEW QUESTIONS

1. What are the objectives of consumer promotion and trade promotion activities?
2. Explain the difference between a pull promotion strategy and a push promotion strategy.
3. What types of coupon distribution are appropriate for the early stages of the product life cycle? For the later stages? What is the relationship between the method of coupon distribution and a promotion's objectives?
4. What are the major reasons that marketing firms use coupons?
5. What benefits come from a manufacturer's implementation of a free sample promotion offer?
6. What elements contribute to the success of a contest offer?
7. Briefly describe the following consumer promotion terms:
   a) Cross-ruff
   b) Redemption rate
   c) Instantly redeemable coupon
   d) Instant win promotions
   e) Rebate
   f) Delayed payment incentive
   g) Slippage
8. What is the objective of a consumer premium offer, and when is the best time (i.e., stage in the product life cycle) to use a premium offer?
9. Briefly explain the nature of a loyalty (frequent-buyer) program.
10. What is the difference between a trade allowance and a performance allowance?
11. What role does cooperative advertising play in the development of a manufacturer's product?
12. Briefly describe the following trade promotion terms:
    a) Retail in-ad coupon
    b) Dealer premium
    c) Collateral material
    d) Branded promotion merchandise

DISCUSSION QUESTIONS

1. "Spending less advertising money directly with consumers, and more advertising money with the trade, will ultimately harm a brand's consumer franchise." Discuss this statement from the manufacturer's viewpoint.
2. Conduct some secondary research on the Canadian coffee market (or another popular market of your choice—soft drinks, laundry detergent, shampoo, etc.) to determine what brands are the leaders in the market. Assume you are the brand manager for Maxwell House roasted coffee (or a popular brand in the other market you chose). What promotion strategies would you recommend to build brand loyalty, considering your market share and stage in the product life cycle? Be specific, and justify your recommendations.
3. Conduct some secondary research on the role and importance of trade shows. Will trade shows play a more prominent role in the marketing mix and marketing communications mix in the future?

NOTES

1. "Coupon Redemption in Canada; Some Interesting Data," Canadian Deals Association, **www.canadaindealsassociation.com**.
2. "Coupon Fact Sheet 2006," Coupon Industry Association of Canada, **www.couponscanada.org**.
3. Katie Little, "Well-off, Educated, and Tech-Savvy: The New Couponer," CNBC, **www.cnbc.comid46556414**.
4. Julie Landry Laviolette, "Digital Coupons Rise in Popularity," *Miami Herald*, November 14, 2014, **www.miamiherald.com**.
5. Lynn Cook, "CPG Slow to Realign Coupon Programs for Growing Popularity of Digital," Greenwood Group, October 9, 2014, **www.greenwoodg.com/news/item/130-cpg-slow-ro-realign-coupon-programs**.
6. "Effective Sampling Strengthens Brands," *GCI Magazine*, September 3, 2008, **www.gcimagazine.com/businessmarketing/27829704.html**.
7. "Stronger Communities Start with Investing in Places We Play," press release, Kraft Canada, May 4, 2015.
8. Liam Lahey, "Roll Up the Rim a Marketer's Dream," *Yahoo Finance*, February 29, 2012, **http://ca.finance.yahoo.com**.
9. Rebecca Harris, "Loyalty Programs: What's in It for Marketers?" *Marketing*, March 31, 2015, **www.marketingmag.ca**.
10. Marina Strauss, "Home Depot Takes Show on the Road," *The Globe and Mail*, October 3, 2003, p. B10.
11. "Promotional Products Industry Profile," **www.brandalliance.com/documents/IndustryProfile.pdf**.
12. Promotion Resource Group, *Important Trends in Branded Promotion Merchandise: A Survey of Buyers and Recipients*, 2006, 2.

CHAPTER 14

Public Relations and Experiential Marketing

© Jonny White/Alamy Stock Photo

Learning Objectives

After studying this chapter, you will be able to

1. Identify the role of public relations, experiential marketing, and event marketing and sponsorships in achieving organizational objectives
2. Describe the various types of public relations activities
3. Identify the steps involved in the public relations planning process
4. Assess the usefulness of a variety of public relations tools
5. Evaluate public relations, experiential marketing, event marketing, and sponsorships as a communications medium
6. Identify the unique considerations involved in the planning and evaluation of event marketing programs

For quite a long time, many organizations considered public relations as an afterthought—something a company got involved with when it faced bad times. It was perceived as a reaction-oriented tactical vehicle for correcting problems that cropped up. How the times have changed! In the age of heightened competition, advancing digital technology, and the lightening speed at which news travels, organizations will employ any form of communications, including public relations, as a means of building and protecting brand or company image.

Given that consumers' media habits are constantly changing, relying on any one medium or a few media could be harmful to a brand or company. An organization must embrace all communications channels and devise an integrated communications strategy to build better relations with customers and to achieve business objectives. Public relations will play a key role in this communications strategy.

Experiential marketing, a form of marketing that includes event marketing and sponsorships, is also growing in importance. Experiential marketing focuses on giving target market customers a brand-relevant experience that adds value to their lives. It involves effective two-way interaction between marketers and consumers on a more personal basis. When consumers are involved with a brand experience or are participating in an event that a brand sponsors, they are actively engaged with the brand, and that engagement can trigger effective word-of-mouth messaging about the brand. This chapter explores the role of public relations and experiential marketing in the marketing communications mix.

Defining Public Relations

Public relations (PR) is defined as "the strategic management of relationships between an organization and its diverse publics, through the use of communication, to achieve mutual understanding, realize organizational goals, and serve the public interest."[1] The word *public* is a crucial aspect of the definition.

The practice of public relations is used to build rapport with the various publics a company, individual, or organization may have. These publics are either internal or external. **Internal publics** are those with whom an organization communicates regularly—employers, distributors, suppliers, shareholders, and customers. **External publics** are more distant and are communicated with less frequently. They include the media, governments, prospective shareholders, the financial community, and community organizations. A good public relations plan involves an open, honest, and constructive relationship with these publics.

Before we proceed with the discussion about public relations, some basic differences between advertising and public relations should be introduced. Essentially, advertising is *paid media* in which message content is controlled or planned by an organization. In contrast, public relations messages are typically unpaid and the media determines the message regardless of what information is supplied by an organization. The media act as a filter for the information a company releases.

Public relations communications are referred to as *earned media*—the quality and importance of the message determines the extent of media coverage. In other words, the story earns its position in the media. In the digital era, people share stories they find interesting with others on social sites such as Facebook, Twitter, and YouTube, a concept referred to as *shared media*. Public relations messages that appear in the news media or in social media offer legitimacy that advertising does not have.

The Role of Public Relations

The role of public relations is varied but generally falls into six key areas: corporate public relations, reputation management, publicity generation, the development of product placement and branded content opportunities, community relations building, and fund-raising (as undertaken by not-for-profit organizations).

CORPORATE PUBLIC RELATIONS

As suggested earlier, public relations can play a vital role in building and protecting the image of a company. A smart company today takes a proactive stance and communicates loudly and clearly the good things it is doing. For example, a company may communicate with its publics in the form of **corporate advertising**. Corporate advertising shows how the resources of an organization can resolve problems by promoting goodwill or demonstrating a sense of social responsibility. A recent study by global PR firm Edelman shows that Canadians support brands that have a high societal purpose associated with them. In fact, 70 percent of Canadians are more likely to recommend a brand that supports a good cause than one that doesn't.[2]

These kinds of messages can be delivered to the public by paid advertising or through public relations. If a company chooses to advertise, it will do so through corporate advertising. Corporate advertising is a form of paid communication that undertakes the task of creating a positive attitude and goodwill toward a company. Corporate advertising does not sell a product but, since the objective is to enhance the image of a company, there could be some long-term and indirect effect on sales. The direct influence of corporate advertising is difficult to measure. Figure 14.1 shows an example of corporate advertising.

REPUTATION MANAGEMENT

Public relations is also a vital form of communication for a company during a crisis. It simply makes good business sense to invest in a program that will protect a reputation that takes years to build and only seconds to lose. A recent survey among Canadians revealed that opinions form quickly when things go wrong for an organization or high-profile individual, and once they are formed they don't tend to change much. From the survey, 61 percent of respondents form an opinion in one day; 92 percent within a week—a true reflection of how 24/7 news coverage and social media exposure has an impact.[3] This particular study looked at several big PR stories from 2013 and assessed how an organization's response influenced public opinion of the organization as a whole. Among the stories were Rob Ford's admission to smoking crack cocaine, lululemon's yoga pants recall (which involved controversial comments about women by its CEO), and BlackBerry's financial losses and layoffs.

How a company manages its public relations during a crisis often influences the final outcome in the public's mind. Do a poor job, and you will suffer the consequences of an unruly public. Punishment can be financially damaging. To demonstrate, consider a recent situation facing Hyundai Motor Co., makers of Hyundai and Kia automobiles. To influence customers to buy its cars, the company used incorrect fuel economy

FIGURE 14.1

An example of corporate advertising

Courtesy of Suncor

numbers on new models. Its comparisons with similar competing automobiles were misleading. Fuel economy is important to many buyers, and when combined with a lower price tag compared to competitor models it was a powerful combination to motivate purchases.

The misleading information undermined the progressive technology positioning strategy that Hyundai was promoting. When caught, the company took appropriate action. Senior executives offered a sincere apology and stated they were committed to making sure the owners of every affected automobile were financially compensated. Through a prepaid credit card, owners were reimbursed for the fuel value of the difference in the combined fuel consumption rating, plus 15 percent.[4] There were more severe financial consequences. The US government fined the company $100 million for violating its Clean Air Act. In announcing the fine, the government stated, "Businesses who play by the rules shouldn't have to compete with those breaking the law."[5]

Early in 2013, the Joe Fresh brand of clothing and its parent company, Loblaw, had to deal with the fallout from the collapse of a Bangladesh garment factory that manufactured its product. With a death toll of over 1100, media coverage of Joe Fresh's connection with the event was constant after the disaster. The Joe Fresh image as a family-friendly brand—good quality at reasonable prices—took a beating once the disaster and connection to exploited workers were exposed. Many Canadians didn't feel good about purchasing or wearing the clothing.

Part of the PR plan to defuse the situation involved sending high-level executives to Bangladesh to explore the circumstances and figure out a way to prevent similar events from occurring in the future. As well, a strong leader, willing to be visible on all issues, is essential. Loblaw chair Galen Weston was front and centre in dealing with the situation. When an organization must react to negative news, it only has one opportunity to get the response right and an extremely short timeframe in which to do it. Therefore, some strategic planning in advance to ensure an organization is ready is crucial. Some important tips on how an organization should handle a crisis situation are included in Figure 14.2.

An organization's leader must be trained to handle the barrage of reporters when he or she is placed in the media spotlight—glaring lights and reporter scrums can be intimidating. Leaders must be prepared to act quickly and show that they have control of the situation. Company presidents and high-level executives must also meet the demands of a more sophisticated and more demanding consumer audience—or suffer the consequences of their wrath.

How well an organization manages a crisis situation has a direct impact on how the public perceives the outcome. Here are some vital tips to ensure effective communications with the public:

TAKE RESPONSIBILITY

If your name is on the problem, take responsibility for it. This is different than accepting blame. The public respects an organization that accepts responsibility.

ONE INDIVIDUAL MUST ASSUME A LEADERSHIP ROLE

People want strong leadership, and to have a sense that decision makers are in charge and have a plan. A strong leader will provide consistency and amplify the essence of the message when necessary.

PEOPLE NEED MORE THAN INFORMATION

They need moral support, a human touch, and a single face with whom to identify and on whom to pin their hopes of recovery.

EMBRACE THE THREE FUNDAMENTALS OF CRISIS COMMUNICATION

- Communicate very clearly what was going wrong
- Communicate what you are doing about it
- Communicate the steps you are taking to ensure it doesn't happen again

REASSURE AND MOVE FORWARD

Once the issue has been contained, advise the public that you are open for business again. The message must offer reassurance and provide proof that appropriate actions have been taken. If the public is satisfied with your efforts, they will forgive you and move on.

FIGURE 14.2

PR tips for handling crisis situations

Sources: Adapted from David Menzies, "Silence Ain't Golden: Media Crisis Dos and Don'ts," *Marketing*, August 1/8, 2005, p. 18; and David Weiner, "The SARS Crisis: Lessons Learned," A public relations advertising feature, *Marketing*, 2003.

PRODUCT PUBLICITY

A primary objective of public relations is to generate news about a product or service that a company is marketing. **Publicity** is news about a product, service, or idea that appears in the print or broadcast media. Essentially, publicity must be newsworthy; what may seem like news to a company may not be news to the media. Newsworthy information includes launching a new product, revealing new information based on research evidence (i.e., a discovery), securing a significant contract that will generate new jobs, or achieving significant sales and profit results.

The traditional means of communicating newsworthy information is to issue a press release or invite the press to a press conference (these tools are discussed in the next section). Information is carefully prepared and distributed to the media in such a way that editors are tempted to run all or parts of the story.

Organizations now directly engage consumers through original content they and their agencies are creating. Automotive companies still use automotive journalists to test drive and report on their new models; automotive magazines and sections of daily newspapers remain a viable means of communication. However, major companies now create their own video content and post it on their website, on YouTube, and in other social media outlets. In doing so, they reach "a wider and more diverse audience than just newspaper or magazine readers." The online audience is there for a reason—they want the content and are expressing interest in the product.[6]

To demonstrate how publicity works, here's a specific example—perhaps an example that breaks all the records for publicity generation. Red Bull planned Felix Baumgartner's jump from the edge of space (a 39 kilometre jump) as millions of people watched online. You were literally right there with him. He shattered the sound barrier and landed safely nine minutes later. Red Bull immediately posted a picture on Facebook of him kneeling on the ground. It generated 216 000 likes, 10 000 comments, and 29 000 shares in 40 minutes. Some 40 television stations in 50 countries carried the live feed, and there were 8 million simultaneous views of a YouTube live stream. These are incredible numbers. One Red Bull fan wrote: "Red Bull gives you wings [Red Bull's advertising slogan]. Debate closed on all fronts." You can judge whether this publicity had an impact on Red Bull's sales.

PRODUCT PLACEMENT, BRANDED CONTENT, AND PRODUCT SEEDING

Product placement is the insertion of brand logos or branded merchandise into movies, television shows, and video games for clear brand exposure. Television viewers these days pay less attention to commercials, so networks and producers of shows have to find new ways to deliver brand messages. Companies that use the product placement strategy believe that products featured in shows have more credibility with viewers and have a better chance of being noticed and remembered. Certainly, the message can't be skipped or muted.

On *Mad Men*, Don Draper, the show's main character, drinks Canadian Club whisky. The brand appeared in the show from its inception. Every time the brand appeared in a scene, it lent Canadian Club a bit of pop culture cachet. The free publicity caused the brand to alter its advertising strategy for a time to connect the brand's past with its future—new ads showed Dad's brand in a free-wheeling 1960s environment, hoping it would appeal to a new generation of rye drinkers. In a market where sales were flat, Canadian Club's sales increased by 8 percent.[7] Other brands that appeared in the show are too numerous to mention, but among them are Smirnoff Vodka, Jaguar, Coca-Cola,

Honda, Heineken, and Life cereal. Don Draper actually pitched a new slogan for the cereal brand: "Eat Life by the Bowlful."[8]

Branded content takes things a step further by weaving the brand into the storyline of a show, movie, or video game. Essentially, branded content is the fusion of advertising and entertainment. Tim Hortons received a boost of celebrity publicity when a fictitious donut (a chocolate Timbit stuffed into a strawberry-vanilla donut) was integrated into the popular sitcom *How I Met Your Mother*. The episode featured famous Canadians, including Jason Priestly, Alex Trebek, and Paul Shaffer (David Letterman's band leader). All of the celebrities mentioned Tim Hortons by name. This is the kind of publicity most brands dream of!

Once it aired, people started tweeting about it and consumers started asking for a Priestly in Tim Hortons outlets. That's when the PR machine kicked into action. Chefs re-created the donut and sent pictures out on Facebook and Twitter. To keep the conversation going, a contest was devised that invited Canadians to submit their own donut flavour inventions via social media. More than 60 000 submissions poured in. Jason Priestly was hired as one of the judges to narrow down the list of finalists. The winning flavour as voted by the public would be sold in Tim Hortons outlets.[9]

The extent to which a brand can and should be integrated into a show is a controversial issue. If there's too much of it, it could turn the viewer off—they see enough commercials already! Thus far, consumers aren't objecting to content integration. Rather, the reaction has been somewhat positive. Apparently, showing cast members doing things with real products or talking about them makes the show more real.

Product seeding involves giving a product free to trendsetters who, in turn, influence others to become aware of the product and, perhaps, purchase the product. Trendsetters create buzz by chatting about the product whenever the opportunity arises—they act as ambassadors for the brand. Marketers can take advantage of their knowledge and their access to consumers, a concept referred to as **word-of-mouth marketing**.

The fact that the product is in the hands of a trendsetter helps create buzz for the brand. For this reason, product seeding is often referred to as **buzz marketing**, though buzz marketing can mean a lot of other things as well. Product seeding campaigns are often implemented just prior to the launch of a new product—the objective being to create some buzz before the launch. There are several advantages to product seeding programs. First, it is a low-cost strategy; the only costs are those of the product given away. Second, product seeding campaigns reach a narrowly defined target. The primary disadvantage relates directly to the product. If it does not meet the expectations of the influencers, they will inform other consumers. Word of mouth can backfire on the brand.

COMMUNITY RELATIONS

In an era of social responsibility, companies are placing high value on programs that foster a good public image in the communities in which they operate. Many companies encourage their employees to give back to the community; some even provide a few hours of work time each week for volunteer involvement. Community relations officers of large organizations arrange community events and often provide funds or other resources to sponsor community events and teams. It's all part of being a good corporate citizen.

Scotiabank is an excellent example of a community-minded company. Among its community initiatives are the Scotiabank Team Community Program and the Scotiabank Employee Volunteer Program. In the Team Community Program, the bank matches funds raised by employee teams (to a maximum of $15 000) that support local causes or groups. In the volunteer program, the bank will offer $1000 to qualifying community-based organizations where employees or retirees volunteered for at least 50 hours a year.

Scotiabank is also actively involved in sponsoring community hockey programs. All branches offer financial support for a local team, league, or association in their community.[10]

FUNDRAISING

Public relations can play a key role in the marketing mix in the not-for-profit sector. Fundraising, for example, relies heavily on public relations. A national organization like the United Way or Salvation Army faces a huge challenge each year. Some people perceive the organization to be a big "money hole" and wonder where all of the donations go. To change this perception, public relations is used to educate the public about how the funds are used, and therefore predispose people to give, solicit commitment, and make people feel good about giving. The goal of fundraising campaigns for the United Way or the Salvation Army is to create a positive image and secure support by sending the public a message that clearly states what the organization is all about. Refer to Figure 14.3 for an illustration.

FIGURE 14.3

A public service announcement with an emotional message encourages understanding and helps raise funds for the Salvation Army.

Courtesy of The Salvation Army and Grey Canada. Photographer: Shanghoon represented by Westside Studio

Public Relations Planning

Public relations should be as closely linked to a company's bottom line as a financial plan or a marketing plan is. Strategic communications planning should be based on the business challenges that lie ahead, marketing needs and strategies, and corporate vision. Any plan that is based on these characteristics must also include a comprehensive public relations program.

Many planners now believe public relations should take the lead in marketing communications campaigns. For certain, public relations practitioners have lead the way in terms of adapting to new technologies and employing new tools to generate better results for organizations. Public relations is a practice that has always thought quickly and acted fast, and as such it is ideally suited for a leading role in the social media era.

The nature of a public relations plan is dictated by the situation at hand. Will it be a proactive plan that can be carefully set out in advance and implemented with precision? Or will it be a reactive plan that is being undertaken only because of some unforeseen circumstance occurring? A public relations plan usually involves five steps: analyzing a situation, establishing objectives, devising a strategy, executing the plan, and evaluating the result. Essentially, the process is very similar to developing an advertising plan, though the tools used and the timeframe can be quite different.

SITUATION ANALYSIS

Before any plan can be devised, a **situation analysis** is conducted to reveal the true nature of the problem to be resolved or the opportunity to be pursued. Clarification is crucial, because a good communications strategy has to be focused if it is to be successful. For example, specific plans may be needed to resolve a crisis situation, launch a new product, or announce company expansion plans or financial results.

ESTABLISHING OBJECTIVES

Public relations objectives must relate specifically to the achievement of marketing objectives. Typically, marketing objectives relate to achieving specific sales, profit, and market share goals. Objectives for launching new products are stated in terms of generating awareness and trial purchase among the target audience over a period of time. For established products, marketing objectives are stated in terms of increasing use among current users. Regardless of the situation or desired outcome, public relations objectives tend to be similar to advertising objectives, because the two disciplines work hand in hand toward a common goal.

Realistic expectations of public relations should be stated in terms of what it can influence. Therefore, objectives such as building recognition, creating a positive image, introducing new products, and engaging consumers with a brand fall within the realm of a public relations plan.

When launching new products, public relations can play a key role. Apple is a master at applying public relations strategies for its new products. Typically the launch is shrouded in secrecy with just enough leaked information (planned PR information) to stir up the rumour mill about what the new product might be—think iPhone, iPad, and so on. There is so much buzz created on social media that there is a pent-up demand. When the product is finally made available, people line up to get it. "Sales exceeded expectations and we couldn't be happier," said CEO Tim Cook of the launch of iPhone 6 and iPhone 6 Plus.[11] There were 4 million preorders in the first 24 hours of availability and a total of 10 million units sold on opening weekend. Refer to the image in Figure 14.4.

FIGURE 14.4

Public relations strategies help create buzz for the launch of new Apple products.

© Justin Sullivan/Getty Images

Publicity objectives can be more sharply focused on a specific task and be quantitative. Publicity objectives should take into account the media through which the message will be transmitted and the target audience they will reach. No matter how targeted an audience might or might not be (in marketing terms), chances are they will be reached by the mass media (e.g., in a news story on television, or a story in a general interest magazine or daily newspaper). If so, gross audience objectives (number of impressions) can be established.

To demonstrate the concept of gross impressions, consider the case of Smirnoff Vodka when it launched a new package and label design in an attempt to attract younger drinkers. A half-page article about the introduction and a picture of the new package design appeared in the *Toronto Star* (the result of a sound public relations plan). At the time, the *Star*'s weekday circulation was 440 000 copies. That figure represents the potential minimum number of impressions the Smirnoff article will achieve. Undoubtedly, a similar article appeared in many other newspapers across Canada.

DEVELOPING THE PUBLIC RELATIONS STRATEGY

Similar to a marketing strategy or an advertising strategy, a public relations strategy considers a common set of variables that include the target market, geographic location, seasonal considerations, and timing. As well, a decision must be made on the most efficient and effective way to reach consumers and cause them to act. A specific task is assigned to public relations (and other communications disciplines) so that the combined efforts are mutually reinforcing and so that all audiences receive the same message.

Strategy deals primarily with how the plan will be implemented. In the case of a new product introduction, for example, public relations may be the initial contact point for consumers and trade customers. The role of public relations is to reach those parties who have the power to influence behaviour, including industry analysts, key media, and consumers classified as innovators and early adopters. The strategic role of public relations should be examined in terms of how well it can do the following:

- Reach opinion leaders (professionals, analysts, trade audiences, and influential media) well in advance of the general public.
- Maximize the news value of new product introductions, new advertising campaigns, and event sponsorships. Messages must be written creatively and visuals must grab attention.
- Time the public relations events to reinforce advertising and sales promotion campaigns and maintain high visibility between campaigns.
- Reach demographic, psychographic, or geographic markets that might not be targeted by advertising.[12]

Strategically, the PR message has to be different from the advertising message. With public relations it's about information and education rather than unique selling points and fancy slogans. Therefore, any claim made in a press release must be substantiated with factual information (e.g., citing consumer research data that confirms a claim or point of view, or explaining an issue thoroughly and accurately).

For publicity-oriented campaigns, product news can be dramatized easily. Without drama and fanfare, the press release will wind up in some editor's recycling box or email trash bin. For the launch of the iPhone 6 and iPhone 6 Plus, Apple focused on two new product benefits—the phones were larger and lighter than previous models. An interesting story can be built around these benefits!

Another option is to employ a **borrowed-interest strategy** to spark interest among editors. A borrowed-interest strategy promotes a newsworthy activity that is related to the product. For example, a product or company is sponsoring an event, or a new contest promotion with a big prize is about to hit the market. Canadian Tire put considerable time and energy into its "We All Play for Canada" initiative. The program was launched with an eight-year sponsorship agreement with the Canadian Olympic Association and partnerships with six other amateur sport groups. Canadian Tire sees the program as a rallying cry to bring back "play" in Canada. It wants Canadian children to be more active, because a country without strong children can't stay strong. The program is designed to foster an emotional

FIGURE 14.5
Canadian Tire uses a borrowed-interest strategy to foster an emotional connection with its customers.

connection between Canadian Tire and its customers and, of course, it presents opportunities to market its play products.[13] Refer to the image (retired creative) in Figure 14.5.

EXECUTING THE PLAN

Executing the plan involves the specific actions and activities that will be used to achieve objectives. In other words, the directives provided in the strategy section of the plan are translated into action plans. The plan will specify what activities will occur, who will perform them, when they will occur, and at what cost. The timing and costs of all activities should be integrated into the marketing plan. The importance of executing details cannot be overemphasized. All things being equal, it is how the information is presented that could differentiate one brand from another. It can make a difference!

To get the message out, public relations has many options, some of which were mentioned earlier in the chapter. The PR arsenal includes press releases, press conferences, annual reports, websites, and social media. These tools are discussed in more detail in the next section of the chapter.

For some specific insight into the role public relations can play in a marketing communications campaign, read the Advertising in Action vignette **Apple's Secret: Good PR**.

EVALUATING EFFECTIVENESS

Like other forms of communication, public relations activities are evaluated through a variety of research methods that can be either qualitative or quantitative. In some way, results achieved should be compared with the objectives that were originally established for the program. There must be an increase in awareness, a change in behaviour, or some kind of financial return. Ketchum Public Relations, a leading international PR agency, has identified three levels for measuring effectiveness: outputs, outcomes, and business results:[14]

ADVERTISING IN ACTION

Apple's Secret: Good PR

Take a moment to think about how you first learned about Apple's latest new product—say the iPhone 6 and iPhone 6 Plus. Chances are you heard about it on social media but knew very little about it. As time passed, more information became available—perhaps a sneak preview of what the product will look like. Regardless, there were lots of bloggers and ordinary people talking about the product.

So the question is, did this situation just happen, or was it part of a master PR plan by Apple to drum up demand for its latest gadget? Apple is the master of PR strategy. By following a few simple techniques, but doing it in such a tantalizing manner, Apple's product launches are always successful.

So what's the plan? First you determine what is newsworthy, and then you leak just enough information on social media to create some buzz. For instance, the iPhone 6 and iPhone 6 Plus were lighter and larger than previous models—features that a story can be built around. Let the rumour mill begin online! A while later journalists and influential bloggers were sent more detailed information and images. Social media exploded with a frenzy of excitement as people shared new information. They couldn't wait to get their hands on the new phone! A big event was held for the launch, where the CEO officially introduced the new phone—the cameras started flashing and photos and stories were placed everywhere. On opening weekend, 10 million iPhone 6 phones were sold!

Why is this approach so successful? Apple adheres to a few basic rules but does so in a sneaky kind of way. It all starts with virtually no information. It's a model of thriftiness. Let the media speculate on what the new product will look like, how it will be different, how it will perform, and so on. This is publicity on steroids, because it's Apple behind everything! When Apple announces something big is coming down the pipe, it rattles the bones of social media. As additional information is released and timelines fall into place, more stories will appear in print media, in online blogs, and in television news broadcasts. Industry analysts will debate the potential merits. It's a gradual build leading up to the big day. The strategy is so successful, competitors don't dare copy it; they just couldn't pull it off the way Apple does!

Once the initial launch is over, Apple embarks on a traditional-style multimedia advertising campaign. Television delivers a simple message but on an emotional level, and print ads in both consumer and business publications deliver important product information in a rational manner—a great combination! While all this is going on, Apple is working on the next great gadget.

© Sean Gallup/Getty Images

- ***Outputs*** measure reach, frequency, visits, tone of message, prominence, and the inclusion of a recommendation or endorsement.
- ***Outcomes*** measure attitude and behaviour change and consider factors such as awareness, comprehension, recognition, credibility, image change, and purchase intentions. Surveys may be required to collect data.
- ***Business results*** are estimated by analytic techniques or from data collected in surveys. Typical measures include sales revenue, new clients secured, market share, purchase intentions, brand value, and reputation value.

Outputs are a measure of exposure, and companies like to know how much exposure was actually received as a result of its public relations activities. This is referred to as **content analysis**. There are organizations that keep track of content. They record what is being reported, where, to how many people, over what period of time, in which media, and how the coverage changes over time.

On social media there is an abundance of analytical information available to measure results of a campaign. Such measures include visits, likes, followers, and the number of active advocates a brand or company may have. Going a step further, an organization can get a feel for the sentiments held by people based on their comments and the general degree of audience engagement.

The Canadian Public Relations Society uses a tool called the Media Relations Rating Point System (MRP) that considers criteria such as type of media, whether a photograph was published in colour or black and white, the tone of the message, or whether a spokesperson was quoted. The MRP template assigns points for things like editorial tone (more points for positive coverage, less for negative). In some ways this system starts to measure return on investment. For more insight into how it works, refer to Figure 14.6.

To illustrate *outcome* measurement, assume the objective was to alter the public's perception about a company (e.g., building a better public image), a focus group could be used before and after the campaign is implemented. Any shifts in attitudes and opinions in the post-campaign group would determine the relative effectiveness of the campaign. Alternatively, a short survey before and after the campaign could measure its effectiveness.

FIGURE 14.6

An illustration of a public relations ratings system

Measuring public relations activity is difficult. This illustration is intended to demonstrate a standardized means of tracking the effectiveness of public relations programs.

The Canadian Public Relations Society (CPRS) recommends that an organization look at the *tone* of the message that appears in the media and then measure the message against a predetermined *list of criteria*. If meaningful criteria have been established, the results can be measured.

The CPRS recommends a 10-point rating system. A maximum of 5 points is awarded for the tone of the piece: positive = 5 points; neutral = 3 points; negative = 0 points. In addition, one point is awarded for each criterion that is met (to a maximum of five criteria).

For this illustration, assume a story was reported in two newspapers and one TV news report. Measuring the articles and report revealed the following results:

	Newspaper 1	Newspaper 2	TV News Report
TONE			
Positive	—	5	5
Neutral	3	—	—
Negative	—	—	—
CRITERIA			
Company/Brand Mention	1	1	1
Photo Included (or Video)	—	1	1
Spokesperson Quote	1	1	—
Prominence/Position	—	1	—
Key Message Delivered	1	1	1
Total Score	**6**	**10**	**8**

Analysis: The article in Newspaper 2 delivered the best results. It delivered exactly what the organization was looking for. For more complete details about this measurement system, refer to the CPRS website, www.cprs.ca.

THE TOOLS OF THE TRADE

The tools available to execute public relations programs are diverse. There are those that are used routinely to communicate newsworthy information and those that are used periodically or on special occasions only. This section discusses those vehicles that are used routinely.

PRESS RELEASES

A **press release** (news release) is a document containing all of the essential elements of the story (who, what, when, where, and why). The release is written in a format that communicates key details early. Copies of the release are mailed to a list of preferred editors, for example those with whom an organization has a good relationship. As well, the release should be distributed to a national wire service and posted on the company's website. Editors receiving the release make quick decisions about what to go with and what to discard. Contact information is always included, should the media require any additional information. A sample news release appears in Figure 14.7.

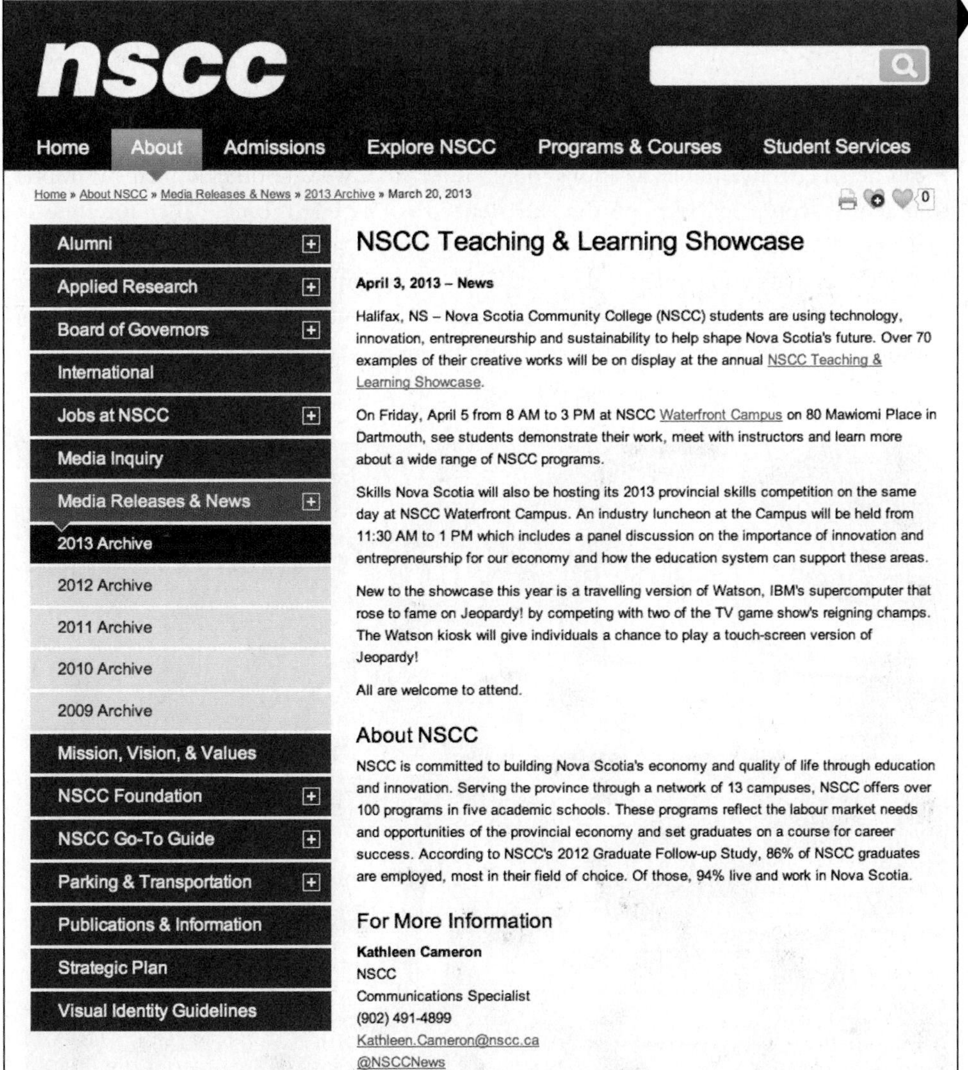

nscc

Home | About | Admissions | Explore NSCC | Programs & Courses | Student Services

Home » About NSCC » Media Releases & News » 2013 Archive » March 20, 2013

- Alumni
- Applied Research
- Board of Governors
- International
- Jobs at NSCC
- Media Inquiry
- Media Releases & News
- 2013 Archive
- 2012 Archive
- 2011 Archive
- 2010 Archive
- 2009 Archive
- Mission, Vision, & Values
- NSCC Foundation
- NSCC Go-To Guide
- Parking & Transportation
- Publications & Information
- Strategic Plan
- Visual Identity Guidelines

NSCC Teaching & Learning Showcase

April 3, 2013 – News

Halifax, NS – Nova Scotia Community College (NSCC) students are using technology, innovation, entrepreneurship and sustainability to help shape Nova Scotia's future. Over 70 examples of their creative works will be on display at the annual NSCC Teaching & Learning Showcase.

On Friday, April 5 from 8 AM to 3 PM at NSCC Waterfront Campus on 80 Mawiomi Place in Dartmouth, see students demonstrate their work, meet with instructors and learn more about a wide range of NSCC programs.

Skills Nova Scotia will also be hosting its 2013 provincial skills competition on the same day at NSCC Waterfront Campus. An industry luncheon at the Campus will be held from 11:30 AM to 1 PM which includes a panel discussion on the importance of innovation and entrepreneurship for our economy and how the education system can support these areas.

New to the showcase this year is a travelling version of Watson, IBM's supercomputer that rose to fame on Jeopardy! by competing with two of the TV game show's reigning champs. The Watson kiosk will give individuals a chance to play a touch-screen version of Jeopardy!

All are welcome to attend.

About NSCC

NSCC is committed to building Nova Scotia's economy and quality of life through education and innovation. Serving the province through a network of 13 campuses, NSCC offers over 100 programs in five academic schools. These programs reflect the labour market needs and opportunities of the provincial economy and set graduates on a course for career success. According to NSCC's 2012 Graduate Follow-up Study, 86% of NSCC graduates are employed, most in their field of choice. Of those, 94% live and work in Nova Scotia.

For More Information

Kathleen Cameron
NSCC
Communications Specialist
(902) 491-4899
Kathleen.Cameron@nscc.ca
@NSCCNews

FIGURE 14.7

A news release distributed to the media and posted on a company website

PRESS CONFERENCES

A **press conference** is a gathering of news reporters invited to witness the release of important information about a company or product. Because the conference is time consuming for the media representatives, it is usually reserved for only the most important announcements. A crisis situation, for example, is usually handled by a press conference. When a professional sports team is about to announce the signing of a star player, a press conference is common. For example, when the Toronto Maple Leafs introduced Mike Babcock (formerly of the Detroit Red Wings) as their new head coach, there was a huge press conference at the Air Canada Centre. Such an important announcement prompted TSN to provide nonstop television coverage of it. Refer to the image in Figure 14.8.

A **press kit** is usually distributed at a conference. The press kit includes a schedule of conference events; a list of company participants, including biographical information; a press release; photographs; copies of speeches; digital material; and any other relevant information. Depending on need, any combination of these materials may be included. The key to developing a good media kit is to evaluate who will use it and what that person is likely to need. For example, the media kit for a new product launch will be very different in tone, style, and content from one needed for a crisis situation.

WEBSITES

Corporate and brand websites are now an integral element of marketing communications. Since the purpose of the website is to communicate information about a company, it can be an effective public relations tool. Visitors to a website quickly form an impression about a company based on the experience they have at the site. Therefore, the site must load quickly and be easy to navigate. Including some kind of entertainment or interactive activity also enhances the visit. The website provides an opportunity to inform the public of an organization's latest happenings. Content can vary from financial information to product information to games and contests. Large companies commonly have

FIGURE 14.8

Press conferences are reserved for important, newsworthy information and announcements.

pages dedicated to specific brands or sales promotions they may be running. All press releases about the company and its brands are linked to the company website, usually in chronological order starting with the newest releases.

SOCIAL MEDIA

Social media comprise the online tools that people use to share content, profiles, opinions, insights, experiences, perspectives, and media itself, thus facilitating conversations and interactions online between groups of people. The emergence of social media has transferred control of the message from the organization to the consumer—the consumer can read the message, formulate an opinion on it, and communicate that opinion to others. Social media has changed communication from monologue (one to many) to dialogue (many to many).

Social media sites have had a significant impact on the way many industries do business, and the impact on PR practitioners has been nothing short of extreme. Furthering the evolution is a shift in the way people relate to news. They don't just read it—they want to interact with it and influence opinions. That explains why many of the most-visited websites are social media sites such as Facebook, YouTube, and Twitter.

Because of the influence of social media, many public relations experts recommend a change in tone and style when delivering company and brand messages. Traditionally, PR messages have been associated with "spin," implying that the organization delivers the message the way it wants. Now, more humility is recommended—organizations need to be as transparent as possible if the goal is to engage the public in the conversation.

Timing is also now a more crucial issue to contend with. Practitioners used to refer to the "Golden 24 hours" they had to prepare and respond to a crisis situation. Now it's called the "Golden hour." Companies have to monitor breaking stories on Twitter that may affect them so that their comments can be offered quickly. To demonstrate the significance of social media, it is now estimated that 50 percent of people have learned about breaking news via social media rather than an official news source.[15]

Social media sites present an opportunity for an organization to post blogs. A **blog** is a frequent, chronological publication of personal thoughts at a website. Blogs are the property and works of people who like to editorialize and, for example, challenge the integrity of an organization. Although an organization cannot control this situation, it must live with the reality that negative things are being said about it. Positive things can also be said, so organizations must network with bloggers and convince them to express positive news about their products. Organizations must recognize that consumer-generated content in a blog carries just as much weight as information presented by corporations and traditional media outlets. "Consumers are in control, and consumers are the media. It's a paradigm shift that's going to change PR forever."[16]

Blogs enable companies to speak directly to consumers, and as a result they are pushing the news media out of their central role in public relations. Many CEOs of large corporations blog; they do so as a means to personalize the structured corporate world they operate in. But, to have an impact and encourage interaction, they must deliver the message in a manner they are unaccustomed to. Since they are speaking directly to the public, they must be more like a journalist. Many companies actively blog today. Advertising in traditional media encourages consumers to follow a company on Facebook, Twitter, Instagram, Pinterest, and other social networks. See Figure 14.9 for an illustration.

Online video-sharing sites are one of the fastest-growing media sectors, with sites such as YouTube attracting millions of visitors daily. Therefore, an organization must evaluate the benefits of broadcasting web videos in the communications mix. A web

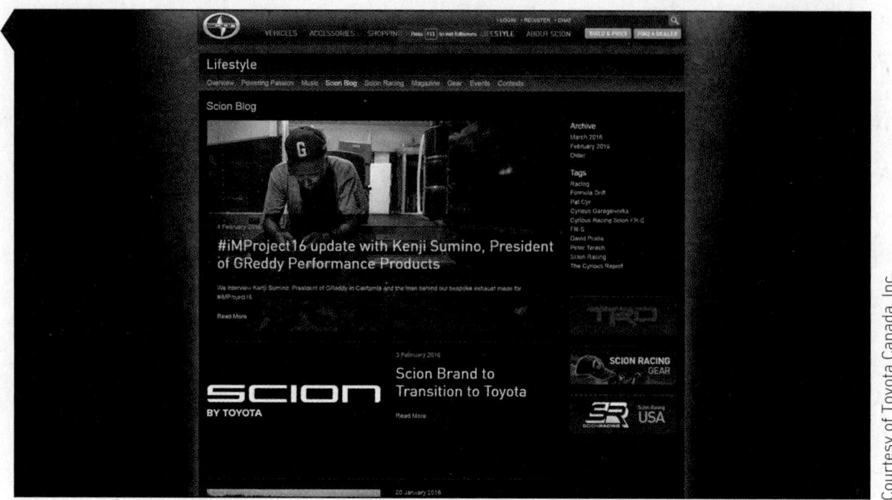

FIGURE 14.9 Companies are using blogs to communicate relevant information about brands to potential customers.

Courtesy of Toyota Canada, Inc.

video is an enticing proposition since production and distribution costs are much lower than creating traditional broadcast material. For smaller businesses that compete with larger businesses, online video helps level the playing field.

Press releases for traditional media were discussed earlier. Social media sites provide an opportunity to communicate more detailed information. A social media news release can include a variety of elements, such as photos and videos, links to blogs, **digital tags**, and RSS feeds.

In summary, social media offers new and innovative ways to help a business achieve its marketing communications objectives. The techniques just described are much less expensive than traditional advertising. When using social media, an organization must consider that some control of the message may be lost. That loss can be weighed against additional exposure and engagement opportunities with potential customers.

ANNUAL REPORTS AND OTHER PUBLICATIONS

The primary purpose of an **annual report**, an annual publication provided by public corporations, is to provide current and prospective investors and stakeholders with financial data and a description of an organization's operations. But the report can do much more to promote the company. It is a good opportunity for the organization to tell the public where the company stands on social and environmental issues, for example. In fact, the annual report is often seen by audiences beyond the primary target—such as the media, community leaders, and employees. Word can spread fast about what a company stands for.

Special interest reports can be integrated into an annual report or can be stand-alone documents. Companies that want to say to the public that there is more to business than a healthy bottom line can issue a special interest report to get a different message out. Special interest reports are designed to appeal to a very selective audience—usually opinion leaders—and focus on issues that affect the organization and the target audience. For example, RBC Financial Group issues a corporate responsibility report each year. The report documents the social responsibility practices of the company and goes a long way in building trust with employees, customers, and clients. The report focuses on issues such as integrity in business and commitment to clients and employees, to diversity, and to the environment. Policies regarding governance, compliance, and ethics are also mentioned.

Public Relations as a Communications Medium

Public relations is only one element in the integrated communications mix, but it can play a key role in specific situations. Those responsible for corporate and brand communications should be aware of the basic benefits and drawbacks of public relations communications.

ADVANTAGES OF PUBLIC RELATIONS

Public relations is often perceived negatively by the consumer—it is associated with terms such as *spin* and *propaganda*. In reality, nothing could be further from the truth. Public relations done properly can be a *credible source of information*. Simply stated, when the message is delivered by an independent third party, such as a journalist or an established blogger (who has influence), the message is delivered more persuasively than any form of advertising. Further, articles appearing in the media are perceived as being more objective than advertisements. With good press coverage, the message is more likely to be believed.

One of the measures of success is PR's impact on business results. A well-planned campaign can *drive up sales*. In 2014, virtually everyone heard about the "Ice Bucket Challenge"—if not, perhaps you were living under a rock somewhere or not a social media participant. The campaign garnered considerable exposure in traditional media and was a viral monster on social media—the concept of shared media. In a one-month period between July 29 and August 20, the ALS Association, a not-for-profit organization fighting Lou Gehrig's disease, raised $31.5 million in donations compared to $1.9 million in the same period the year before. Granted, this is an exceptional example, but it does demonstrate how a PR campaign can impact sales or fundraising goals.[17]

Public relations provides assistance in *building relationships* with consumers and other publics. In the age of social media, consumers voluntarily connect and interact with brands. Good public relations can help build rapport by encouraging ongoing dialogue with consumers. It is a relationship-building tool that can make a difference—it can separate one brand from the rest of the pack. Such a benefit is important, given the rising costs of communicating via media advertising, the fragmentation of the media, and the clutter of commercial messages in all forms of media.

DISADVANTAGES OF PUBLIC RELATIONS

One of the biggest drawbacks of public relations is the *lack of control* over the message by the company. Through press releases, press conferences, and video content posted on social media sites, the company does its best to communicate factual information. Since the media are pressed for time and space, all materials received from companies and selected for use are edited. If only some of the facts are communicated, the story could be misrepresented or presented in a less than desirable manner. Despite this possibility, there are those who believe that any publicity is good publicity!

Catching the eyes and ears of editors is crucial to the success of any public relations program. That is a challenge, considering the enormous amounts of material that flow into media outlets each day. Consequently, the cost of preparing and delivering information may go to *waste*. The senior management of an organization must recognize the waste factor and be prepared to absorb the costs associated with it. Simply stated, what is important to the company and its management group may not be perceived as important by the media. Executives must also be ready for a potential onslaught of negative publicity in social media should they inadvertently step out of line.

Experiential Marketing

Experiential marketing refers to marketing communications programs that allow consumers to be active participants in a brand's marketing effort. Such programs are typically associated with planned consumer events and include such efforts as product sampling and live, hands-on demonstrations that allow consumers to touch or use the product rather than just hearing or reading about it. A well-planned experiential marketing program will engage consumers and spark interest in a brand in an exciting and personal manner. The touchpoint may be something as simple as a free sample distributed at an event or a planned event where the brand is the centrepiece of activity.

The term *experiential marketing* is relatively new, but the fundamental concepts behind it are not. Brands have always employed product sampling, special product promotions, public relations stunts, product seeding, and special events in their marketing arsenal, but it is just recently that the concept of consumer engagement with a brand has taken hold. Engaging consumers requires a carefully designed and emotive experience that often integrates various forms of marketing communications. In an era when traditional media such as television and print are losing their ability to connect with consumers, alternatives such as experiential marketing become more important in the communications mix. Social media has stimulated interest in experiential marketing techniques. To encourage digital participation with a brand, it is now common to post product demonstrations, games, and other interactive content on YouTube and other outlets.

Some of the more common experiential marketing techniques include street teams (e.g., students adorned in brand clothing setting up displays in public places), travelling vehicles (e.g., vehicles specifically designed and decorated in brand colours that travel around distributing samples and demonstrating products), and in-store product demonstrations, which sometimes involve celebrities to attract additional attention.

An experiential event was a key component of the launch of Speed Stick GEAR for men. The new GEAR line of deodorant products is targeted at adventurous millennial males, so the objective of the event was to simulate a sweat-inducing activity that would challenge them. A 60-foot freestanding ice climbing wall was erected in downtown Toronto—a real attention getter! A street team was onsite to hand out samples and encourage people to take part in the climb. More than 200 people scaled the wall over the two-day event. The event created an experience well beyond what a normal deodorant brand could, and it generated national media coverage, social media conversations, and product trial, and provided the backdrop for an international television commercial. Creative for the campaign was developed by Anomaly Toronto, while Free For All Marketing managed the construction and operations of the ice wall. Refer to the image in Figure 14.10.

Tourism and Nova Scotia go hand in hand. As part of Tourism Nova Scotia's "Take Yourself There" advertising campaign, an experiential marketing activity was developed to bring Nova Scotia to another area. Tourism Nova Scotia built a 28-foot tall replica of the famous Peggy's Cove lighthouse at the corner of Bay and Wellington in busy downtown Toronto. Refer to the image in Figure 14.11. Awareness of the event was created by City and *Breakfast Television*, full-page print ads in the *Toronto Star*, geotargeted mobile ads, social media, and street teams. The activity gave Torontonians a genuine taste of what the province was really like.[18]

Organizations are investing more money in experiential marketing, and that investment is justified based on changing market conditions. In the past, an organization was

FIGURE 14.10

An ice climbing experiential event was part of the product launch for Speed Stick Gear for men.

Courtesy of Free For All! Marketing Inc.

concerned about making impressions on people (a staple means for measuring the effectiveness of advertising and public relations communications). Currently, emphasis has shifted so that the objective is to make quality impressions (fewer but better impressions) while engaging the consumer with the brand. Having the consumer interact with the brand helps establish a stronger reason to buy the product and to build a relationship over an extended period. Companies also benefit from any word-of-mouth communications that consumers engage in on either a personal basis or through their social media network.

Experiential marketing is a good fit for the online environment, where consumers are more open and responsive to communications and in many cases take control of communications from the brand. Consumers willingly allow brands into their world, which makes it easier for marketers to engage with them. Leading social media sites such as Facebook, Twitter, YouTube, and Instagram offer significant engagement opportunity.

Event Marketing and Sponsorships

Event marketing and sponsorships are important elements of the marketing communications mix. As discussed in the previous section, a well-planned event will involve consumers with a brand, and once involved they may perceive the brand in a more positive light.

Event marketing is the process, planned by a sponsoring organization, of integrating a variety of communication elements to support an event theme (e.g., a sporting or musical event). For example, Nike plans and executes road races in large urban markets and supports the event with advertising, public relations, and sales promotion activities to achieve runner participation and buzz for the event. To make these events successful, Nike must invest in other forms of communication to generate awareness and encourage participation.

FIGURE 14.11

An experiential marketing campaign brought a bit of Nova Scotia to downtown Toronto.

Courtesy of Communications Nova Scotia

Event sponsorship is the financial support of an event (e.g., an auto race, a theatrical performance, a marathon) by a sponsor in return for advertising privileges associated with the event. Perhaps the most elaborate and expensive sponsorship opportunities are events such as the Olympics and the FIFA World Cup. Global brands such as Coca-Cola, Visa, and McDonald's commit significant funds to sponsor both events. For brands such as Adidas and Nike, sponsorship of FIFA World Cup soccer, national soccer teams, and star soccer players is an essential investment that helps build sales and market share for their soccer equipment and clothing.

© Mark Blinch/The Canadian Press

FIGURE 14.12

BMO is an active sponsor of professional soccer and community soccer programs in Canada. Soccer reaches a diverse target audience—an attractive proposition for the bank.

Event marketing and sponsorships are big business. The sponsorship market in Canada is estimated to be worth $2.85 billion, which is comprised of $1.75 billion in rights fees and $1.1 billion in activation.[19] Activation refers to any form of advertising or other activity that makes people aware of a brand's connection to an event. The event marketing pie is divided among sporting events (which get the majority of the revenue); causes; the arts; festivals, fairs, and annual events; and entertainment. Marketers today are reluctant to rely on traditional means of communication; they realize that television viewing and print media readership are declining each year, so they are investing in alternatives such as event marketing. With event marketing and sponsorships, there is an opportunity for a brand or company to engage with its target market at a sponsored event.

A survey among North American marketing executives indicates that events and sponsorships deliver a return on investment that exceeds that of media advertising. As well, the intangible benefits offer good value; a brand can form an emotional connection with the fans at a sporting event simply by being there and participating (fans expect sponsors at events). For instance, BMO is a strong supporter of soccer in Canada—it supports all three Canadian MLS (Major League Soccer) teams. Toronto FC plays out of the BMO Stadium (the bank holds the naming rights for the stadium), the bank's logo is emblazoned across the front of team jerseys and every ticket sold, and there is significant BMO signage in and around the stadium. BMO is also the lead sponsor of television games broadcast on TSN. Soccer attracts a diverse ethnic audience—an important target market that any financial institution would have in its sights. Refer to the image in Figure 14.12.

SPORTS SPONSORSHIP

Sports sponsorship occurs at amateur and professional levels and can be subdivided into classifications from local events to global events (see Figure 14.13). Sports sponsorships tend to be dominated by certain industries and manufacturers. In Canada, for example, the brewing industry by Molson and Labatt; the financial industry by RBC Financial Group, BMO Financial Group, and Scotiabank; and the restaurant industry by McDonald's and Tim Hortons.

FIGURE 14.13

The various levels of sports event marketing

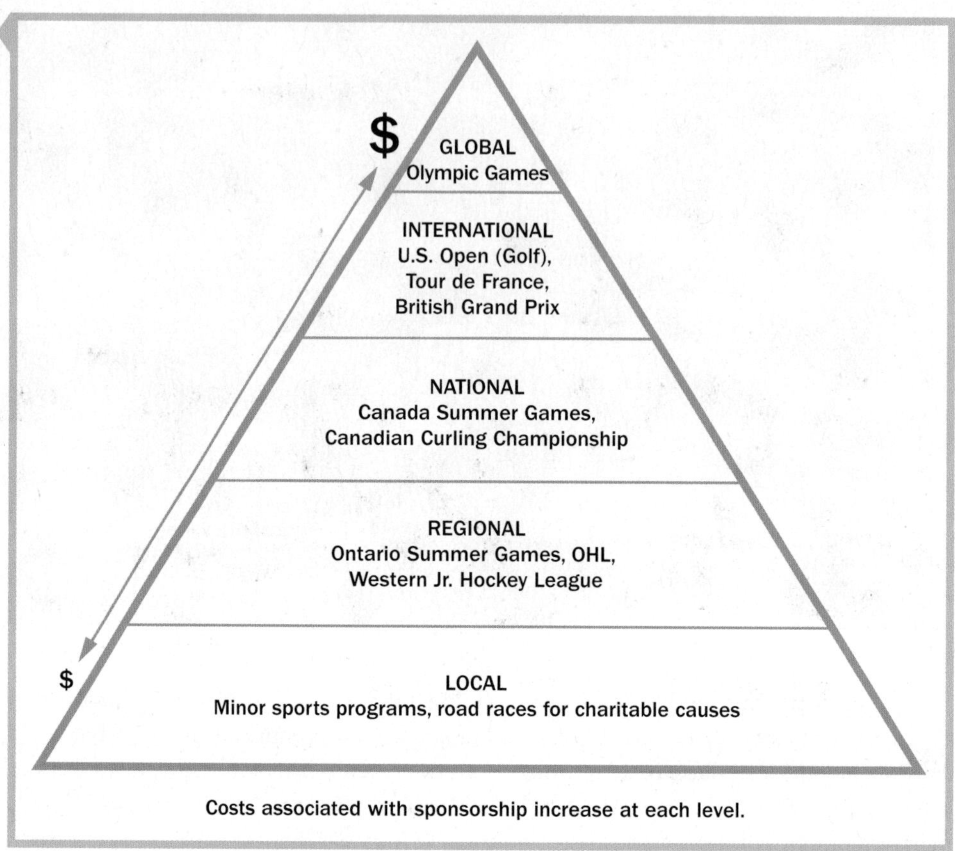

The investment in sports sponsorship increases at each level moving upward on the chart. Organizations choose between spending locally to support community events at relatively low cost, and investing in national and international sponsorships at significantly higher cost. Such decisions are based on how sponsorships fit with other marketing communications strategies and the overall marketing strategy of the organization.

Sponsorships are a key element of BMO's marketing mix. BMO partners with organizations that help create brand exposure nationally while also building regional visibility. As mentioned above, BMO is involved in professional and amateur soccer sponsorships across Canada. At the professional level, it sponsors Toronto FC, Vancouver Whitecaps, and Montreal Impact. At the grassroots level, over 15 000 jerseys carrying the BMO logo are provided to youth soccer leagues. Soccer is a growing sport that appeals to diverse target markets that BMO is interested in.

An organization's involvement in sports sponsorship does not have to be extravagant; involvement and commitment depend on the organization's marketing objectives and its overall strategy. To illustrate, consider that Coca-Cola and McDonald's associate with national and international events, a reflection of their respective status around the world, while Tim Hortons prefers to sponsor local sports programs across Canada. The company's Timbits Minor Sports Program provides team jerseys for community-based youth soccer and hockey leagues. The local sponsorship program fits nicely with the target audience the company is trying to reach.

A recent phenomenon associated with event sponsorship is the practice of ambush marketing. **Ambush marketing** is a strategy used by nonsponsors to capitalize on the prestige and popularity of an event by giving the false impression that they are sponsors. For example, Adidas is the official sponsor of the FIFA World Cup; its investment in the

ADVERTISING IN ACTION

Nike's Ultimate Ambush

To ambush almost seems like an unethical tactic; you catch someone off guard and perhaps do harm to another party. In contemporary marketing, it seems all is fair in love and war. Nike actually has a creative director for the Olympics (Nike does not sponsor the Olympics) whose primary role is to plan and implement strategies that ambush legitimate Olympic sponsors. It's big business with lots of money at stake.

The creative director's focus is on the Nike products that some 3000 Olympic athletes wear on and off the field, from design to deployment. At the 2012 Summer Olympics in London, athletes from many countries wore the same colour. At the Games, Nike's trademark execution was the chartreuse Nike Volt Flyknit shoe—a colour that really stood out in the crowd. Apparently, this combination of green and yellow is the colour most visible to the human eye, so it wasn't selected by accident. Nike acknowledges that the whole point was to create impact—and it did. The shoe garnered all kinds of broadcast, print, and online media exposure during the Games. The result was one of the most iconic images of the 2012 Olympic Games.

Archrival Adidas was an Olympic Games sponsor who paid dearly for the privilege—$155 million. Although Adidas complained about the presence of the shoes and the broadcast coverage Nike was receiving, the company couldn't do much about it. Rather than complain, perhaps Adidas should be spending more time devising programs that make its shoes and apparel stand out. Adidas did not renew its deal for the 2016 Olympics in Rio.

Leslie Smolan, co-founder of Carbone Smolan Agency, says, "Nike's use of the garish shoes was absolutely brilliant. Nike managed to integrate themselves into the Games by showing the product, not just talking about it." Nike has been an Olympic ambusher for a long time. As far back as 1984 at the Summer Olympics in Los Angeles, it ran ads of athletes backed by the Randy Newman song "I Love LA." After those Games, research found that consumers thought Nike was the official sponsor, not Converse, which was the official sponsor.

Fair or foul? Is this good marketing strategy or not? You be the judge.

© Rodrigo Reyes Marin/AFLO/Newscom

Sources: Adapted from Shareen Pathak, "How Nike Ambushed the Olympics with this Neon Shoe," *Advertising Age*, August 20, 2012, p. 1, 19; and Thom Forbes, "Nike Scores with Ambush Products, Ads, PR," *Marketing Daily*, August 13, 2012, www.mediapost.com.

sponsorship is significant, and it expects good value in return. However, Nike, its archrival, mounted an intensive advertising campaign that coincided with the soccer event. Under such conditions consumers get confused as to which brand is the official sponsor. Post–World Cup research on brand recognition revealed that 50 percent of respondents mentioned Adidas as the sponsor. Surprisingly, Nike had a 40 percent response in Brazil and a 33 percent response among US and UK respondents.[20] That's a pretty good ambush! For more insight into ambush marketing and its merits, read the Advertising in Action vignette **Nike's Ultimate Ambush**.

Such tactics have lead to more assertive anti-ambushing strategies by Olympic organizing committees and by organizers of world events such as the FIFA World Cup. For certain, the ethics of the ambushers must be questioned. As well, the practice presents potential financial harm to the sponsorship industry. Properties like the Canadian Olympic Committee, NHL, and NFL are going to command a lot less from sponsors in the future if their rights aren't protected.

Venue marketing, also known as *venue sponsorship,* is another form of event sponsorship. Here, a company or brand is linked to a physical site, such as a stadium, arena, or theatre. In Canada, examples include the Air Canada Centre (home of the Toronto Maple Leafs and Raptors) and the Bell Centre (home of the Montreal Canadiens). Rogers Communications firmly believes in the benefits of arena naming rights, placing its name on three buildings in Canada: Rogers Centre in Toronto (Blue Jays); Rogers Arena (Vancouver Canucks); and Rogers Place (the new downtown arena of the Edmonton Oilers). Refer to the image in Figure 14.14. To illustrate the cost of naming rights in Canada, Air Canada paid $20 million to Maple Leaf Sports and Entertainment to secure the naming rights for the Leafs and Raptors arena.

In the United States, naming rights are much higher. Levi Strauss & Company recently signed a $220 million, 20-year naming rights deal for the San Francisco 49ers's new stadium. The CEO of the 49ers, Jed York, said, "Levi's jeans were designed for the 49ers during the gold rush. It was a good fit for them then and it's a good fit today." To be known as Levi's Stadium, it is the second-highest naming rights deal in National Football League history.[21] The richest naming rights deal in history belongs to the 100 000-seat stadium in Dallas (home of the Dallas Cowboys). The deal is for 20 years at a cost of $400 million. It's called AT&T Stadium.[22]

Besides having their name on the building, most naming rights partners receive a luxury box plus a selection of regular seat tickets; the right to use the team's trademark in advertising, coach, or player appearances; and in-arena displays for their products. It's all a matter of negotiating the right deal.

What's thriving in sports marketing is the concept of *value-added sponsorships*, where hefty doses of public relations and media exposure accompany a marketer's sponsorship agreement.

FIGURE 14.14

Linking a brand name to a venue increases brand exposure and helps build brand image.

The key in this strategy is a lucrative player endorsement. Reebok International has an endorsement deal with hockey sensation Sidney Crosby—a five-year deal worth $2.5 million, more money than any hockey company has ever paid an established star. Sidney Crosby is also a partner with PepsiCo (Gatorade) and Sport Chek (a retail sporting goods and apparel chain).

Adidas, a brand that is struggling to crack the basketball shoe market, recently signed an annual $2 million partnership with rising star Anthony Wiggins (a Canadian who plays for the Minnesota Timberwolves).[23] Assuming Wiggins becomes a real star performer, as he is projected to be, the contract will be renewed at a much higher rate and a shoe model will likely be marketed under the Wiggins brand.

If not with a star, why not partner with a team? General Motors left American football for soccer when it signed a five-year sponsorship deal with Manchester United (a renowned professional soccer team). Manchester United offers worldwide reach that fits with the automaker's desire to make Chevrolet a global brand. In justifying the new direction, Paul Edwards, director of global marketing strategy, said, "We recognized that it's not only the world's biggest sport but also the world's most engaged fans."[24] GM must now leverage the association with Manchester United in its other advertising and marketing communications strategies to fully benefit from the partnership.

Companies and brands must exercise some caution when dealing with sports stars. Any improper or inappropriate behaviour by a star, once it becomes public, could damage the brands the star represents. Many sponsors discontinued their relationships with Tiger Woods (sex scandal), Michael Vick (dog-fighting scandal), and Ray Rice (domestic abuse) once their actions became front-page news. As a form of protection for the sponsor, ethics clauses are built into contractual arrangements with stars.

FESTIVAL AND FAIR SPONSORSHIP

Festivals (film, comedy, and music) offer opportunities to reach a cross-section of adult target audiences. At festivals as popular as the Toronto International Film Festival, there are waiting lists for top-level sponsorships. It seems that companies are eager to align themselves with the movie stars who attend these types of events. Among the lead sponsors are Bell Canada, RBC Financial, L'Oréal, and Visa. Refer to the image in Figure 14.15. The popular Montreal International Jazz Festival attracts sponsors such as TD Bank, Loto-Québec, Bell Canada, Heineken, and CBC Radio-Canada.

Film and other types of festivals are becoming popular with marketers because the festivals offer customized packages suitable to a marketer's needs. The Toronto International Film Festival "approaches sponsorships as true partnerships."[25] It offers a broad spectrum of associations, from corporate entertaining to brand exposure and product sampling opportunities. In 2014, Ford was the automotive sponsor and its vehicles were used to transport A-list celebrities to the red carpet. When the celebrities arrived for their screenings, the cameras started flashing. Celebrity photos appearing in the media included the Ford logo, which was on the side of the vehicle.

Do festivals produce an audience, and is the investment worthwhile? The answer is yes to both questions. There is a saying: "These types of sponsorships reach a 'class' audience rather than a 'mass' audience." The Toronto International Film Festival reaches a "young, urban, affluent" audience: 30 percent are 18 to 34 years old, 77 percent are college or university educated, 60 percent have a household income over $80 000, and all are "culture and experience seekers with high disposable income for entertainment."[26]

FIGURE 14.15

Sponsors of the Toronto International Film Festival reach an upscale audience.

CAUSE MARKETING SPONSORSHIPS

Cause marketing involves a partnership between a company and a not-for-profit entity for mutual benefit. The relationship between the parties has a significant meaning for consumers. This meaning, when associated with a brand or company, can have a positive effect on the consumer's perception of the brand. People like to do business with companies that support their favourite causes. Such is the benefit that CIBC derives from its ongoing title sponsorship of the Canadian Breast Cancer Foundation CIBC Run for the Cure, in which the overall goal is to raise funds to help find a cure for breast cancer. Refer to the image in Figure 14.16. In 2014, the run raised $25 million including $3 million from Team CIBC. Other sponsors of this cause marketing event include Canpar, Dole and Lipton (both PepsiCo brands), The Running Room, and Egg Farmers of Canada.

There are other ways for a company to associate with a worthy cause. For example, the pink ribbon is a recognizable emblem representing efforts to eradicate breast cancer. Brands carrying this emblem donate a portion of their sales to the cause. The Running Room has contributed close to $1 million to the Canadian Cancer Society through the sale of its Pink Ribbon line of clothing.[27]

ARTS AND CULTURE SPONSORSHIP

Arts and cultural event opportunities embrace dance, film, literature, music, painting, sculpture, and theatre. What separates arts and cultural events from other kinds of sponsorships is audience size. Depending on the sponsor, this can be an advantage or a disadvantage. A company such as Molson prefers the mass-audience reach of a sporting event, whereas a financial institution or investment company may prefer to reach a more selective and upscale audience through an arts event. Perhaps only 2500 people attend a particular cultural event, but those people most likely fit the demographic and psychographic profile of the target market. Typically, their education level would be above

The Canadian Breast Cancer Foundation and DARE North America.

FIGURE 14.16

Associating with a worthy cause helps build brand image and trust for a brand with the public.

average, as would their income. To illustrate, BMO is the lead sponsor of the Toronto Symphony Orchestra; RBC Financial Group and Scotiabank are also sponsors.

The primary benefit that companies gain from sponsoring the arts is goodwill from the public. Most firms view this type of investment as part of their corporate citizenship objectives (i.e., they are perceived as good, contributing members of society). For example, in addition to being the lead sponsor of the Toronto Symphony Orchestra, BMO Financial Group is a long-standing sponsor of numerous cultural events and organizations that include the Governor General's Literary Awards, the Stratford Festival, the National Business Book Award, and the National Ballet School.

ENTERTAINMENT SPONSORSHIP

Corporations invest huge amounts of money to sponsor concerts and secure endorsements from high-profile personalities in the hope that the celebrity–company relationships will pay off in the long run. Companies such as Molson, Coca-Cola, and PepsiCo, which are interested in targeting youth and young adult segments, use entertainment sponsorship as a vehicle for developing pop music and youth lifestyle marketing strategies.

An event like the Academy Awards has cachet, and brands that mingle with the stars or show ads on the broadcast stand to benefit. For the past five years, Coca-Cola had been a sponsor, but the company didn't return in 2014, citing a shift in marketing strategy that focused on a younger target. The Academy Awards show has an audience of 40 million in the United States alone—an audience that is 62 percent female, the majority of whom are well educated and affluent.[28] This audience is an ideal fit for sponsor brands like Apple, Samsung, and JCPenney. Advertising insiders refer to the show as the "Super Bowl for women."

Strategic Considerations for Event Marketing and Sponsorships

Advertisers cannot approach event marketing and sponsorships in a haphazard way. Their primary reason for entering into sponsorships is to create a favourable impression with their customers and target groups. To accomplish this, the fit between the event and the sponsor must be a good one. For instance, Nike sponsors professional sports events and employs star athletes associated with those sports in advertising campaigns for its products. Tim Hortons sponsors favourite Canadian pastimes such as hockey and curling. It is the lead sponsor of the Tim Hortons Brier, the national men's curling championship held each year. Generally, event sponsorship is a vehicle for enhancing the reputation of a company and the customer's awareness of a brand. The most effective sponsors adhere to the following principles when considering participation in event marketing:

- ***Select events offering exclusivity*** The need for companies to be differentiated within events they sponsor calls for exclusivity, meaning that direct competitors are blocked from sponsorship. Also, sponsors are concerned about the clutter of lower-level sponsors in noncompeting categories, which reduces the overall impact of the primary sponsor. Typically, sponsorships are offered on a tiered basis with sponsors on lower tiers having fewer privileges.
- ***Use sponsorships to complement other marketing activity*** To maximize impact and achieve marketing objectives, an event or sponsorship must complement a company's other marketing activity. For example, Pepsi-Cola and Frito-Lay (both PepsiCo brands) sponsor the Super Bowl and place several ads during the broadcast. Both brands leverage the Super Bowl sponsorship by implementing a contest for game tickets and other prizes, erecting huge in-store displays to grab consumers' attention, and offering a mail-in rebate for multiple purchases of Pepsi and Frito-Lay products. The integrated strategy embraces event marketing, advertising, and sales promotion (both consumer and trade promotion) across key company brands.
- ***Choose the target carefully*** Events reach specific targets. For example, while rock concerts attract youth, symphonies tend to reach audiences that are older, urban, and upscale. As suggested earlier, it is the fit, or matching of targets, that is crucial. Do the demographics of the event audience match as closely as possible the demographics of the target market?
- ***Select an event with an image that sells*** The sponsor must capitalize on the image of the event and perhaps the prestige or status associated with it. As discussed earlier in the chapter, Coca-Cola and McDonald's bask in the aura of the Olympic Games and the FIFA World Cup. These events have cachet that will make it the cornerstone of a multimedia communications promotion campaign for these brands in the years preceding the games.

- ***Establish selection criteria*** A company evaluating potential events for sponsorship should consider the long-term benefit such sponsorship offers compared with the costs in the short term. For example, being associated with an event that is ongoing, popular, and successful is wise, as there is less risk for the sponsor. A company should also consider whether it is likely to receive communications exposure through unpaid media sources. Events that receive substantial media exposure are very attractive. The company must establish objectives in terms of awareness and association scores (how consumers link the brand to the event), image improvement, increases in sales, and return on investment so the company can properly evaluate its participation in the event.

Measuring the Benefits of Event Marketing and Sponsorship

One reason many companies are reluctant to enter into sponsorship programs is that results are difficult to measure. Large sums of money are spent at one time for a benefit that may be short lived. The basic appeal of event marketing is that it provides an opportunity to communicate with consumers in an environment in which they are already emotionally involved. Beyond this, companies conduct marketing research to determine the impact that sponsorship association has. The following indicators, many of which are obtained from research, are used to measure the benefits of sponsorship:

1. ***Awareness*** How much awareness of the event within the target group is there, and how well do people recall the brand or product name that sponsored the event? If the event is promoted properly, the lead sponsor's name should be top of mind with both attendees and television viewers of an event. For example, when people who are interested in tennis think of our national tennis championships, the Rogers Cup comes to mind. Rogers has been the title sponsor since 2001.
2. ***Image*** What change in image and what increase in consumer perception of leadership or credibility results from the sponsorship? Market research before and after event participation may be necessary to identify this benefit.
3. ***New clients*** How many new clients were generated as a result of the company's sponsoring an event? It is important to include current and prospective customers in the event. For example, inviting customers to view the event from a luxury box and having them enjoy the trappings associated with the box go a long way in solidifying business relationships.
4. ***Sales*** Do increases in sales or market share occur during post-event periods? Participating in an event isn't like dropping a coupon; the actual impact may be longer term. In fact, the real sales benefit may take years to materialize, as it takes time for a sponsor to become closely associated with an event.
5. ***Specific target reach*** Do the events deliver the target constituency? Carefully selected events reach specific targets that are difficult to reach by conventional communications. For example, preteens and teens are difficult to reach through conventional media but can be reached effectively through sponsorship of rock concerts and music tours.
6. ***Media coverage*** What value was derived from editorial coverage? Did the sponsorship result in free publicity for the sponsor? Did participation create any buzz on social media? The industry benchmark for sports sponsorship is currently 4:1, meaning $4 in exposure (e.g., free air time) for every $1 spent on sponsorship and its marketing support.

As mentioned in the public relations section of this chapter, brand exposure (publicity) in the media is measurable and can be compared with advertising exposure.

For sponsorships to be successful, there must be sound business reasons for participating, and the activity must be carefully and seamlessly integrated with corporate marketing and marketing communications plans. For every dollar spent on securing the sponsorship rights, an additional investment of $2 to $3 is needed to promote the association with the event. The organization must leverage the use of its website; incorporate the sponsorship into advertising, public relations, and social media campaigns; and run thematic promotions to get all customer groups (trade and consumers) involved. The various forms of marketing communications must complement each other.

Event Marketing and Sponsorship as a Communications Medium

When assessing whether to be involved with event marketing and sponsorships, an organization weighs the pros and cons of the activity in the context of how well it fits with other marketing and marketing communications strategies. There are numerous advantages and disadvantages of event marketing.

ADVANTAGES OF EVENT MARKETING AND SPONSORSHIP

The primary advantage of event marketing is *target marketing*. Participating in the right event allows an organization to reach its target audience directly and in an environment where the target is receptive to messages (e.g., an auto race where sponsorships are part of the ambience of the event). Sponsorships can also provide *face-to-face access* to current and prospective customers. For example, if a financial services company holds an investment seminar with an open invitation to the public, it will have access to new clients in a noncompetitive environment; at such an event, the message is delivered to a large group at one time. Finally, participation in the right events and sponsorships enhances a company's *public image*. Whether it's involvement with huge events such as the Olympics or just supporting local community events, the effect on image is the same. As cited earlier in the chapter, companies that are perceived to be doing good things are liked better and trusted more.

DISADVANTAGES OF EVENT MARKETING AND SPONSORSHIP

The most prominent disadvantage is *cost*. Any event on a national or international scale involves significant financial commitment, and to enjoy the benefits of such events the commitment is necessary for an extended period. Opting in and out of big events leaves a confusing image with the public. As indicated earlier in the chapter, successful events must be supported with additional spending on advertising and promotion. One complaint commonly raised by event participants is the *clutter* of advertising and signage at events. If there are too many sponsors, the message being delivered by an individual sponsor is diluted; hence, the investment is questionable. As well, the presence of *ambush marketing tactics* by competitors dilutes the product category exclusivity aspect of event participation. Finally, accurately *measuring the effectiveness* of the event or sponsorship in producing sound business results is difficult. It would be nice to know what the return on investment is, but there are so many variables that ultimately contribute to sales and market share performance that the impact of events and sponsorships cannot be isolated.

SUMMARY

Public relations refers to the communications that a firm has with its various publics. Controlled by the media, it is a form of communication for which the organization does not pay, but it is based on information supplied by the organization. Public relations plays a role in developing an organization's image and is an important means of communication in times of crisis.

Two diverse groups are important to an organization, and public relations programs communicate with both of them. Internal publics include employees, distributors, suppliers, shareholders, and regular customers. External publics include the media, governments, prospective shareholders, the financial community, and community groups. Organizations communicate with the various publics through press releases, press conferences, annual reports and publications, social media, and websites. Online communications and social media now play an important role in building corporate and brand image.

Public relations plays a key role in several areas, including corporate advertising; reputation management; publicity generation; product placement, branded content, and product seeding; community relations and public affairs; and fundraising. A public relations campaign is planned much like any other communications plan. It starts with a situation analysis, and then firm objectives and strategies are devised. Once the plan is implemented, research procedures are undertaken to track the effectiveness of the campaign.

Experiential marketing creates an emotional connection with consumers in the form of a brand experience. A key benefit of this tactic is consumer engagement at a time and place where consumers are receptive to brand messages. It is now common for marketers to develop specifically themed events around their brands. Such events tend to have more meaning and impact on consumers than traditional forms of advertising.

Event marketing and sponsorship programs are now an important element of a firm's marketing communications mix, particularly among large Canadian corporations. Sponsorships tend to be concentrated in five areas: sports, festivals and fairs, causes, arts and cultural events, and entertainment. Events and sponsorships can be local, regional, national, or international. The benefits derived from this activity include goodwill and increased awareness as opposed to measurable increases in sales or market share.

Organizations must carefully consider certain criteria before jumping into event marketing. They should look for events that offer exclusivity, complement other marketing communications strategies, closely match their target market's profile, and deliver high levels of media exposure. If the right events are selected and the association with the event is leveraged through advertising and promotion, the organization should enjoy high levels of awareness, an improved image, and stronger sales. The last will likely occur in the long term.

KEY TERMS

ambush marketing 432
annual report 426
blog 425
borrowed-interest strategy 419
branded content 415
buzz marketing 415
cause marketing 436
content analysis 422
corporate advertising 411
digital tags 426
event marketing 429
event sponsorship 430
experiential marketing 428
external publics 410
internal publics 410
press conference 424
press kit 424
press release 423
product placement 414
product seeding 415
publicity 414
public relations 410
situation analysis 417
venue marketing 434
word-of-mouth marketing 415

REVIEW QUESTIONS

1. What are some of the basic differences between public relations and advertising?
2. Identify and briefly explain the role of public relations in the following areas:
   a) Reputation management
   b) Publicity generation
   c) Product placement
   d) Product seeding
   e) Community relations
   f) Fundraising
3. What are the key elements of a public relations strategy?
4. What is a borrowed-interest strategy, and how does it apply to public relations?
5. What is a press kit, and what role does it serve?
6. Identify the basic advantages and disadvantages of using public relations campaigns as a means of communication.
7. What is experiential marketing? Briefly explain and provide a few examples of it.
8. What is the difference between event marketing and event sponsorship?
9. Briefly explain the following event marketing terms:
   a) Ambush marketing
   b) Venue marketing
10. Identify and briefly explain the essential factors an organization should review when deciding to participate in event marketing.
11. What are the primary benefits an organization gains when it invests in event marketing?

DISCUSSION QUESTIONS

1. "Public relations should play a more important role in the communications mix of business organizations today." Discuss the merits of this statement, and provide examples to justify your opinion.
2. Assume you are a public relations consultant, and Unilever has approached you for advice. It wants your recommendation for a celebrity spokesperson to endorse its Dove brand of female personal care products along with a public relations recommendation to announce the signing of the celebrity. Develop a brief plan of action. Be as specific as you can. Provide justification for the celebrity you recommend.
3. "Social media will change the practice of public relations forever." Is this statement true or false? Evaluate this statement, and present an opinion on it.
4. If you were the marketing communications manager for any one of the following products, what events would you sponsor? What benefits would you derive from those sponsorships? Be specific.
   a) Budweiser beer
   b) Gillette personal care products
   c) Hallmark cards
   d) Toyota Lexus
   e) Revlon cosmetics
5. It seems that measuring the effectiveness or return on investment of event marketing and sponsorships is difficult. If so, is it justifiable for companies to invest significant sums of money in event marketing (global, international, and national events)? Do the benefits outweigh the costs? What is your opinion?
6. Is cause marketing a worthwhile endeavour for corporate Canada to invest in? How does a company benefit by being involved in cause-related marketing activities? Explain.

NOTES

1. Flynn, Gregory & Valin, 2008
2. Rebecca Harris, "Canadians Support Brands with Heart," *Marketing*, May 16, 2012, **www.marketingmag.ca**.
3. Rebecca Harris, "Organizations in Crisis Took Reputational Hit in 2013: Survey," *Marketing*, June 10, 2014, **www.marketingmag.ca**.
4. Jeremy Cato, "Hyundai and Kia's Big Black Eye," *Globe and Mail*, November 8, 2012, D10.
5. "United States Reaches Settlement with Hyundai and Kia in Historic Greenhouse Gas Enforcement Case," United States Environmental Protection Agency, Nov. 3, 2014.
6. Michael Bush, "As Media Market Shrinks, PR Passes Up Reporters, Pitches Directly to Consumers," *Advertising Age*, October 26, 2009, p. 9.
7. Susan Krashinsky, "*Mad Men* Serves Canadian Club a Bracer," *Globe and Mail*, April 20, 2012, B7.

8. "Waldorf Stories" Mad Men, AMC, Aug. 29, 2010. Television
9. Susan Krashinsky, "How I Met Your Marketer," *Globe and Mail*, August 2, 2013, B5.
10. Scotiabank, **www.scotiabank.com**.
11. "Apple Announces Record Sales of 10 million iPhone6 and iPhone6 Plus Units in First 3 days," *Apple Insider*, **www.appleinsider.com.**
12. Thomas L. Harris, *Value-Added Public Relations* (Chicago: NTI Publications, 1998), 243–244.
13. Chris Powell, "New Canadian Tire Campaign Bids Us to Go Play," *Marketing*, August 16, 2013, **www.marketingmag.ca**.
14. Ketchum Global Research & Analytics, "The Principles of PR Measurement," **www.ketchum.com**.
15. Orlaith Finnegan, "Social Media Revolutionizes Public Relations," *Social Media Today*, February 20, 2013, **www.socialmediatoday.com**.
16. Kevin Newcomb, "MVW Debuts Blog Marketing Practice," *ClickZ*, **www.clickz.com**.
17. Tom Shapiro, "5 of the Most Effective Campaigns of 2014," *iMedia Connection*, August 21, 2014, **http://blogs.imediaconnection.com**.
18. "Spotted! Tourism Nova Scotia Lights up Toronto," *Media in Canada*, May 21, 2013, **http://mediaincanada.com/2013/05/21/spotted-tourism-nova-scotia-lighthouse**.
19. Susan Krashinsky, "A Blind Faith in Sponsorships," *Globe and Mail*, July 12, 2014, B2.
20. Alicia Andrioch, "World Cup Sponsors Aren't Always Obvious to Consumers," *Marketing*, July 3, 2014, **www.marketingmag.ca**.
21. "Levi's Proposes Stadium Naming Rights," See video at: **http://www.49ers.com/news/article-2/Levis-Proposes-Stadium-Naming-Rights/a2d52c6d-db7a-4040-9ced-a04bc0198eb7**. © Forty Niners Football Company LLC
22. "The Biggest Stadium Naming Rights Deals," *The Richest*, November 20, 2013, **www.therichest.com**.
23. Morgan Campbell, "Rookie Wiggins Not (Yet) Worth $180 Million," *Toronto Star*, July 15, 2014, B8.
24. "GM Backs Manchester after Dropping Super Bowl," *Marketing*, May 31, 2012, **www.marketingmag.ca/new/article/marketer-news/gm-backs-manchester**.
25. Toronto International Film Festival, **http://tiff.net/join/sponsorship-opportunities**.
26. Toronto International film Festival, **http://tiff.net/contents/pdfs/sponsorshipfestival2013.pdf**.
27. Canadian Breast Cancer Foundation, **http://cbcf.org/central/PartnersSponsors/RunSponsors/pages**.
28. Anthony Crupi, "Two of the Oscar's Biggest Sponsors Have Decided Not to Return This Year," *Ad Week*, February 2, 2014, **www.adweek.com/news/television/two-oscars-biggest**.

SCHICK QUATTRO RAZOR

Marketing Background

MARKET SIZE AND GROWTH

The men's grooming market encompasses shaving products, skin care products, hair care products, and fragrances. Combined, these categories represent $720 million in sales annually in Canada. The shaving market is estimated to be worth $320 million at retail. With wholesale and retail margins deducted, the value of the razor market at point of manufacture is estimated to be $225 million.

The grooming market has declined in value marginally in recent years. It has been affected by two basic trends. First, the shaving market has dropped at a faster rate than the overall market. Strong competition among shaving brands produced more promotions and lower retail prices. Second, changing fashions in men's facial hair that favour beards and the "unshaved" look reduced demand for razors and blades.

MARKET SEGMENTS

The razor market is divided between reusable razors and blades, and disposable razors. The reusable segment can be further segmented on the basis of price: regular- or competitively priced razors and premium-priced razors.

In the premium-priced segment, Gillette is the dominant brand with its Fusion ProGlide and Fusion models. In the regular-priced segment, leading brands such as Gillette MACH3, Schick Quattro, and Schick Hydro compete for market share. Private-label brands and purely disposable brands like Bic are also factors in the regular-price segment.

Price is a factor in this market. There are males willing to pay a higher price for each product improvement that comes along, and they tend to be brand loyal. Another group of males always look for the best price available and tend to switch brands frequently.

EXTERNAL ENVIRONMENTS INFLUENCING THE RAZOR MARKET

HEALTH AND WELLNESS There is a growing desire today for men to look and feel healthy.

DEMOGRAPHIC TRENDS Young men and aging baby boomers are concerned with the looking-glass self as well as their own self-image. The goal of older men is to look and feel young. Young urban males who dress well and are socially active are influencing change by making purchases in all grooming categories.

SOCIETAL ATTITUDES General taboos are breaking down; that is, impeccable grooming habits associated with the gay community now transcend all lifestyles. More recently, a more relaxed business environment (fashion and grooming) has resulted in a more masculine "unshaven" look for men.

MARKET SHARE

Even though Gillette dominates market share, the battle between Gillette and Schick is intense. Schick is more aggressive now and has used technology effectively to produce better products. Its investment in advertising has had an impact on market share. The latest market shares are as follows:

Brand	Market Share 2012	Market Share 2015
Gillette	74	70
Schick	17	20
All Other	9	10
Total	**100**	**100**

Schick's market share comprises three brands: Quattro (12%), Xtreme3 (4%), and Hydro (4%).

CONSUMER DATA

Contemporary males of all ages are searching for innovative products that improve appearance. A genuine desire to look and feel better is shaping the male grooming market today.

- Males tend to be brand loyal; once they find the right brand, they stick with it.
- Males prefer basic items that offer tangible benefits; they shun products they perceive as pampering.
- Males' interests now extend well beyond shaving; skin care products are becoming more popular with males of all ages.
- Women frequently purchase grooming products for their male spouse or mate.

COMPETITOR ANALYSIS

The razor market is dominated by Gillette brands. Schick, other brands, and private-label brands are distant followers.

- Gillette's market share is split among three key brands: Gillette Fusion ProGlide, Gillette Fusion, and Gillette MACH3.
- Gillette is a resourceful brand (owned by Procter & Gamble); its key strengths are in technology, product innovation, and marketing.
- The Gillette brand name has an enviable image and reputation among males. It is a well-known male heritage brand.

COMPETITOR ACTIVITY ASSESSMENT

GILLETTE All Gillette brands are marketed by similar means. Each brand receives considerable marketing support, as Gillette's goal is to build and protect market share.

PRODUCT Gillette promises a clean, close, and comfortable shave. Considerable marketing support is directed at the newer Fusion ProGlide razors and blades. Its latest technology, called FlexBall, allows the blade to move from side to side so that it shaves every facial contour in a more comfortable manner.

Gillette Fusion blades are spaced 30 percent closer together, which results in less skin irritation. An enhanced Lubrastrip infused with vitamin E and aloe refines the shaving experience further. Technological advancements keep Gillette in the forefront of razor and blade product development. Male consumers perceive Gillette brands to be reliable.

PRICE The Sensor3 is competitively priced; the MACH3 Turbo is premium priced (about 15 percent more). The Fusion ProGlide and M3 Power razors are higher in price. The additional benefits offered by the M3 Power and Fusion ProGlide razors justify the higher price.

DISTRIBUTION All Gillette brands have extensive retail distribution in drug, grocery, and mass-merchandising stores. Gillette's financial resources allow for significant spending with channel customers to ensure that distribution is maintained.

MARKETING COMMUNICATIONS Gillette brands have significant media advertising support to create awareness and interest. As well, sales promotions are implemented annually across all company brands to generate seasonal interest and to stimulate purchasing patterns. Trial coupons, product sampling, and contests are important elements of Gillette's marketing communications mix.

The Gillette brand has always been associated with sports and sports sponsorships. Gillette is presently a sponsor of Premier League soccer, NASCAR, and over 50 world-class athletes. Gillette summarizes its positioning strategy in all of its marketing communications with the famous slogan: "The best a man can get."

ONLINE COMPETITION

New online shaving services such as the Dollar Shaving Club and Harry's are growing. Their presence has had a negative impact on the sales of traditional brands. Both services offer good-quality replacement blades at lower prices. The Dollar Shave Club offers blades ranging from $3.50 to $9.50, including shipping and handling, for four or five blades and a free handle. Many users claim the blades are just as good as Gillette and Schick. A launch video for the Dollar Shaving Club that claimed "Our blades are f★★king good" was viewed 19 million times on YouTube.

BRAND ACTIVITY ASSESSMENT—SCHICK QUATTRO

PRODUCT The Schick Quattro offers four-blade titanium technology and a design that guarantees a close, comfortable shave. While the Quattro has one less blade than the Gillette Fusion, the impact on the shave is negligible. Quattro Titanium refill blades and Quattro Midnight refill blades are available wherever the razors are sold.

Schick also markets the Quattro Titanium Smooth disposable razor and the Quattro Titanium Sensitive disposable razor. The Titanium Smooth disposables offer four blades on a pivoting head for a smooth shave. The Sensitive disposables offer four blades and a lubricating strip that reduces irritation.

A highly advanced (futuristic-looking) package design draws attention to the revolutionary nature of the Quattro shaving systems.

PRICE The Quattro is priced below the Gillette Fusion ProGlide and Gillette Fusion models. Offering a quality product at a better price than Gillette Fusion systems is desirable for building the brand in the short term.

DISTRIBUTION Quattro has excellent distribution in supermarkets, drugstores, and mass merchandisers. Various consumer and trade promotion activities have produced excellent display activity at point of purchase.

MARKETING COMMUNICATIONS The annual marketing budgets has averaged $2.5 million in recent years. Television and print advertising account for a significant share of the budget and support the brand nationally. Selective use of outdoor advertising has added reach and frequency in key urban markets. Promotional activities, including trial coupons, sampling programs, and contests, contribute to the brand's success.

Marketing Plan

MARKETING OBJECTIVES

1. To increase market share for Schick Quattro from 12 percent to 13 percent in 2016
2. To generate sales revenue of $27 000 000 for Schick Quattro (at point of manufacture) in 2016
3. To continue to position Schick Quattro as a razor that provides a superior shave to any competing product on the market

TARGET MARKET PROFILE

Razor products appeal to all males, but since older age groups exhibit a higher degree of brand loyalty (witness Gillette's dominant position in the market), Quattro will give priority to younger males.

PRIMARY TARGET MARKET

DEMOGRAPHICS

- Males 16 to 35 years old
- Secondary and post-secondary education
- Students, newly employed graduates, career-minded professionals, and businesspeople

PSYCHOGRAPHICS

- Time-pressed daily routines
- Active socially with friends and significant others
- Recreational orientation with an interest in sports viewing and participation
- Very concerned with appearance and health; a strong desire to look and feel good

GEOGRAPHICS

- Across Canada, but metropolitan markets will be given priority

BEHAVIOUR RESPONSE

- These males are looking for products that are reliable, easy to use, and offer superior performance.

SECONDARY TARGET A secondary target comprising males between the ages of 36 and 59 years will also be targeted. While this age group tends to be more loyal and have an established regimen for purchasing shaving products, they are nonetheless interested in innovative products that will improve their self-image. Their psychographic and geographic profile is similar to that of the primary target.

Marketing Communications Strategy

POSITIONING STRATEGY

Schick offers a technologically advanced titanium four-blade system that provides optimal contact over the contours of the face, resulting in the best possible shave.

COMMUNICATIONS MIX

Given the age range of the primary and secondary targets, a combination of traditional media and digital media will anchor the plan. Sales promotion and public relations activities will be added to encourage in-store merchandising activity and to generate buzz among younger males.

BUDGET

The budget for 2016 is $3.0 million for all marketing communications activity.

ADVERTISING OBJECTIVES

1. To achieve a 75 percent awareness level among the primary target market, described as males 16 to 35 years old
2. To encourage trial purchase by members of the primary and secondary target markets
3. To position Schick Quattro as a product that offers customers equal or better performance than the Gillette Fusion razor

Creative Plan

CREATIVE OBJECTIVES

1. To communicate that Schick Quattro offers a close, comfortable, and smooth shave
2. To communicate that the four-blade system provides enhanced performance compared with any other razor

KEY BENEFIT STATEMENT

The Schick Quattro razor offers an incredibly close, smooth shave.

SUPPORT CLAIMS STATEMENT

Numerous tests have been conducted using proper marketing research methods to evaluate and determine the performance level of the Schick Quattro. Tests confirm that the Quattro offers men the best shave possible. As well, the four-blade synchronized system offers technology that is equal to anything offered by competing brands.

Note: Creative objectives are presented in a list format or a key benefit/support claims format. Both options are illustrated above.

CREATIVE STRATEGY

Since Schick Quattro offers equal or better performance, clear, direct, and precise claims will be made in all forms of advertising. The ads will tempt males to compare the Schick Quattro with any other razor system.

IMAGE The consumer should see how easy the product is to use and how reliable it is at providing the key benefit: a close, comfortable shave. Schick Quattro must be quickly perceived as a serious alternative to any Gillette product.

THEME The four-blade synchronized system separates Schick Quattro from all other brands. Therefore, advertising messages will focus on blade technology and the benefits it offers.

TONE AND STYLE All messages will be straightforward, positive, and easy to understand. By showing the razor in action and the satisfaction of the user after shaving (perhaps when he is with a significant other), the choice will be obvious to the consumer.

APPEAL TECHNIQUES Precise appeal techniques will be determined by the ad agency. Any comparisons to Gillette will be implied rather than made directly.

SLOGAN The current tagline, "Free your skin," captures the brand's positioning strategy—its continued use is anticipated.

CREATIVE EXECUTION

All advertising and other forms of marketing communications will deliver the same style of message. It is anticipated that the campaign will embrace 30-second television spots, magazine advertisements, outdoor posters, online banners, and a website. Other integrated marketing activities will include promotion incentives and publicity-generating communications.

Media Plan

BUDGET

From the total budget of $3.0 million, a sum of $2.2 million is allocated to media advertising. The media plan will cover the period January 1, 2016, to December 31, 2016.

MEDIA OBJECTIVES

WHO The primary target market is males 16 to 35 years old, interested in appearance and health (a desire to look and feel good), living in metropolitan markets across Canada. A secondary target market embraces males 36 to 59 years old.

WHAT The message for the Schick Quattro will focus on the benefits offered by the four-blade synchronized shaving system. Such innovation offers males an incredibly close, comfortable shave.

WHEN Advertising will be scheduled throughout the year with a heavier emphasis in the months of February to April (hockey) and August and September (back-to-school).

WHERE The placement of ads will be national in scope with additional coverage in key urban markets.

HOW Since this is a competitive market, reach and frequency will be given equal attention. Continuity issues will be addressed by alternating media and by retaining a media presence at different spending levels throughout the year. An interactive component will engage consumers with the brand.

MEDIA STRATEGY

TARGET MARKET STRATEGY A profile-matching strategy will be employed to reach both the primary and secondary target markets. The primary target spends more time online than the secondary target. A stronger online presence should be included in the media plan. A shotgun strategy is also recommended to improve overall brand awareness and to reach members of the secondary target.

MARKET COVERAGE Schick Quattro is available throughout Canada, so there is a need to employ media that reach a national audience. Key urban markets such as Toronto, Montreal, Vancouver, Ottawa-Gatineau, Edmonton, Calgary, and Halifax will receive additional coverage. Reaching young urban males remains a priority.

TIMING Ads will be scheduled throughout the year using a pulsing strategy. The multimedia campaign will use different media at different times of the year as a means of extending reach and frequency. Higher spending levels are recommended during February, March, and April, when the hockey season is in full swing (to reach sports-minded males), and August and September, a period when young people get back into more rigid schedules and routines (back-to-school months).

REACH/FREQUENCY/CONTINUITY Since brand awareness and trial purchases are immediate objectives, selecting media that maximize reach and frequency will be a priority. Reach will be stressed throughout the entire year, with various media being employed at different times to reach the same target market in different ways. Flights of advertising will be planned to ensure message continuity and maximum impact regardless of the media being employed at any given time.

MEDIA SELECTION RATIONALE A combination of television, magazines, outdoor posters, and online communications is recommended.

a) ***Television*** The most dramatic way to demonstrate the tangible benefits of the Schick Quattro is through television. While males in this age category are watching less television than they used to, television is still the best medium for reaching a large audience. A combination of conventional networks (to reach the mass audience) and sports cable networks (to reach a more targeted audience) will be employed.
b) ***Magazines*** Magazines provide Schick with an opportunity to reach the primary and secondary targets effectively and efficiently. For the younger half of the primary target, titles such as *Maxim* and its clones offer potential. For the older half of the target market, general interest magazines offer effective reach.

c) ***Outdoor Posters*** The target market is time pressed and on the go. Therefore, outdoor posters are an ideal medium for reaching the target audience while they are travelling to and from work or school. The Schick Quattro message will be seen repeatedly through the course of a week. Outdoor advertising enhances reach in key urban markets.

d) ***Online Advertising*** Banner advertising and sponsorships on sports sites are a natural choice, since sports-oriented males in both the primary and secondary target markets visit these sites frequently.

e) ***Website*** A dedicated website (www.schickquattro.ca) provides an opportunity to tell a more complete story about Schick Quattro. The product benefits can be explained in more detail, some entertainment value can be offered, and the target consumer can interact more directly with the brand.

MEDIA REJECTION RATIONALE Radio was not recommended, because the product and package would not be visible. The futuristic design of the product and package are essential elements for achieving awareness and brand recognition objectives. Newspapers were not recommended due to the black-and-white nature of the medium.

MEDIA EXECUTION

For a summary of the media expenditures by medium and time of year, refer to the Exhibits section at the end of this plan. The budget has been effectively allocated between media advertising, sales promotions, and public relations activities.

Sales Promotion Plan

CONSUMER PROMOTION OBJECTIVES

1. To generate awareness and interest for the Schick Quattro among the primary target market
2. To encourage first-time purchases of the Quattro shaving system

TRADE PROMOTION OBJECTIVES

1. To maintain key account listings across Canada
2. To stimulate merchandising support (retail product advertising, special prices, and display activity) at planned intervals throughout the year

SALES PROMOTION STRATEGY

Given the competitive nature of the retail market and the control retailers have over the sale of razor products, equal attention must be given to pull and push strategies. To encourage trial purchases, coupons will be distributed through magazines, and contest incentives will be communicated through in-store advertising.

To protect product listings and encourage merchandising support, adequate funds will be allocated to trade promotions. Funds will also be allocated for the production of point-of-purchase materials that can be used at shelf locations and on displays.

SALES PROMOTION EXECUTION

COUPONS A trial coupon ($2.00 value) will be issued in three waves in *Maxim* and *Maclean's* magazines. This combination reaches the primary and secondary targets nationally.

CONTESTS A contest offer will be communicated through in-store advertising (shelf pads and display cards). In combination with trade promotion funds, this promotion will increase sales volume in the short term and create some excitement at point of purchase.

Contest prizes will be the following:

- Grand prize: Toyota Prius automobile
- Second prize: One of five Sony flat-screen high-definition televisions
- Third prize: One of ten Apple iPads

An online contest will be communicated in conjunction with Rogers Sportsnet. Schick Quattro will be the sponsor of a fantasy league soccer contest called Premiership Predictor. Prizes will be issued weekly, with weekly winners qualifying for a grand prize.

TRADE ALLOWANCES Sufficient funds will be allocated to protect listings in key accounts, increase sales volume, and secure periodic merchandising support throughout the year. A sum of $500 000 is earmarked for trade promotion spending for the year.

POINT-OF-PURCHASE MATERIAL Funds will be allocated for shelf pads, posters, and sundry other point-of-purchase materials that are appropriate for in-store product displays. A budget of $25 000 will be established for this activity.

For a summary of all sales promotion activities, their timing, and costs, refer to the Exhibits section of this plan.

Public Relations Plan

PUBLIC RELATIONS OBJECTIVES

- To generate awareness, interest, and trial usage among the younger portion of the primary target market

PUBLIC RELATIONS STRATEGY

- To employ a group of influencers to help spread the message about the Schick Quattro razor

PUBLIC RELATIONS EXECUTION

To generate some buzz about the Schick Quattro, a product seeding campaign will be implemented among all major Junior A hockey teams across Canada. Junior teams consist of players between the ages of 16 and 20 years. A shaving kit comprising a case, the Schick Quattro shaving system, and two sets of replacement blades will be given to each player on all Junior teams.

The cost of the initial seeding promotion is estimated to be $55 200. See the Exhibits section for details.

EXHIBITS: MEDIA EXECUTION AND OTHER MARKETING COMMUNICATIONS EXECUTION

EXHIBIT 1 **Television Advertising**
All TV spots are 30 seconds in length.

Network	# of Spots	Cost/Spot	Total Cost
CTV—Prime Time	32	$15 000	$480 000
TVA—Prime Time	20	$ 4000	$ 80 000
Rogers Sportsnet	30	$ 5000	$150 000
Total	**82**		**$710 000**

EXHIBIT 2 **Magazine Advertising**
All magazine ads are one-page, four-colour.

Magazine	Frequency	Cost/Page	Total Cost
Maclean's	8	$30 000	$240 000
Maxim	5	$26 000	$130 000
UMM	4	$ 7400	$ 29 600
Cineplex Magazine	4	$16 800	$ 67 200
Le magazine Cineplex	4	$ 7600	$ 30 400
Total	**26**		**$497 200**

EXHIBIT 3 **Outdoor Advertising**
Outdoor ads are horizontal posters (CBS Outdoor).

Market	GRPs	Rate (4 weeks)	Weeks	Total Cost
Toronto	25	$98 600	8	$ 197 200
Montreal	25	$74 100	8	$ 148 200
Vancouver	25	$74 600	4	$ 74 600
Edmonton	25	$19 200	4	$ 19 200
Calgary	25	$21 400	4	$ 21 400
Ottawa-Gatineau	25	$38 100	4	$ 38 100
Halifax	25	$ 6700	4	$ 6700
Total				**$505 400**

EXHIBIT 4 **Online Advertising**
Ads are leaderboards on TSN.ca and Sportsnet.ca (ads directly link to the Schick Quattro website).

Site	Impressions/Month	CPM	Cost/Month	# of Months	Total Cost
TSN	2 000 000	$30	$60 000	5	$ 300 000
Sportsnet	2 000 000	$20	$40 000	5	$ 200 000
Total					**$ 500 000**

EXHIBIT 5 **Media Expenditures by Market**
National media comprise network television, national magazines, and online advertising. Key market media is outdoor advertising.

Market	$ Expenditure	% of Total	% of Key Markets
National Media	$ 1 707 200	77.1	
Key Markets	$ 505 400	22.9	
Total	**$ 2 212 600**	**100.0**	
Key Markets			
Toronto	$ 197 200		39.0
Montreal	$ 148 200		29.3
Vancouver	$ 74 600		14.8
Edmonton	$ 19 200		3.8
Calgary	$ 21 400		4.2
Ottawa-Gatineau	$ 38 100		7.5
Halifax	$ 6 700		1.4
Total	**$ 505 400**		**100.0**

EXHIBIT 6 **Expenditures by Medium**

Medium	Expenditure	% of Total
Television	$ 710 000	32.1
Magazines	$ 497 200	22.4
Outdoor	$ 505 400	22.9
Online	$ 500 000	22.6
Total	**$2 212 600**	**100.0**

EXHIBIT 7 **Media and Marketing Communications Expenditures by Month**
Expenditures include all activities except trade promotions.

Month	Expenditure	% of Total
January	$ 165 900	6.6
February	$ 221 120	8.8
March	$ 379 200	15.2
April	$ 213 400	8.5
May	$ 94 900	3.7
June	$ 94 720	3.7
July	$ 96 900	3.8
August	$ 429 400	17.1
September	$ 379 920	15.8
October	$ 204 600	8.2
November	$ 101 900	4.0
December	$ 114 000	4.6
Total	**$2 495 960**	**100.0**

EXHIBIT 8 **Consumer Promotions—Coupons**

Magazine	Circulation	Frequency	Redemption (%)	Total Cost
Maclean's	371 500	3	2	$49 038
Maxim	115 000	2	2	$10 120
Total	**486 500**			**$59 158**

An on-page coupon with a face value of $2.00 will appear in three issues of *Maclean's* and two issues of *Maxim*. A handling fee of $0.20 must be added to the face value of the coupon.

Costs are calculated as follows:

Circulation × frequency × redemption rate × face value and handling fees = cost of coupon offer

Maclean's: 371 500 × 3 × 0.02 × $2.20 = $49 038

Maxim: 115 000 × 2 × 0.02 × $2.20 = $10 120

EXHIBIT 9 **Consumer Promotions—Contests**

Prize	#Winners	Prize Cost	Total Cost
Grand Prize (Car)	1	$35 000	$ 35 000
TV	5	$ 2 000	$ 10 000
iPad	10	$ 500	$ 5 000
Related Contest Promotion Costs			
Shelf Pads (in-store)			$ 15 000
Posters (in-store)			$ 10 000
Total Cost			**$ 75 000**

EXHIBIT 10 **Total Sales Promotion Expenditures (Including Trade Promotion)**

Activity	Cost
Coupon Offers	$ 59 160
Contest	$ 75 000
Trade Promotions	$500 000
Total	**$634 160**

EXHIBIT 11 **Public Relations—Product Seeding Campaign**

Activity	Cost
Product Seeding—Junior A Hockey	
46 teams × 30 units × $40.00	$55 200

EXHIBIT 12 **Sponsorship Costs—Television and Online**

Sponsorship Activity	Cost
Rogers Sportsnet TV "NHL Hits of the Week" (Wednesdays)	$ 54 000
Rogers Sportsnet.ca "NHL Hits of the Week"	$ 18 000
Rogers Sportsnet.ca—Schick Quattro "Premiership Predictor" Contest	$ 40 000
"Premiership Predictor" Prizes	$ 10 000
Total	**$122 000**

EXHIBIT 13 **Total Marketing Communications Budget**

Activity	Expenditure	% of Total
Media Advertising	$ 2 212 600	73.2
Sales Promotion	$ 634 160	21.0
Public Relations	$ 55 200	1.8
Sponsorships	$ 122 000	4.0
Total	**$ 3 023 960**	**100.0**

EXHIBIT 14 **Plan Budget vs. Actual Budget**

Budget	Budget $
Estimated Budget (Based on Activities)	$3 023 960
Plan Budget	$3 000 000
Expenditure Over Budget	($ 23 960)

Sales and marketing communications budgets will be reviewed quarterly. Adjustments to the budget will be made when necessary.

EXHIBIT 15 **Blocking Chart**

Activity	Jan	Feb	Mar	Apr	May	Jun	Jul	Aug	Sep	Oct	Nov	Dec
Television												
CTV		6	6	6				4	6	4		
TVA	**4**		**4**		**4**			4	4			
Sportsnet	**5**	**5**	**5**							**5**	**5**	**5**
Magazines												
Maclean's	**1**	**1**		**1**		**1**		**1**	**1**			**1**
Maxim	**1**		**1**		**1**		**1**		**1**		**1**	
UMM		**1**			**1**			**1**			**1**	
Cineplex	**1**			**1**			**1**			**1**		
Le Magazine Cineplex	**1**			**1**			**1**			**1**		
Outdoor												
Toronto			↔						↔			
5 Other Markets								↔				
Online												
Sportsnet.ca	←	—	→							←	—	→
TSN.ca				←	—	—	—	→				
Quattro Website	←	—	—	—	—	—	—	—	—	—	—	→
Consumer Promotion												
Ad + Coupons		↔				↔			↔			

Contest								↔				
Public Relations												
Product Seeding									↔			
Sponsorships												
Sportsnet TV	←	—	—	→							←	→
Sportsnet.ca	←	—	—	→							←	→
Sportsnet.ca Contest	←	—	—	→					←	—	—	→

Notes:

Television—Figures indicate the number of spots on each network (prime time).

Magazines—Figures indicate one insertion in each month scheduled (*Maclean's* is a weekly magazine).

Outdoor—Eight-week flight in Toronto and Montreal; four-week flight in Vancouver, Edmonton, Calgary, Ottawa-Gatineau, and Halifax.

Online—Ads placed for 1.5 million impressions on TSN and 1.3 million impressions on Sportsnet each month.

Consumer Promotion—Coupons distributed in three waves in two magazines: *Maclean's* and *Maxim*. The contest will start in August (in-store ads).

Product Seeding—Sample packs distributed to Junior A teams in September.

Sponsorships—The TV ads, internet sponsorships, and an online contest coincide with the regular NHL season, the Premier League soccer season, and the Major League Soccer season.

Website—The Schick Quattro website (www.schickquattro.ca) is maintained by a separate budget.

This marketing communications plan was compiled for illustration purposes. It is designed to show the relationship between various components of marketing communications and how they interact with one another to achieve marketing and marketing communications objectives. The plan also shows the direct relationships among objectives, strategies, and execution for the various subplans within.

APPENDIX II Advertising Regulations

The following is a summary of relevant advertising regulations and information about Advertising Standards Canada, an organization responsible for administering regulations in Canada.

Advertising Standards Canada

Advertising Standards Canada (ASC) is a national industry association committed to ensuring the integrity and viability of advertising through self-regulation. Members of the organization include advertisers, advertising agencies, media organizations, and suppliers to the advertising industry.

The primary codes and guidelines administered by ASC include the Canadian Code of Advertising Standards, Gender Portrayal Guidelines, and the Broadcast Code for Advertising to Children.

The Canadian Code of Advertising Standards is the principal instrument of self-regulation. The Code sets the standards for acceptable advertising and is regularly updated to ensure it remains vital, current, and relevant. It contains 14 clauses that set the criteria for acceptable advertising and is supplemented with interpretation guidelines on the application of the Code's clauses.

Through regional councils, consumer complaints about advertising are accepted, reviewed, and adjudicated. ASC is also responsible for some other self-regulating codes and provides commercial clearance services for food, nonalcoholic beverages, cosmetics, and tobacco products. It also administers guidelines for advertising directed at children.

Canadian Code of Advertising Standards

The Code was first published in 1963. It is periodically reviewed and updated when necessary. The Code sets the criteria for acceptable advertising and forms the basis upon which advertising is evaluated in response to consumer or trade complaints. It is endorsed by all members of ASC.

For the purpose of the Code:

Advertising is defined as any message (the content of which is controlled directly or indirectly by the advertiser) expressed in any language and communicated in any medium to Canadians with the intent to influence their choice, opinion, or behaviour.

Scope of the Code

Authority applies to only the content of advertisements and does not prohibit the promotion of legal products or services or their portrayal in circumstances of normal use. The context and content of the advertisement; the audience actually, or likely to be, or intended to be reached by the advertisement; and the medium/media used to deliver the advertisement are relevant factors in assessing an ad's conformity with the Code.

The provisions of the Code should be adhered to both in letter and in spirit. Advertisers and their representatives must substantiate their advertised claims promptly when requested to do so by any one or more of the councils. The Canadian Code of Advertising Standards includes 14 clauses. These clauses cover the following areas:

- Accuracy and clarity
- Disguised advertising techniques
- Price claims
- Bait and switch
- Guarantees
- Comparative advertising
- Testimonials
- Professional or scientific claims
- Imitation
- Safety
- Superstition and fears
- Advertising to children
- Advertising to minors
- Unacceptable depictions or portrayals

For the complete text of the Code, visit the Advertising Standards Canada website at **www.adstandards.com**.

Gender Portrayal Guidelines

Advertising Standards Canada has established firm guidelines for the portrayal of men and women in advertisements. The guidelines are updated periodically to reflect changes in the social and professional roles of men and women in Canadian society. The current guidelines are not intended to be a "how-to" guide for portraying men and women, but they do provide direction in those areas, which, based on previous consumer complaints, appear to be the most problematic. The guidelines are as follows:

1. ***Authority*** Advertising should strive to provide an equal representation of men and women in roles of authority in actual advertising presentations, including announcers, people doing voiceovers, experts, and on-camera authorities.
2. ***Decision Making*** Women and men should be portrayed equally as single *decision makers* for *all* purchases, including big-ticket items. In joint decision-making processes, men and women should be shown as equal participants, whether in the workplace or at home.
3. ***Sexuality*** Advertising should avoid the inappropriate use or exploitation of both women and men.
4. ***Violence*** Neither sex should be portrayed as exerting domination over the other by means of overt or implied threats or actual force.
5. ***Diversity*** Advertising should portray both women and men in the full spectrum of diversity and as equally competent in a wide range of activities both inside and outside the home.
6. ***Language*** Advertising should avoid language that misrepresents, offends, or excludes women or men.

Broadcast Code for Advertising to Children

Children's advertising refers to any paid commercial that is carried in or immediately adjacent to a children's program, and includes any message that is determined by the broadcaster as being directed to children and is carried in or immediately adjacent to any other program. Some key issues included in the Code are the following:

FACTUAL PRESENTATION

Visual presentations must not exaggerate characteristics such as performance, speed, size, and durability. The relative size of the product must be clearly established.

AVOIDING UNDUE PRESSURE

Children's advertising must not directly urge children to make purchases or urge them to ask their parents to make inquiries or purchases. Direct response techniques that invite purchase by mail or telephone are prohibited.

SCHEDULING

In a 30-minute children's program, a product can be advertised only once. If the program is an hour long, a second commercial may be aired in the second half-hour of the program.

USE OF PROGRAM CHARACTERS, ADVERTISING-GENERATED CHARACTERS, AND PERSONAL ENDORSEMENTS

Puppets, persons, and characters well known to children must not be used to endorse children's products, premiums, or services. The presence of these puppets, persons, or characters in a commercial to establish a theme is acceptable, but they may not handle, consume, mention, or endorse in any way the product being advertised.

SAFETY

Commercial messages, except specific safety messages, must not portray adults or children in unsafe acts or situations.

SOCIAL VALUES

Children's advertising must not encourage or portray a range of values that are inconsistent with the moral, ethical, and legal standards of contemporary Canadian society.

The complete text of the Broadcast Code for Advertising to Children is available at the Advertising Standards Canada website, **www.adstandards.com**.

Other Codes and Guidelines

The following are other codes and guidelines administered by Advertising Standards Canada:

- Guide to Food Labelling and Advertising
- Advertising Code of Standards for Cosmetics, Toiletries, and Fragrances
- Guidelines for the Use of Comparative Advertising in Food Commercials
- Guidelines for the Use of Research and Survey Data in Comparative Food Commercials

- Guiding Principles for Environmental Labelling and Advertising
- Trade Dispute Procedure

The Complaint Process

Consumers who witness advertising that is contrary to the Canadian Code of Advertising Standards must lodge a complaint in writing (emailed complaints are accepted) with one of the national or regional Consumer Response Councils. Complaints can be submitted by letter or by filling in a form that is available at the ASC website. All written complaints are acknowledged and reviewed, and if there appears to be a violation the advertiser will be contacted.

The critical factor in determining whether an advertisement should be reviewed is not the number of complaints received. The fundamental issue is only whether an advertisement appears to contravene the Code.

If there is an infraction of the Code, the advertiser in question is notified. The advertiser can respond to the complaint. If a violation has occurred, the advertiser is asked to amend the advertisement or withdraw it. Once the advertiser has taken either of these steps, the complaint is closed and the complainant is informed in writing of the corrective action. If the complaint is not sustained, the council will explain why to the complainant. Occasionally, an advertiser refuses to take corrective action. In this case, the council will advise broadcasters and publishers carrying the ad. Usually, the media drop the ad in question.

Each year ASC publishes one or more reports on consumer complaints about advertising. The purpose of these complaint reports is to serve, for the benefit of the advertising industry and the interested public, as a guide for the interpretation of the Code as applied to advertising issues that concern the public.

Where to Write

You may obtain a free copy of the Canadian Code of Advertising Standards by writing to ASC in either Toronto or Montreal:

Standards Division
Advertising Standards Canada
175 Bloor Street East
South Tower, Suite 1801
Toronto, ON M4W 3R8
Tel: (416) 961-6311
Fax: (416) 961-7904
Website: **www.adstandards.com**

APPENDIX III Glossary

Account director The senior member of the account management group in an advertising agency who is responsible for the agency's performance in handling client accounts.

Account executive (account planner) The liaison between the agency and client; coordinates the agency's services for the benefit of the client and represents the agency's point of view to the client.

Account management An agency team that offers strategic planning expertise to clients; the team coordinates client projects among various agency departments and presents final recommendations to clients.

Account services group A strategic planning team within an advertising agency that offers clients advice on matters beyond advertising; the team examines the bigger picture before making recommendations to the client.

Account shifting Moving an advertising account from one agency to another.

Account supervisor A mid-level manager in an agency who manages the activities of a group of account executives; generally takes a longer-term perspective on product advertising assignments.

Acquisition strategy A plan of action for acquiring companies or brands that represent attractive financial opportunities.

Ad pads Coupon-sized pads with tear-away sheets describing details of a promotion offer.

Advergaming The integration of brands into video games, including those played online and those purchased directly by consumers.

Advertising A paid form of marketing communication designed to stimulate a positive response from a defined target market.

Advertising agency Service organizations responsible for creating, producing, and placing advertising messages for clients.

Advertising manager Generally, the individual in the client organization responsible for advertising planning and implementation.

Advertising objectives Goal statements for advertisements that include quantitative measures related to behaviour or other relevant issues.

Advertising plan An annual planning document that outlines the advertising activities (creative and media) for the forthcoming year. The plan includes discussion of objectives, strategies, and tactics for both creative and media plans.

Advertising research Any form of research that provides information useful in the preparation or evaluation of creative, of media alternatives, and of media usage.

Advertising share A brand's media expenditure, expressed as a percentage of total product category media expenditures.

Advocacy advertising Advertising that communicates a company's stand on a particular issue (usually one that will affect a company's operations).

Agate line A nonstandardized unit of space measurement in a newspaper equal to one column wide and one-fourteenth of an inch deep.

Agency of record (AOR) A central agency, often used by multiple-product advertisers that use more than one advertising agency, responsible for media negotiation and placement.

Aided recall A research situation in which respondents are provided with certain information to stimulate thought.

AM (amplitude modulation) Refers to the height at which radio waves are transmitted.

Ambush marketing A promotional strategy used by nonsponsors to capitalize on the status and prestige of an event by giving a false impression that they are the sponsors.

Animated banners An internet banner ad that spins or has some form of action.

Animation Using hand-drawn cartoons or stylized figures and settings in an advertisement.

Annual report An annual publication provided by public corporations to shareholders that outlines its operations and financial conditions.

Art director The individual responsible for the visual presentation of an advertisement in print, broadcast, or digital formats.

Assortment media strategy A media strategy in which media dollars are distributed more equitably among several media types.

At-retail media Advertising opportunities available in retail stores that include shelf-talkers, tear-off pads, posters, ads on shopping carts, and digital video screens.

Attitude An individual's feelings, favourable or unfavourable, toward an advertised product.

Audience flow In radio, the change in audience demographics based on the time of day.

Audience fragmentation The splintering of an audience across a greater number of channels (consumers have more channels to choose from).

Backlit poster A luminous sign containing advertising graphics printed on translucent polyvinyl material.

Balance The relationship between the left side and the right side of a print advertisement. Equal weight (left versus right) refers to formal balance, and unequal weight is informal balance.

Banner ad On the internet, an ad that stretches across the page in a narrow band. The viewer clicks on the ad for more information. Banner ads are now available in a variety of shapes and sizes.

Banners In outdoor advertising, large vinyl-painted ads that are framed and mounted on the outside of a building.

Behavioural targeting Refers to a database-driven marketing system that tracks a customer's behaviour to determine his or her interests and then serves ads to that person relevant to those interests.

Behaviour-response segmentation Dividing buyers into groups according to their occasions for using the product, the benefits they require in a product, the frequency with which they use it, and their degree of brand loyalty.

Big box Refers to a webpage ad that is almost a square (300 × 250 pixels) and offers greater width and depth to an ad.

Billboard A common term associated with outdoor poster advertising.

Bleed (bleed page or bleed ad) A situation in which the coloured background of an advertisement extends to the edge of the page so that there is no margin.

Blitz schedule A schedule characterized by heavy media spending in a short space of time (saturation), with spending tapering off over an extended period of time.

Blocking chart A visual document, usually one or two pages long, that outlines all of the details of a media execution.

Blog A website where journal entries are posted on a regular basis and displayed in reverse chronological order.

Body copy Informative or persuasive prose that elaborates on the central theme of an advertisement.

Borrowed-interest strategy To spark interest among editors, a borrowed-interest strategy promotes a newsworthy activity that is related to the product.

Bounce back Advertisements and offers distributed in monthly charge account statements or with the delivery of goods purchased by direct mail.

Brand development index (BDI) The percentage of a brand's sales in a region in relation to the population of the region.

Branded content The inclusion of information about a branded product in the script of a television show or movie.

Brand manager (product manager) An individual who is responsible for the development and implementation of marketing programs for a specific brand or group of brands.

Branded promotion merchandise Useful or decorative products featuring an organization's logo or brand mark that are distributed to existing customers and prospects in appreciation for their business and their loyalty.

Broadsheets A newspaper format with a horizontal centre fold. The page is 10 to 12 inches wide by 20 to 22 inches deep. The majority of Canadian daily newspapers are published in broadsheet format.

Budget The financial resources allocated to a product to support marketing activities.

Build-up schedule A schedule characterized by low initial media weight that gradually builds to an intensive campaign.

Business advertising (or business-to-business advertising) Advertising of finished products and services that is directed at other businesses that can use the advertised items to advantage.

Buzz marketing Activities that generate personal recommendations for a branded product.

Call centre A central operation from which a company operates its inbound and outbound telemarketing programs.

Cash refund A predetermined amount of money returned directly to a consumer by a manufacturer after a purchase has been made.

Catalogues Reference publications, usually annual, distributed by large retail chains and other direct marketing organizations.

Category manager An individual who is responsible for developing and implementing marketing programs for products grouped into the category (e.g., all laundry detergent products).

Cause marketing Marketing that involves a partnership between a company and a not-for-profit entity for mutual benefit.

Central theme (big idea) The glue that binds various creative elements together; it is transferable from one medium to another.

Circulation The average number of copies of a publication sold by subscription, through retail outlets, or distributed free to predetermined recipients.

Circulation list A magazine subscription list that targets potential customers by interest or activity.

Click fraud The practice of artificially inflating traffic statistics by repeatedly clicking on an advertisement.

Click rate A ratio that indicates the success of an advertiser in attracting visitors to click on its ad. The formula is clicks divided by ad impressions.

Clickthrough The number of times users click on a banner ad.

Closing date The deadline for an advertiser to submit the insertion order and material due at a magazine.

Cluster The grouping of commercials in a block of time during a program break or between programs.

Clutter (1) In broadcast advertising, the clustering of commercials together in a short space of time. (2) In print advertising, the extent to which a publication's pages are fragmented into small blocks of advertising.

Collateral materials Visual aids used by sales representatives in sales presentations, such as price lists, sales brochures, and digital materials.

Commission A form of agency compensation in which the agency retains a predetermined percentage of the amount of money a client spends on media advertising.

Compiled list A direct mail list that is prepared from government, census, telephone, warranty, and other publication information.

Concentrated media strategy A media strategy in which the majority of media dollars are allocated to one primary medium.

Consumer advertising Persuasive communications designed to elicit a purchase response from consumers.

Consumer behaviour The acts of individuals in obtaining and using goods and services; the decision processes that precede and determine these acts.

Consumer-generated content Online content, often brand oriented, that is created by consumers for consumers.

Consumer promotions Promotion activity directed at consumers and designed to encourage quicker purchase responses.

Content analysis A process of recording exposure actually received as a result of public relations activities.

Content marketing Involves creating and sharing content to acquire customers.

Contest A consumer promotion technique that involves awarding cash or merchandise prizes to consumers when they purchase a specified product.

Continuity The length of time required to ensure impact on a target market through a particular medium.

Continuity discount A discount based on the purchase of a minimum number of designated spots over an extended period (usually 52 weeks).

Controlled circulation Publications that are distributed free to individuals who fall within a specific demographic segment or geographic area.

Controlled experiment The testing of an advertising campaign in a few local markets to determine its strengths and weaknesses and identify potential changes prior to implementation on a regional or national level.

Conversion A measure of how many people actually took the desired action after exposure to an advertising message distributed online.

Cookie An electronic identification tag sent from a web server to a browser to track a person's browsing patterns.

Cooperative advertising allowance The sharing of advertising costs and materials by suppliers and retailers or by several retailers.

Cooperative direct mail Mailings containing specific offers from noncompeting products (e.g., coupons, samples, subscription offers).

Copywriter The individual responsible for developing the headline, body copy, and signature in an advertisement.

Corporate advertising Advertising designed to convey a favourable image of a company to its various publics.

Corporate discount A discount in print advertising based on the total number of pages purchased by a company (all product lines combined), resulting in a lower page rate for each product.

Corporate objectives Statements of a company's overall goals that take their direction from the mission statement.

Corporate strategies Plans outlining how corporate objectives will be achieved.

Coupons Price-off incentives offered to consumers to stimulate quicker purchase of a designated product. (Coupons are usually product delivered or media delivered.)

CPC (cost per click) A pricing model that determines website advertising costs. Advertisers only pay when their advertisement is clicked on.

CPM (cost per thousand) (1) In print and broadcast media, the cost of delivering a message to 1000 individuals. (2) In interactive media, the cost of displaying an ad 1000 times.

Creative boutique An advertising agency that specializes in the development of creative concepts and executions.

Creative brief A document prepared by the client for the agency, outlining all relevant information pertaining to a new creative development assignment.

Creative concept The central theme or basic sales message that an advertisement communicates through verbal and visual devices.

Creative department The department in an advertising agency that provides creative services such as copy and art.

Creative director The head of the creative department, who oversees the development of all creative generated by the agency.

Creative execution A more precise definition of creative strategy (i.e., tactical considerations regarding the best way to present products for maximum impact, such as using celebrity spokespersons, dramatizations, and colour).

Creative objectives Clearly worded statements that outline the basic content of an advertising message (brand name and benefits that are of high interest to potential buyers).

Creative plan A plan that outlines the nature of the message to be communicated to a target audience; it involves the development of creative objectives, creative strategies, and creative execution.

Creative research Measuring and evaluating the impact of an advertising message on a target market.

Creative strategy Clearly worded statements that provide direction regarding how the message will be presented. Such statements usually consider appeal techniques, tone, style, and theme.

Cross-coupon (cross-ruff) One product carrying a coupon offer for another product (often done by complementary products, such as coffee and biscuits).

Cross-sampling One product carrying a free sample of another product.

Crowdsourcing Using the collective talents of the public at large to complete advertising tasks normally undertaken by a third-party provider.

Customer relationship management (CRM) A practice designed to attract, cultivate, and maximize the return from each customer a company does business with.

Day-after recall (DAR) testing Research conducted the day following the respondent's exposure to a commercial message to determine the degree of recognition and recall of the advertisement, the brand, and the selling message.

Data mining The analysis of information that establishes relationships between pieces of information so that more effective marketing and communications strategies can be identified and implemented.

Daypart A block of time during the day in a station or network's daily programming schedule that is used to distinguish viewing and listening patterns.

Daypart targeting Targeting individuals with online advertising communications based on time of day.

Daytime In television, the daypart that normally runs from early morning (or sign-on) until 4:00 p.m.

Dealer-display advertising Advertising or display materials located in a retail environment to build traffic, advertise a product, and encourage impulse purchasing.

Dealer premium An additional incentive (usually merchandise) offered to a distributor by a manufacturer to encourage special purchase or to secure additional merchandising support from a retailer.

Delayed payment incentive The granting of a grace period during which no interest or principal is paid on a purchased item.

Demographic segmentation The process of dividing a large market into smaller segments on the basis of various combinations of age, gender, income, occupation, education, marital status, household formation, and ethnic background.

Digital sign An outdoor sign that displays digital messages; typically different advertiser messages are rotated on the screen.

Digital strategist A member of the agency team who focuses on technology and is responsible for developing strategies for all forms of new media, be it on laptops, tablets, or smartphones, or in video games.

Digital tags Keywords describing a piece of data, be it a webpage, photograph, or document.

Digital video screens A large format video screen that displays video-style advertising messages.

Dimensional mail Direct mail that can take any form other than the typical flat piece of mail.

Direct mail A form of direct advertising that uses the postal service as the vehicle for delivering the message.

Direct response advertising Advertising through any medium (mail, television, telephone, or internet) designed to generate a response that is measurable.

Direct response communications Reaching an audience of one with a unique message.

Direct response interactive Involves placing ads on the internet that include a call to action.

Direct response print A response-oriented message delivered to prospects via magazine or newspaper advertisements.

Direct response television (DRTV) Television advertising that has two distinct formats: the 30-, 60-, or 120-second spot and the 30-minute infomercial.

Direct segmentation Targeting customers on an individual basis.

Display advertising (1) Advertising that appears anywhere in a newspaper, excluding the classified section. (2) In online advertising, a banner ad.

Display cards Small advertisements located at point of purchase (shelf-talkers, tear-off ad pads, counter posters) that are designed to encourage impulse purchases.

Display shipper A shipping carton that contains a predetermined amount of merchandise and that, when assembled, forms a temporary display at point of purchase.

Divestment strategy Selling off divisions or product lines that no longer fit the strategic direction an organization is taking.

Double targeting Devising a single marketing strategy for both genders or an individual strategy for each of the genders.

Efficiency The relative cost effectiveness of a particular medium, based on CPM.

Endorsement A form of advertising that uses a celebrity (e.g., rock star, television personality, sports star) to present the product message.

Engagement The degree of involvement a person has with the media when he or she is using it.

Engagement (online) A measure of how many people interacted with an advertising message on social media.

Even schedule The purchase of media time and space in a uniform manner over an extended period of time.

Event marketing The process, planned by a sponsoring organization, of integrating a variety of communication elements to support an event theme.

Event sponsorship The financial support of an event by a sponsor in return for advertising privileges associated with the event.

Execution (tactics) Action plans that outline specific details of implementation.

Expandable banner An on-screen ad, not in the banner, employing multiple panels that are launched when the banner is clicked on.

Experiential marketing A form of marketing that creates an emotional connection with the consumer in personally relevant and memorable ways.

Exterior bus poster A poster-type advertisement appended to the side or rear section of a bus.

External publics Those publics that are distant from an organization and are communicated with less frequently.

Eye-movement camera test A test in which a hidden camera records eye movement to gauge the point of immediate contact in an advertisement, how a reader scans the ad, and the amount of time spent reading.

Feature sheet A sheet, commonly used in radio personality announcements, that provides the station with the key benefit and the slogan for the product advertised. The disc jockey develops the specific message wording from the sheet.

Fee system A compensation system primarily based on the amount of time an agency spends on a client's business; hourly rates are assigned to different agency personnel.

Flexform advertising An advertisement that does not conform to normal shapes (e.g., an oddly shaped ad designed to stand out from traditional square advertising spaces in a newspaper).

Flexibility The ability to modify media spending plans throughout the media spending (planning) period.

Flights (or flighting) Refers to the purchase of media time in periodic waves of advertising, separated by periods of total inactivity.

Floating ad An online ad, not in the banner, that moves within a transparent layer over the page and plays within a specific area of the page.

Floor ads Portable floor decals (often called *ad tiles*) that carry advertising messages.

Flow The reader's eye movement (from left to right and from top to bottom) when reading an advertisement.

FM (frequency modulation) Refers to the speed at which radio waves travel, in thousands of cycles per second (kilohertz).

Format A term that, in the context of radio, describes the nature of the programming done by an individual station.

Free-standing insert (FSI) Preprinted ads that are inserted loose into newspapers.

Frequency The average number of times an audience is exposed to an advertising message over a period of time, usually a week. Also called average frequency.

Frequency (online) The number of times an ad is delivered to the same browser in a single session or time period.

Frequency discount A discount based on a minimum number of spots purchased over a specified period of time.

Frequent-buyer (loyalty) program A promotion strategy that provides consumers with a small bonus, such as points or play money, when a purchase is made. These incentives are intended to encourage loyalty toward a product or company.

Fringe time In television, the daypart that normally runs from 4:00 to 7:00 p.m. and 11:00 p.m. to 1:00 a.m. (or sign-off).

Full back An advertisement in the form of a vinyl covering that covers the back of a transit vehicle.

Full-service agency An advertising agency that provides a complete range of services to the client (creative and media planning, marketing research, sales promotion, and even possibly public relations).

Full wrap An advertisement in the form of a vinyl covering that covers both sides and the back of a transit vehicle.

Game (instant win) A promotion that includes a number of predetermined, pre-seeded winning tickets.

Gatefold A printed magazine advertisement that consists of a series of folded pages that conform to the publication's page size.

Geodemographic segmentation Refers to the practice of combining demographic characteristics with geographic characteristics to isolate dwelling areas (e.g., areas within a city) based on the assumption that people seek out neighbourhoods that include their demographic peers.

Geographic segmentation The process of dividing a large geographic market into geographic units (e.g., Canada is divided into Atlantic Canada, Quebec, Ontario, the Prairies, and British Columbia).

Geomapping A database management technique that targets an audience based on demographic, psychographic, and behavioural data.

Grid card A broadcasting price schedule that quotes different price levels, depending on certain criteria such as demand for time, frequency of advertising, volume of advertising, and time of year.

Grocery cart advertising Advertising (small posters) appended to the front of shopping carts that is visible to approaching shoppers in supermarkets.

Gross rating points (GRPs) An aggregate of total ratings in a schedule, as determined by reach multiplied by frequency, usually in a weekly period against a target audience.

Guaranteed position A specific position for an advertisement with a premium rate charged for such positioning.

Headline An initial statement in an ad intended to grab the reader's attention.

Hiatus The period of time between advertising flights.

Hooker The local dealer's name added to national advertisements in newspapers. Also called a tag.

Horizontal publications Publications that appeal to people who occupy the same level of responsibility in a business.

Horizontal rotation The placement of radio commercials based on the day of the week.

Horizontal split A situation in the layout of a print advertisement in which the page is divided across the middle, with an illustration on one half and copy on the other.

House list An internal customer list.

Hybrid team A concept that calls for creative planners from all media platforms to work collaboratively on a client's business.

Impressions (1) In online advertising, the number of times a banner image is downloaded to a page being viewed by a visitor. (2) The total audience reached by a media plan. Often referred to as *total exposures*, impressions are calculated by multiplying the number of people who receive a message (reach) by the number of times they receive it (frequency).

Inbound telemarketing The reception of calls by the order desk, or customer inquiries and direct response calls generated from toll-free telephone numbers.

Industrial advertising The advertising of products that are used to produce and distribute other products.

Infomercial A long commercial (e.g., 30 or 60 minutes in length) that presents in detail the benefits of a product or service.

Inquiry test (split-run test) Placing two different ads for a product in a medium to determine which ad offers the most impact.

Insert A preprinted advertisement (e.g., leaflet, reply card) that is specially placed in a newspaper or magazine.

Insertion order A statement of advertisement specifications sent by an advertising agency to print media, including insertion dates, size, position, and rates.

Insert layout The inclusion of a secondary visual (an insert) in a print layout.

Integrated marketing communications (IMC) The coordination of all forms of marketing communications into a unified program that maximizes the impact on consumers and other types of customers.

Interior cards Print ads in racks above the windows in buses and subway cars.

Internal publics The publics an organization communicates with regularly; can include employees, distributors, suppliers, shareholders, and customers.

International management system A marketing management system calling for uniformity of strategy and execution in all markets; some minor tweaking of strategy may occur to meet local market needs.

Key benefit statement A statement of the basic selling idea, service, or benefit that an advertiser promises a consumer.

Key market plan Purchasing media time on the basis of market priorities (i.e., on a market-by-market basis).

Layout The design and orderly formation of the various elements of an advertisement, within specified dimensions. A layout integrates all copy elements with the illustration to create a complete message.

Leaderboard A webpage banner ad that stretches across the top of a webpage (728 × 90 pixels).

Leaflet A one-page document, printed front and back, containing vital information about an offer.

Lifestyle advertising A form of advertising that attempts to associate a product with the lifestyle of a certain market segment.

Line rate The newspaper advertising rate charged for one agate line.

List broker A company specializing in finding or developing lists for direct marketing purposes. The company finds prospects based on descriptions provided by marketing organizations.

Live action Advertisements that use real-life situations with real people.

Location-based targeting Integrates consumers' location information (based on GPS signals in smartphones) into a marketing strategy.

Logo The distinctive copy style that identifies the company or product.

Long copy advertisement A copy-dominant advertisement that makes little or no use of illustration.

Long-form DRTV Extended commercials lasting from 30 to 60 minutes (also called infomercials).

Make good A rerun of an advertisement at the publisher's expense to compensate for an error in or substandard printing of the original insertion.

Mall poster A form of advertising located inside shopping malls; relies on pedestrian traffic only.

Market coverage (coverage) The identity and number of markets in which advertising occurs over the course of the media plan's execution.

Marketing communications objectives Clearly defined statements that show how advertising and other forms of marketing communications help achieve marketing objectives.

Marketing communications plan A single document that provides details for all the components of a communications plan (e.g., advertising, sales promotion, event marketing, public relations).

Marketing communications strategy A strategic plan that includes a positioning statement, recommended components of the marketing communications mix, and a budget.

Marketing control The process of measuring and evaluating the results of marketing strategies and plans and taking corrective action to ensure objectives are achieved.

Marketing execution Detailed activity plans that contribute to the achievement of marketing objectives.

Marketing mix The four strategic elements of product, price, distribution, and marketing communications.

Marketing objectives Statements identifying what a product will accomplish over a one-year period.

Marketing plan An annual planning document for a product, service, or company that includes background analysis (of the market, the product, and the competition) and objectives, strategies, and tactics for the forthcoming year.

Marketing planning Planning activities that relate to the achievement of marketing objectives.

Marketing research The systematic gathering, recording, and analyzing of data to resolve a marketing problem.

Marketing strategies The process of identifying target markets and satisfying those targets with a blend of marketing mix elements.

Market segmentation The process of dividing a large market into smaller homogeneous markets (segments) according to common needs or similar lifestyles.

Material date The last date for an advertiser to have the production material for an ad at a magazine.

Media billings The total dollar volume of advertising handled by an agency in one year.

Media brief A document prepared by a client for an agency that outlines relevant background information pertaining to the development of a new media strategy and plan.

Media buyer A media specialist who is familiar with the competitive claims of the various media alternatives. The media buyer's primary function is to purchase media time and space for clients as efficiently as possible.

Media buying The process of buying media that will maximize the impact on a target audience at the lowest possible cost to the client.

Media buying service An advertising agency that specializes in media planning and placement.

Media convergence The consolidation of ownership of a variety of media outlets by relatively few companies.

Media-delivered coupons A method of coupon distribution using various media alternatives, including newspapers, magazines, cooperative direct mail, and the internet.

Media director The most senior media position in an advertising agency, this person is responsible for the management of the media department and accountable for media planning and placement for all clients.

Media mix The combination of media used in a media schedule.

Media objectives Clearly worded statements that outline exactly what a media plan should accomplish (who, what, when, where, and how).

Media plan A summary of all the decisions about which media are best suited to reach the target audience in an effective and efficient manner.

Media planner A media specialist who assesses the strengths, weaknesses, costs, and communications potential of various media in order to develop a media plan.

Media planning The preparation of a plan that documents how the client's money will be spent to achieve advertising objectives.

Media research A procedure for accessing relevant media consumption data that will assist a media planner in the development of effective and efficient media plans.

Media strategy Strategic recommendations showing how media objectives will be achieved.

Merge/purge The process of purchasing lists, combining them, and then stripping them of duplicate names.

Microsite An individual webpage or series of webpages that is a supplement to a primary website.

Mid-roll Online video ads placed during a video.

Mission statement A statement of purpose for an organization, usually reflecting the organization's operating philosophy.

Mobile marketing A set of practices that enable organizations to communicate and engage with their audience in an interactive and relevant manner through any mobile device or network.

Motives Conditions that prompt action to satisfy a need (the action elicited by marketing and advertising activity).

Multiple illustration In a print advertisement layout, the use of many individual illustrations, either in sequence or showing a variety of related features and benefits.

Mural banner A hand-painted outdoor ad seen on the side of a building.

Mural (transit) An advertisement in the form of a vinyl covering located on the side of a transit vehicle.

National advertising Advertising of a trademarked product or service wherever that product or service is available.

Needs A state of deprivation—the absence of something useful.

Network advertising Advertising that comes from one central source and is broadcast across the entire network of stations.

New product development strategy A marketing strategy that calls for significant investment in research and development to develop new products.

Noise Competitive advertising messages aimed at a specific target market.

Objectives Statements outlining what is to be accomplished in a plan (corporate, marketing, or advertising plan).

On-demand viewing A service that allows viewers to stream videos for personal viewing at a convenient time.

Online advertising The placement of electronic communications on a website, in email, or over personal communication devices connected to the internet.

Opinion-measure testing A form of research yielding information about the effect of a commercial message on consumers' brand name recall, the extent to which the main idea of the ad is communicated to consumers, and their purchase intentions.

Optimizer A software program that searches a media database to identify media combinations that increase target reach or reduce the cost of buying it.

Outbound telemarketing Telephone calls and faxes a company makes to a customer to develop new accounts, generate sales leads, and even close a sale.

Outdoor advertising Advertising that is directed at vehicular or pedestrian traffic (e.g., posters or billboards, backlit posters, transit-shelter advertising, mall posters).

Pace (television) Designing message content so that it falls within the time parameters of a commercial—usually 15, 30, or 60 seconds.

Package plans Discounted rate plans that combine prime time spots with fringe time and daytime spots.

Paid circulation The total number of copies of a magazine sold via subscription and newsstand sales.

Pass-along reader A person who reads a magazine after having received it second hand.

Payment by results (PBR) system An agency compensation system in which the agency is awarded a predetermined payment when the desired objectives of a campaign are achieved.

Penetration strategy A plan of action for aggressively marketing a company's existing products.

People meter A portable electronic device that identifies which television shows a person watches and for how long.

Perception How individuals receive and interpret messages.

Performance allowance An additional trade discount (beyond a trade allowance) used to encourage retailers to perform a specific merchandising function.

Permission-based email A situation in which an individual agrees to accept email advertising and marketing offers.

Personality A person's distinguishing psychological characteristics, which are influenced by self-perceptions, which in turn are influenced by psychological needs, family, culture, and reference groups.

Personality announcement In radio, a situation in which the disc jockey presents a commercial message in his or her own style.

Personal selling A personalized form of communication that involves a seller presenting the features and benefits of a product or service to a buyer for the purpose of making a sale.

Platform posters Station posters that are located on the subway wall opposite the rider waiting on the platform.

Podcast An audio program downloaded to an iPod or other portable digital media device; listeners can tune in to listen at a convenient time.

Point-of-purchase (POP) advertising Advertising or display materials located in a retail environment to build traffic, advertise a product, and encourage impulse purchasing.

Pop-up coupon A coupon printed on heavier paper stock and stitched into a popular consumer magazine. (It is usually positioned directly before an advertisement for the couponed product.)

Portal A website that serves as a gateway to a variety of services, such as searching, news, directories, email, online shopping, and links to other sites.

Position charge An additional cost for requesting a particular location in a medium.

Positioning The place a brand occupies in the minds of consumers; in other words, the selling concept that motivates purchase.

Positioning strategy statement A summary of the character and personality of a brand and the benefits it offers consumers.

Post-buy analysis An analysis of actual audience deliveries (the actual number of audience members exposed to the ad) calculated after a specific spot or schedule of advertising has run.

Poster (1) A picture-dominant advertisement that uses a minimum of copy. (2) A billboard.

Post-roll Online ads that appear after a video.

Post-testing Evaluating and measuring a message's effectiveness during or after the message has run.

Pre-emption A situation in which a special program replaces regular programming. Advertisers of the regularly scheduled programs are rescheduled for comparable time slots at a later date.

Preferred position A specific position, requested by an advertiser, in a medium.

Premium An item offered free or at a low price to encourage consumers to buy a specific product (offered to consumers in three different forms).

Pre-roll Online ads that appear before the start of a video.

Press conference A gathering of news reporters invited to witness the release of important information about a company or product.

Press kit A folder distributed at a press conference containing materials relevant to the news story.

Press release A document containing all essential elements of a story (who, what, when, where, and why).

Pre-testing Evaluating commercial messages or advertisements prior to final production to determine the strengths and weaknesses of the communications.

Primary reader A person who receives the publication initially or works or lives in the place where the publication is initially received.

Prime time In television, the daypart that normally runs from 7:00 to 11:00 p.m. See also *fringe time* and *daytime*.

Product-as-hero A technique where the advertiser presents a problem situation that is quickly resolved when the product comes to the rescue.

Product demonstration Showing how a product is used in order to identify the benefits it offers.

Product innovation The idea that the product is on the cutting edge of technology or research and development.

Production manager The person responsible for preparing advertisements for all media recommended in a marketing communications plan.

Product life cycle The path a product follows from its introduction to its eventual withdrawal from the market (a four-stage process).

Product placement The visible placement of branded products in television shows and commercial movies.

Product seeding Giving a product free to trendsetters who influence others to become aware of the product and hopefully purchase it.

Profile-matching strategy Matching the demographic profile of a product's target market with a specific medium that has a compatible profile.

Programmatic media buying The practice of using computer algorithms to by media placements for online advertising campaigns.

Psychographic segmentation Market segmentation based on the activities, interests, and opinions (the lifestyles) of consumers.

Publicity The communication of newsworthy information about a product, service, or idea.

Public relations The firm's communications with its various publics (e.g., shareholders, employees, suppliers, governments).

Publisher's statement A statement prepared by a publisher that includes the average paid circulation of a magazine, the number of new and renewal subscriptions, and the geographic breakdown of the circulation.

Pull strategy Creating demand for a product by directing promotional efforts at consumers or final users of the product.

Pulse schedule (pulsing) Grouping advertisements in flights over a predetermined period of time.

Pupillometer test A test that measures the pupil dilation (enlargement) of a person's eye when the person is reading to determine the level of interest in an ad.

Push-down banner An online ad that slides advertising out of the way to reveal additional content rather than covering it up.

Push strategy Creating demand for a product by directing promotional efforts at intermediaries, who in turn promote the product among consumers.

QR (quick response) code A two-dimensional barcode that can be scanned and read by smartphones.

Ratings Audience estimates expressed as a percentage of a population in a defined geographic area.

Reach The total audience (number of people reached) potentially exposed one or more times to an advertiser's message over a period of time (e.g., a week).

Reach plan (total audience plan) A plan that involves rotating a radio commercial through the various dayparts so that the same message can reach different groups of people. In television, commercials are rotated vertically throughout the day and horizontally during the week.

Readers per copy The average number of people who read a single issue of a publication.

Real-time bidding An online auction system in which advertisers bid against each other over ad impressions in real time.

Recall testing Measuring an advertisement's impact by asking respondents to recall specific elements (e.g., the selling message) of the advertisement.

Recency A media advertising model that suggests advertising works best by reminding consumers of a product when they are ready to buy.

Recognition tests Tests that measure a target audience's awareness of a brand, of its copy points, or of the advertisement itself after the audience has been exposed to the message.

Redemption rate Refers to the number of coupons actually redeemed. The rate of redemption for a specific coupon offer equals the number of coupons redeemed divided by the number of coupons distributed.

Reference group (or peer group) A group of people with a common interest who have an influence on the individual members' attitudes and behaviour. It is a group to which a person thinks he or she belongs.

Rebate A predetermined amount of money returned directly to a consumer by a manufacturer after specified purchases have been made.

Regional management system The management of marketing activities based on the needs of consumers in different geographical locations.

Remnant time Unsold TV time inventory available on short notice at a lower cost than usual.

Reply card A type of mail that enables the recipient of direct mail advertising to respond without paying postage (encourages response).

Repositioning Changing the place a product occupies, relative to competitive products, in the consumer's mind.

Response list A list of proven mail-order buyers.

Retail advertising Advertising by a retail store (the advertising of a store name, image, and location, and the re-advertising of branded merchandise carried by the retailer).

Retail in-ad coupon A coupon printed in a retailer's weekly advertising, either via run of press or supplements inserted in a newspaper.

Rich media Internet media that allow for greater use of interaction with animation, audio, and video, and that have advanced tracking and measurement capabilities.

Rifle strategy A strategy that involves using a specific medium that effectively reaches a target market defined by a common characteristic.

ROP (run of press or run of paper) Placing advertisements anywhere within the regular printed pages of a newspaper.

ROS (run of schedule) A discount offered to advertisers who allow the television or radio station to schedule the commercial at the station's discretion.

Rotation plan A selection of radio time slots specified by the advertiser and based on time of day (vertical rotation) and day of week (horizontal rotation).

Rough art The drawing of an advertisement, done to actual size and with the various elements included (i.e., headline, copy, illustration, and signature) to show relative size and position.

Sales promotion Activity designed to generate a prompt response from consumers, distributors, and the field sales force.

Sample Free distribution of a product to potential new users.

Script A document used in the production of television and radio commercials. In the case of television, the script describes the video presentation on one side and the audio on the other. In the case of radio, the audio presentation, sound effects, and music are described.

Search advertising An advertiser's listing placed within or alongside search results in exchange for paying a fee each time someone clicks on the listing in a search situation.

Seasonal discounts (television) Discounts offered to advertisers in traditionally slow seasons. (Television viewership drops in the summer, so additional summer discounts are offered.)

Seasonal schedule A schedule in which media spending is heavier in the preseason (to create awareness) and tapers off during the season of usage.

Selective spot advertising During a network show, some commercial time is not allocated and is left to regional or local stations to sell. Advertisers can purchase this time on a station-by-station basis.

Self-concept An individual's understanding of him- or herself. (In advertising, four categories of consumer self-concept are significant: real self, self-image, looking-glass self, and ideal self.)

Share of voice The amount invested in advertising by one brand expressed as a percentage of the total category investment in advertising

Short-form DRTV Short direct response television commercials lasting from 15 to 120 seconds.

Short rate A charge incurred by an advertiser who does not meet a contractual estimate of advertising time or space.

Shotgun strategy A strategy involving the use of mass media to reach a more loosely defined (i.e., more general) target market.

Showing In outdoor advertising, the purchase of multiple panels in a geographic market to maximize reach.

Signature The part of an ad that closes the selling message. It usually contains the brand name, logo, and slogan. It is often called a tagline.

Situation analysis An analysis of internal and external variables that will impact the development of a marketing communications strategy.

Skip schedule The purchase of media time and space on an alternating basis (every other week, month, etc.), or the use of alternate media types.

Skyscraper A tall, skinny, oblong ad that appears on the side of a webpage (160 × 600 pixels).

Slippage The situation in which a consumer collects proofs of purchase for a refund offer but neglects to follow through and submit a request for the refund.

Social media network A website that connects people with similar interests in a social environment. Such a network may also have a specific focus or topic of interest.

Solo direct mail Individually prepared and distributed direct mail offers. Also called selective direct mail.

Spam Unsolicited email.

Spectacular A nonstandardized outdoor advertising unit constructed according to the customized specifications of the advertiser (often with protruding components, to attract attention).

Split 30s Two 15-second commercials for the same product, one appearing at the start and one at the end of a commercial cluster.

Sponsorship (online) A situation where an advertiser and a website commit to a long-term relationship based on the website's ability to reach the advertiser's target market effectively.

Sponsorship (television) A situation where an advertiser takes advertising ownership of a television show or a segment within a show.

Spot sales The purchase of local broadcast time on a station-by-station basis (sometimes called selective spot).

Starch readership test A post-test recognition procedure that measures readers' recall of an advertisement (noted), their ability to identify the sponsor (associated), and whether they read more than half of the written material (read most).

Statement stuffers Advertisements that are distributed with monthly charge account statements.

Station domination An advertising opportunity where a single advertiser takes control of every advertising space in a subway station.

Station posters Advertisements located on platforms and entrance and exit areas of subway and light rail transit systems.

Storyboard A set of graphic renderings in a television-frame format, accompanied by appropriate copy, depicting what a finished commercial will look like.

Strategic alliance A relationship between two or more companies that decide to work cooperatively to achieve common goals.

Strategic planning The process of determining objectives and identifying strategies and tactics that will contribute to the achievement of objectives.

Strategies Statements that outline how objectives will be achieved.

Street-level unit A rear-illuminated advertising unit typically located on sidewalks, in public squares, and on transit shelters.

Subheadline (subhead) A smaller headline that amplifies the main point of a headline.

Superboard In outdoor advertising, a much larger outdoor poster that is more expensive to produce.

Support claims statement A statement describing the principal characteristics of a product or service that substantiate the promises made about the product in the key benefit statement.

Sweepstakes A chance promotion involving a giveaway of products or services of value to randomly selected participants.

SWOT analysis An evaluation of a brand's (company's) strengths, weaknesses, opportunities, and threats.

Tabloids A newspaper format that is flat and resembles an unbound magazine. The page is 10 to 10 ¾ inches wide by 11 to 14 inches deep.

Tagline An alternative expression for the signature portion of an advertisement. Usually includes the brand name, a distinctive logo, and a slogan.

Target market (or target audience) A specific group of individuals an advertising message is directed at.

Tear sheet A page supplied to an advertiser by a newspaper that carries the advertiser's insertion; the tear sheet verifies that the advertisement ran as scheduled.

Telemarketing Advertising that uses telecommunications to promote the products and services of a business.

Testimonial A form of advertising in which a credible source, usually a typical consumer, presents the product message.

Text messaging The transmission of text-only messages on wireless devices such as mobile phones and tablets.

Thumbnail sketches Small, experimental sketches of a variety of design concepts.

Tip-in An insert that is glued directly onto a page of a magazine; usually the tip-in is attached on top of an ad the advertiser has already placed.

Tipping (in) Gluing items into the seam (gutter) of a magazine (e.g., recipe pamphlets or small catalogues).

Total paid circulation In print, the total of all classes of a publication's distribution for which the ultimate purchasers have paid (single-copy sales plus subscription sales).

Trade advertising Advertising by manufacturers directed at channel members to secure distribution of the advertised product.

Trade allowance A temporary price reduction intended to encourage larger purchases by distributors.

Trade promotions Promotion activity directed at distributors and designed to encourage volume purchases and merchandising support for a manufacturer's product.

Trade show An event that allows a company to showcase its products to a captive audience. Buyers visit trade shows to seek new information; hence, the show is a way for a company to generate leads.

Traffic manager The person responsible for ensuring that the final product (print, digital, or broadcast commercial) reaches the media destination on time.

Transient rate The base rate, or open rate, charged to casual advertisers in a newspaper; it is the maximum rate charged. Also called the casual rate.

Unaided recall A research situation in which respondents are provided no information to encourage thought.

Unity (print) The blending of all elements in a print advertisement to create a complete impression.

Unity (television) The visual and aural flow of a broadcast commercial from the customer's perspective.

Unique selling points (USPs) The characteristics or benefits of a brand that distinguish it from competitor brands.

Upfront buying The selling of advertising time by television networks in advance of the start of a new television season.

Venue marketing The linking of a brand name to a physical site such as an arena, stadium, or theatre.

Vertical publications Publications that reach people with different jobs in the same industry.

Vertical rotation The placement of radio commercials based on the time of day.

Vertical split A type of print advertisement layout in which copy dominates one side and illustration the other—left and right sides are divided by an imaginary line down the middle of the page.

Video advertising Television-style commercials that appear on the internet.

Videostrip An ad that shows a strip of video in the banner space, but when clicked on it expands to reveal the video and accompanying audio in a full-sized panel.

Vinyl wrap An advertising message that can cover various exterior sections of a transit vehicle; a vinyl material containing the message is attached to the vehicle.

Viral marketing A situation in which the receiver of an electronic message is encouraged to pass it on to friends.

Visit A sequence of hits made by one user at an internet site.

Voiceover Spoken copy or dialogue delivered by an announcer who is heard but not seen.

Volume discount A discount that is based on the dollar volume purchased over a 52-week period.

Wallpaper ad An on-screen ad, not in the banner, that is a large image that replaces the web background.

Website A company's presence on the internet. A website provides a company with the opportunity to communicate information about itself, including words, graphics, video clips, and audio clips.

White space The part of an advertisement that is not occupied by any elements.

Wild postings Ads that appear on the sides of hoardings at construction sites (often in downtown areas).

Window ad An on-screen ad, not in the banner, that downloads itself and plays instantly or when a new page is loading.

Word-of-mouth marketing The transfer of a product message by people (often using technology) to other people.

Index

Note: Page references followed by *f* indicate figures.

B

D

E

F

G

P

S

T

U